Intimation of Revolution

Intimation of Revolution: Global Sixties and the Making of Bangladesh studies the rise of Bengali nationalism in East Pakistan in the fifties and the sixties by showcasing the interactions between global politics and local social and economic developments. It argues that the revolution of 1969 and the national liberation struggle of 1971 were informed by the global sixties that transformed the political landscape of Pakistan and facilitated the birth of Bangladesh. Departing from the typical understanding of Bangladesh as a product of Indo-Pakistani diplomatic and military rivalry, this book narrates how Bengali nationalists resisted the processes of internal colonization by the Pakistani military-bureaucratic regime to fashion their own nation. It details how this process of resistance and nation-formation drew on contemporaneous decolonization movements in Asia, Africa and Latin America while also being shaped by the Cold War rivalries between the United Sates, the Soviet Union and China.

Subho Basu is Associate Professor of History and Classical Studies at Montreal, Quebec. His research and teaching interests are South Asian history, history of Bangladesh and Pakistan, subaltern and decolonial studies, international development studies, and democracy and society in India. He is the author of *Does Class Matter? Colonial Capital and Workers' Resistance in Bengal, 1890–1937* (2004). He has also co-authored, with Ali Riaz, *Paradise Lost? State Failure in Nepal* (2007) and co-edited, with Crispin Bates, *Rethinking Indian Political Institutions* (2005).

Intimation of Revolution

GLOBAL SIXTIES AND THE
MAKING OF BANGLADESH

Subho Basu

CAMBRIDGE
UNIVERSITY PRESS

University Printing House, Cambridge CB2 8BS, United Kingdom

One Liberty Plaza, 20th Floor, New York, NY 10006, USA

477 Williamstown Road, Port Melbourne, vic 3207, Australia

314 to 321, 3rd Floor, Plot No.3, Splendor Forum, Jasola District Centre, New Delhi 110025, India

103 Penang Road, #05–06/07, Visioncrest Commercial, Singapore 238467

Cambridge University Press is part of the University of Cambridge.

It furthers the University's mission by disseminating knowledge in the pursuit of education, learning and research at the highest international levels of excellence.

www.cambridge.org
Information on this title: www.cambridge.org/9781009329873

© Subho Basu 2023

This publication is in copyright. Subject to statutory exception and to the provisions of relevant collective licensing agreements, no reproduction of any part may take place without the written permission of Cambridge University Press.

First published 2023

Printed in India by Avantika Printers Pvt. Ltd.

A catalogue record for this publication is available from the British Library

Library of Congress Cataloging-in-Publication Data

Names: Basu, Subho, author.
Title: Intimation of revolution : global sixties and the making of
   Bangladesh / Subho Basu.
Other titles: Global sixties and the making of Bangladesh
Description: Cambridge, United Kingdom ; New York, NY : Cambridge
   University Press, 2023. | Includes bibliographical references and index.
Identifiers: LCCN 2022062149 (print) | LCCN 2022062150 (ebook) | ISBN
   9781009329873 (hardback) | ISBN 9781009329866 (ebook)
Subjects: LCSH: Bangladesh--Politics and government. |
   Bangladesh--History--Revolution, 1971. |
   Nationalism--Bangladesh--History--20th century.
Classification: LCC DS395 .B37 2023 (print) | LCC DS395 (ebook) | DDC
   954.9204--dc23/eng/20230104
LC record available at https://lccn.loc.gov/2022062149
LC ebook record available at https://lccn.loc.gov/2022062150

ISBN 978-1-009-32987-3 Hardback

Cambridge University Press has no responsibility for the persistence or accuracy of URLs for external or third-party internet websites referred to in this publication, and does not guarantee that any content on such websites is, or will remain, accurate or appropriate.

আমার দাদা সৌর, বৌদি সুতপাদি এবং শান্তিনিকেতনকে

To my elder brother, Soura, and sister-in-law, Sutapa, and Santiniketan

Contents

Acknowledgements ix
List of Abbreviations xiii

Introduction 1

1. Nationality Question: Territoriality, Birth of East Pakistan and New Politics of Resistance 28

2. Global Politics and Local Alignment: Cold War Bureaucratic-Military Alliance and Popular Resistance 75

3. Language, Culture and the Global Sixties in East Pakistan 123

4. Praetorian Guards, Capitalist Modernization and the Early Global Sixties: Global Cold War, Empire and the Colonization of East Pakistan 185

5. For Whom the Bell Tolls: Popular Resistance and the Beginning of the Global Sixties in Pakistan 220

6. The Global Sixties and the Coming of Revolution 262

Conclusion 360

Bibliography 370
Index 401

Acknowledgements

My debts are many. Like the workers and peasants of Bengal, I have continued to accumulate them, and, needless to say, I have very little means at my disposal to repay. First, I express my gratitude to those who struggled to establish a democratic polity in East Pakistan and later resisted the military occupation of Bangladesh. Despite all dire predictions, Bangladesh survived the last 50 years and became a relatively prosperous nation. This itself is a tribute to those women and men who fought for her liberation. My mother was born in those parts of Bengal which became East Pakistan. Her family left in 1947 in search of refuge in India. Yet she retained a lifelong interest in Bangladesh and successfully infected me with such interests.

I thank the Gerda Henkel Stiftung Foundation, Düsseldorf, for providing me with a generous grant to conduct this research. McGill University, Montreal, Quebec, granted me a sabbatical for a year which enabled me to visit Dhaka. My colleagues at the university's History Department – Jason Opal, Gavin Walker and Malek Abisaab – helped me in numerous ways throughout my institutional affiliation with McGill. Laila Parsons, Lorenz Luthi, Anastassios (Tassos) Anastassiadis, Elizabeth Elbourne, Kristy Ironside and Judith Szapor read drafts of the first two chapters of this book and commented on them. Ali Riaz, as a good friend, arranged my local sponsor in Bangladesh. My current research questions were born out of many of our discussions at Illinois State University. Zillur Rahman of *Tritiyo Matra* and the Center for Governance Studies, Dhaka, kindly arranged my visa and provided me with an institutional home in Dhaka. Qudrat-e-Khoda and Rumana Nahid Subhan intervened in the last moment to secure my visa.

Aksadul Alam, Mamunur Rashid, Kuhelika (Shahidul Alam) Manzu, Sonia Amin, Utpal Chattopadhyay, Mahmud Ishtiak, Helal Hossain Dhali, Taniya Afrose and other friends made my stay in Dhaka extremely pleasant. Ahsan Habib and Zobaida Nasreen helped me to connect with local scholars and arranged interviews with them. They also introduced me to the treasure trove of the Bangla Academy. At the Bangladesh National Archives, Elias Mohammad Elias Ali offered his excellent hospitality to me. In the reading room at the National Archives, Abdus Salam, a member of staff, helped me obtain documents at a rapid speed. My fellow researcher Niladri Chattopadhyay made the research at the archives extremely pleasant. My research assistant, Nazmul Haque, offered me stellar service. Zillur Rahman again acted as a gracious host. At the invitation of Professor Mesbah Kamal, I went to Barisal by boat from Dhaka. It was a wonderful journey by river. Professor Salimullah Khan invited me to give a lecture at the Center for Advanced Theory, University of Liberal Arts Bangladesh, Dhaka, and commented on my paper. Morshed Shafiul Hasan, a leading Bangladeshi scholar, whose writing influenced me a lot, read my manuscript with avid interest and suggested several alterations. I thank him for his generosity with time.

In Montreal, Suvij Sudershan copy-edited my text and smoothened my language. My friends Sandeep Banerjee, Atreyee Majumder, Auritro Majumder and Shreya Chatterjee engaged enthusiastically with my project and provided me with suggestions. Tarun Chakravorty also turned out to be an excellent friend and interlocutor of Bangladeshi affairs.

In Dhaka, and later in Montreal, my friends Azizul Islam Rasel and Rumana Sharmin Koli opened their home to me, accommodated me as their 'honoured' guest and accepted my odd demands on their hospitality without a murmur of protest. In addition, Rasel kindly went through my drafts, corrected Bangladeshi names and helped me in sorting out myriad information in the footnotes. This book is going to press because of their ardent support. My daughter, Ella, tolerated my absence for six months, and later she was amused by my constant engagement with writing and reading. Her mere presence in the house is a delightful distraction. Mallika Banerjee offered me excellent support. My elder brother, Sauro, and my sister-in-law, Sutapa, always provided me support, encouragement and shelter. We grew up together and inherited the same love and curiosity to know about global culture and society. We are also Santiniketanis at heart and global in thinking. Additionally, I would like to thank my friends Sharoza Nahrin Tanha, Madhulagna Halder and Twisha Singh who helped me in collating information for this book.

I am also grateful to Anwesha Rana, my commissioning editor, and the anonymous referees at Cambridge University Press.

Alas, despite all the support, there may have remained numerous errors in my book. Needless to add, my opinions are mine alone. To prospective readers of my book, as they say in Quebec, *bonne lecture!*

Abbreviations

BNR	Bureau of National Reconstruction
CCP	Communist Party of China
CIA	Central Intelligence Agency
CML	Convention Muslim League
COP	Combined Opposition Party
CPI	Communist Party of India
CPI(M)	Communist Party of India (Marxist)
CPP	Communist Party of Pakistan
CPSU	Communist Party of the Soviet Union
CSP	Civil Service of Pakistan
DAC	Democratic Action Committee
DM	district magistrate
EBDO	Elective Bodies (Disqualification) Ordinance
EPCP-ML	East Pakistan Communist Party (Marxist–Leninist)
EPFDC	East Pakistan Film Development Corporation
EPIDC	East Pakistan Industrial Development Corporation
EPRS	East Pakistan Renaissance Society
IBRD	International Bank for Reconstruction and Development
INC	Indian National Congress
IPTA	Indian People's Theatre Association
NAP	National Awami Party

NDF	National Democratic Front
NSF	National Student Federation
NWFP	North-West Frontier Province
PDM	Pakistan Democratic Movement
PNC	Pakistan National Congress
PPP	People's Party of Pakistan
PRC	People's Republic of China
SAC	Student Action Committee
SEATO	South-East Asia Treaty Organization
UK	United Kingdom
UN	United Nations
US	United States

Introduction

The Idea of the Global Sixties and East Pakistan

The image of the sixties as a transformative, radical era has proved to be enduring. As Tor Egil Førland points out, it is only the sixties, among all the other decades of the twentieth century, that has a journal devoted to its events.[1] This journal, in its 'Aims and Scope', boldly announces, as Førland asserts, that it 'is the only academic, peer-reviewed journal to focus solely on this transformative decade of history'.[2] The key locution here is the word 'transformative'. The era has become associated with revolutionary and radical confrontations, between the forces of the establishment, the global insurgencies and experiments with alternative living in the advanced capitalist world. Throughout the world, successive generations of politicians and social activists have waged cultural wars defending or attacking the radical meanings of the sixties as well as their historical legacy. The decade began with the polarizing, but hugely successful, national liberation struggle in the Caribbean in Cuba. The Cuban Revolution of 1959 appears to announce the beginning of an era that would be volatile and unpredictable, for it did not follow any predetermined master narratives of revolutionary transformation. Intellectually, the global sixties began with the writings of Frantz Fanon,[3] Che Guevara's *foco* theory[4] and Regis Debray's *Revolution in the Revolution*,[5] alongside Mao Zedong's *On Practice and Contradiction*.[6] These texts became central to the art of making revolution and were even read in disparate locations, such as Palestine, Algeria, France, Congo and East Pakistan. Even Jean-Paul Sartre's existentialist perspective on Marxism and Louis Althusser's ruminations on the development of Marx's thought[7] became critical sources for the debates that raged in the dingy and overcrowded 'Madhu's canteen' in Dacca University (present-day University of Dhaka).[8] The decade was marked by the Cultural Revolution in China, the Tet Offensive in Vietnam, a seemingly revolutionary coup and a reactionary counter-coup in Indonesia (culminating in genocidal events), student-led revolutionary activities in Pakistan, the victory of the United Front in West Bengal, combined with the rise of the Naxalite Movement in India, followed by the conclusion of the Algerian War. Furthermore, the beginnings of the Palestinian national liberation struggle; the Prague Spring in Czechoslovakia; the student uprisings in France, Mexico, the United States (US) and West Germany; the civil rights movements in the US; and, of course, the global peace movement, the anti-nuclear weapons campaigns and the rise of the 'new left' transformed the sixties into a decade of hope, protests and rebellion.[9] It was also an era when the new aesthetics emerging in literature, theatre, film and musicals began to create spaces to forge a counter-hegemonic cultural domain among the youth throughout the world. Many among the youths, through such counter-hegemonic cultural discourse, raised questions about modes of governance and the existing ways of doing politics. Since the end of that decade, global approaches to the sixties, and considerations of the 'Global 1968', have become a critical point of intervention in the social sciences. The epistemology of the global sixties starts with Asia, Africa and Latin America. It is now widely accepted that a global analysis of the sixties is untenable without an extended conversation with the historical conditions of the Third World. Fedrick Jameson, a literary scholar, rightly locates 'the beginnings of what will come to be called the 60s in the third world'.[10]

This book looks at the sixties from a location in the Global South. It examines a rather understudied revolution that began in the predominantly agrarian society of the lower Gangetic delta of East Pakistan. It seeks to provide a radical reading of the sixties in East Pakistan and further aims to situate it as an integral component of the global sixties. The story of the global sixties starts with the intellectual flirtations of Bengali student activists with contemporaneous revolutionary texts. In East Pakistan in 1968–69, among the socialist leaning but purely Bengali-nationalist 'nucleus' circle established by Serajul Alam Khan and Kazi Aref Ahmed, the texts of Che Guevara, Regis Debray, Vo Nguyen Giap and Mao were prescribed as essential readings.[11] For these nationalist student revolutionaries, there was much romance to be found in the idea of a Bengali nation state heralding an exploitation-free society.[12] As Jameson maintains, the supposedly unclassed collective entities, such as students, played as much of a role in the making of the East Pakistani global sixties as in other locations. Yet Jameson's oft-quoted observation – that Marxist theory entered a crisis in the global sixties because 'active political categories no longer seemed to be those of social class'[13] – is a generalization based upon a particular reading of specific events which took place in Paris and other Western locations. In fact, throughout the history of East Pakistan, labour unrest had defined the political contour of democratic movements. Unfortunately, much of the historical literature on this subject in Bengali also views these working-class unrests as a prefiguration of a nationalist awakening and thus confines them to the role of a mere appendage to the nationalist movement. However, in East Pakistan, the working classes rejected such a subsumption into a purely nationalist, constitutional autonomy project. They played a critical role as a collective entity in the 1969 mass insurrection, which transformed the general movement into a potent and threatening event against the ruling military junta.[14] Alongside workers, the peasants were also mobilized along class lines based upon the emerging contradictions within the polity and economy, between the rich peasants and the middle peasants. Many among these rich peasants were also constitutionally selected to be power brokers by the military-bureaucratic elites and termed 'basic democrats'. These basic democrats had gained access to developmental funds, while other segments of the 'surplus farmers', namely the middle peasants, did not have access to them.[15] Though admittedly the category of 'middle peasant' is tenuous in the East Pakistani context, Eric Wolf was not far off when he argued that the middle peasants constitute the 'pivotal' group in peasant rebellions of Mexico, Russia, China, Vietnam, Cuba and Algeria. According to Wolf, poor peasants and landless labourers, depending on landlords for their livelihood, have very little 'tactical power' and no independent resources to launch and sustain a rebellion. These middle peasants alone had the necessary 'minimal tactical freedom' to challenge the established order.[16] It was their children who moved into schools, colleges and universities and participated in the radical movements in East Pakistan. Thus, class remained critical to political rebellion in the sixties. Yet it would obviously be simplistic to assume that these antagonistic class contradictions automatically led to a revolution. Hannah Arendt's observation – that the revolutionists watched the disintegration of society and took initiative once the revolution had broken out – is possibly true in the context of East Pakistan of the sixties.[17] Moving a step further, De Nardo, another scholar of revolution, has rightly argued that it was the strategists who had conceptualized the path of revolution, particularly in the case of China and Vietnam.[18] In Pakistan too, a Jacobin-minded pro-Chinese radical Muslim theologian, Maulana Bhashani, played a critical role in the mobilizations of the sixties. He used red flags and red hats as symbols of peasant organization.[19] Thus, the very symbols around which peasants gathered and organized themselves were associated with the communist movement. Class politics, even if the language was crafted by radicals, remained inscribed on the sixties in East Pakistan. Revolutionaries, like Bhashani, despite their own inchoate ideological formulations of Islamic socialism, remained committed towards a radical redistributive agenda.[20]

The term 'long sixties' is conceptualized by Arthur Marwick in the context of what he calls a 'cultural revolution' in Germany, Italy and France, as well as in the United Kingdom (UK) and the US.[21] The significance of this term lies in the acknowledgement that the sixties cannot simply be studied as that time which passed between a pair of historical bookends – that is, 1960–69. Rather, it must be studied in terms of the shared objectivity of a particular historical moment that stretched beyond, but incorporated, events in that decade. The long sixties in East Pakistan began in 1954 with an election that took place in the context of a spasmodic and rickety constitutional process. It was this constitutional process that led to the gaining of a modicum of political power by the politicians of the Awami League. This brief flirtation with 'power' in the Pakistani state led to a split in this pivotal local autonomist organization over questions of Cold War alignment.

For a brief period, when Awami League supremo Huseyn Shaheed Suhrawardy was the prime minister, Pakistan joined the US-backed military blocs of the Baghdad Pact and the South-East Asia Treaty Organization (SEATO). The decision to join such military pacts was guided by the security-related concerns of the emergent military-bureaucratic ruling class in Pakistan, but the League's active support of such a decision led to an internal schism. Radicals, which included both communists and non-communist socialists such as Bhashani, questioned the necessity of a political alignment that violated the basic principles of the Non-Aligned Movement. More importantly, these radicals felt that when political actors and emerging national-liberation struggles in the Middle East and elsewhere in the Muslim world opposed such military blocs, it was imperative that Pakistan should stay away from such formations. Ultimately, these radicals formed a rival political organization, namely the National Awami Party (NAP), based upon a programme of opposition to 'imperial' alignment.[22] The close connection between Cold War military-political alignments and the rise of a pro-Western, supposedly 'modernizing' military junta in Pakistan defined a critical parameter of politics of the 'long sixties'. This parameter was the general tendency to question the cultural politics of national integration as championed by military-bureaucratic regimes. It was also a period marked by growing peasant protests and labour and student militancy in Pakistan. All these movements coalesced around an opposition to the capitalist modernization process, which had increased inequity along class, regional and ethnic lines. These protests were also matched by a deeper social transformation marked by ethnic cleansing, capital flight from the eastern province, the changing dynamics of class formation, the immiseration of the peasantry and the narrowing down of the democratic possibilities of accommodation.[23]

In the sixties, the coup by pro-Western military dictator Ayub Khan gave birth to praetorian capitalism, whereby a garrison state steadily pursued a policy of foreign-aid-driven modernization. Military as an institution secured a pivotal role in the economic process and gave birth to an economy based upon both social inequality and regional inequality. Functional inequality as a necessary condition for economic growth was the new mantra of the regime. Politically, the military secured the loyalty of bureaucracy as a junior partner in the ruling coalition. Furthermore, through basic democracy, military strongman Ayub Khan built up a social coalition of incipient and dependent monopoly of industrial houses and bribed rich peasantry by providing them some control over developmental funds through a constitutional façade of basic democracy. Yet such social coalition did not include the vociferous middle classes, urban working classes and rural subsistence peasantry. More importantly, the suspension of democracy created a phenomenon of minoritization of the majority – namely, the Bengali-speaking population of East Pakistan. The people of East Pakistan could not translate their numerical majority into a parliamentary coalition, and their representation in the ruling military-bureaucratic coalition remained miniscule. They did not have representation among the monopoly industrial houses as well; this then created a situation of internal colonization. In their readiness to escape from a Calcutta-centric internal colonization, Bengali Muslims found themselves in a situation of another colonization where the new colonial rulers acted as distant sovereign, even replicating certain British colonial stereotypes about Bengalis.[24] As the global fifties and sixties witnessed the rise of West-sponsored dictators in Asia, from Syngman Rhee in Korea to Suharto in

Indonesia, there took place also wider resistance culminating in 1968–69 throughout the world, known as the 'high sixties'.[25]

In Pakistan too, over the course of these years, there arose a period of 'high sixties', in 1968–69, marked by students, workers and peasants openly revolting against the military-bureaucratic power edifice. Throughout the Global South and in the Muslim world, the global sixties had its repercussions.[26] So, when did this long period of revolutionary experimentation, cultural interrogations of the status quo and a politics of hope, which were never left unmatched by their dialectical antipodes – fratricidal violence, coups and military dictatorship, and Cold War violence – come to an end? By 1970, the idea of Bangladesh as the land of Bengalis had become more popular than the earlier nationalist notion of Pakistan as a homeland of Muslims.[27] On 26 March 1971, the military crackdown on the radical nationalist movement snowballed into a genocide of East Pakistanis, who were now identified mostly as Bengalis. The guerrilla war of 1971 conducted amid the tensions of the Cold War – with and, in some cases, without Indian assistance – culminated in the liberation of Bangladesh. This book concludes at the beginning of the armed national liberation struggle in 1971, perceiving it as an end of an era. Yet, as Bernardine Dohrn, in a review of a book on the sixties in the US, argued: 'The sixties began in 1954 and the real news is that they're not over yet.'[28]

Contradictions and Contestations: Conceptualizing the Making of Bangladesh as a Product of the Global Sixties

The adumbration of the student revolution and the subsequent national liberation struggle in East Pakistan in relation to the global sixties requires a conceptual reordering of the story of so-called Bengali nationalism. The global frame of reference necessitates a new conceptual approach towards understanding local transformation within a transnational framework – one that is informed by the crosscurrents of multiple geopolitical, ideological, economic and cultural questions. These questions indicate the concurrence of a similar set of actions across diverse geographical locations. For South Asianists, the use of the term 'global sixties' involves an attempt at the thematic exposition of local anti-colonial and wider anti-imperial struggles. Various protest movements made attempts to mobilize class-based social configurations in the Cold War context. But the geopolitics of bipolar power configuration constricted, as it constructed, boundaries and determined the conclusions of these attempts. Despite radical left movements, such as the East Pakistani NAP's efforts over the fifties to transcend the matrices of the Cold War, it was clear by 1971 that the resolution of the 'democratic question' would be unable to escape the whirlwind of geopolitical realities swirling around it. Garry J. Bass' *The Blood Telegram*[29] and Srinath Raghavan's *1971: A Global History of the Creation of Bangladesh*[30] aptly highlight the impact of Cold War alignments in the making of Bangladesh. Yet both these books, and in particularly Raghavan's, despite their strengths, delegitimize and ignore the critical role played by East Pakistani actors in their own liberation, against the backdrop of the multifarious concerns of different powers to Indian policy in the Cold War era. Other works, such as Richard Sission and Leo E. Rose's authoritative account,[31] simply view the process of the birth of Bangladesh as a product of war between India and Pakistan – a perspective that ignores the agency of local actors.[32] Indeed, historians are so dazzled by the gruesome events in 1971, such as genocide, sexual violence and war, that they do not move far enough to explore the evolution of politics in East Pakistan. Most of the insightful works about the birth of Bangladesh is limited to 1971.[33] Many scholars have provided accounts of Ayub Khan's regime ignoring the details of resistance to praetorian rule.[34] Many contemporary accounts merely view the history of Pakistan and Bangladesh through the prism of Islamism. The emphasis on the global sixties, Cold War and the politics of resistance in united Pakistan, in this book, goes against the contemporary perception that the history of Muslim-majority polities in South Asia can only be written through the prism of Islamism. As Saadia Toor has correctly asserted, the overwhelming emphasis on Islam and religious nationalism with Islamist orientations in writing the history of Pakistan blinds us to the complex development of popular movements geared towards securing social justice.[35]

In recent years, new historical research on the making of Bangladesh and even Pakistan focuses primarily on 1971 as a landmark. In a thoughtful and engaging essay, Faisal Devji has called the emergence of Bangladesh as an end of post-colonial state. He points out that the emergence of Bangladesh gives birth to the depoliticized language of humanitarianism, and he puts the example of Kosovo and Bosnia and the question of humanitarian language and international intervention that it involves. He further argues:

> This is not to say, of course, that Bangladesh possesses no political language or imagination, only that the circumstances of its founding have resulted in the emergence of a significant and anti-political

narrative there. This is only exacerbated by the ambiguity if not absence of any national narrative about Bengali Muslims struggling for freedom before 1971, and the problem posed by their participation in the movement for Pakistan before 1947.[36]

Yet, in many ways, this conclusion erases the complex story of internal colonization and the idea of nationalitarian political language that informs the long transition of collective political identity of Bengali Muslims in East Pakistan. Anouar Abdel-Malek outlines in his concept of 'nationalitarian':

> The nationalitarian phenomenon is one in which the struggle against the imperialist powers of occupation has as its object, beyond the clearing of the national territory, the independence and sovereignty of the national state, uprooting in depth the positions of the ex-colonial power – the reconquest of the power of decision in all domains of national life, the prelude to that reconquest of identity which is at the heart of the renaissance undertaken on the basis of fundamental national demands, and ceaselessly contested, by every means available, on every level, and notably on the internal level.[37]

Unpacking this concept, Neil Lazaras quotes from Fanon, who has emphatically asserted that '[It] is the national liberation which leads the nation to play its parts on the stage of history. It is at the heart of national consciousness that international consciousness lives and grows.'[38]

The very cultural imagining that led towards the formation of East Pakistan indicates the complex political imagining of freedom from both formal colonialism and internal colonization in 1947 and international consciousness. While formal colonialism had a negotiated end in South Asia, internal colonization did not end. Neilesh Bose has captured the cultural dynamics of the story of the formation of Bengali Muslim cultural identity in late colonial era.[39] Indeed, the imagining of East Bengal as a Muslim land with its own cultural autonomy and political economic vitality was dashed to ground through another set of internal colonization involving political, identarian and economic modes of management in Pakistan. To revisit Devji, in his important work on the 'Muslim Zion', he also misses the idea of sense of belonging of Bengali Muslims to their land and environment that informed their Pakistani nationalism in the forties. He sweeps this under the carpet because he views Pakistani nationalism solely from the perspective of M. A.

Jinnah and the Muslim League's all-India executive committee.[40] In 1947, at the very moment of the birth of Pakistan, Muslim League leaders in Bengal, Suhrawardy and Abul Hashim, also floated a proposal of united Bengal. Indeed, 1971 was a culminating point of a political journey that started long back. Though in no way such journey was unilinear and unidirectional, it assumed a complex form with various twists and turns. Obviously, no birth of a nation is a process strewn with certitude.

This book engages with this history within a particular global context of the sixties. Pioneering Marxist historian Badruddin Umar[41] has provided a part of this story, and subaltern historian Ahmed Kamal has engaged with the period of the fifties highlighting subaltern anger in East Bengal with insensitive bureaucratic state.[42] Umar's masterly account of the language movement in East Bengal in Bengali provides an analysis of the events in East Pakistan between 1947 and 1952.[43] Furthermore, Tariq Ali has provided an enriching chronicle of the student uprising of 1968–69. He also mentions the local and global contexts of the perennial crisis of legitimacy of the Pakistani state and the political and economic reasons for the same.[44] Nurul Kabir, a well-known Bangladeshi journalist, has written a monograph on the sixties uprising in Bangladesh.[45] Though their treatment is episodic, these texts help us to understand the underlying political events and implicit imagination of student actors in such movements. Three Bangladeshi scholars – Lenin Azad,[46] Morshed Shafiul Hasan[47] and Shekhar Dutta[48] – have produced nuanced and complex accounts of events in the global sixties explaining the role of political economy in such crisis. In addition, Hasan has analysed the intellectual origins of various ideas that informed the process of the making of Bangladesh[49]. As these accounts were in Bengali, they are not readily available to international readers. Given the politics of language in global academia, unless translated, these accounts would remain unknown in the international scholarly circle. Thus, the understanding of a crucial aspect of the global sixties and South Asian history of nation-formation in the post-colonial era would remain a rather skewed, whereby Bengali Muslims would remain in exile to their own history, political imagination and cultural predilections. More importantly, ideological contestations over the implications of the global sixties would remain unknown. This book thereby engages with these aspects.

Indeed, a critical characteristic of the global sixties is the complexities of ideological struggle within the left which took place under the shadow of another 'cold war', namely the Sino-Soviet rivalry. The critical impact of the Chinese Revolution on ideological debates within the left remains an understudied subject. Although China's foreign-policy reach was limited, its critique of Soviet positions had far-reaching effects. Beginning in the late fifties, numerous activists, politicians and intellectuals travelled to China from East Pakistan. Sheikh Mujibur Rahman was one of them. He has recalled his visit to China in elaborate detail in his unpublished autobiography and a travelogue.[50] Bhashani met directly with Zhou Enlai and was deeply impressed by China's agrarian revolution.[51] Indeed, in the fifties, the NAP, of which the Communist Party of Bangladesh was the principal clandestine constituent, emerged as a major alternative to the Awami League, the pivotal advocate for East Pakistan's regional autonomy. However, the NAP lost its efficacy to some degree when the party split in 1967. The seemingly pro-Chinese Bhashani wing of the NAP played a critical role in organizing peasant protests during the 1969 struggle. But the division within the left among the pro-Soviet and pro-Chinese wings, and later, the further fragmentation of the pro-Chinese left into several rival political formations, such as the Communist Party of East Pakistan (Marxist–Leninist) and the Communist Party of East Bengal (Marxist–Leninist), profoundly influenced the outcome of the global sixties in East Pakistan. The internal schisms within the left and, particularly, the pro-Chinese left's growing distance from the nationalist upsurge created a political vacuum within the protest movement. Meanwhile, the pro-Soviet Communist Party became closely aligned with the regional autonomy movement, but the party had no decisive influence due to its relatively smaller membership and instead acted as a battered remnant of the earlier robust, but clandestine, communist network.

Due to the internal paralysis of the left, the Awami League could establish a hegemonic position within the pro-democracy movement. The revolution of 1969 opened up an opportunity to further radicalize the political agenda of Bengali nationalism. However, the left's confusion, arising from their conflicting interpretations of the implications of Chinese geostrategic manoeuvrings in South Asia, rendered them ineffective during the liberation struggle. In post-liberation Bangladesh, Cuba's own contribution to the ideological critique of Soviet Marxism was similarly profound. Many nationalist-minded Bengalis were inspired by Cuba's autonomous brand of Marxism, though they never followed its direct dictum or had links with the Cuban Communist Party. These independent Marxists established a National Socialist Party that sought to develop an independent stance on Bangladeshi politics based on Marxist interpretations as well as an opposition to what they called the Indo-Soviet axis of aggression.[52] Thus, in turn, the fierce competition for ideological hegemony among the Soviet Union, China and Cuba contributed to, in myriad ways, the fragmentation of the left. This, in turn, profoundly impacted the course of events in East Pakistan and Bangladesh. In doing so, the pro-Chinese communists posed a direct challenge to the more established Soviet-aligned centre–left coalition of the Awami League, the Communist Party of Bangladesh and the pro-Soviet NAP. Armed confrontations in post-liberation Bangladesh clearly had a deep historical resonance with similar splits happening elsewhere in the world.

A second theme, crucial in the Pakistani context, is that of internal colonization and the idea of 'national liberation'. These are the elements that lent such rhetorical power to Sheikh Mujib and made Bengali nationalism a new post-colonial force. Bengali nationalism had also sought to explore how other Third World intellectual, political and cultural currents shaped the sentiments, strategies and tactics of building post-colonial cultural identities. Broadly, this meant that the empowerment of the Third World itself served as a driving force towards the realization of Bengali political aspirations. For the left, the pursuit of 'national liberation' required rupturing the compact of US foreign policy and the Pakistani military junta and their political economic policies, which I call praetorian capitalism. The left also made the stranglehold of the military-sponsored financial oligarchs over Pakistan's national resources – a point of contestation. Consequently, the rhetoric of national liberation in East Pakistan, in its more radical forms, envisioned the absolute recuperation of national resources, the elimination of oligarchic control over national resources, complete sovereignty in international relations, particularly in relation to Pakistan and India, and the forging of a 'national consciousness'. Like all nationalisms, the latter had a xenophobic impulse. This was articulated through a thinly disguised hatred towards the Urdu-speaking minority in East Pakistan. Thus, a few within the national liberation struggle aimed at the purging not only of bourgeois desires but also of putative 'non-national' ones. The result was a complicated, but ultimately unsuccessful, process of repression of signs of cultural hybridity by Bengali nationalists. Nationalism thus acted like Damocles' sword on Bangladeshi society.

Vital to the understanding of the complex divisions within the left and nationalist movements is an examination of culture, entailing the exposition of the relationship between politics, national identity and the global counterculture. Indeed, the sixties produced an 'international language of dissent' with a transnational circulation and appropriation of common written texts, films, graphic arts, music and individuals associated with the left. For instance, one must consider here the ideological impact of Nazim Hikmet and Paul Robeson, as well as the songs associated with the US civil rights movement on both sides of Bengal.[53] Indeed, both sides of Bengal had their own robust counter-hegemonic cultural movements grounded in an original understanding of folk music and storytelling combined with avant-garde elements. These cultural movements were by no means 'external' to the debates occurring on the issues related to the empowerment of workers, peasants and the youth. On the contrary, they were in conversation with the struggles against class-based exploitation, state-sponsored religious nationalism and patriarchal familial restraints and individualistic pursuits. The meaning of a presumably given essentialist ethnic identity, in the context of East Pakistan, such as the term 'Bengali', is fraught with tensions and significant contestations. The idea of a linguistic identity that the local population shared with the Indian Bengal did not automatically translate into a plank of cultural and political mobilization. New forms of poetry, music, cultural celebrations and rituals, combined with political readings of linguistic–cultural identity, brought a certain strain of Bengali identity to the consciousness of the emergent middle class. The conception of identity here was wide in its span, recognizing the nearly millennium-long shared cultural existence of a linguistic community, one that had recently been sundered apart due to the colonial drawing of borders.

Importantly, it posited such an identity as a critical platform for political mobilization. Yet this cultural movement too had its own limitations. Central to this politics of culture was the presumption that the student population, comprising largely of middle- and upper-class youth, constituted a revolutionary vanguard. Students in higher-education institutions were perceived as the most important opinion-builders in society and were central to the modernization policies and strategies of nation-formation in Pakistan. In addition, students' selection of music, films, clothing and literature informed the shaping of new social identities. Thus, strategically students and youths were equipped to disrupt these projects of nation-building and could potentially challenge an established political order on the streets as well as at a discursive level.

Analysing Internal Colonization and a Gramscian Interpretation of State Formation in Bangladesh

Though the narrative here focuses on the unfolding of events during the global sixties in Bangladesh, the underlying analysis shares a theoretical framework, with ideas about internal colonization. In analysing politics in East Pakistan and Bangladesh, it is necessary to deal with the idea of internal colonization. Harold Wolpe's conceptualization, utilized here, refers to a situation in which one finds 'within a single nation-state a relationship characteristic of the external relationships between imperialist states and their colonies'.[54] Further, Pablo Casanova has identified seven features of colonialism by defining a colony as the following: (*a*) a territory without self-government (*b*) in an unequal position with respect to the metropolis, where inhabitants do govern themselves, (*c*) and the responsibility for administering which is a concern of the dominant state, and (*d*) whose inhabitants do not participate in elections to higher administrative bodies – that is, rulers are assigned by the dominating country, (*e*) the rights of whose inhabitants, their economic situation and their social privileges are regulated by another state, (*f*) the position of whose inhabitants does not correspond to natural bonds but rather to artificial models, which are the products of conquest or of international concession, (*g*) and whose inhabitants belong to a race, culture and/or linguistic identity different from that of the dominating people.[55] In the East Pakistani context, every point in Casanova's categorization is applicable. This categorization of internal colonization may invite charges of an overtly superficial or functional approach to colonization, understood as a social, economic and political process. But there is a deeper historical reason to refer to East Pakistanis as victims of internal colonization – this experience remained central to the evolution of a national identity in Bengal among Muslims. In the British imperial era, there existed two different modes of governance and colonization in Bengal. While imperial rulers constituted the government that presided over the siphoning of surplus, it partially delegated the management of rural resources in Bengal to intermediary tenure-holders, creating a comprador class. In Bengal, upper-caste Hindu land-holding elites, and associated lower-level service elites, refashioned language and orchestrated a classicization of culture, in a manner that marginalized and ostracized Bengali Muslim cultural sensitivities. This situation became increasingly problematic as the economic marginalization of Bengali Muslims was accompanied by customary discriminations based on the high-caste Hindu rules of purity and pollution. Language also remained a critical marker of difference here. Even as Bengali authors, such as Mir Mosharraf Hossain, searched for alternative venues to classicize Bengali Muslim culture (in his case, by referencing historic events in Arabia), they scrupulously omitted references to colloquially used words in the Bengali Muslim household, including 'Allah'.[56] In the post-colonial era, as a reaction to such cultural marginalization, Bengali Muslim cultural personalities promoted the influence of Urdu vocabulary, and it was no accident that the first seminal cultural organization in Dacca was named Tamaddun Majlish, where both the words are Urdu that were quite uncommon in Bengali. Yet, in many ways, Bengali Muslim culture specifically, and East Bengali culture in general, continued to be perceived even after the partition by Pakistani authorities in an essentially neo-colonial manner. For them, East Bengali culture was at a more primitive level of development, requiring paternal protection by the state's praetorian guards. They regarded Urdu as a shared language of connectivity among Indian Muslims. It is true that from the late nineteenth century onwards, north Indian Muslim elites fought a rear-guard action for the preservation of *nastaliq*[57] as the script of government language in the United Provinces.[58] All over West Pakistan, local elites prioritized the use of Urdu over their mother tongue because of its status as the cultural vehicle of north Indian Islamic civilization. But in Bengal, for nearly 50 years, Bengali Muslim authors invested research in their claims to Bengali culture against the processes of internal colonization by Sanskritic[59] high-cultural considerations.

Abdul Karim Sahitya Bisharad, for example, spent his whole life unearthing Muslim contributions to medieval Bengali culture, in turn significantly modifying the extant history of the society.[60] So the Bengali Muslim cultural question was based on the recognition of difference rather than the erasure of Bengali linguistic tradition. Yet the praetorian guards of the capital and the state precisely mistook this cultural question to be a question of national integration because of their notion of West Pakistan as the primary location of Pakistani polity and economy. In many ways, such cultural obsessions were symptomatic of the absence of a hegemonic social class that could congeal into a historic bloc in power so necessary to preside over what Antonio Gramsci calls the transition from a 'mechanical bloc of social forces often of different races' in pre-capitalist social formations to an organic bloc (if we contextualize 'race' as a signifier of linguistic–cultural groups).[61] In multinational Pakistan, there existed no such organic hegemonic class, and the capitalist class was formed through a military-sponsored economic policy within a context that Ayesha Jalal labels as 'martial-law economics'.[62] The military-bureaucratic compact failed to provide cultural hegemony, rendering this a classic situation of, in the words of Ranajit Guha, 'dominance without hegemony'.[63]

It appears, in many respects, the Awami League was to play the decisive role in consolidating such a historic bloc through 'hybridization', rather than overthrowing, of the colonial state in Pakistan. The inflexible attitude of the military-bureaucratic junta and revolutionary dynamics from below, however, undermined such a neat transition. The military-bureaucratic compact in 1969, in the East Pakistani context, was premised upon an ethno-linguistic divide that bordered on racial exclusivity of the colonial regime. Thus, the revolution of 1969 triggered a crisis in the military-bureaucratic compact. In this period of crisis, a new relationship between structures and superstructures was essential to be forged – one that would correspond with the new constellation of historical forces. Was a new historic bloc formed in Bangladesh, as opposed to Pakistan, which could link the disparate elements of a 'national bourgeoisie' to the residual coercive functionaries of the post-colonial state, bureaucracy and judiciary, police and military? Did Bangladesh, in its respective ways, experience a modernizing 'passive revolution' of sorts, originating in this historical conjuncture? Clearly, the creation of any post-liberation hegemony required more than the conclusion of a political deal to create cohesion and solidarity between old and new elites, those who would then go on to constitute a new political ruling class, whose main function would be to dominate and lead an uneven and fractious alliance of subordinate classes and communities. Yet, given the hyper-mobilized state of the Bangladeshi society and the ideological polarization among radical political activists, no mechanism was available to achieve hegemony. This is because the new state did not merely have to assimilate the intellectuals inherited from the praetorian neo-colonial state and its institutions, but also recruit those 'organic' intellectuals whose links to the masses and to civil society were not exclusively formal or bureaucratic.[64] As Gramsci stresses, it is necessary for the intellectual not just to 'know' but to 'understand and feel' his or her relation to the people. Herein lies the significance of a re-conceived civil society that includes the whole domain of culture, discourses and language, literature, folklore and, indeed, the whole universe of symbolic representation to be found in the popular culture, or rather popular cultures, of the land.[65] Gramsci argues that the revolutionaries had to wage a 'war of position', a long struggle on the terrain of civil society with the aim of changing what is understood as the 'common sense' of doing politics.[66]

Here, to understand the pattern of state-formation in the post-liberation context, we can put Gramsci into dialogue with Fanon. Fanon clearly warns, in his posthumously published *The Wretched of the Earth*, that if the post-colonial nations failed to produce socially committed elites, then the state might lead towards a culture of racketeers who would simply be a caricature of their Western mentors,[67] or, in the case of Bangladesh, to paraphrase Fanon, the earlier military-bureaucratic compact. In such a context, liberation struggles could become one-party regimes, and there could emerge a 'modern form of bourgeois dictatorship, without mask, without make-up, without scruple and cynical'.[68] And a path to 'tribalist dictatorships' would also come into existence, bolstered by the masters of yesterday.[69] Bringing this analysis together with Gramsci's, it becomes apparent that the failure to congeal an ideological hegemony through a war of position heralded a Bangladesh where the warnings of Fanon, the foremost revolutionary of the global sixties, would become tragically true.

Towards Chapter Planning

The first chapter in this book discusses the process of imagining a nation and the fragility of the nation state as a political entity in the Global South. The contradiction between the desire for national sovereignty and the crucial limits in the way of exercising this sovereignty generated tensions that informed and influenced politics in the post-colonial world. These tensions, coupled with the uneven and combined development of national polities in the Global South, transformed the national question into a perennially unresolved problem. In a multilingual political entity such as united Pakistan, the central government's perceptions of threats to its security clashed with demands for the empowerment of territorially distributed nationalities. This became more acute in the context of East Pakistan. The rise of religious nationalism in eastern India was described as a fallout of the class struggle that had resisted the internal colonization of the Muslim peasantry of East Pakistan. But the very formation of a territorially compact and culturally near-homogeneous political entity gave rise to other means of imagining a perennial community in the context of Pakistan. Given the uneven development within the context of Pakistan, a new form of internal colonization defined the relationship between East Pakistan and West Pakistan. The central government prioritized the survival of the political centre over that of its constituent units. A critical fallout of this centralizing drive, premised upon a hastily constructed notion of South Asian Muslim identity, was the cultural introspection that slowly led towards assertions of Bengali identity.

The second chapter picks up the political story that evolved in the context of this greater cultural reconfiguration and deals with the history of political mobilization for autonomy in East Pakistan as it took place under the shadow of the Cold War. In 1954, the elections to the provincial legislature exposed the limitations of the constitutional structure of governance in East Pakistan. The rise of the military-bureaucratic compact as the ruling power bloc in Pakistan was accompanied by Pakistan's growing imbrication into Cold War alignments, specifically, with the US-sponsored military blocs. This led to a fissure within the Awami League over the question of the efficacy of this Cold War alignment. The shadow of global conflict informed local party-political alignments, and with this, East Pakistani politics entered the stage of the revolutionary global sixties. The situation was complicated by the emergence of direct military-bureaucratic control over the state.

The third chapter deals with the Bengali cultural identity in East Pakistan. The idea of being 'Bengali', and the identarian movement associated with it, was about a century long. Internal colonization and cultural marginalization defined the existence of the vast majority of Muslims in Bengal. In the colonial period, a significant minority of the Muslim middle classes tried to develop a standardized Bengali language to serve as a vehicle of cultural articulation for the Muslim masses. The use of Sanskrit-standardized Bengali as the medium of writing also heightened these notions of difference. This construction of a separate cultural register for Bengali Muslims was a source of debate for many intellectuals in East Pakistan. The announcement of Urdu as a national language, and the concomitant declaration that Bengali was an inappropriate cultural medium for a nation established through the Muslim nationalist movement, created a space for oppositional activity among Bengali students. Furthermore, this did not exhaust debates over the distinctiveness of Bengali culture in East Bengal. Was the cultural heritage of Bengal clearly defined? Was Rabindranath Tagore, a pre-eminent Bengali poet and writer, whose language was permeated with non-Muslim imageries, appropriate for Pakistani culture? Can Tagore's songs be considered appropriate for the articulation of intimate feelings such as love, devotion and patriotism in a predominantly Muslim cultural milieu? What is the relationship between the vast corpus of folk literature that is suffused with pre-Islamic heritages and the official cultural policy of the state? There took place a significant degree of cultural struggle in terms of forms, themes and structures of poetry, novels, songs and even mediums of public entertainment such as cinema and theatre. At the forefront of this cultural introspection was a group of writers, poets, cultural activists and film-makers who sought to define a counter-hegemonic cultural sphere. Many of them were persuaded by the idea of socialism, and some of them had active links with the global revolutionary movements, while a few were themselves global peripatetic revolutionaries. The efforts of these artists led to the rise of a positive self-perception of being Bengali in East Bengal. Their cultural work emphasized a shared history of community-formation and cultural traditions among Bengalis of all religions for nearly a thousand years. From films based on folk culture to the celebration of the writings of Tagore, Kazi Nazrul Islam and Jibanananda Das to the those of Jasim Uddin, Shamsur Rahman, Al Mahmud and Nirmalendu Goon, Bengal witnessed a complex synthesis of Bengali identity and Muslim cultural ethos. Unlike the official ideology of the Pakistani state, they did not put these two critical selves into a confrontational mode.

The class alignment in Pakistan under the military-bureaucratic regime acquired the characteristics of state-sponsored capitalistic development; the state assisted in the process of capitalist accumulation and brought into existence a 'bourgeois' class that was subservient to the interests of the regime. Gradually, the military as an institution acquired a distinctive corporate presence in the economy. The state utilized international patronage to augment its armament industry and military stockpile. The fourth chapter focuses on the making of praetorian state. In the early sixties, under praetorian guards, Pakistan was pursuing a process of capitalist modernization in alliance with the US. There existed a deep political–ideological symbiosis between the policies of the Pakistani military-bureaucratic regime, the US policy makers and influential academics connected with the political establishment. With massive aid from Western donors, followed by encouragement from the US administration and the Harvard-based American advisors, military rulers adopted a growth-oriented economic policy between 1958 and 1969. During this decade, Pakistan witnessed an expansion in its industrial base concomitant with the rise of a large working class. Ayub Khan also initiated an economic policy through the Fauji Foundation that allowed the transfer of ownership of state land to the army, as well as the retraining of military personnel who sought jobs in the private sector at state expense, and the unhindered circulation of military officers from the army to private industry. This established the foundation of military control over the economy and the new form of capitalistic development in Pakistan that could be termed praetorian capitalism. Yet such growth-oriented strategies were not accompanied by an attention to social equity. Consequently, despite growth, economic and social inequalities between the two wings, as well as different social classes, deepened. The impact of such policies on East Pakistan transformed it into an internal colony. These policies provided little benefit to the poor peasants, expanding urban working classes and salaried middle classes in East Pakistan; the dialectics of response to these policies resulted in both the groundswell of revolutionary anger from below and the counter-revolutionary military reactions producing a similar violent reaction from above. Hereby, the US acted with the same Cold War calculations, culminating in the bloody events of 1971.

The fifth chapter deals with the radical shift within the popular student and workers' struggles, as well as peasant movements, towards a democratic struggle in Pakistan. In 1958, when Ayub Khan staged his coup d'état, the streets of the towns of East Pakistan remained calm. Nearly after a decade of palace intrigues, the formation of unstable ministerial coalitions and a veritable musical chair among politicians for the position of prime minister and chief minister, the suppressions of the popular electoral verdict had alienated people from political processes. Soon, radical ideas of revolution, now further informed by global politics of wars of national liberation in Africa and Asia, gained credence. Social coalitions forged through popular movements enabled new political leaders to embrace novel methods of resistance. The dialectics of politics marked by state-sponsored guided democracy and student resistance defined the early stage of the global sixties in East Pakistan. Soon the growing social inequality brought into existence a labour movement. Increasingly, labour militancy and strikes undermined the complacency of the military-bureaucratic regime. Ayub Khan engineered a victory for his candidature against combined opposition through the system of basic electorate. Yet opposition to his regime led him to a military adventure in Kashmir that generated a war-induced nationalism to strengthen his regime.

The sixth chapter deals with the rise of the autonomy movement in East Bengal; in the absence of old stalwarts such as Suhrawardy, Sheikh Mujib became the new leader of the organization. Based upon the old 21-points programme of the United Front of 1954 and the formulation of the doctrine of two economies for a bi-territorial state of Pakistan, Sheikh Mujib and his associates developed a shorter six-points programme that outlined a plan for a confederate structure in Pakistan with a weaker centre. In 1966, Sheikh Mujib tried to place his new programme before the people. His subsequent arrest and trial on a sedition charge gave him much more political publicity, along with the ongoing students, workers and peasants' movements, with Bhashani as the most visible representative, adding importance to Sheikh Mujib's release from prison. Yet the Sino-Soviet rivalry and heuristic debates among Maoists over revolutionary strategies led to innumerable splits in the rank of leftists in East Pakistan. While Bhashani became an isolated political figure, Sheikh Mujib gained enormous political dividend from his imprisonment and stubborn fight for the six-points programme. As Ayub resigned and Yahya Khan, his successor, declared martial law with the promise of elections, Sheikh Mujib became the voice for the autonomy movement, riding a strong undercurrent of student radicalism. Students awarded him the title 'Friend of Bengal' and constructed his iconic status. His rise subsequently altered the parameters of Bengali nationalism. In the elections in 1970, following a marauding cyclone, Sheikh Mujib-led six-point Awami League emerged victorious with an outright majority in the new national assembly of entire Pakistan. There were clear signs of a military confrontation, with the military regime amassing its military might, forestalling any possibility of a democratic negotiation. Sheikh Mujib launched a non-violent movement to secure a transfer of power. The militarily unprepared Bengali nationalists rushed towards an escalation of conflict, with Sheikh Mujib holding the balance through his formidable negotiation skills. Yet determined military rulers cracked down on the movement. This started a new phase of violent crackdown, and the subsequent guerrilla movement, accompanied by the Indian intervention, finally led to the birth of Bangladesh. Thus, in a longer perspective, it was far from certain that Bengali nationalism would have resulted in the establishment of an independent nation state. Even Bengali identity was not a given plank of mobilization; it was a product of the coalescing of different types of movements against the background of the sixties.

Notes

1. Tor Egil Førland, 'Cutting the Sixties Down to Size: Conceptualizing, Historicizing, Explaining', *Journal for the Study of Radicalism* 9, no. 2 (2015): 125–48, p. 126.
2. *The Sixties: A Journal of History, Politics and Culture*, cited in Førland, 'Cutting the Sixties Down to Size', p. 126, https://www.tandfonline.com/action/journalInformation?show=aimsScope&journalCode=rsix20 (accessed on 27 January 2020).
3. See Frantz Fanon and Anthony Appiah, *Black Skin, White Masks*, trans. Richard Philcox (New York: Grove Press, 2008 [1952]); Frantz Fanon and Adolfo Gilly. *A Dying Colonialism*, trans. Haakon Chevalier (New York: Grove Press, 1967); Frantz Fanon, *The Wretched of the Earth*, trans. Constance Farrington (London: Grove Press, 1968 [1961]); Frantz Fanon, *Toward the African Revolution: Political Essays*, trans. Haakon Chevalier (New York: Monthly Review Press, 1967).
4. See Che Guevara and David Deutschmann, *Che Guevara Reader: Writings by Ernesto Che Guevara on Guerrilla Strategy, Politics & Revolution* (Melbourne: Ocean Press, 1997).
5. See Regis Debray, *Revolution in the Revolution?: Armed Struggle and Political Struggle in Latin America* (Harmondsworth, Middlesex: Penguin Books, 1968).
6. See Mao Zedong, *On Practice and Contradiction*, with an introduction by Žižek Slavoj (London: Verso, 2007).
7. See Jean-Paul Sartre, *No Exit, and Three Other Plays* (New York: Vintage International, 1989); Louis Althusser, *For Marx* (London: Verso, 1990).
8. For details, see Ananta Yusuf, 'The Legacy of Madhu's Canteen', Daily Star, 13 September 2013, https://www.thedailystar.net/news/the-legacy-of-madhus-canteen (accessed on 27 November 2022).
9. For details regarding the global nature of the sixties, see Christopher Connery, 'The End of the Sixties', *Boundary 2* 36, no. 1 (2009): 183–210.
10. Fredric Jameson, 'Periodizing the 60s', *Social Text* 9, no. 10 (1984): 178–209, p. 180.
11. Aref Ahmed Kazi (with Abdur Rajjak and Serajul Alam Khan), *Bangalir Jatio Rastro* (Dhaka: Ankur Prokashoni, 2014), pp. 61–62.
12. The most crucial ideologue of such a vision was Serajul Alam Khan, who argued in terms of three resurrections of Bengali culture and society from the times of Shri Chaitanya and Sultan Alauddin Hussain Shah

to nineteenth-century Bengal renaissance and the establishment of the Bengali nation state in 1971. Serajul Alam Khan, *Swadhinata-Sososhtro Songram ebong Agamir Bangladesh* (Dhaka: Ankur Prokashoni, 2019), pp. 1–14.
13. Jameson, 'Periodizing the 60s', p. 205.
14. Mesbah Kamal, *Unosottorer Gonoobbuththan: Shahid Asad o Shreni Rajniti Prosonge* (Dhaka: Shrabon Prokashoni, 2006), pp. 69–70, 81–82; Badruddin Umar, *Ekattorer Swadhinota Juddher Pothe* (Dhaka: Jatio Sahitya Prokash, 2015), pp. 20–21; Mahbub Ullah, *Shater Doshoker Chatro Andolon o Onyanyo Prosongo* (Dhaka: Islam Gyan Bitoroni, 2001), pp. 35–38; Lenin Azad, *Unosottorer Gonoobbuththan: Rastro Somaj o Rajniti* (Dhaka: Jatio Sahitya Prokash, 2019 [1997]), pp. 449–51, 458–59, 463–64, 469–74, 475–76, 532–33, 586, 601–02.
15. Umar, *Ekattorer Swadhinota Juddher Pothe*, pp. 21–23; Kamal, *Unosottorer Gonoobbuththan*, pp. 50–51.
16. Eric Wolf, 'Peasant Rebellions', *International Social Science Journal* 21, no. 2 (1969): 286–93.
17. Hannah Arendt, *On Revolution* (New York: Viking Press, 1963), p. 259.
18. James DeNardo, *Power in Numbers* (Princeton, NJ: Princeton University Press, 1985), p. 11.
19. Peter Custers, 'Secular Democracy, Socialism and Bhasani', *Frontier Weekly* 41, no. 11 (2008), https://www.frontierweekly.com/archive/vol-number/vol/vol-41-2008-09/vol-41-11-14%20Sep%2028-Oct%2025%202008/bhasani-41-11-14.pdf (accessed on 15 March 2020).
20. Zillur R. Khan, 'Leadership and Political Opposition in Bangladesh', *Asian Affairs* 5, no. 1 (1974): 41–50.
21. Arthur Marwick, 'The Cultural Revolution of the Long Sixties: Voices of Reaction, Protest, and Permeation', *International History Review* 27, no. 4 (2005): 780–806.
22. For details, see Sumanta Banerjee, 'Bangladesh's Marxist-Leninists: I', *Economic and Political Weekly* 17, no. 32 (1982): 1267–71. For further details, see M. Rashiduzzaman, 'The Awami League in the Political Development of Pakistan', *Asian Survey* 10, no. 7 (1970): 574–87. There also exist several eyewitness accounts and analyses from participants. These will be analysed further in the book.
23. The most prescient analysis along this line can be found in secret diplomatic correspondences of the British High Commission. For example, a draft of the report on internal political situation in Pakistan in October

1969 briefly states: 'In East Pakistan the economic situation continues to deteriorate steadily and the outlook is bleak. No new investment has been coming forward and many Pakistani businessmen have been transferring assets to West Pakistan. Despite signs of official awareness of the urgent need to tempt more private capital to the East, the budget contained no new incentives specifically aimed at doing this.' FCO 37/474 1968/69, Confidential FSP 1/1 444A Foreign and Commonwealth Office Department, South Asian FSP1/1, Part 1, Pakistan Political Affairs (Internal): Internal Political Situation.
24. The term 'distant sovereign' is borrowed from the work of Sudipta Sen in another context. Sen, following the footsteps of Eric Stokes and Ranajit Guha, has argued that the British edifice of colonial state was exported from England. I am using the term in a limited sense to indicate how metropolitan power in Pakistan exported the constitution-making process to East Pakistan. Sudipta Sen, *Distant Sovereignty: National Imperialism and the Origins of British India* (New York: Routledge, 2002).
25. Richard Sission, and Leo E. Rose, *War and Secession: Pakistan, India, and the Creation of Bangladesh* (Berkeley: University of California Press, 1990).
26. See, for example, Shu-Mei Shih, 'Race and Relation: The Global Sixties in the South of the South', *Comparative Literature* 68, no. 2 (2016): 141–54; Burleigh Hendrickson, 'March 1968: Practicing Transnational Activism from Tunis to Paris', *International Journal of Middle East Studies* 44, no. 4 (2012): 755–74.
27. In a diplomatic report to the secretary of state, on 23 March 1971, N. A Burrows wrote: 'The President's broadcast speech of 6 March in which by implication he put most of the blame for the crisis on a "handful" of troublemakers in East Pakistan and expressed his determination – and that of the army – to maintain the integrity, solidarity and sovereignty of Pakistan may well have confirmed Mujib in his intention to implement civil disobedience campaign and to show the martial law regime just where the power really lay in what was now almost always referred to as "Bangla Desh", the land of Bengal. The point seems to have taken by the President because by Tuesday, 9 March, he initiated a series of conciliatory moves.' Restricted/Confidential/Secret/Foreign and Commonwealth Office Diplomatic Report, Department of South Asia, Dispatch from BHC Islamabad to Secretary of State, 23 March 1971; FCO file reference FSP1/2, Title of Paper: Pakistan's Political Crisis 'The March Days'; HM Diplomatic Service Dept or Post South Asian File NO F8 P1/1 Part A,

Title: Political Situation in Pakistan 5C/72 FCO37/870. After the 1970 election, Frank Sargeant, a British diplomat in Dacca, in a confidential letter, on 21 December 1970, to Sir Cyril Pickard, the then British High Commissioner stationed in Rawalpindi, wrote: 'Since the birth of Pakistan, the Bengalis of East Pakistan have been politically frustrated by their association with West Pakistan. To Bengalis, who had representative government to a considerable degree under the British, their political developments appear to have been throttled while they have had to wait for the people of West Pakistan to emerge from feudalism.' FCO 37/684 FSP 1/7, General Elections in Pakistan.

28. Bernardine Dohrn, 'Sixties Lessons and Lore', *Monthly Review* 53, no. 7, December 2001, p. 12.
29. Garry J. Bass, *The Blood Telegram: India's Secret War in East Pakistan* (New York: Random House, 2013).
30. Sreenath Raghavan, *1971: A Global History of the Creation of Bangladesh* (Cambridge, MA: Harvard University Press, 2013).
31. Sisson and Rose, *War and Secession*.
32. Sisson and Rose, *War and Secession*.
33. Nayanika Mookherjee, *The Spectral Wound: Sexual Violence, Public Memories and the Bangladesh War of 1971* (Durham: Duke University Press, 2015); Yasmin Saikia, *Women, War, and the Making of Bangladesh: Remembering 1971* (Durham, NC: Duke University Press, 2011); Salil Tripathi, *The Colonel Who Would Not Repent: The Bangladesh War and Its Unquiet Legacy* (Connecticut: Yale University Press, 2016).
34. Lawrence Ziring, *The Ayub Khan Era: Politics in Pakistan, 1958–1969* (Syracuse, NY: Syracuse University Press, 1971); Karl J. Newman, Heinz Pankalla and Robert Krumbein-Neumann, *Pakistan under Ayub Khan, Bhutto and Zia-Ul-Haq* (München: Weltforum Verlag, 1986); Herbert Feldman, *From Crisis to Crisis: Pakistan 1962–1969* (London: Oxford University Press, 1972); Karl von Vorys, *Political Development in Pakistan* (Princeton, NJ: Princeton University Press, 2016).
35. Saadia Toor, *The State of Islam: Culture and Cold War Politics in Pakistan* (London: Pluto Press, 2011).
36. Faisal Devji, 'End of the Postcolonial State', *Economic and Political Weekly* 56, no. 44 (October 2021): 67–72.
37. Anouar Abdel-Malek, *Nation and Revolution*, trans. Mike Gonzalez (*Social Dialectics*, vol. 2) (Albany, NY: State University of New York Press, 1981), pp. 13, 222.

38. Franz Fanon, *The Wretched of Earth*, trans. Constance Farrington (New York: Grove Press, 1968), pp. 247–48, quoted in Neil Lazarus, 'Disavowing Decolonization: Fanon, Nationalism, and the Problematic of Representation in Current Theories of Colonial Discourse', *Research in African Literatures* 24, no. 4 (1993): 69–98, https://jstor.org/stable/3820255 (accessed on 28 April 2020).
39. Neilesh Bose, *Recasting the Region: Language, Culture, and Islam in Colonial Bengal* (New Delhi: Oxford University, 2014).
40. Faisal Devji, *Muslim Zion: Pakistan as a Political Idea* (Cambridge, MA: Harvard University Press, 2013).
41. Badruddin Umar, *The Emergence of Bangladesh*, vol. 1: *Class Struggles in East Pakistan, 1947–1958* (Karachi: Oxford University Press, 2004). Also see Badruddin Umar, *The Emergence of Bangladesh*, vol. 2: *The Rise of Bengali Nationalism,1958–1971* (Karachi: Oxford University Press, 2006).
42. Ahmed Kamal, *State against the Nation: The Decline of the Muslim League in Pre-Independence Bangladesh, 1947–54* (Dhaka: University Press Limited, 2009).
43. Badruddin Umar, *Purbo Banglar Bhasha Andolon o Totkalin Rajniti* (Tritio Khondo) (Dhaka: Subarna, 2013).
44. Tariq Ali, *Pakistan: Military Rule or People's Power* (New York: William Morrow and Company, 1970).
45. Nurul Kabir, *Deposing of a Dictator Revisiting a Magnificent Mass Uprising after 50 Years* (Dhaka: Samhati Publications, 2020).
46. Azad, *Unosottorer Gonoobbuththan*.
47. Morshed Safiul Hasan, *Swadhinotar Potobhumi: 1960r Doshok* (Dhaka: Anupom Prokashoni, 2014).
48. Shekhar Dutta, *Shaater Doshoker Gono Jagoron: Ghotona Pobaho Parjyalochona Probhab* (Dhaka: Somaj Bikash Prokashoni, 2015).
49. Morshed Safiul Hasan, *Purbo Banglay Chinta Chorcha 1940–70: Dwondwo o Potikria* (Dhaka: Anupom Prokashoni, 2017), p. 465.
50. Sheikh Mujibur Rahman, *Asomapto Atmojiboni* (Dhaka: University Press, 2018); Sheikh Mujibur Rahman, *Amar Dekha Noya Chin* (Dhaka: Bangla Academy, 2020*)*.
51. For an access to Bhashani's ideas about China, see 'Record of Conversation between Zhou Enlai, Chen Yi, and Head of Pakistan's Delegation Participating in the PRC's National Day Celebration, Maulana Abdul Hamid Khan Bhashani', https://digitalarchive.wilsoncenter.org/document/121573.pdf (accessed on 23 June 2021).

52. For details, see Lawrence Lifschultz and Kai Bird, *Bangladesh: The Unfinished Revolution* (Asia Series, vol. 2) (London: Zed Press, 1979).
53. Poet Subhas Mukhopadhaya translated Hikmet's poems into Bengali. Those poems are collected in two anthologies, titled *Nirbachita Nazim Hikmet* (Selected Poems of Nazem Hikmet) (1952) and *Nazem Hikmet er Aro Kobita* (More Poems of Nazem Hikmet) (1974).
54. Harold Wolpe, 'The Theory of Internal Colonization: The South African Case', in *Societies of Southern Africa in the 19th and 20th Centuries*, vol. 5, pp. 105–120 (London: Institute of Commonwealth Studies, University of London, 1974).
55. Pablo Gonzalez Casanova, 'Internal Colonialism and National Development', *Studies in Comparative International Development* 1 (1965): 27–37.
56. Mir Mosharraf Hossain published *Bishad Sindhu* (Oceans of Sorrows) in three parts in 1885, 1887 and 1891. Based on both Persian sources and *punthi* literature in Bengal, he narrated the story of the death of Imam Hossain and Imam Hassan in Karbala. These songs were transmuted into folk songs known as 'Jari Gaan', which were sung as devotional songs in rural Bengal and thus familiarized rural Muslim devotees with tales of Muharram. For details, see Mou Banerjee, 'The Tale of the Tailor: Munshi Mohammad Meherullah and Muslim–Christian Apologetics in Bengal, 1885–1907', *South Asian Studies* 33, no. 2 (2017): 122–36, p. 123.
57. *Nastaliq* is the default Arabic script variant for the Urdu language, also used for Persian and other languages in Afghanistan, India, Iran and Pakistan.
58. For a succinct summary of the conflict which attracted major scholarly attention, see Robert D. King, 'The Poisonous Potency of Script: Hindi and Urdu', *International Journal of the Sociology of Language* 150 (2001): 43–59.
59. Sanskritic refers to Sanskrit-based, upper-caste Hindu high culture.
60. For details, see, for example, Bose, *Recasting the Region*, p. 128.
61. Antonio Gramsci, 'Note 18: History of the Subaltern Classes', in *Quaderni del Cacere* (Prison Notebooks), vol. 3, ed. V. Gerratana (Turin: Giulio Einaudi Editore, 1975). Also see Antonio Gramsci, *Selections from the Prison Notebooks of Antonio Gramsci*, ed. and trans. G. Nowell (New York: International Publishers, 1971), pp. 242–43.
62. Ayesha Jalal, *The State of Martial Rule: The Origins of Pakistan's Political Economy of Defence* (Cambridge South Asian Studies) (Cambridge: Cambridge University Press, 1990).

63. Ranajit Guha, *Dominance without Hegemony: History and Power in Colonial India* (Cambridge, MA: Harvard University Press, 1997).
64. I use here Kate Crehan's understanding of organic intellectual based on Gramsci's writing. She argues: 'Organic intellectuals are not a particular kind of intellectual. They are the form in which the knowledge generated out of the lived experience of a social group with the potential to become hegemonic achieves coherence and authority.' Kate Crehan, *Gramsci's Common Sense: Inequality and Its Narratives* (Durham, NC: Duke University Press, 2016), pp. 29–30.
65. For a detailed exposition of Gramsci's ideas, see Arun K. Patnaik, 'Gramsci's Concept of Common Sense: Towards a Theory of Subaltern Consciousness in Hegemony Processes', *Economic and Political Weekly* 23, no. 5 (January 1988): PE2–PE5, PE7–PE10.
66. Gramsci, *Selections from the Prison Notebooks*, pp. 34, 201–02, 419–72. For a detailed exposition of this point, see Mark Rupert, 'Globalising Common Sense: A Marxian–Gramscian (Re-)Vision of the Politics of Governance/Resistance', *Review of International Studies* 29 (December 2003): 181–98. See his discussion of war of position on p. 185.
67. Fanon, *The Wretched of the Earth*. See the third chapter 'The Pitfalls of National Consciousness', which is particularly relevant in this discussion.
68. Mireille Fanon-Mendès France, and Donato Fhunsu, 'The Contribution of Frantz Fanon to the Process of the Liberation of the People', *The Black Scholar* 42, nos. 3–4 (2012): 8–12.
69. Fanon, *The Wretched of the Earth*.

1

Nationality Question

Territoriality, Birth of East Pakistan and New Politics of Resistance

Tired by a long walk, I now sat down on a lonely mountain top and started observing the surroundings. I could see the never-ending Turkish military camps in front of us and heard the noises of canon firing from the side of Silivri. In my immediate vicinity, small *chiba* shrubs were moving like waves in the evening breeze. This scene reminded me of the coming of dusk over green fields and villages in Bengal. In my mind, I could hear the melodious tune sung by cowherds and peasants. Songs of birds and beauties of nature during spring in Bengal flashed in my mind's eye. I immediately started singing, 'Oh my golden Bengal, I love you.'[1]

So wrote Syed Abu Mohammad Ismail Hossain Siraji, a Bengali writer and a poet, who went to Ottoman Turkey as a member of the Indian medical delegation to assist the Khilafate during the first Balkan War in 1912. Siraji narrated the experience of his journey to Turkey in an epistolary form, which was serialized in the noted Bengali magazine *Mohammadi* in 1912. He later published these letters as a travelogue. In the description here, he is drawing a distinction between home and abroad. His zeal for the pan-Islamist cause brought him to the Balkans, and yet, here, in the midst of the war and noises of canon firing, he remembered Bengal. This sense of belonging to a global *ummah* Islamia and the simultaneous romantic invocation of Bengal as a homeland were complementary. As a devout Muslim, Siraji possibly could not associate with the deified form of 'mother Bengal', a powerful symbol in Indian nationalist Hindu political tradition;[2] yet Siraji was moved by the abstract image of 'mother Bengal' portrayed by Rabindranath Tagore in his song.

The intellectual journey of this patriotic song in Bengal is tied up with the cultural imagining of a homeland in different spatial and temporal contexts. In 1905, Bengal was gripped by the colonial decision to partition the province. The Hindu landowning gentry and professional elites were aghast at this decision. Feelings were ambiguous among Muslim Bengalis, who mostly inhabited the riverine tracks of eastern Bengal. A few among them joined the anti-partition agitation, but many remained silent, and over the months they welcomed the idea of a Muslim-majority province of Eastern Bengal and Assam.[3] In the midst of this polarizing moment, Tagore, as a pre-eminent poet and public intellectual, highlighted the idea of united Bengal in his patriotic songs. These songs were sung in meetings and political marches. He also transformed the Hindu ritual of Rakhi Bandhan – whereby sisters of all ages tie a talisman called *rakhi* around the wrists of their brothers to symbolically protect them from unforeseen dangers – into a social event by tying *rakhi* around the wrists of Muslims as a mark of brotherhood.[4] His creative impulse drew him to evoke the myth of a golden Bengal in a song entitled 'Sonar Bangla' (Golden Bengal), published in the Bengali literary journals *Bangadarshan* and *Baul* simultaneously in September 1905. Imagining a nation as a mother obviously has a masculine underpinning, whereby the map and space acquire an affective female dimension.[5] Yet the symbol of 'golden Bengal' communicates to Bengalis an image of a land of prosperity and abundance. It is a construct that is timeless and classless.[6]

In 1905, when Tagore wrote the song, his nephew Abanindranath Tagore drew the paintings of Banga Mata, the personification of an undivided Bengal that was soon to be divided to serve colonial administrative ends. In the younger Tagore's painting, the Hindu deity Laxmi is clad in a saffron sari[7] like an ordinary Bengali woman and appears to be holding in her four hands a book, sheaves of paddy, a piece of cloth and a rosary. Originating in the Tagore family, inflected with *swadeshi* patriotism of the anti-partition movement, the song and the painting have two different political journeys as the symbols of Bengali and Indian landscapes. While the painting had a different reincarnation in the form of a deified figure of 'Mother India' – Bharat Mata[8] – the first two stanzas of the song became the symbol of the predominantly Muslim Bengali nationalism in Bangladesh during the liberation struggle in 1971 and were later adopted as the national anthem, even though Tagore was a sharp critic of nationalism as a political phenomenon.[9] The song's adoption as a national anthem did not go unquestioned in Bangladesh,[10] but the emotive appeal of the song continued to move millions in the country as it bridges the territoriality of a nation state with an emotive sense of belonging.

This idea of territoriality in Bengal was, doubtless, a product of colonial capitalism. However, contrary to the unilinear understanding of territorialized nationalism and colonial cartography in the region, according to which 'Mother India' stands for South Asia,[11] I propose that the colonial map did not evoke the image of a spatialized geo-body of an Indian nation in Bengal and, even more particularly, in Eastern Bengal. Yet the sense of belonging to Bengal, among Muslim Bengalis, could not be reduced to an abstract notion of 'Muslim Zion' or to that of a nation state that was territorially neutral. Faisal Devji conceptualizes 'Zion' as a political form that declines hereditary connections between ethnicity and soil in favour of membership based on nothing but an idea of belonging.[12] This again produces a reductionist view of the Pakistan movement. The production of space comprises complex affective but also economic and political processes across different temporalities through which Muslim Bengalis dialectically adopted, imagined and deployed their strategies of making a 'community and nation'. Such strategies were embedded in the spatio-temporal contexts of given historical moments. Space was produced in interaction with the political and economic forces as well as the social structuration that informed the historical processes behind these politics.[13]

This chapter explores the interaction between the processes of the production of space and political articulation in that particular temporal context. It investigates the experience of subaltern social classes during the formative years of Pakistan as a nation state, with a focus on their relations to territoriality. It demonstrates that with the partition of Bengal and India in 1947, a contradictory political process came into existence. The territorialization of East Pakistan as a bounded political entity led to a gradual etiolation of justifications of Pakistani nationalism. The hold of Hindu landlordism and Brahmanical hierarchical culture that reminded Muslim peasants of their humiliating subaltern status and provided popular legitimacy to Pakistani nationalism lost its raison d'être in post-colonial Pakistan, as the state in East Pakistan altered colonial economic linkages, class structure and political economy. The 'nationalization' of territory and population under conditions of post-colonial nation-building brought into existence endemic border conflict and vicious sectarian riots. The rupture of complex networks of movement of commodities, capital and labour over the space of a united Bengal and Assam also ushered in severe economic dislocation. A constant threat of hunger became the condition of life for the poor peasants in East Bengal. The continuation, and, in many instances, strengthening, of colonial bureaucratic governance dashed to the ground the euphoria of liberation from both formal colonial rule and conditions of internal colonization by Hindu landlords.

The fear of the ubiquitous presence of India remained imprinted on the East Pakistani psyche; at the same time, the peculiar territorial location of East Bengal, later rechristened as East Pakistan, also confirmed the necessity of cross-border ties. The centralized state of Pakistan appeared to be a remote administrative apparatus that institutionalized bureaucratic domination. New national bureaucracy, to paraphrase Frantz Fanon, 'had nothing to do with transforming the nation; it consists, prosaically, of being the transmission line between the nation and a capitalism, rampant though camouflaged, which today puts on the mask of neo-colonialism'.[14]

Soon a new form of affective nationalism arose, which sought to transform the bureaucratic administrative state into an imagined community having roots in local culture with a 'nationalitarian' potential.[15] This dynamic dance between hopes and frustrations led towards an exploratory beginning of a new nationalistic politics that inscribed an affective belonging to Bengal within the territorial and ethno-demographic reality of post-colonial Pakistan. The 1954 popular elections led to the dismantling of the Muslim League–led government in East Bengal, which marked a new phase in East Pakistani politics. This chapter studies the period between 1947 and 1954 as a critical era that saw Pakistani nationalism lose its legitimacy in East Bengal.

The Politics of Border-Making: Trade and Territoriality of East Pakistan

Tajuddin Ahmad, a 22-year-old Muslim League activist from East Bengal, meticulously kept daily journals in his youth. On 14 August, the day before independence, an excited Tajuddin wrote in his diary: 'Today at midnight British rule is going to end and Indians will start governing themselves.'[16] He described in vivid details the events of 15 August 1947, the day Pakistan came into existence as an independent state.[17] The decorated city of Dacca (present-day Dhaka), with its gates and streets illuminated between Babubajar Bridge and Mogultully, thrilled Tajuddin. Friendship and amity prevailed among Muslims and Hindus, and an atmosphere of gay merriment prevailed in the town. Despite there being rains on the previous few days, the day of independence was sunny and unusually warm. There were people in all open spaces of the town, including the mosques and the railway station, Tajuddin observed. In the morning, around 10.30 a.m., the chief justice, Akium, administered the oath of office to the prime minister, Khawaja Nazimuddin, and two other ministers, Nurul Amin and Hamidul Haq Chowdhury. The last British governor, Frederick C. Bourne, was also sworn in. At 3.30 p.m. a long procession started. Nazimuddin, the premier of East Bengal, along with the nawab of Dacca, headed the procession in a car. Around 4 p.m. the procession reached Victoria Park, where the flag of Pakistan was hoisted. The meeting started amidst chanting from the Koran. At night there was a display of fireworks.[18] As a young Muslim Leaguer, Tajuddin was definitely elated at the establishment of a Muslim 'homeland' in his beloved Bengal. Tajuddin's sentiment was shared by millions in East Bengal that day.

Yet, as soon as the celebration of independence from colonial rule was over, the grim reality of the partition became manifest. The making of an international border would sever critical politico-economic sinews that had evolved over the last century with colonial capitalist penetration. The area that came to constitute East Pakistan was not only densely populated, but also expanding in terms of spatial limits through the export of rice and jute cultivation, as well as through the colonization of virgin land in neighbouring Assam. This migration was assisted by the introduction of steamer and railways. The colonial intervention to restrict the flow of immigrant settlers through the line system had led to confrontations between the settlers and the various segments of local population. Now, on the other hand, an international border had transformed Bengali settlers into foreigners.[19] In the north-east, many Bengali peasants were settling further deeper into the native states of Tripura and expanding the ecological frontier of dynamic rice-based agriculture.[20] There also existed a symbiotic relationship between the economies of the hill people and the inhabitants of the river delta in the plains. Directly to the north of East Bengal, relationships with those from the Khasi, Garo and Jayantia hills were structured through diverse forms of trades and commodity exchanges.[21] These ties were further strengthened through the existence of nested communities of the hill people in various locations in north Bengal, such as the Garos, Hajongs, Khasis and Lushais.[22] More importantly, tea plantations located in the Assam valley and in Sylhet were connected with the port of Calcutta (present-day Kolkata) and Chittagong (present-day Chattogram), partly through steamer lines and partly via railways.[23] In the west, the province was connected with Calcutta, which remained the centre of economic life in colonial Bengal. The most vital cash crop, jute, was processed and exported through the city of Calcutta to overseas destinations. The jute trade was controlled by a British cartel – the Indian Jute Manufacturer's Association – and its Marwari intermediaries.[24] Jute remained the most important source of cash in rural Bengal.[25] The political economy of East Bengal remained integrally related to this vast and complex spatial network of production and consumption.

Partition and border-making disrupted this complex and integrated Bengali spatial expanse that had come into existence, particularly since 1857.[26] The political sovereignty of East Pakistan crucially hinged on the enforcement of this border. But the spatial logic of political–economic ties dictated otherwise. This contradiction between, on the one hand, the political logic of border-making and the territorialization of the state-space and, on the other, the economic force of a century-long process of spatial integration and linkage clashed with each other. As a consequence, the post-partition border became a site of conflict, fragmentation and contestation. In 1947, tensions flared up on all sides of the border. Even the remote Noakhali, on the south-eastern border of East Bengal with the princely state of Tripura, which joined India in 1947, witnessed a significant degree of tensions. A Pakistani officer's report describing an incident on the Tripura border provided a theatrical quality to an instance of such confrontation. According to the report, on 6 October 1948, around 11 armed men from Tripura state forcibly crossed into the Pakistani border, with a doctor and a court sub-inspector riding on an elephant. These people were ostensibly returning from an inquest and took a short route through the East Bengal territory to their headquarters in Belonia town in Tripura. Even though there existed a long circuitous route through the forested regions within Tripura, the Pakistani officer grumbled, they preferred a straight path through the East Bengal territory. On the way, inside East Bengal, these Indian officials arrested three Pakistanis on the ground that they were grazing cattle and cutting forest produce in Tripura state without permit.[27] This arrest produced discontent among villagers, and the Pakistani official recorded the ensuing confrontation in great detail:

> This wrongful arrest of their fellow villagers aroused intense indignation amongst the local people and an alarm was raised, with the result that when the Tripura Party reached village Nijkalikapur also in Noakhali, they were confronted by an angry crowd of some 150 villagers who

demanded the release of their prisoners. The five prisoners made a break for freedom, and the armed personnel then opened fire, injuring two of them. They beat a retreat taking with them one of the injured men among another of the prisoners but leaving behind the elephant and its mahut, which were seized by the local people and handed over to the police.[28]

The conflict thus did not simply evolve around the innocuous transgression of the border. Rather, such a contestation involved making claims over the produce of the land and, significantly, took place between the peasants and the newly constituted post-colonial state authority. The exercise of sovereignty over the state-space by the officials of the Tripura court here infringed on the routine quotidian political economy of marginal people living in the borderland. Hence, it provoked violent resistance from the subaltern population. The border created a new spatial hierarchy that impacted the subsistence economic activity of the people who lived on the margins of the society and who discovered their locations on another new margin: that of a 'nation'.

As a meeting point between the state and the people, border politics in this instance involved struggles over the economic and political rights in a newly turned foreign land. The superintendent of the police in Tippera district (Comilla) candidly wrote in his report:

> It appears that the Pakistani Muslims of the area on the border of the state mostly depend for the livelihood either on the land situated within the [Tripura] state territory or on the products of the reserve forest belonging to the [Tripura] state. A system of permits exists by which all people living in Pakistan have to pay a scheduled rate of taxes for bringing any of the permissible products of the reserve forests, for grazing cattle and also for harvesting paddy belonging to their own land in the state's territory. For sometimes past these scheduled rates have been increased inordinately which has affected the poor people on the border very seriously. Reports have been received that of late the state authorities have prohibited the harvesting and removal of aus paddy from such lands.[29]

In the context of the rice economy on East Pakistan's border, Malini Sur recently hypothesized that 'as locations of strife and political actions, borders enable anthropology to rethink the relationship between politics and mobility'.[30] However, while the border tension around rice cultivation became the new normal after partition, there took place multifarious dislocations in the previously integrated regional economies along the newly drawn border lines. At the bottom level there were mundane police reports from the Tripura and East Bengal border which indicate how local petty officials' actions disrupted a routine economy. One report described in detail such an instance:

> In the 3rd week of April last [year], Harish Chandra De, head forest guard, detained 33 cows of Pakistani people of P. S. Kotwali on the ground that they had entered the teak forest. He released the cows after realizing Rs. 3 per cow, although these persons had valid grazing permits from the state.[31]

Notwithstanding the petty corruption of state officials on both sides of the border, this instance simply indicated the altered spatial practice of governance in quotidian life. This was recognized by district officials on both sides. Exasperated by the complaints of their respective citizens, officials of both East Pakistan and Tripura met at the Dewan's place in Agartala on 12 January 1949 and decided that 'no useful purpose will be served by discussing such incidents in details [sic] as both sides had a long list of complaints against the other and joint enquires [will] be conducted into major incidents only'.[32] This decision indicated that local officials could not resolve a conflict that had an extra-local dimension. The solution of quotidian problems of peasants, woodcutters and grazers now classified as 'Pakistani' had to be resolved at the national level in East Pakistan through a spatial reorganization of political economy.

The impact of the newly constituted border became all-pervasive on inter-dominion economic activity. Railway transportation of goods was marked by intense and prolonged custom checks at the border. Trucks carrying perishable commodities were stopped for inordinate durations at the new boundary line.[33] Ironically, there was a typical Bengali twist to such disputes over the movement of goods reflecting the commonality of their culinary culture. Generally slow and reluctant, the East Bengal government responded promptly only when the government of West Bengal complained about fish being held at Hili border for long hours.[34] Otherwise, newly constituted border patrols, vigilante groups and overzealous police often delayed and hampered cross-border mobility of labour, commodities and capital.[35] A dispute over the Indian decision to devalue currency in 1949 brought the inter-dominion trade to a halt.[36] The resulting impasse undermined the complex economic network of spatially integrated relationships. Coal, which remained the first item of trade to be modernized in Bengal, was now imported at a prohibitive expense from South Africa so that the steamer and rail network in East Bengal did not remain paralyzed.[37] Many everyday items of consumption, including kerosene and tinned goods, disappeared from the market.[38] At the same time, the local products of East Bengal, such as fish, jute, hides and skins, and other commodities, were now restricted to state-space within its borders.[39] The new state-space of East Pakistan thus remained in a state of siege without an alternative spatial outlet. The jute trade that constituted the economic lifeline of the peasant economy suffered the worst damages. As the row over the devaluation of currency between India and Pakistan had led to a standstill in trade between the two dominions, except for the smuggling across the porous border, the government of Pakistan acted with alacrity and established a jute board to direct trade. This was accompanied by the establishment of the National Bank of Pakistan even prior to the scheduled date in order to provide a price-guarantee system for jute, as well as to finance storage facilities to prevent distress-selling of jute by peasants. More importantly, the Pakistani government, in partnership with private capital from West Pakistan, modernized the mechanisms for jute production and helped in the establishment of the pioneer Adamjee mills in Narayanganj. While this benefited East Pakistan enormously, East Bengal still produced jute far in excess of the need. As a consequence, jute smuggling remained a powerful feature of the economic life of East Bengal till 1958, when the deployment of trained border guards, military units and harsh repression undermined the cross-border trade.[40]

Meanwhile, border conflicts over *char*s, or river islands, which came into existence through slit deposits, intensified in the absence of clear boundary lines to delineate ownership over such vagaries of nature. A typical example of such conflicts could be found in a telegram of an exasperated Bidhan Chandra Roy, the chief minister of West Bengal, on 4 September 1948, to Khwaja Nazimuddin, the chief minister of East Bengal:

> I regret I have to differ from you regarding the meeting of officers. The officers' meeting in Dacca cannot obviously find out where truth lies nor can they settle the boundary except after a local survey by officers competent in surveying.[41]

To complicate matters, each side routinely arrested police or law enforcement officials of the other when they crossed the putative border line.[42]

Search for an Organic Nation: Nationalization of Population, Ethnic Cleansing and the Making of East Pakistan

As the border continued to transform the space of East Bengal into a nationalized space, there took place an impulse towards the nationalization of the population on both sides of the border.[43] In India and East Bengal, at the time of the birth of the successive nation states, there emerged among elites what Michael Mann called 'organic conceptions of nation'.[44] As the idea of 'organic nation' – composed of a desirable ethno-religious category – became prominent in the worldview of bureaucrats, state personnel and dominant communities, ethnic cleansing of the perceived minority became a distinct political possibility. More importantly, the very deployment of the term 'minority' reflected an attempt to classify and push people to the margins of society based on an ascriptive ethno-religious identity. This has a historical parallel with the 'Jewish question' in Europe. Aamir Mufti points out how, under conditions of modernity, the situation of Jewish assimilation into the emerging European national societies mirrors the minoritization of Muslims within the context of colonial–national modernity in India.[45] The same observation could also be applied to Muslims in post-colonial India and Hindus in post-colonial Pakistan.

Sectarian conflicts and the refugee exodus had begun before the actual partition. By the summer of 1947, according to one estimate, 'over a million of Hindu refugees had made their way across the Bengal border to Calcutta and perhaps half as many Muslims had fled West Bengal, Assam and Bihar and crossed into East Bengal'.[46] Yet both the governments of India and Pakistan tended to treat East Bengal and the adjoining regions of Assam, West Bengal and Tripura differently from the Pakistani provinces of Sindh and Punjab and the adjoining regions of north-western India. In the east, the governments of India and Pakistan did not confiscate the properties of the evacuees or of the people who took shelter across the border during the riots.[47] It was not expected that there would take place such a drastic population exchange as in north-western India and West Pakistan. Yet the violence continued in Bengal, and by 1950 it had turned into a widespread ethnic cleansing. To understand the process of ethnic cleansing, I shall use two critical instances that shed light on the broad general patterns of the nationalization of identity of a population. The first case refers to the migration of Muslims from West Bengal by examining the microhistory of an ethno-religious conflict in Nadia district, and the second dissects the anatomy of violence in both Bengals in 1950.

The first story starts in Nadia district, which was awarded to West Bengal under the Radcliffe proclamation.[48] Within this district, Santipur was a known centre of weaving which had traditionally produced fine-quality hand-spun clothes. It was a predominantly Hindu town with a few exclusively Muslim neighbourhoods embedded in it. As the partition of Bengal approached, tensions between the Hindu and Muslim populations became endemic in the town. In October 1946 there occurred quite a few minor fracases between the two communities. In January 1947 there took place a bomb attack on a mosque.[49] A local organization with a strange name, the Bombard Military Samity, which had been active since 1937 in extortion and other petty crimes, suddenly became an anti-Muslim 'patriotic' paramilitary organization. They started harassing poor Muslims who lived on the margins of the society. These everyday harassments and humiliations caused a slow but steady exodus of Muslims from Santipur and Nadia to Jessore, Khulna, Kushtia and Pabna districts in East Bengal.[50]

Many such poor Muslims of peasant background wrote petitions to the district magistrate (DM) of Pabna for compensation for the petty crimes they had faced in West Bengal. Written in formulaic Bengali, possibly assisted by a professional writer, these petitions stated their harassments in India. Many petitioners gave thumb impressions rather than written signatures as they were not literate. Most of them were harassed by their neighbours, who also belonged to similar marginal communities among Hindus. Asif Ali Sikdar, for example, narrated how his pair of bullocks was snatched by neighbouring Hindus of a milkmen caste. Another person, Yasin Rari, claimed that local Bagdis (members of untouchable communities) had come and destroyed his paddy fields and snatched his only cow and four *maund*s of paddy. He had left his property worth 1,650 rupees in West Bengal and demanded to be compensated.[51] Some of them accused the Bombard Military Samity of entering their households without proper notice at ungodly hours. The latter searched their premises, took away little valuables and harassed the women of their household. The police did not help them and in many instances appeared to be complicit with their persecutors.[52] This quotidian harassment matched Mann's observation: 'Ethnic hostility rises where ethnicity trumps class as the main form of social stratification in the process of capturing and channeling classlike sentiments towards ethnonationalism.'[53]

Within this context of quotidian tension there took place, in July 1948, an explosion of ethno-religious violence in the midst of the month of Ramadan when Muslims were preparing for religious festivity. The official account of the West Bengal government, as per *The Statesman*, an English newspaper from Calcutta, put it as follows.

> A press note issued by the West Bengal government states that on July 19 a band of Muslim hooligans are alleged to have attacked three Hindu school girls at Santipur and molested one of them. Their cries for help attracted Hindus of the locality. Some of the miscreants were caught by members of the public and taken to the police station where a case was lodged against them. The hooligans, in turn, made counter-allegations of assault etc against certain Hindus and a case was also started on their complaint.

> These incidents, the press note continues, were followed by a certain amount of communal tension in Santipur. On July 20, the head of a cow was found stuck on a bamboo clump in Santipur. Thereupon a mob of infuriated Hindus, variously armed, attacked some neighbouring Muslim houses, resulting in the death of one person and injuries to seven others.

> Armed police forces were rushed to the spot and order was restored. Curfew was imposed and section 144 Cr. PC, promulgated. Goondas of both communities were rounded up.[54]

The long communique reflected bureaucratic myopia. It described the incident as a sudden outburst without highlighting the pre-existing tensions in the area or the slow exodus of Muslims from the town and its vicinity. Across the border in East Bengal, the incident raised furore as the trickle of refugees turned into a torrent. Pakistani officials obviously tried to disprove the official narrative of the West Bengal government and sought to blame them for partisan behaviour. One missive pointed out that it was unclear why Muslims, who were at the receiving end of political violence in India, and placed in an already tense situation, would like to put a cow's head on public display. Muslims were perfectly aware that such an act would provoke massive retaliation from Hindus and worsen their already precarious situation. It could have been a work of an *agent provocateur,* mused one official.[55] It is needless to say that there existed some justification in Pakistani officials' explanations here.

The details, as they appeared from various eyewitness accounts, indicated a much more perilous situation for Muslims. On 19 July there were several attacks on mosques in the area, some of which were plundered, and a few Muslims were killed. On 20 July the DM arrived in Santipur with police forces and guarded the Muslim localities. But two Muslim localities, Ramnagore and Topkhanapara, were left unprotected. A Hindu mob armed with bamboo staves, spears, guns and draggers attacked the Muslim neighbourhood. Nearly 10 Muslims were killed on the spot, and many were injured. An old lady fled through the jungle and reached the DM. After hearing of the attack from her, the DM arrived there with police, though by then the rioters had left. Following the riot, the area remained tense. Local businesses boycotted Muslims. Muslims said that even the Hindu doctors refused to treat Muslims injured in the riot.[56] Pakistani officials claimed that injured Muslims were not even admitted to the hospital.[57] In such circumstances many Muslims panicked and left the town. They took shelter in several neighbouring districts in East Bengal.

In East Bengal, Muslims arriving from Nadia started circulating rumours exaggerating the incident. A. Majid, an alarmed DM of Rajshahi (Rampur Boalia) in East Bengal, noted on 26 July 1948:

> There is considerable agitation in the town here and a meeting was also held by Moulavi Nadar Bux, MLA, as a sort of protest. There seems to be some idea of 'Economic boycott' of Hindus. In any such action Muslims themselves are likely to suffer and that may lead to more serious happenings.[58]

These incidents were endemic after the partition on both sides of Bengal. They led to a slow but steady process of population exchange. The ethno-religious demography of Nadia district, for example, underwent radical transformation in the period between 1947 and 1951. Before the partition nearly 37.38 per cent of Nadia's population were Hindus and 61.25 per cent were Muslims. The Radcliffe line divided Nadia into two parts: Nadia came into West Bengal, and Kushtia was awarded to East Bengal. Even after the partition in 1947, Nadia remained a Muslim-majority district whereby Muslims constituted 52.65 per cent and Hindus formed 45.07 per cent of the population. However, within four years, in 1951, as Subhashri Ghosh demonstrates, Hindus came to constitute 77.03 per cent and Muslims were reduced to 22.36 per cent of the population.[59] The reversal of the ethno-religious demographic composition spoke to a literal process of minoritization.

In the fifties, riots engulfed both sides of Bengal. Barisal, a district in south-western Bengal, became the epicentre of such violence. According to *Modern Review*, a premier periodical in Calcutta, the riots in Barisal led to the death of 'nearly 2,500 and in East Bengal total casualties were estimated in the neighbourhood of 10,000'.[60] The events in Barisal and East Bengal did not simply reflect the *modus operandi* of ethnic cleansing; it also brought to fore the assumptions about the relationship between territoriality and the identity of the population in India and East Bengal.

The genealogy of this explosion of ethnic cleansing in Barisal could be located in the peasant resistance to police in rural East Bengal. In East Bengal, the Communist Party of Pakistan (CPP) (East Pakistan Provincial Committee) had been involved in organizing poor peasants in various pockets, and the Pakistani state was determined to erase the communist influence in East Bengal. A vast majority of communist activists in East Bengal came from a non-Muslim background. Consequently, clashes between communist activists and the police were pregnant with possibilities of being reinterpreted as ethno-religious confrontations. In the inflammable post-partition political environment, such riots had the potential to lead towards ethnic cleansing. This is what happened in a village named Kalshira in Khulna district. In this *namasudra*-dominated village, the police came to arrest a communist activist. They entered his household and tried to rape a woman. Angry villagers attacked them. The police then sought help from Muslim villagers and later returned with a larger reinforcement. They started systematically persecuting the villagers. Alarmed *namasudra* villagers started leaving Khulna for a safe haven across the border.[61] In a public speech in Calcutta on 15 January 1950, the Indian home minister, Vallabhbhai Patel, who was then himself engaged in the repression of communists, accused East Bengal of deliberately erasing its ethno-religious minority.[62] He thus provided a more sectarian reading of the events in East Bengal. Yet Patel might have had a wider political canvas in mind. This was a period when Jawaharlal Nehru was exploring the possibility of a no-war pact with Pakistan despite troubles in Kashmir and Hyderabad. He and Liaquat Ali were engaged in epistolary diplomacy against the wishes of Patel.[63] So India's wily home minister's statement could be read as an articulation of his frustration at a different political process.

Patel's speech prompted furious media denunciations of Pakistan. Indian newspapers started reporting events in Kalshira from 20 January onwards as an instance of simple communal violence rather than a botched attempt to repress communists in East Bengal that had turned into Dalit repression.[64] Taking cue from Patel's speeches, the Hindu Mahasabha (a right-wing Hindu-supremacist organization) held public meetings in various parts of West Bengal which contributed towards the escalation of tensions.[65] This process created the perfect environment for sectarian hatred. Anti-Muslim pogroms began in Calcutta. Taya Zinkin, a British reporter from *The Guardian*, described in detail the horror of riots in the Adamjee jute mill of Howrah. Her horror increased manyfold when she discovered living humans in a pile of dead bodies. In poignant language she described the scene:

> The dead were mixed up with the living. In front of me a woman squatted, immobile. She had lost an arm, severed from the shoulder which dripped from a huge blood clot. On her lap lay the body of an infant cut into two at the waist. But she, the mother, was alive.[66]

The American periodical *News Week* dramatically titled its news report as 'Blood in Bengal'. It described how the refugees from West Bengal ignited communal riots in East Bengal.[67] Then the riots again spread to different parts of West Bengal.

By February, pogroms against non-Muslims had begun in East Bengal. Badruddin Umar is correct in asserting that prominent newspapers in Dacca orchestrated an anti-India campaign in a barely concealed sectarian rhetoric.[68] There took place a series of debates in the legislative assembly between Hindu members of the Pakistan National Congress (PNC) and the government. In a debate on 7 February 1950, Basanta Das, the leader of the PNC, demanded an international inquiry into the sectarian violence in East Pakistan. This debate animated public opinion. Even Tajuddin Ahmad, a young Muslim Leaguer of moderate views, wrote in his dairy, on 10 February 1950, that although the innocence and civic commitment of the members of the legislative assembly had led them to raise the demand for an international inquiry into the riots, this had displeased even the extreme liberals.[69] The demand was unacceptable to the Muslim East Bengalis as it had been raised by the PNC.

The very existence of the PNC, as a Hindu organization, reminded the Muslim masses in East Bengal of pre-independence conflicts between the

Indian National Congress (INC) and the Muslim League. Indeed, soon after independence the Hindu politicians had wanted to disband the INC and join a non-sectarian national organization. According to Abul Mansur Ahmad, it was the Muslim League leaders who coerced the East Bengal Congress leaders into continuing the Congress organization. Ahmad speculates that Muslim League leaders possibly did so in order to keep the old political polarization alive in a newer political environment.[70]

This debate between the Muslim League and the INC further animated the situation. Nurul Amin, the premier of East Bengal, gave a highly provocative speech on 9 February 1950. This was the time of inter-dominion meetings, and the chief secretary of the West Bengal government was visiting Dacca on 10 February. Soon clerks of the central secretariat in Dacca took out a procession to the Indian High Commission. This procession led to the beginning of massive communal violence in East Bengal. Tajuddin Ahmad, nonetheless, blamed Bihari refugees from India for the violence.[71]

On 13 February, a rumour circulated in Barisal that A. K. Fazlul Huq – the last premier of united Bengal, popularly called Sher-e-Bangla (Lion of Bengal) – had been killed by a Hindu mob, and riots flared up in the entire Bakerganj district. On 13 February, the DM organized a meeting between prominent Hindus and Muslims to keep peace in the province.[72] But a riot flared up in the interior. Many Hindu leaders pointed fingers at the *ansar*s, an ill-trained auxiliary volunteer force, for their involvement in riots. In many instances, lower-level police officials remained inactive or were complicit in riots. Indeed, in Muladi, Hindus were massacred at a police station. Women were raped in large numbers. Similar incidents happened in the port area of Barisal town where the Hindus were instructed by an officer in charge of the police station to gather in warehouses. The news of such a gathering leaked, and a violent mob attacked and massacred these Hindus.[73] *Maulavi*s (Muslim religious scholars) were involved in preaching violence, and Zinkin mentions a curious case in which a *maulavi* allegedly instructed tenants of a Hindu lady, P. L. Roy, to either convert her or kill her. The presence of an infidel in their midst would damn their soul, warned the aforementioned *maulavi*.[74] In Mymensingh, a landlord of French descent, Pierre Delauney, told Zinkin of a massacre on train. While crossing a bridge, the driver had intentionally slowed down the train, and a mob attacked members of the Hindu community. Hundreds of thousands of non-Muslims trekked to the border to avoid being killed, dispossessed and/or raped. Zinkin also observed a mass migration of Bengali Muslim refugees from Assam whose condition, she asserted, was as pitiable as that of Hindus from East Bengal.[75] Yet it would be wrong to simply categorize refugees from East Bengal into a homogeneous Hindu grouping. A majority of East Bengal Hindus were Dalits. Even the 'notorious' minority commissioner of East Bengal, N. M. Khan, admitted as much in his conversation with Zinkin.[76] One of their leaders, Jogendranath Mondal, from Barisal, who was the law member of the Pakistan cabinet, was already frustrated. His compatriots had been bringing grievances to him regarding the political situation in East Bengal. He resigned from his position while he was visiting Calcutta. To a great extent, the riots of 1950 undermined the claims of Dalit politics in East Bengal. Sectarian riots opened up another dimension of the politicization of ethnicity in East Bengal. During an interview with Aziz Ahmad, the Punjabi chief secretary to the government of East Bengal, Zinkin noticed that he had a colonial attitude towards East Bengalis. Ahmad accused Muslim Bengalis of not being proper Muslims. He said that they generally offered *namaz* (prayer) in Bengali instead of Arabic and often swore in the name of a Hindu goddess. Zinkin similarly found a deep resentment of Punjabis during an interview with Zakir Hussain, a Bengali inspector general of police. Even in the midst of an anti-Hindu pogrom, she thus noticed another latent ethnic conflict evolving in East Bengal.[77]

The sectarian tensions in both Bengals lay not in any ingrained hatreds among Bengalis, but in the schematics of nationalism and nation-state formation in the late colonial and post-colonial eras. In the case of East Bengal, the uncertainty about territoriality, sovereignty and even the very existence of the state brought to the fore an organic concept of nation within the territorial context. Yet diverse ethnic fault lines contested the process and contributed to the anxiety of both national elites, print media and locally embedded powerful actors. Nehru's proposal of a pact regarding 'minorities' in both nations after a year-long negotiation of a no-war pact also came as a de facto territorial recognition of Pakistan.[78] 'Minorities' were nationalized in both countries. Yet, in both West and East Bengal, the tragedy of such epic proportions had a humane dimension. Their trauma remained deeply embedded in the victims' minds. In a letter to the DM of Rajshahi, dated 24 July 1948, Kutubuddin Ahmad, for example, wrote:

> I have seen with my own eyes the killing of 8 or 10 Muslims with daggers and spears.

Kutubuddin narrated his experience of ethnic cleansing in Nadia in formal Bengali. Yet he became emotional while recording his experience.[79] In Barisal, Nani Gopal Babu, a Hindu survivor of the riot, recalled to a researcher, Anasua Basu Mallick, in vivid detail the evening of the attack, 50 years later. He spoke of how the riots had picked up momentum after the local Muslims joined hands with Bihari refugees. Hindu villagers approached the local leader, Altafuddin Mohammad, also a Muslim, to save them. Altafuddin agreed to guard his Hindu neighbours with weapons. An irate Muslim mob first chopped Altaf, and Nani Gopal Babu recalled the details of what followed:

> When they were chopping Altaf, my father and brother-in-law were hiding in the same room. My brother was also in that room. They asked for my brother-in-law's wristwatch after killing Altaf. As he refused, they cut his hand with that watch. He had something else. He refused to hand it over also; so they beheaded him. I was saved as I was in the next room. They killed my sister's husband in front of her. My father was trying to stop them; so they stabbed him on his neck also. So much blood everywhere! I can't forget that scene still now. Whenever I close my eyes, I can see that scene.[80]

M. R. Akhtar Mukul, a famous journalist and writer, recalled the Indian steamers that were sent to Barisal in East Bengal to take Hindu refugees to Calcutta. In his mind's eye, he claimed, he could hear a shrill cry, 'Ma go' (Oh my mother), coming from those steamers as they started moving.'[81] Territorializing the nation state and nationalizing population had a very high price tag attached to them.

Agrarian Question, Political Economy of Starvation and Popular Disquiet

In the midst of the riots in Dacca, Zinkin went to meet a professor of Hindu descent. As he packed to leave for Calcutta, he described to her his sense of insecurity in the new political environment. Among the many other things that caused him to be anxious, he said: 'Yesterday when my tenants [rural peasants] came to pay their rent, they did not leave shoes out on the doorstep. Tomorrow, who knows they may and come and kill me.'[82] This made Zinkin wonder whether the land reforms looming large in the horizon had motivated the tenants to skip the payment of rent. She was unable to understand her interlocutor's discomfort for what she missed was implicit in the conversation: a lament for the death of the older colonial regime in Bengal. The professor, as a landholding elite, was a beneficiary of the Permanent Settlement Acts introduced by the British colonial rulers. Like many Bengali upper-caste Hindus, he combined income from the land with employment in the service sector. His worldview was premised upon feudal hangovers: rent collection and his identity as landlord which entailed the subservience of the peasantry class. He was, no doubt, disturbed by the tragic violence against Hindus, but he was equally distressed by the disappearance of quotidian norms of obeisance on the part of the peasants. Yet the very loss of his power was a mark of a new form of democratization of society and the appeal of the Pakistan movement in Bengal. The latter was an ethno-religious articulation of the aspiration of the peasant classes for freedom from landlordism. Such class aspirations of the Muslim subsistence peasants, however, were hardly matched by land reforms in the new state.

The biggest disappointment came with the land-reform legislation of 1950. On 7 April 1948, Hamidul Haq Chowdhury, the finance minister of the East Bengal government, initiated a draft bill on land reforms in the legislative assembly. After nearly two years of debates the bill was passed into law as the East Bengal State Acquisition and Tenancy Act on 16 December 1950.[83] Though the Muslim League ministers claimed that the Act would usher in a revolution in East Bengal, in reality it fell far short of benefitting the poor peasantry. Under this Act, the government acquired the interests of all rent-receivers, above that of the cultivator. The Act, however, defined 'cultivator' as a farmer who cultivated land with the help of labourers or sharecroppers (*bargadars*).[84] It did not recognize sharecroppers as tenants.[85] Ironically, according to the Floud Commission appointed in 1938–40, nearly 17 per cent of the total cultivated area was brought under plough by sharecroppers, and probably 7 per cent of cultivation was done with the assistance of agricultural workers.[86] In 1944–45, A. H. M. Ishaque, the development commissioner, conducted a plot-to-plot enumeration of land cultivation in Bengal. This study was entitled *Agricultural Statistics by Plot-to-Plot Enumeration in Bengal 1944–45*.[87] According to Ishaque's sample survey of 77 villages with a total of 3,213 families, as many as 961, or 29.9 per cent, were entirely landless labourers. More importantly, Ishaque's report points out that if those possessing less than an acre of land (including homestead) and those who were heavily dependent on the land they took in on a sharecropping basis were to be included in the aforementioned number, the total comes to 1,586, or just under 50 per cent of the total population.[88] Yet the Act regarded the sharecroppers as landless labourers and thus paved the way for their eviction at will. This left a large segment of the rural society vulnerable to the pressure of surplus farmers.

The second much-vaunted goal of the Act was the redistribution of land. This was negligible. According to the Act, the lands of all persons (including land cultivated by sharecroppers) in excess of 33.3 acres per family or 10 *bigha*s per member of the family, whichever was larger, plus the area of homestead land up to a maximum of 10 *bigha*s, were to be acquired by the government. These ceilings were relaxed for tea, coffee, sugarcane and rubber plantations, cassia leaf gardens, orchards and large-scale farming by the use of power-driven mechanical appliances.[89] Yet the ceiling was too high relative to the average size of holdings. Even after the Land Reforms Act of 1964, the total amount of excess land obtained under the Act was very low – around 163,741 acres. Since net cropped area in East Bengal was 19.2 million acres in 1947–48, the land made available for redistribution by the state acquisition operation was a little less than 1 per cent.[90] It was clear that the redistributive impact of this Act was quite negligible. Obviously, such steps did not benefit poor cultivators. Even in 1976, the ownership of land in rural East Pakistan was highly concentrated, where 20 per cent of the farm households of Bangladesh owned 53 per cent of the total cultivable land area.[91]

The Act enabled the state to transfer a portion of the agricultural surplus from a numerous and dispersed class of intermediaries to the provincial government. Except for the elimination of illegal exactions (*abwab*s), the cultivating tenants, particularly subsistence farmers, did not gain any benefits from the Act. Indeed, the state income from land revenue increased from 17.4 million in 1947–48 to 67.5 million in 1957–58 and jumped to 130.5 million in 1958–59.[92] Theoretically, tenants might have benefitted if the government were committed, or at least inclined, to spending this surplus for agricultural improvement, but as the East Bengal government was starved for cash, the possibility of such expenditure was negligible. Rather, the state expanded its bureaucratic networks, in particular the police force, with the help of such surplus. Thus, the Act laid the foundation for the creation of a state-centric salaried class through the appropriation of surplus from peasantry.

More importantly, Abu Abdullah, a developmental economist, argues that the *tahsildar*s, or officers responsible for revenue collection, turned out to be as rapacious as *naib*s (estate managers of *zamindars*) and *gomostha*s (rent-collecting agents of *zamindars*).[93] In many areas, tenants did not recognize any remarkable transformation in their lives after the transition from the parasitic landlord regime to a surplus-extracting bureaucratic regime. According to S. A. Quadir, who studied the economic life of a village in rural East Bengal, the majority of peasants told him that before the abolition of *zamindari* they could leave their rent in arrears for three to four years, but now rent had to be paid up promptly every year with an additional development tax. In case of a default, the government was prompt in filing a case under certificate procedure for the attachment of the land for which rent had fallen in arrears.[94] However, the reference to an apparently relaxed *zamindari* system of rent collection, in comparison to the modern rapacious bureaucrats, was borne out of a severe case of presentism. In the twentieth century, the power of the *zamindars* had declined in the face of growing peasant resistance and governmental pressure. By the middle of the twentieth century, *zamindars* remained creatures of the past without much clout in the present and had virtually no future. The new bureaucratic state, in the form of a national government, had a much better reach in the rural society and appealed to peasants; thus, it was easy to see the state as more rapacious, but in their heydays, the *zamindars* were known for their heinous exactions. Nonetheless, it would be equally wrong to underestimate the devastating impact upon the peasants of the corrupt practices of low-level officials and the state's merciless extraction of surplus from subsistence peasants. This process deprives the subsistence peasants of any illusions they might have had about the newly formed bureaucratic nation state. This disillusionment among peasants increased further when the new state of East Pakistan failed to intervene meaningfully to ward off a food crisis. At the time of partition, there were telltale signs of such a food crisis in the offing.

On 15 August 1947, according to one estimate, the granaries in East Bengal held not more than a fortnight's supply, and the annual shortfall in grain production in East Bengal amounted to 5 per cent in proportion to the population, despite 7.8 million tonnes of rice production.[95] The immediate crisis was avoided by importing wheat from West Pakistan and rice from Burma (present-day Myanmar), as well as by adopting an extraordinarily stringent rice-procurement policy that involved dividing the country into four rice-procurement zones.[96] Nonetheless, the food crisis and associated hunger and starvation in rural East Bengal raised doubts about government statistics. Both the leaders of the opposition, and even some political activists within the ruling Muslim League, raised questions about the statistics of food shortages. They blamed persistent hoarding by traders as the reason behind such problems. In 1948–49 and 1951 hunger and starvation stalked East Bengal. Opposition members demanded that certain regions be declared as impacted by famines. The government hid behind the technicalities of the legal definition of famine and thus refused to issue such a declaration.[97]

The government imposed a cordoning system to restrict food movement from deficit districts. They also ordered the levying of food from surplus farmers. But the rickety administrative structure, the corruption in the lower level of bureaucracy and the cooperation between surplus farmers and government officials prevented effective implementation of the policies of cordoning and procurement. Many surplus farmers had been able to evade the levy through bribes and political connections.[98] In some instances, the state was powerless to prevent rice trade across international borders to India. Van Schendel recorded an incident from 1948 that demonstrated the might of the powerful and orchestrated lucrative rice trade across the border. The border area of Murshidabad opposite Rajshahi was known as a rice-deficit distressed area and thus attracted the flow of rice from Rajshahi. On 11 January 1948, nearly 500 boats laden with paddy travelled on the river Atrai in Rajshahi to India. They ignored the police order for a halt, and the police were too few in number to stop them. On 12 January, next day, after being tipped off about a large assemblage of boats, the cordoning officer tried to deploy force to prevent the movement of the rice fleet. But in the afternoon, a number of boats, guarded on the riverbanks by approximately 60 armed men, tried to break through the police cordon. The boatmen and their guards refused to show their permits to the officer when ordered. Instead, they chased him and nearly apprehended him mid-river. Police fired in all directions to enable the officer to escape, and the officer fled by swimming across the river. But the paddy boats bypassed the police, collected about 20 of their injured compatriots and four dead bodies, and then moved towards the border.[99]

Meanwhile, the burden of levy disproportionately fell upon the vast majority of subsistence peasants and Hindu landholders, traders and moneylenders who lost their old political connections. However, while the Hindu landholders still had a powerful lobby in the assembly, the subsistence peasants remained unrepresented.[100] Rather than remaining and starving in East Bengal, many of them started to move towards Assam in India.[101] Rural footloose working classes thus started vetoing with their feet the idea of a territorialized nation state. By the fifties, draconian laws were enacted to evict Bengali Muslim peasants from Assam. The ruthless enforcement of these laws compelled these migrants to return to Bengal. The territorial state had imprisoned the rural working poor, and the border remained the symbol of such imprisonment.

Bureaucratic Governance, Peasant Discontent and Political Resistance

In a polyethnic trans-territorial state like Pakistan, the bureaucratic centralization of the political system was fraught with danger. In East Pakistan, the ruling faction in the Muslim League had an alliance with the bureaucratic elites of West Pakistan. Yet as pogroms, economic crises and the near-famine situation persisted in East Pakistan, the new post-colonial governing elites groped in the darkness. Both the ruling Muslim League and the bureaucratic elites were afraid of a rebellion from below. Their main fear in the founding years of East Bengal was the rebellion of agricultural workers, sharecroppers and marginal farmers organized by the CPP (East Pakistan Provincial Committee) and its peasant front, the Bangiya Pradeshik Krishak Sabha. The communist movement in Bengal, though established by Muslims, gained popularity through the conversion of imprisoned Hindu *bhadralok*[102] revolutionary nationalists to Marxist ideology. Prominent communist leader Muzaffar Ahmed, popularly known as Kakababu, who hailed from the East Bengal peasantry, played a crucial role in converting these *bhadralok* nationalist revolutionaries to the communist cause.[103] Thus, despite the presence of Muzaffar Ahmad, Abdul Halim and Abdullah Rasul, three pivotal figures of the Bengal communist movement, in East Bengal most communists came from a Hindu *bhadralok* social background. The social structuration of East Bengal approximated a fourfold classification. At the apex of the society, there stood a class of landholders and various types of intermediate tenure holders, in the middle there were surplus farmers who were known as *jotedar*s in local parlance, below them were peasants who relied on family labour for farm activities, and at the bottom of the social pyramid were located the subsistence peasants, sharecroppers and agricultural workers. While the overwhelming majority of *zamindar*s in East Bengal were upper-caste Hindus, most *jotedar*s were Muslims, with a sprinkling of the Hindu peasant castes. A significant section of the subsistence peasants, sharecroppers and agricultural workers were the Santhals, Rajbangshis and various other historically poor labouring communities. In north Bengal, the widespread prevalence of sharecropping led towards the rise of a sharecroppers' movement from 1937 onwards.[104] To take the movement to new heights, in September 1946, the Krishak Sabha launched the *tebhaga* agitation. *Tebhaga* meant that the *bargadar*, or sharecropper, would take home the entire crop and hand over one-third to the landlords. This call reversed the conventional arrangements whereby the *bargadar* transported the entire harvest to the landlord's house, where it was divided. The movement thus challenged the superior status of landlords and sought to reverse the hierarchical structure of rural society.[105] As a vast majority of these sharecroppers belonged to the socially ostracized marginal groups in Hindu society, the attempt by the upper-caste Hindu *bhadralok* to mobilize the rural poor also spoke to their aspirations of social mobility through various reformist movements.[106] The movement reached its height in 1946–47, when it touched the lives of nearly six million peasants in rural Bengal.[107] When Huseyn Shaheed Suhrawardy, the premier of Bengal, declared that there would be law recognizing the claim of *bargadars*, it further stimulated the movement. The movement now spread from its core constituency of Dalits and Advasis to poor Muslim peasants. However, the bill was shelved due to lobbying by *jotedars* within the Muslim League, and the alarmed government now decided to suppress the movement through police repression.[108] According to Bhabani Sen, a communist leader, nearly 10,000 peasants were arrested, and 50 of them were killed in the course of the movement.[109] By 1948, the *tebhaga* movement was officially called off by the Communist Part of India (CPI).

The other area where the CPI had success in Bengal was in Mymensingh district. From 1937 onwards, Moni Singh, a communist, sought to organize peasants in the Durgapur–Susang area of Mymensingh against the *tanka* system.[110] The *tanka* system was a particular type of tenancy that involved the payment of a fixed amount of produce as rent. This was known as *dhankarari* in most parts of Bengal. Throughout the forties, Hajongs struggled against the *tanka* system, and during the Second World War, the area became a liberated zone of the Krishak Sabha.[111] By 1947 these movements had coalesced into a powerful resistance. In Barisal, too, communists organized social movements under the leadership of Manoroma Basu and Ghulam Kibria.[112] Thus, at the very moment of the Pakistan state's foundation in East Bengal, there took place a massive peasant upsurge. There were nearly 20,000 members of the CPI at the time of partition, a majority of whom were located in East Bengal.[113]

In 1948 there took place a critical shift in the CPI's political strategy. Taking his cue from a 1947 speech by Andrei Aleksandrovich Zhdanov[114] which was delivered at the founding meeting of the Information Bureau of the Communist and Workers' Parties, commonly known as Cominform,[115] and which addressed the international situation, B. T. Ranadive, the new general secretary of the CPI, moved towards a more revolutionary line at the Second Congress held in February–March 1948 in Calcutta and, in 1949, adopted political theses to that effect.[116] The move towards a revolutionary line led the CPI to launch an offensive in East Bengal with the slogan 'This is a sham independence'. Revolutionary attempts by the CPI during this period were met with severe repression; these included an attempt to revive the *tebhaga* peasant base, to organize a Hajong rebellion, as well as to support a new rebellion among the Santhals in present-day Chapai Nawabganj district. Ila Mitra, who, among others, organized a Santhal peasant uprising in the Nachole area, was captured and faced savage sexual repression in prison.[117] Rebel women were perceived through a sexual lens by many among the law enforcement officials, and the violent patriarchy legitimized their sexual savageness. In many ways these officers believed that violating a woman's honour would stigmatize the woman rather than the male policemen who were responsible for such savage attacks. In Hajong areas, the remnant of *tanka* movement was suppressed with heavy hands.[118] Similarly, Nankar peasants who had to perform forced labour in return for food revolted in the greater Sylhet region against *zamindar*s and were supressed ruthlessly by the East Pakistan police and Ansars. Again, many of these peasants came from historically poor, former-untouchable communities. The indifferent administration viewed these peasant uprisings as a law-and-order problem and ignored their social content.

Communist-sponsored rebellions of marginal peasants from ritually poor non-Muslim tribalized communities thus ended in failure. The slogan of 'sham independence' did not appeal to a vast majority of the population who had gained independence so recently from colonial rule. While the Muslim League regime started losing its popular legitimacy as a ruling political party, the vast majority of the peasantry refused to experiment with radical political transformation. Bureaucrats and police further encouraged social divisions based on religion to isolate and defeat communists.[119] Many among the radicals regarded these rebellions as a non-Muslim reaction against the establishment of a Muslim-majority state.[120] Yet the masses, irrespective of their religious orientations, wanted a respite from the authoritarian-bureaucratic state run by a political party which did not engage in any democratic dialogue with the people. For example, even a demand for the clearing of the drainage of a moribund river became a source of conflict between the peasants and the bureaucracy in the Madarsha Union in Chittagong district where people took the initiative to dig canals in Haldi River to avoid flooding. The bureaucracy was so afraid of this people's initiative that when 3,000–4,000 people beating drums and playing *sanai*[121] marched towards the canal to be dug, the DM, apprehending an attack on the police force, ordered an open firing, resulting in the death of 10 persons.[122] The firing in Madarsha became a symbol of the bureaucratic high-handedness of the regime. Discontent brewed further against a one-party regime backed by an insensitive bureaucracy.

This alternative to official Muslim League politics came from within the organization. In the late colonial era, the Muslim League had been a broad platform with diverse political tendencies within it. A significant number of Muslim League cadres in Bengal came from the *proja* (tenant) movement. Hailing from rich and middle-class peasant families, they went for formal schooling, and some obtained university education.[123] These educated young women and men aspired to employment in government services and the expanding service sectors. They joined politics to end the domination of landholding classes. Ideologically, these men held a liberal view of social restructuring through normative, reformist democratic structures. Their aim was to create a thriving market-driven property regime. Most of them were inclined towards various types of populism. Despite the predominance of surplus-producing (as opposed to subsistence-level) peasants in the support base, the top brass of the Muslim League came from large landholding families, such as the nawab family of Dacca, and a few business magnates like the Ispahani family. It remained a patrimonial coalition of rich men who had embraced politics as a quest for power and for safeguarding their influence and heritage as members of the landholding *ashraf* class (traditionally members of an aristocratic, Urdu-speaking social formation). Thus, Muslim League politics remained trapped in two contradictory pulls of fundamentally antithetical political orientations: the elites wanted to preserve their property interests, while the bourgeois reformists, with their aspirations to be middle classes, dreamt of a moderate degree of social transformation.

Factional problems within the Bengal Muslim League became more acute when, between 1943 and 1945, these young men were brought into the Muslim League organization by Abul Hashim, a radical scholar of Islamic theology. He built up the Muslim League organization in *mufassil* towns[124] with offices and regular secretaries. He also introduced free membership to the Muslim League and created a democratic environment and structure in the party, whereby aspiring middle-class youths could establish their presence in the party hierarchy.[125] Shaheed Suhrawardy, an Oxford-educated scion of an elite landholding family from West Bengal, who played a role in organizing the Muslim workers of Calcutta, made an alliance with Abul Hashim. Though this duo had different political goals among themselves, together they represented a coalition of those younger party members who wanted a liberal-bourgeois democratic future for Pakistan and perceived themselves as progressives.[126] As these two leaders backed the United Bengal thesis in April 1947, and since they both hailed from West Bengal, the duo remained hesitant to migrate to East Bengal in the initial years after independence.

In July 1947, the Nazimuddin group outmanoeuvred the Suhrawardy–Hashim group in an election for the position of the prime minister of Bengal among Muslim League assembly members. This new faction wanted to consolidate its hold over both the party's political apparatus as well as the government. Except for a fierce display of Muslim nationalism, it actually sought to retain the political status quo in East Pakistan. Allied with the central party leadership, this ruling clique in the East Pakistan government sought to exclude from the organization younger entrepreneurial party activists close to the Suhrawardy–Hashim coalition.[127] As the Nazimuddin group, led by veteran Muslim League politician Maulana Akram Khan, consolidated its grip over the administration, it excluded Suhrawardy, Hashim and their followers from levers of power. These younger members gathered at a Muslim League office at 150 Mogultully in Dacca, and this office became the new centre for opposition politics in East Bengal within the framework of Pakistani nationalism. These young cadres floated many plans for new organizations, but only a few smaller political groups came into existence. Youth and student activists such as Sheikh Mujibur Rahman, Tajuddin Ahmad, Kamruddin Ahmad, Oli Ahad and others explored the path of opposition politics.[128] It was on the question of state language (*rashtra bhasha*) that the opposition among the students came into focus.[129]

Yet, for two years, the ruling clique within the Muslim League regime in Dacca did not face any serious challenges as the stalwarts of Muslim nationalist politics remained in India. Fazlul Huq, though not connected with Muslim League politics at that time, chose to reside in Calcutta. His close confidant, Abul Mansur Ahmad, also stayed in Calcutta for a while.[130] Even

Maulana Bhashani, a radical populist leader of immigrant Muslim peasants in Assam, remained incarcerated in India.[131] It was as if the new territorial division did not become evident to them. After his return to East Bengal, Bhashani contested in a by-election in Tangail, but his victory was declared null and void on the appeal of Khurram Khan Panni, a local *zamindar*. This led to further activities in the opposition circle within the Muslim League. The opposition groups put up a candidate named Shamsul Huq in the Tangail by-election who defeated the official Muslim League candidate. Alarmed, the government tried to close avenues for a democratic articulation of politics and suspended all by-elections.[132]

The growing censorship, imprisonment of political activists critical of the government, and persistence of hunger, sectarian violence and bureaucratic indifference led towards the formation of a new party-based political organization in 1949. The activists of the 150 Mogultuly group issued a call for a conference of workers of the Muslim League in a house called Rose Garden in Dacca on 23 and 24 June 1949. This conference gave birth to an organization known as the Awami Muslim League under the presidentship of Bhashani. In Urdu, *awam* means 'people'; the new organization was implying that it was a *people's* Muslim League. Indeed, the manifesto of the new party had the same ideological tenor of Muslim nationalism.[133] The political programme of the new party, however, indicated a slightly more radical orientation by including the demands for the abolition of the *zamindari* system without compensation, the holding of elections on the basis of universal franchise, a judicial investigation into the alleged corruption in the cabinet, the release of student leaders from jail and the introduction of compulsory universal primary education. The new organization also advised the government to hold an all-party food conference to discuss how to relieve the hardships of the food crisis.[134]

The office bearers of the Awami Muslim League included Bhashani as president, Shamsul Huq as general secretary and two youth leaders, Sheikh Mujibur Rahman and Khondakar Mostaq Ahmad, as assistant general secretary.[135] Sheikh Mujib was then in jail. The organization also appointed a provincial committee composed of 40 members. However, many youth activists stayed away from the new party as it included the word 'Muslim' in its name and thus could not shed communal identity.[136] The formation of this new political party indicated the beginning of a type of political polarization in East Bengal which was different from the older, and now redundant, political division between the INC and the Muslim League. It also opened up an avenue for an oppositional outlet against the government beyond revolutionary politics of the CPP (East Pakistan Provincial Committee). In the early fifties, the Muslim League encountered significant opposition from another source. The students of Dacca University (present-day University of Dhaka) and other higher educational institutions opposed the idea of the introduction of Urdu as the national language. On 21 February 1952, students confronted the police and faced their firing. The evolution of the language movement and the cultural assertions of East Bengalis will be treated more elaborately in Chapter 3. But this much was clear: the Muslim League government had become isolated from the most vocal segment of the youth. The more the government felt challenged politically, the more it relied on bureaucracy, police violence and repression.

This bureaucratization had another problematic aspect: its upper echelon came from West Pakistan. According to the *New York Times*, Mahmud Husain Khan, a Muslim League minister, said that 'the situation became so bad that one could walk through the secretariat and not find a single Bengali among the secretaries in the ministries'.[137] Many of these officials were said to have a colonial attitude towards the local population. The absence of Bengali officials at the top levels became a source of complaints among Bengali politicians. Added to this was the accusation that though exports of jute had given Pakistan a considerable amount of hard currency, East Bengal had not received benefits proportionate to its area's total revenue contribution.[138] There were also allegations about the uneven distribution of foreign aid between two wings.

At the grassroots level, the absence of democratic avenues, and the branding of all propaganda, even that of the Awami Muslim League, as 'communist conspiracy', created a suffocating environment. Local Muslim League officials exhorted the police to take action against Awami Muslim League activists for organizing campaigns.[139] Muslim League leaders also doubted the patriotism and sincerity of Bhashani's commitment to Pakistan. Soon Suhrawardy joined Bhashani. These two leaders had significant differences in terms of their political orientation: Suhrawardy was an advocate of parliamentary politics and was partial towards an international alliance with the United States (US). Bhashani, a radical populist, was oriented towards peasant populism and regarded the US as an enemy of the newly emancipated Asian and African peoples.[140] That these two leaders made a common cause against the Muslim League indicated how far the latter had alienated public opinion in Bengal. In 1953, it became clear that the government might call for elections soon. The Awami Muslim League's provincial council met together in a convention between 3 and 5 July. The new general secretary of the party, Sheikh Mujib, placed the organizational report. The organization refused to shed from its nomenclature the word 'Muslim'. This led to fierce debates.[141]

Elections came to East Bengal on 8 March 1954. Fazlul Huq, the veteran politician, resigned from his official designation of advocate general of the East Bengal government before the elections and floated a new organization called the Krishak Shramik Party.[142] There were a few other Islamic political parties in the fray too. The most prominent political organization was, of course, the Awami Muslim League, but it was also experiencing a significant political debate within its ranks. Sheikh Mujib opposed a demand for a United Front with other opposition parties. However, popular mood among party activists swung in favour of a United Front. [143]

With this, the election essentially became a referendum on the Muslim League government. It was clear that a popular wave against the Muslim League was sweeping through the province. Abul Mansur Ahmad, a Mymensingh-based Awami League leader, was given the responsibility of drafting the manifesto of the United Front. He drafted a 21-point manifesto; he used the number 21 as a deliberate mark of identification with the Language Martyrs' Day on 21 February.[144] Students became involved in the campaign for a United Front in very large numbers, and the vote itself was a festive occasion. Bengali Muslim peasant women, who did not move outside their villages without *pardah*,[145] came out to vote in significant numbers. Male relatives held mosquito nets over their female family members and walked for miles in such a state to cast their votes.[146] Abul Mansur Ahmad recalled a curious incident on the day of election. His opponent was his friend Abul Kalam Shamsuddin, the editor of the pro-Muslim League Bengali daily, *Azad*. Looking at the voting trends, both Ahmad and Shamsuddin realized that the latter would lose the election miserably and would therefore have to forfeit his deposit. So they both requested the electorate to cast a few votes for Shamsuddin, just to save the money that he had deposited with the government because of electoral law. People told them that while they had no problem in saving up and collecting the deposit money for Shamsuddin, they would not vote for a Muslim League candidate under any circumstances. As a consequence, Shamsuddin lost his deposit – he secured only 1,600 votes out of 31,000 total votes cast.[147] The depth of anger against the Muslim League became particularly evident in the defeat of Nurul Amin, the chief minister of the province and a veteran Muslim League leader, at the hands of a political neophyte, Khaleq Newaj, a law student.[148] The results indicated a clean sweep for the United Front. Table 1.1 provides a party-wise break-up of the seats in the East Bengal legislative assembly elected on the basis of separate electorate.

The United Front ministry developed fissures soon after it was born. Meanwhile, the Communist spectre had also come to haunt the political elites of East Pakistan. According to one estimate, around 50–60 of the Muslim seats alone (from a total of 237) were held by communist or pro-communist members clandestinely.[149] The situation became more complicated in May 1954, when an emotional Fazlul Huq, during a visit to Calcutta, declared that in removing the barriers which existed between the two Bengals, he 'would not take note of the fact that there was a political division of the province of Bengal into East and West Bengal'.[150] Not surprisingly, the speech caused a furore in West Pakistan. In East Pakistan, on 22 and 23 March, there took

Table 1.1 Results of the 1954 provincial election in East Bengal

Party	Total seats won
Total Muslim seats	237
Constituents of the United Front	
Awami Muslim League	140
Krishak Shramik Party	34
Nizam-e-Islam	12
Youth League	15
Ganatantri Dal	10
Total seats of the United Front	215
Independents	12
Muslim League	9
Khilafat-e-Rabbani	1
Total Hindu seats	72
Scheduled Caste Federation	27
Pakistan National Congress	24
United Front (minority)	10
Communist Party of Pakistan (East Pakistan Provincial Committee)	5
Ganatantri Dal (minority)	2
Buddhist	2
Christian	1
Independent (caste Hindu)	1
Total	307

Source: Based on information supplied in Richard L. Park, 'East Bengal: Pakistan's Troubled Province', *Far Eastern Survey* 23, no. 5 (1954): 70–74, pp. 71–72.

place an unexpected riot in the Karnaphuli paper mill in Chittagong between Bengali and non-Bengali workers, and on 15 May another similar kind of riot rocked the newly constructed Adamjee jute mill in Narayanganj, an industrial suburb of Dacca. Recent micro-histories of the riot have indicated a more complex picture of the confrontation between labour and administration, rather than simply a Bengali–non-Bengali conflict.[151]

On 29 May, the governor general of Pakistan, Ghulam Muhammad, dismissed Fazlul Huq's cabinet under Section 92A of the interim Constitution. Iskandar Mirza, the major general and defence secretary of the government of Pakistan, replaced Chowdhury Khalequzzaman. Over the next three days, the Pakistan government sent 10,000 troops to East Bengal. Additionally, the Royal Pakistan Navy frigate *Sind* was dispatched with munitions and additional troops on 29 May. The government placed Fazlul Huq under house arrest.[152] As usual the CPP (East Pakistan Provincial Committee) was blamed for the industrial violence, and by 5 July the government declared the party an unlawful association. Iskandar Mirza ordered arrests of a total of 1,047 persons, including at least 11 members of the legislature.[153]

The government gained new supporters from among the newly elected politicians. Ghulam Sarwar, who was the prime accused in the Noakhali riots of 1946, issued a leaflet on 20 June 1954, welcoming the dissolution of the Fazlul Huq military and accusing him of being anti-national. Addressing Bhashani as 'comrade', in effect implying that Bhashani was a communist, Sarwar held him responsible for the decline in the political environment of East Bengal. At the end of his leaflet, he declared that the people of East Pakistan were Pakistani and Muslims, and not Bengali. Thus, Sarwar initiated a new ideological debate which hinted at the incompatibility between a Pakistani Muslim identity and a Bengali one. No doubt, Sharwar, an astute political player, thought this was a meaningful way to be in the good books of the administration, and he was not far off. N. M. Khan, a seasoned bureaucrat, wrote in an approving manner to Aziz Ahmad, the cabinet secretary of the Pakistan government, on 10 July 1954:

> He is the same person who was at one time accused of starting the Hindu-Muslim riots in Noakhali. His present statement is, however, very appropriate in the situation which faces us.[154]

The government of East Bengal was baffled by the rise of Bengali nationalism and thus became very nervous. Any display of Bengali nationalism, even across the border, became suspect in the eyes of the government. For example, even an unknown play called *Bengalee*, written by Brajendra Kumar De, published in Calcutta, was proscribed in East Bengal in 1955. The play was written against the background of Emperor Akbar's invasion of Bengal during the reign of a Pathan ruler. The Pathan ruler was upset by the activities of one of Akbar's tyrannical revenue officials and wanted to end the Delhi government's intervention. He went to the battlefield against Akbar, and his forces were annihilated by the Mughal army. The official reviewer claimed that 'the drama preaches Bengal is for Bengalis and advocates for secular sovereign Bengal', which were grounds for its proscription. On 17 February 1955, the governor proscribed the play by applying the Press Act of 1931, which was enacted by the erstwhile British government to suppress the civil disobedience movement in India.[155] In the perception of Pakistani bureaucrats, a new threat had been added to Pakistan's existence – an attraction among Bengalis to the idea of an 'independent sovereign secular Bengal'.

Conclusion

This turn of events ended a phase in the history of East Bengal's integration with the Pakistani political system. The partition of Bengal undermined the older spatial economics of an expanding region. It severed the old colonial space of production and consumption and reoriented the geography of transportation. The resultant dislocation in the economic life caused a situation of persistent hunger in East Bengal. The problem became more acute with pogroms of the putative minorities on both sides of the border. The suppression of communist rebellion in the end undermined the bargaining power of the rural working poor. In addition, the new ruling class of rich farmers enacted a land reform that remained insensitive to the needs of the poor peasants. More importantly, the bureaucratic (mis)management of vital ecological problems rendered Pakistan into a mere administrative state without any democratic dialogue between the people and their ruling elites.

Consequently, mere fractional fighting within the ranks of the Muslim League became a significant source of ideological conflict and led towards the rise of a critical opposition to the national ideology and the state. The intolerance towards any form of dissent led Pakistani political elites to disregard the democratic verdict of the people. As a consequence, the administration created a new challenge before themselves: an incipient but potentially attractive Bengali 'nationalism'.

For the next four years, between 1954 and 1958, the democratic experiment continued in East Pakistan in the midst of intrigues, factional squabbles and hopes of a constitutional transformation. At the same time, there took place a split in the Awami League as the organization witnessed the exit of the populist radicals and the left. The next chapter will deal with this four-year period, the most crucial years in the final phase of the quasi-democratic civilian regime, when East Pakistan was expecting the coming of constitutional reforms and a general election. Such hopes were dashed to the ground by the sudden suspension of politics with Ayub Khan's military coup.

Notes

1. Syed Abu Mohammad Ismail Hossain Siraji, *Turaska Bhraman* (Calcutta: Sahjahan Company, 1913), p. 118 (translation mine).
2. The most important symbol of deified form of Bengal and later India was Bankim Chandra's song 'Vande Mataram'. The song often repelled Muslim youth from the nationalist movement. Muzaffar Ahmad, a well-known leader of the Communist Party of India (CPI), wrote in his autobiography that despite his inclination to join Indian revolutionary nationalist movement, he felt alienated by the use of the song. Muzaffar Ahmad, *Amar Jibon o Bharater Communist Party* (Calcutta: National Book Agency, 1969), p. 2. For details of the evolution of the song into battle cry during communal riots or nationalist agitations, see Sabyasachi Bhattacharya, *Vande Mataram: The Biography of a Song* (New Delhi: Primus Books, 2013).
3. For details of the Bengali response to the partition in 1905, see Sumit Sarkar, *The Swadeshi Movement in Bengal 1903–1908* (New Delhi: People's Publishing House, 1973).
4. S. Sarkar, *The Swadeshi Movement*.
5. Nayanika Mookherjee, 'Gendered Embodiments: Mapping the Body-Politic of the Raped Woman and the Nation in Bangladesh', *Feminist Review* no. 88 (2008): 36–53.
6. Meghna Guhathakurta, 'Sonar Bangla: Inspiration, Illusion and Extortion', *Humboldt Journal of Social Relations* 23, nos. 1–2 (1997): 197–217.
7. A sari is a long piece of cloth wrapped around the body, worn by women in South Asia.

8. Sumathi Ramaswamy, *The Goddess and the Nation: Mapping Mother India* (Durham, NC: Duke University Press, 2010).
9. According to Tanika Sarkar, for Tagore 'nationalism was invariably a project of power and self-aggrandisement, of exclusion and incipient imperialism: whereas patriotism or the love of the country is a project of care and nurture, of love for people, land, and for the earth'. Tanika Sarkar, 'Rabindranath's "Gora" and the Intractable Problem of Indian Patriotism', *Economic and Political Weekly* 44, no. 30 (2009): 37–46.
10. In 2000, Aftab Ahmed, a professor of Political Science of Dhaka University, was reported to have questioned how 'Sonar Bangla' could be the national anthem of independent Bangladesh given that it was originally composed to protest against the British plans to partition Bengal in 1905. For the debates in Bangladesh over the adequacy of the song as a national anthem, see Dina M. Siddiqi, 'In Search of Sonar Bangla (Golden Bengal)', *Himal*, May 2003, http://www.himalmag.com/component/content/article/146/18u-In-Search-of-Shonar-Bangla.html (accessed on 3 February 2011). Also see Nayanika Mookherjee, 'The Aesthetics of Nations: Anthropological and Historical Approaches', *Journal of the Royal Anthropological Institute* 17, no. 1 (2011): S1–S20. Recently, Prince Mahmud, known as 'Noble Man', a pop singer from Bangladesh, posed a similar question. More seriously, Mufassil Islam, a Dublin-based academic accused Tagore of being 'Hindutwa fanatic' and thus argued that Tagore's song should not be the national anthem of Bangladesh. Mufassil Islam, 'Rabindranath, Jatiyo Songit o Dhormo', YouTube, https://www.youtube.com/watch?v=rU17IsWSmqw (accessed on 26 August 2019). Similar podcasts and tirade against Tagore abound on YouTube. It is difficult to estimate the popularity of such views.
11. The theme of national spatial construction, based on the colonial science of mapping, has informed the current historiography of nation-space in India. The relationship between space and nation also occupies the central focus of Manu Goswami's writings. Goswami has explored the relationship between British surveying and mapping and Indian imagining of state-space as the putative space of nation. In a similar manner, Sumathi Ramaswamy's recent work on the imagining of maps as a mother goddess vividly portrays gendered identity of maps as geomorphic figures. Ramaswamy acknowledges sensitivities among Muslims towards such geomorphic depictions of the Indian map but does not engage with Muslim intellectuals' alternative imaginings of the map of India, territoriality and nation. Ramaswamy, *The Goddess and the Nation*.

12. Faisal Devji, *Muslim Zion: Pakistan as a Political Idea* (London: Hurst & Company, 2013).
13. Following Bob Jessop, I use the term 'space' as comprising of 'the socially produced grids and horizons of social life. It offers a whole series of strategically selective possibilities to develop social relations that stretch over space and time.' Bob Jessop, 'Gramsci as a Spatial Theorist', *Critical Review of International Social and Political Philosophy* 8, no. 4 (2005): 421–37, p. 424.
14. Frantz Fanon, *The Wretched of the Earth*, trans. Constance Farrington (London: Grove Press, 1968 [1961]), p. 152.
15. Neil Lazaras used Anouar Abdel-Malek's term to indicate Fanon's commitment to a different form of internationalist nationalism. I quote here from Lazaras' analysis: 'Fanon commits himself to precisely such a "unisonant" view of the decolonized state in distinguishing categorically between bourgeois nationalism and another would-be hegemonic form of national consciousness – a liberationist, anti-imperialist, nationalist internationalism, represented in the Algerian arena by the radical anti-colonial resistance movement, the Front de Liberation Nationale (FLN), to whose cause Fanon devoted himself actively between 1956 and 1961, the year of his death. Of this latter – "nationalitarian" (the term is Abdel-Malek's) – form of consciousness, Fanon wrote that it "is not nationalism" in the narrow sense; on the contrary, it "is the only thing that will give us an international dimension.… it is national liberation which leads the nation to play its part on the stage of history. It is at the heart of national consciousness that international consciousness lives and grows.' Neil Lazarus, 'Disavowing Decolonization: Fanon, Nationalism, and the Problematic of Representation in Current Theories of Colonial Discourse', *Research in African Literatures* 24, no. 4 (1993): 69–98, p. 72, https://jstor.org/stable/3820255 (accessed on 28 April 2020). Fanon, *The Wretched of the Earth*, pp. 247–48.
16. Tajuddin kept his diaries in the English language between 1946 and 1956. He handed them over to historian Badruddin Umar when the latter was writing the history of language movement in Bengal. Umar returned to him the diaries of the year 1946 and 1956, but he kept with himself his daily journals between 1947 and 1953. Tajuddin later told Umar that he lost the diaries of those years during the Pakistani military invasion. He further added that given his uncertain lifestyle, Umar should keep his journals for their safekeeping. After Tajuddin's death in the hands of right-wing

military coup plotters in 1975, Umar handed over Tajuddin's diaries to the latter's family. Though Tajuddin wrote in English, this account is based on the printed Bengali version of his daily journal. See Tajuddin Ahmad, *Tajuddin's Diary*, vol. 1, ed. and trans. Simin Hossain Rimi (Dhaka: Protibhas, 2014 [1999]), entry of 14 August 1947, pp. 48–49.

17. Pakistan celebrates its Independence Day on 14 August though according to the Indian Independence Act, 1947, the real handover of power took place on 15 August 1947. However, in 1947 the ceremonies for the transfer of power were held a day earlier in Pakistan so that the last British viceroy, Lord Mountbatten of Burma, could attend the ceremonies in both Pakistan and India. In Dacca the ceremonies took place on 15 August 1947. Yet K. K. Aziz, a Pakistani historian, is extremely critical of the practice of describing 14 August 1947 as the Independence Day of Pakistan. See K. K. Aziz, *The Murder of History: A Critique of History Textbooks Used in Pakistan* (Delhi: Renaissance Publishing House, 1998).

18. Based on T. Ahmad, *Tajuddin's Diary*, entry of 15 August 1947, pp. 49–52.

19. Debarshi Das and Arupjyoti Saikia, 'Early Twentieth Century Agrarian Assam: A Brief and Preliminary Overview', *Economic and Political Weekly* 46, no. 41 (2011): 73–80. Also see Jayeeta Sharma, *Empire's Garden: Assam and the Making of India* (Durham, NC: Duke University Press, 2011). Udayon Misra, 'Immigration and Identity Transformation in Assam', *Economic and Political Weekly* 34, no. 21 (1999): 1264–271. Also see Sanjib Baruah, *India against Itself: Assam and the Politics of Nationality* (Philadelphia: University of Pennsylvania Press, 1999), pp. 49–56.

20. L. S. Gassah, 'Trade Routes and Trade Relations between Jayantia Hills and Sylhet District in the Pre-Independence Period', in *Proceedings of North East India History Association*, 9th session, Gauhati University, Guwahati, 1988, pp. 202–08 (Shillong: North East India History Association, Department of History, North-Eastern Hill University, 1988); B. B. Kumar, 'The Border Trade in North-East India: The Historical Perspective', in *Border Trade: North-East India and Neighbouring Countries*, edited by Gurudas Das and R. K. Purkayastha (New Delhi: Akansha Publishing, 2000); Jayanta Bhusan Bhattacharjee, 'Genesis and Patterns of British Administration in the Hill Areas of North Eastern India', *Proceedings of the Indian History Congress* 36 (1975): 409–30.

21. Thomas Costa and Anindita Dutta, *The Khasis of Bangladesh: A Socio-Economic Survey of the Khasi People*, edited by Philip Gain and Aneeka Malik (Dhaka: Society for Environment and Human Development

[SEHD], 2007); Md Kayum Shikdar, Amitkumar Biswas and Ripon Mollick, 'The Socio-Economic Background of Khasia Ethnic Community of Bangladesh', *IOSR Journal Of Humanities And Social* 7, no. 4 (January–February 2007): 58–72.
22. Azizul Rasel, 'Experiencing the Border: The Lushai People and Transnational Space', in *Borders and Mobility in South Asia and Beyond*, edited by Reece Jones and Md. Azmeary Ferdoush, pp. 81–97 (Amsterdam: Amsterdam University Press, 2018).
23. Das and Saikia, 'Early Twentieth Century Agrarian Assam', pp. 73–80.
24. Subho Basu, *Does Class Matter? Colonial Capital and Workers' Resistance in Bengal, 1890–1937* (New Delhi: Oxford University Press, 2004).
25. For details, see Tariq Omar Ali, *A Local History of Global Capital: Jute and Peasant Life in the Bengal Delta* (Princeton, NJ: Princeton University Press, 2018).
26. Tirthankar Roy, 'Where Is Bengal? Situating an Indian Region in the Early Modern World Economy', *Past & Present* 213, no. 1 (November 2011): 115–46.
27. 'Procedure of Correspondence between Assistant Trade Commissioner and the Government of East Bengal', 31 C-7/49, Political Branch, B Proceedings, Bundle No. 1, January–November 1950, Home Department, Government of East Bengal, National Archives of Bangladesh.
28. 'Procedure of Correspondence between Assistant Trade Commissioner and the Government of East Bengal', 31 C-7/49, file titled 'Tripura State Border Matters', Political Branch, B Proceedings, Bundle No. 1, January–November 1950, Home Department, Government of East Bengal, National Archives of Bangladesh.
29. 'Procedure of Correspondence between Assistant Trade Commissioner and the Government of East Bengal', 31 C-7/49, file titled 'Copy of Report of Additional Superintendent of Police, Tippera, Dated 12.11.48', Political Branch, B Proceedings, Bundle No. 1, January–November 1950, Home Department, Government of East Bengal, National Archives of Bangladesh.
30. Milani Sur, 'Battles for the Golden Grain: Paddy Soldiers and the Making of the Northeast India–East Pakistan Border, 1930–1970', *Comparative Studies in Society and History* 58, no. 3 (July 2016): 804–32, pp. 807.
31. 'Procedure of Correspondence between Assistant Trade Commissioner and the Government of East Bengal', 31 C-7/49, file titled 'Tripura State Border Matters'.

32. 'Procedure of Correspondence between Assistant Trade Commissioner and the Government of East Bengal', 31 C-7/49, file titled 'Extracts from the Minutes of the Conference Held at the Residence of the Dewan of the Tripura State Agartala, at 2:30 p.m. on 12th January, 1949', Political Branch, B Proceedings, Bundle No. 1, January–November 1950, Home Department, Government of East Bengal, National Archives of Bangladesh.
33. 'Procedure of Correspondence between Assistant Trade Commissioner and the Government of East Bengal', 31 C-7/49, file titled 'Harassment of Travellers – Detention of Trains, Border Searches Dates and Details', Political Branch, B Proceedings, Bundle No. 1, January–November 1950, Home Department, Government of East Bengal, National Archives of Bangladesh.
34. 'Procedure of Correspondence between Assistant Trade Commissioner and the Government of East Bengal', 31 C-7/49, file titled 'West Bengal's Complaints Regarding Hili Rail Station', Political Branch, B Proceedings, Bundle No. 1, January–November 1950, Home Department, Government of East Bengal, National Archives of Bangladesh.
35. One such instance of vigilante groups was that of the Kirit Vikram Bahini by Habul Chandra Banerjee who was expelled from Comilla on the district magistrate (DM)'s order. Habul Chandra had some connections in the past with revolutionary nationalists. The Bahini sought to check the migration of peasants from the East Bengal territory across Tripura border. 'Procedure of Correspondence between Assistant Trade Commissioner and the Government of East Bengal', 31 C-7/49, file titled 'Inside Tripura State', Political Branch, B Proceedings, Bundle No. 1, January–November 1950, Home Department, Government of East Bengal, National Archives of Bangladesh.
36. From the midnight of 19 January 1950, the government of India prohibited selling of tickets to any East Bengal railway station. Passengers travelling to East Bengal were asked to travel to the border and then board a different train from the border upon purchasing a separate ticket. 'Bengal Obstacles to Rail Travel', *The Times*, Friday, 20 January 1950, p. 3.
37. Richard D. Lambert, 'Factors in Bengali Regionalism in Pakistan', *Far Eastern Survey* 28, no. 4 (1959): 49–58. DOI: 10.2307/3024111.
38. 'Indo-Pakistan Trade', *The Times*, 2 January 1950 p. 5.
39. Lambert, 'Factors in Bengali Regionalism in Pakistan'.
40. Lambert, 'Factors in Bengali Regionalism in Pakistan'.

41. 'Procedure of Correspondence between Assistant Trade Commissioner and the Government of East Bengal', 31 C-7/49, file titled 'Copy of Telegram from Hon'ble B. C Roy to Hon'ble Khawaja Nazimuddin, Premier East Bengal Dated the 4th September 1948', Political Branch, B Proceedings, Bundle No. 1, January–November 1950, Home Department, Government of East Bengal, National Archives of Bangladesh.
42. 'Procedure of Correspondence between Assistant Trade Commissioner and the Government of East Bengal', 31 C-7/49, file titled 'Copy of Telegram from Hon'ble B. C Roy to Hon'ble Khawaja Nazimuddin, Premier East Bengal Dated the 4th September 1948'.
43. The Indian English term 'communalism' does not explain critical process of ethnic cleansing that accompanied the border-making in post-colonial states of India and Pakistan.
44. The notion of organic nation is borrowed from Mann's understanding of the concept. He argues: 'Murderous ethnic cleansing is a hazard of the age of democracy since amid multiethnicity the ideal of rule by the people began to entwine the demos with the dominant ethnos, generating organic conceptions of the nation and the state that encouraged the cleansing of minorities.' Michael Mann, *The Dark Side of Democracy: Explaining Ethnic Cleansing* (New York: Cambridge University Press, 2005), p. 3.
45. Aamir R. Mufti, *Enlightenment in the Colony: The Jewish Question and the Crisis of Postcolonial Culture* (Princeton, NJ: Princeton University Press, 2007).
46. Joya Chatterji, 'Secularisation and Partition Emergencies: Deep Diplomacy in South Asia', *Economic and Political Weekly* 48, no. 50 (2013): 42–50.
47. Chatterji, 'Secularisation and Partition Emergencies', p. 44.
48. The Radcliffe proclamation, on 17 August 1947, finalized the dividing line between India and Pakistan both in the west and in the east.
49. 'Migration of Muslims from Nadia on Account of Hindu Persecution and Killing of Muslims and Burning of Muslim Homes', 31 C-7/49, file titled 'Letter to the District Magistrate, Jessore, through the Relief Officer Dated 2nd August 1948, Mahiuddin Ahmed on Behalf of Refugees of Santipore, Memo no. 1149, Copy Submitted to Chief Secretary to the Government of East Bengal, Dacca District Magistrate, Jessore, 3.8.48', Political Branch Bundle, January–November 1950, List 119, List 112 B, 306–35, Home Department (CR), Government of East Bengal, National Archives of Bangladesh.

50. 'Migration of Muslims from Nadia on Account of Hindu Persecution and Killing of Muslims and Burning of Muslim Homes', 31 C-7/49, file titled 'To the Secretary to the Government of Pakistan Ministry of Foreign Affairs and Commonwealth Relations, Karachi, Subject: Communal Violence and Killings of Muslims Santipur, District Nadia (West Bengal)', Political Branch Bundle, January–November 1950, List 119, List 112 B, 306–35, Home Department (CR), Government of East Bengal, National Archives of Bangladesh.
51. 'Migration of Muslims from Nadia on Account of Hindu Persecution and Killing of Muslims and Burning of Muslim Homes', 31 C-7/49, file titled 'To D. L. Power Esq, PAS, Dy Secretary to the Government of East Bengal Home (Political) Office of the District Magistrate Pabna 700c Dated Pabna the 10th July 1948 42, Petitions from Sadek Ali Mondal and Others', Political Branch Bundle, January–November 1950, List 119, List 112 B, 306–35, Home Department (CR), Government of East Bengal, National Archives of Bangladesh.
52. 'Migration of Muslims from Nadia on Account of Hindu Persecution and Killing of Muslims and Burning of Muslim Homes', 31 C-7/49, file titled 'To D. L. Power Esq, PAS, Dy Secretary to the Government of East Bengal Home (Political) Office of the District Magistrate Pabna 700c Dated Pabna the 10th July 1948 42, Petitions from Sadek Ali Mondal and Others'.
53. Mann, *The Dark Side of Democracy*, p. 5.
54. *The Statesman*, Calcutta, 24 July 1948.
55. 'Migration of Muslims from Nadia on Account of Hindu Persecution and Killing of Muslims and Burning of Muslim Homes', 31 C-7/49, file titled 'To the Secretary to the Government of Pakistan Ministry of Foreign Affairs and Commonwealth Relations, Karachi, Subject: Communal Violence and Killings of Muslims Santipur, District Nadia (West Bengal)'.
56. 'Migration of Muslims from Nadia on Account of Hindu Persecution and Killing of Muslims and Burning of Muslim Homes', 31 C-7/49, file titled 'Letter to the District Magistrate, Jessore, through the Relief Officer Dated 2nd August 1948, Mahiuddin Ahmed on Behalf of Refugees of Santipore, Memo no. 1149, Copy Submitted to Chief Secretary to the Government of East Bengal, Dacca District Magistrate, Jessore, 3.8.48'.
57. 'Migration of Muslims from Nadia on Account of Hindu Persecution and Killing of Muslims and Burning of Muslim Homes', 31 C-7/49, file titled 'Top Priority Radiogram, H. H. Nomani, District Magistrate, Jessore, Memo No. 1085C, District Office, Jessore, the 22nd July 1948, Best Copy

Forwarded to the Chief Secretary, Government of East Bengal, Dacca', Political Branch Bundle, January–November 1950, List 119, List 112 B, 306–35, Home Department (CR), Government of East Bengal, National Archives of Bangladesh.

58. 'Migration of Muslims from Nadia on Account of Hindu Persecution and Killing of Muslims and Burning of Muslim Homes', 31 C-7/49, file titled 'Secret Memo No. 1023, G. Rajshahi, Magistrate, Dated 25th July 1948', Political Branch Bundle, January–November 1950, List 119, List 112 B, 306–35, Home Department (CR), Government of East Bengal, National Archives of Bangladesh.

59. Subhasri Ghosh, 'The Working of the Nehru Liaqat Pact: A Case Study of Nadia District, 1950', *Proceedings of the Indian History Congress* 68, no. 1 (2007): 853–62, p. 855. The statistics are collected from R. A. Dutch, *Census of India, 1941*, vol. 4: *Bengal* (Delhi: Manager of Publications, Government of India, 1942), p. 211; Constituent Assembly of India, *Population of India According to Communities Based on the 1941 Census* (Delhi: Government of India, 1947), pp. 10, 12; Asok Mitra, *Census of India, 1951: District Census Handbook* (Delhi: Manager of Publications, Government of India, 1953).

60. Kedar Nath Chatterji (ed.), *The Modern Review: A Monthly Review of Miscellany*, vol. 88 (July–December 1950), p. 345, cited in Ghosh, 'The Working of the Nehru Liaqat Pact', p. 854.

61. Moni Singh, *Jibon Songram* (Prothom Khondo) (Dhaka: Jatio Sahitya Prokashoni, 1983), p. 157.

62. Badruddin Umar, *Purbo Banglar Bhasha Andolon o Totkalin Rajniti* (Dwitio Khondo) (Dhaka: Subarna, 2011), pp. 266–67.

63. Pallavi Raghavan, 'The Making of the India–Pakistan Dynamic: Nehru, Liaquat, and the No War Pact Correspondence of 1950', *Modern Asian Studies* 50, no. 5 (2016): 645–78.

64. The story of Dalit repression was clear in the letters written to Jogendranath Mondal, the leader of the Scheduled Caste Federation. For details, see Dwaipayan Sen, *The Decline of the Caste Question: Jogendranath Mandal and the Defeat of Dalit Politics in Bengal* (Cambridge: Cambridge University Press, 2018), pp. 198–99.

65. Umar, *Purbo Banglar Bhasha Andolon* (Dwitio Khondo), pp. 266–67.

66. Taya Zinkin, *Reporting India* (London: Chatto & Windus, 1962), p. 37.

67. 'Blood in Bengal', *Newsweek*, New York, 10 April 1950, p. 41.

68. Umar, *Purbo Banglar Bhasha Andolon* (Dwitio Khondo), p. 270.

69. Tajuddin Ahmad, *Tajuddin's Diary*, vol. 2, ed. and trans. Simin Hossain Rimi (Dhaka: Protibhas, 2014 [1999]), pp. 74–76.
70. Abul Mansur Ahmad, *Amar Dekha Rajnitir Ponchas Botsor* (Dhaka: Prothoma, 2018), pp. 258–59.
71. T. Ahmad, *Tajuddin's Diary*, vol. 2, pp. 74–76.
72. Bundle List No. 119, December to January 1952–1953, File No. CR2B-3 of 1950, Proceedings 1024 to 1028 B July 1952, Home Department, Government of East Bengal, National Archives of Bangladesh.
73. Bundle List No. 119, December to January 1952–1953, File No. CR2B-3 of 1950, Proceedings 1024 to 1028 B, July 1952, Letter from C. C. Biswas, Minister for Relief and Rehabilitation, to Dr. A. M. Malik, dated 5 September 1950', Home Department, Government of East Bengal, National Archives of Bangladesh. In Barisal, 330 cases were lodged and 2096 persons were arrested. However, only one police officer of sub-inspector (SI) rank and six constables were prosecuted. Md Barkatulla, Report of District Magistrate 13.11.1950, Bundle List No. 119, December to January 1952–1953, File No. CR2B-3 of 1950, Proceedings 1024 to 1028 B, July 1952, National Archives of Bangladesh.
74. Zinkin, *Reporting India*, pp. 39–53.
75. Zinkin, *Reporting India*, pp. 39–53.
76. Zinkin, *Reporting India*, pp. 39–53.
77. Zinkin, *Reporting India*, pp. 39–53.
78. Raghavan, 'The Making of the India–Pakistan Dynamic'.
79. 'Migration of Muslims from Nadia on Account of Hindu Persecution and Killing of Muslims and Burning of Muslim Homes', 31 C-7/49, file titled 'Letter to District Magistrate Rajshahi, Ranibazar, 24.7.48', Political Branch Bundle, January–November 1950, List 119, List 112 B, 306–35, Home Department (CR), Government of East Bengal, National Archives of Bangladesh.
80. Anasua Basu Raychaudhury, 'Nostalgia of "Desh", Memories of Partition', *Economic and Political Weekly* 39, no. 52 (2004): 5653–660.
81. M. R. Akhtar Mukul, *Ponchaser Doshoker Rajniti o Sheikh Mujib* (Dhaka: Bikash Mudron, 2011), p. 30.
82. Zinkin, *Reporting India*, pp. 44–45.
83. Umar, *Purbo Banglar Bhasha Andolon* (Dwitio Khondo), p. 113. Also see I. N. Mukherji, 'Agrarian Reforms in Bangladesh', *Asian Survey* 16, no. 5 (1976): 452–64.

84. J. Russel Andrus and Azizali F. Mohammed, *The Economy of Pakistan* (London, Karachi and Dacca: Oxford University Press, 1958), p. 120.
85. M. H. Khan, *The Role of Agriculture in Economic Development: A Case Study of Pakistan* (Wageningen: Centre for Agricultural Publications and Documentation, 1966), p. 130.
86. Abu Abdullah, 'Land Reform and Agrarian Change in Bangladesh', *Bangladesh Development Studies* 4, no. 1 (1976): 67–114, pp. 73–74.
87. A. H. M. Ishaque, *Agricultural Statistics by Plot-to-Plot Enumeration in Bengal 1944–45* (Calcutta: Department of Agriculture, Forest and Fisheries, Government of Bengal).
88. Abdullah, 'Land Reform and Agrarian Change in Bangladesh', pp. 72–74.
89. Abdullah, 'Land Reform and Agrarian Change in Bangladesh', pp. 80–84.
90. Abdullah, 'Land Reform and Agrarian Change in Bangladesh', p. 83.
91. F. Tomasson Jannuzi and James T. Peach, 'Note on Land Reform in Bangladesh: The Efficacy of Ceilings', *Journal of Peasant Studies* 6, no. 3 (1979): 342–47, p. 343.
92. Abdullah, 'Land Reform and Agrarian Change in Bangladesh', p. 86.
93. Abdullah, 'Land Reform and Agrarian Change in Bangladesh', p. 86.
94. S. A Quadir, *Village Dhaniswar: Three Generations of Man-Made Adjustment in East Pakistan Village* (Comilla: Pakistan Academy for Village Development, 1960), p. 112.
95. 'Bengal Partitioned', *The Times*, 26 July 1948, p. 5.
96. 'Bengal Partitioned', *The Times*.
97. Umar, *Purbo Banglar Bhasha Andolon* (Dwitio Khondo).
98. Ahmed Kamal, *State against the Nation: The Decline of the Muslim League in Pre-Independence Bangladesh 1947–54* (Dhaka: University Press Limited, 2009), p. 69.
99. 'Report of the Executive Enquiry on the Firing Resorted to by the Armed Police Party Posted at Chanchkoir on 12.1.48' (Police P5R-10/48 [10–48]), cited in Willem van Schendel, 'Working through Partition: Making a Living in the Bengal Borderlands', *International Review of Social History* 46, no. 3 (2001): 393–421, p. 411.
100. Umar, *Purbo Banglar Bhasha Andolon* (Dwitio Khondo), p. 47.
101. Umar, *Purbo Banglar Bhasha Andolon* (Dwitio Khondo), pp. 55–56.
102. *Bhadralok* refers to wealthy, successful, well-educated people, usually from Bangladesh or West Bengal, who are considered to have high social status.

103. David M. Laushey, *Bengal Terrorism & the Marxist Left: Aspects of Regional Nationalism in India, 1905–1942* (Calcutta: Firma K. L. Mukhopadhyay, 1975).
104. Goutam Kumar Dey, 'The Formation of Bengal Provincial Kisan Sabha and the Roll of Communist Party', *Proceedings of the Indian History Congress* 75 (2014): 623–27.
105. D. N. Dhanagare, 'Peasant Protest and Politics: The Tebhaga Movement in Bengal (India), 1946–47', *Journal of Peasant Studies* 3, no. 3 (1976): 360–78.
106. Jnanabrata Bhattacharyya, 'An Examination of Leadership Entry in Bengal Peasant Revolts, 1937–1947', *Journal of Asian Studies* 37, no. 4 (1978): 611–35.
107. Muhammad Abdullah Rasul, *Krishak Sabhar Itihas* (Calcutta: Nobojatok Prakashan, 1969), p. 154.
108. Bhattacharyya, 'An Examination of Leadership Entry'.
109. Bhabani Sen, 'Banglay Tebhaga Andolon', in *Tebhaga Smarak*, Calcutta, pp. 14–15, cited in Kamal, *State against the Nation*, p. 112.
110. Singh, *Jibon Songram* (Prothom Khondo).
111. Bhattacharyya, 'An Examination of Leadership Entry'.
112. Moni Singh, *Jibon Songram* (Dwitio Khondo) (Dhaka: Jatio Sahitya Prokashoni, 1992), p. 11.
113. Marcus F. Franda, 'Communism and Regional Politics in East Pakistan', *Asian Survey* 10, no. 7 (1970): 588–606, p. 588.
114. Zhdanov was a Soviet politician and cultural theorist. After the Second World War, he was regarded as the successor-in-waiting to Soviet leader Joseph Stalin but died before him.
115. Cominform was founded at a conference of communist parties from across Europe in Szklarska Poręba, Poland, in September 1947.
116. John H. Kautsky, 'Indian Communist Party Strategy Since 1947', *Pacific Affairs* 28, no. 2 (1955): 145–60, pp. 149–50.
117. Kavita Panjabi, '"Otiter Jed" or Times of Revolution: Ila Mitra, the Santals and Tebhaga Movement', *Economic and Political Weekly* 45, no. 33 (2010): 53–59.
118. For details of the repression of communist rebellion and politics in tribal borderland of Mymensingh, see Sur, 'Battles for the Golden Grain'.
119. Kamal, *State against the Nation*, pp. 120–28.
120. Oli Ahad, *Jatio Rajniti 1945–75* (Sixth Edition) (Dhaka: Bangladesh Co-Operative Book Society Limited, 2015), p. 100.

121. *Sanai* is Bengali for the Indian classical musical instrument *shehnai*, a double-reed conical oboe made of wood except for a flaring metal bell attached to the bottom of the instrument. It is similar to the flute.
122. 'Assembly Question Regarding Firing Incident on 29th September 1948 at Madrassa Village in the District of Chittagong', P3I-9/55 B158 SL 152, Home Department, Government of East Bengal, National Archives of Bangladesh.
123. Harun-or-Rashid, *The Foreshadowing of Bangladesh: Bengal Muslim League and Muslim Politics, 1936–1947* (Dhaka: Asiatic Society of Bangladesh, 1987).
124. *Mufassil*, or *mofussil*, refers to the regions outside the three East India Company capitals of Bombay, Calcutta and Madras in colonial India – in other words, parts of the country outside its major urban centres.
125. Shila Sen, *Muslim Politics in Bengal, 1937–1947* (New Delhi: Impex India, 1976), pp. 181–86.
126. Harun-or-Rashid, *The Foreshadowing of Bangladesh*.
127. Umar, *Purbo Banglar Bhasha Andolon* (Prothom Khondo), pp. 203–10.
128. Umar, *Purbo Banglar Bhasha Andolon* (Prothom Khondo), pp. 210–37.
129. Umar, *Purbo Banglar Bhasha Andolon* (Prothom Khondo), pp. 210–37.
130. Ahmed, *Amar Dekha Rajnitir Ponchas Botsor*, p. 187.
131. Bhashani was in prison. He came to east after he was released. Syed Abul Maksud, *Maulana Abdul Hamid Khan Bhasani* (Dhaka: Agami Prokashoni, 2014), p. 91.
132. Ahad, *Jatio Rajniti*, p. 89.
133. Umar, *Purbo Banglar Bhasha Andolon* (Prothom Khondo), pp. 210–37.
134. Umar, *Purbo Bnaglar Bhasha Andolon* (Prothom Khondo), pp. 210-237.
135. Harun-or-Rashid, *Mul Dharar Rajniti: Bangladesh Awami League Council 1949–2016* (Mainstream Politics: Bangladesh Awami League Council 1949–2016) (Dhaka: Bangla Academy, 2019), pp. 3–4.
136. Notable among them were Tajuddin Ahmad and Oli Ahad. They objected to the inclusion of 'Muslim' in the name of the organization and preferred a more non-sectarian organization.
137. *New York Times*, 8 July 1954, cited in Stanley Maron, 'The Problem of East Pakistan', *Pacific Affairs* 28, no. 2 (1955): 132–44, p. 133.
138. Richard L. Park, 'East Bengal: Pakistan's Troubled Province', *Far Eastern Survey* 23, no. 5 (1954): 70–74.
139. 'Anti Government Propaganda and Communist Slogans by the Organizers of Awami League at Gopal Gunj, Faridpur', Bundle 51, B Proceedings,

May–September 1949–50, 3R-50/49, Home Department, Government of East Bengal, National Archives of Bangladesh.
140. This would become evident when the two parted ways in an acrimonious manner in 1956–57. For details, see M. Rashiduzzaman, 'The National Awami Party of Pakistan: Leftist Politics in Crisis', *Pacific Affairs* 43, no. 3 (1970): 394–409.
141. Harun-or-Rashid, *Mul Dharar Rajniti*, pp. 15–16.
142. Ahmad, *Amar Dekha Rajnitir Ponchas Botsor*, p. 266.
143. Harun-or-Rashid, *Mul Dharar Rajiniti*, pp. 21–22.
144. Ahmad, *Amar Dekha Rajnitir Ponchas Botsor*, pp. 267–71.
145. *Pardah*, or *purdah*, refers to the state and practice of seclusion or concealment among Muslim women.
146. Ahmad, *Amar Dekha Rajnitir Ponchas Botsor*, p. 273.
147. Ahmad, *Amar Dekha Rajnitir Ponchas Botsor*, p. 274
148. Ahmad, *Amar Dekha Rajnitir Ponchas Botsor*, p. 274.
149. Park, 'East Bengal', p. 73.
150. Richard L. Park and Richard S. Wheeler, 'East Bengal under Governor's Rule', *Far Eastern Survey* 23, no. 9 (1954): 129–34, p. 131.
151. Layli Uddin, '"Enemy Agents at Work": A Microhistory of the 1954 Adamjee and Karnaphuli Riots in East Pakistan', *Modern Asian Studies* 55, no. 2 (2021): 629–64.
152. Park and Wheeler, 'East Bengal under Governor's Rule', p. 132.
153. Park and Wheeler, 'East Bengal under Governor's Rule', p. 133.
154. 'Home Poll Leaflet Statement of Shah Syed Ghulum Sarwar, MLA, Regarding the Present Situation in East Bengal', List 118, Bundle 25. DO no. 5998 Poll, 4L-3/54, October 1955, Home Department, Government of East Bengal, National Archives of Bangladesh.
155. Political Branch, B Proceedings 110, List No. 118 B, February 1955, 362–363, Home Department, Government of East Bengal, National Archives of Bangladesh.

2

Global Politics and Local Alignment

Cold War Bureaucratic-Military Alliance
and Popular Resistance

Layli Uddin, a British scholar of Bengali descent, recalls how an 84-year-old peasant, Burhan Uddin, told her with conviction that Bhashani used to fly 'over trees on his boat protected by an ambush of tigers and … the thwack of his *lathi* [walking stick] reverberating across the entire subcontinent'.[1] This attribution of supernatural powers to a political leader, who captured the imagination of subaltern classes, was not unprecedented in the annals of Indian social movements. Shahid Amin notes similar rumours circulating among peasants in the United Provinces, in India, during the Khilafat–non-cooperation movement of the twenties; here, too, the peasants imagined M. K. Gandhi as possessing supernatural powers.[2] Like Gandhi, who was a masterful politician of twentieth-century South Asia, Bhashani neither held a formal position of authority in the power structures of state nor evinced any desire for such formal trappings. Born in a peasant family, he was more interested in translating his moral capital, earned as a social activist and religious interlocutor, into political capital for the construction of collective resistance of subaltern communities. Though he appeared inchoate and inconsistent to many among his opponents, Bhashani sought to pit a morally grounded communitarian ideology of labour against the colonial process of surplus accumulation across both colonial and seemingly post-colonial temporalities in East Bengal. In this process, he engaged with various ideological apparatuses of the international socialist movements and, ultimately, as a peasant populist, was drawn to the emotional appeal of Chinese agrarian socialism.

In the fifties, Bhashani's opposition to the West Pakistani regime was grounded in the demand for proportional elected representation according to the population distribution in different provinces. He combined this demand with constitutional autonomy. Admittedly, regional autonomy was also the goal of the constitutionalists in the Awami League. The crucial difference between Bhashani and his fierce critics drawn from the moderate constitutionalists in the Awami League was this: Bhashani attempted to fuse these demands while also opposing Pakistan's closeness to the Western military bloc. He deciphered, in the formation of military bloc, a crucial hindrance towards the global movement for decolonization. As the president of the Awami League, Bhashani did not want the organization to be a party to such an 'imperial alliance'. His rejection was based on the fact that, in his opinion, the imperial powers were engaged in suppressing national liberation struggles in South-West Asia in particular and Asia and Africa in general.[3] Bhashani became a far more vocal critic of the US-sponsored military alliance in the wake of the Suez Crisis (1956–57). As a post-colonial Muslim nation, Pakistan could ill-afford to ignore the massive demonstration of public support for Egypt during the Suez Crisis.

In order to excavate the roots of this debate, this chapter analyses the patterns in the formation of post-colonial polity in Pakistan. In the process of transition to the post-colonial Pakistani 'nation state', the Muslim League, the premier political party, was expected to play a decisive role in the 'hybridization' of the colonial state. To this end, the Muslim League would empower popular classes in subjugating the residual functionaries of the post-colonial state, whose previous role had been mainly coercive: the bureaucracy and judiciary, the police and the military. However, it failed miserably in performing such tasks. Clearly, the emergence of any centralized post-partition political hegemony required more than the conclusion of a deal between the political elites of two wings. It required cohesion and solidarity between the elites of all ethnicities in order to make up a new political ruling class whose function would be to not simply dominate but also lead an uneven and fractious alliance of subordinate classes and communities.

Yet the social conditions were not present to achieve such fusion. In West Pakistan powerful quasi-feudal landholding elites, who had a critical presence in the party-political apparatus, army and, to a lesser extent, bureaucracy – the residual coercive apparatuses of colonial state – did not have the political will or even the capacity to carry out reforms. As a consequence, instead of being subjugated to the representatives of popular social classes, coercive colonial institutions gained a new lease of life within the post-colonial polity. In East Pakistan, in contrast, the emergent 'middle class' actually entered the political stage through a struggle against the residual landlordism which was instituted by the colonial regime.

As a consequence, in Pakistan the new state had failed not only to assimilate the intellectuals inherited from the colonial state and its institutions but also to recruit those 'organic' intellectuals whose links to the masses and civil society were not simply formal or bureaucratic.

Thus, the democratic aspirations of the 'middle-class' political activists of East Pakistan, where a majority of Pakistanis resided, clashed with the political power configurations of West Pakistan, the epicentre of power in the post-colonial situation. Increasingly composed of an emerging bureaucratic-military[4] oligarchy, the political elites of West Pakistan, whose origins could also be traced to landed elites, sought external-aid-driven growth so as to bypass any internal socio-economic reforms or democratic institutional transformations.

The fifties witnessed a critical consolidation of military alliances, sponsored by the US, whose sole aim was to encircle the Soviet Union and the People's Republic of China (PRC) and contain the spread of global communist movements. Within Pakistan, military leaders and politicians, recruited primarily from landowning classes, sought an alliance with the US in order to obtain funding for their military and industrial regeneration. At the same time, most political activists from East Pakistan, including those belonging to the Awami League, were committed to keeping the Cold War outside South Asia. However, the constitutionalists within the Awami League, who, in the fifties, came to share power at both central and provincial levels through popular movements, also hoped that a general election would enable them to extend popular control over the state and its coercive apparatus.

In contrast to the constitutionalists, Bhashani and his political associates (among peasant populists, socialists and communists) deciphered that such a global military alliance would further enhance the power of bureaucratic-military oligarchy in the country. They felt that the membership of this international military alliance would commit Pakistan to Cold War alignments. A policy of non-alignment, based upon Afro-Asian solidarity, would, in their perception, possibly relate the pro-democracy movement in East Pakistan to the global decolonization struggles. As part of this later internationalist commitment, Bhashani lent political support to the poor peasants' demand for agrarian reforms, to workers' movements for industrial democracy and to a cultural conference tracing the roots of East Bengali culture to a common South Asian heritage. This emphasis on the commonality of the origin of South Asian culture led many of his opponents within the constitutionalist faction to brand him an 'Indian agent'.[5] They sought to soft-pedal the issue because they did not want to destabilize the structure of governance which they had become a part of – at both the centre and state levels – despite being aware of the limited power civilian governments wielded. Yet the dispute between internationalists and constitutionalists within the Awami League became so bitter that Bhashani and his associates ultimately opted for a new political party in 1957 – the National Awami Party (NAP). In many ways, the emergence of Bhashani's NAP represented a critical ideological link between the global political alignment and its local political manifestation. The terms 'local' and 'global' are used here to signpost the mutuality of local–global political spheres as they co-determined the struggle for autonomy in East Pakistan, and Pakistani politics in general, in the Cold War era. The imbrication of local and global politics presaged the coming of the sixties in Pakistan.

Agrarian Class Structure and Military-Bureaucratic Axis in Post-Colonial State in Pakistan between 1947 and 1954

To a large degree, the class structure of agrarian landlordism directed the West Pakistani politics of the fifties. The domination of landlords in West Pakistan's agrarian structure impacted not only the quotidian politics of governance but also more macro aspects, such as the overall developmental priorities of the state. Reaching deep into political and military nexuses, this landlordism forms the backdrop to Pakistan's inability to implement land reforms, extract surplus from agrarian sector or make sectoral transfer of resources towards industrialization. Such agrarian reforms could have enhanced tenurial security in rural areas, increased agricultural productivity and also expanded an internal market. Indeed, wherever one finds instances of successful state-based development, such as in the East Asian economies of South Korea and Taiwan, one also notices the presence of pre-industrialization land reforms. In many ways, Pakistan was much closer to the Latin American countries – caught in an early stage of industrialization where agrarian reforms were restricted by a landed oligarchy – and sought to become a developmental state with very moderate success.[6]

A cursory glance at the West Pakistani society of the fifties would confirm the deep stranglehold exercised by landholders over economy and polity. According to agricultural statistics four-fifths of the cultivated land in Sind, nearly half of the cultivated land in Punjab and a little less than half in the North-West Frontier Province (NWFP) were owned by big landlords. About 7,000 of them in Sind owned more than 500 acres each. Even in Punjab, where the number of very big owners was comparatively small, ownership extending over 3,000 acres was not rare.[7] Before the land reforms of 1959, introduced by martial-law administration, land legislation in West Pakistan remained patchy and varied from region to region. No doubt then that in 1950 the NWFP, the Punjab and Sind passed provincial tenancy Acts. These Acts sought to provide security of tenure and regulate rental shares. In some cases, they restricted certain cesses imposed by landlords on tenants. However, despite these efforts, an overwhelming majority of the tenants remained dependent on landed elites in West Pakistan.[8]

The political system that flourished within such a landlord-dominated social matrix obviously reflected their hegemony. In the Muslim League Council, out of a total membership of 503, as many as 163 were landlords. Interestingly, the next largest constituent group in the Council was that of the lawyers, who numbered around 145.[9] Their legal certifications, however, were mere sheepskin, for many among this group, too, drew an income from land ownership and did not actively practice law. Individually and collectively, these landed elites sought to preserve landholding interests and were not susceptible to party-political disciplines. This dependence on landlords was reflected in the workings of the provincial assemblies of West Pakistan. Talukder Moniruzzaman, a political scientist from East Pakistan, notes the popular saying that 'the key to Pakistan politics is to be found in a little official publication for restricted circulation by the Government of India before 1914 ... entitled The Landed Families of the Punjab'.[10] The applicability of this saying is as clearly visible in the dynamics of West Pakistan of the fifties as in '1914' – for parliamentary politics still operated in terms of rivalries among different coteries of landlords.

This landlord domination generated a particular form of clientelist politics. As per Luis Roniger, 'clientelism involves asymmetric but mutually beneficial relationships of power and exchange, a non-universalistic quid pro quo between individuals or groups of unequal standing'.[11] This implies a mediated and discriminatory access to resources and markets. In the landlord-dominated politics of West Pakistan, mostly landholding elites 'provided selective access to goods and opportunities that placed themselves or their supporters in positions from which they can divert resources and services in their favor'. These landholding elites' decisions to distribute resources were governed more by localized customary practices than party-political disciplines. Such observations, at the same time, are not meant to imply that the patron–client relationship is only a characteristic of the so-called traditional societies. Indeed, as early as 1968, Alex Weingrod clearly conceptualized the contrast between the traditional 'dyadic patronage' and modem 'party-directed clientelism' in terms of the degree of segmentation or integration of local sectors within nation states.[12] By taking into consideration such differential models of clientelism, we can argue that the landlord domination created an explicit form out of a particular kind of personalized resource control. This form potentially threatened the existence of the state, whose creation had already been marked by a high degree of precarity in 1947.

M. A. Jinnah, the undisputed leader of the Pakistan movement and the first governor general of the country, was aware of the self-engrossed clientelism of the quasi-feudal Muslim League local bosses. A terminally ill and overworked leader who was also a lonely political personality, Jinnah did not have the time or luxury to innovate upon methods of governance. Engaging in classic acts of path-dependency, Jinnah continued the colonial vice-regal system in order to overcome the deeply entrenched system-vested interest groups. This proved to be an institutionalized continuation of colonial governance, which thereby allowed the top bureaucrats to exercise power without the supervision of elected politicians.

Thus, from the very inception of Pakistan as a polity, members of the Civil Service of Pakistan (CSP) exercised significant influence over the administration of the constituent provinces. They kept the central government informed of provincial affairs by dispatching fortnightly reports to the office of governor general. After Jinnah's demise, under Liaquat Ali Khan, civil servants sacked elected provincial ministers.[13] While both Jinnah and Liaquat Ali enjoyed a significant degree of popular legitimacy, their successor Khawaja Nazimuddin lacked both popular legitimacy and political finesse. In 1951, when Nazimuddin decided to step down from the position of governor general in order to (rather unconstitutionally) become prime minister, he selected Ghulam Muhammad, a former bureaucrat in colonial audit and accountancy service, to become the governor general. Ghulam Muhammad was a finance minister in Liaquat Ali's government, but it was speculated that

Liaquat Ali might dispense with Ghulam Muhammad's service due to his ill health.[14] Nazimuddin's selection of Ghulam Muhammad was possibly based upon the shrewd calculation that since Ghulam Muhammad was physically enfeebled (due to his continued illness), he would be unable to use the power of his office against the prime minister.

Ironically, the power of the CSP reached its height under governor general Ghulam Muhammad. In April 1953, Ghulam Muhammad summarily dismissed prime minister Nazimuddin, despite the fact that the latter enjoyed the confidence of a majority of the members of the Constituent Assembly. Mohammad Ali Bogra, a diplomat, was brought in as his replacement.[15] Bogra, otherwise a lacklustre politician, devised a constitutional formula for power-sharing between two wings and placed it before the Constituent Assembly on 7 October 1953. His plan envisaged a bicameral federal assembly with two houses – the House of Unit and the House of People – and an inbuilt parity for the two wings. His plan further stipulated that the two houses of the legislative assembly would form the electoral college for the presidential elections, and the president was to be elected for a term of five years.[16] Emboldened by the success of the Constitution-making formula, on 21 September 1954 the Constituent Assembly challenged the power of the unelected governor general's office, ultimately divesting the position of its authority to dismiss the government. A panicked Ghulam Muhammad dismissed Pakistan's Constituent Assembly on 24 October 1954 and selected his council of 'all talents', a euphemism that was deployed to hide the impropriety of his act. The army chief, Ayub Khan, and the general, Iskandar Mirza, backed this dismissal, and Ayub Khan, the serving commander-in-chief, became the defence minister. Chaudhry Muhammad Ali, who had been a civil servant, worked as secretary general and cabinet secretary under Liaquat Ali and had later become the finance minister under Nazimuddin and continued as finance minister.[17] The tactics of the dissolution smacked of a palace coup whereby prime minister Bogra, who was summoned back from the US, found himself a virtual prisoner on his landing at the Karachi airport. A nervous Bogra was then compelled to announce on radio the dismissal of the Constituent Assembly. For his cooperation with this 'grand conspiracy' he was allowed to continue as the prime minister of Pakistan.[18] It was a process that was not entirely free from foreign intervention. British constitutional expert William Ivor Jennings provided legal justifications of the dismissal, and it was clear that his reasoning was premised upon the vice-regal system of colonial governance.[19]

General Mirza, Ghulam Muhammad's successor and a soldier-turned-civil-servant, provided the ideological justification for such an authoritarian system of governance. He argued that in a society where the majority of population were illiterate, politicians, as their elected representatives, produced anarchy, and thus a fully functioning democracy remained unsuitable for such societies.[20] This kind of arrogantly colonial perspective could only be articulated in such a candid manner because the popular representatives were neither popular nor very representational. West Pakistani politicians treated the peasantry, who constituted an overwhelming majority of the population, as their tenants rather than citizens.[21] Thus, they lacked the ability and political willingness to mobilize the peasant masses who alone could provide popular legitimacy to democratic representational rule. Indeed, all elections that were held in West Pakistan were marked by low turnouts and little popular enthusiasm.[22] The quasi-feudal political leadership allowed the bureaucracy to continue as the more powerful stakeholder in the polity, and political leaders negotiated their interests through backroom deals with bureaucrats. This rise of bureaucracy in Pakistan occurred in the early fifties because of the way the social structure conditioned interactions between popular leaders and the colonial institutions of the state. It was hardly a case of an overdeveloped state.

Yet it would be wrong to imagine that 300 elite members of the CSP in the fifties represented a 'modernizing developmentalist elite force' that would deliver land reforms and industrialization and alter the social structure so as to create the conditions for the rise of a developmental state in Pakistan.[23] In other words, they did not constitute a developmental bureaucracy that could operate above the interest-group dynamics emanating from the social structure or minimize rent-seeking activities. Though these civil servants had their origins in a middle-class social milieu and arrived at their jobs through a system of meritocracy, they desired a social relationship with these landholding elites and, more importantly, remained ideologically committed to the preservation of the agrarian status quo. In other words, because of the presence of such a powerful social class of landlords, it would have been impossible to deliver state-based development involving a redistribution of their assets. In terms of quotidian governance, members of the CSP relied on the carefully constructed colonial image of district officers as *mai–baap*, or loco parentis, of the rural folk.[24] Lacking popular legitimacy or the political will to engage in a radical social programme, they were a bastion of conservatism in Pakistan. Indeed, the colonial philosophy of paternalist despotism, based upon an alliance with landed elites, continued in post-colonial Pakistan, and people were confined to, to quote Dipesh Chakrabarty's memorable phrase, the 'waiting room of history'.[25]

The ultimate coercive power in Pakistan, as in all other sovereign states in the world, belonged to military. The weak nature of democratic control over the state apparatus of Pakistan, and the declining popular legitimacy of politicians, created a significant degree of autonomy for the army to take its place as the key institution of the state – for the military, unlike the top echelon of bureaucracy, was also the most crucial social institution in the region. It offered the second-largest source of employment outside of the agricultural sector in Punjab, the largest and most important province of West Pakistan.[26] In the late colonial era, the army had its own presence in the patron–client network in rural areas. After the First World War, worried about the loyalties of the troops, colonial officials embarked upon a policy of securing the soldiers' homes from seditious political persuasions. In Punjab, according to Tan Tai Yong, this was mainly accomplished through the merging of the civil and military authorities in the province, particularly through the post-war institution of the District Soldiers' Boards. These boards functioned as welfare institutions. In Punjab and in various pockets of West Pakistan, there came into existence a class of military officers from among landholding elites. In the forties, the vast majority of these soldiers were recruited from the Muslim-majority districts, because Sikhs were perceived to be influenced by communists and nationalists and therefore neglected by colonial military recruiters.[27]

This process was informed by a masculinist military culture. As argued by Prem Chowdhry, who has written in the context of south-east Punjab (which is equally applicable to north-west Punjab), the combination of marital race status, land ownership and good physique ideologically oriented these officers towards a militarized masculinity. This militarized masculinity was buttressed by legal and administrative measures, which had been, apparently, adopted in deference to certain popular cultural practices.[28] More importantly, despite their roots among rural landholding elites, military leaders in the late forties and early fifties were more exposed to global affairs than the civilian landholding elites. Many officers had commanded soldiers outside South Asia during the Second World War and enjoyed a close rapport with their superior British officers.[29] As independence approached, a select few among these officers were trained in the British military academy at Sandhurst. They were groomed as future leaders of the Pakistani army, and British officers selected them on their supposed loyalty to British strategic interests in the Middle East.[30] No doubt, the army officers' crop, with international experience and Western connections, and sharing an ideology of militarized masculinity, regarded themselves as natural leaders of the society.

From a very early stage in its existence, the Pakistani polity developed a model of power-sharing with the military. Though the army was under the control of civilian leaders during the brief period when Jinnah and Liaquat Ali exercised supreme control, it retained its autonomy. British generals who officered the army retained their independence; and after the indigenization of the army, the defence department remained in the hands of armed forces. Mirza, who had been a commissioned officer in the colonial army, became the defence secretary of independent Pakistan. It was true that Mirza was more of a bureaucrat than a military officer, but he carried the rank of major general and could appear as an insider–outsider in the army. It was Mirza, a Sandhurst trained officer, who, in 1951, supported the promotion of Ayub Khan to the position of commander-in-chief of the army, the first Pakistani to hold the post. He did so, however, under the mistaken assumption that Ayub Khan was the least politically ambitious among all the other contenders. As commander-in-chief, Ayub Khan undertook an independent state visit to Turkey in 1953, a crucial military partner of the US. He also visited the US in order to press for a military treaty in the same year, bypassing civilian leaders.[31] It was clear that with the transition to a Pakistani commander-in-chief, the army had assumed a far more proactive role in the administration. In 1954, when Ghulam Muhammad mounted a constitutional coup, he invited Ayub Khan, the serving commander-in-chief, to be the defence minister. This institutionalized the army's presence in the administration, and Tayyab Mahmud calls this praetorianism, or the beginning of the military's presence as the dominant partner in a country's government.[32]

Army officers coveted their connections with the West and saw in Western aid the solution to their resource crunch, in terms of both the supply of arsenal and the underwriting of civilian reconstruction projects. The strategic location of West Pakistan, the long-standing loyal service by the Indian and Pakistani armies to colonial causes and the relative immunity of the armies from 'civilian control' were appreciated by the Anglo-American political establishment and military leaders. What was interesting was that four main players in Pakistani politics in the fifties were all loyal colonial bureaucrats: Ghulam Muhammad, Chaudhry Muhammad Ali, Iskandar Mirza and Ayub Khan. These people had barely any connection with the

Pakistan movement or the general trajectories of the Indian independence struggle. Thus, the very structure of society in West Pakistan, its peculiar landlord domination, impacted the institutional alignment of the state and created conditions for an incomplete decolonization in Pakistan.

Cold War, the Military-Bureaucratic Axis and Internal Colonization, 1954-58

Within the West Pakistani state, the army and its bureaucratic allies, rather than the quasi-democratic political leaders, saw in the Cold War a solution to their resource crunch in terms of both the regeneration of the military and funds for civilian developmental programmes. While both the United Kingdom (UK) and the US had a positive assessment of the Pakistani army, in terms of its capability to perform 'imperial firefighting' missions in the Middle East, they were uncertain about arming Pakistan for Cold War purposes. Though Pakistan was located in strategic proximity to the region and shared the same religion, the state's security focus was on India and remained crucially embedded in South Asian geopolitics. The British Commonwealth office knew that India would not view arming the Pakistani army in positive terms, despite favourable signals from a few British military leaders who served in the Pakistani army.[33] In contrasts to the UK, the US was more concerned about the growing political instability in the areas surrounding the oil-rich Gulf countries and worried by the turn of events in South-West Asia and North Africa. The British plan to develop a security organization centred around Egypt lost its credibility after the Free Officer's Crop gained access to political power on 22 July 1952.[34] Soon, the entire region from Syria to Iran became embroiled in anti-imperial nationalist upsurges. The US became convinced that they had to act before the oil-rich region slipped out of control. Pakistan was regarded as a more reliable country having an effective colonial military structure and supposedly willing to contribute towards the defence of the region from Communist forces.[35] However, the UK held the view that unless there took place a clear resolution of the Kashmir issue,[36] any military alliance with Pakistan would deteriorate into the morass of regional conflicts. Indeed, the British Commonwealth relations office found Donald Kennedy's (undersecretary to South-East Asia desk in the Truman administration) argument, that the UK was standing in the way of Pakistan's willingness to contribute towards the defence of the Middle East, ignorant of the real nature of Pakistan's defence needs. The Commonwealth office was aware that prime minister Liaquat Ali had rejected a British proposal for a Middle East defence deal in April 1949 because he had wanted assurances about regional threats to Pakistan. In 1951, when approached on this issue, Liaquat Ali told Gordon Walker (British secretary of state for Commonwealth affairs) that he could not do anything until the Kashmir issue was resolved.[37]

UK officials were correct in their prediction that there existed a fragile peace in South Asia behind which lay an ongoing arms race between India and Pakistan. The predicament for the UK was that if it did not sell arms to Pakistan, others would step in the vacuum. More importantly, as far as lucrative arms trade went, there existed a fierce competition between the UK and the US. At the same time, the UK was also concerned about Pakistan's ability to meet its payment needs. A telegram from the foreign office in London to the British embassy in Washington mentions clearly:

> Pakistan had a good run financially since 1950 until the fall in raw material prices. But the present prospects are most doubtful. She is already running into an adverse balance of payments and her capital budget is to be met from cash balances. 54 million dollars are certainly beyond her earning capacity even if the rupee equivalent could be provided in her budget. Defence has accounted for over half of the budget running at approximately pound 125 million per annum (1952/53 estimates).... Pakistan is nevertheless a sovereign state and is determined to spend money on defence at the present level. This being so it is much preferable economically that she should spend her money in the Sterling area than in the United States or France.[38]

This global competition for the procurement of arms in the context of the regional 'cold war' had significant implications for the political economy of the 'inter-wing' disparity within Pakistan. The increasing 'raw material' prices that the British document referred to were that of jute. Indeed, in the early fifties, during the Korean War, Pakistan earned foreign exchanges by exporting gunny bags.[39] Jute was produced and processed primarily in East Bengal, and in 1951, East Bengal was in the second spate of a food crisis.[40] Yet the government of Pakistan was siphoning resources from the subsistence-oriented peasant agriculture in East Bengal in order to procure arms in the international market.

Even American officials, despite their enthusiasm for including Pakistan in a military alliance, realized that it was difficult for them to pay for their ambitious armament procurement plan. Indeed, Kennedy, according to a British document, admitted to British officials:

> He [Kennedy] had already pointed out to Pakistanis that it would be embarrassing to United States Administration if in trying to obtain a grant of wheat which Pakistan wanted, they were to argue that Pakistan could not afford to pay for it while at the same time Pakistan was proposing to pay $15 million a year for three years on armaments.[41]

Yet while the government of Pakistan was spending resources from East Pakistan on defence needs, the defence doctrine that the first Pakistani commander-in-chief, Ayub Khan, promoted had very little to offer to East Bengal. Ayub Khan argued in a public meeting that West Pakistan offered the best defence positions against any assaults on Pakistan. Abul Mansur Ahmad, a moderate Awami League politician, recalled a frank but bitter debate with Ayub Khan during a conference in Murree between 7 and 14 July 1955. Ayub Khan informed Ahmad that East Pakistan could not be defended, and so if the Indian army occupied East Pakistan, the West Pakistan-based Pakistani army would attack India and capture Delhi. To Ayub Khan, this was the only viable way to defend East Pakistan. In response to Ahmad's suggestion that the Pakistani government should then station half of its army in East Pakistan where the majority of Pakistanis resided, Ayub Khan retorted that that would completely weaken the military forces and indicated laughingly that only a civilian unlettered in military affairs could suggest such a thing. Ayub Khan also negated the importance of the guerrilla warfare, in cases of asymmetrical military strength, for the defence of a country.[42] The implication of Ayub Khan's military doctrine, as outlined in this exchange, revolved on two claims: (*a*) the army had a more coherent perception of the security needs of the country than civilian politicians and (*b*) East Pakistan did not matter in the overall defence planning of Pakistan except as a resource provider. This construction of a garrison state would have crucial implications for the resource-scarce political economy of Pakistan, as well as the dynamics of inter-regional resource distribution.

The military establishment in Pakistan was fortunate because the US perception of instability in its immediate neighbourhood trumped concerns within the US over the South Asian regional conflicts. Since 1945, the

US developed a vision of national security geared towards combatting the influence of communism. This vision included, according to Melvyn P. Leffler,

> a strategic sphere of influence within the Western Hemisphere, domination of the Atlantic and Pacific oceans, an extensive system of outlying bases to enlarge the strategic frontier and project American power, an even more extensive system of transit rights to facilitate the conversion of commercial air bases to military use, access to the resources and markets of most of Eurasia, denial of those resources to a prospective enemy, and the maintenance of nuclear superiority.[43]

The installation of the new Dwight D. Eisenhower administration in 1953 sought to translate that vision into reality more aggressively. This led assertions of American freedom from British tutelage in South Asian affairs. John Foster Dulles, the new secretary of state, toured South-West Asia with mutual security administrator Harold E. Stassen. Dulles floated a proposal that Turkey, Pakistan, Iraq and Iran could constitute the core of an American security cordon against the Soviet Union.[44]

In the meantime, on 30 September 1953, Pakistani commander-in-chief, Ayub Khan, and not the civilian head of the administration, met the secretary of state, Dulles. Ayub Khan directly asked for assistance for Pakistan's army. Many within the Western diplomatic circle regarded the Pakistani army as less susceptible to popular sentiment.[45] Dulles welcomed Ayub Khan and assured the general that he was prepared to provide military assistance to Pakistan, notwithstanding Indian opposition. Apart from Dulles, vice-president Richard Milhous Nixon weighed in by declaring that 'Pakistan is a country I would like to do everything for. The people have less complexes than the Indians. The Pakistanis are completely frank, even when it hurts. It will be disastrous if the Pakistan aid does not go through.'[46] Nixon was referring to India's foreign policy of non-alignment and her subtle rebuff to American overtures during his visit to the region. With support from two key figures in his administration, president Eisenhower assented to the programme in January 1954. In April 1954, Pakistan and Turkey concluded a mutual assistance agreement. The US and Pakistan formally signed a Mutual Defence Assistance Agreement on 19 May 1954, and in September 1954, Pakistan became a signatory to the Manila Pact,[47] thus becoming a founding member of the South-East Asia Treaty Organization (SEATO).

The following year, on 23 September 1955, it joined the Baghdad Pact[48] with Iraq and Turkey. Iran joined in October. Soon the UK, too, moved into the Baghdad Pact.[49]

It is ironic that just before joining the Baghdad Pact, Iran had a coup that deposed the democratically elected Mohammad Mosaddegh government and was engineered by the Central Intelligence Agency (CIA) of the US and British foreign intelligence that feared communist influences in Iran.[50] In Pakistan, too, there took place a coup in 1958. Similarly, recent research suggests that the US had plenty signals indicating conditions for a coup in Turkey in 1960.[51] All three regimes – Iran, Pakistan and Turkey – claimed to have initiated 'progressive', 'modernizing' measures to transform the country's political economy. Two of them, Pakistan and Iran, encountered social revolutions of very different kinds, both of which transformed political power equations in their respective regions. In Iraq, the monarchical regime and the pro-British prime minister Nuri al-Said faced both popular opposition and military revolt; ultimately the monarch, his family members and the prime minister were tragically assassinated. The suddenness of the coup surprised the Anglo-American leadership, which even considered invading Iraq.[52] The Baghdad Pact, rather than bringing peace and stability to the region, escalated political instability. Simmering ethnic conflicts accompanied by internal colonization within the respective nation states, such as the Kurds in Iraq and Turkey and the Bengalis in East Pakistan, made a mockery of the idea of 'collective security' in the 'free world' of Turkey, Iraq and Pakistan.

Politics in Pakistan: Political Leaders, Palace Intrigues and the Formation of the Government

At the very moment that Pakistan was signing the US-sponsored multilateral defence treaties, the central government was dismissing the democratically elected government of East Bengal. Zinkin records how Mirza, who had been deputed to East Bengal as a governor, summed up his governing philosophy: 'I am used to running natives. I have done it before under the British.'[53] The government decided to arrest members of opposition parties. Sheikh Mujib, who was known to be a courageous leader and a gifted organizer, was arrested as soon as the United Front ministry in East Bengal was dismissed.[54] The government, naturally, arrested members of the left-leaning political parties, such as the Ganatantri Dal (Democratic Party), widely believed to be one of many fronts of the Communist Party of Pakistan. For the first time the Communist Party of Pakistan was banned. Though the previous Muslim League government had ruthlessly suppressed communists, it had never declared the Communist Party illegal.[55] Mirza did it, possibly, with an eye towards convincing the US government of their anti-communist credentials. Members of the bureaucratic-military oligarchy used their anti-communist rhetoric to cloak their essential intolerance of even the most normative forms of liberal democratic governance. Many within the ranks of British and American diplomatic corps were suspicious of the communist presence in East Pakistan.[56] Mirza's move of arresting the elected left-leaning members no doubt established his 'democratic credentials' to the sponsors of the Cold War. One should view his words about shooting Bhashani (the left-leaning populist provincial president of the Awami Muslim League) in the same light.[57] To understand this situation, and the state of formal party politics, it is necessary to examine both the nature of the political leadership in East Bengali society and the pattern of 'palace politics' in Pakistan.

In the final years of colonial rule and the early years of Pakistan, parliamentary politics in East Bengal, like in West Pakistan, were dominated by three aristocratic figures: Fazlul Huq, Suhrawardy and Nazimuddin. They defined party-political activities in East Bengal in an era of transition from colony to post-colony. All three leaders came from Urdu-speaking *ashraf* families. Nazimuddin – the scion of a nawab family in Dacca, who had been educated at Dunstable Grammar School in Bedfordshire, UK, held a law degree from Trinity Hall, University of Cambridge, a true favourite of the colonial ruling elites and British business interests in Bengal, and the second unelected prime minister of Pakistan – had, by 1952, rendered himself into a pedestrian political figure among the middle classes in East Bengal by aligning himself with the Urdu cause.[58] In contrast to Nazimuddin, Fazlul Huq and Suhrawardy could rightly sense the growing significance of the nascent middle class, and they appealed to East Bengali youths from this economic stratum, who were steeped in the regional culture and language. This 'middle class' was defined by its boundaries. It excluded big landlords, subsistence peasants, manual workers and big merchants. From the early twentieth century onwards, many from among the ranks of the East Bengali surplus farmers began to consider education as a source of upward mobility. After completing college or university, these folks joined the white-collar professions of law, journalism and teaching, or, after independence, obtained clerical ranks in government offices. With the departure of Hindu government officials and clerical employees, these middle-class governmental positions opened up substantially to Bengali Muslims. Not surprisingly, both Fazlul Huq and Suhrawardy directed their politics to appeal to this nascent rural middle class.

Among these two, Fazlul Huq was the older one. Trained in the sciences at Calcutta University, he opted for a life in law and was called to the bar in 1897. Huq's political acumen was reflected in his support for the aspirations of surplus farmers, from whose rank the new rural middle class was coming into existence. In 1937, Huq found an opportunity to implement his socio-political agenda, when the expansion of franchise, alongside the provision of separate electorates for Muslims, enabled him to steer his peasant-and-tenant party (the Krishak Praja Party) to political power in a provincial election, albeit in an alliance with the Muslim League. During the six years of his premiership of Bengal (1937–43), Huq provided immense relief to the peasants through three signature legislations: the Bengal Agricultural Debtors' Act (1938), the Money Lenders' Act (1938) and the Bengal Tenancy (Amendment) Act (1938).[59] He thus became instrumental in bringing politics to the rural middle class, especially to those belonging to the ranks of surplus farmers.

Yet Huq was not a radical politician and had no fondness for grassroots-based movements. Elected in 1913 to the Bengal assembly, Huq never directly affiliated himself with the nationalist mass movement. In the twenties, when the entire Muslim Bengal was in political ferment over the Khilafat issue, Huq remained unmoved and even opposed agitational politics.[60] He selected the colonial legislative assembly as his primary arena of political activism and was familiar with the operations of these deformed colonial–democratic institutions. Not surprisingly, in 1954, when the central authority in Pakistan dismissed his government and placed him under house arrest, he refused to initiate any movements against the central government and risk going to prison. In a meeting with the leading United Front legislators in the East Bengal assembly, he advised that they adopt an ultra-radical course of action, which included visiting their constituencies and organizing revolutionary activities against the state. Abul Mansur Ahmad, a long-time associate of Huq, correctly guessed that his friend was anxious and possibly trying to find a way to negotiate with the central government.[61] This silence and compliance did not produce immediate results. Bogra, the former ambassador to the US who subsequently assumed the position of prime minster, in a radio address on 16 June 1954, called Huq 'a traitor who confessed his crime'.[62]

Nonetheless, to the ruling elites of Pakistan, Huq was known for his populist political eclecticism. They were aware that Huq placed himself above party-political discipline. In his long career he had served as an office bearer of both the INC and the Muslim League, and at the height of his influence, he had changed his political partners from the Muslim League to the INC and even to the Hindu Mahasabha. He moved the Lahore Resolution in 1940 as the elected premier of Bengal, the largest Muslim-majority province in colonial India. Yet he did not support the partition of Bengal, or even the partition of India, and maintained a tacit silence during the entire partition process.[63] Given his unpredictable nature, the Pakistani government was of the view that Huq could be made to change his position. In the aftermath of the palace coup of October 1954, when Ghulam Muhammad dismissed the Constituent Assembly, the governor general, sensing political reprisals against him, started soft-pedalling on Huq. He issued a statement before coming to Dacca where he said that he did not consider Huq a traitor to the nation. He also approached Ataur Rahman Khan, the Awami League leader of East Bengal, through another emissary.[64] On 14 November 1954, governor general Ghulam Muhammad came to Dacca, and both Ataur Rahman and Huq rushed to the airport to garland him, with the expectation that democracy would be restored to East Bengal.[65] Yet democratic rule was not restored. Rather, the unelected bureaucrats and generals of the Pakistani government deployed another trick to rope in Suhrawardy.

The Awami Muslim League's pivotal leader, Suhrawardy, was a politician of similar predilections as Huq. Like the older politician, Suhrawardy sought to build up a nascent middle-class base in Bengal's politics. Born in a wealthy landlord family from Medinipur in West Bengal, Suhrawardy was also an Urdu-speaking *ashraf*, though, unlike Huq, he never made Bengali his principal medium of political communication. Educated at the University of Oxford and called to bar at Grey's Inn, London, Suhrawardy started his political career in Calcutta Corporation as an ally of Bengal's Congress leader Chittaranjan Das. As a politician he, too, was more attuned to operating within the cloistered circles of the colonial institutional arena than to leading a mass movement.[66] He also had an eye for spotting young political talents. In 1938, for example, Suhrawardy and Fazlul Huq visited Gopal Gunj, a small town in East Bengal. Local Muslims organized a massive reception for political leaders, despite opposition from the INC. On his way to the local school, Suhrawardy spotted a young organizer named Sheikh Mujibur Rahman and asked him, in pidgin Bengali, whether there were any local

Muslim League organizations. When the young Sheikh Mujib explained in detail the local situation, an impressed Suhrawardy asked him his name, address and family background, and ordered an accompanying officer to note them down. He later sent Sheikh Mujib a note from Calcutta thanking him for his support during the visit. Impressed by this gesture to an unknown rural middle-class boy, Sheikh Mujib became a political protégé of Suhrawardy.[67] An interesting paradox of Pakistani politics was that though Suhrawardy was an Urdu-speaking *ashraf* from West Bengal who had selected Karachi as his new home, he remained popular among members of the emergent East Bengali middle class and was much distrusted for that reason within the circles of the West Pakistani political establishment. The Awami Muslim League provided him with a platform and a mass base to substantiate his claims to political leadership in Pakistan, and in return Suhrawardy, as a West Pakistani, sought to negotiate East Pakistan's demands for autonomy. Like an *ashraf* landholding gentry, Suhrawardy regarded his party as his political fief rather than perceiving himself as a leader of a democratic organization.[68]

In the summer of 1954, around the time when the unelected bureaucrats were busy dismissing the newly elected East Bengal government, a physically ill Suhrawardy was convalescing in Zurich, having undergone a medical procedure there. In October of that year, governor general Ghulam Muhammad, uncertain about the reception of his second palace coup, started searching for new allies. He approached the Awami Muslim League leader of East Bengal, Ataur Rahman, through Muhammad Osmani, who was the leader of the Awami Muslim League in West Pakistan. Ghulam Muhammad told Osmani that if the Awami League did not support him, the governor general would transfer power to the army.[69] Osmani and Ataur Rahman were disciples of the same *pir* (spiritual guide) and thus had a close relationship. Ataur Rahman immediately visited Suhrawardy in Zurich with the news that their political rivals, namely the Muslim League, had now been decimated. The governor general, with the tacit approval of the army, had dissolved the Constituent Assembly and requested for the Awami League's support, with the alternative being military rule. Even Suhrawardy, who had by then been politically active for nearly 25 years, could not comprehend why the military had *now* entered politics formally. He returned to Pakistan on 11 December 1954 with expectations of becoming prime minister in return for his support. But his dreams were dashed to the ground by the quotidian reality of palace politics. Two generals, Ayub Khan and Mirza, who had been the most powerful players within Ghulam Muhammad's ruling coterie, objected to Suhrawardy's accession to power. Suhrawardy thus had to join Ghulam Muhammad's 'cabinet of talent' as a law minister.[70] His close political confidants from East Bengal opposed the move in no uncertain terms. Sheikh Mujib even told him to his face that he now wondered whether he made a mistake by accepting Suhrawardy's leadership.[71] It was plausible that Suhrawardy, as a veteran of the cloistered circle of colonial institutional politics, had realized that if he spent too much time in political exile, it would mean an end to his career. It was particularly true in the Pakistani context, where there was no constitutionally charted democratic path to access political power. To his followers Suhrawardy confessed that he was not an 'ideological person but a person with ideas'.[72] The Awami Muslim League was obviously uncomfortable with Suhrawardy's presence in a cabinet that was presided over by an unelected bureaucratic-military oligarchy. Their discomfort increased manifold when Abu Hossain Sarkar, a protégé of Huq, was inducted to the central government as well. Meanwhile, distrusting Huq and anticipating a conspiracy to marginalize the Awami Muslim League, Sheikh Mujib, in February 1955, sought to dislodge Huq from the post of United Front chairperson.[73] Suhrawardy indirectly endorsed the move by publicly branding the United Front as nothing but a mere conglomeration of different political parties.[74]

Meanwhile, a bizarre twist of events led towards the further consolidation of the military's grip on power. At the end of the summer of 1955, Ghulam Muhammad, who had suffered a debilitating stroke, had to move to the UK for treatment. On 7 August 1955, major general Mirza – who, under the governor general, Ghulam Muhammad, had experienced a meteoric rise in Pakistani politics – was selected as acting governor general. On 6 October 1955, Mirza returned his gratitude for this rapid promotion by dismissing his benefactor, the paralytic Ghulam Muhammad, from power.[75] In a situation where there existed no Constitution, backroom wheeling and dealing mattered the most. As soon as Mirza moved up to the position of chief executive of the state, he indulged in a new game of coalition-building. He dismissed Muhammad Ali, his other benefactor, from the position of prime minister and made him to return to his old position of ambassador to the US. Mirza's final macabre touch was to lend the impression that Suhrawardy would soon be invited to become the prime minister of Pakistan. Ultimately, Muhammad Ali, a competent and possibly the only democratically inclined bureaucrat in the bureaucratic-military oligarchy, became prime minister.[76] Apparently, Muhammad Ali had secured the support of the Muslim League and the Krishak Shramik Party of Huq. Huq himself scored a victory over his Awami Muslim League rivals by entering into an alliance with the Muslim League, a party that he had professed to detest.[77] As a reward, he was offered the position of home minister in the new government of Pakistan, and on 5 June 1955, his Krishak Shramik Party formed a very fragile ministry in East Bengal, in alliance with the PNC.[78] On 23 March 1956 the government enacted a Constitution based on parity and 'one-unit formula' whereby all the provinces in West Pakistan were transformed into one province. This was done with a view to deny East Bengal any added parliamentary advantage arising from its larger demographic size. The name of East Bengal was also changed to East Pakistan, and Pakistan officially became an Islamic republic.[79] Mirza happily entered the new era by getting himself elected as the first president of Pakistan. He immediately reneged many of the compromises reached during the Murree Conference on the issue of provincial parity in the matters of government appointment and military recruitment. A frustrated Awami League boycotted the Constituent Assembly session during which the Constitution was accepted.[80] Interestingly, among the Awami League members, only Suhrawardy did not participate in that walkout. As Muhammad Ali sought to consolidate his position in the government, Mirza became increasingly envious. In the unstable world of the Pakistani 'palace politics' of the fifties, fortune only smiled upon the politicians for a few months. Mirza had very little intentions of following the parliamentary norms of non-intervention in political process and upholding the newly enacted Constitution. Rather, he engaged in a new conspiracy to weaken the party-political formations. He had a close rapport with Khan Saheb of the NWFP. He proposed his name as the chief minister of West Pakistan. As their political partnership grew, Khan Saheb floated the Republican Party on 12 September 1956. It was a party of landed elites. The new party engineered multiple defections from the Muslim League, reducing it to a mere rubble.[81]

Palace politics continued with its own logic of intrigues, backdoor wheeling and dealing, coalition-making and coalition-breaking, Constitution-making and Constitution-flouting processes. Yet, among all the political parties in Pakistan, the Awami League was the only one that had an identifiable popular base in East Pakistan. Most of its activists were recruited from among the middle classes, and it was from among these ranks that the next generation of East Bengali leaders came, such as Ataur Rahman, Abul Mansur Ahmad, Sheikh Mujib and Oli Ahad, to name a few. All of them had been born outside the privileged circle of landed-elites and had spent their early lives fighting the residues of the Permanent Settlement. Of the influential trio of Ataur Rahman, Sheikh Mujib and Abul Mansur Ahmad, the latter was a veteran of INC politics and had some idea of grassroots-level organization. He was a democrat who had wanted to secure a constitutional regime for Pakistan.[82] Sheikh Mujib, as mentioned earlier, was a youth activist and a gifted organizer who believed that a strong party organization was the precondition for the smooth functioning of a constitutional democracy.[83] Ataur Rahman was an able administrator and skilful negotiator and was waiting for an opportunity to access political power.[84] In the fifties moment, all three of them were staunch Muslim nationalists, troupers of the Pakistan movement and firm believers in the unity of Pakistan. But they also believed that the unity of Pakistan could be best secured through a constitutionally guaranteed autonomy for East Pakistan.

Subaltern Protests: Bhashani, Secularization of the Awami League and New Political Configuration in Pakistan

Bhashani, the president of the Awami Muslim League, was a crucial exception among these aristocratic and middle-class leaders. He belonged to a peasant background and had become politically prominent by organizing the peasantry.[85] Born in 1885 and orphaned at a young age, Bhashani, formerly named Abdul Hamid Khan, grew up in a rural east Bengal marked by poverty, landlordism and famine. From among his memories of childhood, he recalled very clearly the great Indian famine of 1898–99 in which thousands of rural Bengalis had perished. Hamid Khan even lost his playmates, who succumbed to hunger. He was amazed by the fact that the rich had hoarded food during a mass starvation in order to satisfy their greed for surplus.[86] David Arnold has shown how, in many respects, the peasants' response to subsistence crisis and famine closely paralleled a peasant insurgency.[87] Such an event leaves an indelible mark on the consciousness of the peasantry, as it had on the mind of Hamid Khan. The formation of peasant-based collective resistance remained the hallmark of his politics. While his childhood experiences transformed Bhashani into a peasant activist, his exposure to Islamic theology at an early age constituted the basis of his moral conviction in politics.

In his teenage years, a Sufi preacher, Nasiruddin Baghdadi, took Hamid Khan under his wing and brought him to his *khanqah* (shrine) in Jalseswar, located in what was then the Goalpara district in lower Assam. Baghdadi trained Bhashani to read Arabic and Persian and familiarized him with exegeses on the Koran, the Hadith and the Fiq. At his request, Bhashani joined the Darul Uloom, an Islamic theological seminary in Deoband, Uttar Pradesh.[88] Though Barabara Metcalf, who studied the institutional history of Deoband, stresses that its fame as a theological seminary was due to its non-political and bureaucratized educational structure, Bhashani seemed to have found his radical political predilections at Deoband.[89] Here, Bhashani was influenced by Mahmud al-Hasan, popularly known as Shaykh al-Hind, who played a critical role in the anti-colonial movement in the NWFP.[90] Islam and radical interpretations of the Koran became critical hallmarks of his politics. In the fading years of his life, Bhashani wrote about his Islamic belief system. In 1974, in an essay entitled 'Rabubiyater Bhumika' (The Role of Rabubiyah), Bhashani recorded his ideals about Islamic social justice. He used the concept of *hukumat-i-rabbani* (the just order of god) to characterize the divine ethical order, as opposed to *hukumat-i nafsdnyiat* (the order of the tyrants). For Bhashani, the *hukumat-i-rabbani* was not a theocratic Islamic state that rigidly applied Islamic law but, rather, a godly government where people would not starve. Bhashani claimed that the *rabubiyat* (an attribute of Allah or divinity) advocated the abolition of private ownership and that the state should distribute things in proportions based on need.[91] Thus, trained in Islamic jurisprudence, and inheriting the peasant consciousness of resistance, where the spiritual and the material remained fused in an integral form of moral vision, Bhashani promoted his own ideals of equality in search for a just society.[92] Farid Esack, in a later South African context, pointed out how Islamist theologians had chalked out a hermeneutical methodology that rendered basic Koranic concepts relevant to the contemporaneous social and political situation.[93] Similarly, exposed to theological training in the Koran both under a Sufi *pir* and at Deoband, Bhashani deciphered in theological training the emancipatory possibilities of political utopia.

Bhashani had had a brief encounter with both the revolutionary nationalist secret society movement and the INC-sponsored mass nationalist movements in the twenties,[94] but he became an activist-organizer in the circles of peasant politics in Assam. In the late nineteenth century, Assam was a sparsely populated frontier region between South and South-East Asia. Colonial rulers embarked upon a capitalist reconstruction of the economy through tea-plantation estates that linked Assam's economy with global market. The construction of railways and steamer lines connecting Brahmaputra valley, through the neighbouring Bengal delta, with the ports of Calcutta and Chittagong, integrated Assam with the pan South Asian colonial state-space. Over time, Assam became a complex ethnic mosaic with immigrants pouring in from all over South Asia. The most numerous of these immigrants were Bengalis. Escaping from the oppressive land tenure structure in the heavily populated land-scarce region of East Bengal, a large number of Muslim Bengali peasants settled on river islands and banks formed by the Brahmaputra's silt deposits. They reclaimed this uninhabitable, forest-covered, virgin land for agriculture.[95] The influx of immigrants and their reclamation activities led to a rise on the prices of land in Assam. Local landlords benefitted from land speculation. But the rising Assamese middle class and the local tenants complained of land seizures by immigrants. In response to such criticisms, in 1920, the colonial state devised a border system, which entailed revenue officials drawing lines on the map within which immigrants would have to restrict their economic activities.[96] This attempted segregation fuelled new political confrontations between the representatives of the immigrant Bengali peasants, who wanted to abolish the border system, and the INC. Under the leadership of a primarily Assamese-speaking middle class, the INC sought to defend this border system.[97]

In such a politically charged environment, Bhashani became an important organizer of the immigrant Bengali peasants. In 1929 he settled down at Ghagmari in the present-day Dhubri district of Assam. He also had an establishment in a silt island in the Brahmaputra, which was known as Bhashanir *char* (Bhashani's river island) and which helped immigrant Bengali peasants to find a place to settle down. It was his identification with the peasant immigrants in Bhashanir *char* that earned him the sobriquet Bhashani. Dressed in a simple lungi (a long piece of clothing wrapped around the hips and reaching the ankles) and *punjabi* (a shirt without collar), he would go from one Bengali Muslim settlement to another, organizing by propagating peasants' rights. The historian Amalendu Guha hints at this image of a pious renunciant politician among the immigrant Bengali Muslim peasants:

> The itinerant Maulana, with his simple and pious habits and great organizing abilities, was accepted by the rural folk not only as a political leader, but also as a *pir*, believed to be possessed of occult powers.[98]

This image of the sacred renunciant–politician transformed Bhashani into an organic social activist of the peasant community. Between 1932 and 1947, he organized multiple movements against the border system. In the meantime, in 1947, the INC government in Assam tried to demolish the villages of immigrant Bengali Muslim peasants in order to compel them to move back into East Bengal. Bhashani, who was actively protesting against the system, was arrested in 1947. The government of Assam released him, but only on the condition that he move to Pakistan. In East Bengal, the Muslim League did not welcome him, and he became the president of the Awami Muslim League (as discussed in the previous chapter). During his frequent imprisonment as an Awami Muslim League politician, Bhashani came into contact with members of the Communist Party of Pakistan. Though he never became a communist, Bhashani developed a close rapport with the communists and socialists.[99] In 1954, when the United Front government was dismissed in East Bengal, he was attending a peace conference in Stockholm. As the Pakistani government did not allow him to enter East Pakistan, Bhashani remained in exile in London. However, due to changes in the political circumstances, he left London and reached Bombay on 5 January 1955. From Bombay he reached Calcutta, along the way becoming increasingly anxious about the Hindu refugee exodus to West Bengal. He sent a letter to Oli Ahad, one of his young political colleagues, requesting him to organize a campaign in order to prevent such an exodus. He said that if this exodus continued, the Bengalis would soon become a minority in Pakistan.[100] Concerned with the issue of religious polarization, he became an advocate of secularizing the polity. On 15 April 1955 Bhashani was allowed to enter East Pakistan. In the Awami Muslim League's council convention (held between 21 and 23 October 1955 in Dacca), Bhashani led the debate towards opening up the Awami Muslim League to members of all religious communities and promoted dropping the word 'Muslim' from its nomenclature. Suhrawardy, a veteran Muslim League politician, opposed the move. Sheikh Mujibur was torn between his political loyalty towards his mentor, Suhrawardy, and the overwhelming urge of party activists to secularize the organization. Finally, on 22 October 1955, Suhrawardy withdrew his opposition against the secularization drive.[101] This seminal move by Bhashani and numerous ordinary political workers transformed the Awami League into a mass organization of all segments of Bengali people in East Pakistan.

In May 1956, East Pakistan faced a massive food crisis. In the midst of this food crisis, Bhashani started observing a hunger strike from 7 May onwards in order to obtain a financial grant for East Pakistan from the Pakistani government. From May 1956 onwards, hunger marches became a regular feature of public life in East Bengal. Huq, the then governor of East Pakistan, allowed the formation of a ministry by Sarkar of the Krishak Shramik Party. Sarkar was Huq's protégé, and so the ministry enjoyed gubernatorial support, but it did not have the support of a majority in the East Pakistan legislative assembly. Sarkar avoided calling an assembly session and did not even place the annual budget before the assembly, in fear of losing the trust vote. Finally, on 30 August, Mirza instructed Huq to prove that he commanded a majority in the East Pakistan assembly. A nervous Sarkar resigned from his position on the same date. Meanwhile, the food crisis had created a volatile political situation in the province. On 4 September 1956, hunger marchers again assembled in villages nearby Dacca and tried to enter the city. Government troops opened fire on the hunger march, killing four people. The city of Dacca was on the precipice of a full-scale rebellion. The students and working classes of Dacca took to the streets. Bhashani and Sheikh Mujib led a massive procession in Dacca, and the city witnessed a complete breakdown of governmental authority. A nervous Huq called Bhashani on the 5 September and requested that the Awami League form a government.[102] The Awami League appointed Ataur Rahman as the leader of its provincial assembly party. He became the new chief minister of East Pakistan on the 6 September.[103] Thus, a subaltern rebellion brought about a change of regimes in East Pakistan. Both Mirza and Suhrawardy were in Dacca when the new ministry was sworn in. President Mirza was already planning his next move in palace politics. Impressed and alarmed by the rebellion, he returned to Karachi with Suhrawardy by the same plane on the 6 September. The next day, rumours were afloat in the capital city that Suhrawardy would be the next prime minister of Pakistan.[104]

In this game of musical chairs for the post of prime minister, Suhrawardy remained the last prominent personality associated with the Pakistan movement who had yet to hold that office. He was also on a weak political turf. His party commanded only 13 seats in the parliament. He had to rely on the Republican Party to provide support to his ministry and thus became beholden to Mirza, who was the moving spirit behind the party. More importantly, Suhrawardy's primary mass base was in East Pakistan, even though he did not live there. He also personally believed that he was a West Pakistani and, as a consequence, sought to impress upon West Pakistanis that he was the only honest broker who could negotiate with East Pakistanis and make them accept political deals that were seemingly unpalatable to them. To the East Pakistanis he became an articulate politician with a foothold in West Pakistani establishment. He convinced them that he could represent them more sympathetically. On the 12 September 1956, Suhrawardy became the prime minister of Pakistan through a political deal with the Republican Party and with the tacit approval of Mirza. Abul Mansur Ahmad, a veteran of the tenancy movement in East Pakistan, became the industry and commerce minister. The Awami League became a member of ruling coalitions at both the centre and in East Pakistan, the most populous province in the country. Yet the matter did not end amicably within the Awami League.[105] On 17 September, Suhrawardy came to Dacca, and on the next day, he and Bhashani attended a massive public meeting. In the meeting, according to Suhrawardy-loyalist Kamruddin Ahmad, Bhashani took out a whip and said to the audience that if Suhrawardy did not abide by the 21-point manifesto of the United Front, then he would be whipped in public. This act obviously hurt the sentiments of a Suhrawardy-loyalist like Tofazzal Hossain, popularly known as Manik Miah, the influential editor of *Ittefaq*, the largest-circulating daily in East Pakistan.[106]

To conclude, Bhashani, born in a peasant family and leading the life of an itinerant rustic theologian-turned-social-activist, made a decisive intervention in East Pakistani politics by transforming the largest political platform, the Awami League, into an open, secular forum; Suhrawardy, an Oxford-trained barrister, was reluctant to endorse such secularization. It was the hunger marches on the streets, led by Bhashani and his associates, that culminated in the changes at the government level. Clearly, the Machiavellian calculations of the president, Mirza, played a role in the toppling of the Sarkar ministry. However, the mass protests decisively dented the popular legitimacy of the Kirshak Shramik Party government that had been appointed through palace intrigues. Thus, there existed two trends within the Awami League: one emphasized constitutional norms and reforms, while the other prioritized the organized movements of popular social classes for the democratization of polity and society. These two trends were not mutually exclusive, but they did cluster around separate political personalities. Suhrawardy came to represent the first – the constitutional parliamentary wing – while Bhashani became distinctly associated with the second trend – grassroots-level political movements.

The Pakistani Government, the Suez Crisis and the Birth of the NAP

The Awami League ministers in the central government of Pakistan sought to bring transparency to government dealings, to develop an ethos and practice of accountability to their constituents and to reform inter-wing disparities, as well as to foster close cooperation with the elected government of East Pakistan. Indeed, as a step towards further transparency, Mansoor Ahmad opposed corruption in the field of coastal navigation by drawing attention to the powerful vested-interest group in the shipping industry that was backed by Mirza (who, naturally, opposed these moves).[107] In East Pakistan, with central funding, the Awami League government dealt decisively with the food crisis within a short period of time. It initiated a planned development of the economy, the infrastructure and the irrigation systems. It began constructing a new plant that had the capacity to produce chemical fertilizers, as well as improving the productive capacity of a cement factory.[108] The government planned to deepen land reforms and remove the vestiges of the Permanent Settlement. It released all political prisoners unconditionally, and the Awami League ministers even went to the gates of the prisons to felicitate those released. On the other hand, there existed problems of coordination among individual leaders, which often resulted in internecine, factional squabbles. Sheikh Mujib, who was the general secretary of the party, demanded that the government should be completely subservient to the party organization. Ataur Rahman, the chief minister, claimed that the government should have a certain degree of autonomy from the party's dictates.[109] Many believed that Sheikh Mujib was eying the chief ministership himself.[110] But it was not these internal party squabbles, or the differences arising from the rise of military rule in Pakistan, that led to the split in the party. Instead, the split came due to an ideological issue of international importance – the Suez Crisis.

As a regionalist political party in Pakistan, the Awami League was committed to obtaining more resources for the province. Since the army was primarily a West Pakistani organization, an increase in the military budget was viewed with suspicion in the Awami League circles. As a member of the newly formed Constituent Assembly–turned-parliament, Abul Mansur Ahmad asserted that nearly 62 per cent of the government budget was spent on defence even as none of this was invested in East Pakistan. According to him, this was making West Pakistan more prosperous and East Pakistan poorer.¹¹¹ Implicit in such an assertion was the hint that the military budget was also draining the surplus produced regionally in East Pakistan. The general populace in East Pakistan shared such concerns about the army. Even the troops that were deployed to protect East Pakistan from India were viewed by some as occupying forces that bore no connection with the local population. Writing in 1959, Richard Lambert, an American professor of sociology commented:

> The seeming reluctance of the Pakistan central government to recruit heavily from Bengal and, when it did so, to send Bengali troops outside of Bengal, made the troop detachments in East Bengal take on the character of a military occupation force.¹¹²

This view was further confirmed when, in 1954, additional troops were deployed to suppress the democratically elected popular government. For these reasons, an international pact that would bring military investment remained an unattractive proposition to East Bengal and its largest political organization. No doubt, the Awami League passed resolutions condemning the Baghdad Pact and the Manila Pact in its council session on 19 and 20 May 1956. An angry Suhrawardy, who supported such pacts, called on Oli Ahad, a left-leaning youth leader and office-bearer of the organization, and demanded an explanation.¹¹³ Despite Suhrawardy's displeasure, opposition to the Baghdad Pact remained alive within the Awami League.

The opposition to UK- (and US-) sponsored military pacts had much wider political support in East Pakistan. In the early fifties, the East Bengal government had ruthlessly suppressed communists and left-wing organizations. Initially, the communists had looked for an opportunity to organize a broad platform to articulate their views. Since the Awami Muslim League had a specific religio-communitarian orientation, the communists sought to establish a non-sectarian progressive party. In 1951 there came into existence the East Pakistan Youth League (Yuba League). The aforementioned Oli Ahad had played a crucial role in organizing the first session and soon became the organization's secretary.¹¹⁴ Meanwhile, the left-leaning students gave birth to the Chhatro Union, a radical student organization, in Dacca in 1952.¹¹⁵ The next year, the communists played a crucial role in establishing a leftist political platform, known as Ganatantri Dal. Popular peasant leader Haji Ahmad Danesh became its president and the general secretary was Mahmud Ali.[116] During the election campaign in 1954, the communists and the Awami Muslim League moved politically closer, and Oli Ahad, by then the leader of the Youth League, joined the Awami League.[117] These ties were strengthened in the aftermath of the election, when the Pakistani government dismissed the election results and unleashed repressive measures against the democratic movement. By 1955, when the Awami League emerged as the broadest and most active secular political organization in East Pakistan, many communists joined the party to steer it leftwards. Sardar Fazlul Karim, a communist, was even selected to be the Awami League's representative to the Pakistani Constituent Assembly.[118] Besides the communists, there were a significant number of left-leaners within the Awami League. Many of them clustered around Bhashani.[119] They were apprehensive about becoming entangled with the Cold War camp for fears of becoming alienated from the Non-Aligned Movement.

By 1956, as the events surrounding the Suez Crisis gradually unfolded, these radicals felt more and more alienated. Pakistan's involvement with the Baghdad Pact, right on the eve of the Suez Crisis, capped the long history of disappointments that had characterized the relationship between the Pakistani ruling elites and the Arab nationalist leadership. Since its formation, Pakistan had seriously tried to court the Arab countries. But while Pakistan championed Islamic solidarity, many among the younger generations of Arab nationalists perceived this Islamic appeal as detrimental to the evolution of a national identity and cold-shouldered Pakistan. Even before the rise of Gamal Abdel Nasser and the Free Officers to power, the Egyptian foreign minister, Salah al-Din Pasha, had announced in November 1951 that Egypt looked to India for 'moral support in her struggle for national liberation'.[120] The conservative monarchs and oil barons of the smaller sheikhdoms were more responsive to Pakistan's overture. They had far more to lose from nationalist revolutions, which aimed at land reforms, nationalization of resources, republicanism and Arab unifications.

Arab nationalists particularly frowned upon Pakistan when it entered into an alliance with Britain, Turkey, monarchical Iraq and Iran. The Arab League, where Egypt played a pivotal role, did not approve of this plan. The coincident events of an Israeli raid on the Gaza strip and the formation of the Baghdad Pact, which had the UK as a signatory, made Nasser unsympathetic to Pakistan.[121] But Egypt was not among the Arab countries having such a view of the Baghdad Pact. Nasser had particularly angered Pakistani leaders by developing close ties with India during the Bandung Conference in 1955. Pakistani leaders projected the deeply unpopular regime of Nuri al-Said of Iraq as an example of Arab support to the pact and the way forward to Arab unification.[122]

Given such international circumstances, there existed in East Pakistan a popular resentment regarding Pakistan's enthusiasm for a military pact. Such popular sentiments did not escape the attention of the US or even that of the Soviet Union. So much so that the US ambassador to Pakistan, Horace Hildreth, travelled to Dacca and addressed East Pakistanis through a speech on the radio on 24 January 1956. In this address, Hildreth criticized the politics of neutrality. He announced frankly that if Pakistan wanted US military aid, it would have to continue in pro-Western military blocs. The *New York Times* reported that the address caused a stir in Pakistani official circles as well. The event was also reported in the Communist Party of the Soviet Union's daily newspaper, *Pravda*. The *Pravda* report was titled 'A Legitimate Question'. As soon as this report was published, it caught the attention of the British embassy in Moscow. In secrecy, the British embassy personnel dispatched an English translation of the report to their embassy in Karachi.[123] Thus, the debates in Dacca concerning the Baghdad Pact and the SEATO gained international attention.

Meanwhile, international politics in South Asia had become far more complicated. Even before the Suez Crisis, in private conversations with foreign leaders, the Pakistani leaders had never concealed their animosity towards Nasser. On 21 September 1955, Mirza, the governor general of Pakistan, told the British high commissioner, Alexander Symon, that the Egyptians hated Pakistanis.[124] Nasser courted the further displeasure of Pakistani ruling elites when, along with Nehru, he participated in the formal declaration of the Non-Aligned Movement, which took place in the island of Brijuni in Yugoslavia on 19 July 1956.[125] But public opinion in the Middle East turned in Nasser's favour as soon as he announced the nationalization of the Suez Company on 26 July 1956. Even in far-flung Morocco on the Atlantic coast, George W. Shepherd Jr, a pioneering American-Africanist scholar, noted:

> The day I arrived in Rabat, the capital of Morocco, the streets were almost empty and the city was quiet. Everything had been shut down by a general strike called by the Istiqlal Party in sympathy with the Egyptians over the nationalization of the Suez canal.[126]

The critical problem before Pakistani leaders was that they were in alliance with the UK, an imperial power that was perceived as the archnemesis of Arab nationalist ambitions towards national independence and unity. From Algeria to Lebanon to Iraq, everywhere on Arab streets there was widespread disapproval of the former imperial powers – primarily, the UK and France. It was in the midst of this growing tension between Pakistan and Arab nationalists that Suhrawardy became the prime minister of Pakistan.

To deflect attention from the Middle East, Suhrawardy kicked off his foreign policy programme with a bold step: visiting the PRC. Quite apart from foreign-policy concerns, he was well aware that in the East Pakistani political circles, China was held in high esteem. US ambassador Hildreth had warned him of 'communist wiles' and had asked him to avoid the sort of publicity that could damage US–Pakistan ties, specifically of the kind that would turn off the newspaper readers in the US. To this, 'Mr. Suhrawardy had apparently replied that he was well aware that the "new look" in communist tactics did not carry with it any change in their intentions, and (in effect) he was as wily as they'.[127] After returning from China, Suhrawardy sent a letter to US president Eisenhower, making it clear that he would like to act as an intermediary between the US and the government of China over the sensitive issue of the release of American prisoners captured during the Korean War.[128] Hildreth, ever on the lookout for allies and enemies, observed in a telegram to Eisenhower:

> Obviously Suhrawardy wishes an attempt to replace Nehru as intermediary between Chou [Zhou Enlai, the first premier of the People's Republic of China] and US and in conversation said Chou told him he, Chou, mistrusted both Nehru and Nehru's influence with US Government and felt he, Suhrawardy, could [have] more influence with US Government than Nehru.[129]

Hildreth was worried about Zhou's impending visit to Pakistan on 20 December 1956 and sought instructions from Eisenhower.[130] Suhrawardy's visit to China, and his attempt to establish a relationship with China, raised his popularity among left-wing Awami League workers in East Pakistan. On 2 November 1956, in a teacher-training college in Dacca, the left-leaning Awami League members established the Pak–China Friendship Society. Bhashani became its patron; Ataur Rahman, the chief minister of East

Pakistan, became its president; and Zahur Hossain Chowdhury, an editor of the left-leaning journal *Dainik Sombad*, was elected its general secretary. Oli Ahad, the leader of the left-leaning Youth League, became its principal organizer.[131] Zhou visited Dacca in the last week of his tour of Pakistan. The Pak–China Friendship Society arranged a reception for the Chinese premier in Dacca's Gulistan cinema hall.[132]

Notwithstanding Suhrawardy's efforts in improving the Sino-American relationship, the political flare-up in the Middle East had tied Suhrawardy's hands. According to a plan prepared by France, the UK and Israel, the newly formed state invaded the Suez Canal region. On 29 October 1956, Israel escalated matters by launching an air attack, thus triggering an international crisis. For Suhrawardy, the situation became an emotive issue that could explode the unity of his party and undermine his base in East Pakistan. Pan-Islamic and pan-Asianist anti-imperial sentiments led to a spontaneous, almost frenzied, reaction on the streets of East Pakistan. Dacca became a city of processions and demonstrations. At one point an angry mob set fire to a building that formerly housed the British Information Service, in Purono Paltan, on 3 November, in the old part of the city. On 9 November 1956, Bhashani declared 'Egypt day' in East Pakistan and the provincial Awami League government declared the date a holiday.[133]

Suhrawardy was aware of this groundswell of anger. Yet he also knew that any anti-Western utterings would upset the Pakistani military and bureaucratic elites and that they would not hesitate to throw him out of power. Besides, he was a committed supporter of the Baghdad Pact. He wrote in *Foreign Affairs* in 1957:

> These by-elections occurred at the same time that I, as Prime Minister, restated in definitive terms Pakistan's foreign policy, which avoids the equivocations of neutralism and aligns us squarely on the side of the free democracies and the upholding of principles of responsibility in world affairs. It was a difficult time for such a test. Spurred by the autumn's complex developments in the Suez area, passions seemed to be running high. Yet the people listened and by their votes sustained the rational course rather than passions and shibboleths.[134]

He was thus in a deep dilemma. To further increase his anxiety, the Indian prime minister, Nehru, had written him a letter on 2 November that asked him to stand united with Afro-Asian efforts against the invasion of Egypt. A few days later, Nehru sent an invitation to Suhrawardy to attend the Colombo Powers[135] meeting in New Delhi on 12 November for that purpose. Suhrawardy refused to attend the meeting and made it clear that he had another meeting of the Baghdad Pact countries.[136] Implicit in his refusal was the hint that the Colombo Powers were marginal to Pakistan's national interests in comparison to the Baghdad Pact meeting. The problem for Suhrawardy was that Nasser regarded Pakistan, Iraq and Turkey as official allies of Britain through the Baghdad Pact. He therefore decided to avoid any diplomatic bonhomie with Pakistan and refused to accept Pakistani presence in the United Nations' (UN) Emergency Force in Egypt. This shocked Suhrawardy's supporters. Kamruddin Ahmad, a Bengali follower of Suhrawardy and a member of the Pakistani diplomatic corps at the UN, felt insulted when he found out from United Nations secretary general, Dag Hammarskjöld, that Nasser had personally removed Pakistan's name from the list of countries contributing to the UN Emergency Force.[137]

In the wake of the Suez Crisis, Mirza attended a meeting of the Baghdad Pact.[138] Suhrawardy went with him and offered to visit Cairo to meet Nasser. Angered by Iraq and Turkey's role in the Suez Crisis, Nasser turned down the request of a meeting with another member of the Baghdad Pact.[139] Suhrawardy had further increased his own dilemma. In the US, in a televised interview, Suhrawardy voiced his intention to mediate, along with US, in bringing the Israelis and the Arabs together. In Egypt this news was not received cordially.[140] But even under such pressure, Suhrawardy stuck to his guns in a speech at Dacca University on 9 December 1956 and defended the Baghdad Pact and Pakistan's pro-Western foreign policy.[141]

With such political gestures, Suhrawardy soon lost his popularity among the left youth circles in East Pakistan. During the Suez Crisis there took place a steady radicalization of the youth and students in East Pakistan. This radicalization was reflected in a youth festival organized in the town of Rangpur between 4 and 7 January 1957. Oli Ahad was the principal sponsor of this festival, although Awami League ministers were also present at what was primarily a Youth League festival.[142] On 7 and 8 February, Bhashani called for an Awami League council meeting at Kagmari in Tangail district. This convention at Kagmari was accompanied by an Afro-Asian cultural conference on 9 February. It also involved a social gathering of writers from India and Pakistan. The list of Indian literary figures included

Tarashankar Bandyopadhaya, Abdul Odud, Humayun Kabir, Probodh Sanyal and Radharani Debi. Bhashani also planned the construction of 'commemorative gates' to honour South Asian political leaders, such as Gandhi, Jinnah, Chittaranjan Das, Subhas Chandra Bose, Hakim Ajmal Khan, Nehru and Mirza. To irritate right-wing politicians, he also had a gate dedicated to the Chinese communist leader Mao Zedong and the Soviet leader Joseph Stalin.[143] The event had an international impact. On the eve of the UN discussions about Kashmir, the Indian delegation there distributed photos of the event and claimed that there was no need for a discussion of the Kashmir issue since there prevailed peace between the two countries. However, Suhrawardy ordered the Pakistani entourage to stick to the scheduled discussion on Kashmir, and on 24 January 1957, the UN Security Council passed Resolution 122.[144] According to this document, the state's Constitution was invalidated from being its ultimate legal disposition. To Pakistani nationalists, this was a significant success for Suhrawardy's foreign policy.[145]

Prior to the conference, Oli Ahad published a booklet called 'East Pakistan Awami League and Foreign Policy'.[146] Despite such preparations by the party's left wing, Bhashani and Suhrawardy concluded a 'deal' before the council meeting to not press for a resolution on foreign-policy matters. As a consequence, the Awami League council did not place a resolution in the conference regarding Pakistan's withdrawal from the Baghdad Pact or the SEATO. Among the council members, only Oli Ahad voted against the resolution. The next day, the pro–Awami League daily *Ittefaq* published this news in its front page. However, on 7 February 1957, Bhashani gave a speech against the government's foreign policy, which concluded with a warning for the Pakistani central government. Bhashani said that if the government did not provide adequate representation to East Pakistan, he might bid farewell to Pakistan.[147] This was the first direct and public call for the secession of East Pakistan by a prominent leader. On 18 March, Bhashani informed his young political fellow traveller, Oli Ahad, that he would like to resign from the post of the Awami League's president and instructed him to personally give his letter of resignation to Zahur Hossain Chowdhury of *Dainik Sombad*.[148] The Awami League Working Committee of East Pakistan called a session on 30 March. The latter half of this meeting was held in the chief minister's room in the provincial legislature, during which Abul Mansur Ahmad, the commerce and industry minister of Pakistan, moved a resolution asking for the expulsion of Oli Ahad as the organizing secretary of the Awami League. Of the 30 members present at the Awami League meeting, 14 supported and 9 opposed this resolution. The dissenting members also resigned from their respective positions in the organization.[149] This event initiated the process of a split in the party.

Soon Bhashani made it clear that he was considering floating an alternative to the Awami League. But on 13 June 1957, in an Awami League council meeting, both Suhrawardy and Bhashani debated foreign-policy alignments.[150] After Bhashani left the meeting, Sheikh Mujib moved a resolution supporting the Pakistani government's foreign policy, and this was accepted by a majority vote. Meanwhile, Bhashani, in alliance with Mian Iftikharuddin, G. M. Syed, Abdul Ghaffar Khan and Muhammad Osmani of West Pakistan, planned an all-Pakistan convention of 'leftist political activists'. On 25 and 26 July 1957, a new NAP came into existence. Tofazzal Hossain, the editor of *Ittefaq*, sarcastically dubbed the new party the 'Nehru Aided Party'.[151] The National Awami Party was backed by the Communist Party of East Pakistan, though most of its popular figures were ethno-nationalists from West Pakistan, who also turned out to be big landlords. In contrast, NAP leaders from East Pakistan were members of the middle classes. Despite having two different social constituencies in the two wings of Pakistan, the NAP became the largest left-leaning political formation in the country, with an agenda based upon non-alignment and a reluctance to identify with any military bloc.[152]

Despite the Awami League's expressed hostility towards the new organization, its hold of government machinery proved to be ephemeral even as Suhrawardy expected national elections to be held immediately. Soon, Mirza, engaged in a new conspiracy, compelled Suhrawardy to resign on 17 October 1957. Suhrawardy's bonhomie with the pro-Western president did not prevent the consolidation of the bureaucratic-military forces within the state machinery. But he kept his hopes up for 15 April 1958, the date on which the general election was supposed to be held in Pakistan. It was a naive hope. On 8 October 1958, he had declared a national emergency by dissolving the Constituent Assembly. However, Ayub Khan, who was appointed the martial law administrator, staged a second coup by dismissing Mirza on 26 October 1958. This transformed the bureaucratic-military domination into a military-bureaucratic dictatorship. The democratic forces in East Pakistan had failed to recognize a simple fact: the politics of military pacts facilitated the rise of military-bureaucratic forces.

Conclusion

Pakistani politics was shaped by an articulation that lay between the dominant form of the West Pakistani mode of production and the colonial inheritance of a military-bureaucratic political structure. The landed elites, who dominated political parties in West Pakistan, remained engrossed in rent-seeking activities. Jinnah, the founding figure of Pakistan, had followed a vice-regal structure of governance, which had mutated into a form of bureaucratic-military oligarchy. It was not an overdeveloped state but, rather, the *only* form of state structure that existed as a legacy of the colonial period. In East Pakistan, the newly emerging middle class struggled to establish democratic structures that could help stave off a situation of internal colonization. Yet their interests clashed with the military-bureaucratic elites and semi-feudal landowners in West Pakistan. The military and bureaucratic elites had found their salvation in the political climate of the Cold War and eagerly sought an alliance with the US and the UK in order to pursue a policy of aid-driven economic growth that required no painstaking structural reforms. The flow of aid strengthened the state's military apparatus, while the imperial alliance sought to use Pakistan's highly trained military to bolster its interests in the increasingly revolutionary nationalist environment of the Middle East. Meanwhile, in East Pakistan, the middle-class leadership sought a compromise with the democratic façade that the military-bureaucratic authorities kept up by playing into the belief that Pakistan would move towards a constitutional democracy. This convenient myth was shattered by the political storm that the Suez Crisis brought to Asia and Africa. The man who read into this revolutionary possibility was Bhashani, a self-proclaimed peasant populist and rural theologian who had built up a coalition of peasant populists, socialists and communists within the Awami League. He could not avoid the Awami League's split, but he left a critical instance of far-sighted resistance to the military-bureaucratic junta and their representatives.

Bhashani's particular brand of articulating regional nationalism spoke to the wider current of decolonization and national liberation struggles in the Global South in the mid-fifties. His ideas were similar to what Malek outlines in his concept of 'nationalitarian'. According to Malek,

> the nationalitarian phenomenon is one in which the struggle against the imperialist powers of occupation has as its object, beyond the clearing of the national territory, the independence and sovereignty of the national

state, uprooting in depth the positions of the ex-colonial power – the reconquest of the power of decision in all domains of national life, the prelude to that reconquest of identity which is at the heart of the renaissance undertaken on the basis of fundamental national demands, and ceaselessly contested, by every means available, on every level, and notably on the internal level.[153]

Unpacking this concept, Neil Lazarus quotes from Fanon, who has emphatically asserted:

[I]t is national liberation which leads the nation to play its part on the stage of history. It is at the heart of national consciousness that international consciousness lives and grows.[154]

To Fanon, an auto-critique of nationalism could take place only through a lively dialogue with the global process of decolonization. Indeed, the sweeping breadth of decolonization that was taking place in the fifties – from South-East Asia through South Asia and South-West Asia via Africa all the way to Latin America – constituted a global theatre of action for the majority of the world. Over the course of these years, the world witnessed the rise of the non-alignment movement, and the concept of Afro-Asian solidarity gained credence. These were also the years of the Bandung Conference, the Algerian War of Independence and the impending national liberation of Ghana. The Bandung Conference, in particular, signified a critical moment in the national liberation movements in Asia. In the words of Vijay Prasad, the 'Bandung Spirit' came to mean 'that the colonized world had now emerged to claim its space in world affairs, not just as an adjunct of the First or Second Worlds, but as a player in its own right'.[155] Thus in the fifties, Bhashani, in alliance with the communists and peasant populists, was making an ideological intervention that, to a certain extent, anticipated the coming of the global sixties.

Notes

1. Layli Uddin, 'Lessons of Freedom', *Daily Star*, 12 December 2016, https://www.thedailystar.net/opinion/tribute/lessons-freedom-1328605 (accessed on 1 May 2020).

2. Shahid Amin, 'Gandhi as Mahatma: Gorakhpur District, Eastern UP, 1921–2', in *Selected Subaltern Studies*, ed. Ranajit Guha and Gayatri Chakravorty Spivak, pp. 288–342 (New York: Oxford University Press, 1989).
3. On 30 November 1967, in a speech at the National Awami Party's (NAP) special session in a presidential address, Bhashani spelled out his position more clearly. He said that people in Asia, Africa and Latin America, through their national independence struggle against US-sponsored imperialist powers, understood the real nature of American imperialism. Syed Abul Maksud, *Maulana Abdul Hamid Khan Bhasani* (Dhaka: Agami Prokashoni, 2014), p. 815.
4. I have used the term 'bureaucratic-military' to distinguish it from military-bureaucratic domination from 1958 onwards. This is to highlight my differences with Hamza Alavi's thesis of military-bureaucratic domination. See Hamza Alavi, 'The State in Post-Colonial Societies: Pakistan and Bangladesh', *New Left Review* 1, no. 74 (1972): 59–81; Hamza Alavi, 'Class and State in Pakistan', in *Pakistan: The Unstable State*, ed. Hassan N. Gardezi and Jamil Rashid, pp. 40–93 (Lahore: Vanguard, 1983); Hamza Alavi, 'Authoritarianism and Legitimation of State Power in Pakistan', in *The Post-Colonial State in Asia: Dialectics of Politics and Culture*, ed. Subrata Kumar Mitra, pp. 19–71 (New York: Harvester Wheatsheaf, 1990).
5. For details, see Uddin, 'Lessons of Freedom'.
6. Cristóbal Kay analyzed the comparative case of Latin America and East Asia and thus established an archetype of Latin American case. Cristóbal Kay, 'Why East Asia Overtook Latin America: Agrarian Reform, Industrialisation and Development', *Third World Quarterly* 23, no. 6 (2002): 1073–102, https://jstor.org/stable/3993564 (accessed on 13 May 2020). For different types of land reforms, see Andrew W. Horowitz, 'Time Paths of Land Reform: A Theoretical Model of Reform Dynamics', *American Economic Review* 83, no. 4 (1993): 1003–10, https://jstor.org/stable/2117592 (accessed on 17 May 2020). For land reforms in East and South-East Asia, see Peter Dorner and William C. Thiesenhusen, 'Selected Land Reforms in East and Southeast Asia: Their Origins and Impacts', *Asian-Pacific Economic Literature* 4, no. 1 (1990): 65–95.
7. Mushtaq Ahmad, 'Land Reforms in Pakistan', *Pakistan Horizon* 12, no. 1 (1959): 30–36, https://jstor.org/stable/41392253 (accessed on 4 May 2020).
8. Ronald Herring and M. Ghaffar Chaudhry, 'The 1972 Land Reforms in Pakistan and Their Economic Implications: A Preliminary Analysis',

Pakistan Development Review 13, no. 3 (1974): 245–79, https://jstor.org/stable/41258246 (accessed on 4 May 2020).

9. M. Shahid Alam, 'Economics of the Landed Interests: A Case Study of Pakistan', *Pakistan Economic and Social Review* 12, no. 1 (1974): 12–26. www.jstor.org/stable/25824782 (accessed on 4 May 2020).
10. Talukder Moniruzzaman, 'Group Interests in Pakistan Politics, 1947–1958', *Pacific Affairs* 39, nos. 1–2 (1966): 83–98, p. 85.
11. Luis Roniger, 'Political Clientelism, Democracy, and Market Economy', *Comparative Politics* 36, no. 3 (2004): 353–75.
12. Alex Weingrod, 'Patrons, Patronage and Political Parties', *Comparative Studies in Society and History* 10, no. 4 (1968): 377–400.
13. Khalid B. Sayeed, 'The Political Role of Pakistan's Civil Service', *Pacific Affairs* 31, no. 2 (1958): 131–46, DOI: 10.2307/3035208.
14. Sayeed, 'The Political Role of Pakistan's Civil Service'.
15. For details of this palace intrigue, see Kamruddin Ahmad, *A Social History of Bengal* (Dacca: Raushan Ara, 1970), pp. 115–16.
16. Syed Azhar Ali, 'Unicameralism in United Pakistan: Why and How?', *Pakistan Horizon* 48, no. 3 (1995): 69–80, www.jstor.org/stable/41393529 (accessed on 8 July 2020).
17. Sayeed, 'The Political Role of Pakistan's Civil Service', pp. 133–34.
18. K. Ahmad, *A Social History of Bengal*, p. 117.
19. H. Kumarasingham, 'A Transnational Actor on a Dramatic Stage: Sir Ivor Jennings and the Manipulation of Westminster Style Democracy in Pakistan', in *Constitution-Making and Transnational Legal Order* (Comparative Constitutional Law and Policy Series), ed. Gregory Shaffer, Tom Ginsburg and Terence C. Halliday, pp. 55–84 (Cambridge: Cambridge University Press, 2019), DOI: 10.1017/9781108561792.003.
20. Sayeed, 'The Political Role of Pakistan's Civil Service', p. 134.
21. Moniruzzaman, 'Group Interests in Pakistan Politics, 1947–1958', pp. 83–98.
22. Tahir Kamran, 'Early Phase of Electoral Politics in Pakistan: 1950s', *South Asia: Journal of South Asian Studies* 24, no. 2 (July–December 2009): 257–82.
23. The number 300 is collected from Shahid Javed Burki's essay on Pakistan bureaucracy. Shahid Javed Burki, 'Twenty Years of the Civil Service of Pakistan: A Re-evaluation', *Asian Survey* 9, no. 4 (1969): 239–54, DOI: 10.2307/2642543.
24. Sayeed, 'The Political Role of Pakistan's Civil Service'.

25. Dipesh Chakrabarty, *Provincializing Europe: Postcolonial Thought and Historical Difference* (Princeton, NJ: Princeton University Press, 2008 [2000]).
26. Rajit K. Mazumder, *The Indian Army and the Making of Punjab* (New Delhi: Permanent Black), pp. 2–3.
27. Tan Tai Yong, 'Maintaining the Military Districts: Civil–Military Integration and District Soldiers Boards in the Punjab, 1919–1939', *Modern Asian Studies* 28, no. 4: 833–74, DOI: 10.1017/S0026749X00012555
28. Prem Chowdhry, 'Militarized Masculinities: Shaped and Reshaped in Colonial South-East Punjab', *Modern Asian Studies* 47, no. 3 (2013): 713–50.
29. Mazumder, *The Indian Army and the Making of Punjab*, p. 38.
30. For details, see Ayesha Jalal, *The State of Martial Rule: The Origin of Pakistan's Political Economy of Defence* (Cambridge South Asian Studies) (Cambridge: Cambridge University Press, 1990), pp. 117–119.
31. Ayesha Jalal, 'Towards the Baghdad Pact: South Asia and Middle East Defence in the Cold War, 1947–1955', *International History Review* 11, no. 3 (1989): 409–33.
32. Tayyab Mahmud, 'Praetorianism and Common Law in Post-Colonial Settings: Judicial Responses to Constitutional Breakdowns in Pakistan', *Utah Law Review* 4 (1993): 1225–1305.
33. Jalal, 'Towards the Baghdad Pact', pp. 415–18.
34. Robert J. McMahon, 'United States Cold War Strategy in South Asia: Making a Military Commitment to Pakistan, 1947–1954', *Journal of American History* 75, no. 3 (December 1988): 812–40.
35. McMahon, 'United States Cold War Strategy', p. 821.
36. The India-controlled union territories of Jammu and Kashmir and Ladakh were part of the princely state of Jammu and Kashmir before independence. However, India and Pakistan entered into a military conflict over the region in 1947–48. The Indian army cleared the state of 'Pakistani tribal invaders' and claimed that the Maharaja of Kashmir acceded to the Indian Union, and Pakistan refused to accept the accession. The United Nations (UN) passed a resolution for plebiscite provided both countries withdrew their armies, but neither side withdrew its armies, and the plebiscite became a dead issue. In the fifties, the UK still expected a resolution of the Kashmir dispute through peaceful means.
37. FO J. D Murray, South-East Asia Department, to B. A. B Burrows, Counselor, British Embassy, Washington, 8 January 1950. D3300/30.

38. FO UK Telegram no. 693, 23 June 1952, Arms supplies for India and Pakistan, FY 1192/12, Ministry of Defense.
39. Parvez Hasan, 'Balance of Payments Problems of Pakistan', *The Pakistan Development Review* 1, no. 2 (1961): 15–48, p. 24, https://jstor.org/stable/41258033 (accessed on 9 July 2020).
40. *Nao Belal*, 2 August 1951.
41. FO UK Telegram to Sir O. Franks, No. 1443, 28th July 1952, from Washing to Foreign Office.
42. Abul Mansur Ahmad, *Amar Dekha Rajnitir Ponchas Botsor* (Dhaka: Prothoma Prokashan, 2018), pp. 296–99.
43. Melvyn P. Leffler, 'The American Conception of National Security and the Beginnings of the Cold War, 1945–48', *American Historical Review* 89, no. 2 (April 1984): 346–81, p. 379.
44. McMahon, 'United States Cold War Strategy', p. 821.
45. A typical example of Western apprehension was reflected in an observation made by W. Norris, a British diplomat at High Commission, that various Muslim militant organizations put pressure on the Pakistani government to foster a Muslim bloc that would hold aloof from the Soviet Union and the West. Despite discomfort, Zafarullah Khan, the foreign minister of Pakistan, demonstrated that Pakistani government was on the side of Muslims in Iranian and Egyptian dispute, and yet he withstood pressures to join a neutral bloc. FO FY1023/6/4, Letter from W.G. Norris, British High Commission in Karachi, to T. E. Bromley, British Embassy in Baghdad, 5 April 1952.
46. McMahon, 'United States Cold War Strategy', p. 837.
47. The Manila Pact was signed in September 1954 in Manila, Philippines, which led to the foundation of the South-East Asia Treaty Organization (SEATO). SEATO was a defence organization formed to resist the expansion of communism in South-East Asia. The organization comprised of eight member countries: Australia, France, New Zealand, Pakistan, the Philippines, Thailand, the UK and the US. It was dissolved on 30 June 1977 as many members lost interest and withdrew.
48. The Middle East Treaty Organization (METO), also known as the Baghdad Pact and subsequently known as the Central Treaty Organization (CENTO), was a military alliance of the Cold War. It was formed on 24 February 1955 by Iran, Iraq, Pakistan, Turkey and the UK. Though the US played a crucial role in forming the alliance, it was not a member. The alliance was dissolved on 16 March 1979.

49. McMahon, 'United States Cold War Strategy', p. 838.
50. Mark J. Gasiorowski, 'U.S. Perceptions of the Communist Threat in Iran during the Mossadegh Era', *Journal of Cold War Studies* 21, no. 3 (2019): 185–221.
51. For details of US tolerance of the coup, see Christopher Gunn, 'The 1960 Coup in Turkey: A U.S. Intelligence Failure or a Successful Intervention?', *Journal of Cold War Studies*,17, no. 2 (2015): 103–39.
52. Stephen Blackwell, 'A Desert Squall: Anglo-American Planning for Military Intervention in Iraq, July 1958–August 1959', *Middle Eastern Studies* 35, no. 3 (1999): 1–18, DOI: 10.1080/00263209908701276.
53. Taya Zinkin, *Reporting India* (London: Chatto & Windus, 1962), p. 40.
54. A. M. Ahmad, *Amar Dekha Rajnitir Ponchas Botsor*, p. 204.
55. Moni Singh was the general secretary of the Communist Party of East Pakistan. He mentioned this in vivid details in his autobiography. Moni Singh, *Jibon Songram* (Dwitio Khondo) (Dhaka: Jatio Sahitya Prokashani, 1992), p. 24.
56. The Central Intelligence Agency (CIA) estimated that there were roughly 1,500 communists and their fellow travellers in Pakistan in the fifties. Communists had their main presence in East Pakistan, and they had representations in the provincial assembly of East Pakistan and the national assembly pf Pakistan. They identified Bhashani as a fellow traveller of communists. CIA Archives, 'Probable Developments in Pakistan', National Intelligence Estimate Number 52–56, 13 November 1956, p. 9, https://www.cia.gov/library/readingroom/docs/CIA-RDP79R0 1012A007900030001-3.pdf (accessed on 22 June 2021).
57. See CIA Archives, 'Probable Developments in Pakistan', p. 9.
58. For details, see Oli Ahad, *Jatio Rajniti*: *1945 theke 1975* (Fourth Edition) (Dhaka: Bangladesh Co-operative Book Society, 2004), pp. 126–30.
59. Sana Aiyar, 'Fazlul Huq, Region and Religion in Bengal: The Forgotten Alternative of 1940–43', *Modern Asian Studies* 42, no. 6 (2008): 1213–49, www.jstor.org/stable/20488062 (accessed on 9 July 2020).
60. For details, see Rajat K. Ray, 'Masses in Politics: The Non-Cooperation Movement in Bengal 1920–1922', *Indian Economic & Social History Review* 11, no. 4 (1974): 343–410, DOI: 10.1177/001946467401100401.
61. A. M. Ahmad, *Amar Dekha Rajnitir Ponchas Botsor*, p. 206.
62. A. M. Ahmad, *Amar Dekha Rajnitir Ponchas Botsor*, p. 206.
63. Joya Chatterji, *Bengal Divided: Hindu Communalism and Partition, 1932–1947* (Cambridge: Cambridge University Press, 1994), pp. 191–219.

64. Singh, *Jibon Songram* (Dwitio Khondo), pp. 26–27.
65. Ahad, *Jatio Rajniti*, pp. 194–95.
66. Kenneth McPherson, *The Muslim Microcosm, Calcutta, 1918 to 1935* (Beitrage Zur Sudasienforschung) (Wiesbaden: Steiner, 1974), pp. 95–96.
67. Sheikh Mujibur Rahman, *Asomapto Atmojiboni* (Dhaka: University Press, 2018), p. 11.
68. In 1955, in response to a question by journalists regarding differences of opinion in the Awami League, Suhrawardy apparently said: 'Awami League! What is Awami League, I am Awami League'. He was implying that without him the organization did not exist. Ahad, *Jatio Rajniti*, p. 195.
69. K. Ahmad, *A Social History of Bengal*, p. 117.
70. K. Ahmad, *A Social History of Bengal*, pp. 118–19. Abul Mansur Ahmad, a close follower of Suhrawardy, explicitly discussed how Suhrawardy was promised the prime minister's position and was later duped. A. M. Ahmad, *Amar Dekha Rajnitir Ponchas Botsor*, pp. 294–95, 302–05.
71. Rahman, *Asomapto Atmojiboni*, p. 286.
72. K. Ahmad, *A Social History of Bengal*, p. 119.
73. A. M. Ahmad, *Amar Dekha Rajnitir Ponchas Botsor*, pp. 289–90.
74. Ahad, *Jatio Rajniti*, p. 197.
75. This observation was based on Sayeed's essay 'The Political Role of Pakistan's Civil Service'. Also see K. Ahmad, *A Social History of Bengal*, pp. 123–26.
76. A. M. Ahmad, *Amar Dekha Rajnitir Ponchas Botsor*, p. 308.
77. A. M. Ahmad, *Amar Dekha Rajnitir Ponchas Botsor*, pp. 315–16.
78. A. M. Ahmad, *Amar Dekha Rajnitir Ponchas Botsor*, p. 315.
79. A. M. Ahmad, *Amar Dekha Rajnitir Ponchas Botsor*, p. 322.
80. A. M. Ahmad, *Amar Dekha Rajnitir Ponchas Botsor*, p. 322.
81. K. Ahmad, *A Social History of Bengal*, pp. 123–26.
82. Abul Mansur Ahmad took pride in the fact that after his speech in the parliament on 9 January 1954, he was compared with Edmund Burke in a telegram from East Bengal. A. M. Ahmad, *Amar Dekha Rajnitir Ponchas Botsor*, pp. 315–16.
83. Rahman, *Asomapto Atmojiboni*, pp. 218–20, 236.
84. Ataur Rahman Khan, *Ojarotir Dui Botsor: Mukhkho Montritter Dinguli, 1956–1958* (Dhaka: Prothoma, 2017).
85. Maksud, *Maulana Abdul Hamid Khan Bhasani*, pp. 30–31.
86. Abid S. Bahar, 'The Religious and Philosophical Basis of Bhashani's Political Leadership', PhD dissertation, Concordia University, Montreal,

2003, pp. 43–45, https://spectrum.library.concordia.ca/id/eprint/2294/ (accessed on 6 August 2018).
87. David Arnold, 'Famine in Peasant Consciousness and Peasant Action: Madras, 1876–8', in *Subaltern Studies: Writings on South Asian History and Society*, vol. 3, ed. Ranajit Guha, pp. 62–115 (New Delhi: Oxford University Press, 1984).
88. Maksud, *Maulana Abdul Hamid Khan Bhasani*, p. 35.
89. Barbara Metcalf, 'The Madrasa at Deoband: A Model for Religious Education in Modern India', *Modern Asian Studies* 12, no. 1 (1978): 111–34, p. 111.
90. For Mahmud al-Hassan's role in spreading Deobandi thoughts, see Muhammad Fahim Khan, 'The Life and Times of Ḥaji Sahib of Turangzai', *Islamic Studies* 16, no. 1 (1977): 329–41. For Mahmud al-Hassan's impact on Bhashani, see Syed Irfanul Bari, 'Asamprodaikota o Maulana Bhashani', in *Nanan Matray Maulana Bhashani* (Dhaka: Papyrus, 2018), p. 16.
91. Maksud, *Maulana Abdul Hamid Khan Bhasani*, p. 717.
92. In many ways, Bhashani's ideology represents what Karl Marx called 'the expression of real suffering and the protest against real suffering. Religion is the sigh of the oppressed creature, the heart of a heartless world, and the soul of soulless conditions.' Karl Marx, 'Contribution to the Critique of Hegel's Philosophy of Right', in *Early Writings*, p. 244 (New York: Vintage, 1974).
93. Farid Esack, *Qur'an, Liberation and Pluralism: An Islamic Perspective of Interreligious Solidarity against Oppression* (Oxford: Oneworld Publications, 1997).
94. Many Muslim young men were attracted towards revolutionary secret society movements in Bengal. Yet their overt use of Hindu Kali-worshipping rituals as initiation ceremonies in secret societies repelled them. Famous communist leader Muzaffar Ahmad recalled his own predilection towards revolutionary nationalist societies and his uneasiness for their overt use of Kali-worshipping rituals as initiation ceremonies. Muzaffar Ahmad, *Amar Jibon o Bharater Communist Party* (Calcutta: National Book Agency, 1969), p. 4.
95. Writing in 1927, B. C. Allen, a commissioner of Assam, recorded: 'Near the river the land as a rule is low and is covered with reed jungle, much of which has in recent years been taken up by hardy immigrants from Bengal, who are trained to snatch a living from places which an up-countryman would consider to be quite unfit for human.' B. C. Allen, 'Assam', *Journal of the Royal Society of Arts* 75, no. 3892 (1927): 764–86, p. 765.

96. Debarshi Das and Arupjyoti Saikia, 'Early Twentieth Century Agrarian Assam: A Brief and Preliminary Overview', *Economic and Political Weekly* 46, no. 41 (2011): 73–80. Also see Jayeeta Sharma, *Empire's Garden: Assam and the Making of India* (Durham, NC: Duke University Press, 2011).
97. The INC leaders also planned an alternative colonization by bringing in Bihari Hindus in order to counter the growing presence of Bengali Muslims. Amalendu Guha, 'East Bengal Immigrants and Maulana Abdul Hamid Khan Bhashani in Assam Politics, 1928–47', *Indian Economic and Social History Review* 13, no. 4 (1976): 419–52.
98. Guha, 'East Bengal Immigrants', p. 426.
99. Maksud, *Maulana Abdhul Hamid Khan Bhasani*, p. 104.
100. Ahad, *Jatio Rajniti*, pp. 197–98.
101. Ahad, *Jatio Rajniti*, pp. 202–03.
102. Ahad, *Jatio Rajniti*, pp. 210–12.
103. Kamruddin Ahmad, *Banglar Ek Modhyobitter Atmokahini* (Dhaka: Prothoma Prokashon, 2018), pp. 60–62.
104. K. Ahmad, *Banglar Ek Modhyobitter Atmokahini*, p. 62.
105. K. Ahmad, *Banglar Ek Modhyobitter Atmokahini*, pp. 63–64.
106. K. Ahmad, *Banglar Ek Modhyobitter Atmokahini*, pp. 63–64.
107. A. M. Ahmad, *Amar Dekha Rajnitir Ponchas Botsor*, pp. 274–78.
108. A. M. Ahmad, *Amar Dekha Rajnitir Ponchas Botsor*, pp. 294–318, 328.
109. K. Ahmad, *Banglar Ek Modhyobitter Atmokahini*, pp. 119–120.
110. A. M. Ahmad, *Amar Dekha Rajnitir Ponchas Botsor*, p. 328.
111. A. M. Ahmad, *Amar Dekha Rajnitir Ponchas Botsor*, p. 235.
112. Richard D. Lambert, 'Factors in Bengali Regionalism in Pakistan', *Far Eastern Survey* 28, no. 4 (1959): 49–58, p. 54, DOI: 10.2307/3024111,
113. Ahad, *Jatio Rajniti*, p. 211.
114. Ahad, *Jatio Rajniti*, pp. 119–22.
115. Singh, *Jibon Songram* (Dwitio Khondo), pp. 15–16.
116. Singh, *Jibon Songram* (Dwitio Khondo), pp. 17–18.
117. Ahad, *Jatio Rajniti*, pp. 181–84.
118. Singh, *Jibon Songram* (Dwitio Khondo), pp. 34–35.
119. Harun-or-Rashid, *Mul Dharar Rajniti: Bangladesh Awami League Council 1949–2016* (Mainstream Politics: Bangladesh Awami League Council 1949–2016) (Dhaka: Bangla Academy, 2019), pp. 52–53.
120. S. M. Burke, *Pakistan's Foreign Policy: An Historical Analysis* (London: Oxford University, 1973), p. 67, cited in Sohail H. Hashmi, '"Zero Plus Zero Plus Zero": Pakistan, the Baghdad Pact, and the Suez Crisis',

International History Review 33, no. 3 (2011): 525–44, p. 527, www.jstor.org/stable/23033197 (accessed on 6 June 2020).

121. Hashmi, '"Zero Plus Zero Plus Zero"', pp. 525–44.
122. Yehoshua Porath, 'Nuri al-Sa'id's Arab Unity Programme', *Middle Eastern Studies* 20, no. 4 (2006): 76–98, DOI: 10.1080/00263208408700600.
123. United Kingdom Foreign and Commonwealth Office, DY 10345/1, British Embassy, Moscow, 1 February 1956 (Restricted 1195/13/56); *Pravda*, 30 January 1956.
124. United Kingdom Foreign and Commonwealth Office with the Complement of Constitutional Department, 11 October 1955, FO 371 DY 1022/2, 'Record of an Interview between Sir Alexander Symon and Governor General of Pakistan dated 21 September 1955'.
125. Aleksandar Životić and Jovan Čavoški, 'On the Road to Belgrade: Yugoslavia, Third World Neutrals, and the Evolution of Global Non-Alignment, 1954–1961', *Journal of Cold War Studies* 18, no. 4 (2016): 79–97, DOI: 10.1162/JCWS_a_00681.
126. George W. Shepherd Jr, 'Suez: Touchstone of Colonialism', *Africa Today* 3, no. 5 (1956): 6–7, www.jstor.org/stable/4183826 (accessed on 4 July 2020).
127. United Kingdom Foreign Office, DY 1632/5, British Embassy, Washington, DC, 22 October 1956, FO 371, Bottomley to J. O. McCormick, South-East Asia Department, Foreign Office, London.
128. National Archives of the United States, Department of State, Central Files, 611.93/12–1256, Secret, Priority.
129. National Archives of the United States, Department of State, Central Files, 611.93/12–1256, Secret, Priority.
130. National Archives of the United States, Department of State, Central Files, 611.93/12–1256, Secret, Priority.
131. Ahad, *Jatio Rajniti*, p. 217.
132. Ahad, *Jatio Rajniti*, p. 217.
133. Ahad, *Jatio Rajniti*, pp. 217–18.
134. Huseyn Shaheed Suhrawardy, 'Political Stability and Democracy in Pakistan', *Foreign Affairs* 35, no. 3 (1957): 422–31, p. 431, DOI: 10.2307/20031239.
135. John Kotelawala, the then prime minster of Sri Lanka, hosted a conference of the prime ministers of Burma, India, Indonesia and Pakistan. This launched a new five-power grouping called the Colombo Powers. This group stood for Afro-Asian solidarity in foreign policy sphere.
136. Hashmi, '"Zero Plus Zero Plus Zero"', pp. 541.

137. K. Ahmad, *Banglar Ek Modhyobitter Atmokahini*, p. 73.
138. United Kingdom Foreign Office, DY 1632/3, Inward Telegram to Commonwealth Relations Office, President's Movements in November.
139. Mohammed Ahsen Chaudhri, 'Pakistan and the Muslim World', *Pakistan Horizon* 10, no. 3 (1957): 156–66, www.jstor.org/stable/41392316 (accessed on 4 July 2020).
140. Hafeez-ur-Rahman Khan, 'Pakistan's Relations with the U.A.R', *Pakistan Horizon* 13, no. 3 (1960): 209–26, www.jstor.org/stable/41392373 (accessed on 4 July 2020).
141. Ahad, *Jatio Rajniti*, p. 221.
142. Ahad, *Jatio Rajniti*, p. 219.
143. Ahad, *Jatio Rajniti*, p. 226.
144. K. Ahmad, *Banglar Ek Modhyobitter Atmokahini*, p. 99. Kamruddin, however, was wrong in stating that they persuaded United Nations delegates that the gate erected in honor of Chinese leader Mao Zedong was only to impress Chinese delegation to the UN. In the UN in 1950, Chinese delegation represented the nationalist republic of China, and not people's republic.
145. K. Ahmad, *Banglar Ek Modhyobitter Atmokahini*, pp. 102–03.
146. Ahad, *Jatio Rajniti*, p. 222.
147. Ahad, *Jatio Rajniti*, p. 223.
148. Ahad, *Jatio Rajniti*, p. 227.
149. Ahad, *Jatio Rajniti*, pp. 227–31.
150. Ahad, *Jatio Rajniti*, p. 231.
151. Ahad, *Jatio Rajniti*, pp. 231–34.
152. M. Rashiduzzaman, 'The National Awami Party of Pakistan: Leftist Politics in Crisis', *Pacific Affairs* 43, no. 3 (1970): 394–409.
153. Anouar Abdel-Malek, *Nation and Revolution*, trans. Mike Gonzalez (*Social Dialectics*, vol. 2) (Albany, NY: State University of New York Press, 1981), pp. 13, 222.
154. Franz Fanon, *The Wretched of Earth*, trans. Constance Farrington (London: Grove Press, 1968 [1961]), pp. 247–48, quoted in Neil Lazarus, 'Disavowing Decolonization: Fanon, Nationalism, and the Problematic of Representation in Current Theories of Colonial Discourse', *Research in African Literatures* 24, no. 4 (1993): 69–98, https://jstor.org/stable/3820255 (accessed on 28 April 2020).
155. Vijay Prashad, *The Darker Nations: A People's History of the Third World* (New York: New Press, 2007), p. 45.

3

Language, Culture and the Global Sixties in East Pakistan

In 1971, from the ruins of polyethnic Islamic Pakistan, Bangladesh emerged as the only linguistic nation state in South Asia. Though South Asia has always been a multilingual region with different linguistic communities concentrated in distinct territories, political divisions, based on claims to putative nationhood, centred around the two larger religious entities of the Hindus and the Muslims.[1] Unlike Europe, language played a relatively minor role in influencing South Asian nationalisms unless linguistic identities became part of broader religious conflicts. Indeed, the South Asian subcontinent had been characterized by sectarian violence along Hindu–Muslim religious lines since the early decades of the twentieth century.[2] In many ways such violence was informed by colonial engagement with the construction of 'history' and identities of South Asians.[3] The birth of Bangladesh, based upon a shared language among Muslims and Hindus, symbolized a post-colonial journey in culture and politics. The student movement for the declaration of Bengali as one of the national languages of Pakistan in 1952 was the starting point of this journey. Police firing on the students' movement caused the first critical public expression of disenchantment among students with the idea of Pakistan. In Dacca, Bengali cultural activists invented a tradition of celebrating martyrs' day on 21 February, memorializing the death of students and ordinary pedestrians in police firing.[4] The martyrs' column, erected two days after the event, symbolized the making of a 'secular sacred space' reflecting a putative nation's emotional longing. This very act inscribed the language movement on the collective memory of Bengali speakers in East Pakistan.[5] In 1969, at the height of the global sixties, the Awami League, the principal regional organization, raised the emotive slogan 'Brave Bengali pick up arms and liberate Bangladesh'.[6] There was an assumption in extant literature that linguistic identity automatically trumped over religious–national identity among Bengalis. Such a discourse raises a question: why did Bengali culture and linguistic identity, which had been shared among both Muslims and Hindus, outplay religious national identity of Pakistan? This was more surprising particularly because the Pakistan movement had had such a big support among Bengali Muslims in late colonial India; in fact, the organization that spearheaded the Pakistan movement in Bengal had argued that East Pakistani cultural and literary activities should start afresh in order to break from Hindu-influenced modern Bengali literature. Indeed, the nature of contestation over Bengali identity was informed by debates about Bengali culture, and many Muslim nationalists among the Bengali literati wanted to depart from this 'Hindu' orientation of Bengali culture.

In order to understand the significance of culture in the Bengali world, I begin this intellectual journey with Andrew Sartori's exploration of the word 'culturalism'.[7] According to Sartori, Bengal witnessed a birth of culturalism under the sign of capital. As capital emerged as a globally transformative force in the eighteenth and nineteenth centuries, intellectuals in different locations of the world engaged with the philosophy of liberalism, the supposed political expression of capitalist property relations. Thus, when Bengal entered the global political economy of exchange of commodities, Bengali intellectuals became familiar with its attendant idioms of rule of law, freedom and equality, or liberal political philosophy. Intellectuals such as Rammohun Roy and Dwarkanath Tagore engaged with liberal political philosophy as a political articulation of capitalism. Yet the global financial crisis of 1847–48 pushed Bengalis out of circuits of capital accumulation[8] and gave birth to an imperial economy whereby India got locked into a dual role as a captive market for British manufactured goods and as a producer of raw materials for export. As a consequence, Bengali liberal concerns retreated into an 'alternative ideological paradigm centred on the concept of culture'.[9] Sartori offers an interesting reading of pioneering modern Bengali litterateur Bankim Chandra Chatterjee, who in the 1860s and 1870s articulated a liberal vision but by the 1880s moved to 'a characterization of liberal subjectivity as itself a quintessentially Western norm incongruous with being native'.[10] Sartori emphasizes that Bankim Chandra's 'new humanism' was founded on the concept of *anushilan*, or 'culture', that laid the foundation of culturalism.[11] Bankim Chandra sought to elevate Hinduism as a civic religion of a putative nation. This culturalism actually became a critical signifier of

Bengal's identity and cast a long shadow over Bengal's political and literary developments associated with middle classes. The severe nativist turn towards Hindu nationalism, of which Bankim Chandra remained the most articulate and elegant representative, played a critical role in shaping the journey of Bengal in the twentieth century.[12]

The birth of culturalism as a signifier of Bengali identity led to momentous contestations along religious lines in the twentieth century. Though in Sartori's writing there is little reference to class, it cannot be ignored that Bengali literary activity was the crucial hallmark of a newly emerging colonial salaried class, rooted in the layers of intermediate tenure holders in rural East Bengal. Indeed, they could take advantage of colonial educational system because of their access to surplus from land. Many among these late nineteenth-century Bengali Hindu writers were imbued with the idea of a regeneration of Hindu society. They uncritically accepted the colonial epistemology of Aryan Vedic origin of Indian civilization.[13] Most of them perceived Muslim society as trapped in a medieval religious value system. Muslim rulers in India were condemned as tyrannical and bigoted.[14] Since census operations from 1871 made it clear that Bengal proper had a slight Muslim majority, Bengali Hindu *bhadralok* sought to deny Bengali identity to their Muslim compatriots, who were largely peasants in the landed estates of Hindu intermediate tenure holders.[15]

The late nineteenth century was also the period when upwardly mobile peasants from the deltaic region of East Bengal took advantage of changes in the global political economy and began to participate in the cultivation of cash crops such as jute.[16] As they became relatively financially independent, these Muslim surplus farmers mounted a stiff resistance to the intermediate tenure holders, predominantly composed of upper-caste Hindu elites.[17] A new group of intellectuals emerged from their midst. Many among these intelligentsia felt that there persisted a situation of internal colonization in rural east Bengal. Neilesh Bose has recently asserted that the Bengali Muslims intelligentsia developed a literary tradition which highlighted their distinctive notion of being both Muslims *and* Bengali.[18]

Bengal witnessed the emergence of, to quote Hugh McLennan's Canadian novel, 'two solitudes'.[19] There were obvious exceptions to this trend. In the early decades of the twentieth century, Bengali poet Kazi Nazrul Islam transcended the void between two solitudes. He highlighted commonalities among Bengalis in terms of their struggle against colonial rule. He also spoke to the experience of class oppression among peasants and workers across religious lines.²⁰ In the twenties and thirties, there emerged a movement known as 'emancipation of intellect' (*buddhir mukti andolon*) among Bengali Muslims in Dacca. Pioneered by the Shikha (Fire) group, these writers questioned the given assumptions about tradition among Muslims.²¹ Nonetheless, over the course of the forties, these experiments with cultural forms and themes underwent a metamorphosis with the evolution of popular Pakistan movement.

In extant literature it had been argued that Pakistan movement in Bengal emerged as a peasant utopia.²² Yet there existed distinct cultural movements among Muslim middle classes that sought to highlight the demand for Pakistan in cultural terms. In 1942, the East Pakistan Renaissance Society (EPRS) sought to promote Pakistani nationalism in literature and culture. The East Pakistan Literary Association, founded in Dacca in 1943, similarly sought to encourage Pakistani nationalism in the literary sphere in East Bengal.²³ Thus, the global moment of the retreat of European empires in East Bengal was characterized by a euphoria about a pan-South Asian Muslim nation. More importantly, religious nationalism permeated the cultural world of Bengali intelligentsia as well. They sought to distinguish themselves as Muslims from overarching Bengali identity.

Borrowing from Fanon's notion of national liberation struggle as 'a panorama on three levels',²⁴ I argue that Pakistani nationalism in East Bengali literature between 1947 and the early fifties represented, in a rather qualified sense, an assimilationist stage, as Fanon asserted.²⁵ While using the word 'assimilationist', I do not argue that such a moment was characterized by a uniform surrender to diktats from an 'outside colonial power'. Rather, I argue that such moments of political decolonization were pregnant with many possibilities and trends. In the period immediately preceding independence, the ideology of a pan-Indian Muslim League nationalism, based on the two-nation theory, resonated with an assertive Bengali Muslim nationalism and could align with Bengali perception of *desh* (homeland) as Purbo Pakistan (East Pakistan). The idea of Pakistan thus became coterminous of two nationalisms at the moment of her birth: Pakistani Muslim nationalism based upon the two-nation theory and the rather undefined and inchoate Bengali Muslim nationalist quest for homeland. In the post-independence period in the newly independent Pakistan, pan-South Asian Muslim nationalism could temporarily subsume within its fold Bengali Muslim nationalism.

However, as soon as the new Pakistani state came into existence, there took place a peculiar conflation of Muslim identity with the Urdu language in the Pakistani officialdom. This official attitude also side-lined the history of the Muslim literati's involvement with Bengali language for nearly 800 years.[26] Among public intellectuals of Bengal this hostility of officials triggered a rethinking about the role of literature and language in the making of a Muslim community in Bengal. As Nira Yuval-Davis argues, the notion of belonging is politicized and firmly enunciated only when a particular community perceives some form of threat and thus prioritizes certain aspects of identities in order to highlight their sense of belonging to this community.[27] Among the Bengali Muslim literati, two kinds of pressures thus informed and influenced the making of Bengali identity: the internal marginalization by the Hindu landed aristocracy and the upper-caste Sanskritic cultural entrepreneurs influenced the rise of a Muslim nationalist perception. And yet the Pakistani ruling social coalition's rejection of Bengali Muslim cultural claims led to the formation of an overarching Bengali cultural identity encompassing Bengali Hindu writings. These two trends survived among the emerging literati and intellectuals in East Pakistan and left an indelible mark on the making of popular culture and perception of Bengali identity in general. These two tends sometimes converged and sometimes stood in stark opposition to each other.

It was the cultural movement of the fifties and the early sixties that helped in developing a resistance 'culture' in East Pakistan. I borrow the term 'resistance culture' from the works of Selwyn Cudjoe[28] and, more importantly, the work of Barbara Harlow.[29] Expanding on Cudjoe, Harlow perceived resistance as a combination of actions that aimed at liberating people from their oppressors over a larger space. For Harlow, 'resistance literature' came into being as a crucial component of an organized struggle against oppression, and it was through literary and cultural struggle that oppressed people were able to emancipate themselves from the cultural hegemony and domination of oppressors.'[30] It is, however, not claimed here that such a resistance in East Pakistan constituted a monolithic homogenous totality. Neither is it denied that in some ways such acts of literary and cultural resistance were also partly complicit in the wider statist nationalist project that it sought to resist. As a colonizing power, the military bureaucratic junta in Pakistan came from a post-colonial society that had also been involved in cultural introspection. Modern Urdu literature contained a vibrant progressive strand that highlighted the everyday struggles of working women and men and questioned divisive religious nationalism.[31] Yet the statist agenda of internal colonization remained separate from dissenting Pakistani Urdu-speaking intellectuals' inclusive cultural articulations.

Facing state hostility, there took place a critical introspection of Bengali culture in the fifties and early sixties. It symbolized what Fanon recognized as a phase just before the anti-colonial battle.[32] As processes of internal colonization deepened in East Pakistan, radical poets, novelists, singers and playwrights confronted a state-sponsored nationalist ideology that claimed a shared post-colonial religious nationalist identity with the majority of their subjects, but in practice disenfranchised them on the issue of quotidian governance. In the realm of culture, a suspicion of the Bengali language as un-Islamic, because it borrowed its vocabulary from Sanskritic sources, persisted among officials of the state and even among a section of the Bengali literati. Yet as Ngũgĩ wa Thiong'o claimed in the African context, writing in a mother tongue is the first act towards decolonization, since it involved an inner struggle concerning the articulation of feelings.[33] In East Pakistan, Bengali writers debated among themselves about the nature of the Bengali language that could articulate their Muslim-ness and whether they ought to depart from the literary tradition of Bengali that existed earlier. Ultimately, they prioritized articulating their views in their 'mother tongue' and claimed their heritage to nearly a century-old tradition of Bengali writing that had evolved from Rammohan Roy to Kazi Nazrul Islam.

This debate and assertion of rights to articulate in the mother tongue gradually became a cultural movement encompassing poetry, music, paintings and film-making. The Bengali literati, as elsewhere, in their early moments of nationalist stirring, turned their attention to folk culture for authenticity. This phase involved, per Fanon, the re-narration or reinterpretation of past times and old legends, or a return to folk traditions and cultures of the people, among the literati. Bengali artists looked towards recovering a syncretic tradition of paintings on earthen plates, or *sora* art, in rural East Bengal and scroll paintings known as *patua* art.[34] The production of Urdu films in Dacca was gradually complemented by the making of Bengali films. Bengali film-makers, when they made movies in Bangla, started tracing their roots in distinctive folk tales that drew upon syncretic Bengali practices.[35] This became part of the language of resistance against the praetorian state sponsored cultural nationalism. It was within this cultural domain that a newly imagined community of a distinctive Bengali Muslim nation was born in the sixties and entered a dialogue with its political articulation. In other words, the conversation between popular discontent on the street and the cultural movement established the parameters of this cultural introspection. In the words of Auritro Majumder, such a dialogue fosters insurgent imaginations.[36] This is a phase that, following Gramsci, I understand, is characterized by a war of position by Bengali cultural activists. Gramsci conceptualized the idea of a 'war of position' in the context of liberal democracies, where the authority of the state or political society was firmly rooted in civil society. In liberal democracies, the ruling classes reinforced such control through civil society. For Gramsci, the liberal democratic state thus exercises not dominance but political hegemony whereby control is exercised through both consent and coercion.[37]

This led towards the high sixties, during which there was a confident assertion of Bengali cultural processes. As Fanon postulated, the final stage of national liberation struggles arrived when full-blown cultural assertion took place among oppressed nationalities. This third phase in East Pakistan was marked by the emergence of a national revolutionary literature through which the literati, in unison with the masses at the moment of national liberation, became 'the mouthpiece of a new reality in action'.[38] It was the second phase that had been characterized by, in Gramscian terminology, a war of manoeuvre. The idea of a 'war of manoeuvre', as Gramsci conceptualizes it, involves physically overwhelming the coercive apparatus of the state. However, the success of this strategy depends on the nature of the state's hegemony – that is, its position within civil society.[39] By 1970, through a long-drawn cultural struggle, Bengali autonomy activists could build up a hegemonic notion of a democratic Bengali ethno-linguistic state as opposed to Pakistani nationalisms' idea of a unified homeland for South Asian Muslims protected and guided by the praetorian guards.

The presentation of the language issue as a step-by-step move towards the national liberation struggle would invite the charge of a teleological prioritization of the nation state, which was constructed as a 'realization' of previous efforts and fit into a linear narrative. The end journey of such a narrative is the emergence of the nation state. As Prasenjit Duara claims, 'linear History, by understanding the past through the linguistic signs of the present, reduces or sublets the past to the present'.[40] More importantly, Chakrabarty has argued that such a history of the nation state and quest for citizenship prioritizes a historical meta-narrative that privileges a 'hyperreal' Europe and thus reduces the very historical process to a mimetic act of European history.[41] Yet the multiple processes that contributed towards the making of the first linguistic nation state in South Asia does not confirm

Chakrabarty's observation. It was premised upon a complex transformation in the notion of collective self with internal contradictions, with twists and turns that did not lend themselves so easily to a linear narrative. The birth of a linguistic state through a revolution is not an end in the ongoing process of social transformation, but it certainly constitutes a crucial milestone. The contours of such an imagined community did change in different circumstances and may change in a future with different circumstances.

Moment of Independence: Pakistanism in the Bengali Cultural World

In the forties, Bengal witnessed the collapse of the colonial regime under the impact of the Second World War. When Japan entered into a pact with the Axis powers in September 1940, nobody anticipated that the war would reach the Bengal frontier within two years. But on 14 December 1941, Japanese forces emerged victorious in the Malay Peninsula and attacked British Burma. The Japanese air force also started bombing Calcutta in April 1942. Panic gripped the city and its environs. Meanwhile, hasty retreat of colonial forces from Burma led towards the Japanese occupation of Rangoon. From February 1942 there took place a mass exodus from Burma, and a vast number of Indians and Burmese moved towards British-held territories in Assam and Bengal in search of shelter. Anisuzzaman, a Bengali writer, who in his younger years lived on Congress Exhibition Road in the Park Circus area of Calcutta, recorded his impression of the arrival of Burmese refugees in Calcutta. One day, he noticed, a large number of Burmese refugees in tattered clothes moving through the street in front of his apartment. His neighbour, a Burmese family, sheltered some of these refugees, and others moved on to some unknown destination amidst tears and sadness.[42] Many of the refugees from Burma, who were of Bengali origins, brought back tales of the rapid collapse of the British Raj in the face of Japanese attacks.[43] The very image of invincibility of the British army suffered a jolt.

With the Japanese occupation of Burma, Bengal became a frontline province in the Second World War. Allied troops comprising Chinese, Americans and British were stationed in Calcutta, which increased pressure on the depleting resources of the province.[44] The fall of Burma also caused a shortfall in the supply of rice, and the government of India's policy of putting trade barriers in eastern India contributed towards shortages of supply.[45] The government of India's war-finance policy exerted an inflationary pressure on the economy as '[m]oney flowed into Bengal paying for war products and the effect was to force the price of scarce consumer goods upwards as increased spending power chased fewer goods, a circle from which the poor were excluded'.[46] Amartya Sen argued that this failure of exchange led to a decline in the relative price of labour-power vis-à-vis food, which jeopardized the survival of those who lived by selling their labour.[47] To exacerbate this disastrous situation, Bengal witnessed a massive cyclone and floods, which further disrupted the normal flow of goods.[48] Soon famine had broken out in rural Bengal and millions perished, while the colonial government initially paid scant attention to this dire situation. Many rural working poor came to Calcutta in search of food. Dead bodies piled up on the streets of the colonial megapolis.[49] The moral fabric of the society had been torn asunder. The middle classes sought to immunize their sensitivities from the daily occurrence of mass death, selling of children and wives by men, and deliberate abandonment of the old and infirm. The situation reminded people of an impending apocalypse, and it remained inscribed on public memory.[50]

The combination of close proximity of the collapse of the colonial regime, the apocalyptic situation of famine and the related epidemics, and the intensification of class struggle in rural Bengal with the poor facing the squeeze in the flow of credits and starvation[51] created a climate for imagining a socially meaningful future. In the wake of this, two movements came into existence which exercised a critical influence over culture in East Pakistan. The first cultural movement was headed by communists who approached the conscience of middle classes and indigent intelligentsia through songs, poems, short stories, innovative photojournalism, paintings, sculptures and plays on famines and struggles of workers and peasants,[52] while the second encompassed Muslim nationalist attempts to imagine, articulate and conceive a putative Muslim nation in Bengal and its relationship with other Muslim communities in South Asia. Muslim nationalists envisaged Pakistan as a bridge between the past and the future transforming the dreary present. Eleven veteran journalists, who gathered to establish the East Pakistan Renaissance Society, consciously used the term 'renaissance' in order to indicate that they aimed at total cultural autonomy of Bengali Muslims. By cultural autonomy they implied a complete freedom from what they claimed to be the blind emulation of Bengali Hindu writers. This cultural movement in their perception would usher in a modernity and an intellectual revolution.[53] The East Pakistan Renaissance Society was obviously embedded in a very specific temporality of the collapse of the colonial regime in the midst of war, death and devastation. The future of Pakistan was uncertain. Members of this society thus sought to spell out the meaning of Pakistan for Muslims of eastern India in social, cultural and geopolitical terms and to assert that Hindus and Muslims constituted two different nations.[54]

Ideologically, the East Pakistan Renaissance Society made it clear that India harboured many nations which were artificially welded into a subcontinental state by the British Empire. As colonial rule was coming to an end, these nations had the right to self-determination. Almost echoing the Leninist notion of national liberation, the East Pakistan Renaissance Society demanded the right to self-determination for Bengal. Radical humanist M. N. Roy and communist writers and scholars entered into dialogue with members of the East Pakistan Renaissance Society.[55] After holding a series of meetings, the East Pakistan Renaissance Society held an important conference in Calcutta on 5 May 1943. On behalf of the welcoming committee of the conference, president Abul Mansur Ahmad gave a speech about the location of culture in Pakistan in Bengali Muslim terms. However, he claimed that Bengali Muslims constituted not only a different nation from Bengali Hindus but also a different nation from Muslims of north-western India.[56] Later in another conference of the East Pakistan Renaissance Society on 1 and 2 July, Abul Mansur Ahmad made categorical claims that modern Bengali literature that evolved from Ishwar Chandra Vidyasagar and Bankim Chandra to Sarat Chandra Chattopadhyay and Rabindranath Tagore could not be regarded as the literature of East Pakistan. This literature, he claimed, was not created by Bengali Muslims and did not appeal to Bengali Muslims. It did not reflect a Muslim spirit. In his perspective, Bengali Muslim writings had to break completely free from their Hindu moorings, and he thus directed attention to *puthi* literature of Bengal.[57] He claimed that *puthi* literature constituted a treasure in Bengali Muslim literature.[58] As a symbol of a new beginning, members of the East Pakistan Renaissance Society imported unused Arabic and Persian words in Bengali language. For example, soon after the partition, Syed Sajjad Hossain wrote an article titled 'Mashreki Pakistane Bhashar Swarup'. In that article he made it clear that if Bengali language had to become the vehicle of the articulation of Muslim *tamaddun* (culture), then people would have to use Arabic and Persian *alfaz* (sentences) and consciously purge those words which did not reflect the spirit of Islamic *tamaddun*.[59]

There is no doubt that the Bengali language, as it evolved in the pre-colonial period, had come to contain a significant number of Persian words. In the course of the long nineteenth century, colonial rulers made an attempt to standardize written Bengali language and selected Bengali pundits, or upper-caste literati, to write textbooks in Bengali. In the process many Persian words were substituted with Sanskrit vocabulary known as *tatsamo* words by the upper-caste Hindu writers associated with the colonial institution of Fort William College. The government school textbooks in the late-nineteenth-century Bengal followed the prose style pioneered by writers associated with the aforementioned college. Bengali Hindu writers who dominated the newly emerging Bengali literature followed this highly Sanskritized style of writing.[60] Sanskritized Bengali not only erased Persianate expressions, but also developed a distance with colloquial Bengali which was increasingly regarded as the language of women confined to the interior of households or peasants living in rural areas. In the nineteenth century there came into existence a gendered critique of such formalized Bengali as a male language.[61] The evolution of this male-centric formal language was the indirect result of colonial capitalism producing a standard language as part of administrative convenience and business operations. As Etienne Balibar has argued, capitalism requires a standardized language to create a market.[62] A critical result of such experimentation was the evacuation of Muslims from their Bengali identity. Thus, the cultural erasure of Persianate expressions alienated the sensitivities of mid-twentieth-century Bengali Muslim writers.

Writers and journalists associated with the East Pakistan Renaissance Society thus promoted an environment of new nationalism in literature in Islamic terms. An emotional identification with Pakistani nationalism found particular expressions in Bengali poetry composed by such nationalists in the late forties. Kamal Chowdhury, for example, wrote in a poem in the *Mohammadi* magazine on 17 December 1944:

Jalimer taja khun pie jage bharoter Muslim
Noyone tahar herar alo odhore ei Rahim

Drinking the fresh blood of tyrants, Indian Muslims had woken up
Divine light lit up their eyes and their lips utter God's name[63]

Or consider Talim Hossain writing in the *Mahe Nao* magazine:

Pakistaner hukomote elhiate
Islam pher hobe abad duniate

Milbe abar piara nobir millate
Noya jomanar Musolman

Under the command of Pakistan
Islam will regain her position
In our prophet's congregation
Muslims of new age will assemble again[64]

Written in a language mixed with Persian words, these nationalistic poems extolled the virtue of Pakistan as the source of new hope for Indian Muslims. An overwhelming majority among emerging Muslim middle classes in Bengal supported Pakistan. Even teenagers conducted a letter-writing campaign for Pakistan. As the INC and the communists formed their respective party-affiliated organizations for teenagers, *Azad*, the mouthpiece of the Bengal Muslim League, formed a separate unit of nationalistic organization for such youths, known as Mukul Bahini, literally translated as 'Budding Force'.[65]

The East Pakistan Renaissance Society also popularized a putative map of East Pakistan. Abdus Sadeque, an economist and a member of the East Pakistan Renaissance Society, drew a map of East Pakistan at the end of his article on the political economy of East Pakistan. According to his map, the new East Pakistan would include the entire region of Bengal to the east of the Bhagirathi River and Assam (including Assamese Hindu-majority districts), except for the overwhelmingly Hindu-majority Burdwan division. During the first major conference of the East Pakistan Renaissance Society, an artist was commissioned to draw a coloured political map of this putative East Pakistan, which was then displayed as a backdrop to the main stage for speakers.[66] The proposed territorial limit in the map included Hindu-majority districts of Khulna, 24 Parganas and the city of Calcutta.

Soon it became clear that Hindus and Muslims lived in two different imagined future 'nation states' in the city of Calcutta. For the Muslim middle classes, Calcutta would be an integral part of the province of East Pakistan, and to the Hindus, Calcutta would obviously be included in India. On 16 August 1946, the Muslim League proposed Direct Action Day to press forward the demand for Pakistan. On that day, the Muslim League organized processions and mammoth meetings in Calcutta, but soon these were attacked, and massive sectarian violence engulfed the city. In a Hindu-majority city, Muslims had borne the brunt of the attack, and the Calcutta violence was avenged in Noakhali in the interior of Bengal, while the violence in Noakhali provoked violence in Bihar. These violent riots accelerated the process of partition despite a last-ditch attempt by Hashim, Suhrawardy, Sarat Bose and Kiran Shankar Ray to avoid the division through the proposal of a united Bengal.[67] The partition further created a new environment of violence in the region. Oli Ahad, a student activist and writer, described the situation during the partition in following words:

> The fruit of Indian independence movement was partition: Punjab was divided, Bengal was amputated and Assam was curved up. Caravans of millions of people left their homeland for another country. During the journey many died, many became paupers within their own country, some lost their homes and others their ancestral properties. Their prosperous past mocked at them. Only an eyewitness can feel the pain of such events. I have seen these events with my own eyes, felt the pain in my heart but could not do anything to alter the course of events. The poisonous environment paralysed us. Empathy, conscience and education all were rendered invalid. Bestiality was praised and regarded as a display of valour.[68]

The Language Question in the East Pakistan Literary Circle

Interestingly, in the midst of this sectarian polarization along Hindu–Muslim lines, the partition of Bengal and India were accompanied by another controversy involving the language of Pakistan. On 17 May 1947, at a conference of Itehad-e-Muslimeen in the princely state of Hyderabad, Chowdhury Khalequzzaman, a prominent Muslim League leader from Lucknow, declared that Urdu alone would be the national language of Pakistan.[69] Khalequzzaman spoke in the context of the politics of the United Province, where nearly a century-old, bitter language controversy threatened the cultural identity of the Muslim literati. This conflict was known as Urdu–Hindi controversy. Urdu is written in the Persian *nasta'liq* script, which, in turn, is based on the Arabic calligraphic style called *naskh*. Its vocabulary contains a significant number of Persian, Turkish and Arabic loan words, though its origin could be traced back to Hindui, or Hindvi.[70] During the 1830s, the East India Company replaced Persian with English as the official language at the higher levels of administration, while the local vernaculars were used for daily transactions of official businesses at the lower level. But this involved recognizing a particular local vernacular in a polylinguistic society like that of India. Thus, in the NWFP and elsewhere in north India, Urdu replaced Persian as the official language.[71] Again, here colonial capitalism was interested in creating a standardized vernacular that was not associated with older ruling elites. Thus, they decided to replace Persian with Urdu which dominated the educational curriculum, local court communication and exchanges in the lower-level administrative circles.

In contrast to Urdu, Hindi is written in the Nagri script with high inputs of Sanskrit vocabulary. In the nineteenth century, demand for the use of Sanskritized Hindi, at the local level again, originated from the pundits of Fort William College, and in the later decades of the nineteenth century it gained popularity among upper-caste Hindu elites in the United Province. These upper-caste Hindu elites demanded that Hindi should replace Urdu as the language of administration. From 1900 both Urdu and Hindi were used as official languages of the United Province. A common bridge between the two languages was a more colloquial version known as Hindustani spoken in the bazaars of north India. Though traditionally many Hindu elites were well versed in Urdu as well as Hindi, at the time of independence many INC politicians preferred Hindi as the official language of the United Province and promoted it also as the national language of India. Both Gandhi and Nehru opined in favour of Hindustani.[72] But cultural polarization informed by rival religious nationalist projects pushed the cause of Hindustani into oblivion. It survived only in the movie industry of Bollywood. This bitter controversy over language had transformed Urdu, in the mind of north Indian Muslims, as the symbol of Islamic cultural identity, though many Hindus continued to learn Urdu, and many prominent litterateurs in Urdu were Hindus.

The acceptance of Urdu by the Punjabi Muslim literati as their own language was more instructive in telling us about the hold of Urdu over the imagination of the Muslim literati in north India. As mentioned earlier, with the assumption of colonial control, Urdu replaced Persian as the language of the court and everyday official transactions at a lower level from 1851 onwards. Again, the colonial capitalist regime was in search of a standardized language to communicate with the local population and to facilitate the smooth functioning of the local education system. In colonial official circles it was believed that though Punjabi was widely spoken by the rural population of the province, Punjabi did not have standardized written language to be promoted as the vernacular medium of instruction, and hence colonial officials promoted Urdu. Yet the colonial designs of producing a uniform language did not always work smoothly in a multi-ethnic, multi-religious society having complex local processes of ethno-religious collective self-making among its population.

As the United Provinces witnessed the Hindi–Urdu controversy, the Punjabi Muslim literati overwhelmingly sided with the cause of Urdu. When P. L. Chatterjee, the Bengali Hindu vice chancellor of Lahore University in Punjab, in 1908, proposed that Punjabi should replace Urdu as the vernacular language, the Muslim literati protested against such a move.[73] Eventually, Punjabi as a vernacular language came to be written in the Gurumukhi script by Sikhs, the Nagri script by Hindus, and the Shahmukhi, or modified Perso-Arabic, script by Muslims. Urdu became the principal language of print media in Punjab. The status of Urdu, as a standardized written language, gained hold in Punjab where it was not the first language of the population. It was thus not absurd for Muslim League leaders from north India to expect Urdu to be declared as the national language of Pakistan on the eve of independence. The very idea of a 'one language, one religion' policy had been premised upon a modernizing bourgeois perception of the making of the European nation state along the French model.[74] As a self-proclaimed 'modernizer', Jinnah believed that the selection of Urdu as the national language would be synchronous with the perception of a common language among Muslims in Pakistan.[75] What he ignored was the complex regional dynamics between language and cultural identity formation in different corners of the South Asian subcontinent.

Yet in Bengal, for nearly five decades, the Bengali Muslim literati had sought to curve out a regional identity as Bengali Muslims, and they were invested in making the Bengali language an official language in Pakistan. A young writer, Abdul Huq, wrote a series of four essays in Bengali periodicals on the national language of Pakistan in 1947.[76] He made an implicit argument that Bengali Muslims had more of a claim to the Bengali language, and thus it would be the appropriate national language of Pakistan. Soon, Ziauddin Ahmad, a noted mathematician and the vice chancellor of Aligarh Muslim University, demanded in a conference in Hyderabad that Urdu alone be declared the national language of Pakistan.[77] In 1947 Muhammad Shahidullah, a noted linguist and a professor of Sanskrit at Dacca University, in an article in *Daily Azad*, argued for two national languages in Pakistan, Bengali and Urdu. Shahidullah was an advocate for the Bengali language since 1918. In that year, in an academic discussion over the future national language of India in a meeting presided by the poet Rabindranath Tagore, at Santiniketan, Shahidullah had spoken of declaring Bengali the national language of India.[78]

Soon many Bengali litterateurs came to defend the proposition that Bengali should be the national language of Pakistan. Noted among them was the young poet Farrukh Ahmad who was an ardent advocate of the Pakistan movement and believed that Bengali literature should make a new beginning in East Pakistan in order to move out of its Hindu moorings. Yet he opposed the declaration of Urdu as the national language of Pakistan. In a journal article, he wrote that those who believed that if Bengali became the national language Islam's position would be undermined suffer from an ugly defeatist mentality.[79] Soon after the partition, the Tamaddun Majlis, a cultural organization of East Bengal issued a booklet entitled 'National Language of Pakistan: Bengali or Urdu?' The Tamaddun Majlis was established on 1 September 1947 in order to promote Islamic cultural values and was deeply influenced by the ideas of the East Pakistan Renaissance Society. It became the earliest promoter of the idea of the Bengali language as the national language of Pakistan. In the booklet were featured three authors of varied political positions: Abul Kashem, a professor of physics at Dacca University and an Islamist cultural activist; Abul Mansur Ahmad, a Muslim League politician, lawyer and writer; and Qazi Motahar Husain, a professor of physics, mathematics and statistics at Dacca University but also noted for his association with the emancipation-of-intellect movement. As far as literature and culture went, both Mansur Ahamad and Kashem believed that Bengali literature in East Pakistan should break free from its Hindu moorings, but Motahar Husain held the firm belief that Bengali literature was a common heritage of both Bengals and there was no need for any sharp rupture. Yet, despite their diverse political positions, they closed their ranks to oppose the declaration of Urdu as the sole national language of Pakistan.[80] At the same time, the newly established Democratic Youth League in Dacca gave a call for the declaration of Bengali as the national language of Pakistan.

A little while later, at the Sylhet Sahitya Sansad convention, Syed Mujtaba Ali, a famous essayist and disciple of Tagore, gave a call for the declaration of Bengali as the national language of Pakistan. Later Mujtaba Ali published his address in the Calcutta-based journal *Chaturanga*. A year later Mujtaba Ali was invited to preside over a literary meeting in Bogra on 12 December 1948, and he was soon offered the position of principal of Azizul Huq College, Bogra, which he joined in early 1949. In the college annual magazine, some students wrote articles against the police repression of students who had taken part in the language movement in Dacca. Though the materials for the magazine were selected long before Mujtaba Ali had taken over, he was still accused of inciting students for writing articles against the Pakistani government. The magazine was banned, and all its copies were confiscated. Mujtaba Ali fled to Calcutta in order to avoid arrest.[81] On 31 December 1948 and 1 January 1949 at the Curzon Hall of Dacca there took place the first convention of the East Pakistan Literary Association. At the convention, well-known linguist Shahidullah, in his presidential address, declared: 'It is true that we are Hindus and Muslims but it is more true that we are Bengali. Mother nature had stamped this truth on our appearance. This could not be hidden in the Hindu garb of garland, pigtail and vermillion mark on the forehead or Muslim dress of lungi and skull cap.'[82] At the meeting, the Urdu-speaking Pakistani bureaucrat Fazl Ahmad Kariim Fazli was present, and he was an enthusiast for introducing the Perso-Arabic script for the Bengali language. He protested against Shahidullah's speech and said that there should not be any link between the language spoken in West Bengal with that spoken in East Bengal. This led to an exchange of sharp words between Bengali union minister and writer Habibullah Bahar and Kariim Fazli. The latter left the meeting in a huff.[83]

Thus, from the very beginning of Pakistan as an independent 'nation state', the language controversy generated an uneasiness in the relationship between the two wings of the country. Alongside the British colonial policy of essentializing Muslim identity on the basis of separate languages, the Pakistani elite harboured a notion of developing a bourgeois state premised upon the model of one standardized language, modified in this context through a reference to Islam. But such project encountered critical resistance in East Pakistan. This did not imply that those members of the literati who claimed that Bengali should be the national language of Pakistan had a ready-made identity of being a Bengali. Rather, the Muslim literati in East Bengal had to engage in a complex negotiation between the contradictory pressures for the absorption of their identity in an overarching notion of Bengaliness encompassing two Bengals and the Pakistani state's attempt to erase their Bengali identity. While a segment of the Muslim literati resisted an attempt to integrate themselves in the overarching Bengali identity – comprising both Hindus and Muslims in cultural terms – collectively a vast majority of the Bengali literati, irrespective of their politico-cultural positions, protested against the Pakistani attempt to erase their linguistic identity in the process.

Thus, the process of the construction of a unilingual nation state in a polylingual society complicated the hold of the overarching ideology of religious nationalism. The complex coexistence of two nationalisms – pan-South Asian Muslim nationalism and regionally entrenched Bengali Muslim nationalism – started witnessing fissures right at the moment of the birth of the nation.

Student Movement and the Language Martyrs' Day

Students constituted a critical political force in the resource-poor societies of the Third World. In a vastly preliterate society, with entrenched oral traditions, students with their cultural capital enjoyed a privileged social status as intellectual interpreters between rural society of oral tradition and political society rooted in colonial traditions of written documentation. Students also acted as interpreters between the growing capitalist direction taken by governance and the vastly subsistence peasant economy. Finally, they constituted a bridge in cultural terms between the urban world of entertainment and folk traditions in rural society. In a fast-changing postcolonial society, despite being increasingly trapped in a situation of internal colonization, students in East Bengal thus constituted interpreters of the signs of bourgeois modernity to the subaltern social classes. To many parents, who belonged to the middle peasant stratum in rural society, college education constituted the key to the future and had the potential of unlocking the doors of social mobility. Between 1947 and 1971, East Pakistan witnessed a significant expansion of its student population. Most of these Bengali Muslims came from peasant households in rural areas.[84]

University students constituted a critical social constituency in the East Pakistani society at the time of formal decolonization by the British Empire. Students were aware of their socially privileged role as multifarious interpreters of the signs of political, economic and sociocultural modernity in a polity engaged in experimentations with capitalist transition. This was particularly true for Dacca University where students were concentrated in the political nerve centre of governance. These students, located in dorms, sharing the same curricula and having a much wider perspective of the country and its future, had a deeper 'collective conscience', to use a Durkheimian phrase elaborated by his student Maurice Halbwachs.[85] The character of this collective consciousness was also conditioned by mnemonic encoding. The collective memory of students' role in the Pakistan movement provided them with a moral entitlement in the political affairs of the nascent nation. Many of these students were writers in the Bengali language and thus had an intimate relationship with the emerging literary world and print media. Some were also genuinely worried about their future career and job prospects. As the state, the main source of coveted jobs, recruited through competitive exams, students were concerned that they had to compete with West Pakistani students who were far more familiar with the Urdu language than Bengalis. Thus, concerns about their career, alongside their deeper identification with the mother tongue and literary activities in the Bengali language, prompted them to initiate action.

From 1948 onwards students organized movements for the declaration of Bengali as the state language of Pakistan alongside Urdu. Muslim League–affiliated student bodies remained divided into two factions. The faction loyal to Suhrawardy, along with left-leaning student groups, tried to establish an organization separate from the official Muslim League-affiliated student body. They also distanced themselves from the CPP (East Pakistan Provincial Committee)-affiliated student organizations. This group came to be known as the East Pakistan Muslim Student League. There took place an internal debate within the newly established student body as to whether they should drop the word 'Muslim', and Sheikh Mujib, a young moderate student activist, after a fierce argument, persuaded radical Oli Ahad to accept the word 'Muslim' in the nomenclature.[86] On 25 February 1948, Dhirendranath Dutta, a Hindu member of the Pakistani Constituent Assembly, demanded the introduction of Bengali as a national language. His motion was opposed by prime minister Liaquat Ali. But in East Pakistan, on 27 February 1948, a few students and political activists formed a committee of action for state language.[87] On 11 March the state action committee decided to observe a 'direct action day' for the Bengali language. Police severely cracked down on student protests and arrested many student activists, including Sheikh Mujib and Oli Ahad.[88] This contributed to the intensification of the movement, and the government, on 15 March, signed an agreement with student activists and released all prisoners.[89] A left-leaning group of students protested against governor general Jinnah when he visited Dacca between 19 and 22 March. In a closed-door meeting, student representatives argued with Jinnah when he asserted that Urdu alone should be the national language of Pakistan.[90]

The student movement for the declaration of Bengali as a national language was not always popular with the wider populace. The original inhabitants of Dacca regarded students with suspicion, and many among them believed that they were conspiring to destroy Pakistan.[91] Yet the movement got a new lease of life when Fazlur Rahman, the Bengali education minister of the central government, on 27 December 1948, declared in a teachers' convention that Bengali should be written in the Arabic script. On 7 February 1949 he further explained the necessity of such a project in a meeting of the national advisory board on education. In December 1948, during a national convention of the educational advisory board, it was expected that the government might introduce a change to the scripts of the Bengali language, but that did not materialize. The attempt to introduce the Arabic script in writing Bengali language fizzled out after a failed attempt to introduce adult education through Arabic script.[92] On 27 November 1948, when Liaquat Ali visited East Bengal, the general secretary of Dacca University's students' union, Golam Azam, read a felicitating speech in which he demanded the introduction of Bengali as one of the national languages of Pakistan. Liaquat Ali skilfully avoided addressing this burning question, but in Rajshahi, a rural town, he faced student unrest. The unrest in Rajshahi was suppressed by the police with a heavy hand. This galvanized the student community. On 10 January 1949 students observed a day of protest against police atrocities, which was addressed by youth leader Sheikh Mujib. This movement pushed the East Pakistan Muslim Student League to the forefront of the student struggle.[93]

As the student movement webbed and waned, there persisted an uneasy lull on the language issue. On 1 April 1951, the Dacca University State Language Action Committee (Dhaka Bishwobidyalay Rastro Bhasha Songram Committee) sent a memorandum to all members of the Pakistani Constituent Assembly. But Pakistani politics underwent a sea change with the assassination of Liaquat Ali. Nazimuddin, who had become the governor general in the wake of Jinnah's death, now became the prime minister of the country after Liaquat Ali's demise. Though Nazimuddin came from Dacca, he belonged to the Urdu-speaking *ashraf* community. On 27 January 1952, he declared in a public meeting in Dacca that Urdu would be the sole national language. He further informed the audience that the attempt to write Bengali in Arabic script had been successful in 21 adult educational centres, and people were inspired by the success. To protest against Nazimuddin's speech, on 30 January 1952, an All-Party State Language Action Committee was formed. At a session of the East Bengal provincial legislative assembly, it was decided to hold an all–East Bengal strike on 21 February 1952, alongside a mass student demonstration in the city. On 6 February 1952 there took place a meeting of the All-Party State Language Action Committee, in which majority of the members expressed their opinion against holding a mass student rally on 21 February defying the government prohibition of public gathering. Bhashani, who was presiding the meeting, however, condemned such a decision and told fellow members that if the government banned lawful protest in the country, such a resolution of obedience would strengthen the hands of autocracy.[94] Meanwhile, students held meetings on 4, 11 and 13 February subsequently for the massive demonstration on 21 February. In response to student activism, the East Bengal government decided to clamp Section 144 in Dacca. Section 144 was a colonial legislative clause that prohibited public gatherings in a given territorial jurisdiction. This constitutional provision empowered any executive magistrate to impose the said law during anticipated emergencies.

The All-Party Language State Action Committee urgently met in the central office of the Awami Muslim League. However, Bhashani was not present in Dacca, and so veteran former Muslim League politician Abul Hashim presided over the meeting. The meeting resolved not to violate Section 144, but the Dacca University State Language Action Committee and Dacca Medical College's student union voted against this resolution. This obviously implied that radical students from Dacca University had decided to move forward with their own action. Oli Ahad and other radical student leaders decided to gather in the Arts and Humanities complex of Dacca University on 21 February.[95]

In Dacca University, on 21 February 1952, the dean of the Arts faculty, Zubery, along with proctor and professor Muzaffar Ahmad Chowdhury and the head of the department, Newman, met with the vice chancellor, Syed Moazzem Hossain. All of them requested students not to hold any demonstration defying Section 144.[96] At 12 noon, students started their meetings in Dacca University's Arts and Humanities complex. Their meeting at Dacca University's campus resolved that they would continue to violate Section 144 in a peaceful manner. Oli Ahad compared the situation with Gandhi's call for non-violent revolution during the Rowlatt Satyagraha.[97] As students progressed to the gate to peacefully defy the prohibition on public gathering, some students started pelting the police with stones. Organizers dubbed it the handiwork of agent provocateurs. Attacked by students, police fired tear gas into the campus. As the student and police confrontation went beyond control, the district magistrate on duty, Muhammad Qureshi, ordered firing into the unarmed student crowd around 3 pm. The first casualty of police firing was a student of political science named Barkat. Soon another student, Rafiuddin, and Salam, an employee of the Central Secretariat in Dacca, died. As the news of the police firing circulated, employees of the Central Secretariat, journalists and the staff of the Dacca radio station, and later on railway workers, went into strike. Rickshaw pullers, street vendors and subaltern segments of Dacca's population actively protested. East Bengal national assembly members, Maulana Abdur Rashid Tarkabagish and even Abul Kalam Shamsuddin, a Muslim League loyalist, journalist and the organizer of the East Pakistan Renaissance Society, resigned from the Muslim League. Shamsuddin, too, resigned from the East Bengal national assembly. On 23 February Shamsuddin presided over a meeting in an empty land beside Dacca University where students died in police firing.[98] Syed Haidar, a student at a medical college, designed a temporary martyrs' column to commemorate the martyrdom of students.[99] The emerging Bengali middle-class honeymoon with the Muslim League suffered a severe jolt after the police firing on the student-led language movement. Though many died in peasant uprisings in rural areas earlier in East Bengal, the death of students impacted the middle-class mentality deeply. Students were visual symbols of social mobility and were regarded as the future of the nation. The location of the conflict in Dacca, the capital city, in the premier university of East Bengal ensured that the event had a detailed and immediate news coverage. The news shocked the middle classes profoundly. Thus, the death of students in the police firing transformed the event into an act of public mourning.

Extant historical literature in the English language underestimated the seminal importance of the student unrest in East Bengal and the emotional rupture it caused in the Pakistani nation-building project. Richard Sisson and Leo Rose traced the origin of 'secession of East Pakistan' in the war between India and Pakistan.[100] Similarly, Srinath Raghavan, in a remarkable account of the making of Bangladesh, highlighted Indian diplomatic efforts to obtain support for the liberation war, ignoring earlier student movement.[101] Gary Bass, in a spectacular account of the events related to the independence of Bangladesh, focused his attention on the US involvement in supporting Pakistan despite evidence from American diplomatic staff, but he also bypassed the emotional rupture of 1952.[102] In a pioneering investigation into the decline of popular legitimacy of Pakistani nationalism in East Bengal between 1947 and 1954, Ahmed Kamal ignored the language movement.[103] He focused on the subaltern alienation rather than middle-class disenchantment with Pakistani nationalism. Umar, who wrote the most detailed and elaborate account of the language movement in Bengali, bypassed the event in his English-language narrative in order to explain the class dynamics of Bengali nationalism in East Pakistan.[104] The emerging middle class, which remained the cultural carriers of the Pakistan movement, became disenchanted with the Muslim nationalist utopia of Pakistan as a land of 'eternal Eid' after the students' martyrdom over the language question. 'My Brothers' Blood-Spattered 21 February', a song composed by Abdul Gaffar Chowdhury, on 28 February 1952 – and tuned by Altaf Mahmud, a renowned composer who was martyred during the liberation war – captured the emotion of middle classes:

> They fired at the soul of this land
> They tried to silence the demand of the people
> They kicked at the bosom of Bengal
> They did not belong to this country
> They wanted to sell away her good fortune
> They robbed the people of food, clothing and peace
> On them we shower our bitterest hatred
> Wake up today, the twenty-first February
> Do wake you please.[105]

Cultural Resistance to the Pakistan Project in East Pakistan, 1952 to 1961: A War of Position

Culture and language remained a contested political field in East Pakistan. Many believed that the Bengali language had to be reformed in order to be used as a language appropriate for Pakistani Muslim culture. With this purpose in mind, the government formed the East Bengal Language Committee on 9 March 1949. The committee recommended that the Sanskritization of the language had to be avoided and that Bengali grammar had to be freed from the influence of the Sanskrit language, and proposed a drastic modification of the Bengali writing system.[106] Ganesh Charan Basu,[107] who was the head of the Bengali and Sanskrit department in Dacca and also a member of the aforementioned committee, raised mild objections to such sweeping changes. Shamsuddin, who was a member of the committee, recalled that Ganesh 'Babu' was reminded by other members that they did not regard Bengali as a descendant language of Sanskrit and the main aim of the committee was to erase the influence of Sanskrit from the Bengali language, and thus a

Sanskrit professor should remain silent in the affairs of the committee.[108] The committee's prescription, however, could not be implemented, because of the reluctance among the general body of Bengali scholars to engage in such a state-engineered transformation of the Bengali language. But such views of the reform of the Bengali language and literature along a perceived Islamic cultural tradition prevailed among those Bengali writers and poets who were ideologically oriented towards Pakistani nationalism. Poet Golam Mostafa even advocated editorial corrections to Nazrul's writings for his widespread use of 'Hindu' imageries which he believed was not appropriate for Pakistani culture.[109]

Yet, in East Bengal, there prevailed a contrapuntal cultural tradition too. This was most evident in the novels written in this period. Syed Waliullah, a young writer, published his novel *Lal Salu* (Red Cloth) in 1948. He offered a trenchant critique of the practice of *pir*-ism (*pirbad*) in rural Bengal in the novel. The story revolves around a semi-literate man, Majid, who during the famine of 1943 left his natal village and settled down in a new village. Here, Majid becomes the custodian of an uncared grave which he claimed to be that of a spiritual preceptor (*pir*) and cultivates his influence among the villagers as a religious preceptor too. He wards off threats to his position when another *pir* appears in the village. He also sabotages an effort to establish a school in the village by another young man, Akkas. Majid undermines the efforts of Akkas by pointing out that since Akkas was a clean-shaven young man, he could not be a pious Muslim. A similar social theme characterized the writings of Abu Ishaque, who, also in 1948, published his novel *Surjya Dighal Bari* (A Cursed House). The novel depicts social life in rural Bengal against the background of the Bengal famine and the partition. It is a novel that projects how a divorced woman, Jaigun, struggled against conservative Muslim social mores in rural Bengal and remained resilient in the face of all social opposition. Thus, two of the most important literary creations of the late 1940s, soon after the partition and independence, indicate the persistence of creative social criticism among Bengali writers of Muslim background despite the apparent triumph of Muslim nationalism.

Contrapuntal literary and cultural efforts also manifested in organized cultural activities and literary conventions. Indeed, soon after the partition, in the port town of Chittagong, there came into existence two cultural organizations known as Sanskriti Parishad and Prantik. Many of the members of these cultural organizations were associated with the CPP (East Bengal Provincial Committee) and belonged to the tradition of the Indian People's

Theatre Association. On 16 Match 1951, they held a literary convention in Chittagong. Poet Sufia Kamal presided over this organization, and in his presidential address Abdul Karim Sahitya Bisharad explicitly asserted:

> We believe that literature is not simply a reflection of society and culture but also a device to improve society. Writers and artists have a responsibility to save social life from hunger, unemployment and social strife and to ensure social progress. We trust a literature that talks about social welfare and social progress.[110]

In Dacca University, too, there came into existence an organization called Cultural Convention (Sanskriti Sansad). This organization staged progressive plays such as Bijon Bhattarcharrya's *Joban Bondi* (Testimony) and Tulsi Lahiry's *Pathik* (Traveller).[111] Written against the background of the famine, *Joban Bondi* spoke of the plight of a peasant family. Lahiry was a playwright from Rangpur in north Bengal, and his play, *Pathik*, spoke of the journey of the modern world and depicts class repression as an all-encompassing experience of modern society. In 1951 another organization named Agrani challenged the religious nationalist framework of culture propagated by the ruling elites. Then, in 1952, there came into existence the Pakistan Sahitya Sansad (Pakistan Literary Association). Many of this organization's members were associated with the CPP (East Pakistan Provincial Committee) and played a pivotal role in developing socialist realism as a cultural tool. The literary association also sought to promote non-communal progressive cultural values. Kazi Motaher Hossain, who was associated with the emancipation-of-intellect movement was the president of the organization, and Faiz Ahmad was the general secretary.[112] The language movement of 1952 and the avant-garde cultural movements radicalized many student activists. For instance, Anisuzzaman, who was a refugee from West Bengal and a devoted Muslim, started his life as an ardent defender of Pakistan in his teenage years. He gradually became involved in the language and cultural movement.[113] His experience of the language movement eroded his faith in formal religion. Over time he was drawn to the CPP (East Pakistan Provincial Committee). The publication of progressive literature from West Bengal deeply impacted the students of Dacca University. Progressive students like Anisuzzaman read Debiprasad Chattopadhaya's popular but scholarly exposition of Marxism. The Anil Sinha-led New Literary Association introduced students to Soviet and alternative Marxist developments in science.¹¹⁴ Anisuzzaman was not alone. Many from his generation became involved in the cultural movement associated with the left.¹¹⁵

Organization of literary conventions became a part of the cultural movement in East Bengal. The Pakistan Literary Association promoted discussions on Maxim Gorky, a Soviet writer, and Sukanto, a Marxist poet from West Bengal who died in his teenage years.¹¹⁶ Students also became involved in promoting peace conferences. In 1952 Pakistan sent a delegation to the communist-influenced World Peace Council's conference in the newly established People's Republic of China. A young Sheikh Mujib was one of the members of the delegation that went to China.¹¹⁷ In the World Peace Conference in Beijing, Sheikh Mujib befriended Indian-Bengali delegate Manoj Basu and told him that Pakistan had introduced a passport to travel between the two Bengals so that Hindus in East Pakistan would become scared and leave the country. In turn, they would encourage migration of Urdu speakers from India. As a consequence, Bengalis would become a minority in Pakistan.¹¹⁸ This idea of Bengalis becoming a minority in Pakistan because of the exodus of Bengali Hindus to India and the influx Urdu-speaking refugees from India had also been a concern of Bhashani.¹¹⁹ True to his Bengali autonomist political convictions, Sheikh Mujib delivered his speech in Bengali at the conference organized by the World Peace Council in Beijing. In Dacca, the Pakistan Peace Association organized a reception for him, and he won the hearts of young listeners through his down-to-earth speech.¹²⁰ Though not a communist, Sheikh Mujib, as a Bengali autonomist, established a powerful presence among secular cultural activists. Thus, the progressive movement became the natural political constituency for Bengali autonomists in East Bengal.

Members of the Pakistan Literary Association sought an alliance with progressive Urdu writers. In Dacca, Urdu writers invited Anisuzzaman to address their convention about medieval Bengali *puthi* literature, and Anisuzzaman presented a long article in the English language for the Urdu-speaking audience and established a rapport with them.¹²¹ In 1954, after the victory of the United Front, writers from West Bengal visited East Bengal during literary conventions organized by the Pakistan Literary Association. In 1954, Indian writers such as Subhas Mukhopadhyaya, Debiprasad Chattopadhyaya, Radharani Devi, Kazi Abdul Wadud and Manoj Basu attended the Pakistan Literary Association's meeting. The *Azad* newspaper criticized this invitation of Indian writers, but the pro–Awami League daily,

Ittefaq, supported this literary meet. Despite acrimonious debate in the public sphere, old friendships between the Bengalis of two Bengals rekindled. During the meeting, Mukhopadhyaya met with his friend Farrukh Ahmad, a poet who was known for his opposition to such literary conventions.[122] Authorities even allowed, though under heavy police surveillance, Mukhopadhyaya and Chattopadhyaya to visit Ila Mitra, the famous communist leader of East Bengal. Ila Mitra was then in prison hospital due to inhuman police torture on her. Sitting at her bedside, Mukhopadhyaya read his translation of Nazim Hikmat to Ila Mitra. Anisuzzaman accompanied them as a young volunteer. Later Anisuzzaman, as a young communist, reported the incident to his assigned senior mentor from the party, one comrade Ramzan Miah, who asked him in detail the condition of Ila Mitra. Long after the incident, Anisuzzaman came to know that Ramzan Miah was actually Ila Mitra's husband and a senior communist, Ramen Mitra, who was then underground and had assumed an alias.[123] Yet the success of the convention did not silence its critiques. Newspapers loyal to the Muslim League created a storm of protests against the convention. Thus, an attempt to form a permanent committee to hold such conventions annually failed in the face of protests from Pakistani nationalists.[124]

Writers and poets also undermined the legitimacy of the undemocratic Muslim League regime through plays and poems. These cultural activities altered the parameters of literary writings and established a link between protest literature and aesthetics in East Bengal. The most important of such literary endeavours was communist writer and literary critic Munier Chowdhury's play *Kabar* (Grave). After the actions in 1952 of the language movement, Chowdhury was arrested along with other cultural activists. In the Dacca Central Jail, political prisoners were seldom allowed free time to interact. But in one exceptional ward in the prison, because of scarcity of space to accommodate so many political prisoners, nearly 80 odd prisoners were locked up. The other half of that ward was used as a mosque. On Fridays, Muslim political prisoners from all the separate cells and yards were brought here, and they used the opportunity to meet their colleagues and exchange opinions. During one such Friday meeting, political prisoners conveyed the request of this ward's inmates to Chowdhury to write a play on the events of 21 February.[125] A fellow communist and a well-known journalist, Ranesh Dasgupta, also encouraged Chowdhury to write such a play. Chowdhury promptly wrote the play and named it *Kabar*. Political prisoners who requested him to write the play performed it in jail.[126]

Kabar had deep resemblances to Jewish pacifist American writer Irwin Shaw's anti-war play, *Bury the Dead*, written and enacted in New York in 1936. Shaw's play was translated into Bengali in Calcutta by Utpal Dutt, a famous theatre personality, and in Dacca, it was translated by Jamal Uddin Hossain. It was later staged under the direction of Ataur Rahman, who was also known in Dacca as *mancha sarothi* (charioteer of proscenium).[127] *Kabar* was thus not very original in its format. Chowdhury located the story of the drama in a graveyard. It begins with an influential political leader of the ruling party (Muslim League) and a loyal police officer drinking from a bottle to overcome their fear in an uncanny and eerie atmosphere late at night while supervising the surreptitious burial of those who died in police firing. But the grave diggers refuse to obey their orders to bury these bodies without proper funeral rituals. But then comes the magical moment in the play when a *murda faqir*, or 'ascetic of the dead', appears and calls for the resurrection of the dead. To the horror of the leader and police officer, the dead bodies rise with their ghastly wounds and refuse the leader's plea to go back to eternal sleep. The police officer, who turns out to be more resourceful, calls the mother of one of the victims and wife of another to persuade them to return to their eternal sleep. But the ascetic of the dead intervenes and threatens to march into the streets of Dacca with the dead bodies. Fortunately, for the officer and leader, the daybreak comes, and the ghosts melt away in daylight. Soon the grave diggers inform them that the burial is complete. The duo realizes that they were hallucinating in an inebriated state. By creating a surrealist moment in the play, the playwright tries to convince the audience the immorality of the act of killings by the police in Dacca. Introducing the ascetic of the dead, as a custodian of the conscience of living, the playwright hints that the regime that killed innocent people illegally would become a haunted regime forever. It posed a challenge to the legitimacy of Muslim League rule in East Bengal. The play was a landmark in the protest literature against the Muslim League regime.

Alongside *Kabar*, Hasan Hafizur Rahman, an emerging young poet, published a new anthology of poems, essays and short stories known as *Ekushe* (Twenty-One), in memory of the students' martyrdom on 21 February 1952. Anisuzzaman, who was associated with the production of the book, recorded in his memoir that East Bengal's communist leader Khoka Roy sent an essay from prison entitled 'All Languages Had Equal Status'. It was published under a pseudonym, Ali Ashraf. Anisuzzaman contributed a short story alongside Sirajul Islam who also contributed a short story. The editor included Shamsur

Rahman's poem which was recently published in a left-leaning Calcutta-based magazine known as *Parichoy*. Various young poets such as Abdul Gani Hazari, Anis Chowdhury, Fazle Lohani, Ataur Rahman, Abu Zafar Obaidullah, Alauddin al-Azad, Burhanuddin Khan Jahangir, Syed Shamsul Haque, Jamauluddin and Hasan Hafizur Rahman contributed poems. Songs of Abdul Gaffar Chowdhury and Tofazzal Hossain were included. Aminul Islam drew the front cover, and Bijan Chowdhury and Bashir Ahmad contributed sketches. For publication, the authors contacted the famous journalist M. R. Akhtar Mukul and Mohammad Sultan's press known as Punthi Potro (Books and Letters). However, due to financial shortage they could not publish the book on 21 February 1953. It was published in March 1953, and the book was proscribed in April 1953. The press accumulated huge debt, and the owner of the press verbally abused the editor, Hasan Hafizur Rahman, for this. Rahman went back to his village, sold his land and repaid the debt.[128] Despite the brief life of the book in the market, it assumed a cult status in East Bengal. The book was distributed through clandestine networks and became so popular that it was publicly reprinted in 1965 and 1968 under the full gaze of the military regime. The recitation of these poems during processions and public meetings and in literary gatherings became hallmarks of protests. These songs were also sung on many occasions and gained immortality in public life. As literary conventions and cultural meets became the norms of resistance, Bhashani transformed literary conventions and cultural meets into public festival during Kagmari convention in 1957. Organizing the Afro-Asian cultural festival in the wake of the Bandung Conference and the Suez Crisis, Bhashani created a carnival of the masses.[129] He placed the question of cultural rights within the wider context of Afro-Asian solidarity movement and decolonization of the Third World. By then it had become clear that the state language could not be imposed from above in the name of religious nationalism. In 1956 the government of Pakistan recognized Bengali as one of the national languages.

The partisans of Bengali culture and its heritage, spearheaded by communist-minded intellectuals, launched a form of cultural struggle against the regime. From a Gramscian perspective these intellectuals engaged in a 'war of position' to undermine the legitimacy of the state. In the early 1950s, Pakistani ruling elites did not function in a democratic set-up, and it would be a stretch to suggest that they enjoyed an ideological hegemony over social apparatus in East Pakistan. Yet the collective memory of the struggle for Pakistan provided a semblance of legitimacy to the regime.

Cultural resistance offered by Bengali literary activists tended to undermine that partial legitimacy through the 'war of position' within civil society. This cultural resistance slowly built up the strength of the social foundations of a newly imagined community of a linguistic nation by creating alternative intellectual resources. As articulated by Gramsci, issues of culture lay at the heart of a revolutionary project; culture crucially informs how people see their world, and, more importantly, 'it shapes their ability to imagine how it might be changed, and whether they see such changes as feasible or desirable'.[130] Bengali cultural activists, though they were a minority, engaged in such a struggle against Pakistani state-sponsored cultural polices and dominance. To go back to Fanon, it marked the first stage of a rupture with the continuation of the colonial edifice of the government by the Pakistani bureaucratic-military axis in the fifties.

Global Sixties and the Changing Paradigm of Bengali Culture: From War of Position to War of Manoeuvre

The coming of the sixties altered the dynamics of resistance in East Pakistan against the ruling military-bureaucratic axis. The cultural movement, the tone and mode of writings in East Pakistan, and the social mores of thinking within the literati underwent a radical shift. Increasingly the cultural resistance entered a dialogue with growing movements on the streets of Dacca and other towns in Bengal. The dialogue between social movements on the street and cultural activities acquired an organized form by the late sixties. This cultural and intellectual challenge steadily undermined the political legitimacy of the Pakistani military junta-sponsored religious nationalism in the Eastern wing of the country. The movement for cultural recognition of a Bengali collective identity started with an unusual figure for revolutionary resistance – Rabindranath Tagore.

Tagore was globally known for his contributions to Bengali literature. In 1961 Bengalis all over the world were preparing for the celebration of his birth centenary. Yet, throughout his life, Tagore was as much admired as he was unjustly criticized. Tagore's reception in East Pakistan was not an exception. Poets and writers who showered praises on Tagore before partition now criticized him for lack of originality. Golam Mostafa, a well-known poet, had hypothesized before the partition that Tagore's musical poems (*giti-kobita*) had touched the truest spiritual inclination of Islam. Yet, after the partition, in 1960, he argued that Tagore had lacked a creative spirit and was completely mired in religious superstition.[131] Many Islamist cultural activists tried to establish Nazrul's greatness at the expense of Tagore. In 1951 Syed Ali Ahsan, later a professor of Bengali in Dacca University, and also in the University of Karachi, wrote in an article entitled 'Purbo Pakistaner Bangla Sahityer Dhara' (Bengali Literary Tradition of East Pakistan) that after partition, Bengali culture should not be equated with the earlier cultural traditions of undivided Bengal. He argued that a new literature should derive its sustenance from Islamic traditions by incorporating Musalmani *puthi* writings in the mainstream of Bengali literature, with rural life as its new focus. Castigating the emancipation-of-intellect movement as a reflection of a demented mentality that insulted Islamic ethical foundations of culture, he further argued that for the sake of unity of the Pakistani nation state, East Bengalis were prepared to reject Tagore's legacy in Bengali literature.[132] Ali Ahsan later changed his stand completely on the cultural issue.

However, it was not simply the Muslim nationalists who criticized Tagore. In 1949 Bhavani Sen, a communist theoretician, characterized the works of the Bengali renaissance figures such as Rammohan, Vivekananda and Tagore as reactionary. Such an evaluation did not go uncontested in communist circles. Historian Sushobhan Sarkar, a fellow Marxist, provided a robust defence of the Bengal renaissance. Young communist writers in East Pakistan, organized under the banner of the Pragati Lekhak o Shilpi Sangha (Progressive Writers and Artists Association), such as Munier Chowdhury, Akhlaqur Rahman, Abdullah al-Muti, and Alauddin al-Azad accepted the view that Tagore was a bourgeois reactionary. The president of the organization, Ajit Kumar Guha, a professor in prestigious Jagannath College, alongside well-known journalist Ranesh Dasgupta, disputed the official position, but they were a minority.[133]

Given such a political climate, it was not unusual that praetorian rulers of Pakistan would reject the celebration of Tagore's birth centenary. Sensing the views of the governing elites, the Bangla Academy in Dacca decided not to go ahead with the celebration. Three public committees had been formed for the celebration, and they coordinated their activities under the leadership of Justice Ghulam Murshid. Despite pressure from the government, Murshid was not dissuaded from heading the centenary celebration. In order to avoid the charge that the Indian High Commission was funding the events, Murshid told the committee members that he would provide the funding. Later it was revealed that the fund was clandestinely collected by A. K. M.

Hafizuddin, a person no less than the inspector-general of police in East Pakistan!¹³⁴ The celebration of the birth centenary did not remain free from controversy. *Azad*, a conservative magazine, portrayed Tagore as a Hindu chauvinist and a friend of British imperialism, while Awami League–affiliated *Ittefaq* and pro-communist *Sombad* defended Tagore's legacy in East Pakistan. Soon there came into existence a cultural organization called Chayanat (named after a raga in the classical Indian music tradition).¹³⁵ This cultural organization sought to promote Bengali cultural activities in East Pakistan, including the celebration of Tagore's and Nazrul's birthdays and the Bengali New Year.

Tagore's legacy in East Pakistan entered into crisis again in the wake of the India–Pakistan war of 1965. During the war, Radio Pakistan and television broadcasts stopped airing Tagore's songs because of their 'Indian' origin. But in 1967 the government decided to ban the airing of Tagore's songs on Radio Pakistan, since his ideas were perceived to be contrary to those of Pakistan, on the order of the information and broadcasting minister, Khwaja Sahabuddin. On Anisuzzaman's request, Munier Chowdhury drafted a protest statement. Anisuzzaman organized a signature campaign on this statement. It was due to Anisuzzaman's tireless efforts that a statement by 19 writers, scientists, painters, and teachers appeared in the newspapers on 25 June 1967.¹³⁶ The statement termed the government's decision 'very unfortunate', claiming Tagore as 'an integral part of the cultural existence of the Bengali-speaking Pakistanis' and that 'the significance of this fact should be respected' in the framing of governmental policy. In private, the famous scientist Muhammad Qudrat-i- Khuda, while signing the statement, commented to Anisuzzaman that the condemnation was not strong enough. Despite the prevalence of widespread opposition to the government's decision, 40 intellectuals also signed a counter-petition supporting the government's position. They declared that Tagore's values were not conducive to Pakistani cultural ethos. Shamsuddin and Abul Mansur Ahmad were among these 40 people. Yet the counter petition in favour of the government's decision did not dampen the enthusiasm of the admirers of Tagore. The latter held a meeting at poet Jasimuddin's house and threatened to launch a movement against the ban. In July 1967 these protestors gave birth to an organization named Committee for the Protection of Cultural Rights. Throughout East Pakistan, cultural activists opposed the ban on Tagore's songs. The committee celebrated Tagore's legacy for three days on the occasion of Tagore's death anniversary in 1967. Even the state-funded Islamic Academy, under its director Abul Hashim, protested the government's policy. Hasan Hafizur Rahman, now associated with the Writers' Guild in East Pakistan, held a five-day celebration in remembrance of great poets: Tagore, Michael Madhusudan, Ghalib, Iqbal and Nazrul. The celebration started with Tagore, though the government decided to telecast only the last four days, ignoring the celebration of Tagore. Meanwhile, Anisuzzaman and his associates concentrated on publishing an anthology of the works of East Pakistani scholars on Tagore. Nearly 30 writers, poets, scientists and scholars contributed to this anthology. Famous East Pakistani painter Zainul Abedin drew the front cover for it.[137]

Under pressure from public opinion, minister Khawaja Shahabuddin announced that he did not consider Tagore's songs to be opposed to the spirit of Pakistan, but also qualified his statement by saying that he *would* consider restricting only those songs which directly contradicted the spirit of Pakistan. This was regarded as a victory by Tagore enthusiasts in East Bengal. In 1968–69, at the height of the global sixties, student and worker revolts throughout Pakistan toppled the military dictatorship. As the students increasingly adopted a radical stance in relation to Bangladeshi independence, Tagore's song 'O amar Sonar Bangla / Ami tomai bhalobasi / Chirodin tomar akash / Tomar batash amar prane bajay bashi' ('O my Golden Bengal / I love you / Forever your skies / Your air set my heart in tune as if it were a flute') became a popular emblem of the movement, and after independence, it was not accidental that this song became the national anthem of Bangladesh. Tagore enthusiasts included Bengali nationalists, communists and even moderate Islamists in East Pakistan. While cultural movements surrounding Tagore drew people from wide crosscurrents of people, Dacca had a strong undercurrent of communist-sponsored cultural activities that often drew upon the radicalism of the long sixties and wider global socialist culture.

In the sixties, Dacca city became a fertile ground for avant-garde cultural activities that questioned the framework of an exclusivist religious nationalism. Communist cultural activists played a crucial role in such events. In 1960 there came into existence the Srijoni Sahityk Gosthi (Creative Literary Clan). This organization published anthologies on the events of 21 February as well as on the international workers' day on 1 May. In 1967 it published an anthology of essays titled *Jayodhwoni* (Sound of Victory) celebrating the 50 years of the existence of the Soviet Union.[138] In 1968 two playwrights, Mozzammel Hossain Montu and Sulaiman, provided a dramatic form to Maxim Gorky's 1906 novel *The Mother*, and staged the play for

Dacca audiences on the occasion of Gorky's hundredth birth anniversary.[139] The CPP (East Pakistan Provincial Committee) in 1967 underwent a split when the Maoists decided to form a separate political organization. In 1966, however, the Maoist cultural activists established a new organization called Kranti (Revolution), which included seven members: Rafiqul Islam, Kamal Lohani, Zahurul Islam, Sheikh Abdul Jabbar, Mahasin Sastropani and Abdus Samad Khan Mukul.[140] Kranti staged a cultural festival delivering *gono sangeet* (people's songs) on 22 and 23 February 1967. Amanul Haque, a dance director, directed a dance drama entitled *Jwolche Agun Khete Khamare* (Ember Is Burning in Farms and Fields). The novelty of the theme, for a dance drama, had been widely appreciated by the audience. In 1967 Kranti published a new anthology of poems, essays and short stories on the occasion of the Bengali New Year in the month of April. Kamal Lohani published short-length books on Mao's writings. In the same year Kranti also published a booklet welcoming the new Bengali year, 1374. Describing its ideology in that booklet, Kranti again referred to the events of the global sixties, such as the war in Vietnam and the 'forward march of people three continents – Asia, Africa, and Latin America'.[141]

In March 1968, due to inner-party schisms, there came into existence a new cultural organization known as Unmesh Sahitya o Sanskriti Sansad (Pioneer Literary and Cultural Association). In April 1968 this group staged a play called *Alor Poth Jatri* (Travellers on Enlightened Path) in the house of its secretary, Indu Saha. On 24 April 1968 they organized a small procession from Baitul Mukarram, the central mosque in Dacca, to the river port in old Dacca, in remembrance and protest of the killings of communist political prisoners on 24 April 1950 in Rajshahi Jail.[142] On 30 January 1970 this group staged a popular play called *Biplober Pododwoni* (The Footsteps of Revolution) commemorating the student revolutionaries of 1967–68. On the occasion of the Bengali New Year in 1970, an anti-colonial play, *Expeditioners of Dawn* (Bhorer Obhijatri), was enacted, and finally when a devastating cyclone stuck East Pakistan in November 1970, the group staged a play *Shober Michile Jiboner Joygan* (Song of Life in the Procession of Dead Bodies). It was written by Mohosin Shastropani and directed by Amir Khasru. On the eve of the military crackdown on 23 March 1971, the group staged a poster drama condemning military rule.[143] The military crackdown silenced this cultural organization, and its founding president, Zahurul Islam, disappeared forever when the Pakistani army invaded the village he was residing in on the banks of Buri Ganga near Dacca.[144]

In the interior of East Pakistan there also came into existence cultural organizations affiliated with communist groups. The most well-known among these was Sandipon, in Khulna, established in 1963. It was an organization that emphasized the singing of agitprop songs, otherwise known as people's songs. Khalid Rashid Guru was the founding member of this organization. In April–May 1971 the Pakistan army assassinated Rashid Guru.[145] In Jessore there came into existence an organization known as Surbitan. Though established in 1952, the organization became prominent in the sixties by staging patriotic songs and organizing festivals commemorating the Language Martyrs' Day. Most of these organizations drew their volunteers from Maoist communist groups in rural Bengal.

The largest left-leaning cultural organization in East Pakistan, however, was Udichi. It was established by Satyen Sen, a pioneering communist writer and novelist from the pro-Soviet fraction of the CPP (East Pakistan Provincial Committee). He penned the famous novel *Koibarto Bidroho* (Koibarta Rebellion) against the background of the Pal Empire in the late eighth century. Koibartas were a low-caste peasant community, and their republic attracted the attention of historians. The inspiration for the establishment of the organization came from Ranesh Dasgupta, a famous communist journalist. Golam Mohammad Edu, Manzurul Ahsan Khan, Mostofa Wahid Khan, Kamrul Ahsan Khan, Ekram Ahmed, Akhtar Hossain and Rizia Begum were among the first group of organizers who travelled in the interior of the country and recruited cultural activists in the face of torture and deprivation. The organization followed a broad spectrum of cultural activities dedicated towards non-sectarian secular nationalist ethos. Several plays such as *Alo Aschhe* (Light Is Coming) and *Shapath Nilam* (We Have Taken Oath) had an emotional impact on the audience during the halcyon days of the student and workers' uprisings of 1968. A significant number of intellectuals of the country took part in the public awareness campaign of Udichi. Writers, poets and artists from wide walks of life took part in the organization, and it eventually became the largest among all cultural fronts in independent Bangladesh.[146]

Throughout the sixties, East Pakistan witnessed a transformation in the themes, content and writing styles of poems, novels and short stories. The most notable shift was in the genre of poetic literature. In the sixties there emerged a new crop of poets who employed different imageries, metaphors and poetical language. They moved away from the hyperbolic Muslim nationalist rhetoric of the late forties. Foremost among them was poet

Shamsur Rahman, a graduate of English literature from Dacca University in 1953, who clearly steered Bengali poetry towards a new direction. Influenced by well-known Bengali poets of the thirties and forties, such as Buddhadev Bose and Jibanananda Das, he composed his first anthology of poems, *Pratham Gan Dwitiya Mrittur Age* (First Song before a Second Death), in 1959, and since then he became a prolific poet of nature and love with a keen eye for spotting extraordinary details in the midst of the ordinary. Through his magical lyrics, he transformed the quotidian drudgery of urban life, melancholy of sheer poverty and even mundane objects like traffic lights into urbane and elegant verse.[147] He also wrote the most profound political poems of the sixties and the early seventies. In a famous poem on the revolution of 1969 known as 'Asader Shirt' (Asad's Shirt), he transformed the frazzled, blood-stained shirt of a young communist demonstrator, killed in police firing, into a banner of the freedom struggle. In 'Amar Dukhini Bornomala' (My Sorrowful Alphabet), he articulated his passionate repudiation of the proposition made by the Hamoodur Rahman Commission in the sixties, that Bengali could only be 'integrated' into the Pakistani nation if it was written in the Arabic or Latin scripts.[148] Finally, during the liberation struggle of Bangladesh in 1971, he escaped from Dacca city into his natal village. One afternoon he observed the fun and joy of a little girl swimming in the pond and, inspired by the freedom and happiness of the girl, he penned his poem 'Swadhinota' (Liberty), which became one of the most poignant portrayals of the liberation struggle of Bangladesh:[149]

> Liberty you are my mother's white sari
> Fluttering in the breeze in the yard.
> Liberty, you are the red colour of *mehndi*[150]
> On the lender palm of my sister.
> Liberty, you are a bright red poster like stars in a starlit sky
> In my friend's hand.
> Liberty, you are the thick black
> Loose hair of my wife
> Flowing in the wind.
> Liberty, you are the coloured shirt
> On my son,
> The play of sunlight on
> My daughter's cheek.
> Liberty, you tire my garden,

> The song of the cuckoo,
> The rustling leaves
> Of an ancient banyan tree,
> The note book where I write my verses
> Just as I choose.[151]

The poem was smuggled out of the border of East Pakistan to Calcutta and was published in a literary journal.[152] In independent Bangladesh, Islamic fundamentalists entered Rahman's apartment in Dacca to murder him; he was saved by his wife. Later he declared in an interview to *Statesman*, a leading daily of Calcutta: 'A poet has no religion.' He further added: 'His true religion is to protest against anti-human activities. I believe in democracy.'[153]

Rahman was not alone among the new generations of poets who moved away from the slogans of religious nationalism to a more imaginative lyrical portrayal of quotidian life in Bengal. Many others were involved in this quest for a more meaningful investigation into life embedded in quotidian mundane things. Al Mahmud, who later became an admirer of Islamic mysticism, in the sixties, composed his first poetical anthology, *Kaler Kalosh* (The Pitcher of Time).[154] He combined wit with passionate nostalgia about the lost landscape of rural East Bengal. Nirmalendu Goon, a popular Marxist poet, wrote angrier and directly political poems condemning the occupation of his land.[155]

In many East Pakistani Bengali poems of the sixties, critics discern the influence of the French nineteenth-century poet Charles Baudelaire. Many poets shared a manifesto of sadness, and some of them believed that, like Baudelaire, there existed constant tussle between God and Satan and that humans had an indeterminate existence.[156] Among these poets, Abdul Mannan, a poet, was lost in surrealist imageries. He thus wrote:

> Satan is pulling my one hand and God the other
> What a great festivity among these two are over me.
> I am food for these two
> In the middle of these tug of war my two hands got torn.[157]

Though many criticized these poets for their 'non-political poetry' in the midst of the halcyon days of the global sixties, this philosophy of doubt, sadness and indeterminate existence of humans was reflected in political positions too. A deep sense of alienation from 'state' conditioned expression in verse, as Shahid Qadri wrote unambiguously:

> The word state reminds me
> of tanks displayed on the Independence Day.
> State reminds me of the fence at the racecourse
> Of Curfew and the clause of 144.[158]

Finally, in a rather direct poetic political writing, on the eve of the liberation struggle, poet Shamsul Haq wrote:

> See, I am unarmed, but
> I have a kind of weapon that is
> Never exhausted, which with every use
> Only grows sharper and sharper –
> My life.
> I don't have only
> One life,
> But millions and millions of lives.
> See, I do not have a flag
> In my hand,
> But the flag I possess
> Is not raised on the mast
> Of some braggart –
> My flag is my mother's face.
> I do not have only one mother,
> But millions and millions of mothers.[159]

In many ways, as Thomas Newbold asserts: 'Quite simply, the new poets resisted the straightforward equivalence that literary Pakistanism had drawn between lexical choices and Muslim identity. They favoured instead a poetic theory that prized the aesthetic autonomy of the individual poet and enjoined a more creative relationship between poets and the symbols they used.'[160]

Bengali novels, too, underwent a similar transformation in terms of themes and structure. Syed Waliullah's *Chander Amabosya* (Etiolating Moon) and Zahir Raihan's *Hajar Bochor Dhore* (For a Thousand Years) explain the anatomy of rural life, poverty and the frustrations of educated youth and class repression. Communist novelist Satyen Sen's *Podochihno* (Footprint) explain the insecurity and slow transformation of life in a Hindu village in rural Bengal from prosperity to misery. Finally, Shahidullah Kaiser's *Sareng Bou* (Wife of Sailor) depicts the struggle of a village housewife against the designs of local rich peasants, amidst the destruction brought by a tidal wave in a seaside village. All these landmark novels depict social transformation, class struggle, patriarchal dominance and the sad consequences of the partition. Thus, novels of the sixties highlight rural life within the wider context of the time and through a social realist portrayal.[161]

The cultural transformation of the political landscape also found its echo in the world of paintings and art form. Shashi Bhushan Paul established in 1904 the Maheshwarpasha School of Fine Art, which was the first fine arts institute in East Bengal. The school offered a four-year degree course and organized annual exhibitions from 1917 onwards.[162] Yet the institutionalized learning of painting in East Pakistan centred around the efforts of Zainul Abedin and his associates from the Government College of Art and Craft, Calcutta, such as Quamrul Hasan, Safiuddin Ahmed and Anwarul Haque.[163] In 1948 they established the Dacca Institute of Art, and in 1950 they organized the first fine arts exhibition of East Bengal at Lytton Hall in Dacca. In 1956 a full-fledged building, planned and executed by Abedin and Mazharul Islam, one of the stalwart architects of East Pakistan, came into existence. Mofidul Hoque, a student of Dacca Art College, later recalled that in the fifties, the members of the art college consciously tried to develop a distinct art tradition putatively different from the art tradition of Calcutta, where many of these faculties studied in their early life.[164]

Abedin, who was a central figure in this effort to build up an art institution in Dacca, was a student of Government College of Art and Craft, Calcutta, and later he became a faculty member in the same institution. Rejecting the oriental style of painting of Bengal Arts College, Abedin was attracted to the quotidian life of ordinary people. He thus concentrated on drawing Calcutta's industrial areas and then rural areas. He drew pictures of harvest and leisure in rural Bengal. It was the devastating famine of 1943 that attracted him towards social realist paintings. He drew sketches of famished and uprooted peasant families.[165] Along with communist artist Chittoprosad's sketches, and Sunil Jana's photos, these drawings became immortal through their stark expressions of bitter reality in the famine years.[166] Abedin later experimented with various art forms but again returned to line drawing and social realism on the eve of liberation struggle.[167]

In February 1970, in the midst of political upheaval, Abedin exhibited an elaborate scroll to celebrate the annual harvest festival at the Dacca Art Institute. The scroll was sixty-five-feet long. It was drawn in wax, black ink and watercolour. Abedin titled the scroll *Nabanna*, the Bengali word for the festival of new harvest, and, incidentally, it was the name of a play that marked the beginning of the Indian People's Theatre Association (IPTA) movement in Bengal in 1943 in the midst of the famine. The artist almost revisited the struggle of those younger years in late colonial Bengal.[168] The scroll contains three key themes in three different frames. In the first, uprooted, emaciated villagers slog over a dilapidated countryside, and vultures loom over their deserted rural habitats. The second depicts life in East Pakistan (Bangladesh), a depiction of rural life. The third communicates collective tending of earth and a golden harvest; in this frame, peasants are seen resting amidst their bountiful yield and boatmen fastening their boats. These images of struggle, labour and leisure constitute an epic montage of the political celebration of rural 'Bangladesh', the birth of a new society. Abedin invited exhibition visitors to sign the scroll as if everybody, audience and artist included, was participating in the quotidian life of peasant society.

In 1968–69, while Bhashani was drawn into the mass uprising and the struggles of rural peasantry, alongside that of the industrial workers and the student movement of Dacca University, Abedin's radical folk realism in *Nabanna* echoed this harnessing of the rural and the political. The act of making the scroll itself was becoming an allegory of arrival.

The drawing of this scroll was preceded by Abedin's drawings of 'Palestinian War Refugee' series in 1969–70, reflecting a return to his distinct personal language of social realism.[169] The drawing of Palestinian war refugees was also a reflection of the influence of the global sixties and the revolutionary quest for freedom of the majority world from variants of colonialism and occupation.

Abedin drew *Manpura '70*, a huge 30-foot long scroll depicting the coastal storm of 1970, which killed thousands of people in November of that year. The storm became a controversial event in the relationship between East Pakistan and the military junta of Pakistan. In an emotional speech in public in 1971, Bhashani drew attention to the callous negligence of East Pakistan by the West Pakistani military junta. East Pakistani politicians and Sheikh Mujib further understood the relief distribution as the crucial test of Pakistani goodwill for East Pakistani people. By the time of the storm, at least in public rhetoric, East Pakistan had ceased to exist. Rather, the term 'Bangladesh' was widely used. Abedin visited the island of Mainpura after the storm and witnessed the devastation with his own eyes. A profoundly disturbed Abedin then drew the aforementioned scroll, which itself represented an act of political resistance and collective struggle.¹⁷⁰ The artist empathized with the suffering masses of East Pakistan and expressed his willingness to stand with them in that moment of their despair. This was an emotional outburst of creative energy that symbolized the birth of a new society out of the ruins of an old one, comparable to the famine of Bengal in the final years of colonial rule. These two processes of decolonization were united through the mediation of the popular upsurge of the global sixties.

Abedin was not alone in searching for a distinct artistic expression that articulated a separate identity through the celebration of quotidian plebian life in rural Bengal. Ordinary and mundane, folk culture and syncretism became the source of defiance against the statist promotion of culture by the praetorian guards of Pakistan. One such artistic idiom was the attempt to revitalize the folk artform of *sora*, or decorated earthen plates. But the most explicit political articulation in art came from the drawings of Quamrul Hassan. Inspired by paintings of Jamini Roy and Nandalal Bose, Hassan concentrated on drawing lives in rural Bengal. He was known for his unique blending of the traditional scroll painting styles of rural Bengal with the twentieth-century avant-garde cubist art form pioneered by Georges Braque and Pablo Picasso.¹⁷¹ Like Abedin, Hassan also had ties with the IPTA movement in the late forties. He was also involved with the popular uprising of 1969 and the movement of Sheikh Mujib in 1971. On 23 March 1971, on the eve of military crackdown, he drew ten posters depicting the face of Yahya Khan, the military dictator of Pakistan. This combination of a satire on the viciousness of the expression of the military dictator presented in the idiom of folk artform became the leitmotif of the liberation struggle of Bangladesh. Thus, Bengali intelligentsia moved from the stage of war of position to war of manoeuvre whereby they could establish a new framework of commonsensical understandings of the collective cultural-self and launch a victorious struggle for liberation from cultural colonization.

Popular Art Medium and the Register of Political Transition

The most popular creative medium was obviously films. The process of film-making, content of the movies and their themes underwent a transition in East Pakistan in the sixties. This had a direct bearing on the commonsensical understanding of homeland and the articulation of love and sorrow for said homeland. This section surveys a history of film-making in East Pakistan to understand the complex process of shift in the content, themes, and cinematic language.

The initiative to make films began in Dacca in 1927–28. Younger members of the famous nawab family of Dacca launched a new production house called the Dacca East Bengal Cinematograph Society. In 1927–28 they produced *Sukumari*, a short film of four reels. In 1931 they produced a full-length film of 12 reels, titled *The Last Kiss*. Ambuj Gupta, a physical instructor of Jagannath College, directed this movie.[172] In 1946, on the eve of independence of the South Asian subcontinent from British colonial rule, Obaidul Huq directed a movie entitled *Dukkhe Jader Jibon Gora* (Those Whose Life Is Made of Misery). It was a pioneering attempt by a Bengali Muslim to direct a movie. Yet film-making did not take off among East Pakistani Bengalis.

In Dacca, after the formation of Pakistan, Nazir Ahmad made a documentary film on governor general Jinnah's 10-day visit to East Pakistan in 1948, entitled *In Our Midst*. In Bengali it was known as *Purbo Pakistane Dos Din*, and in Urdu as *Hamrohi*. Ahmad took the help of Calcutta's Aurora film studios though he edited the movie himself. Between 1949 and 1952, Ahmad worked at the British Broadcasting Corporation (BBC) in London, and he frequented the Movietone film studio and learnt the art of making movies. During his visit to London, Nurul Amin, the chief minister of East Pakistan, invited Ahmad to establish a film unit in East Pakistan.[173] In 1953 the UK government provided a 300,000 rupees grant to the Pakistani government to build a film studio, and by 1954 Ahmad had made a new documentary, *Salamat*, which was printed and processed in the Shahnur studio of Lahore. *Salamat* was a futuristic documentary about Dacca city where the eponymous Salamat, a mason, could envisage the new buildings replacing the old and declining city. After *Salamat*, the Pakistani government granted (to Ahmad) 136,000 rupees to establish a film studio, which he built up in the Tejagaon industrial estate of Dacca in 1957.[174] In many ways, while the movie studio was born through the cooperation of the Pakistani government, it had the symbolic imprint of Bengali nationalism too. The person who was instrumental in steering the Bill for the East Pakistan Film Development Corporation (EPFDC) in the provincial legislative council on 3rd April 1957 was Sheikh Mujib, the young industry and commerce minister of the only Awami League ministry during the Pakistan era. Shiekh Mujib was an iconic figure among Bengali nationalists.

The first Bengali talkie was, however, produced before the establishment of the EPFDC studio. The departure in the direction of making of a Bengali movie in East Pakistan came with the release of *Mukh o Mukhosh* (Face and the Mask) based on a play called *Dakat* (Robber) written by Abdul Jabbar Khan. The story involved the torture of an innocent and injured young boy by a group of bandits who capture him during a raid. Ultimately, the boy is rescued by righteous-thinking people.[175] In 1954 Jabber Khan, an engineer by profession and playwright by passion, along with Mohammad Modabber, a writer and journalist, and Mohiuddin, involved in the Calcutta film industry, formed Iqbal Films in 1954. They also did not want to utilize the Indian film studios located in Calcutta. In *Mukh o Mukhosh*, local amateur actors, Inam Ahmed and Purnima Sen, acted in the movie without fees.[176] Nonetheless, the director faced hurdles when it came to processing and printing the movie.

In the early years of Pakistan, the foundation of the nascent movie industry in Dacca was characterized by anecdotes about Hindu discrimination against the Muslim movie crew in the nearby Calcutta film studios. According to one anecdote, Q. M. Zaman, who used to work as an assistant under the Hindu pseudonym of Kiran Dey at the New Theatres in Calcutta in the early forties, on one occasion, touched the movie camera for some reason and had to face the usual Hindu opprobrium: 'How come a Muslim's son has the courage to touch the camera? Who brought him here?' Zaman allegedly lost his job from the studio for this violation of caste prejudice among Hindus.[177] Though there existed no evidence to support this anecdote, Alamgir Kabir, a pioneering Bengali movie critique, also mentions that in Dacca two prominent film personalities in the fifties, Muhiuddin and Fateh Lohani, tried to work on movie production in Calcutta under the (Hindu) pseudonyms of Mohini Chowdhury and Kiran Kumar.[178] The very use of Hindu pseudonyms reflected a bias against Muslims among Bengali Hindus of that period. Thus, no doubt, in the foundational years there persisted a significant degree of discomfort about Indian Bengalis in Dacca. Determined to avoid Calcutta, Jabber Khan sent the movie to Shahnoor Studio, in Lahore, for editing and printing. After finishing the processing of the movie, the customs of West Pakistan restricted him from taking the prints with him for alleged lack of permission to leave the country. Finally, after a personal meeting with the home minister of Pakistan, Jabber Khan was able to bring the prints to his native East Pakistan. Yet his hurdles were not over. At a time when the local theatres were dominated by Indian, Urdu and Hollywood movies, most distributors and movie theatre owners did not show any interest in screening the East Pakistani Bengali-language movie.

Anisuzzaman recalls in his autobiography that in the fifties in Dacca, two theatres called Manasi and New Pictures House used to show Indian Hindi films. Two other theatres, Rupmahal and Mukul, used to run Bengali movies mainly produced in Calcutta. Another movie hall, New Paradise, showed weekly English films.[179] Finally, Jabber Khan was able to release the film in the Rupmahal movie theatre where Sher-e-Bangla Fazlul Huq was present as the chief guest at the film's premier.[180] Zakir Hossain Raju, a historian of Bangladeshi cinema, has dubbed the movie as the first step towards Bengali Muslim cultural modernity.[181] He particularly asserts that the long shots of rural scenery and the modernist portrayal of a version of Indian classical dance in the movie represent an association with Bengali Muslim social life in rural areas.[182] Thus, the making of the pioneering East Pakistani Bengali movie witnessed a contestation over the identity of the region. The rejection of Bengali *bhadralok* and the sneering attitude of Pakistani governmental authorities, combined with the unpreparedness of local movie theatres to show a home-made movie, actually acted as a constraint on the East Bengali film-makers to produce and articulate their own cultural ambition.

The situation improved when, in 1959, with the active patronage of Nazir Ahmad, Fateh Lohani made two films: *Akash ar Mati* (Sky and Soil) and *Asiya*. In the second movie, Kabir noted the influence of Satyajit Ray's *Pather Panchali* (Song of the Road) though the focus was on the landscapes of East Pakistan. The movie reflected a deeper identification with rural East Bengal.[183]

In the late fifties and throughout the sixties, East Pakistan produced a number of Urdu films through cross-wing collaboration.[184] This was partly due to the presence of a wider market for such films and partly because there was little confidence among movie directors that Bengali movies could compete with Urdu movies and Indian-made Bengali movies. On a positive note, movie directors were aware of the complex and varied regional linguistic traditions of Pakistan, and thus they made Urdu movies.[185] Indeed, one of the most successful movies produced in East Pakistan was made in both Bengali and Urdu – *Jago Hua Sabera* (The Day Shall Dawn), focused on the lives of boatmen of the Padma River. It borrowed part of the theme from Manik Bandopdhay's *Boatmen of Padma*, though the director A. J. Kardar gave the credit of writing the film narrative to Faiz Ahmad Faiz. The movie received an award at the Moscow International Film Festival.[186] Thus, Urdu movies, focusing on life in rural Bengal and its landscape, enjoyed a representational success. In the early sixties, a number of Urdu commercial movies were produced in East Pakistan, but interestingly, they did not become box-office successes in West Pakistan.[187] The market for Urdu movies made in East Pakistan remained limited, and commercial viability was at stake.

Yet the first commercial success with Bengali movies came with those that combined a folkloric mode with tales of rural lives in the sixties. Jabber Khan's movie *Joar Elo* (Tide Has Arrived) depicts a bucolic Islam, with a focus on the mixture between supernatural and natural. Following Jabber Khan's box-office success, Salahuddin, who earlier made movies on urban life, turned to fairy-folktales and made a movie called *Rupban*. A simple narrative based on the tradition of roving folk operas, called *jatra* (journey), proved to be an instant box-office success.[188] The return to folk narratives in films was a reflection of what Fanon noted about the discovery of the roots of indigenous cultures in a colonized nation. Facing internal colonization and competition from Urdu movies, as well as smuggled Indian movies, film-makers turned to the folk traditions of Bengal. The result was spontaneous endorsements by ordinary folks in East Pakistan. The folk theme also influenced Zahir Raihan, the most versatile director of East Pakistan, to make another movie in 1966 based on the folktale of Behula. Though the story was associated with 'Hindu' goddess Manasa, it was presented as a folktale on celluloid screen, and it enjoyed a significant commercial success. The movie also started the film career of popular Bengali actor Razak.[189]

Raihan had been a member of the crew in Kardar's team that had made the movie that revolutionized film-making in East Pakistan. A younger brother of communist writer and journalist Shahidullah Kaiser, Raihan made a number of Urdu and Bengali movies in East Pakistan that reflected the cultural and social ethos of the land. Unfortunately, both these brothers were martyred in the closing days of the Pakistani military occupation of Bangladesh in 1971.[190] In Dacca, with the rise of Bengali nationalism, as a form of political protests against the military junta, the production of Bengali movies began to outnumber Urdu movies. The hunger for Bengali movies produced in West Bengal became evident when the audience rioted for a ticket to view Satyajit Ray's movie *Mohanagar* (The City) during the international film festival in Dacca in 1966. In 1970 Raihan made a new movie, *Jibon theke Neya* (Collected from Life), a political satire on the military dictatorship of Ayub Khan. In the movie, an autocratic woman exercises strict control over her family members:

her husband, two brothers and the servants. The movie employs an allegory in a comic fashion. It imagines the tyrannical character in the household as the military dictator and other members of the house as people of East Pakistan. The turn towards nationalism did not imply a complete absence of world influence. On the contrary, in 1969 the global influence became manifest in political life. Students and intellectuals were aware of the happenings in the world. Kabir himself participated in the Algerian War of Independence and established connections with the Palestinian Liberation Organization.[191] Avant-garde cultural events, as discussed earlier, engaged with themes of the Vietnam War, the Cultural Revolution in China and the student revolution in Paris. Films there reflected the rising popular movements throughout the world. The streets of Dacca heard distant echoes of 1968–69 and the Cold War.

Yet it would be wrong to imagine that the cultural streams of thoughts were unidirectional. Rather, between 1966 and 1971, East Pakistan witnessed the production of Masud Rana novels, a popular genre of pulp-fiction spy thrillers written by Qazi Anwar Hussain. In his novels, written between 1966 and 1971, Anwar Hussain sought to promote Pakistani nationalism by highlighting the mischievous and marauding activities of Bengali-speaking Indian agents who were countered by Masud Rana, a Bengali-speaking agent of the Pakistan Counter Intelligence Service. His novels *Dhansho Pahar* (Hills of Destruction) and *Bharatnatyam* (The Indian Dance) highlighted the threats posed by Bengali Indian agents to East Pakistan in alliance with some rogue Bengali elements from East Pakistan itself. In the third novel, the villain turned out to be a Bengali Hindu of Pakistani origin. These novels drew upon international political alignment in South Asia whereby American scientists and the Chinese were shown as allies of Pakistan, while Indians, particularly Bengali Hindus, were villains in both these novels.[192] The context, settings and temporalities in these early novels of the Masud Rana series reflect a clear attempt to establish a common ground between the two wings of Pakistan against the evil designs of Indian Bengalis. As Projit Bihari Mukherjee points out, it was an attempt to sever the spatial location of East Pakistan from its surroundings in order to create a hyperreal national space.[193] The popularity of these novels reminded the complexity of transformation in popular consciousness among the literati in a period of social revolution.

If Cold War spy thrillers offer a critical insight into one aspect of popular mentality, the other aspect could be gleaned through folksongs that were composed by ordinary peasants to register their understanding of social developments. Popular Bengali folksongs, like Mexican raps recapturing events of the barrios in a form of ballad, referred to seminal events of social protests. Abu Saeed Zahurul Haque, in a seminal article, refers to a series of songs reflecting different temporalities of struggles in East Bengal for cultural liberation.[194] I draw upon his article to reconstruct the popular mentality of struggle as a dialectical antipode to the techno-spatial articulations of Cold War spy thrillers.

In 1952, soon after the language movement, a song composed by singer, lyricist and composer Abdul Latif referred to the student struggle:

They want to take away the words of my mouth.
They chain my hands and feet whenever I try to speak
The language that my grandfather spoke,
The language that my father speaks.
Tell me, brother, how can I forget that, and speak another language?[195]

Or a peasant song refers to the gradual etiolation of trust in 1954 between the two wings of Pakistan through a reference to the riverine life in East Bengal and the imagery of boat. Folk poets sang:

O my beloved, if I knew [your nature] earlier
I would never have embarked upon your damaged ship.
You took me on board in the name of Islam,
Now you deceive me, and I am in mortal danger.
…
Allah is my patron, and saint Gazi is my helper.
You will never get hold of me again.[196]

Finally, during the high sixties, at the moment of the revolt against Ayub Khan's regime, folksongs sarcastically referred to the dictator:

I tell you honestly
I am sorry for poor Ayub Khan
He created twenty-two rich families
None of them comes to his rescue now
Zalem [Oppressor] Ayub is surely approaching his doom

We are out in the fields and streets to bring his downfall
He behaved like a mighty king, and now he looks like a frightened goat
O my dear, I am sorry to death[197]

These songs sung in villages, and in weekly markets known as *haat*s in Bengali, formed the other end of popular consciousness. Thus, the cultural struggle altered the paradigm of collective imagination of homeland.

Conclusion

The intellectual and cultural journey of the East Pakistani literati, from their birth to the rise of the high sixties, reflects a complex story of transitions in collective identity. It was a product of the post-colonial process of state formation, cultural oppression and a rediscovery of self-identity. Internal colonization within Pakistan, the painful journey of the country towards capitalist modernity under the old colonial praetorian guards, and the Cold War climate of 'superpower blocs' forced regional conflicts into a broader contradiction between capitalism and socialism. The result was attempts by Bengali Muslim literati to go back to their roots in the face of cultural oppression and then the rejection of the superficial patina of pan–South Asian Muslim nationalism. They went back to their indigenous roots of a peasant Islam of Bengal and then expanded this deeply agrarian culture by borrowing from global resources. The revolutionary environment of the high sixties played a huge role in providing the latter particular direction to such a culture.

There obviously existed deeper ambiguities in this intellectual and cultural journey. The resistance to pan-Bengali identity persisted among Bengali Muslim intellectuals. The memory of landlord oppression, the air of cultural superiority by Bengali Hindu gentry and their quotidian practice of purity and pollution based on caste hierarchy obviously informed and influenced their cultural quest. Yet they also realized this was a product of colonial social and economic transformation. Their quest for a Bengali identity also aimed to transcend colonial social constructions and build up a new identity which sought to become Muslim and Bengali and also more inclusive of global influences. They engaged in a quest for a form of politically informed cultural modernity. In that process they invented and reinvented cultural imaginings of a nation in the making.

Notes

1. In an influential tome, Peter van der Veer argues that 'religious nationalism in India has a history of its own, which cannot be reduced to the master narrative of European modernity'. Yet he admits these two trends are deeply impacted by 'colonial-orientalist impact'. According to van der Veer, the colonial state and its governmental practices promoted the idea of 'Hindu majority' and the 'Muslim minority' as social and political categories. Peter van der Veer, *Religious Nationalism: Hindus and Muslims in India* (Berkeley and Los Angeles: University of California, 1994), p. 193.
2. The Indian term 'communalism' is used to refer to sectarian religious violence. In an influential book, Gyanendra Pandey charts out the idea behind the term and sociopolitical issues that underpin Hindu and Muslim struggles. Gyanendra Pandey, *The Construction of Communalism in Colonial North India* (New Delhi: Oxford University Press, 2006 [1990]).
3. Peter Gottschalk discusses complexity of identity formation but also points out that the power of classifying categories and the scientific European notion of knowledge informs and influences the construction of sectarian identity. Gottschalk demonstrates how ascendant European notions of science, along with assumptions about India's essentially religious character, fundamentally informed the knowledge produced about India and Indians during the colonial period. Peter Gottschalk, *Religion, Science, and Empire: Classifying Hinduism and Islam in British India* (New York: Oxford University Press, 2013).
4. Based on constructivist approaches towards identity, Charles L. Briggs argues that 'traditions are created in the present, thus reflecting contestations of interest more than the cultural essence of a purportedly homogeneous and bounded "traditional" group.' Charles L. Briggs, 'The Politics of Discursive Authority in Research on the "Invention of Tradition"', *Cultural Anthropology* 11, no. 4 (1996): 435–69, p. 435, www.jstor.org/stable/656664 (accessed on 14 August 2020). E. J. Hobsbawm and Terence Ranger argue: 'Invented tradition is taken to mean a set of practices normally governed by overtly or tacitly accepted rules and of a ritual or symbolic nature, which seek to inculcate certain values norms, or behaviour by repetition which automatically implies continuity with the past.' E. J. Hobsbawm and Terence Ranger (eds.), *Invention of Tradition* (Cambridge: Cambridge University Press, 1983).

5. The commemoration of the event started from the following year in Dacca and then spread throughout East Pakistan. It was a classic act in which the memorialization of street protests is transformed into a public event of national mourning. For more about the use of political events on street as a source of collective memory, see Michael Hebbert, 'The Street as Locus of Collective Memory', *Environment and Planning D: Society and Space* 23, no. 4 (August 2005): 581–96.
6. Kamal Lohani, a veteran journalist and cultural activist, recalls how at a crucial meeting on 7 March 1971, during the historic speech of Sheikh Mujib, activists raised the slogan 'Brave Bengali pick up arms and liberate Bangladesh'. Kamal Lohani, 'Bir Bangali Ostro Dhoro/Bangladesh Swadhin Koro', *Ittefaq*, Dhaka, 1 March 2017, Wednesday.
7. Andrew Sartori, *Bengal in Global Concept History: Culturalism in the Age of Capital* (Chicago Studies in Practices of Meaning) (Chicago: University of Chicago Press, 2008).
8. Here, Sartori borrows from the writings of Blair B. Kling's work on Dwarkanath Tagore. Blair B. Kling, *Partner in Empire: Dwarkanath Tagore and the Age of Enterprise in Eastern India* (Berkeley: University of California Press, 1976).
9. Sartori, *Bengal in Global Concept History*, p. 76.
10. Sartori, *Bengal in Global Concept History*, p. 108.
11. Sartori, *Bengal in Global Concept History*, p. 110.
12. Ahmad Safa, a notable novelist and essayist of Bangladesh, forcefully argues this point in one of his books. He recognizes Bankim Chandra's genius but also argues the latter's contribution towards the making of Hindu nationalism. Ahmad Safa, *Shotoborsher Pherari: Bankim Chandra Chattopadhaya* (Dhaka: Khan Brothers and Company, 2009). For a detailed analysis of the impact of Bankim Chandra's nativist ideas, see Sandeep Banerjee, *Space, Utopia and Indian Decolonization: Literary Pre-Figurations of the Postcolony* (Edinburgh South Asian Studies Series) (London: Routledge, 2019).
13. For details, see Subho Basu, 'The Dialectics of Resistance: Colonial Geography, Bengali Literati and the Racial Mapping of Indian Identity', *Modern Asian Studies* 44, no. 1 (2010): 53–79.
14. For detailed discussion of such views, see Sandeep Banerjee and Subho Basu, 'The City as Nation: Delhi as the Indian Nation in Bengali Bhadralok Travelogues 1866–1910', in *Cities in South Asia*, ed. Crispin Bates and Minoru Mio, pp. 125–142 (London: Routledge).

15. For example, Rajani Ghosh writes without ambiguity that among inhabitants of Bengal, Hindus spoke Bengali and Muslim gentlemen spoke Urdu. He further maintains that lower-caste Hindus and Muslims of Cachar, Sylhet, and Chittagong spoke very corrupted and low-quality (*kadarja*) Bengali. Rajani Ghosh, *Bhugol Vidyasar (Core of Geographic Knowledge)*: *Containing a General Account of Asia, Europe, Africa, America and Oceania, A Detail of India, Great Britain, Ireland and a Particular Description of Bengal Especially, with an Appendix of Ancient Names of the Countries and Towns and Compiled from Recent Authorities* (Kati Para, Jessore: Rajcumar Ghosh, 1871), p. 131, quoted in Subho Basu 'The Dialectics of Resistance'.
16. For the changes in rural economy of Bengal, see Tariq Omar Ali, *A Local History of Global Capital: Jute and Peasant Life in the Bengal Delta* (Princeton, NJ: Princeton University Press, 2018).
17. Partha Chatterjee, 'The Colonial State and Peasant Resistance in Bengal, 1920–1947', *Past & Present* 11, no. 1 (February 1986): 169–204.
18. Neilesh Bose, *Recasting the Region: Language, Culture, and Islam in Colonial Bengal* (New Delhi: Oxford University Press, 2014).
19. As in Hugh MacLennan's work, where French and English residents of Canada did not interact with each other, Hindus and Muslims became two solitudes in colonial Bengal. Hugh MacLennan, *Two Solitudes*, ed. Michael Gnarowski (Montreal: McGill-Queen's University Press, 2018).
20. Nazrul Islam is an iconic figure among Bengalis across the border. Celebrated as a rebel poet, Nazrul occupies a central place in modern Bengali culture and literary tradition. Numerous articles have been written in Bengali on Nazrul and his contribution to modern Bengali culture and literary tradition. In independent Bangladesh, Nazrul is accorded the status of national poet. See, for example, Priti Kumar Mitra, *The Dissent of Kazi Nazrul Islam: Poetry and History* (New Delhi: Oxford University Press, 2007).
21. Shahadat H. Khan. *The Freedom of Intellect Movement (Buddhir Mukti Andolan) in Bengali Muslim Thought, 1926–1938* (Lewiston, NY: Edwin Mellen Press, 2007).
22. It was Taj ul-Islam Hashmi who popularized the idea of Pakistan as a peasant utopia based on the popular reception of the idea among Muslim peasants. Taj ul-Islam Hashmi, *Pakistan as a Peasant Utopia: The Communalization of Class Politics in East Bengal, 1920–1947* (Boulder, CO: Westview, 1992).

23. Humayun Azad, 'Bhasha Andoloner Sahityik Potobhumi (Literary Background of Language Movement)', vol. 5, in *Bhasha Andoloner Artho Samajik Potobhumi (Socio-Economic Background of Language Movement)* (Combined 5 Volumes) (Dhaka: University Press, 2000), pp. 1–2.
24. Frantz Fanon, *The Wretched of the Earth*, trans. Constance Farrington (London: Grove Press, 1968 [1961]), p. 178.
25. Fanon, *The Wretched of the Earth*, p. 176.
26. Abdul Kairm Sahitya Bisharad focused his attention on the Muslim contribution to Bangla literature in the pre-colonial era. He dedicated his life in collecting old Bengali manuscripts (called *puthi*s). In 1920–21, the Bangiya Sahitya Parishad, a pivotal Calcutta-based Bengali literary establishment, published his catalogue of Bengali manuscripts entitled *Bangala Prachin Punthir Bibaran* in two volumes. The Dhaka University Library and the Varendra Research Museum, Rajshahi, hold his collections in a special section. His lifelong effort symbolizes Bengali Muslim intellectuals' love for their language and literature and their historic awareness of their contribution to the language and culture over 800 years.
27. Nira Yuval-Davis, 'Belonging and the Politics of Belonging', in *Contesting Recognition: Culture, Identity and Citizenship*, ed. Janice McLaughlin, Peter Phillimore and Diane Richardson, pp. 20–35 (New York: Palgrave Macmillan, 2011), cited in Tulshi Kumar Das, Ritupurna Bhattacharyya and Pranjit Kumar Sarma, 'Revisiting Geographies of Nationalism and National Identity in Bangladesh', *Geojournal* 87 (2022): 1099–1120.
28. Selwyn Cudjoe defined resistance as any act or complex of acts that are designed to get rid of the oppressors whether they are slave masters or planters of multinational corporations. He further states that his book examines the artistic form that carried forward the ideology of resistance. Selwyn Reginald Cudjoe, *Resistance and Caribbean Literature* (Athens, OH: Ohio University Press, 1981).
29. Barbara Harlow, *Resistance Literature* (New York: Methuen, 1987).
30. Harlow, *Resistance*, p. 30.
31. Hafeez Malik provides an early account of progressive writing in the Urdu language in Pakistan. Hafeez Malik, 'The Marxist Literary Movement in India and Pakistan', *Journal of Asian Studies* 26, no. 4 (1967): 649–64, DOI: 10.2307/2051241. Kamran Asdar Ali provides interesting insights into debates concerning national culture among Urdu writers through a critical engagement with Saadat Hasan Manto's writings. Kamran Asdar

Ali, 'Progressives and "Perverts": Partition Stories and Pakistan's Future', *Social Text* 29, no. 3 (2011): 1–29.
32. Fanon, *The Wretched of the Earth*, p. 222.
33. Ngũgĩ wa Thiong'o, *Decolonising the Mind* (London: Heinemann, 1986).
34. Quamrul Hassan, a well-known painter and a modern artist, developed interests in folk forms of art and came to be known as Patua Quamrul Hassan. *Patua* art was a folk artform popular in the eastern region of India. It depicts stories from the Ramayana, the Mahabharata and Sufi tales of Bengal. Through these tales it builds up narratives about contemporary life in rural Bengal and the eastern Indian region.
35. A critical instance of such a movie was Zahir Raihan's *Behula*. Released in 1966, it is based on a folktale from East Bengal that also incorporates Hindu mythology. For Urdu films made in Bengal, Lotte Hoek made a detailed analysis of such cross-wing cultural activities. Lotte Hoek, 'Cross-Wing Filmmaking: East Pakistani Urdu Films and Their Traces in the Bangladesh Film Archive', *BioScope: South Asian Screen Studies* 5, no. 2 (2014): 99–118.
36. The concept of insurgent imagination is explored in detail in the work of Auritro Majumder. Auritro Majumder, *Insurgent Imaginations: World Literature and the Periphery* (Cambridge: Cambridge University Press, 2020).
37. For details of the analysis of the term, see Daniel Egan, 'Rethinking War of Maneuver/War of Position: Gramsci and the Military Metaphor', *Critical Sociology* 40, no. 4 (2014): 521–38.
38. Fanon, *The Wretched of the Earth*, p. 179.
39. See Egan, 'Rethinking War of Maneuver/War of Position'.
40. Prasenjit Duara, *Rescuing History from the Nation: Questioning Narratives of Modern China* (Chicago and London: University of Chicago Press, 1998), pp. 48.
41. Dipesh Chakrabarty, *Provincializing Europe: Postcolonial Thought and Historical Difference* (Princeton, NJ: Princeton University Press, 2008 [2000]).
42. Anisuzzaman, *Kal Nirobodhi* (Dhaka: Sahitya Prokash, 2019 [2003]), p. 53.
43. For details of the refugee exodus from Burma during the Second World War, see Sanjay Bhattacharya, *Propaganda and Information in Eastern India 1939–45: A Necessary Weapon of War* (Richmond, VA: Curzon Routledge, 2001). The most important literary rendering of this event is Amitav

Ghosh's novel *The Glass Palace*. Amitav Gosh, *The Glass Palace* (New York: Random House, 2001).
44. Richard Stevenson, *Bengal Tiger and British Lion: An Account of the Bengal Famine of 1943*. (Bloomington, IN: iUniverse, 2005), p. ix. Also see Manish Sinha, 'The Bengal Famine of 1943 and the American Insensitiveness to Food Aid', *Proceedings of the Indian History Congress* 70 (2009): 887–93, http://www.jstor.org/stable/44147736 (accessed on 17 January 2021).
45. Auriol Law-Smith, 'Response and Responsibility: The Government of India's Role in the Bengal Famine, 1943', *South Asia: Journal of South Asian Studies* 12, no. 1 (1989): 49–65.
46. Auriol, 'Response and Responsibility', pp. 54–55.
47. Amartya Sen, 'Starvation and Exchange Entitlements: A General Approach and Its Application to the Great Bengal Famine', *Cambridge Journal of Economics* 1, no. 1 (1977): 33–59.
48. Paul R. Greenough, *Prosperity and Misery in Modern Bengal: The Famine of 1943–1944* (Oxford: Oxford University Press, 1982), p. 273.
49. Anisuzzaman recorded how his sister started cooking gruel for starving rural working-class people who came to their neighbourhood for food. But their number increased, and they gathered in front of their house in such large numbers that their father feared that they would break the door. He ordered Anisuzzaman's sister to stop cooking for them and also made sure that all windows of the house remained closed so that they did not have to view the sufferings of the people. Anisuzzaman, *Kal Nirobodhi*, pp. 55–56.
50. The visual representation of the Bengal famine haunted Bengalis. Zainul Abedin immortalized the famine through his sketches, and Sunil Jana took photographs of the famine for *Swadhonota*, the journal of the CPI. Novelist Manik Bandyopadhyay lamented the famine victims not forcefully snatching food from shops ('Why did they not grab and eat?' (Chhiniye khayni keno?) Manik Bandyopadhyay, *Granthaboli*, vol. 8 (Calcutta: Granthalaya, 1963), pp. 634–43. Later, two Bengali film-makers, Satyajit Ray and Mrinal Sen, made films about the famine: *Ashani Sanket* (Distant Thunder) by Ray and *Akaler Sondhane* (In Search of Famine) by Sen.
51. Rajender Kaur, 'The Vexed Question of Peasant Passivity: Nationalist Discourse and the Debate on Peasant Resistance in Literary Representations of the Bengal famine of 1943', *Journal of Postcolonial Writing* 50, no. 3 (2014): 269–81, DOI: 10.1080/17449855.2012.752153.
52. For details, see Anuradha Roy, *Cultural Communism in Bengal, 1936–1952* (New Delhi: Primus Books, 2014).

53. These journalists and writers were Abul Kalam Shamsuddin, Mohammad Habibullah Bahar, Mujibur Rahman Khan, Syed Sadekur Rahman, Mohammad Khairul Anam Khan, Mohammad Modwaber, Abdul Hi, Zahur Hossain Chowdhury, Anwar Hossain, Fazlul Karim Khan and Mosharrof Hossain. Abul Kalam Shamsuddin, *Otit Diner Smriti* (Memories of Old Days) (Dhaka: Khosroj Kitab Mohal, 2019 [1968]), pp. 169–71.
54. Shamsuddin, *Otit Diner Smriti*, pp. 169–71.
55. M. N. Roy, Ellen Roy, Rajani Mukherjee and Arati Mukherjee, and several other radical humanists, visited the office of *Azad*, and in that meeting M. N. Roy declared his support for Muslim rights for national self-determination. They were followed by communist writers and activists, Bankim Mukherjee, Somenath Lahiri, Golpal Halder and Anil Kanjilal. Shamsuddin, *Otit Diner Smriti*, p. 172.
56. Abul Mansur Ahmad, *Amar Dekha Rajnitir Ponchas Botsor* (Dhaka: Prothoma Prokashan, 2018), pp. 203–04.
57. *Puthi* literature is a literary genre characterized by works written in a mixed vocabulary drawn from Bangla, Arabic, Urdu, Persian and Hindi. It was in vogue during the eighteenth and nineteenth centuries, and its composers as well as readers were Muslims. The word *puthi* (or *punthi*) is derived from *pustika* (book). However, only a particular type of writing dating from the aforementioned time period is known as *puthi*.
58. Azad, 'Bhasha Andoloner Sahityik Potobhumi', p. 5.
59. Mohammadi Magh, 'Mashreki Pakistane Bhashar Swarup Masik', 1356/1949, cited in Morshed Safiul Hassan, *Purbo Banglay Chinta Chorcha 1940–70: Dwondwo o Potikria* (Dhaka: Anupom Prokashoni, 2017), p. 465.
60. Jnanabrata Bhattacharyya, 'Language, Class and Community in Bengal', *South Asia Bulletin* 7, nos. 1–2 (1987): 56–63.
61. Anindita Ghosh, 'Valorising the "Vulgar": Nationalist Appropriations of Colloquial Bengali Traditions, c. 1870–1905', *Indian Economic & Social History Review* 37, no. 2 (June 2000): 151–83.
62. Etienne Balibar, 'The Nation Form: History and Ideology', *Review (Fernand Braudel Center)* 13, no. 3 (1990): 329–61, http://www.jstor.org/stable/40241159 (accessed on 20 April 2021).
63. Azad, 'Bhasha Andoloner Sahityik Potobhumi', p. 20.
64. Azad, 'Bhasha Andoloner Sahityik Potobhumi', p. 20.
65. Anisuzzaman, *Kal Nirobodhi*, pp. 75–77, 94–95.

66. Shamsuddin, *Otit Diner Smriti*, pp. 179–83.
67. Joya Chatterji, *Bengal Divided: Hindu Communalism and Partition, 1932–1947* (Cambridge: Cambridge University Press, 1994).
68. Oli Ahad, *Jatio Rajniti: 1945 theke 75* (Fourth Edition) (Dhaka: Bangladesh Co-Operative Book Society, 2004), p. 31 (translation mine).
69. Abdur Rauf Chowdhury, *Swayotto Shashon, Swadhikar o Swadhinota* (Dhaka: Kotha Prokash, 2010), pp. 40–41.
70. According to Shamsur Rahman Faruqi, a scholar of the Urdu language, Urdu was previously known as Hindvi, Hindi, Dihlavi, Gujri, Dakani and Rekhtah. Indeed, the name 'Urdu' seems to have been used for the first time, at least in writing, around 1780. Shamsur Rahman Faruqi, 'A Long History of Urdu Literary Culture', in *Literary Cultures in History: Reconstructions from South Asia*, ed. Sheldon Pollock, part-i.î (Berkeley: University of California Press, 2003), p. 806.
71. Christopher King, 'The Hindi–Urdu Controversy of the North-Western Provinces and Oudh and Communal Consciousness', *Journal of South Asian Literature* 13, nos. 1–4 (1977–78): 111–20.
72. David Lelyveld, 'The Fate of Hindustani: Colonial Knowledge and the Project of a National Language', in *Orientalism and the Postcolonial Predicament: Perspectives on South Asia*, ed. Carol A. Breckenridge and Peter van der Veer, pp. 189–214 (Philadelphia: University of Pennsylvania Press, 1993).
73. Tahir Kamran, 'Punjab, Punjabi and Urdu the Question of Displaced Identity: A Historical Appraisal', *Journal of Punjab Studies* 14, no. 1 (2008): 11–25, p. 12.
74. Albert Doujot, *Le Patois* (Paris: Librairie Delagrave, 1946), quoted in Ephraim Nimni, 'Marx, Engels and the National Question', *Science & Society* 53, no. 3 (1989): 297–326.
75. See the debates between Jinnah and the student representatives of Dacca University in 1948. Ahad, *Jatio Rajniti*, p. 70. In debate with Dhirendranath Dutta, prime minister Liaquat Ali stated: 'Pakistan is a Muslim state and it must have as its *lingua franca* the language of Muslim nation.... [P]akistan has been created because of the demand of a hundred million Muslims in this subcontinent and the language of the hundred million Muslims is Urdu. *It is necessary for a nation to have one language and that language can be Urdu and no other language*', quoted in Hasan Hafizur Rahman (ed.), *History of Bangladesh War of Independence Documents*, vol. 1 (Dhaka: Government of Bangladesh, 1982), p. 55 (emphasis mine).

76. These articles were published in the *Ittehad* on 22 and 29 June 1947, the *Dainik Azad* on 30 June 1947 and the *Saptahik Begam* on 3 August 1947.
77. *Dainik Azad*, 19 May 1947.
78. *Moslem Bharot* (Prothom Borsho) (Prothom Khondo), Boishakh 1327, cited in A. R. Chowdhury, *Swayotto Shashon*.
79. *Saogat*, Aswin 1354, quoted in A. R. Chowdhury, *Swayotto Shashon*, pp. 43–44.
80. A. R. Chowdhury, *Swayotto Shashon*, pp. 44–51.
81. Syed Muazzem Ali, 'Syed Mujtaba Ali – a pioneer of our Language Movement', *Daily Star*, 11 February 2009.
82. Hassan, *Purbo Banglay Chinta Chorcha*, p. 59.
83. Hassan, *Purbo Banglay Chinta Chorcha*, p. 59.
84. According to a sample survey, conducted in 1957, among university and college students in Dacca, 93 per cent of students identified themselves as Bengali Muslims, and nearly 77 per cent of them came from villages. Approximately half of the respondents' fathers were semi-literate or illiterate. A. N. M. Muniruzzaman, *The Living and Working Conditions of Students of the University and Colleges of Dacca 1957* (Dacca: University of Dhaka, 1961), tables II-2, II-6, II-14.
85. Barbara A. Misztal, 'Durkheim on Collective Memory', *Journal of Classical Sociology* 3, no. 2 (2003): 123–43.
86. Ahad, *Jatio Rajiniti*, p. 84.
87. Sheikh Mujibur Rahman, *Asomapto Atmojiboni* (Dhaka: University Press, 2018), p. 92.
88. S. M. Rahman, *Asomapto Atmojiboni*, pp. 92–93.
89. S. M. Rahman, *Asomapto Atmojiboni*, pp. 92–93
90. Ahad, *Jatio Rajniti*, pp. 70–72
91. S. M. Rahman, *Asomapto Atmojiboni*, p. 92.
92. Rafiqul Islam, 'The Bengali Language Movement and the Emergence of Bangladesh', *Contributions to Asian Studies* 11 (1978): 145–46, https://proxy.library.mcgill.ca/login?url=https://www-proquest-com.proxy3.library.mcgill.ca/scholarly-journals/bengali-language-movement-emergence-bangladesh/docview/1307833941/se-2?accountid=12339 (accessed on 7 July 2021).
93. Ahad, *Jatio Rajniti*, pp. 78–83.
94. Ahad, *Jatio Rajniti*, p. 132.
95. Ahad, *Jatio Rajniti*, pp. 137–39.
96. Ahad, *Jatio Rajniti*, p. 138.

97. Ahad, *Jatio Rajniti*, p. 139.
98. Shamsuddin, *Otit Diner Smriti*, p. 249.
99. Anisuzzaman, *Kal Nirobodhi*, p. 179.
100. Richard Sisson and Leo E. Rose, *War and Secession: Pakistan, India, and the Creation of Bangladesh* (Berkeley: University of California Press, 1990).
101. Srinath Raghavan, *1971: A Global History of the Creation of Bangladesh* (Cambridge, MA: Harvard University Press, 2013).
102. Gary J. Bass, *The Blood Telegram: India's Secret War in East Pakistan* (New York: Random House, 2013).
103. Ahmed Kamal, *State against the Nation: The Decline of the Muslim League in Pre-Independence Bangladesh, 1947–54* (Dhaka: University Press Limited, 2009).
104. Badruddin Umar, *The Emergence of Bangladesh*, vol. 1: *Class and Political Struggles in East Pakistan, 1947–1958* (Karachi: Oxford University Press, 2004); Badruddin Umar, *The Emergence of Bangladesh*, vol. 2: *The Rise of Bengali Nationalism, 1958–1971* (Karachi: Oxford University Press, 2006).
105. Henry Glassie and Feroz Mahmud, *Living Traditions* (Cultural Survey of Bangladesh Series, vol. 11) (Dhaka: Asiatic Society of Bangladesh, 2008), pp. 578–79 (translated from Bengali into English by Kabir Chowdhury).
106. *East Bengal Language Committee Report* (Dacca: Government of Bangladesh, 1949), pp. 102–03.
107. Ganesh Charan Basu was the head of the department of Bengali and Sanskrit in Dacca University. He left Dacca in 1950 in the wake of anti-Hindu riots in East Pakistan. Anisuzzaman, *Kal Nirobodhi*, p. 151.
108. Shamsuddin, *Otit Diner Smriti*, p. 251.
109. Hassan, *Purbo Banglay Chinta Chorcha*, p. 604.
110. Mohosin Shastropani, *Lal Potakar Niche Sanskritik Andolon* (Cultural Movement under the Red Banner) (Dhaka: Porua, 2017), p. 59.
111. Shastropani, *Lal Potakar Niche*, p. 58.
112. Anisuzzaman, *Kal Nirobodhi*, p. 189.
113. Anisuzzaman, *Kal Nirobodhi*, pp. 167–84.
114. Anisuzzaman, *Kal Nirobodhi*, pp. 187–88.
115. Shastropani, *Lal Potakar Niche*, p. 58.
116. Anisuzzaman, *Kal Nirobodhi*, p. 223.
117. Sheikh Mujib recorded his impression of China in his travelogue, *Amar Dekha Noya Chin* (Dhaka: Bangla Academy, 2020).
118. Manoj Basu, *Chin Dekhe Elam* (Dwitio Porbo) (Calcutta: Metropolitan Printing and Publishing House Limited, 1955), p. 196.

119. After 1954, Bhashani went on self-exile in Europe. He later returned to Calcutta. From Calcutta he wrote to Ahad that the latter could collect his passport and should come immediately to Calcutta. 'The massive exodus of people from East Pakistan to districts in West Bengal would make us a minority in Pakistan. It would also create panic among Hindus in East Pakistan,' Bhashani said. The letter was dated 28 March 1955. Oli Ahad, *Jatio Rajniti*, p. 198.
120. Anisuzzaman, *Kal Nirobodhi*, pp. 192–93.
121. Anisuzzaman, *Kal Nirobodhi*, p. 232.
122. Anisuzzaman, *Kal Nirobodhi*, pp. 236–41.
123. Anisuzzaman, *Kal Nirobodhi*, pp. 240–24.
124. Anisuzzaman, *Kal Nirobodhi*, pp. 241–43.
125. Hasanuzzaman Khan, 'Political Prisoners First Performed the Drama "Kabar"' (letter to editor), *Daily Star*, 30 December 2014, https://www.thedailystar.net/political-prisoners-first-performed-the-drama-kabar-57588 (accessed on 2 April 2021).
126. Shastropani, *Lal Potakar Niche*, p. 57.
127. Shastropani, *Lal Potakar Niche*, p. 57.
128. Anisuzzaman, *Kal Nirbodhi*, pp. 208–09.
129. Layli Uddin, '"We Are the 95%": Bhashani and the Kagmari Festival', *Daily Star*, 12 December 2020.
130. Kate Crehan, *Gramsci, Culture and Anthropology* (Berkely: University of California Press, 2002), p. 71.
131. Golam Mustafa, 'Amar Chintadhara' (Dacca: Ahmad Publishing House, 1968), pp. 25, 38, 213, 232, cited in Hassan, *Purbo Banglay Chinta Chorcha*, pp. 585–86.
132. Ali Ahsan, 'Purbo Paksitan Bangla Sahityer Dhara', cited in Hassan, *Purbo Banglay Chinta Chorcha*, p. 65.
133. Anisuzzaman, 'Claiming and Disclaiming a Cultural Icon: Tagore in East Pakistan and Bangladesh', *University of Toronto Quarterly* 77, no. 4 (2008): 1058–69.
134. Anisuzzaman. 'Claiming and Disclaiming a Cultural Icon'.
135. Shaila Sultana, 'Problematising the Popular Discourses about Language and Identity of Young Adults in Bangladesh', *3L: Language, Linguistics, Literature* 18, no. 4 (2012): 49–63.
136. Anisuzzaman, *Kal Nirbodhi*, pp. 436–41.
137. Anisuzzaman, *Kal Nirbodhi*, pp. 436–41.
138. Shastropani, *Lal Potakar Niche*, p. 64.

139. Shastropani, *Lal Potakar Niche*, p. 64.
140. Shastropani, *Lal Potakar Niche*, pp. 65–66.
141. Shastropani, *Lal Potakar Niche*, p. 66.
142. Shastropani, *Lal Potakar Niche*, pp. 68–69.
143. Shastropani, *Lal Potakar Niche*, p. 69.
144. Shastropani, *Lal Potakar Niche*, p. 70.
145. Shastropani, *Lal Potakar Niche*, p. 72.
146. Ekram Ahmed, 'Udichi', in *Banglapedia: National Encyclopedia of Bangladesh*, ed. Sirajul Islam and Ahmed A. Jamal (Dhaka: Asiatic Society of Bangladesh, 2012 [2003]).
147. Ghulam Murshid, 'Indian Sub-Continent: Bangladesh – Modern Bangladeshi Writing', *Wasafiri* 10, no. 21 (1995): 66–69. Also see Baitullah Kaderi, *Shater Doshoker Kobita Bishoy o Prokoron* (Poems of the 1960s: Subject and Structure) (Dhaka: Nobojug Prokashoni, 2009); Nazneen Ahmed, 'The Poetics of Nationalism: Cultural Resistance and Poetry in East Pakistan/Bangladesh, 1952–71', *Journal of Postcolonial Writing* 50, no. 3 (2014): 256–68.
148. William Radice, 'Shamsur Rahman: Visionary Poet of Bangladesh's Freedom Struggle, without Vanity or Affectation', *Guardian*, 15 September 2006.
149. Interview with N. N. Tarun Chakrabarty, a close associate and disciple of poet Shamsur Rahman, in Montreal on 9 March 2021.
150. *Mehndi* is a type of red-brown dye made from henna, which is used to apply a temporary design to a person's skin, especially on the occasion of weddings.
151. Translated by Kabir Chowdhury.
152. Interview with N. N. Tarun Chakrabarty, Montreal, 9 March 2021.
153. Radice, 'Shamsur Rahman'.
154. Murshid, 'Indian Sub-Continent: Bangladesh', pp. 66–69.
155. Murshid, 'Indian Sub-Continent: Bangladesh', pp. 66–69.
156. Kaderi, *Shater Doshoker Kobita Bishoy o Prokoron*, pp. 55–56.
157. Abdul Mannan, 'Pagol Ei Ratrira' (Those Mad Nights), cited in Kaderi, *Shater Doshoker Kobita Bishoy o Prokoron*, p. 78.
158. Shahid Kadri 'Tomake Obhibadon Priotoma' (Salute You My Darling), cited in Kaderi, *Shater Doshoker Kobita Bishoy o Prokoron*, p. 90.
159. Kabir Chowdhury, 'Liberation War and Creative Writing', Muktomona, 16 December 2006, https://mm-gold.azureedge.net/Special_Event_/16December/kabir_chowdhury161206.html (accessed on 27 April 2021).

160. Thomas Newbold, 'Beyond the Break with the Past: Reckoning with Literary Pakistanism in East Bengal', *Economic and Political Weekly* 56, no. (44): (2021): 60–66.
161. For detailed analysis of the novels of the sixties, see Rafique Ullah Khan, *Bangladesher Uponyas ebong Shilporup* (Dhaka: Bangla Academy, 1997), pp. 7–138.
162. Mohammad Emdadur Rashed, 'The Emergence and Development of Academic Fine Arts: Perspective Bangladesh', *Thespian Magazine* 4, no. 1 (September–October 2016): 34–39.
163. Sanjukta Sunderason, 'Shadow-Lines: Zainul Abedin and the Afterlives of the Bengal Famine of 1943', *Third Text* 31, nos. 2–3 (2017): 239–59.
164. Mofidul Hoque, 'River, Boat and Artistic Investigation of Qayyum Chowdhury', *Anyadin* (Special Eid Festival Issue), 2001, pp. 516–19, cited in Zakir Hossain Raju, *Bangladesh Cinema and National Identity: In Search of the Modern?* (Routledge Contemporary South Asia Series) (London: Routledge, 2015), p. 127.
165. Sunderason, 'Shadow-Lines', pp. 239–59.
166. Rajarshi Dasgupta, 'The People in People's Art and People's War', in *People's Warrior: Words and Worlds of PC Joshi*, ed. Gargi Chakrabartty, pp. 443–56 (Kolkata: Tulika, 2014).
167. Sunderason, 'Shadow-Lines', pp. 239–59.
168. Sunderason, 'Shadow-Lines', pp. 239–59.
169. Sunderason, 'Shadow-Lines', pp. 239–59.
170. Sunderason, 'Shadow-Lines', pp. 239–59.
171. Lala Rukh Selim, 'Art of Bangladesh: The Changing Role of Tradition, Search for Identity and Globalization', *South Asia Multidisciplinary Academic Journal* 9 (2014): 10–19.
172. Md Mohiuddin, 'Film Business in Bangladesh: A Historical Account', *Journal Of Humanities and Social Science* 19, no. 1 (2014): 33–36.
173. Faqrul Hassan 'Najir Ahmed Purbobonger Chalachitra Bikasher Udoktya' (Najir Ahmad: A Pioneering Film-Maker in East Bengal), *Ittefak*, 1 April 2017.
174. F. Hassan 'Najir Ahmed'.
175. Sabiha Huq and Srideep Mukherjee, 'Guns in Bangla Cinema across Borders: Perspectives on Cultural Evolution', *Palgrave Communications* 6, no. 1 (2020): 1–12, https://www.nature.com/articles/s41599-019-0379-6 (accessed on 28 April 2021).
176. Huq and Mukherjee, 'Guns in Bangla Cinema across Borders'.

177. Raju, *Bangladesh Cinema and National Identity*, p. 127.
178. Alamgir Kabir, *Cholochitro o Jatio Mukti: Rochona Songroho* (Films and National Emacipation: Collected Works) (Dhaka: Agami Prokashoni, 2018), p. 67.
179. Anisuzzaman, *Kal Nirobodhi*, pp. 195–96.
180. Fayeka Zabeen Siddiqua, 'Talking about Our First Talkie', *Daily Star*, 6 November 2015.
181. Raju, *Bangladesh Cinema and National Identity*, p. 124.
182. Raju, *Bangladesh Cinema and National Identity*, p. 136.
183. Kabir, *Cholochitro o Jatio Mukti*, p. 67.
184. Hoek, 'Cross-Wing Filmmaking'. Also see Lotte Hoek, 'Urdu for Image: Understanding Bangladeshi Cinema Through Its Theaters', in *South Asian Media Cultures: Audiences, Representations, Contexts* (Anthem South Asian Studies), ed. Shakuntala Banaji, pp. 73–90 (London: Anthem Press, 2010), p. 73.
185. Sabiha Huq, 'A Liminal Bengali Identity: Film Culture in Bangladesh', in *Media Culture in Transnational Asia: Convergences and Divergences*, ed. Hyesu Park, pp. 162–80 (Rutgers: Rutgers University Press, 2020).
186. Kabir, *Cholochitro o Jatio Mukti*, pp. 68.
187. Kabir, *Cholochitro o Jatio Mukti*, pp. 78–79.
188. Kabir, *Cholochitro o Jatio Mukti*, pp. 78–79.
189. Muhammed Shahriar Haque, 'Early Life of an Accidental Actor: Before Nayak Raj Razzak', *East West Journal of Humanities* (Special Issue) 6–7 (2016–17): 121–36, p. 131.
190. M. S. Haque, 'Early Life of an Accidental Actor'.
191. Salimullah Khan, 'Alamgir Kabirer Ogyan, othoba "Ami Mukti Juddhoke Bujhte Pari Ni" (Alamgir Kabir's Unconscious, or 'We Do Not Understand Liberation War!'), in Kabir, *Cholochitro o Jatio Mukti*, pp. 20–21.
192. Projit Bihari Mukherjee, 'Technospatial Imaginaries: Masud Rana and the Vernacularization of Popular Cold War Geopolitics in East Pakistan, 1966–1971', *History and Technology* 31, no. 3: 324–40.
193. Mukherjee, 'Technospatial Imaginaries'.
194. Abu Saeed Zahurul Haque, 'The Use of Folklore in Nationalist Movements and Liberation Struggles: A Case Study of Bangladesh', *Journal of the Folklore Institute* 12, nos. 2–3 (1975): 211–40, DOI: 10.2307/3813927.
195. A. S. Z. Haque, 'The Use of Folklore', pp. 217–18.
196. A. S. Z. Haque, 'The Use of Folklore', pp. 217–18.
197. A. S. Z. Haque, 'The Use of Folklore', p. 222.

4

Praetorian Guards, Capitalist Modernization and the Early Global Sixties

Global Cold War, Empire and the Colonization of East Pakistan

In the early sixties, under praetorian guards, Pakistan was pursuing a process of capitalist modernization in alliance with the US. There existed a deep political–ideological symbiosis between the policies of the Pakistani military-bureaucratic regime and the US policymakers and influential academics connected with the political establishment. The military-bureaucratic regime of Pakistan constituted a critical component of the US' Cold War imperialism and was regarded as an experimental ground for 'modernization' theory. With massive aid from Western donors and encouragement from US administration and Harvard-based American advisors, military rulers adopted a growth-oriented economic policy between 1958 and 1969. During this decade, Pakistan witnessed an expansion in its industrial base concomitant with the rise of a large working class. Yet such growth-oriented strategies were not accompanied by an attention to social equity. As a consequence, despite growth, economic and social inequalities between the two wings, as well as different social classes, deepened.[1] The experiment with Basic Democracy, a brainchild of Ayub Khan, turned out to be a coalition of economically powerful rural and urban social classes under the patronage of a ruling military-bureaucratic axis.[2] This ruling social coalition incorporated the large industrial and banking houses and landed magnates of West Pakistan combined with the rich peasants in the countryside of East Pakistan under the institutional hegemony of the military-bureaucratic edifice. In the process, approximately 40 business houses exercised significant stranglehold over the economy of Pakistan.[3] More importantly, Ayub Khan initiated an economic policy through Fauji Foundation that allowed the transfer of ownership of state land to the army, retraining of military personnel who sought jobs in the private sector at state expense and the unhindered circulation of military officers from the army to private industry.[4] This established the foundation of military control over the economy and the new form of capitalistic development in Pakistan that could be termed as praetorian capitalism. It was similar to the Latin American trajectory of development of praetorian capitalism under the patronage of the US and US-based corporate houses in the Cold War era, and the consequent violence stemming from it in both contexts was also identical. As Gilbert M. Joseph has put it,

> the dynamics of the Latin American Cold War are embedded in a particularly ferocious dialectic linking reformist and revolutionary projects for social change and national development and the excessive counterrevolutionary responses they triggered in the years following World War II. This dialectic, which shaped regional life in the late twentieth century and conditioned the region's prospects for the new millennium, played out in overlapping and interdependent domestic and international fields of political and social power.[5]

The consequence of such policies on East Pakistan transformed it into an internal colony. These policies provided little benefit to the poor peasants, expanding urban working classes and salaried middle classes in East Pakistan; the dialectics of response to these policies ranged from the groundswell of revolutionary anger from below and the counter-revolutionary military reactions producing a similar violent reaction from above. Here also the US acted with the same Cold War calculations, culminating in the bloody events of 1971.

The Revolution from Above: The Military-Bureaucratic Regime, Basic Democracy and the Constitution

In 1954, Ayub Khan, recently appointed as the chief of armed staff of Pakistan and later defence minister, expressed in a letter to president Eisenhower the desire of the Pakistani military officers to serve US strategic interests in much the same way that they had served the British imperial interests prior to independence.[6] Indeed, in 1961 president Ayub Khan declared in the US that Pakistan was the only country in the world where the US armed forces could land at any time freely to defend the free world.[7] There was no doubt that members of the US republican administration of the Eisenhower era admired the general's candour and his offer of service. After the coup of October 1958, when Iskandar Mirza was still not deposed by Ayub Khan, secretary of state John Foster Dulless in a letter to president Mirza wrote:

> It is, of course, with a certain sadness that one sees constitutions suspended and the rule of men substituted, as it were, for the rule of law. Nevertheless, it is never possible to generalize about these matters and I know that you and General Ayub have a selfless dedication to the welfare of your country, so that what under other circumstances would be dangerous can, under these circumstances, be benign.[8]

The letter, though written in a guarded language, is widely interpreted as evidence of US support for the coup in Pakistan. Lawrence Ziring, who studied politics in Pakistan and Bangladesh, asserts that at the time of the coup of 1958, general elections were a few months away, and it was anticipated that the newly elected government might alter its policy of Cold War involvement.[9] The US administration regarded any democratic experiment in Pakistan as a risk, particularly, because the US invested substantial amount of money in arming the Pakistani army.[10] Thus, the republican administration in the US tacitly endorsed the coup. US attempts to build up a Cold War empire had ideological implications for the economic policy formulations too. Indeed, widely prevalent ideas of modernization theory in the US policy circles also created a more congenial climate for the acceptance of a highly authoritarian model of governance dedicated to modernization in a 'transitional society'. In 1960 Walt Whitman Rostow published his notable work *The Stages of Economic Growth: A Non-Communist Manifesto*, which was based on an earlier essay by him also entitled 'Stages of Economic Growth'. He presented his treatise as an alternative to Marxist interpretations of economic history.[11] The 'non-communist manifesto' of Rostow emphasized technicist reasons for industrial take-off. He explains that the preconditions for sustained industrialization involve a build-up of a social overhead of capital, notably in transport, technological revolution in agriculture, an expansion in imports financed by more efficient production process and marketing of natural resources. These essential changes, Rostow concludes, would enable initially small enclaves of modern industrial activity in a country to expand, which could afterwards be self-sustained mainly through the ploughing back of profits.[12] What is remarkable in this analysis is the absence of any focus on the social distribution of resources and unequal access to such resources among different social classes and communities in any given society. Sociologically, too, this was the high noon of modernization theories as proposed by Daniel Lerner's *The Passing of Traditional Society: Modernizing the Middle East*, published in 1958.[13] In this work there is an easy equation between modernity and urban society. In modernization theory, it has been generally argued that if modernizing elites were interested in the articulation and supervision of development strategies for their countries, and remained engaged with the task of 'nation-building' – that is, of creating viable national societies from their culturally diverse populations – then there would be a steady progress towards industrialization.[14] A noted Pakistani developmental sociologist, who was then studying in the US, recorded in his article:

> In fact the prevailing wisdom in America at the time seemed to favour the rise of authoritarian military regimes in developing countries. Such regimes, it was argued, promoted political stability, a prerequisite for development, and provided suitable nurturing grounds for badly needed 'modernising elite'.[15]

Karl Wittfogel wrote a book which, following Marx's despatch to the *New York Daily Tribune* on 25 June 1853, was called *Oriental Despotism*. It was fondly quoted by Harry Feldman, and yet Feldman failed to recognize that oriental despots were partly the creatures of Western foreign policy.[16] American policy makers, particularly during Eisenhower's time, regarded Ayub Khan and his associates in the army as ideal modernizers. Later, in 1967, Samuel Huntington, a political scientist who specialized in studying political order and had deeper influence in policymaking circle, wrote appreciatively: 'More than any other leader in a modernizing country after World War II, Ayub Khan came close to filling the role of a Solon or Lycurgus or Great Legislator on a Platonic or Rousseauian Model.'[17]

What were Ayub Khan's policies that earned him praise from US policy makers and academics? How did he actualize his role as a modernizer? In 1958 Ayub Khan consolidated his coup through a series of repressive measures. He instituted special military courts throughout the country. Presidential decree authorized these courts to provide wide ranging punishments 'except death, transportation, or imprisonment exceeding one year or whipping exceeding fifteen stripes'. He ordered arrests of politicians associated with the previous regime. The elderly among them were placed under house arrests. In 1959 the government promulgated the Public Conduct Scrutiny Ordinance, the Scrutiny Ordinance, and the Public Offices (Disqualification) Order. These Ordinances empowered review boards to judge misconduct of public officials. Military officers had a decisive say in these review boards. By July 1959 approximately 1,662 officials had been punished, and 813 among them were dismissed. Not satisfied with such sweeping measures, Ayub Khan further issued, on 6 August 1959, the Elective Bodies (Disqualification) Ordinance, instituted special tribunals to try former political leaders for their 'misconduct' and banished 7,000 people from politics.[18] In East Pakistan all prominent Awami League leaders such as Abul Mansur Ahmad, Sheikh Mujib, Mansur Ali, Korban Ali, Hamidul Haq Chowdhury and Nuruddin Shaben Chowdury faced false cases regarding corruption and were sent to prison, though a high court later threw out such ridiculous cases against them.[19] As a consequence, in January 1962, the government further reinforced prohibitions on the attendance and address of any meeting or procession and, on 30 January, arrested civilian ex-prime minister Suhrawardy, who was immensely popular in East Pakistan.[20] Ayub Khan then amended the Security of Pakistan Act, 1952, to rescind writs of habeas corpus of political detainees from the jurisdiction of the courts. On 2 April 1962, prior to the withdrawal of the martial law, the government even threatened to intrude in mosques if they held political meetings under the garb of religious congregation.[21] Ayub Khan peppered these coercive measures with whirlwind tours in different parts of the country and presented his coup as a revolution geared towards the institution of a constitutional democratic regime appropriate for the 'genius of Pakistani people'.[22]

Ayub Khan no doubt had a 'vision' of political system appropriate for Pakistan. In 1954, after becoming the defence minister of the country, he clearly stated his vision in a document entitled 'Present and Future of Pakistan' for a highly centralized presidential form of government, whereby the president would be perceived to be in charge of both executive and legal functions. He specifically mentioned that laws would be operative if only they were certified by the president, except on rare occasions when they would be passed by a three-fourth majority. There could not be any amendment of the Constitution unless agreed to by the president.[23] He also envisaged, in that document, an indirect system of electorate. The document reflected a continuation with the idea of vice regal authority as instituted by Jinnah, the founding leader of the country.[24] As a military officer who was trained in colonial army, Ayub Khan had a romantic vision of rural society that was supposedly isolated from the outside world. He retained a fond memory of rural society in the NWFP where he was born.[25] He obviously wanted to sideline the newly emerging urban middle class who were enamoured with the idea of a parliamentary democracy. Though the façade of parliamentary rule in the fifties benefitted the old landholding families of West Pakistan, these families had little to fear from Ayub Khan's penchant for centralized modernist regime that would essentially continue with a colonial format of governance. They expected such top–down form of governance to benefit their interests too.

In the early sixties, when Ayub Khan looked beyond Pakistan to his South Asian neighbourhood, he obviously noticed that the Nepali monarch had disbanded parliamentary democracy on 15 December 1960.[26] Ayub Khan, who himself was absolutely determined to institutionalize the authoritarian regime he established, was no doubt inspired by these political developments. As he packaged his coup as a revolution, he euphemistically termed his first crucial efforts to institutionalize his political system 'Basic Democracy'. He chose the first anniversary of his coup as the occasion for the introduction of Basic Democracy and introduced the system on 27 October 1959.[27] In East Pakistan the system was similar to the Village Self Government Act which was introduced in 1919 during the colonial era.[28] The previous colonial Act had created a two-tier village government through the Union Board and the District Board. The system of Basic Democracies created a five-tier arrangement of councils. At the lowest rung were the Union Councils. Under this system, five or more villages, with a total population of 10,000–15,000, were grouped into one constituency, electing one Union Council representative for every 800–1,500 inhabitants through universal adult franchise.[29] The candidates thus elected would comprise two-thirds of the Union Council's total membership, with the balance being appointed members. The Union Council was empowered to elect a chairman from among its own membership. The chairmen played an important part in the new setup, for they were ex-officio members of the councils at the next higher level, the Tahsil Councils, which had powers of supervision over all the actions taken by the Union Councils.[30] Some of these ex-officio members qualified for nomination to councils at higher levels so that ultimately these chairmen of Union Councils could reach the top of the administrative pyramid by obtaining a seat in the Provincial Council.

The second tier consisted of the Thana, or Tehsil Councils. Their jurisdiction extended over an area of about 10 Union Councils. These bodies primarily acted as a communications link through which public policy was directed to the Union Councils. The next tier, the District Councils, constituted the most important unit in Basic Democracy. These District Councils under the Basic Democracy were responsible for, among other important subjects, agriculture and food security.[31] The Divisional Councils, the fourth tier, were merely a coordinating body, and, lastly, the Provincial Councils had no power; they were simply thought to be a poor substitute for a provincial legislative body.[32]

Behind the façade of this so-called democratic setup, the bureaucracy, mainly high-ranking officials from the CSP, played a crucial role. The divisional commissioner, a high-ranking bureaucrat, could determine the number of members of the Union Council. The sub-divisional officer and district commissioner, a rank lower than division commissioner, had been empowered to appoint nominated members. The de facto chairman of the Tehsil Council was the sub-divisional officer and, in his absence, the circle officer, an ex officio member of the Council. Government officials, specified by the divisional commissioner, were 'official' members of the District Council, and the chairman of the District Council was the deputy (district) commissioner.[33] The political system under Basic Democracy, in effect, placed the sub-divisional officers, deputy (district) commissioners and (divisional) commissioners in charge of rural development administration. In 1965, the Ayub Khan regime decreed that all members of the Union Council would be elected, but this did nothing to reduce the power of bureaucrats, who pulled the strings from behind and controlled the funding through works programme in the villages.[34] Thus, Basic Democracy could be termed as a method of incorporating bureaucrats as junior partners in the governance of the country.

In 1959, 40,000 Basic Democrats were elected from East Pakistan and West Pakistan each. Eight thousand units of Basic Democracy were created for electing 10 members who, in turn, constituted the electoral college for the presidential election.[35] This system of election with its indirect pyramidical structure continued till the dismantling of the Ayub Khan regime in 1969. Who were these Basic Democrats in East Pakistan? Rashiduzzaman provides a picture of the nature of rural society and the position of Basic Democrats in rural social hierarchy. According to a survey cited in his work, nearly 77.78 per cent of elected members of the Union Councils were agriculturalists, around 16.96 were contractors and the rest 5.6 per cent were lawyers, doctors or school teachers.[36] In a survey of 3,675 members of the Union Board chairmen, it was found that nearly 61.12 per cent of chairmen had an annual income of 4,000 rupees and above, around 28.79 had an annual income between 2,000 and 4,000 rupees, and only 9.69 per cent claimed an income less than 2,000 rupees per annum.[37] In this period, 85.7 per cent of the rural population had an annual income of less than 2,000 rupees per year. Apart from income, in terms of the size of their landholdings, nearly 42.40 per cent of the Basic Democrats in East Pakistan had more than 13.5 acres of land. Around 40.41 per cent of Basic Democrats had 5–7.50 acres of land. In terms of average rural landholding size in East Pakistan, 62.81 per cent of Basic Democrats were holders of large farms.[38] It can be concluded that large numbers of Basic Democrats were recruited from the class of surplus farmers who could be classified as rich peasants. However, at the district level in 1964, 24 per cent of the Basic Democrats were contractors and businessmen.[39] In other words, at the lowest level the Ayub Khan regime recruited rich peasants. Since the British period, colonial rulers' search for collaborators in local societies had led them towards recruiting rural notables. Ayub Khan's regime was no exception. The military-bureaucratic order under Ayub Khan represented a class coalition of rural magnates, rich peasants and big businesses, but excluded the poor and middle peasants, urban working classes and the burgeoning middle classes.

Ayub Khan had another utility for the Basic Democracy system. Soon after the first election of the Basic Democrats on 13 January 1960, he called for a referendum on his regime by the Basic Democrats. This decree also enabled him to initiate a constitution. An election was held among the Basic Democrats on 14 January 1960. The ballot paper was printed in a way so that it would only allow a 'yes' vote. Each ballot was numbered and registered for a specific voter in order to enable the government to identify the ballots of the people. Such a 'democratic' electoral exercise yielded a verdict of 75,282 votes for the president out of a total 78,720 votes. On 17 January, Ayub Khan assumed the position of the president of Islamic Republic of Pakistan, relinquishing his old title of martial law administrator.[40]

He then appointed the Constitution Commission comprising 11 'constitutionalists', including two retired judges, a lawyer and two prominent businessmen. A retired chief justice of Pakistan, Mohammad Shahabuddin, was appointed the president of the commission. The commission completed its work on 29 April 1961.[41] It consulted major political figures in the country through questionnaires and thus claimed that it consulted a significant section of opinion makers among the elites, including former prime minister Bogra. Ayub Khan then appointed special committees to further amend the proposals and completely altered the draft prepared by Shahabuddin. The last stage of Constitution-making commenced with the governors' conference in Dacca opened on 23 October 1961.[42]

The Constitution that was formally adopted by Ayub Khan can be termed as presidential tyranny tempered by the electoral college of Basic Democrats. Despite this, the Ayub Khan regime maintained a farce of democracy through the creation of a national assembly. The national assembly of Pakistan consisted of only one house, having 156 members, with a half of them elected through the electoral college from East Pakistan and the other half similarly elected from West Pakistan. Again, Basic Democrats formed the electoral college.[43] The president could summon and prorogue and even dissolve the assembly. There was one important restriction: if the president dissolved the national assembly, he himself was obliged to seek re-election within 120 days from the date of the dissolution. The president could not also dissolve the national assembly within the first 120 days of its formation or if a formal notice of impeachment of the president had been served, though the right to impeach the president ultimately belonged to the Basic Democrats.[44] According to the new constitutional provisions, the finance minister had to present the budget to the national assembly, and yet the Constitution had made it clear that the national assembly of Pakistan had effective control *only* over that part of the budget that dealt with new expenditure. Recurrent expenditure was not brought under the purview of the national assembly although there were demands for such a scrutiny by the national assembly among politicians. Almost entirely following the colonial practice between 1921 and 1947, the 1962 Constitution divided the budget into votable and non-votable portions, and the national assembly could only vote for a small percentage of the budget.[45] Through this Constitution, Ayub Khan successfully disenfranchised the urban middle classes, squashed any possibilities of popular articulation through legislative process, even though the national assembly often refused to abide by his dictates, and stamped the army's authority on the governance of Pakistan for an indefinite period.

The vexed question of the status of East Pakistan no doubt drew the attention of Ayub Khan. Indeed, in his autobiography, written nearly six years after the shambolic process of Constitution-making in 1961, he observed:

> East Bengalis who constitute the bulk of the population probably belong to very original Indian races. It would be no exaggeration to say that up to the creation of Pakistan, they had not known any real sovereignty. They have been in turn ruled by caste Hindus, Moguls, Pathans or the British. In addition, they have been and still are under considerable Hindu cultural and linguistic influence. As such they have all the inhibitions of the down-trodden races and have not yet found it possible to adjust psychologically to the requirements of newborn freedom. Their popular complexes, exclusiveness, suspicion, and a sort of defensive aggressiveness probably emerge from this historical background. Prudence, therefore, demands that these factors should be recognized and catered for and they helped so as to feel equal partners and prove an asset. That can be done if they are given considerable measure of partnership.[46]

With these patronizing words, the president actually spelled out the constitutional arrangement for East Pakistan as a province. It was clear that he did not want them to have a greater say in the administration of Pakistan because they constituted the majority of the population. But to be fair to Ayub Khan, neither did he give the people of West Pakistan any meaningful say in his administration. His new Constitution for East Pakistan turned out to be a gubernatorial autocracy moderated by presidential 'viceregal' control. The governor was not an elected official, and he served at the pleasure of the president. The provincial governor's ministers and parliamentary secretaries required prior presidential approval, and the governor had to report to the president alone.[47] The governor in the provinces did not have to abide by the legislature in making legislation, and even if the legislature passed a legislation by a two-third majority, the governor could veto it. If the legislature continued to pass the legislation in opposition to the governor for a second time with a two-third support, the governor could request the president to refer the matter to the national assembly. Only if the national legislature approved the Bill, it might then become a law.[48] Political powers were distributed among three categories – federal, concurrent and provincial – but in an emergency the national legislature had supreme authority to legislate in all matters, and the federal government commanded residual power over the concurrent lists.[49] Thus, Ayub Khan successfully brushed the issue of provincial autonomy under the carpet.

Praetorian Capitalism and Internal Colonization: The 'Decade of Development' and Growing Economic Inequity

In 1947, at the time of her birth, Pakistan inherited the world's largest irrigation system from the colonial rulers.[50] This was primarily located in West Pakistan. However, the industrial inheritance of Pakistan from colonial India was meagre. The geographic location of Pakistan was such that only 9.6 per cent of the total number of industrial units (1,414 out of 14,677), 5.3 per cent of the electric capacity (72,700 kilowatts out of a total capacity of 1,375,000 kilowatts) and only 10 per cent of the known mineral deposits fell into the territory designated under Pakistan.[51] Most of the industrial units were small-scale, usually simple home-based production. Indeed, out of 451 textile factories and 160 sugar factories of British India, only 16 and 5, respectively, were located in Pakistan. Even East Pakistan, which was a jute-growing area, had none of the 91 jute mills located within its boundaries. Yet, in the 15 years between 1949–50 and 1964–65, the manufacturing sector of Pakistani industries increased at nearly 15 per cent per year, though the rate of increase in real per capita income in Pakistan was less than 1 per cent per year.[52] At the same time, it has been observed that the level of per capita income was at least 30 per cent higher in West Pakistan than in East Pakistan in 1964–65, though this difference had been only 10 per cent higher in West Pakistan's favour in 1949–50.[53] What factors accounted for this remarkable industrial growth and unremarkable transformation in the per capita income for ordinary Pakistanis? Why did the income gap between East and West Pakistan increase so rapidly? How far did the Ayub Khan regime, with its developmental imperatives, produce equitable development for Pakistan?

The economic transformation in Pakistan and growing inequality between East Pakistan and West Pakistan required an understanding of the operation of industrial policy in Pakistan. The industrial policymaking in Pakistan in the fifties actually facilitated the stranglehold exercised by few West Pakistani mercantile houses over the entire economy. Import–export control became a very powerful tool to shape the industrialization policy and guide the resource allocation process. The government preferred to grant import licenses to migrant bourgeoisie during 1950–52, and the bureaucracy controlled the investment and production for political purposes. West Pakistani bureaucrats who occupied pivotal position in the government granted such licenses to largely immigrant Gujarati trading communities. From the beginning, the government emphasized cooperation with the private sector. The Pakistan Industrial Development Corporation, which was established in 1952, to facilitate industrialization, had a heavy representation of incipient industrial houses of West Pakistan. Pakistan also decided from early stage of its industrialization to sell public-sector industries to the private sector.[54] As a consequence, in 1961, 17 industrial houses from West Pakistan controlled 30 per cent of gross fixed assets and 20 per cent of the total sales of large manufacturing sectors.[55] Most of these families were Gujarati-speaking Khoja, Bohra and Memon families who moved from India to Pakistan and settled down in Karachi and its environs. Two Punjabi mercantile houses, Saigol and Colony, also figured prominently.[56] Even in East Pakistan six houses – namely Adamjee, Dawood, Karim, Bawani, Ispahani and Amin – controlled 40 per cent of the total assets in the manufacturing sector and 32 per cent of the production in large-scale manufacturing sectors.[57] Except for Ispahani, which was originally a Calcutta-based trading house of Iranian origin, all these groups belonged to either Karachi-based Gujarati immigrant families or Punjabi families. East Pakistani local mercantile houses were nowhere near in establishing themselves in the industrial scenario of their own province. As the Karachi-based industrialists established their stranglehold on jute, *the* pivotal industry in East Pakistan, these industrial houses could siphon surplus from East Pakistan to West Pakistan and initiated a process of industrialization in the city of Karachi and its environs. Thus, two processes operated simultaneously: the rise of quasi-monopolistic control and regional and class-based inequities in society.

Yet, from the mid-fifties the boom initiated by the Korean War through the export of raw jute and cotton came to a halt. In 1955 Pakistan devalued the rupee,[58] but there did not take place any significant expansion in the domestic market, and this acted as a constraint on the industrialization process. With the devaluation of the rupee, it became extremely costly to import machines to set up new industries. More importantly, the Pakistani government had to invest a significant amount of capital to bolster its defence arrangement. A cursory glance at the government spending in the economy indicated that the government prioritized defence spending. In 1947–48, the government spent nearly 50 per cent of its expenditure on defence budget; in 1950 it increased to 51 per cent, and in 1961 it increased to 58.7 per cent.[59] The threat to this crucial aspect of a garrison state, based upon the old colonial institutional arrangement of viceregal governance, actualized the army's direct intervention. The military accessed political power in order to disenfranchise the popular constituencies that were threatening to undermine the overall system of the bureaucratic-military structure.

The military-bureaucratic regime under Ayub Khan made a strategic intervention in the economy to bolster up a process of industrialization. The Ayub Khan regime rescinded the licensing system of the import substitution era in the fifties. As a consequence, industrial houses could import raw materials and expand their productive capabilities. The military-bureaucratic regime also circumvented the high exchange rate of rupees by formulating a bonus voucher system providing exporters of manufactured goods an 'export bonus' through an additional access to foreign exchange in hard currencies. With these policies, the Ayub Khan regime no doubt ushered in a process of rapid industrialization. In the first half of the sixties there took place a 17 per cent expansion in the large industrial sector. The gross national product of Pakistan rose by 5.5 per cent, and throughout the sixties the per capita gross national product increased by 3 per cent.[60] Between 1959 and 1969, East Pakistan also witnessed rapid industrialization. In 1962 the Pakistan Industrial Development Corporation, a government concern, invested to set up 21 industrial units. These included 12 jute industrial units, one cotton textile unit, two paper mills, two ship repairing units, two sugar refineries and one fertilizer factory. In 1962 the government constituted the East Pakistan Industrial Development Corporation (EPIDC). The EPIDC invested in 38 industrial units including steel factory. Thus, between 1959 and 1968 the number of government-sponsored industrial units increased from 1,524 to 3,538. Between 1958–59 and 1964–65 the industrial progress in East Pakistan increased to 14.02 per cent, but between 1963 and 1964 and 1968–69 it again fell to 6.69 per cent despite heavy investment.[61] Interestingly, according to Lenin Azad, while large industrial units between 1963 and 1964 struggled to maintain their existence, small industrial units maintained a steady pace of expansion of an annual 4.37 per cent. In fact, in terms of sales statistics, since 1963–64 small industrial units sold more products comparatively than large industrial units, and they had a significantly higher profit margin despite much smaller degree of state help.[62] This obviously indicates that smaller industrial units had a different dynamism of growth which had a different implication in terms of the pattern of class formation in East Pakistan.

In the early sixties there took place a critical expansion among the small industrialist class in East Pakistan. A class of industrialists emerged from the ranks of traders. The government provided foreign exchange certificates to East Pakistani traders based in Dacca and Chittagong. Various industrial schemes facilitated the rise of a small industrialist class mostly recruited from the Bengali traders. While many among them supported the industrial drive of the military-bureaucratic regime, they also faced a significant degree of competition from the West Pakistan-based large industrial houses. They were thus ambivalent in their political support to the military-bureaucratic regime and remained sympathetic to the constitutional movement for autonomy in East Pakistan and the transformation towards democracy.

This industrialization was possible through various forms of aids, soft loans and credits offered by the government to the already existing large industrial houses. Between 1958 and 1970, M. H Khan noted that the Pakistan Industrial Credit and Investment Corporation lent 45 per cent of its loans to 13 monopoly industrial houses.[63] Similarly, the Industrial Development Bank of Pakistan, which provided small loans, lent 32 per cent of its loans to 30 monopoly houses.[64] According to Mushtaq Khan, these state-controlled industrial banks 'allocated about a fifth of industrial investment during this period', and among the 17 privately owned banks, 7 were directly under the control of the very same large business houses.[65] The result, as Pakistani economist Rashid Amjad argued, was that the top 18 groups controlled 35 per cent of the industrial assets, while the top 44 houses controlled around 50 per cent.[66] A crucial feature of this industrialization was the suppression of real wages of the workers. In 1954 the share of wages in the value-added manufacturing industry was 45 per cent, but it dropped to 25 per cent by 1967.[67] There is no doubt that data are scanty regarding real wages of workers in Pakistan. Yet, in an article written in 1967, Azizur Rahman Khan guessed that in East Pakistan the wage rate declined from 1955 to 1959 fairly rapidly and then recovered a good deal, but even in 1963 it was lower than in the base year of 1955.[68] Thus, industrialization without redistribution created a significant degree of class differentiation. More importantly, it expanded the number of industrial workers who were concentrated in large conurbations in Pakistan. In East Pakistan they were concentrated in Dacca and Chittagong, and this enabled industrial working class to be a critical factor in the politics of the province.

Pakistan achieved this remarkable industrialization through foreign aid. Obviously, a significant amount of foreign aid in 1954 was received by the Pakistani army. The US provided 250 million dollars' worth of arms and ammunitions to Pakistan. Top military officials were provided training in the US.[69] In 1955, when Pakistan introduced the first Five-Year Plan, the US provided generous grants and helped establish the Pakistan Institute of Development Economics. Edward Mason, Gustav Papanek and Stephen Lewis, known as the Harvard advisory group, came to Pakistan as government advisors. Their plan to reduce West Pakistani dependence on Indian water became a significant success through the Indus Basin Development project in 1960 as the US, the UK, Australia, Canada, New Zealand, West Germany and the International Bank for Reconstruction and Development (IBRD) agreed to invest 867 million dollars (including 632 million dollars in foreign exchange) in West Pakistan over a 10-year period.[70] In 1960 the IBRD acceded to Pakistan's request and formed a consortium of foreign-aid-supplying countries. This consortium, at its second meeting in June 1961, committed another 320 million dollars of aid for 1961–62.[71] On 14 October 1961, the US further agreed to provide 621 million dollars' worth of agricultural commodities stretched over another four years and to accept non-convertible rupees in payment under the Public Law 480 scheme.[72] Finally, on 24 and 25 January 1962, the consortium further provided 625 million dollars.[73] Responding to US loans, the Soviet Union also granted an aid of 30 million dollars for oil exploration, and even the PRC provided 66.9 million dollars without any interest.[74] Thus, the ready availability of foreign aid actually bankrolled this industrial expansion, whereby, in the words of Papenek, Pakistani 'robber barons' could establish a presence on the industrial map. They also acquired surplus through squeezing the peasant subsistence agriculture.[75] As the terms of trade between the industrial sector and the agricultural sector were heavily biased in favour of the latter, the subsistence peasants had to bear the burden of industrialization.

Apart from the overall implications of sharpening class differences, this industrialization had significant effects on regional imbalances. While both West and East Pakistan benefitted from the industrialization driven by foreign aid, East Pakistan became a captive market for West Pakistani goods. In return, East Pakistan exported raw materials necessary for the industrialization of West Pakistan. Between 1964–65 and 1969–70 the exports of finished industrial products from West Pakistan to East Pakistan increased by 93.9 per cent. In rupee terms they increased from 85.2 crores to 165.2 crores. During this period, trade surplus in favour of West Pakistan expanded by 132.2 per cent, or, in rupee terms, from 31.6 crores in 1964–65 to 73.6 crores in 1969–70.[76] According to Shahid Javed Burki, West Pakistan imported approximately 8.8 per cent of primary commodities from East Pakistan in 1964–65, and within five years the volume of import from East Pakistan doubled to 17.7 per cent. Thus, the trading pattern between West Pakistan and East Pakistan reflected a situation of internal colonization. According to John Thomas Woodward, the net transfer of resources from East to West Pakistan, and the expenditure of only about one-third of Pakistan's development resources in East Pakistan, led towards stagnation in the economy. As a consequence, in the 23 years of united Pakistan's existence, the per capita income of East Pakistan rose by only two dollars.[77] The social coalition of monopoly industrial houses, landlords and rich peasants, buttressed by an institutional arrangement of military and bureaucracy, constituted the most remarkable feature of praetorian capitalism that flourished at the expense of the rural poor, urban industrial working classes and segments of middle classes. This praetorian capitalism also contributed towards regional imbalances that matured into the internal colonization of East Pakistan.

Population, Growth, Agriculture and Rural Poverty

East Pakistan is located in a fertile alluvial plain fed by the three mighty river systems of the Ganges, the Meghna, and the Brahmaputra, which discharges every year 650,000,000 cubic metre of water.[78] Seasonal monsoon adds to this massive flow of water. As the fertility of the soil produces an abundance of rice crops, the region recorded massive population growth. As per the 1961 census, nearly 95 per cent of East Pakistan's 50 million people resided in some 65,000 villages, and the overall density approached closely to 1,000 people per square mile.[79] Between 1951 and 1961, the census data recorded an annual average population growth rate of over 2 per cent. With this heavy dependence on agriculture, approximately 80 per cent of the agricultural labour force was made up of owner-cultivators or unpaid family labour.[80] Yet these overall statistics of population growth hide a crucial factor. According to Rehman Sobhan, a noted economist, in 1951, approximately 83.51 per cent of the people in East Pakistan depended on agriculture. In 1961 the overall percentage increased to 85.26 per cent. In West Pakistan there took place, during this period, despite an overall population increase, a decline in the number of people engaged in agriculture from 65 per cent to

59.31 per cent.[81] Thus, a regional disparity persisted in the political economy of the development.

More ominously for East Pakistan there also existed a tendency towards an increase in the number of landless agricultural workers. Moving back to the slightly earlier era of the late fifties and the early sixties, Swadesh Ranjan Bose argues that between 1951 and 1961, while the agricultural labour force increased by 33.8 per cent, the number of landless workers increased by 63.6 per cent.[82] From 1961 to 1974, the male labour force in Bangladesh increased by 27 per cent. The labour force, who work for hire, expanded by 42 per cent during 1961–74 compared to the growth rate of 27 per cent in the fifties.[83] The population pressure also led to a decline in the size of farms. According to Mohiuddin Alamgir, the average size of farms in East Pakistan declined from 3.5 acres in 1960 to 3.2 acres in 1967–68. He further asserts that the average size of holdings did not vary much in the different regions within the country.[84] The pressure of steady population growth contributed towards subdivision and fragmentation of farms. The law of inheritance pushed towards the small sizes as well, and this was further supplemented by the natural pauperization process under the pressure of money lenders. Yet population growth was not the only reason for the decline of the living conditions of the rural poor.

Sobhan drew a picture of abject poverty and exploitation by rich peasants, or the so-called surplus farmers. In East Pakistan, Sobhan maintains, only 37 per cent of households in rural areas had domestic livestock. On the other hand, the top 10 per cent landholders controlled 37 per cent of all work animals in East Pakistan.[85] Nearly 64 per cent of the villages reported that they did not have enough work animals to till the land.[86] One-third of all holdings reported that they did not have access to ploughs. The number of ploughs increased as holdings became larger.[87] As a consequence, these small farmers depended on large farmers for credit, ploughs and even food. This resulted in high levels of indebtedness among small farmers. At the end, when they could not repay their debts and remained hard-pressed for everyday livelihood, they sold their land and joined the ranks of landless workers.

Indeed, poverty was so pervasive that 87 per cent of rural people had an annual income of 366 Pakistani rupees.[88] According to Sobhan's survey, 67 per cent of the monthly budget of the average peasant household was spent on food, primarily consisting of rice and cereal. Even fish, which was the principal source of protein for East Pakistani peasants, were not part of regular diet.[89] Nearly 6.3 per cent was spent on clothing and footwear, 14.5 per cent on household items and 12.3 per cent on miscellaneous items.[90] Nearly 60.3 per cent of the peasants interviewed by Sobhan and his team answered that they could not support themselves from their landholdings in a 'good' year, and this number increased to 84.4 per cent.[91]

Village Society, Agrarian Structure and Social Classes

The classic village structure in the sixties, according to an anthropologist studying rural East Bengal, corresponded more to Clifford Geertz's description of villages in rural Indonesia:

> In no sense ... corporate territorial unit(s) coordinating all aspects of life in terms of residence and land ownership, as peasant communities have commonly been described, but [they are] rather a compound of social structures, each based on a different principle of social affiliation.[92]

This compound social structure was revealed in social organization, fluid ritual-based social stratification and changing landholding pattern indicating the sharpening of class polarization in the rural economy in the sixties. In a rather insightful observation, Peter J. Bertocci has drawn the picture of social organization in the villages. For Bertocci, who conducted the anthropological study of two villages in Comilla in the sixties, the typical village, called *gram* in Bengali, consisted of homestead clusters. The leadership of these villages came from affluent lineages that were called *sardari* lineages, and their members were known as *sardar*s (also *matabbar*s).[93] In a single village there existed several subgroupings whose members were variously loyal to one or the other of several *sardar*s. These groupings were designated locally in Comilla *reyai*, which in quotidian parlance meant 'protégé'. Several *sardar*s from different *gram*s constituted a formal council of elders who decided disputes involving members of this larger multi-village community.[94] Collectively for the villagers this entire assemblage was called *samaj*, meaning society or community in Bengali. It was obviously a symbolic community as the *samaj* did not have a definite territory and operated through networks surrounding the local market.[95] Bertocci also found that though caste did not constitute an elaborate social organization in rural East Bengal among Muslims, there are certain genealogies associated with names that indicate affiliation to social status based upon a secular affiliation with pre-colonial governmental positions or religious work. These names were regarded with respect in rural Muslim society, and some people were referred to as *uccha bongsho* (high-status lineage), others as *majhari bongsho* (middle-status lineage) and rest as *nichu bonghsho* (low-status lineage), though most were referred to as *grihastha*, or householder.[96] Yet, after a careful observation, Bertocci concludes with a quote from Max Weber: '... while property and status did not always coincide and yet in the long run they tended to do so with extraordinary regularity.'[97] Thus it brings forth the issue of class division in rural Bangladesh.

The term 'class' obviously does not indicate a critical watertight vertical compartmentalization of rural society. André Beteille has cautioned us against using the terms 'rich peasants', 'middle peasants' and 'poor peasants', and he also argued that the term *jotedar* does not indicate a homogenous category of an exploiting, landholding social class.[98] Yet, in his miniscule study of two villages in Comilla, Bertocci confirms the existence of a class structure in rural Bengal, though it is not similar to the Leninist categorization of 'rich peasants', 'middle peasants' and 'poor peasants'. According to Bertocci, nearly 50 per cent of the peasants in the villages he studied were poor and landless, 39 per cent were marginal and subsistence peasants and 11 per cent were surplus farmers. It was these surplus farmers who were categorized by Bertocci as 'middle peasants'.[99] Harry Blair maintains that the possession of 3–4 acres would enable the owner to attain 'middle peasant' status – that is, a peasant who will have some surplus available for the market, will employ some labour off the farm and will derive some of his income from activities outside agriculture.[100] While there is no doubt that the 'middle peasants' dominated in Bangladesh politics both socially and economically, the upper layers of these surplus farmers, as many economists call them, were rich peasants who controlled far more amount of land than the ordinary middle-peasant farms of 3–4 acres. In a co-authored article, Abu Abdullah, Mosharaff Hossain and Richard Nation have maintained that farms comprising 12.5 acres constituted a dividing line between 'large' and 'medium' holdings. In 1961, according to their estimate then, large farms constituted only about 3.5 per cent of all farms but operated 19 per cent of the total farm area. However, farms possessing land of 25 acres and above were only about 0.5 per cent of all farms.[101] This finding matches to some extent with the findings of Sobhan, who maintains that 3 per cent of the farms controlled 19 per cent of the cultivated area, 10 per cent of the farms controlled as much as 36 per cent of cultivated area and 51 per cent of the farms were under 2.5 acres in size.[102] Sobhan, from his detailed survey, concluded that while the class of landlords disappeared from East Pakistan, the overall shortage of land compelled poorer farmers to rent land from big farmers for bare survival.[103] Politically, this class of big farmers had dominated the structure of Basic Democracy. For example, as Rashiduzzaman has demonstrated, out of 329 Union Councillors elected in East Pakistan, as per his survey, 42 per cent held 12.5 acres of land and only 2.29 per cent held land of less than 2.5 acres.[104] Ayub Khan's reforms thus actually tried to recruit the upper layer of these surplus farmers as they possessed much higher amounts of land.

Basic Democracy, Cold War Empire and Rural Development

Did the condition of middle peasants, small peasants and agricultural workers improve under Ayub Khan? The answer to this question depends on the relationship between peasant economy and the outside world. The relationship with the outside world was structured through two important nexuses: the state and peasant economy on the one hand and, on the other, the market as the conduit of surplus produced by peasants. We shall first study the impact of the state and then turn our attention to the market.

The state's relationship with the peasant economy was through land revenues, and the state extracted a significant amount of land revenue from subsistence peasant economy. For example, the land revenue in East Pakistan in 1957–58, amounted to 67.5 million rupees, but it increased to 150 million rupees in 1968–69.[105] This was a significant burden on subsistence agriculture.

Nonetheless, the government invested back into agriculture through the Rural Public Works Programme during the Basic Democracy era. According to Woodward, who studied the programme, between 1962 and 1969 the government of Pakistan invested 168 million dollars in the programme in East Pakistan. This amounted to 8 per cent of the annual developmental budget in East Pakistan.[106] Here, again, the Cold War imperial presence of the US was evident. The money for the programme came from the Public Law 480 aid provided by the US.

In 1961 Akhter Hameed Khan, a Gandhian, a former Indian Civil Service officer and the director of the Village Agricultural and Industrial Development programme, developed a model of integrated rural development for the East Pakistan Academy for Rural Development. Hameed Khan was an unusual director who was known for his integrity, commitment and dedication to the cause of eradication of poverty from rural society. The Comilla model involved pilot projects for flood control, drainage of water and local irrigation, the formation of cooperatives, extension of loans to women for animal husbandry and the use of family-planning devices for women. In an article, Tariq Omar Ali traces how the programme was tied to the modernization theory and the Cold War liberal empire of the US.[107] The use of pre-existing Gandhian Abhoy Ashram as the headquarter for the programme was embedded in the countryside and the Kotbari constructed by Constantinos Doxiadis, who developed his architectural style as a blend of modernity with tradition and symbolized the liberal free-market architectural style as opposed to the Soviet central planning.[108] The programme thus symbolized US-sponsored technological solutions to the problems of social inequity and resource scarcity. Technological solutions imported from the outside and imposed from above without recognizing the agency of the local population and social structure remained part and parcel of the Cold War-induced imperial model of growth without social equity. Indeed, the leadership of cooperatives sponsored by the Comilla project remained in the hands of rich and middle peasants. They also befitted from the irrigation facilities. Many of them were engaged in subsidiary activities outside agriculture and could thus diversify their incomes.[109]

Yet, despite such planning, foreign involvement and the investment of the East Pakistan government in the rural development programme during the Basic Democracy era, the efficacy of the programme remained doubtful. Woodward blamed the mismanagement after 1965 on the political intervention of Ayub Khan-loyalist governor Monem Khan's administration in East Pakistan.[110] Sobhan severely criticized the Rural Public Works Programme. According to Sobhan, even in Comilla where the government supervised the integrated rural work programme, the number of people earning less than Pakistani 1,000 rupees had increased between 1957–58 and 1963–64 from 38.9 per cent to 52.4 per cent.[111] Overall the ranks of the upper-income group had swelled up, but a far larger number of people were moving down in terms of annual income, and, according to Sobhan, the incidence of pauperization among a vast number of peasants increased.[112] To move back to the issue of taxation, it seems that heavy increase in taxations did not bring tangible benefits to the peasants, except adding to their misery. The real beneficiaries of these programmes were the rich peasants, who, as a social class, expanded their stranglehold on the rural economy at the expense of the subsistence peasants.

This did not diminish the necessary requirement for technological transformation. Indeed, it was an urgent necessity in East Pakistan in the context of water management for irrigation and flood prevention. The irrigation programme also originated within this imperial context of uplifting Third World agriculture in order to avoid a social revolution. In 1957, at the invitation of the East Pakistani government, a team of experts under general Julius Albert Krug, a former head of the US Army Corps of Engineers, visited East Pakistan and informed the establishment of a new autonomous agency of water management outside the existing rigid administrative system. Aid-giving agencies strongly supported their recommendation and, consequently, Ordinance No. 1 of 1959 brought into existence the East Pakistan Water and Power Development Authority to provide centralized control of water resources and power development.[113] The new agency enjoyed significant powers to plan and construct water-resource and power projects, establish rates and collect revenues. The aid donors viewed the autonomous agency as a neat administrative device to enable them to assist the recipient country towards a clear objective. In 1964 the Pakistan Water and Power Development Authority (WAPDA) presented a master plan, for a 20-year programme containing 51 large projects with a total estimated cost of 17.6 billion rupees (3.2 billion dollars) with 46 per cent of the cost, or 1.5 billion dollars, as the estimated foreign exchange requirement. Individual projects ranged in cost from 14.7 million rupees (3.1 million dollars) to 1291 million rupees (271 million dollars).[114] However, political developments interfered with the plan's development. It seems that without democracy, in a situation of internal colonization within the political framework of military-bureaucratic dictatorship, the Cold War mission of imperialistic benevolence collapsed under the quotidian realities of the rural political economic structure.

The dismal picture of the rural development programme contributed to the atmosphere of distrust and hatred towards the Basic Democrats and the corrupt council chairmen among the rural population. It was not easy to assess the reactions of the peasantry to various developmental initiatives of the modernizing military-bureaucratic regime. One can sense their despair through the their response to Sobhan's survey questionnaire. In 1964 Sobhan and his team interviewed 1,816 inhabitants scattered over nearly 40 police precincts (*thana*, the lowest administrative territory in India and the then Pakistan). Nearly 70.4 per cent of the respondents felt they were worse off then than they were 1957.[115] The march of poverty in rural areas continued throughout the Pakistani period. In fact, Kirsten Westergaard argues that in 1963–64 in East Pakistan only 4 per cent of the population were regarded as extreme poor, but in the early seventies nearly 40 per cent were regarded as such. Scholars of political economy categorized the agrarian system in the early seventies as 'below poverty-level equilibrium trap'. The term 'poverty line' refers to the per capita expenditure barely necessary to purchase food and related items adequate for the minimum needs of a person, and 'famine line' represents the level of consumption below which death is much closer.[116] Thus, the much-touted developmental decade of Ayub Khan was marked by a decrease in the living standard of the most vulnerable segment of the population in East Pakistan. Yet noted sociologist and modernization theorist Edward Mason, an American advisor to the Pakistani government, claimed that these programmes were 'probably the most successful attempt to use effectively the services of underemployed agricultural workers that has been undertaken in any less developed country'.[117] The ideologues of the Cold War empire sometimes remained imprisoned in their own imagination.

Islam, Martial Prowess and Praetorian Capitalist Modernization

Like any other post-colonial political entity, the relationship between religion and state, and its implications in politics and even quotidian life, was never worked out fully, and there already existed a notion of 'Muslim becoming' in Pakistan. Pakistan came into existence as a Muslim homeland, and Jinnah, as the pivotal leader of Pakistan, believed that he would be able to steer the country towards a secular polity whereby religious differences would be confined to private space. In his address to the national assembly on 11 August 1947, he made a strategic declaration to that effect.[118] Obviously, Jinnah's various utterances could be interpreted in a contradictory manner, but this speech inspired those who believed that religion should be separate from politics. Many among Bengali litterateurs in East Pakistan highlighted the speech as a critical foundational principle of the Pakistani state. In 1954, after the victory of the United Front in East Bengal (the name East Pakistan was introduced in 1956), Mofazzal Haidar Chaudhury, in an op-ed in *Dainik Millat*, argued that the separation Jinnah had advocated indicated that Pakistan would be founded as a democracy and not a theocracy.[119] Indeed, during the Ayub Khan regime in 1966, Abdul Haq, a Bengali writer, in an article entitled 'Muslim Nationalism: A Reinvestigation' (Muslim Jatiota

Punorniriksha), published in the Bengali *Samakal* magazine, stated that if in united India the rise of Hindu nationalism was anathema to Muslims, then why in Pakistan would religious nationalism would be an acceptable force? He equated religious nationalism with sectarianism (*samprodaikota*).[120] There were obvious counter-arguments among Bengali intellectuals in East Pakistan, but the topic aroused a lot of debate.

Ayub Khan sought to project his identity as a Muslim modernizer along the lines of Muhammad Ali of Egypt, Mustafa Kemal Atatürk of Turkey, Reza Shah of Iran and Amanullah Khan of Afghanistan. Most soldiers who were socialized in the military circle had a secular orientation towards life. The version of Islam that the military-bureaucratic regime projected was in harmony with praetorian capitalism. Saadia Toor has demonstrated how the Harvard International Development specialists and the US government encouraged the Pakistani establishment to use Islam as a specific kind of ideology to enforce labour discipline and anti-communism.[121] As part of this project, the Pakistani government encouraged in particular the ideological training of army personnel along martial interpretations of Islam, which contradicted the inherent commonsensical humane values associated with the religion.

Yasmin Saikia thus maintains that in 1960, the general headquarters of armed forces in concurrence with the ministry of defence decided to use the ideal of jihad and the notion of *mujahid* (one who engages in jihad) to bolster the morale of the army. Confronting the enemy with gallantry and the spirit of sacrifice for the defence of a Muslim state was emphasized in these programmes as *afzal* (superior) to all other forms of service. The government devised a programme of training soldiers that stressed a special mission combined with regular lectures on nationalism based on religion. It utilized various media of communications, such as the military journal *Daily Hilal* and periodic radio broadcasting, exhibitions, lectures and discussions to instil the spirit of jihad.[122]

Education became another crucial artefact to retrain the nation and homogenize the identity of Pakistanis. In 1952 the government reviewed the education system of Pakistan and formulated a national plan for education. In 1957 the Educational Reforms Commission for East Pakistan also made recommendations, but there did not yet exist a comprehensive programme for education. In 1958 the Ayub Khan government instituted the National Commission of Education under the chairmanship of S. M. Sharif. The commission stressed the ideals of Pakistan as a Muslim nation that had a national purpose of the pursuit of modernity based upon Islamic identity. In 1960 there came into existence the Central Institute of Research which was renamed the Islamic Research Institute in 1962. Its director, Fazlur Rahman, advised educating the *ulema* (body of Muslim scholars) through setting up an academy known as the Department of Awqaf, and, in 1963, Al-Jamia al-Islamiya was established as a university on the model of the Al-Azhar University in Cairo. At the same time there took place an attempt to Islamize Pakistan's history and culture.[123]

This attempt to reconcile Islam with the purpose of developing a praetorian capitalism confronted two critical hurdles in East Pakistan. For many among the middle-class literati in West Pakistan, such an emphasis on Islam often regarded Bengali culture as synonymous with Hindu tradition, and this ahistorical claim had led to the marginalization of East Bengali culture. The false equation of culture with religion had been criticized by the Bengali literati. Indeed, Ahmad Sharif, a professor of medieval Bengali at Dacca University, wrote in an article:

> Naoserwa, Janjan, Shareer [pre-Islamic mythical figures from the Middle East] were non-Muslims from foreign land and Vikramaditya, Bhojraraj were our neighbors. If infidel foreigners Shahnuriman, Rostam-Sohrab had become our relatives, then it is difficult to think that our neighbors Bhismo, Dron-Kripo or Bhimarjun [figures in the Mahabharata] were not close to us. This is a self-delusion and an act of self-hatred to a gigantic proportion.[124]

While a sizeable section of the intelligentsia among Bengali middle classes were alienated by the emphasis on the construction of a citizen of a modern state through an Islamized identity based upon north Indian Muslim martial values, Ayub Khan's attempt to foster capitalism also contradicted the values of bucolic Islam existent among peasants.

Here we revisit Comilla academy, the showpiece of US-sponsored praetorian capitalist developmental programmes in rural Bengal, as an example. Omar Ali describes how the academy imagined peasant objections that modern technology interfered in 'God's Will'. The academy identified village *ulema*s as the main culprit in peasant Islam. Akhter Hamid Khan, the dedicated director of the academy, spoke of the contradictory role of *ulema*s in rural society. He held village *ulema*s to be responsible for holding together a sober, morally conscious community that could bear natural adversity with patience; at the same time, he held *ulema*s to be responsible for 'medieval ideas and customs'.[125] According to Hamid Khan, 'ulemas condemned artificial irrigation, or insect control, or chemical fertilisation as arrogant defiance of God's laws which would soon bring His vengeance. And indeed, when the floods came they were proclaimed as the retribution for listening to the Academy's sinful suggestions'.[126] Omar Ali lists the academy's efforts to modernize rural Islam by recruiting *kabiyal*, or village bards, to perform *kabi gan* (rural bard's recital of poems) privileging the academy's perspective, through Hamid Khan's writings in the academy's journal quoting traditional authorities on Islam and organizing tours of Kotbari by the village clergy and even a reorientation training.[127] Of course, the academy's family-planning programme encountered trouble because the contraceptives and intrauterine devices used by the academy caused physical discomfort to women.[128] Yet the village women's troubles were blamed on their superstitions. Ironically, as Omar Ali correctly observes, it had been the bucolic iteration of Islam that had popularized the Pakistan movement in rural Bengal.

Thus, it seems that the praetorian modernism and the US' pedagogic project of producing modernity collapsed under the quotidian realities of rural East Pakistan.

Conclusion

The peculiar programmatic alignment between the Cold War imperial project and the praetorian capitalism of the Pakistani military-bureaucratic regime produced a significant thrust towards industrialization and rural development projects in both wings of Pakistan. Yet the developmental project initiated by the military-bureaucratic regime, with scant regard to social equity, accelerated both industrial development and social inequality. The stranglehold exercised by a handful of West Pakistani business houses over the economy, the fall in the real wages of a burgeoning working class and the persistence of absolute poverty in rural East Pakistan actually exposed glaring social fault lines in Pakistan. More importantly, despite increasing investment in East Pakistan, the military-bureaucratic regime further consolidated the process of its internal colonization, both economically and culturally. Politically, the military-bureaucratic regime institutionalized the dominance of a social coalition of West Pakistan-based monopoly trading houses and landed magnates and rich peasants of East Pakistan. The so-called Basic Democracy obviously consolidated the grip of the army and the elite CSP cadres of bureaucracy over the process of governance, and the army also emerged as a significant economic institution with a role in the production process. Yet the system left the articulate urban salaried social classes and the disgruntled working classes outside the ruling coalition. Rural peasants in East Pakistan remained trapped in poverty. Ideologically, a modernizing praetorian version of masculine Islam left outside its fold both the conservative *ulema*s and progressive middle classes. The condition in East Pakistan was ripe for a social revolution, but objective circumstances of the revolution were not alone sufficient for revolutionary upsurge. The revolution depended on the subjective agents who must be ready to revolt and set fire to a combustible social situation.

Notes

1. Omar Noman, *The Political Economy of Pakistan 1947–85* (London: KPI Limited, 1988), pp. 27–32, 35–43.
2. For details of the analysis of this military-bureaucratic ruling edifice and social coalition, see Hamza Alavi, 'The State in Postcolonial Societies: Pakistan and Bangladesh', in *Imperialism and Revolution in South Asia*, ed. Kathleen Gough, and Hari P. Sharma, pp. 145–73 (New York: Monthly Review Press, 1973). Though I disagree with certain findings of Alavi, it remains one of the most theoretically informed discussions of political economic development of Pakistan.
3. These 22 families exercised control over nearly 66 per cent of the industry, 97 per cent of the insurance and 80 per cent of the banking industry. Noman, *The Political Economy of Pakistan*, pp. 35–43.
4. Ayesha Siddiqa, in her pioneering work on the military's role in economy, evolved a concept of 'milbus', arguing that it involves two aspects: the increasing privatization of security apparatus in developing countries and military engaging in non-traditional economic activities such as farming and running businesses like hotels and airlines. For details, see Ayesha Siddiqa, *Military Inc.: Inside Pakistan's Military Economy* (London: Pluto Press, 2007), p. 6. Also see Chaitram Singh, 'Military Coups in Pakistan and the Corporate Interests Hypothesis', *Journal of Third World Studies* 28, no. 1 (2011): 47–59.

5. Gilbert M. Joseph, 'What We Now Know and Should Know: Bringing Latin America More Meaningfully into Cold War Studies', in *In from the Cold: Latin America's New Encounter with the Cold War*, ed. Gilbert M. Joseph and Daniela Spenser (Durham, NC: Duke University Press, 2008), p. 4.
6. Khan Abdul Ghaffar Khan, *My Life and Struggle: Autobiography of Badshah Khan* (as narrated to K. P. Narang), trans. Helen Bouman (New Delhi: Hind Pocket Books, 1969), p. 134.
7. Zulfiqar Ali Bhutto, *The Myth of Independence* (Oxford: Oxford University Press, 1969), p. 1.
8. Department of State, Central Files, 790D.00/10–1758, Personal and Confidential, https://history.state.gov/historicaldocuments/frus1958-60v15/d330 (accessed on 12 May 2021).
9. Lawrence Ziring, *Pakistan in the Twentieth Century: A Political History* (Karachi, New York, Delhi: Oxford University Press, 1997).
10. Overall, during the Eisenhower administration, Pakistan received a total of 7,921 million dollars of economic aid and 3,130 million dollars of military aid. This was the highest amount of US aid offered to the country between 1947 and 2016. Murad Ali, *The Politics of US Aid to Pakistan: Aid Allocation and Delivery from Truman to Trump* (Routledge Studies in South Asian Politics) (Abingdon, Oxon: Routledge, 2019), p. 33.
11. Walt Whitman Rostow, 'The Stages of Economic Growth', *Economic History Review* (New Series) 12, no. 1 (1959): 1–16, DOI: 10.2307/2591077.
12. Rostow, 'The Stages of Economic Growth', p. 5.
13. Daniel Lerner, Lucille W. Pevsner and David Riesman, *The Passing of Traditional Society: Modernizing the Middle East* (New York: The Free Press, 1964).
14. The the essence of this argument can be found in Francis Bator, Richard Blackmer, Richard Eckaus, Everett Hagen, Daniel Lerner, Max Millikan, Ithiel de Sola Pool, Lucian Pye, Paul Rosenstein-Rodan and Walt Whitman Rostow, 'Economic, Social, and Political Change in the Underdeveloped Countries and Its Implications for United States Policy', a study prepared for the Senate Committee on Foreign Relations, MIT Center for International Studies, Massachusetts Institute of Technology, Cambridge, MA, 30 March 1960.
15. Hassan N. Gardezi and Soofia Mumtaz, 'Globalisation and Pakistan's Dilemma of Development [with Comments]', *Pakistan Development Review*

43, no. 4 (2004): 423–40, http://www.jstor.org/stable/41260697 (accessed on 4 June 2021), p. 425.
16. Karl Wittfogel, *Oriental Despotism: A Comparative Study of Total Power* (New Haven: Yale University Press, 1957), p. 38.
17. Samuel P. Huntington, *Political Order in Changing Societies* (New Haven: Yale University Press, 2006), p. 251.
18. This is based upon the description provided by Karl von Vorys, *Political Development in Pakistan* (Princeton, NJ: Princeton University Press, 1965), pp. 189–91.
19. Abul Mansur Ahmad, *Amar Dekha Rajnitir Ponchas Botsor* (Dhaka: Prothoma Prokashan, 2018), pp. 460–65.
20. A. M. Ahmad, *Amar Dekha Rajnitir Ponchas Botsor*, pp. 466–67.
21. Vorys, *Political Development in Pakistan*, pp. 190–91.
22. 'It is revealing that Ayub, while visiting the rural areas of West Pakistan to explain the system of Basic Democracy in his railroad train called the Pak Jamhuriyat Special (Democracy Express), said that: "It was his desire to see the country as organized as her army"'. Khalid B. Sayeed, 'Pakistan's Basic Democracy', *Middle East Journal* 15, no. 3 (1961): 249–63, p. 250, http://www.jstor.org/stable/4323370 (accessed on 28 May 2021).
23. The text of the memo is reproduced in Vorys, *Political Development in Pakistan*, appendix A, pp. 296–306.
24. Elliot Tepper first mentioned Jinnah's preference for vice regal authority in his article on Pakistan after the departure of Bangladesh. Elliot L. Tepper, 'The New Pakistan: Problems and Prospects', *Pacific Affairs* 47, no. 1 (1974): 56–68, p. 57.
25. Ayub Khan was born in a village called Rehana in the NWFP in British India and came from a family of military servicemen. His father served as Risaladar Major in Hodson's Horse in the British Indian army. He was thus not exposed to urban life till he came to Aligarh in Uttar Pradesh, in present-day India, to study. Mohammad Ayub Khan, *Friends Not Masters: A Political Autobiography* (New York: Oxford University Press, 1967), pp. 2–6.
26. Leo E. Rose and Margaret W. Fisher, *The Politics of Nepal: Persistence and Change in an Asian Monarchy* (New York: Cornell University Press, 1970), p. 53.
27. R. L. Mellema, 'The Basic Democracies System in Pakistan', *Asian Survey* 1, no. 6 (1961): 10–15, p. 10. DOI: 10.2307/3023605.

28. Kirsten Westergaard, *State and Rural Society in Bangladesh: A Study in Relationship* (London: Curzon Press, 1985), p. 51.
29. Sayeed, 'Pakistan's Basic Democracy', pp. 250–51.
30. Harry J. Friedman, 'Notes on Pakistan's Basic Democracies', *Asian Survey* 1, no. 10 (1961): 19–24, p. 21.
31. Sayeed, 'Pakistan's Basic Democracy', pp. 250–55.
32. Vorys, *Political Development in Pakistan*, p.199. Altaf Gauhar also discusses why provincial legislatures were weakened. Altaf Gauhar, *Ayub Khan: Pakistan's First Military Ruler* (New York: Oxford University Press, 1996), p. 83.
33. Commenting on the predominance of officials, Sayeed surmises: 'The fear still remains that, in Basic Democracy, not even Lord Ripon's objective of substituting outside control for inside interference may be achieved because district officers cannot only control Divisional and District Councils in which the officials predominate, but also Union Councils through their nominees'. Sayeed, 'Pakistan's Basic Democracy', p. 254.
34. Lenin Azad, *Unosottorer Gonoobbuththan: Rastro Somaj o Rajniti* (Dhaka: Jatio Sahitya Prokash, 2019 [1997]), p. 90.
35. Yasmin Saikia, 'Ayub Khan and Modern Islam: Transforming Citizens and the Nation in Pakistan', *South Asia: Journal of South Asian* Studies 37, no. 2: 292–305, p. 299.
36. M. Rashiduzzaman, *Politics and Administration in the Local Councils: A Study of Union and District Councils in East Pakistan* (London and Karachi: Oxford University Press, 1968), table 8(iv), p. 37, cited in Azad, *Unosottorer Gonoobbuththan*, p. 91.
37. Azad, *Unosottorer Gonoobbuththan*, pp. 91–94.
38. Azad, *Unosottorer Gonoobbuththan*, pp. 91–94.
39. Westergaard, *State and Rural Society in Bangladesh*, p. 53.
40. Vorys, *Political Development in Pakistan*, p. 202.
41. Vorys, *Political Development in Pakistan*, p. 209.
42. Vorys, *Political Development in Pakistan*, pp. 211–21.
43. M. Rashiduzzaman, 'The National Assembly of Pakistan under the 1962 Constitution', *Pacific Affairs* 42, no. 4 (1969): 481–93, p. 482, DOI: 10.2307/2754129.
44. Rashiduzzaman, 'The National Assembly of Pakistan', p. 482.
45. Rashiduzzaman, 'The National Assembly of Pakistan', p. 485.
46. M. A. Khan, *Friends Not Masters*, p. 187.

47. Vorys, *Political Development in Pakistan*, pp. 227–28.
48. Vorys, *Political Development in Pakistan*, pp. 227–28.
49. Vorys, *Political Development in Pakistan*, p. 226.
50. William Easterly, 'The Political Economy of Growth without Development: A Case Study of Pakistan', Paper for the Analytical Narratives of Growth Project, Kennedy School of Government, Harvard University, 2001, p. 1.
51. Yu V. Gankovsky and L. R. Gordon-Polonskaya, *A History of Pakistan, 1947–1958* (Lahore: People's Publishing House, 1972), pp. 99–100.
52. Stephen R. Lewis, *Economic Policy and Industrial Growth in Pakistan* (London: Allen & Unwin, 1969), p. 1.
53. Lewis, *Policy and Industrial Growth in Pakistan*, p. 1.
54. Rashid Amjad, 'Industrial Concentration and Economic Power', in *Pakistan: The Roots of Dictatorship: The Political Economy of Praetorian State*, ed. Hasssan N. Gardezi and Jamil Rashid, pp. 228–69 (London: Zed Press, 1983), p. 236.
55. Amjad, 'Industrial Concentration and Economic Power', p. 232.
56. Amjad, 'Industrial Concentration and Economic Power', p.234.
57. Amjad, 'Industrial Concentration and Economic Power', p.232.
58. Jamil Rashid and Hassan N. Gardezi, 'Independent Pakistan: Its Political Economy', in *Pakistan: The Roots of Dictatorship: The Political Economy of Praetorian State*, ed. Hassan N. Gardezi and Jamil Rashid, pp. 4–11 (London: Zed Press, 1983), p. 7.
59. Bilal Hashmi, 'Dragon Seeds: Military in the State', in *Pakistan: The Roots of Dictatorship: The Political Economy of Praetorian State*, ed. Hassan N. Gardezi and Jamil Rashid (London: Zed Press, 1983), p. 159.
60. Noman, *The Political Economy of Pakistan*, pp. 35–43.
61. Azad, *Unosottorer Gonoobbuththan*, pp. 102–06.
62. Azad, *Unosottorer Gonoobbuththan*, p. 106.
63. Mushtaq Khan, 'The Political Economy of Industrial Policy in Pakistan 1947–1971', Working Paper No. 98, Department of Economics, School of Oriental and African Studie (SOAS), University of London, February 2002, p. 24, https://eprints.soas.ac.uk/9867/1/Industrial_Policy_in_Pakistan.pdf (accessed on 7 April 2021).
64. M. Khan, 'The Political Economy of Industrial Policy in Pakistan 1947–1971', pp. 24–25.
65. M. Khan, 'The Political Economy of Industrial Policy in Pakistan 1947–1971', pp. 24–25.

66. Rashid Amjad, *Private Industrial Investment in Pakistan 1960–1970* (Cambridge: Cambridge University Press, 1982), p. 47.
67. Hamza Alavi, 'Class and State' in *Pakistan: The Unstable State*, edited by Hassan N. Gardezi and Jamil Rashid, pp. 40–93 (Lahore: Vanguard, 1983), p. 82.
68. Azizur Rahman Khan, 'What Has Been Happening to Real Wages in Pakistan?', *Pakistan Development Review* 7, no. 3 (1967): 317–47, p. 327.
69. Jamil Rashid, 'Pakistan in a Debt Trap', in *Pakistan: The Roots of Dictatorship: The Political Economy of Praetorian State*, ed. Hasssan N. Gardezi and Jamil Rashid, pp. 173–91 (London: Zed Press, 1983), p. 178.
70. Vorys, *Political Development in Pakistan*, p. 180.
71. Vorys, *Political Development in Pakistan*, p. 180.
72. Vorys, *Political Development in Pakistan*, p. 181.
73. Vorys, *Political Development in Pakistan*, p. 181.
74. Rashid, 'Pakistan in a Debt Trap', p. 180.
75. Gustav F. Papanek, 'Squeezing the Peasant', in *Pakistan's Development: Social Goals and Private Incentives* (Karachi: Oxford University Press, 1968).
76. Shahid Javed Burki, 'Fall of East Pakistan: Some Economic Consequences', *Pakistan Economic and Social Review* 10, no. 1 (1972): 9–16, http://www.jstor.org/stable/25824725 (accessed on 8 June 2021).
77. John Thomas Woodward, 'Development Institutions, Projects, and Aid: A Case Study of the Water Development Programme in East Pakistan', *Pakistan Economic and Social Review* 12, no. 1 (1974): 77–103, p. 78, http://www.jstor.org/stable/25824787 (accessed on 22 June 2021).
78. Willem van Schendel, *A History of Bangladesh* (Cambridge: Cambridge University Press, 2013 [2009]), p. 4.
79. Warren C. Robinson, '"Disguised" Unemployment Once Again: East Pakistan, 1951–1961', *American Journal of Agricultural Economics* 51, no. 3 (1969): 592–604, p. 593, DOI: 10.2307/1237911.
80. Robinson, '"Disguised" Unemployment Once Again', p. 593.
81. Rehman Sobhan, *Basic Democracies Works Program and Rural Development in East Pakistan* (Dacca: Bureau of Economic Research, Dacca University and Oxford University Press, 1968), pp. 2–3.
82. Swadesh R. Bose, 'Trend of Real Income of the Rural Poor in East Pakistan, 1949–66', *Pakistan Development Review* 8, no. 3 (1968): 452–88, p. 460, http://www.jstor.org.proxy3.library.mcgill.ca/stable/41981663 (accessed on 14 June 2021).

83. M. Mahmud Khan, 'Labour Absorption and Unemployment in Rural Bangladesh', *Bangladesh Development Studies* 13, nos. 3–4 (1985): 67–88, http://www.jstor.org/stable/40775791 (accessed on 14 June 2021).
84. Mohiuddin Alamgir, 'Some Aspects of Bangladesh Agriculture: Review of Performance and Evaluation of Policies', *Bangladesh Development Studies* 3, no. 3 (1975): 261–300, p. 207, http://www.jstor.org/stable/40794100 (accessed on 11 June 2021).
85. Sobhan, *Basic Democracies Works Program*, p. 10.
86. Sobhan, *Basic Democracies Works Program*, p. 10.
87. Sobhan, *Basic Democracies Works Program*, p. 10.
88. Sobhan, *Basic Democracies Works Program*, p. 13.
89. Sobhan, *Basic Democracies Works Program*, p. 15.
90. Sobhan, *Basic Democracies Works Program*, p. 15.
91. Sobhan, *Basic Democracies Works Program*, p.15.
92. Clifford Geertz, 'Form and Variation in Balinese Village Structure', *American Anthropologist* 61, no. 6: 991–1012, p. 991, cited in Peter J. Bertocci, 'Elusive Villages: Social Structure and Community Organization in Rural East Pakistan', PhD thesis, Department of Anthropology, University of Michigan, 1970, p. 11.
93. Peter J. Bertocci, 'Community Structure and Social Rank in Two Villages in Bangladesh', *Contributions to Indian Sociology* 6, no. 1 (1972): 28–52, p. 30, DOI: 10.1177/006996677200600102.
94. Bertocci, 'Community Structure and Social Rank in Two Villages in Bangladesh', p. 30.
95. Bertocci, 'Community Structure and Social Rank in Two Villages in Bangladesh', p. 31.
96. Bertocci, 'Community Structure and Social Rank in Two Villages in Bangladesh', p. 40.
97. Bertocci, 'Community Structure and Social Rank in Two Villages in Bangladesh', p. 41.
98. André Beteille, 'Class Structure in an Agrarian Society: The Case of the Jotedars', in *Studies in Agrarian Social Structure*, pp. 117–41 (Delhi: Oxford University Press, 1974).
99. Bertocci, 'Community Structure and Social Rank in Two Villages in Bangladesh', p. 37.
100. Harry W. Blair, 'Rural Development, Class Structure and Bureaucracy in Bangladesh', *World Development* 6, no. 1: 65–82, DOI: 10.1016/0305-750X(78)90025-6.

101. Abu Abdullah, Mosharaff Hossain and Richard Nations, 'Agrarian Structure and the IRDP Preliminary Considerations', *Bangladesh Development Studies* 4, no. 2 (1976): 209–66, p. 210, http://www.jstor.org/stable/40794132 (accessed on 22 June 2021).
102. Sobhan, *Basic Democracies Works Program*, p. 5.
103. Sobhan, *Basic Democracies Works Program*, p. 7.
104. Rashiduzzaman, *Politics and Administration*, table 8 (iv), p. 37, cited in Azad, *Unosottorer Gonoobbuththan*, p. 91.
105. Abu Abdullah, 'Land Reform and Agrarian Change in Bangladesh', *Bangladesh Development Studies* 4, no. 1 (January 1976): 67–114, p. 86.
106. John Thomas Woodward, 'The Rural Works Programme in East Pakistan', in *Development Policy*, vol. 2: *The Pakistan Experience*, ed. Walter P. Falcon and Gustav F. Papanek, pp. 186–236 (Cambridge: Harvard University Press, 1971), p. 187.
107. Tariq Omar Ali, 'Technologies of Peasant Production and Reproduction: The Post-Colonial State and Cold War Empire in Comilla, East Pakistan, 1960–70', *South Asia: Journal of South Asian Studies* 42, no. 3 (2019): 435–51, DOI: 10.1080/00856401.2019.1590788.
108. T. O. Ali, 'Technologies of Peasant Production and Reproduction', pp. 443–45.
109. Westergaard, *State and Rural Society in Bangladesh*, pp. 106–07.
110. Woodward, 'The Rural Works Programme in East Pakistan', p. 196.
111. Sobhan, *Basic Democracies Works Program*, p. 229.
112. Sobhan, *Basic Democracies Works Program*, p. 231.
113. Woodward, 'Development Institutions, Projects, and Aid'.
114. Woodward, 'Development Institutions, Projects, and Aid', p. 82.
115. Sobhan, *Basic Democracies Works Program*, p. 18.
116. Westergaard, *State and Rural Society in Bangladesh*, p. 104.
117. Edward S. Mason, 'Economic Development of India and Pakistan', Occasional Paper No. 13, Harvard Center for International Affairs, Cambridge, MA, September 1966, p. 56, cited in Woodward, 'The Rural Works Programme in East Pakistan', p. 187.
118. Pervez Hoodbhoy, 'Jinnah and the Islamic State: Setting the Record Straight', *Economic and Political Weekly* 42, no. 32 (2007): 3300–03.
119. Mohammad Maniruzzaman (ed.), *Mofazzel Haider Chowdhury: Rochonaboli* (Prothom Khondo) (Dhaka: Bangla Academy, 1982), cited in Morshed Safiul Hassan, *Purbo Banglay Chinta Chorcha 1940–70: Dwondwo o Potikria* (Dhaka: Anupom Prokashoni, 2017), p. 526.

120. Cited in Hassan, *Purbo Banglay Chinta Chorcha*, p. 526.
121. Saadia Toor, *The State of Islam: Culture and Cold War Politics in Pakistan* (London: Pluto Press, 2011).
122. Saikia, 'Ayub Khan and Modern Islam'.
123. Saikia, 'Ayub Khan and Modern Islam'.
124. Ahmad Sharif, *Bichit Chinta* (Dacca: Agami Prokashoni, 1968), pp. 19–20, cited in Hassan, *Purbo Banglay Chinta Chorcha*, p. 544.
125. T. O. Ali, 'Technologies of Peasant Production and Reproduction'. Particularly see the discussion on religion, pp. 445–51.
126. T. O. Ali, 'Technologies of Peasant Production and Reproduction', 445–49.
127. T. O. Ali, 'Technologies of Peasant Production and Reproduction', 445–49.
128. T. O. Ali, 'Technologies of Peasant Production and Reproduction'. Particularly see the discussion on women, pp. 449–51.

5

For Whom the Bell Tolls

Popular Resistance and the Beginning of the Global Sixties in Pakistan

In 1958, when Ayub Khan staged his coup d'état, the streets of East Pakistani towns remained calm. After nearly a decade of palace intrigues, with its unstable ministerial coalitions, its game of political musical chairs for the positions of prime minister and chief minister and its suppression of popular electoral verdict, people were alienated from political processes. This was also a period of political transition when pivotal figures of Bengal politics – Fazlul Huq, Suhrawardy and Khawaja Nazimuddin – passed away in the consecutive years of 1962, 1963 and 1964. In 1965 a coalition of opposition political parties made their last desperate bid to uninstall the Ayub Khan regime through the shambolic presidential election instituted by Ayub Khan. The combined opposition parties selected Fatima Jinnah, sister of Mohammad Ali Jinnah, the founder of Pakistan, as their candidate. Fatima Jinnah would have been a formidable consensus candidate if Pakistan had had a universal adult franchise, but under conditions of the Basic Democracy regime, Fatima Jinnah had to win over the 'Basic Democrats' who were beholden to Ayub Khan for access to the position of power. The defeat of Fatima Jinnah foreclosed the possibility of removing the military-bureaucratic regime through lawful constitutional opposition and electoral mobilization.

Under the shadow of the garrison state, politics in East Pakistan evolved both within the framework of the Constitution of Pakistan and clandestine plans to liberate East Pakistan through armed revolution. In 1960 the world witnessed a radical re-alternation of the global political order with the independence of African colonies. In 1960 alone, 17 independent states emerged in Africa. Most of these newly independent states experienced political convulsions emanating from the contestation between various forms of socialist movements and dying colonial imperialism. Congo, for example, entered a political crisis with the assassination of Patrice Lumumba, and Algeria witnessed a prolonged revolution. Radical ideas of revolution informed by a global wave of national liberation in Africa and Asia impacted students' movements in East Pakistan. A tacit understanding between the Awami League and the CPP (East Pakistan Provincial Committee) produced a united front among those students who were against the military-bureaucratic regime. Students mounted a stiff resistance to the military-bureaucratic regime, and they were joined by urban working classes. The alliance between the Awami League and the communists produced the most powerful popular movement against the military-bureaucratic regime in East Pakistan.

This new social coalition, forged through popular movements among students and workers, paved the way for wider confrontations with the military-bureaucratic regime. The dialectics of a politics, marked by state-sponsored religious nationalism and geared towards sectarian violence and war, were matched by the resistance to and questioning of hyperbolic masculine religious nationalism, particularly when it became clear that East Pakistan was left unguarded during the war between India and Pakistan in 1965. The nature of the resistance shifted from the demand for the restoration of parliamentary democracy to that of complete autonomy for East Pakistan. Highlighting the contradiction between the West Pakistan-based monopoly industrial houses and the labouring masses of East Pakistan, a young Awami League leader, Sheikh Mujib, revived the Awami League organization as a principal party for regional autonomy. Despite war and anti-minority pogroms, the early sixties were marked by students and workers' resistances. Yet there did not exist a popular political programme for the masses.

Military Rule and Party-Political Formations: Political Movement for the Restoration of Democracy

Even in 1958, mass involvement in politics remained muted. Internecine conflicts among various constituents of the United Front of 1954, the squandering of the popular verdict for access to political power and the blatant opportunism displayed by political leaders alienated masses from political process. Historic compromises, even on the question of the autonomy of Bengal, and cynical political calculations of allying with unelected bureaucratic captains of the central government of Pakistan further contributed towards this disillusionment with political parties. Though the Awami League government, for a brief while, brought improvement to the living standards of the people, it remained stuck in the quagmire of internecine quarrels between chief minister Ataur Rahman and the organizing secretary of the party, Sheikh Mujib.[1] Meanwhile, the foreign policy of the Awami League government, headed by Suhrawardy, supported Pakistan's joining the military blocs formed by the UK and the US. During the halcyon days of the Suez Crisis, this policy had caused a rift between the progressive sections of the party, under the leadership of Bhashani, and the mainstream Awami League, led by Suhrawardy. The new political formation, the NAP, remained closely aligned with the underground CPP (East Pakistan Provincial Committee). The split in the Awami League caused confusion within the progressive movement in East Pakistan and undermined the move towards securing autonomy. While it is true that, in 1958, the provincial legislative assembly passed a unanimous resolution for the complete autonomy of East Pakistan, Suhrawardy restrained the Awami League from organizing a movement for this autonomy as he jokingly said: 'The English language, the PIA [Pakistan International Airlines] and I are the only links between East and West Pakistan.'[2] This witty assertion indicates how he perceived his role in Pakistani politics. Yet by supporting the two-unit policy, he also shelved the demand for the federal reorganization raised by Pathan, Sindhi and Baluch political activists. The pursuit of their personal interests and the opportunism of political leaders, combined with the mushrooming of political parties, further contributed towards the political apathy among the masses. Thus, political parties lost their popular legitimacy to resist martial law by 1958. A few intellectuals, such as Abul Kalam Shamsuddin, who was associated with the East Pakistan Renaissance society in the forties, welcomed military takeover and the suspension of a spasmodic democracy.[3] Indeed, Ataur Rahman, the chief minister of the recently dissolved Awami League ministry in East Pakistan, wrote:

> When arrested leaders like Sheikh Mujibur Rahman, Abul Mansur Ahmad and others were produced before the court, thousands of people gathered in the open ground next to the court to observe the fun. They were in an exalted mood and clapped, whispering that these leaders were justly punished and shouted, 'Long live martial law'.[4]

Ataur Rahman could have exaggerated the reaction in his description, as he was obviously at loggerheads with Sheikh Mujib and had surrendered to the Elected Body Disqualification Ordinance enacted by martial law, but his words contained some truth. People were either hostile or apathetic to the fate of political leaders. Many prominent personalities welcomed the imposition of martial law. Indeed, in Karachi, the capital of the country, Fatima Jinnah told *Morning News*:

> A New era has begun under General Ayub Khan and the armed forces have undertaken to root out the administrative malaise and anti-social practices, to create a sense of confidence, security and stability, and eventually to bring the country back to a state of normalcy.[5]

Ironically, it was Fatima Jinnah who became the candidate of the combined opposition against Ayub Khan in the shambolic 1965 presidential election.

Nonetheless, the military-bureaucratic regime did not have complete sway over the political system. Basil J. Green Hill, the British deputy high commissioner in Dacca, wrote to a colleague that his talk with brigadier Sahib Dad had revealed that the latter was facing a passive resistance from the Bengali civilian administration.[6] While the brigadier attributed this attitude to a tiny minority of the Bengali middle class, at the popular level the declaration of martial law and the draconian rules of the government were greeted with what the deputy high commissioner termed as malicious rumours. The government responded by declaring that such rumour-mongers would be severely punished.[7] Indeed, a government information bureau report on Sheikh Mujib recorded:

> It is ascertained on secret enquiry that Sheikh Mujibur Rahman, General Secretary of the East Pakistan Awami League (since dissolved), before his arrest on 12-10-58, gave instructions to some of his trustworthy party workers to the effect that they should remain completely passive during the Martial Law Administration in the country but must bear in mind to launch a 'Secret Whispering Campaign' amongst the people of the following lines:
>
> (i) Martial Law is a prelude to the establishment of the Punjabi Rule in East Pakistan. Bengali language is finished
> (ii) East Pakistan will be made a colony of West Pakistan
> (iii) East Pakistan is doomed forever.[8]

Notwithstanding such passive resistance, two Pakistani military officials, Sahib Dad, the sub-administrator of martial law in Dacca city, and colonel Niazi,⁹ the martial law administrator of Chittagong, confided that they were looking forward to a semi-autocratic rule for 25 years along the lines of military rule in Turkey. They also opined that provincialism, by which they implied Bengali demands for autonomy, had to be wiped out. They confided to the British deputy high commissioner that they aimed to provide, like colonial rulers, cheap food, basic amenities and some measures of social justice to Bengalis.¹⁰ This admission in a casual conversation revealed the callously anti-democratic colonial attitude of these military officials. The perceptive British deputy high commissioner noted that 'there are some signs that a more difficult period may be on the way'.¹¹

Hill was not far off the mark in his comment. Though many political leaders were put behind bars soon after the coup, Suhrawardy remained outside the prison. He made efforts to contest the imprisonment of political leaders, by the military rulers, on the charges of corruption. He travelled throughout Pakistan fighting court cases to obtain the release of his political colleagues. He asked his close confidant, Abul Mansur Ahmad, who had been an INC man before independence and had participated in the Khilafat movement, to prepare a blueprint of mass democratic agitation against the military regime.¹² Though physically exhausted and ageing fast, Suhrawardy emerged as a focal point of the established political leaders' opposition to the military regime. On 24 January 1962, he met with political leaders of Pakistan in a closed-door meeting.¹³ He emphasized the restoration of parliamentary democracy as the goal of the anti–military-bureaucratic regime movement. He announced that until the restoration of democracy, party political differences would have to be jettisoned and all political parties would have to work in a united front. Suhrawardy also advised political activists to participate in national assembly elections under a new Constitution, but he cautioned that nominations would have to be provided to those candidates who would remain loyal to their democratic principles.¹⁴ Many doubted the political efficacy of such a programme. Despite Suhrawardy's moderate political programme and opposition to the regime on strictly constitutional terms, the government decided to arrest him on 30 January 1962. Military rulers branded Suhrawardy as an unpatriotic self-centred political leader who was conspiring with anti-national forces to destabilize Pakistan.¹⁵ His arrest sparked off student protests in East Pakistan, though Suhrawardy maintained his distance from the radical student movement that continued throughout 1962.

Meanwhile, the government continued preparing for elections to national and provincial assemblies based on the Basic Democracy constitution. On 14 April 1962, seven leaders from different political parties published a statement in East Pakistani newspapers questioning the legitimacy of the elections. These political leaders expressed doubts about the representative character of the elections, given the tiny size of the electorate. They also pointed out that the elections were taking place at a time when prominent political leaders and student activists had been incarcerated. These leaders were Nurul Amin (the Muslim League), Ataur Rahman (the Awami League), Hamidul Haq Chowdhury (the Krishak Shramik Party), Syed Azizul Huq, Mahmud Ali (the NAP) and Pir Mohosin Uddin.[16] The government continued with preparations for an election despite the expressions of concern by major politicians. On 24 March the government published the candidate list and announced that only elected Basic Democrats would constitute the electorate for the national assembly election.

Sadness descended on Bengal when, on 27 April, Fazlul Huq, popularly known as the Lion of Bengal, passed away. Notwithstanding the departure of this great leader, the government held the national assembly on 28 April, and on 6 May, members of the provincial assemblies were elected.[17] Despite the election being a lowkey affair because of the limited nature of the electorate, political discussions took place in the election meetings, quite apart from the monetary transactions for votes.[18]

Once the elections were completed, on 8 June 1962 the military-bureaucratic regime withdrew martial law. On the same day the government promulgated a new Constitution and inaugurated the session of a new national assembly.[19] Nonetheless, the military government continued with an ordinance that particularly restricted the activities of the political parties. On 24 June, in East Pakistan, nine political leaders, including Nurul Amin, Ataur Rahman, Hamidul Huq Chowdhury, Abu Hossain Sarkar, Mahmud Ali, Yusuf Ali Chowdhury, Pir Mohsin Uddin, Syed Azizul Huq and Sheikh Mujib, issued a statement.[20] Sheikh Mujib had then just been released from prison. In order to pacify public opinion, on 15 July 1962 Ayub Khan passed an Act allowing political parties to resume their activities. The Act demanded that political parties be loyal to Islamic ideology, respect the integrity and the security of Pakistan and not receive money from a foreign country. The Act also made it clear that if the Supreme Court found any party in violation of the fundamental clauses of the Act, that party would be banned and its funds and property would be confiscated by the central government. People who were disqualified under the Elected Bodies Disqualification Order, 1959, were prohibited from joining any political party as members or office-bearers for six years. If any disqualified politician associated themselves with any political party, they could suffer imprisonment for up to two years and might have to pay hefty fines.[21]

With the passage of this Act, faith-based political parties immediately restored their party organizations. The most important faith-based political organization in Pakistan was the Muslim League. Previously, it had been the only party with a national organization and had been associated with the Pakistan movement. The president of the Muslim League, Abdul Qayum Khan, was in jail, and the ageing Maulana Akram Khan, vice-president of the pre-1958 League, had announced a League Council meeting in Dacca, but he was criticized by Ayub Khan and his cabinet member Zulfiqar Ali Bhutto for this decision. Under pressure from the government, Maulana Akram Khan cancelled the meeting. A section of Muslim League leaders held a convention in Karachi on 4 September 1962, under the presidentship of veteran Muslim League leader Chowdhury Khalequzzaman. The initiative in reviving the party was taken by the Ayub Khan-appointed government ministers. On 15 December 1962, the leadership of the Convention Muslim League (CML) (a splinter group of the Muslim League) was offered to Ayub Khan, who promised to consider it after the party had been reorganized based on elections. Ayub Khan joined the party in May 1963 and became its president the following December. Thus, the CML became the party of the government.[22]

As the CML endorsed the Elective Bodies (Disqualification) Ordinance (EBDO) disqualifications and supported the government, the 'Ebdonians' boycotted the CML. They initiated a meeting of the Muslim League Council on 27 October 1962. The prime movers of the Council were Mian Mumtaz Muhammad Khan Daultana of Lahore and Fazlur Rahman of Dacca. Sardar Bahadur Khan, Ayub Khans's brother, became one of its organizers. Khawaja Nazimuddin was selected as the president.[23] The Council Muslim League, as it was called, opposed the military government. Thus, the old Muslim League had now become a divided house, and both its former constituent political parties existed on paper only.

The other major faith-based political party, Jamaat-e-Islami, revived its organization on 16 July 1962. The Jamaat-e-Islami had a grassroots level organizational network, ideologically committed leadership and a loyal though limited following. The Jamaat stood for the establishment of an Islamic state based on the Koran and the Sunnah. They also demanded a parliamentary form of government based on universal adult franchise and periodically held free and fair elections with the right of every group to propagate their views. The Jamaat was the only party whose organizational apparatus and leadership had not suffered under martial law.[24] The other smaller faith-based organization was the Nizam-e-Islam, which was reactivated on 6 August 1962. Primarily based in East Pakistan, the party demanded the conformity of all existing laws to Islamic tenets, the restoration of the prefix 'Islamic' to the title of the state, the removal of restrictions on politicians under EBDO handicaps and the freedom of speech and association. It had a small presence in Pakistani politics.[25] Law minister Mohammad Munir, in an interview with the British high commissioner, Morrice James, expressed his apprehension about the revival of these two Islamist political parties, and James dryly noted his diplomatic observation:

> It was the characteristic of a society like Pakistan's that when political life began on a mass scale it should express itself first in terms of religious fanaticism, since the people were so much more religiously than politically minded.[26]

Yet James was wrong-footed in his orientalist preconception about Muslim societies, as these faith-based political parties remained on the margins of Pakistani politics, both in the East and in the West.

The main opposition to martial law, including secular political formations, revolved around Suhrawardy. On his release in August, Suhrawardy called upon the opposition politicians to form a national front with the single purpose of the restoration of democracy. His efforts led to the formation of the National Democratic Front (NDF) – a loose alliance of the entirety of the opposition forces, from both East and West Pakistan, which included the Council Muslim League, Awami League, the National Awami Party, the Krishak Sramik Party, the Nizam-e-Islam, the Jamaat-e-Islami and the Republican Party. The NDF was launched in October 1962. Suhrawardy emphasized that the NDF was not a political party struggling for power but a movement for achieving the democratic rights of the people. When launching the movement, Suhrawardy, characteristic of his moderate politics, kept the door of negotiation with the government open and even pleaded with the president to initiate a round-table conference to discuss possible amendments to the Constitution.[27] Ayub Khan asserted that the Constitution 'suits our condition best' and any changes would have to proceed through the assembly, whereas holding a round-table conference with political leaders would be a violation of the Constitution.[28] The NDF with Suhrawardy at its helm continued a lacklustre campaign for direct elections based on universal adult franchise and constitutional amendments directed to increase the power of the legislature and the independence of the judiciary in order to counterbalance the powers of the executive. Suhrawardy argued that democracy had never been put into practice in Pakistan, and the Constitution of 1956 had never been given the chance of a 'democratic implementation', thus implying that the claim that democracy had failed in Pakistan was factually incorrect.[29]

The opposition leaders, including Suhrawardy, toured extensively all over Pakistan. In West Pakistan, NDF leaders were not welcomed, and Suhrawardy was the target of an assassination attempt. In one public meeting, miscreants, possibly encouraged by the government, threw stones at Sheikh Mujib that hit his spectacles, and at the Karachi railway station there was a bomb attack on NDF leaders.[30] The movement for the restoration of democracy met with more success in East Pakistan. It was decided that in January 1963, leaders of the NDF would meet in Karachi. But Suhrawardy, the main proponent of the NDF, suffered a heart attack in December 1962. He went to London for treatment, and the British were apprehensive that he would indulge in anti-government protests, though he spent most of his time in the company of his nephews and cousin.[31] He returned to Beirut, where he passed away in a hotel on 6 December 1963. In Suhrawardy's absence the NDF lost much of its political relevance.

Suhrawardy was the last politician who had a considerable following in both wings of Pakistan. He had hoped that the restoration of democracy would establish a strong union between the two wings. With his death there did not remain a honest broker who could negotiate with and command the respect of both wings of Pakistan, and the chasm between the two deepened. This was known to general Ayub Khan, who, in a letter to Kamruddin Ahmad, a member of Pakistani diplomatic service who had served in UN missions in New York, India and Burma, wrote in reference to East Pakistan:

I am trying to do my best to ameliorate the situation to the extent possible, but the neglect of centuries cannot be put right in a day and furthermore without the willing cooperation of the people. This unfortunately is not forthcoming because of the pathologically hostile attitude towards West Pakistan and a feeling that salvation of East Pakistan lies in some sort of separation.[32]

Though Ayub Khan blamed East Pakistanis for their 'pathological hatred' of West Pakistan, he refused to acknowledge that it was the absence of democracy that was contributing to this growing chasm between the people of East Pakistan and the military-bureaucratic regime based in West Pakistan.

With Suhrawardy's death, Sheikh Mujib now moved forward to establish his leadership in East Pakistani politics. Though Sheikh Mujib was a protégé of Suhrawardy, he differed from him on two different counts. First, he was always wedded to the party-political organization and believed that the Awami League should play a pivotal role in organizing the pro-democracy movement. He had little faith in a broad united front of political parties belonging to opposite ideological orientations and was also concerned that the Muslim League and the Jamaat-e-Islami, once fully revived, would exploit the political vacuum in the absence of the Awami League. Second, for Sheikh Mujib, democracy in Pakistan was a step towards securing autonomy for East Pakistan. His end goal was thus different from that of his political mentor, who regarded democracy as a means towards strengthening the union of Pakistan. On 9 January 1964, Sheikh Mujib, as the general secretary of the Awami League, issued a circular to the members of the working committee and secretaries and presidents of the reconstituted district committees for a meeting on 25 January 1964 at his house in Dhanmandi, Dacca. On 25 January, nearly 23 members of the working committee and 16 presidents and secretaries of district committees met at Sheikh Mujib's residence. In the meeting, Tajuddin Ahmad proposed the revival of the party organization, and Mashiur Rahman of Jessore seconded it.[33] Old guards of the Awami League, Ataur Rahman and Abul Mansur Ahmad, opposed the revival of the party organization and emphasized that the NDF should be given the priority in order to restore democracy.[34] Sheikh Mujib believed that the Awami League should play a pivotal role in the politics of East Pakistan and that autonomy should be its goal. Thus, the party leadership passed into the hands of a new generation of leaders epitomized by Sheikh Mujib and Tajuddin.

On 5 March 1964 the national working committee of the Awami League met and declared that the League had been revived as a political organization. On 6 March the Awami League convened a council session under the presidentship of Abdur Rashid Tarkabagish. On 7 March the defining tone of the party was set by Sheikh Mujib acting as the general secretary of the party. Emphasizing the necessity of autonomy for East Pakistan, Sheikh Mujib argued that the League was the only organization that drew attention to the discrimination and exploitation of East Pakistan by West Pakistani industrialists. Implicitly acknowledging that the NDF was a rather tame movement, he asserted that there was a need for a strong and committed party organization to back up the NDF activities, as it was not possible to dislodge 'reactionaries' from power through petition and statements. This was why the Awami League had been revived.[35] In other words, Sheikh Mujib transformed the Awami League into a party for regional autonomy, highlighting popular grievances against the capitalist modernization process which had contributed to the regional imbalance between the two wings. Even the political resolution of the Awami League prioritized two different economies for two regions of Pakistan. Thus, the Awami League, under Sheikh Mujib, became an organization dedicated towards the realization of autonomy for East Pakistan. With the new generation of politicians, a new political agenda came into existence – namely, the autonomy of East Pakistan within, or even outside, the union of Pakistan.

The Global Sixties and the Schemes of Revolutionary Emancipation of 'Purbo Bangla'

While official NDF-led pro-democracy movement remained a moderate and rather tame force against the government, there existed an undercurrent of more radical protests. Two revolutionary events impacted radicalism in East Pakistan: the Algerian War of Independence (1954–62) and the Cuban Revolution (1958). In the fifties, the entire Afro-Asian world was gripped by the Algerian War. Algeria had exercised a significant influence over Fanon in the conceptualization of his theories of revolution. Similarly, the Cuban Revolution had established connections with the Algerian War. Fidel Castro sent a large consignment of American weapons, captured during the abortive Bay of Pigs invasion, to Algeria. In December, at the UN General Assembly, in a speech, Che Guevara referred to the 'tragic case of the Congo' and denounced the Western powers' 'unacceptable intervention'. Che Guevara then undertook a tour of African states, travelling to Algeria, Mali, Congo-Brazzaville, Senegal, Ghana, Dahomey, Egypt and Tanzania. These events left indelible marks on radical youths and students in or from East Pakistan.

In 1963 Alamgir Kabir, a student residing in London, became part of a clandestine organization known as the East Bengal Liberation Front. They ran two journals, one in English and the other in Bengali, respectively known as *Asian Tide* and *Purbo Bangla* (East Bengal). Kabir also underwent training in the use of light arms and prepared himself for armed insurrection.[36] As a Londoner, Kabir was familiar with the Cuban Revolution, the Algerian War and the Palestinian resistance movement. In fact, he was close to both Algerian and Palestinian revolutionaries.[37] Meanwhile, the radicalism of the Chinese Communist Party (CCP), the Cuban Revolution and the national emancipation movements in Africa had attracted the attention of the left-leaning student community. *Sombad*, a left-leaning newspaper, reported critical revolutionary events throughout the world and radicalized the student movement.

Haidar Akbar Khan Rono, Rashed Khan Menon and Kazi Zafar Ahmed, three student leaders, left their own accounts of how global protests- and revolutionary movements had influenced their radicalism. Rono recalled how communist student activists clandestinely used to meet in room numbered 180 in Salimullah Hall of Dacca University, where they discussed the international revolutionary movement.[38] Events in India also attracted their attention. They were angry at Nehru's highhanded removal of the elected communist government in Kerala. Ironically, Rono, who obtained a scholarship named after the SEATO treaty, donated the money to the communist-inclined cyclostyled journal *Shikha* (Flame), a name based on *Iskra*, the foundational journal of Marxists in the Russian Social Democratic Party in the early years of the twentieth century.[39] Kazi Zafar also mentioned how Patrice Lumumba and the Algerian revolutionaries had inspired the student movement in East Pakistan.[40] Asad Chowdhury, a student, now an established poet, published in *Sombad* a poem titled *Itihaser Ar Ek Nayok* (Another Hero of History), written on Lumumba. Azad Sultan, a student writer, edited a special anthology titled *Africar Hridoye Surjyodoy* (The Rise of the Sun in the Heart of Africa).[41] In the sixties, students came to know about international political situations, the national emancipation movements in Asian and African nations and the complexities of the Cold War situation. In 1966 Vietnam Day was celebrated with large gatherings and protests.⁴² Indeed, even though ephemeral and very incipient, Kazi Zafar and his associates also established a Bengal Liberation Association.⁴³ In 1962, during the student movement at Dacca University, Rono met with captain Abdul Halim Chowdhury, a Bengali officer of the Baluch regiment. Halim Chowdhury told student leaders that if the student movement aimed at the independence of East Pakistan, Bengali officers would turn their guns against their Pakistani colleagues. Rono replied that for such an event they would have to wait for another 10 years.⁴⁴

With the radical tenor of the global sixties surrounding the youth in Bengal, clandestine preparations continued for armed struggle in East Pakistan. In Dacca, another group known as the 'inner group', led by Moazzem Chowdhury, sought to demand the independence of Bangladesh. Moazzem Chowdhury had been active in the CPP (East Pakistan Provincial Committee) organization in Sylhet district in Dacca before independence, and later he was aligned with the Abul Hashim group within the Muslim League. He became disillusioned when East Pakistan did not become an independent sovereign state in the spirit of the Lahore resolution.⁴⁵ His organization was inspired by the nationalist revolutionary traditions of the anti-colonial independence struggle in Bengal in the early twentieth century, and they modelled their activities along the line of those of Subhas Chandra Bose, a Bengali leader of the Indian independence struggle. Political activists and Bengali civil service members constituted the core of this group. In 1960, 'inner group' leader Moazzem Chowdhury persuaded Sheikh Mujib to cross the border and seek Indian assistance to organize an armed struggle in East Pakistan.⁴⁶ As per the plan, Moazzem Chowdhury escorted Sheikh Mujib beyond the border of Tripura, a former princely state in the north-east of India. But India was then not prepared to interfere in the internal affairs of Pakistan for a different reason.

In 1960 Nehru had reasons not to meddle in the 'internal affairs' of Pakistan. On 30 March 1959, the Tibetan religious leader and temporal head of the Tibetan government, the Dalai Lama, had escaped from Lhasa and reached India on 18 April 1959. Pakistan was keenly observing the decline of the relationship between India and China. Mohammad Ali, the Pakistani ambassador to Japan, said on 20 April 1959: 'The Tibetan issue has jolted Asian people out of their complacency. The Tibetan revolt should have more impact on Asia than the invasion of Hungary by Russia. The Chinese have followed the same pattern, which should open the eyes of Asia to the danger of red imperialism.'⁴⁷ On 24 April 1959 president Ayub Khan offered a joint defence agreement with India.[48] This suggestion was welcomed by Jayaprakash Narayan and Kodandera Madappa Cariappa.[49] On 4 May 1959 Nehru had announced in the Lok Sabha: 'I am all for settling our problems with Pakistan and living normal, friendly and neighbourly lives. But we do not want to have a common defence policy which is almost some kind of military alliance. I do not understand against whom people talk about common defence policies.'[50] However, Nehru was aware that India was facing a critical situation north of its border. Under such circumstances Nehru would not take the risk of disturbing the apparent peace between India and Pakistan by supporting rebels in East Bengal, particularly in a circumstance where there was no visible sign of unrest in East Pakistan.

From the Indian side, a few overenthusiastic Bengali diplomats, bureaucrats and personnel of the intelligence services were involved in encouraging East Pakistani dissidents. Yet Indians were unprepared for Sheikh Mujib's arrival. Sheikh Mujib wanted to go to London and organize propaganda activities from there, but Indians wanted him to remain in Agartala, the state capital of Tripura, and conduct his anti-Pakistan campaign from there. In a rather different version of the event, the chief minister of Tripura, Sachindra Lal Singh, later claimed that Sheikh Mujib had come to Tripura in 1963, but in the wake of India's defeat at the hands of China, Nehru had refused to support Sheikh Mujib's propaganda work in Tripura.[51] Sheikh Mujib was disappointed, and he returned home dejected.[52] In 1964 the 'inner group' tried to send Sheikh Mujib to London during the Commonwealth Summit so that he could meet Nehru there, but the latter passed away before the session.[53] These events indicate two important factors: the growing importance of Sheikh Mujib in East Pakistani politics and Sheikh Mujib's support for revolutionary efforts to shred ties with Pakistan.

In 1958, the East Bengal Liberation Party, under the leadership of Ali Asad and Abdur Rahman Siddiq, was also among the first organizations to visualize national independence. These leaders also visited India and sought Indian assistance.[54] Ali Asad, the leader of the group, was involved in the language movement of 1952 and had been active in the Awami League. After Ayub Khan's military coup, they felt that there was little opportunity to realize autonomy for East Bengal within the framework of a united Pakistan. The leaders of the group approached the Indian High Commission in Dacca through Abul Mansur Ahmad, a senior leader of the Awami League. The involvement of Abul Mansur Ahmad was surprising as he was known to be a firm supporter of united Pakistan and a loyalist of Suhrawardy. Indian officials at the embassy did not assure them of Indian assistance and asked them to go to Calcutta to talk to Indian politicians. In India they were arrested for a little while on the suspicion of being Pakistani spies and did not secure much assistance. But this organization left a critical impression in East Pakistan by circulating leaflets and putting up posters calling for secession from Pakistan. Their posters were marked by a red star indicating a vague association with the global socialist movement. Yet treachery and defection led to the arrests of the key leaders of the party, and one among them died due to torture.

In 1962 another organization of young high school and college students, known as the Banga Bahini, sprang up in different neighbourhoods of Dacca. But far more widely known was an organization called Opurbo Sansad (Wonderful Assembly).[55] This was a codename for the future independent government of Bangladesh, and the organization consisted chiefly of academics, though it operated in a clandestine manner with a strict code of conduct. This organization published three manifestos between 1963 and 1965. The first manifesto, published on 21 December 1963, was titled 'What Do Bengalis Want?' (Bangali ki Chay?). Though the question was posed rhetorically, the answer was implicit in the question, namely 'independence'. On 1 January 1964 the second manifesto, 'Bengal Again under Attacks by Jackals and Vultures' (Shakun Shrigaler Abar Bangla Akromon), detailed the attacks on the Bengali language and culture by the martial law regime. The third manifesto, 'Bengali in History' (Itihaser Dharay Bangali), detailed why Bengalis desired independence. It was written by Ahmad Sharif, a noted specialist on medieval Bengali literature and a Marxist professor at Dacca University. They distributed their manifestos and leaflets in trains and railway stations. This organization also promoted Tagore's famous song 'O My Golden Bengal' as the future national anthem of Bengal.[56]

There also came into existence a clandestine organization known as the Bengal Nucleus in English and as the Swadhin Bangla Biplobi Parishad in Bengali. This student group followed the old nationalist revolutionary traditions of secret society movements in Bengal. Yet they had a reading and discussion list which included the works of Che Guevara, Regis Debray and Mao Zedong.[57] The impact of the global sixties was imprinted on the functioning of this group, and such organizations developed their political strategies outside the formal setup of the CPP (East Pakistan Provincial Committee)-affiliated organizations. The collection of such organizations can be seen as an emergent New Left in East Pakistan.

Indeed, in 1961 there took place a series of clandestine meetings between communist leaders Moni Singh and Khoka Roy, and Sheikh Mujib and his associate, the noted journalist Tofazzal Hossain. The CPP (East Pakistan Provincial Committee) was initially bewildered by the fact that the pro-American Suhrawardy's confidants, Tofazzal Hossain and Sheikh Mujib, sought a meeting with them. The party's secretariat approved the meeting, and Singh and Roy placed a demand charter before Sheikh Mujib and Tofazzal Hossain. This included demands such as autonomy of East Pakistan, the scrapping of West Pakistan as a unit, the restoration of provincial autonomy in West Pakistan, the release of political prisoners, an increase in the wages of industrial workers, a reduction of taxes on the peasantry and a non-aligned anti-imperialist foreign policy.[58] Instinctively anticipating the rise of the New Left and global student unrest, during the meeting Singh, the general secretary of the East Pakistan unit of the Communist Party, specifically asserted that students were the most organized political constituency, and in the absence of an organized workers' movement, students could provide an effective challenge to the military-bureaucratic regime.[59] Both Singh and Sheikh Mujib agreed to launch a movement for the restoration of democracy, the ending of military rule and the release of political prisoners, as well as the circulation of leaflets concerning the demands of workers and peasants. They differed on the issue of a non-aligned foreign policy. Sheikh Mujib wanted to press forward the demand of the independence of Bangladesh. Singh and Roy were reluctant to endorse such demands on ideological grounds. Arguing that it would be a premature move, the communist leaders persuaded Sheikh Muijb to wait for a future tide of events. Sheikh Mujib responded: 'I accept your opinion today but my words will remain.'[60] It appeared that Sheikh Mujib could rightly sense the principal contradiction in Pakistani politics. By adopting an uncompromising stand against the West Pakistan-based military dictatorship and praetorian capitalism, Sheikh Mujib touched upon the incipient nationality question in East Pakistan. Nonetheless, both Singh and Sheikh Mujib agreed that the Chhatro Union, the communist student organization, and the Chhatro League would work together to organize the movement in Dacca University.[61] This agreement between the communists and the Awami Leaguers became a turning point in the movement for the restoration of democracy.

Thus, in the early sixties, the imposition of martial law and the absence of a democratic venue for the articulations of grievances paved the way for an underground revolutionary movement. Sheikh Mujib emerged as a crucial figure in such movements towards national autonomy both in organized politics and in clandestine revolutionary preparations. Among the established politicians he alone acted as a bridge between these spheres of the struggle. The clandestine understanding between the regional autonomist Awami League and the CPP (East Pakistan Provincial Committee) enabled student rebellion in East Pakistan and provided a sustainable basis for mass movements against the military-bureaucratic regime.

Student Rebellion and the Challenge to the Martial Law Regime

Among the students, two groups organized resistance to martial law. Established as the Muslim Chhatro League in 1948, the Chhatro League was an organization affiliated to the Awami League. The Chhatro Union, the other popular student organization born in the wake of the language movement among students on 26 April 1952, remained a student association close to the left movement in East Pakistan, headed by the CPP (East Pakistan Provincial Committee).[62] The Chhatro Union was a successor organization to the All-India Student Federation, an organization affiliated with the CPI before independence in colonial India. Between 1952 and 1954, it was expected that the Chhatro League and the Chhatro Union would merge to form a new united progressive student organization, but the foreign policy of the Awami League government in 1956 led towards a confrontation between the League and the Union over international issues. The Union remained steadfastly opposed to Pakistan's participation in the SEATO and the Baghdad Pact and gained popularity among students at the expense of the League.[63] To counter the growing popularity of the Union, the League started showing documentaries on the Soviet intervention in Hungary. Both organizations remained at loggerheads during these years.[64] The conflict between the two groups reached its height when the Union leaders prevented Awami League leader Sheikh Mujib from entering Dacca University.[65] In 1958, however, when pro-US Ayub Khan assumed political power and suspended democracy, both the League and the Union faced a significant degree of restrictions.

After the clandestine meeting between Sheikh Mujib and Moni Singh, based on the understanding between the CPP (East Pakistan Provincial Committee) and the Awami League, Chhatro Union leader Mohammad

Farhad took initiative in organizing a meeting with the representatives of the Chhatro League on 30 December 1961. Yet the two organizations had divergent perspectives on the political events within Pakistan and beyond. League leaders aimed at establishing parliamentary democracy, and Union representatives wanted to highlight the issue of the right to national self-determination in the colonized world. The joint meeting resolved that despite certain fundamental differences, the two organizations would start movements against the military dictatorship from 21 February 1962.[66] Nonetheless, the arrest of Suhrawardy on 30 January provided an immediate cause to protest the military regime.

On 29 January, at midnight, a meeting was called involving student organizations of all parties including the pro-Ayub Khan National Student Federation (NSF) and the conservative Chhatro Shakti (Student Power). The meeting was arbitrarily suspended by Mohammad Farhad for lack of agreement. This was a strategic move by Farhad to misguide the pro-establishment student organizations who were in touch with the police intelligence. He later reconvened the meeting with the Chhatro League, and they jointly decided to organize protests the next day.[67] Meanwhile, NSF leaders assured the police and the military intelligence that there would not be any student protests the next day. But the next morning there took place a spontaneous strike in Dacca University.[68] As newspapers did not publish the news of the strike, student militants demonstrated against government-sponsored newspapers, and at one point they symbolically burnt several copies of newspapers in front of the Press Club.[69] On 3 February, when the foreign minister of the Ayub Khan administration, Manzur Qadir, visited Dacca University to deliver a speech, he was grilled about the possibility of two different economic policies for two different wings of Pakistan. Angry students also physically attacked him. Finally, the police came and rescued Qadir from among the students.[70]

Nervous about the rise of student militancy, on 5 February the government announced a sine die to university activities till further notice. On 6 February a few thousand students gathered to protest against the decision and marched through the streets. General Ayub Khan was then visiting Dacca, and so the police were cautious about the possibility of students disrupting his schedule. Meanwhile, students even chased the car of the general commanding officer of the army in Dacca as his car passed through a street where the students were holding a rally. Student processions reached Old Dacca where ordinary people welcomed them.[71] On 7 February militant students decided to surround

Ayub Khan himself in order to restrict his movements in Dacca. Guessing the students' intentions, both the army and the police surrounded Dacca University campus. To scare the students, two field guns were placed near the campus. Yet the students somehow managed to bring their processions outside the campus and reached Old Dacca. But the police started beating up students with staves (*lathi* charge), and they were scattered in the face of police violence.[72] The army, aided by the police, surrounded the campus and ordered all students to vacate college halls and dorms. It took nearly a week to vacate all the students from the campus. The army was waiting to arrest student leaders, but torrential rain enabled student leaders to escape the military dragnet. However, the mass arrests of student leaders, which according to newspaper reports numbered 229, undermined the morale of students in Dacca.[73] The movement then spread to the small towns of East Pakistan. Governor Azam Khan, an associate of Ayub Khan and one of the primary architects of the coup of 1958, however, was sympathetic to the demands for democracy in East Pakistan and did not unleash full-fledged military oppression.[74] The student movement became the first challenge to the martial law regime in Pakistan, and the undercurrent of anger against the authorities among the urban populace found expression in solidarity with the students when they marched to the population centre of Old Dacca. Yet the student movement could not inspire the overall population to revolt against the martial law regime.

Student political activists continued to remain dissatisfied with the military regime in Pakistan. Soon the government held a farcical election of the national assembly through the Basic Democracy system on 28 April 1962, and later, on 6 May 1962, they held elections to the provincial legislative assembly. Radical students, belonging primarily to the Chhatro Union, decided to visit the houses of prominent political personalities who had been elected to the national assembly to dissuade them from joining the cabinet of Ayub Khan and to articulate the demands of East Pakistan. Rono, who was one of the members of those student delegations, recalled the hypocrisy of the established politicians. For example, when the student delegation visited the house of former prime minister of Pakistan, Mohammad Ali Bogra, the latter assured the students that he would never join the cabinet of Ayub Khan. Abdus Sabur Khan, another former prominent Muslim League leader, told the student delegation that they had come to the wrong person as he had no desire to join the cabinet. He had faced torture under the British police during the colonial days, and it would be unthinkable that he would surrender to Ayub Khan.[75] Within a week of reaching Karachi, both these leaders rushed to join Ayub Khan's cabinet.

On the day of the national assembly members' departure, student militants marched to the airport. They found a few members of the national assembly in the VIP (very important person) lounge of the airport. Kazi Zafar, the then leader of the Chhatro Union, appealed to them to oppose the Ayub Khan government. Mashiur Rahman, popularly known as Jadu Mian, supported student demands and even raised the slogan 'Down with the Ayub regime'.[76] But not everybody was willing to agree with the students. Monem Khan, a pro-Ayub Khan politician who had earlier issued a statement that political prisoners were traitors to the country, announced that he would remain loyal to his principles. Students harassed him and even physically assaulted him. Finally, Tofazzal Hossain, also known as Manik Mian, the prominent editor of *Ittefaq*, a pro-Awami League newspaper, intervened to enable Monem Khan to board the plane.[77] Soon after this incident, Ayub Khan appointed Monem Khan as the governor of East Pakistan. Mohammad Farrukh, the relatively moderate governor, was removed from his position.[78]

The student movement was revived again in September 1962, and this time it became a mass student movement against the education policy of the Ayub Khan government. Ayub Khan sought to reform and transform the education system of Pakistan in order to push forward his ideas of modernization along free market lines. On 30 December 1958 he announced his purpose of reforming education and appointed S. M. Shariff, a former professor and secretary, to the education department of the Pakistani government as the chairman of the commission. On 5 January 1959, Ayub Khan inaugurated the commission comprising a total of 10 members, with 6 from West Pakistan and 4 from East Pakistan. The commission submitted its report on 26 August 1959 to Ayub Khan,[79] proposing a comprehensive rehaul of the education system and arguing that the secondary school curriculum should include a core of compulsory subjects along with a few optional ones, with an emphasis on technical and vocational subjects. This was related to the vision that the purpose of education was to create productive workers rather than usher in comprehensive social development. More controversially, it recommended that courses of both the regular and honours undergraduate curricula should be of three years duration. Echoing Ayub Khan's notion of unfettered free-market modernization, the Sharif Commission considered the idea of free education meaningless and viewed it as an expensive service commodity. Not surprisingly, the commission proposed that the government and the community should equally share the cost of primary education, and that three-fifth of the cost of secondary education should come from fees. In higher education, the community should bear a larger portion of the cost than before.[80] This implied a hike in fees and a restriction of opportunities.

For students in East Pakistan, this implied the closing of the door to higher education. Despite a higher degree of enrolment in primary schools, due to the lack of investment in the educational sector and the transfer of resources from the east to the west, East Pakistan produced far fewer number of graduates.[81] Additional fees and extra years in the university, combined with uncertain job prospects, made the recommendations of the commission a bitter pill to swallow for the student community. Thus, the student protests this time did not remain confined to student militants but spread across wider cross sections of the student community and incorporated mass students.

Student protests started from Dacca College, the oldest college established in East Pakistan. On 10 August 1962, high school and undergraduate students of Dacca College gathered in a meeting presided by Chhatro Union leader Kazi Faruk Ahmed. They formed a non-partisan student organization, called the Degree Student Forum, to lead the struggle.[82] In that meeting, the students decided to observe strikes all over East Pakistan on 15 August, a day after the Independence Day of Pakistan. On that day the students organized a massive procession in which even school children participated. Between 15 August and 10 September, students held several meetings and rallies. The Degree Student Forum now expanded into the East Pakistan Student Forum. However, the government warned students that they would face severe police action if they held their rally. The government also imposed a prohibition on public gatherings. The students withdrew the call for a public meeting. The Student Forum decided to postpone their rally on 10 September but called for a strike again on 17 September. They even established contacts with the Merchant Association, the Government Employee's Federation and the Rickshaw Driver's Union, as well as different trade unions of industrial workers.[83] As the students prepared for a showdown with the authorities, the situation took a new turn on 16 September.

On 10 September, Suhrawardy was released from prison, and he visited Dacca on 16 September. Known for his moderate position and scrupulous adherence to constitutional propriety, Suhrawardy was apprehensive about the growing student militancy. Meanwhile, the Chhatro League and the Chhatro Union organized a procession from the airport to receive Suhrawardy, a stalwart of the pro-democracy movement. Suhrawardy, however, did not like the slogans raised in his reception. He particularly disliked the slogan that talked about scrapping the Constitution, since he preferred reforming the Constitution in order to secure democracy.[84]

Meanwhile, on 17 September, a huge number of students had gathered in the university area by 9 a.m. News came that the police had fired at a student procession in Nababpur area of Dacca. Excited students immediately brought a procession, which marched through the streets and passed the Dacca High Court. Many ordinary people were joining the procession when suddenly the police fired at the back of the procession. Two participants died immediately, and a third succumbed to his injuries the next day.[85] As the procession marched on despite the police firing and reached Old Dacca, another procession by protestors also arrived from another direction. The police and the army barricaded the road so that the two processions could not meet. Then they started firing teargas and a few rounds of bullets. Students threw bricks at the police, but soon the systematic use of teargas left the students in disarray. By the evening, the army took control of the city and clamped Criminal Procedure 144, which enabled them to prohibit the assembly of four or more people in an area. The government issued arrest warrants against student leaders.[86] Even in the interior of East Pakistan, the police opened fire on students in Jessore.[87]

A few student leaders risking arrests went to meet Suhrawardy at the house of Muslim League leader Nurul Amin.[88] According to communist student leader Rono, Suhrawardy was then reading a statement condemning the firing. To Rono, it seemed more like a legal brief rather than a political statement. The last sentence of the statement read something like, 'If this situation persists then we shall not remain a silent spectator.' Suhrawardy then asked the assembled leaders, 'Do you realize the significance of this statement?'[89] An angry Kazi Zafar intervened at this moment and told Suhrawardy that while students were facing bullets, these leaders were preparing bulletins. Students demanded that the leaders give a call for another strike. However, Suhrawardy did not agree with this demand, since he feared that red students were leading the movement towards a revolutionary direction.[90] Suhrawardy proposed to meet the governor to secure their demands through discussions. He also criticized the students for burning the copy of the Constitution of Pakistan in the shade of a mango tree (*am tola* in Bengali) of Dacca University.[91] An irritated Zafar told Suhrawardy that students had obtained his release from prison by agitating from the same mango shade, and if the students so wished they could also politically bury him in the same spot.[92]

Suhrawardy remained unmoved and told Zafar that he was not a politician to be dictated by kids.⁹³ Suhrawardy even refused to attend the prayer held in the honour of the martyrs the next day.⁹⁴ He, however, met governor Faruk and secured the demands of students. On the other hand, rumours circulated in Dacca that Suhrawardy had been sent to the city by the Ayub Khan administration in order to diffuse the situation.⁹⁵ Notwithstanding the real motive of his visit, he could stall the mass democratic struggle against the martial law regime and was thus able to delay the student upsurge. There took place a divergence between the AwamiLeague-affiliated Chhatro League and the communist-dominated Chhatro Union over the latter's verbal duel with Suhrawardy. Students, belonging to all political fractions, organized a mass meeting on 24 September in Paltan Maidan in Dacca, where the movement against the Sharif Commission unofficially ended. The students' struggle in 1962 was the first significant challenge to the Ayub Khan regime.

Despite the culmination of the movement against the Sharif Commission on 24 September, the student struggle did not come to an end in 1962. Agitations took place in the Agricultural University and the Dacca Polytechnic Institute on various student issues. The government followed a similar strategy of repression comprising sine die adjournments of events and arrests of student leaders. Students from Dacca University expressed political solidarity with the agitating students of the Agricultural University.⁹⁶ On 27 December 1962, Monem Khan, the new governor of East Pakistan, tried to visit the Dacca College campus in order to inaugurate a week-long educational event, but the students demonstrated against him. A few student leaders, including the left-wing ones, such as Farhad and Rono, had been arrested, but the court released them because of lack of evidence.⁹⁷ Meanwhile, the state government formed a committee to investigate into the reasons for the student unrest. Mahmood Hossain, the vice chancellor of Dacca University, was appointed as the chairman of the committee. The report of the committee expressed sympathy with the student movement. To a visiting group of government officials, including a minister from Pakistan, Hossain stated that the students basically wanted the end of Ayub Khan's dictatorship. Soon after this statement, Hossain was removed from the position of vice chancellor of Dacca University.⁹⁸

Monem Khan, the newly appointed governor of the province, turned out to be the bête noire of the student movement. Both in 1962 and 1964 he tried to visit the campus of Rajshahi University to attend the student convocations and faced massive protests. On 22 March 1964, when the governor tried to attend the convocation of Dacca University as a chancellor, students boycotted the convocation and clashed with the police. Dacca University's student union proposed that the chancellor should be a non-political academic luminary rather than a governor. The police resorted to stave-beating of the students and surrounded the campus. As night fell, the police arrested 150 students from residential halls and closed the university for an indefinite period. The government also sponsored a student union – the NSF – even though the students accused that this organization was filled with non-student anti-social elements.

Soon the students protested throughout the province against the mistreatment of Dacca University students. The government closed down all educational institutions in the province and arrested over 1,200 students, expelled many students from the university and took away the degrees of opposition student leaders.[99] The government issued warrants against left-wing student activists Rono, Zafar and Menon. Top-ranking student leaders of the Chhatro League, such as Serajul Alam Khan and Shah Moazzem Hossain, also met with the same fate. Those newspapers which reported the student unrest were issued with show-cause order and were asked to submit deposits with the government. Three newspapers, *Ittefaq*, *Sombad* and *Azad*, kept their front pages blank in protest against this.[100] On 22 September all the important student organizations framed a 22-point student charter. Prominent among these points was the demand for phase-wise introduction of free education, the establishment of schools and colleges in rural districts and the opening of night courses in the established colleges, education through the native language and the modernization of Madrasah education. On 15 December the government appointed a new commission under the chairmanship of Hamoodur Rahman. The new commission was officially known as the Commission for Student Problems and Welfare. Though the report of the commission cautioned the government against taking harsh measures against students and requested that it consider student demands with patience, the commission also criticized student organizations and rejected the proposal for free education and education through the native language; the students rejected this commission as well.[101]

By 1965 students had emerged as the most vocal and active opponents of the military-bureaucratic regime and its praetorian capitalist modernization of East Pakistani society. The united student movement, based upon the alliance of the Chhatro League and the Chhatro Union, challenged the might of the military-bureaucratic regime. Students in the sixties constituted a political force that acted as a surrogate working class in an agrarian society, just as Moni Singh, the secretary general of the CPP (East Pakistan Provincial Committee), had told Sheikh Mujib in 1961.

Workers' Movement and Social Coalition from Below against the Ayub Khan Regime

In 1947, the industries in East Bengal comprised nine cotton factories, 50 jute baling presses of all types, 58 rice mills, 3 sugar factories, 2 small oil mills, 2 tiny glassworks and 1 cement factory.[102] This meagre industrial sector provided employment to a small number of workers. The railways employed a segment of the workers, but there existed only 1,418 miles of railway tracts, and even most of these remained inoperable.[103] Nonetheless, in the fifties, during the Korean War, the increased international price of jute had played a crucial role in the industrial development of East Pakistan. Jute exporters, who made a significant profit from the jute trade, invested in jute baling presses. The government also invested in the jute industry. In 1951 there were 333 factories in East Pakistan that provided employment to only 66,648 workers.[104] This situation altered by the sixties, when the Pakistan Industrial Development Corporation invested in 21 new industrial concerns. In 1962, with the establishment of the East Pakistan Industrial Development Corporation, the pace of industrialization picked up further, and in 1964–65, the number of factories in East Pakistan increased to 3,538.[105] The most important industries were jute and cotton textiles, and they were followed by the chemical industry, copper works, metal industry, ship repairing and printing press. This led to the expansion in the size of the industrial workforces. In Dacca, too, there took place an expansion of the industrial centre, with two major industrial centres emerging near the city: Narayanganj and Tongi. In 1950, Calcutta-based Muslim entrepreneurs Adamjee Brothers set up the Adamjee jute mill which had the reputation of being the largest jute mill in Asia. Besides, the Bawa Group also established a jute mill in Narayanganj. Narayanganj also hosted a number of cotton hosiery units, with the most famous among them being the Dhakeshwari Cotton Mill of Narayanganj, established by Surya Kumar Bose. Ramesh Chandra Roy Chowdhury established the Luxmi Narayan Cotton Mill in 1929. The Dhakeshwari opened a second mill in 1937. The Chittaranjan Cotton Mill, also established in Narayanganj, was the principal hosiery manufacturing centre of Bangladesh.[106] In Tongi there came into existence several cotton textile factories and a jute mill called the Nishat jute mill. Most prominent among them were Meghna, Kaderia, Ashraf and Satrong cotton textile mills. The Tongi industrial estate employed thousands of workers. The port of Chittagong also witnessed massive industrial development. Pakistan Oxygen, Chittagong Steel Mills, Gandhara Motors, among others, were housed in Chittagong. Besides, Chittagong was the largest port in East Pakistan that also had a ship repairing workshop. Similarly, Khunla, which is located north of the Mongla port, witnessed expansion in the industrial sector. The major industries comprised jute, chemicals, fish and seafood packaging, power generation and ship repairing.[107] In addition, there existed a number of tea plantations in Sylhet and Chittagong districts.[108]

As a consequence of the fast pace of industrialization there came into existence a large working class concentrated in the three large cities of Dacca, Chittagong and Khulna. Most workers were first-generation industrial workers who had migrated from rural areas. They still retained their ties with their natal villages. As a result of the partition and communal violence in the mill towns of Bengal, a significant number of Urdu-speaking Muslim workers had migrated from India and found employment in industrial centres.[109] Besides, there existed older migrant working classes in the already-existing factories and industrial concerns. Tea plantations employed largely Adivasi workers who had migrated nearly a hundred years ago from the Chota Nagpur plateau in West Bengal and present-day Jharkhand, while a few workers were also Khasis.[110] The working classes remained cosmopolitan and heterogeneous. As a consequence, during moments of industrial unrest, there also took place riots along linguistic and religious fault lines. The infamous Bengali–Urdu speakers' riots in the Adamjee jute mill and the Karnaphuli paper mill in 1954 reflected the complexity of political organization in the industrial centres of East Pakistan.[111]

Trade unions existed mostly on paper, and the few trade unions that functioned remained dominated by outside political activists, while both general political awareness and trade union consciousness remained low. Left-leaning political parties concentrated primarily on highlighting peasant demands, as East Bengal had a long-standing history of peasant mobilization against landlordism. The CPI and the Revolutionary Socialist Party were well-versed in organizing among incipient working classes. Nonetheless, in 1947 there came into existence the East Pakistan Trade Union Federation, with A. M. Malik as its chair. Yet Malik's decision to join the Muslim League ministry in 1948 led to dissensions within the federation. Leftists, mainly loyal to the CPP (East Pakistan Provincial Committee), protested against the decision, and differences between them arose with respect to the railway strike notice served to the government on 16 March 1949. The federation expelled the left-leaning East Bengal Railroad Workers' Union, the Dacca District Textile Workers' Union, the Dacca Rickshaw Drivers' Union and the Barishal Bidi Shramik Union from the federation.[112] In 1949 there came into existence the All-Pakistan Trade Union Federation, even as various schisms, along personal lines, were developing within the official trade union organizations. There also existed the East Pakistan Mazdoor Federation, a combination of left-wing trade union organizations. Veteran communists Mohammad Toaha and Abdus Samad played critical roles in the left-leaning trade union organization.[113] After the declaration of martial law, trade union activities came to a halt, and the trade union federation witnessed a three-way split among three personalities: Aftab Ali, Faiz Ahmad and K. M. M. Qadir, each of whom formed their own trade union federations.[114]

In such circumstances, trade unionists and political activists, formerly loyal to a Marxist political formation known as the Revolutionary Socialist Party, formed a trade union organization among the jute mill workers known as the Chatkal Shramik Federation.[115] On 2 July 1964, in the midst of martial law, Chatkal Shramik Federation called for a strike with the demand of an increase of the minimum wage from 65 to 81 rupees. They calculated the minimum wage on the basis of the price of rice. K. A. Abdul Kader, Sydur Rahman and Abdul Mannan led the strike. Kader was arrested soon after the strike started, entered into talks with governor Monem Khan and called for the withdrawal of the strike. But the strike continued. According to the *New York Times*, five jute mills of East Pakistan were involved in the strike. The industry suffered a loss of 2 million dollars.[116] These five jute mills included Adamjee, Dacca, Karim and Rawa. On 22 July the government entered into an agreement and increased the wage in average by 8 rupees.[117] This enhanced the prestige of the Chatkal Shramik Federation and emboldened the working classes to confront the martial law authorities through collective bargaining with the employers. In 1965 the workers entered into another prolonged strike as inflation eroded their wage gains. This time the much more prolonged strike spread to 55 jute mills. There were internal dissensions among unions as the communist-influenced Chittagong-based union signed a separate agreement with Yahya Bawani and Ispahani.[118] This led to the arrest of Abdul Mannan, but Sydur Rahman remained active and became a rallying figure among the workers in East Pakistan. Labour unrest soon spread to the Tejgaon industrial area in Dacca and the left-wing student activists who had participated in the 1962 student movement now moved towards organizing industrial workers.[119] This led to the establishment of a social coalition comprising students and workers resisting from below the Ayub Khan regime in East Pakistan.

Communal Riots, Shambolic Election and the India–Pakistan War

On 27 December 1964, Moi-e-Muqaddas Nabwi (holy relic of the Prophet's hair) had been reported missing from the Hazratbal shrine in Srinagar.[120] The presence of the Prophet's hair in Kashmir was regarded by Muslim Kashmiris as a blessing. Many felt the presence of such a sacred relic had almost elevated Kashmir to the status of Medina: 'Kashmir Medina ba-shud az moi-e-nabi'.[121] As the news about the disappearance of the holy relic spread, Kashmiri Muslims organized massive protests. The government of India immediately took steps to restore the holy relic though they remained cautious about declaring its restoration.[122] Meanwhile, on 2 January, in the industrial district of Khulna, communal violence flared up; and on 3 January the CML, which enjoyed the patronage of Ayub Khan in Pakistan, announced Kashmir Day to protest the incident, and a general strike was declared in Khulna which had a significant concentration of Hindus. Abdus Sabur Khan, a minister in the East Pakistani government, addressed a huge gathering in the Daulatpur industrial area in the outskirts of Khulna. Bihari Muslim workers who were evicted from India during previous communal violence primarily attended the meeting. Soon after the meeting, the crowd launched attacks in Hindu areas.[123] Mostly Bihari Muslim workers of Khulna Shipyard, Dada Co., Ispahani Co., and Kata Co. Soleman participated in the rioting, and soon the violence also spread to the Mongla port, another concentration of working classes.[124] On 13 January riots hit Dacca. Again, Bihari Muslim industrial workers were involved in the attack on trains in Tejgaon industrial areas. Riots flared up particularly in Naryanganj areas where the mill owners distributed arms among workers to organize attacks on Hindu-dominated areas.[125] Riots did spread to Dacca city where again Bihari Muslim workers led the communal violence.[126] But violence took a different turn when rioters attacked physical training colleges and harassed Bengali Muslim girls. On 15 January rioters killed a Bengali litterateur and cultural activist, Amir Hossain Chowdhury.[127] Rioters stabbed to death a 28-year-old American teacher,

Richard Novak, of Notre Dame College of Dacca when he went to the mill areas of Narayanganj to take photographs of mass violence against Hindus.[128]

Meanwhile, riots in East Pakistan provoked attacks on Muslims in India. Riots spread to Calcutta in West Bengal and Assam.[129] The Pakistani government claimed that nearly 100,000 thousand refugees arrived from Assam, Tripura and West Bengal in East Pakistan.[130] The influx of Bengali Muslim refugees coincided with the settlement of these refugees in Garo areas of East Pakistan, and attacks on the Garo settlement led to an exodus of Garos to the Garo Hills (in present-day Meghalaya) in India on 5 February 1964.[131] This event also had international repercussions as European and American powers perceived it as an attack on the Christian community.

The ferocity of riots and the international nature of the crisis surprised the leaders of the Bengali regional autonomy movement.[132] On 14 and 15 January 1964 pro-Awami League newspaper *Ittefaq* wrote editorials against the riot. Sheikh Mujib risked his own life in saving riot victims.[133] On 16 January Bengali regional autonomists formed a committee of 19 members and issued an appeal titled 'Purbo Pakistan Rukhia Darao' (East Pakistan Resist), and *Ittefaq* published an editorial to that effect. Radical students, communists and Awami Leaguers became active in preventing riots. They opened an office in Topkhana Road, Dacca, to monitor the situation and send assistance to riot victims.[134] Khoka Roy, a communist leader of Hindu descent, claimed that this preparation prevented further rioting.[135] Nonetheless, communist student activist Rono lamented that they did not have strength everywhere, and thus on a rescue mission in the industrial areas of Savar in Dacca's outskirts they discovered dead bodies of women and men.[136]

According to the Constitution that Ayub Khan gifted to the people of Pakistan, presidential election had to be held every three years. In 1964 Ayub Khan initiated a constitutional amendment engineered through a defection of nine members from opposition even in the shambolic national assembly and brought forth the date of the election to January 1965.[137] On 31 May 1964 he also released Sheikh Mujib from prison. On 12 July various opposition political parties observed Anti-Autocracy Day.[138] On 24 July all political parties, except Ayub Khan's CML, formed an electoral alliance called the Combined Opposition Party (COP). On 19 August the CML nominated Ayub Khan as a candidate for the presidential election. At the same time the COP nominated Fatema Jinnah as their candidate. Soon after this declaration, Khawaja Nazimuddin, who hoped that he would be nominated as the candidate of COP, passed away on 23 October 1964. With his death three prominent old guards of Bengal politics – Fazlul Huq, Suhrawardy and Nazimuddin – passed away, ending a political generation of Muslim nationalism.

The election did not enthuse radical student leaders, and many opposition political figures such as Bhashani remained rather dissatisfied with the selection of the candidate. The COP included faith-based radical political organizations such as the Jamaat-e-Islami, who opposed the family reforms of Ayub Khan, a progressive measure that sought to change polygamy as a social institution and women's inheritance within the family. The presence of former Muslim League leader Nurul Amin, who was the chief minister of East Pakistan during the student movement of 1952, also disheartened Bhashani and his associates. Bhashani issued a separate pamphlet demanding the release of political prisoners, debt cancellation measures for the peasantry, redistribution of surplus land and state-owned land among landless workers and marginal peasants, cancellation of the practice of leasing rural markets and swamps to highest bidders, determination of lowest minimum price of jute and sugar cane, ending of communalism and allowing religious minorities to sell their properties, and protection of cottage industries. He asked votes for the COP based upon this demand charter.[139] Despite blatant state support for Ayub Khan, Fatema Jinnah evoked positive response in public meetings in East Pakistan. Ayub Khan released a huge amount money to Basic Democrats and convinced the Basic Electorate that if Fatema Jinnah won the election, then the Basic Democracy system would be cancelled and Basic Democrats would lose their position. In the end she secured 46.5 per cent votes in East Pakistan among Basic Democrats in East Pakistan, indicating a growing slide in popularity of Ayub Khan even among rich peasants, a social stratum that he nurtured most through the allocation of developmental funds.[140]

Meanwhile, alongside sliding popularity, the Ayub Khan regime faced cooling down of the US' relationship with Pakistan. Ayub Khan stepped up his criticism of the US when the latter offered military aid to India in the wake of the 1962 war. His foreign minister, Zulfiqar Ali Bhutto, encouraged him to develop relationship with China. Pakistani public opinion expressed dismay with Ayub Khan for his pro-Western stand when it was announced in Washington, DC that 525 million dollars in military aid would be extended to India.[141] More importantly, Pakistan now sought to settle her border with China. Both countries reached an 'agreement in principle' on 28 December 1962 in relation to the location of the border with China in Pakistan-occupied Kashmir. The relationship warmed further when the first Sino-Pakistani

Trade Agreement was signed in Karachi on 5 January 1963. This treaty provided for an exchange of Chinese manufactured goods for Pakistani cotton, jute and leather goods.[142] Pakistan and China also signed a Boundary Agreement with provision for a Joint Boundary Demarcation Commission on 2 March 1963.[143] The US viewed Pakistan's growing proximity to China with suspicion and expressed its dissatisfaction through various diplomatic gestures. President Lyndon B. Johnson even directly accosted Pakistani foreign minister Bhutto when the latter met him on 29 November 1963, after the death of president John F. Kennedy.[144]

Ayub Khan, under prodding from his foreign minister, meanwhile visited China in March 1965 and established closer ties of Pakistan with it. He followed this with a visit to the Soviet Union. He was diversifying Pakistan's relationship with global players. The US obviously did not like Ayub Khan's close proximity to China and viewed the increasing role of his foreign minister Bhutto with suspicion. President Johnson communicated this to Ayub Khan and cancelled Pakistan's president's visit to the US.[145]

Meanwhile, Pakistan and India both became involved in armed skirmishes over the small uninhabitable salt marsh of Rann of Kutch, lodged between the Indian state of Gujarat and the Pakistani region of Sindh, in April 1965. As the territory was advantageous to Pakistan, Pakistan could overrun Indian military posts.[146] The failure of the Indian army convinced Ayub Khan and his close advisors that after the defeat in the hands of the Chinese army, Indian people and forces remained so demoralized that they lost the appetite to fight. The massive protests in the Kashmir Valley during the Hazrat Bal incident further convinced Ayub Khan that Kashmiris were ready to revolt. He prepared a plan of two-staged armed intervention in Indian-held Kashmir. The first was known as Operation Gibraltar, which would involve infiltration of Kashmir by regular members of armed forces masquerading as Kashmiri militants. These soldiers would encourage locals to revolt and occupy Srinagar. They would then appeal to the international community to recognize the Kashmir government established by Pakistanis. The success of this operation would lead towards the second phase of the military operations whereby the Pakistani army would directly attack Akhnur which constituted a key link in Jammu.[147] Ayub Khan expected that this external expedition would reverse his declining political status in Pakistan and even the wayward province of East Pakistan would support his endeavour. Meanwhile, Ayub Khan expected, as in the Rann of Kutch, the international community or global powers would intervene in the war.

Ayub Khan was right in thinking that such a strategy would win public approval even in East Pakistan. Indeed, *Ittefaq* started reporting the success of the 'Mujahedeen' army in Kashmir during Operation Gibraltar.[148] After the Indian counterattack in the direction of Lahore on 6 September, entire East Pakistan witnessed massive nationalist outpouring. Writers, poets and musicians all condemned the Indian invasion. Stories of divine interventions in favour of the Pakistani army circulated during the war.[149] The East Pakistan regiment stationed in the Sialkot sector provided stiff resistance against the advancing Indian army.[150] Even Anisuzzaman, a progressive writer who was then in England, admitted his lowkey but definite support to the Pakistani cause. Indeed, Anisuzzaman, in his characteristic humorous way, described how both Indian and Pakistani Marxists defended their respective nations using same logic.[151] Celebrated communist writer Munier Chowdhury participated in a popular pro-Pakistan radio programme called 'Hing Ting Chot', named after a famous phrase coined by Calcutta-based Bengali writer Sukumar Roy. Sufia Kamal, a progressive woman writer, led a women delegation to governor Monem Khan after a gathering at the Baitul Mukarram mosque. Hasan Hafizur Rahman, a noted Bengali writer, who was associated with the 21 February language movement, wrote a book called *Simanto Shibir* (Border Post), and Munier Chowdhury, Syed Shamsul Haque and Rafiqul Islam, three distinguished figures, wrote a book called *Ronangon* (Battlefield).[152] Sheikh Mujib, Ataur Rahman and other opposition leaders met with governor Monem Khan to express solidarity. In a public speech Sheikh Mujib blamed the UN for its failure to resolve the Kashmir issue.[153] Bhashani even called for Pakistan to withdraw from the UN. Yet, true to his left-leaning political orientation, he called for scrapping all treaties with the US.[154]

The Hindu community of East Pakistan also suffered during the war. On 12 February 1964 the government banned the selling of property by Hindu owners without state permission. In 1965 the state could acquire the property of Hindus under the provisions of the Enemy Property Act. The famous Mohini Mill of Kushtia had been brought under the control of the East Pakistan Industrial Development Corporation.[155] Many Hindus left the country, and there took place little protests against this. War unified two wings of Pakistan and religious nationalism had its heyday.

As soon as war came to an end, the differences in the political response to the peace treaty manifested sharply in two wings. Political leaders based in East Pakistan welcomed the peace treaty, but in West Pakistan people rioted against the treaty. It was widely propagated in West Pakistan that they had won the war but lost in diplomatic negotiations. More importantly, it became clear that during the war East Pakistan remained unprotected. There did not exist any relationship with the outside world and people did not have independent means to judge news of the war. Then it became known that East Pakistan did not have adequate food grains stored in the government warehouses. The East Pakistan State Bank did not have enough hard foreign currency to buy goods from the international market.[156] Despite massive investment in defence expenditure in Pakistan, East Pakistan was left unprotected. Soon political differences between East Pakistan and West Pakistan witnessed sharp polarization. Political leaders felt betrayed by the Pakistani military regime. In the end, hyper-nationalist war propaganda strengthened the demand for autonomy in East Pakistan.

Conclusion

Politics in the early years of the sixties witnessed a dialectical movement. The opening years of the decade witnessed massive protests by students and workers against the martial law regime. The national independence movement against colonial regimes and radical protests of the global sixties impinged on the consciousness among student radicals and labour activists. Revolutionary movement to decolonize East Pakistan from internal colonization remained compromised by the political establishment's loyalty to the ideal of Pakistan.

The NDF's aim of amendment of the Constitution through the national assembly turned out to be a mirage. Similarly, the COP's support for Fatima Jinnah did not dislodge Ayub Khan from power through the system of Basic Electorate which turned out to be a shambolic exercise. Ayub Khan could manipulate the Basic Electorates to win the election. Despite such political withering of opposition, it seemed a change was looming in the horizon. Old political guards with their memories of colonial rule and commitment to the Pakistan movement gradually passed away. Among the old guards Fazlul Huq was revered as a statesman, but he was burdened with old age and then passed away. Nazimuddin rendered himself a pedestrian in East Pakistani politics through his support for Urdu as a national language and died before the presidential election. It was Suhrawardy's death that removed the possibility of constitutional limits of the movement and deep loyalty to the idea of Pakistan. Increasingly, this void was filled up by Sheikh Mujib who constituted a bridge over the chasm between the revolutionary underground and open pro-democracy popular movement and constitutional electoral politics.

While popular movements against the regime gained momentum, attacks against religious minorities also increased, sometimes with patronage of the military regime. The government manipulated events in India and democratic struggles in Kashmir for the self-government to step up the ethnic cleansing of minorities. War with India, as planned by the military regime, provoked surging religious nationalism uniting two wings in extraterritorial loyalty towards the military regime of Pakistan, and yet East Pakistan was left unprotected by the same military regime. Once the high-tide religious nationalism emanating from war was over, the Bengali autonomy movement leaders again became aware of the process of internal colonization. What lacked in this context was a clear political programme that articulated aspirations of the people of East Pakistan and could unify them in an action. It was the political programme and a decisive leadership that would create a new leap in East Pakistani politics.

Notes

1. Kamruddin Ahmad, a Pakistani diplomat and a historian close to the Awami League, recalled an incident in 1958. He was then posted as a deputy high commissioner in Calcutta. Sheikh Mujib called him and informed him that he would have lunch at his place. Kamruddin Ahmad waited for Sheikh Mujib to arrive next afternoon at his place. But Sheikh Mujib appeared at his house in a very agitated manner around 1 p.m. the next day, accompanied by two of his colleagues. He even refused to have lunch, but then, at Ahmad's wife's request, he settled down a little. He informed them that Atatur Rahman had transferred the DM and the police superintendent of Sheikh Mujib's native district, Faridpur, because of Mohan Mian's (another politician) requests. An angry Sheikh Mujib told Ahmad that he would arrange for the toppling of the ministry within a week. Ahmad booked a return flight to Dacca for Sheikh Muijib but also realized that the days of the Rahman ministry were numbered. Within a week Ahmad got the news that nine members of the NAP had withdrawn support from the Rahman ministry. Kamruddin Ahmad, *Banglar Ek Modhyobitter Atmokahini* (Dhaka: Prothoma Prokashon, 2018), p. 192.

2. Rizwan Ullah Kokab and Mahboob Hussain, 'National Integration of Pakistan: An Assessment of Political Leadership of Huseyn Shaheed Suhrawardy', *Journal of Political Studies* 24, no. 1 (2017): 315–31.
3. Abul Kalam Shamsuddin wrote in his autobiography that the political unrest and anarchy caused such a bitterness among people that prohibition on political parties was welcomed by them. See Abul Kalam Shamsuddin, *Otit Diner Smriti* (Memories of Old Days) (Dhaka: Khosroj Kitab Mohal, 2019 [1968]), p. 266 (translation mine).
4. Ataur Rahman Khan, *Swaiiracharer Dosh Botsor* (Dacca: Naoroj Kitabistan, 1970), p. 68.
5. Cited in Lawrence Ziring, *The Ayub Khan Era: Politics in Pakistan, 1958–1969* (Syracuse, NY: Syracuse University Press, 1971), p. 10.
6. Foreign and Commonwealth Officer Papers, DO 134/26, Deputy High Commissioner Basil J. Greenhill to R. W. D. Fowler, 3 November 1958.
7. Foreign and Commonwealth Officer Papers, DO 134/26, Deputy High Commissioner Basil J. Greenhill to R. W. D. Fowler, 3 November 1958.
8. IB Report, East Pakistan, F/N-606-48, PF Part 9, p. 28.
9. Later, lieutenant general Niazi surrendered to the allied army of liberation force of Bangladesh and India on 16 December 1971.
10. Foreign and Commonwealth Officer Papers, DO 134/26, Deputy High Commissioner Basil J. Greenhill to R. W. D. Fowler, 3 November 1958.
11. Foreign and Commonwealth Officer Papers, DO 134/26, Deputy High Commissioner Basil J. Greenhill to R. W. D. Fowler, 3 November 1958.
12. Abul Mansur Ahmad, *Amar Dekha Rajnitir Ponchas Botsor* (Dacca: Prothoma Prokashan, 2018), p. 466.
13. The meeting was attended by Ataur Rahman, Abu Hossain, Hamidul Huq, Tofazzal Hossain, Sheikh Mujib and Yusuf Ali Chowdhury (Mohan Mian), a representative of Nurul Amin. Shyamali Ghosh, *Awami League 1949–1971*, trans. Habib ul-Alam (Dhaka: University Press Limited, 2007), p. 60.
14. Ghosh, *Awami League*, pp. 60–61.
15. Ghosh, *Awami League*, p. 61.
16. Ghosh, *Awami League*, p. 64.
17. Ghosh, *Awami League*, p. 65.
18. Karl von Vorys, the political scientist who attended the election campaign, observed: 'Four separate campaigns that I personally observed from close quarters suggest the following pattern. First, claims of associations with the defunct parties were frequent themes. Second, political problems,

especially the issue of universal suffrage, regularly entered the discussions between candidate and electors. There were also formal negotiations for votes, either in terms of money or future favors. Finally, although to a somewhat lesser extent than in West Pakistan, ascriptive identifications were ever-present and remained of critical importance.' Karl von Vorys, *Political Development in Pakistan* (Princeton, NJ: Princeton University Press, 1965), p. 236.

19. Susheela Kaushik, 'Constitution of Pakistan at Work', *Asian Survey* 3, no. 8 (1963): 384–89, DOI: 10.2307/3023649.
20. *Dawn*, 25 June 1962. Also see Rashed Khan Menon, *Ek Jibon: Swadhinotar Surjoday* (A Life: Dawn of Independence) (Dhaka: Batighor, 2021), pp. 80–81.
21. For details, see Saleem M. M. Qureshi, 'Party Politics in the Second Republic of Pakistan', *Middle East Journal* 20, no. 4 (1966): 456–72, http://www.jstor.org/stable/4324059 (accessed on 22 August 2021).
22. Saleem Qureshi has offered a detailed explanation of Pakistani politics, and this section is based upon his explanation of politics. Qureshi, 'Party Politics in the Second Republic of Pakistan', pp. 456–72. Also see Mughees Ahmed, 'Relationship between Political Parties and Non-Political Powers: An Analysis with Reference to Pakistan', *Pakistan Journal of Social Sciences* 29, no. 1 (2009): 107–15.
23. Qureshi, 'Party Politics in the Second Republic of Pakistan', pp. 456–72.
24. Qureshi, 'Party Politics in the Second Republic of Pakistan', pp. 456–72.
25. Qureshi, 'Party Politics in the Second Republic of Pakistan', pp. 456–72.
26. Foreign and Commonwealth Office Records, 'Revival of Political Parties in Pakistan', DO/134/29, Record of the Talk with Mohammad Munir Rawalpindi on 11 August 1962.
27. *Dawn*, 5 October 1962.
28. The *Dawn* published the president's letter on 11 October 1962.
29. *Dawn*, 29 October 1962. Abul Mansur Ahmad, a veteran Awami League leader and Suhrawardy's follower, further elaborated this point in his autobiography. He claimed that the old leaders of Pakistan used to say: 'We understand the right to vote by people but we shall not organize election.' Ayub Khan said it more directly to the people that the people of Pakistan did not know how to use their franchise, and thus he did not give them the right to vote and that suited Pakistani genius. Ahmad claimed that there was no distinction between the two claims; there did not exist democracy in Pakistan. A. M. Ahmad, *Amar Dekha Rajnitir Ponchas Botsor*, p. 475.

30. K. Ahmad, *Banglar Ek Modhyobitter Atmokahini*, pp. 428–29.
31. Shaista Suhrawardy Ikramullah, *Huseyn Shaheed Suhrawardy: A Biography* (Karachi: Oxford University Press, 1991), pp. 108–10.
32. Cited in K. Ahmad, *Banglar Ek Modhyobitter Atmokahini*, pp. 426–27.
33. Harun-or-Rashid, *Mul Dharar Rajniti: Bangladesh Awami League Council 1949–2016* (Mainstream Politics: Bangladesh Awami League Council 1949–2016) (Dhaka: Bangla Academy, 2019), p. 74.
34. Kamruddin Ahmad hinted at this in his autobiography. See K. Ahmad, *Banglar Ek Modhyobitter Atmokahini*, p. 190.
35. Rashid, *Mul Dharar Rajniti*, pp. 76–79.
36. Salimullah Khan, 'Alamgir Kabirer Ogyan Othoba Muktijuddhoke Amra Bujhte Parini', in Alamgir Kabir, *Cholochitro o Jatio Mukti: Rochona Songroho* (Films and National Emacipation: Collected Works) (Dhaka: Agami Prokashoni, 2018), pp. 20–21.
37. Salimullah Khan, 'Alamgir Kabirer Ogyan Othoba Muktijuddhoke Amra Bujhte Parini', pp. 20–21.
38. Haidar Akbar Khan Rono, *Shotabdi Perie* (Dhaka: Tarafdar Prokashani, 2012), pp. 28–29.
39. Rono, *Shotabdi Perie*, pp. 28–29.
40. Kazi Zafar Ahmed, *Amar Rajnitir 60 Botsor: Joar Bhatar Kothon* (Sixty Years of My Politics: Stories of Ebb and Flow) (Dhaka: Torofdar Prokashoni, 2017), p. 98.
41. Rono, *Shotabdi Perie*, pp. 148–50.
42. Menon, *Ek Jibon*, p. 195.
43. K. Z. Ahmed, *Amar Rajnitir 60 Botsor*, p. 99.
44. Rono, *Shotabdi Perie*, p. 38.
45. Morshed Safiul Hasan, *Swadhinotar Potobhumi: 1960r Doshok* (Dhaka: Anupom Prokashoni, 2014), p. 226.
46. Hasan, *Swadhinotar Potobhumi*, pp. 227–28.
47. J. N. Dixit, *India–Pakistan in War and Peace* (London: Routledge, 2002), pp. 127–29.
48. Dixit, *India–Pakistan in War*, pp. 127–29.
49. Norman D. Palmer, *South Asia and United States Policy* (Boston, MA: Houghton Mifflin, 1966), pp. 206–07.
50. Dixit, *India–Pakistan in War*, pp. 127–29
51. Hasan, *Swadhinotar Potobhumi*, pp. 229–30.
52. Hasan, *Swadhinotar Potobhumi*, p. 229.
53. Hasan, *Swadhinotar Potobhumi*, p. 230.

54. Afsan Chowdhury, 'Bangladesher Swadhinatar Andoloner Dharabahikota: East Bengal Liberation Party 1958', *Samakal*, 25 June 202, p. 13.
55. Hasan, *Swadhinotar Potobhumi*, pp. 236–37.
56. Hasan, *Swadhinotar Potobhumi*, pp. 237–38.
57. Kazi Aref Ahmed, *Nucleus, BLF, Swadhinota: Bangalir Jatio Rastro* (Dhaka: Ankur Prokashoni, 2014), p. 61.
58. Moni Singh, *Jibon Songram* (Dwitio Khondo) (Dhaka: Jatio Sahitya Prokashoni, 1992), pp. 57–58.
59. Singh, *Jibon Songram* (Dwitio Khondo), p. 58.
60. Manoranjan Roy, *Songramer Tin Doshok* (Dhaka: Jatio Prokashoni, 1986), p. 182.
61. Singh, *Jibon Songram* (Dwitio Khondo), p. 59.
62. Mahfuj Ullah, *Purbo Pakistan Chhatro Union: Gourober Dinguli* (Dhaka: Adorn Publications, 2012), p. 14.
63. Mohammad Hannan, *Bangladesher Chatro Andoloner Itihas, 1830–1971* (Dhaka: Agami Prokashoni, 2013), pp. 208–10.
64. Hannan, *Bangladesher Chatro Andoloner Itihas*, pp. 208–10.
65. Hannan, *Bangladesher Chatro Andoloner Itihas*, pp. 208–10.
66. Hannan, *Bangladesher Chatro Andoloner Itihas*, pp. 238–39.
67. Rono, *Shotabdi Perie*, p. 32.
68. Rono, *Shotabdi Perie*, p. 32.
69. Rono, *Shotabdi Perie*, pp. 32–33.
70. Menon, *Ek Jibon*, pp. 59–60.
71. Hannan, *Bangladesher Chatro Andoloner Itihas*, pp. 238–39.
72. Hannan, *Bangladesher Chatro Andoloner Itihas*, pp. 239–40.
73. Hannan, *Bangladesher Chatro Andoloner Itihas*, pp. 239–40.
74. For details of the activities, see Vorys, *Political Development in Pakistan*, pp. 193–95.
75. Rono, *Shotabdi Perie*, pp. 46–48.
76. Rono, *Shotabdi Perie*, pp. 46–48.
77. K. Z. Ahmed, *Amar Rajnitir 60 Botsor*, pp. 114–15.
78. K. Z. Ahmed, *Amar Rajnitir 60 Botsor*, p. 115.
79. Hasan, *Swadhinotar Potobhumi*, p. 73.
80. Pakistan Commission on National Education, *Report, January–August 1959* (Karachi: Manager of Publications, 1961), pp. 82–86.
81. Mohammad Niaz Asadullah, 'Educational Disparity in East and West Pakistan, 1947–71: Was East Pakistan Discriminated Against?', *Bangladesh Development Studies* 33, no. 3 (2010): 1–46.

82. Hannan, *Bangladesher Chatro Andoloner Itihas*, p. 250.
83. Hannan, *Bangladesher Chatro Andoloner Itihas*, p. 252.
84. *Dainik Ittefaq*, Tuesday, 21 August 1962.
85. Hannan, *Bangladesher Chatro Andoloner Itihas*, p. 253.
86. Rono, *Shotabdi Perie*, p. 55.
87. Menon, *Ek Jibon*, p. 90.
88. Kazi Zafar recalled in his memoir that the meeting took place in the house of Ataur Rahman Khan, the former Awami League chief minister of East Pakistan. K. Z. Ahmed, *Amar Rajnitir 60 Botsor*, p. 125.
89. Rono, *Shotabdi Perie*, pp. 55–56.
90. K. Z. Ahmed, *Amar Rajnitir 60 Botsor*, p. 125.
91. K. Z. Ahmed, *Amar Rajnitir 60 Botsor*, p.125.
92. Rono, *Shotabdi Perie*, pp. 55–56.
93. Rono, *Shotabdi Perie*, pp. 55–56.
94. Rono, *Shotabdi Perie*, pp. 57.
95. Hannan, *Bangladesher Chatro Andoloner Itihas*, p. 252.
96. Hasan, *Swadhinotar Potobhumi*, pp. 76–77.
97. Hasan, *Swadhinotar Potobhumi*, p. 77.
98. Hasan, *Swadhinotar Potobhumi*, p. 77.
99. Hasan, *Swadhinotar Potobhumi*, pp. 78.
100. Hasan, *Swadhinotar Potobhumi*, pp. 79.
101. Hasan, *Swadhinotar Potobhumi*, p. 81.
102. Nafis Ahmad, 'Industrial Development in East Bengal (East Pakistan)', *Economic Geography* 26, no. 3 (1950): 183–95, p. 184.
103. Sergei Stepanovich Baranov, *East Bengal: Characteristics of Economic Development, 1947–1971*, trans. Tajul Islam, Abaul Barakat, Abdus Sabur, Abdul Momin, Kairul Hossain, Shoeb Ali Shikdar and Bau Naser Khan, ed. Tajul Islam (Dhaka: Jatiya Sahitya Prakashani, 1986), pp. 10–11.
104. Central Statistics Office, *Economic Survey of East Pakistan* (Karachi: Government of Pakistan, 1957), p. 29.
105. *Statistical Digest of Bangladesh*, no. 8, Dhaka, table No. 51, pp. 70–71.
106. Abu Hanifa Md Noman, Md Aslam Mia, Hasanul Banna, Md Sohel Rana, A. S. A. Ferdous Alam, Chan Sok Gee, Che Ruhana Isa and A. C. Er, 'City profile: Narayanganj, Bangladesh', *Cities* 59 (November 2016): 8–19.
107. See Sumel Sharafat, 'Mongla Port Capacity Expanding', *Prothom Alo*, http://en.prothom-alo.com/economy/news/132991/Mongla-port-capacity-expanding (accessed on 12 February 2021). Istiaque Ahmed, Khandaker

Asif Mahmud and Shaila Islam, 'A Study on Historical Transformation of the Urban Integration Core of Khulna City, Bangladesh', *International Journal of Innovation and Applied Studies* 8, no. 4 (2014): 1410–17.
108. G. M. R. Islam, M. Iqbal, K. G. Quddus and M. Y. Ali, 'Present Status and Future Needs of Tea Industry in Bangladesh', *Proceedings-Pakistan Academy of Sciences* 42, no. 4 (2005): 305–14.
109. Anindita Ghoshal, 'The Invisible Refuges: Muslim "Returnees" in East Pakistan, 1947–1971', *Journal of the Asiatic Society of Bangladesh (Humanities)* 63, no. 1 (2018): 59–89, pp. 70–71.
110. Faisal Ahmmed and Md Ismail Hossain, *A Study Report on Working Conditions of Tea Plantation Workers in Bangladesh* (Dhaka: ILO Country Office for Bangladesh, 2016), pp. 15–16.
111. Layli Uddin, '"Enemy Agents at Work": A Microhistory of the 1954 Adamjee and Karnaphuli Riots in East Pakistan', *Modern Asian Studies* 55, no. 2 (2021): 629–64, DOI: 10.1017/S0026749X19000416.
112. Kamruddin Ahmad, *Labour Movement in East Pakistan* (Dacca: Progoti Publishers, 1969), p. 36.
113. K. Ahmad, *Labour Movement*, p.44.
114. K. Ahmad, *Labour Movement*, p. 50.
115. Nirmal Sen, *Amar Jobanbondi* (Dhaka: Ityadi Grontho Prakashani, 2012), p. 247.
116. *New York Times*, Monday, 27 July 1964, p. 31.
117. Sen, *Amar Jobanbondi*, pp. 246–47.
118. Sen, *Amar Jobanbondi*, p.249.
119. Student leaders Rono, Zafar and Menon played a crucial role in developing the labour movement in the Tongi industrial area from 1966 onwards.
120. Idrees Kanth, 'The Social and Political Life of a Relic: The Episode of the Moi-e-Muqaddas Theft in Kashmir, 1963–1964', *Himalaya: The Journal of the Association for Nepal and Himalayan Studies* 38, no. 2 (Article 10, 2018): 61–75.
121. Kanth, 'The Social and Political Life of a Relic', pp. 61–75.
122. Kanth, 'The Social and Political Life of a Relic', pp. 61–75.
123. Sachi G. Dastidar, *Empire's Last Casualty: Indian Subcontinents' Vanishing Hindu and Other Minorities* (Kolkata: Firma KLM, 2008), p. 170. Nonetheless, Dastidar sometimes exaggerates the impact without much factual evidence.
124. Kali Prasad Mukhopadhyay, *Partition, Bengal and After: The Great Tragedy of India* (New Delhi: Reference Press, 2007), p. 58.

125. Rono, *Shotabdi Perie*, p. 78.
126. Priti Kumar Mitra, 'Bangladesher Mukti Songramer Itihas 1958–1966', in *Bangladesher Mukti Sangramer Itihas 1947–1971*, ed. Salahuddin Ahmad, Monem Sarkar and Nurul Islam Monjur, pp. 82–150 (Dhaka: Agami Prokashoni, 2013), p. 107.
127. Mitra, 'Bangladesher Mukti Songramer Itihas 1958–1966'.
128. Michael Novak, 'The Day My Brother Was Murdered', *American Spectator*, 24 December 2012, https://spectator.org/42533_day-my-brother-was-murdered (accessed on 15 January 2021).
129. Mayurakshi Das, 'Calcutta Cauldron: City-Life during the January 1964 Riots', *Proceedings of the Indian History Congress* 78 (2017): 1147–54.
130. *London Times*, 20 January 1964.
131. Milani Sur, 'Battles for the Golden Grain: Paddy Soldiers and the Making of the Northeast India-East Pakistan Border, 1930–1970', *Comparative Studies in Society and History* 58, no. 3 (July 2016): 804–32.
132. Rono, *Shotabdi Perie*, pp. 77–79.
133. Mozaharul Islam, *Bongo Bondhu Sheikh Mujib* (Dacca: Bangla Academy, 1974), pp. 228–29.
134. Rono, *Shotabdi Perie*, pp. 77–79.
135. Roy, *Songramer Tin Doshok*, p. 78.
136. Roy, *Songramer Tin Doshok*, pp. 77–79
137. Roy, *Songramer Tin Doshok*, p. 78. G. P. Bhattacharjee, *Renaissance and Freedom Movement in Bangladesh* (Calcutta: Minerva Associates, 1973), p. 202. Also see Sharif al-Mujahid, 'Pakistan's First Presidential Elections', *Asian Survey* 5, no. 6 (1965): 280–94.
138. Sekhar Dutta, *Shaater Doshoker Gono Jagoron: Ghotona Probaho Parjyalochona Probhab* (Dhaka: Somaj Bigyan Prokashoni, 2015), p. 195.
139. Rono, *Uttal Shater Doshok* (Dhaka: Punthi Niloy, 2016), p. 36.
140. The figure 46.5 per cent is a calculation from al-Mujahid, 'Pakistan's First Presidential Elections', p. 292.
141. George. J. Lerski, 'The Foreign Policy of Ayub Khan', *Asian Affairs* 1, no. 4 (1974): 255–73.
142. Klaus H. Pringsheim, 'China's Role in the Indo-Pakistani Conflict'. *China Quarterly* 24, no. 24 (1965): 170–75, pp. 171–72.
143. Pringsheim, 'China's Role in the Indo-Pakistani Conflict', pp. 171–72.
144. Pringsheim, 'China's Role in the Indo-Pakistani Conflict', pp. 172–73.
145. Pringsheim, 'China's Role in the Indo-Pakistani Conflict', pp. 172–73.

146. Farooq Bajwa, *From Kutch to Tashkent: The Indo-Pakistan War of 1965* (London: Hurst, 2013), pp. 73–95.
147. Bajwa, *From Kutch to Tashkent*, pp. 98–100.
148. *Ittefaq*, 30 August 1965.
149. Hasan, *Swadhinotar Potobhumi*, p. 100.
150. Ishfaq Ilahi Choudhury, '1965 Indo-Pak War: Busting the Myth', *Daily Star*, 8 September 2014.
151. Anisuzzaman, *Kal Nirobodhi* (Dhaka: Sahitya Prokash, 2019 [2003]), pp. 413–14.
152. Hasan, *Swadhinotar Potobhumi*, pp. 100–01.
153. Hasan, *Swadhinotar Potobhumi*, p. 97.
154. Hasan, *Swadhinotar Potobhumi*, pp. 97–99.
155. Dhirendranath Dutta, *Shahid Drindronath Dotter Atmokotha*, edited by Anisuzzaman, Rashid Haidar and Minar Mansur (Dhaka: Bangla Academy, 1995), p. 138, cited in Hasan, *Swadhinotar Potobhumi*, p. 104.
156. Kamruddin Ahmad, *Swadhin Banglar Obhyudyoy Ebong Otopor* (Dhaka: Dhrupad Sahityoangon, 2018), p. 75.

6

The Global Sixties and the Coming of Revolution

The popular upsurge of the sixties in Pakistan was a product of the interaction among global, regional and local politics. It was not a unilinear movement towards the rise of Bengali nationalism but, rather, several complex twists and turns in global and local politics, and the atmosphere of the global sixties transformed nationalist imaginings in East Pakistan. The image of Ayub Khan's military-bureaucratic regime was seriously tarnished by his inability to wrest Kashmir from Indian control. Propaganda during the 1965 war had convinced the Pakistani people that they had emerged victorious from the war. Yet the Tashkent peace accord belied such claims. This resulted in popular anger at home as Ayub Khan could not explain why he had been unable to secure in Tashkent what he had claimed to have won on the battlefield. Meanwhile, the war also involved Ayub Khan's regime in intense Cold War diplomacy. During the war, China had proclaimed open support to Pakistan while the US had stopped the supply of weapons to the latter as soon as the war started. However, after the war Ayub Khan moved closer to the US, since he knew that China could not meet the economic needs of his model of foreign-aid-driven praetorian capitalism. He also compelled the long-time member of his kitchen cabinet, the pro-Chinese Zulfiqar Ali Bhutto, to resign. Bhutto raised the banner of revolt on the high moral ground of independence for Kashmir, installation of parliamentary democracy and policies tuned towards Islamic socialism. It was a timely move on Bhutto's part. Consequently, divisions appeared among the ruling elites of Pakistan, and Ayub Khan became estranged from the very institution that had supported him, namely the army. As the ruling elites became fragmented, the war unleashed inflationary pressure on the economy, and people embarked on protests. Glaring class inequality and regional imbalance fuelled unrest. Soon global revolutionary waves hit Pakistan.

George Katsiaficas, a participant social historian of the global 1968, calls this the 'eros effect' of the global wave of revolution.[1] The eros effect refers to the movement of transnational waves of transformative social movements. During this moment, popular social upheavals dramatically challenged established social orders, and the basic assumptions of patriotic nationalism. The authority of the government, hierarchy and the subjugation of labour were intensely questioned.[2] During the eros effect, popular movements could not only imagine a new way of life, but millions of people lived according to transformed norms, values and beliefs. It was a secular millenarian moment at which the dawn of a new society could be perceived. Between 1968 and 1971, East Pakistan experienced this global moment of social emancipation, during which the radical alliance between students and workers unleashed protests against Ayub Khan's model of praetorian capitalism. Soon workers, students and middle peasants burst into mass protests. Bhashani, an octogenarian peasant populist leader with Maoist leanings, symbolized this struggle to a great extent. Yet his attempts were enfeebled by dissensions among the communists. 'Drawing on the narrative theories of Hayden White and Northrop Frye', James Krapfl demonstrates in the context of Czechoslovakia in 1989 that 'successive and rival interpretations of unfolding history not only reflected participants' perceptions; they were political instruments by means of which participants strove to shape the course of history'.[3] This was true of the 1969 revolution in East Pakistan whereby participants' rival interpretations of history and competing recollections provide clues to the complex historical processes that unfolded in East Pakistan in 1969.

Nervous about radical popular rebellion, the military junta compelled Ayub Khan to resign and released high-profile political prisoners like Sheikh Mujib. The new martial law administrator, Yahya Khan, declared that the first general election (based on the principle of 'one person, one vote') would be held in Pakistan, and seats to different provinces would be allotted in proportion to the population.[4] Sheikh Mujib, the leader of the Awami League, now released from prison, drew his legitimacy from popular support. Unfettered by any opposition from the fractionalized and competing groups of pro-Chinese communists, he became a populist national hero who concentrated his political programme on the unresolved nationality question in East Pakistan. He was also assisted by pro-Soviet communist factions in his campaign and faced weak opposition from conservative political parties that had a very limited mass base.

In other words, in a situation of the decomposition of various existing party-political formations, the masses supported a leader who promised national emancipation based on regional linguistic identity. This campaign provided the final shape to the idea of linguistic nationalism. In the process of this electoral campaign an emotive idea of independent Bangladesh was born. This was the moment of the birth of a truly counter hegemonic discourse of nationalism. In Fanonian terms, anti-colonial consciousness reached its apex.[5] In 1970, the massive devastation unleashed by the Bhola cyclone in East Pakistan and the delay in the flow of aid further alienated East Pakistani people from the West Pakistani military junta. In many ways, a revolution occurred in the political common sense of the majority of East Pakistanis during the election campaign. The idea of a linguistic homeland trumped Pakistani nationalism, and Sheikh Mujib's emergence as a symbol of the newly imagined Bangladesh, as well as the great expectations concerning his leadership among the masses, made him a prisoner to the dreams of millions. Thus, in the face of military intransigence to negotiate a fundamental premise for a Constitution based on the six-point programme, he remained absolutely committed to his stand. Popular forces in the two wings of Pakistan thus adopted a diametrically opposite stand. More importantly, Yahya Khan, the new martial law administrator, was emboldened by the fact that he enjoyed the tacit support of president Richard Nixon and his national security advisor, Henry Kissinger, who considered Yahya Khan's role indispensable in their clandestine negotiations for rapprochement with China. This strengthened Yahya Khan's resolve to crush the opposition in East Pakistan through military means. Soon severe repression unleashed by the army led towards an armed liberation struggle by the people of Bangladesh. From 26 March 1971, the majority of people in East Pakistan embraced Bangladesh as their new homeland. Mass popular uprising during the global sixties led to a process of decolonization from the hold of praetorian capitalism in East Pakistan, and the complexities of global political circumstances also enabled a particular strand of that nationalism to emerge victorious. Thus, the global sixties transformed the political landscape of Pakistan.

War, International Diplomacy and Changing Dynamics of the Pakistani Policy

The war of 1965 embroiled Pakistan in the international politics of the Cold War, and the military administration of Ayub Khan developed fissures in response to such involvement. In the early sixties, Pakistan had developed a close diplomatic relationship with China, a development of which the US administration was wary. President Johnson indicated to Pakistan his deep displeasure with the pro-China tilt of the Ayub Khan administration.[6] During the 1965 war, the US secretary of state, Dean Rusk, had announced the suspension of military supplies to India and Pakistan on 8 September.[7] In contrast, on 7 September, China had condemned 'Indian aggression' and expressed 'firm support for Pakistan in its just struggle against aggression'. China also accused India of violating the India–China border.[8] On 19 September 1965 China once again announced that India had violated the Indo-Chinese border and further stressed that it was conducting the gravest armed provocation since the 1962 war.

This sabre rattling by China alarmed the US and the Soviet Union. Between 18 and 20 September both the US and the Soviet Union issued a warning against any Chinese involvement.[9] But in Pakistan the public opinion swelled in support of China, and the US became very unpopular. The following is an excerpt from a CIA report which grudgingly admits Chinese popularity in Pakistan:

> Recent events have shown him that his China policy was largely a failure: fear of China did not deter India from striking back at Pakistan; and India did strike back, it became apparent to Ayub that Chinese intervention would create for Pakistan more problems than it would solve. However, public opinion is in favor of working with China, and Ayub probably will not make any move to break existing ties.[10]

Notwithstanding this development, Ayub Khan sought to retain ties with the US. Throughout the India–Pakistan war of 1965, Ayub Khan remained in touch with the US administration through the US embassy.[11] Western powers encouraged him to negotiate peace with India, and the UN Security Council resolved on 20 September that both India and Pakistan had to withdraw all armed personnel back to the positions held by both the states before 5 August 1965. Ayub Khan resented this proposal as it did not mention Kashmir and called for a return to the status quo. He rightly sensed that the omission of the Kashmir issue would undermine his legitimacy as a military leader among army officers. In Karachi, rioting erupted in response to the proposal. Mobs threw stones at the US embassy and snatched the American flag. British and Canadian embassies were also attacked. US sources alleged that despite the heavy presence of the police, stoning was allowed to progress for a while.[12] Ayub Khan's finance minister, Muhammad Shoaib, a well-known economist, told the US embassy that Ayub Khan had been almost persuaded to accept the peace. He requested the US to maintain reassurances and encouragement to Ayub Khan, because, in Shoaib's own words, 'we must prevent this thing from going the Chinese way'.[13] Shoaib was afraid that Pakistan would lose economic support from the US, and as such Pakistan's ambitious plan to revitalize its economy would be jeopardized.[14] In contrast to Shoaib, foreign minister Bhutto, the architect and advocate of the pro-China policy of the Pakistani government, earned the ire of the US administration. A document by the CIA mentions:

> Karachi has also – at the expense of its good relations with the West – pursued other anti-Indian efforts. In particular, led by its anti-Western Foreign Minister Z. A Bhutto, it has lined up in international forums with such radical, anti-western states as Indonesia, Ben Bella's Algeria Cuba and China. While it has done so probably to gain more diplomatic allies against India – whose international outlook has become generally moderate and conciliatory – it has nonetheless endorsed the most extreme and irresponsible anti-American positions.[15]

Ayub Khan, meanwhile, confided to the Iranian foreign minister that he would be happy to be a 'satellite of the US' as long as the US did not ask him to be a 'satellite of India'.[16] Meanwhile, the shah of Iran, a close ally, and an outspoken supporter of Pakistan during the war, informed the US embassy that he had sent a delegation to persuade Pakistan to accept the UN proposal. Otherwise, Iran indicated, it would suspend aid to Pakistan. From the American perspective, Ayub Khan's flirtation with the Chinese had pushed him into a corner.[17] Indeed, Pakistan's closest allies were Turkey and Iran, who were also close allies of the US. Finally, foreign minister Bhutto read Ayub Khan's order of ceasefire in the UN, whereby Ayub Khan stated his disaffection with the ceasefire statement in following terms:

> Pakistan considers Security Council Resolution 211 of 20 September as unsatisfactory. However, in the interests of international peace and in order to enable security to evolve a self-executing procedure which will lead to an honorable settlement of the root causes of the present conflict,

namely the Jammu and Kashmir dispute, I have issued the following order to the Pakistan armed forces: You will stop fighting as of 3 a.m. on 23 September – 2200 GMT 22 September, and from that time you will not fire on an enemy unless fired on.[18]

Ayub Khan thus registered his protest with the ceasefire resolution as it did not address the Kashmir issue. He made it very clear to his officers and to the international community that he would not compromise his position on the Kashmir issue for which he went to war. At the same time, he signalled to the US that he abided by their request to end the war. While Ayub Khan primarily weighed pros and cons in terms of Pakistan's relationship with the US and China, the Soviet Union had not been lying dormant with regards to these events taking place in their neighbourhood. In early September and again on 13 September 1965, the Soviet Union offered to arrange a meeting of the leaders of India and Pakistan to engage in peace talks.[19] On 17 September, the Soviet prime minister offered to take part in this meeting and proposed that the meeting be held in Tashkent or any other city in the Soviet Union.[20] The Indian prime minister accepted the Soviet offer in principle. Soon after the war, Pakistan approached the US government for its view.[21] On 15 November president Ayub Khan announced in the Pakistan national assembly that he had accepted the ceasefire 'because Big Powers – particularly the US, the Soviet Union and the UK – assured that they would use their influence to reach a settlement of the Kashmir dispute'.[22] Meanwhile the Soviet Union refused to support the resolution adopted on 5 November 1965, on grounds of procedural differences. British diplomats registered their concerns over the fact that the big four – the US, the UK, the Soviet Union and France – had failed to agree.[23]

Responding to Soviet overtures and also to create pressure on the US, foreign minister Bhutto visited Moscow on 23 November 1965.[24] Meanwhile, the UK complained of Soviet refusal to cooperate in the summit between the big four. A British diplomatic cable to the UK embassies in Tokyo, Rawalpindi, Washington, DC, and Moscow on 14 October cryptically commented that Pakistanis might meet with India under Soviet auspices and speculated:

> [I]f such meeting took place before withdrawal had been started, the Soviets could cash in on the situation and achieve a cheap diplomatic triumph over withdrawal. On the other hand, if the Tashkent meeting

took place after withdrawals had begun, the Soviets would be forced to risk burning their fingers over a long-term Kashmir settlement.[25]

In other words, the West had not objected to the meeting in Tashkent because they would like to put the onus on the Soviets, which would help them avoid direct responsibility for diplomatic failure to secure peace. The Soviets, on the other hand, made such attempts because of their expanding conflicts with China and the growing Chinese influence in Pakistan.

The US observed Soviet interventions in South Asian affairs with slight concern and softened its stance towards Pakistan. Ayub Khan, according to the CIA, recognized that if the fighting continued, his forces would be worn down and defeated by India's larger ones. As a CIA memorandum puts it:

> President Ayub clearly agreed to a ceasefire only after considerable hesitation and with considerable anguish. He did so for two principal reasons: (1) he was aware that if the fighting continued his forces would be worn down and then defeated by India's larger ones, and (2) he saw that the only way to offset India's military superiority was through a major Chinese military attack on India. Even assuming that China was willing to launch such an attack, which is unlikely, Ayub was clearly unwilling to cast his lot completely with China.[26]

Ayub Khan thought that the only way to offset India's military superiority was through a major Chinese attack. But such an attack might create a significant international problem, and it was not clear as to whether Chinese forces would truly launch an attack on India.[27] The Americans, on the other hand, hoped that Ayub Khan would recognize his dependence on the West in general, as the Soviet Union would not, and communist China could not, supply the military and economic needs of Pakistan.[28] Ayub Khan's problems became acute, as according to the CIA report, very few people were aware of Pakistan's deteriorating military position, though many civilian and military officials wondered why Pakistan had stopped fighting if it was doing militarily as well as it was claimed. But popular expectations had been aroused, and Ayub Khan could not tell the truth about the war as it would inevitably raise questions as to why he had embarked on such a course of action. This would undermine his rule and the CIA feared that, as Bhutto threatened, Pakistan would withdraw from the UN, join hands with China and engage in an endless war with India – a war that they might not win. The

CIA considered Ayub Khan a safer bait than the rise of Muslim nationalism or pro-Chinese communism.[29]

The US lobbying and Ayub Khan's own inclination towards the US finally had borne fruits. Ayub Khan wanted to sound the US administration before going to Tashkent for a peace discussion with India. Between 12 and 16 December 1965, he visited the US to mend his relationship with the American administration. His warm reception at the White House signified that the US still viewed Ayub Khan as a critical ally. Ayub Khan quite categorically asked Johnson whether the US would stand aside if India attempted to force an inequitable settlement of the two countries' problems.[30] Johnson assured Ayub Khan that that would not be allowed to happen, though he cautioned the latter that Pakistan had to genuinely be a victim, and it could not be making use of the tactics put recently into practice in Kashmir. Johnson also made it clear that the US did not have capability to impose a settlement of the Kashmir situation on India.[31] Ayub Khan also assured Johnson that Pakistan did not have a secret understanding with China.[32] In the Western diplomatic circle Pakistan's relationship with China weighed quite highly. There were concerns about Bhutto, who was believed to be an unpredictable pro-China dark horse in the Pakistani cabinet. Indeed, when Ayub Khan, on the way back from the US, visited Bonn in December to discuss possible German military assistance to Pakistan, British diplomatic correspondence concentrated on Bhutto. Needless to add, Bhutto was already unpopular in Western diplomatic circles.[33] A British officer gleefully commented that Bhutto played a minor role in the talk with the German chancellor and the Pakistani embassy staff virtually ignored him.[34] A British diplomat named Nixon cautioned the embassy of their enthusiasm about Bhutto's fall, though his language too revealed a severe dislike of Bhutto:

> As to the significance of his [Bhutto] minor role we are unable to make any confident judgements. He is such a slippery man that he changes his spots to suit the occasion and will normally be restrained when President Ayub is present. His imminent downfall has frequently been predicted before, during what turned out to be only a temporary and possibly a deliberate eclipse. We do not see any strong reasons for thinking that his position has changed significantly. Nevertheless, much will depend upon the outcome of the Tashkent talks and their possible effect on Sino-Pakistan relations since Bhutto is the main advocate of close links with China.[35]

Diplomatic correspondence among Western powers revealed their preference for Ayub Khan, provided he disassociated Pakistan from communist China. Ayub Khan obviously had to perform a critical balancing act in international politics as he was dependent on US aid to run the course of development along the lines of praetorian capitalism, and yet he could not sideline China, then regarded as the centre of world revolution, because of the popularity of China among people in Pakistan. In domestic politics, too, he had to reclaim his stature in West Pakistan as a powerful military leader. At the same time, he had to cut Bhutto's wings, who sensed Ayub Khan's weakening grip over Pakistani politics and had started putting pressure on him. Nonetheless, Ayub Khan could not afford another costly military confrontation with India, which might again evoke hostile reactions from the US. It was precisely to avoid another unwinnable war with India and diplomatic isolation from the West that Ayub Khan agreed to come to terms with India. In Tashkent, thus, Ayub Khan agreed to the Soviet peace proposal with India precisely to maintain the flow of aid from the West and to avoid another disastrous war.

Bhutto launched a tirade against Ayub Khan and, according to Altaf Gauhar, Ayub Khan's information secretary, Bhutto spread the rumour that there were secret clauses in the Tashkent agreement.[36] In contrast to Ayub Khan, Bhutto followed a path of populist nationalism with certain inclinations towards the global socialist movement. From 1963 onwards he had steered Pakistan's foreign policy towards pro-socialist revolutionary forums in global politics. His shrewd reading of the local political situation and the pent-up frustration of the urban working class under conditions of praetorian capitalistic development prompted him to play the role of the opposition leader in the closing days of Ayub Khan's military dictatorship. He obviously spiced it up with virulent anti-India rhetoric. Thus, there appeared a fracture within the Ayub Khan administration due to international diplomatic pressure. The logic of aid-driven praetorian capitalism and populist nationalism clashed in West Pakistan against the background of the global tide of protests and subaltern anger. A military dictator presiding over uneven capitalistic development could hardly involve people in the process of governance, and Ayub Khan's Basic Democracy system was based upon the principle of selective mobilization in the place of mass involvement. In short, Ayub Khan was afraid of the masses; yet war time compulsions had led him to flirt with popular nationalist mobilizations. Now the people demanded accountability and transparency from the regime, but Ayub could ill afford to be transparent. Thus, he faced protests.

As soon as the Tashkent accord was signed, protests took place on the streets of West Pakistani cities. It was clear that Pakistan had agreed to return to the status quo and there had been no mention of the Kashmir issue in the accord. India suffered a shock as prime minister Lal Bahadur Shastri died in Tashkent from a heart attack. Soon the widows of the soldiers killed in the battlefields organized a procession in Lahore. These women rhetorically posed a question to Ayub Khan: why did he send their husbands to death for nothing?[37] On 14 January 1966 a large procession took place in Lahore against the Tashkent accord, and the police had to resort to firing to scatter the assembled crowd.[38] Popular anger on the streets increased further because the war had imposed a financial burden on Pakistan. West Pakistani military leaders tried to distance themselves from Ayub Khan. His inability to win the war and his acceptance of the Tashkent accord made him a liability in the eyes of many soldiers, politicians and bureaucrats. Gauhar, his close ally and political secretary, quite aptly complained that establishment political figures played a crucial role in undermining Ayub's regime and the political order he constructed from within.[39]

While the regime faced such an internal crisis, Ayub Khan's model of foreign-aid-driven praetorian capitalism encountered another crucial problem: the impact of massive inflation on everyday life. The price of sugar and flour went up rapidly. The rationing of food led to long queues in front of ration shops.[40] As asserted by economic historian Omar Noman, Ayub Khan's model of the economy deliberately ignored distributional issues and inflation eroded the real wages of the burgeoning working class.[41] Ayub Khan tried to civilianize the rule of the military and the upper echelon of the bureaucracy, engineered into existence a monopoly capitalist oligarchy and also made the wealthy peasantry a distant junior partner in the ruling social coalition that he expected to act as the popular basis of his constitutional order. But in the face of revolutionary anger from below, fissures in the political establishment led to his fall from power. Friendship with revolutionary China came at a small price: China, the self-proclaimed revolutionary centre of the world, sent literature on Marxism–Leninism–Mao Zedong thought in large quantities, and these books were available in bookshops all over the country. The idea of a peasant revolution captured the attention of many among students and youth activists.[42] Not surprisingly, among many other factors, the youth in West and East Pakistan became radicalized by such exposure.

East Pakistan and Popular Resistance: The Idea of Provincial Autonomy

Surrounded by India on three sides, East Pakistan remained isolated from the rest of the world during the war.⁴³ It had also remained undefended during the 17 days of war.⁴⁴ The war halted trade with India and the prices of essential food items started skyrocketing. Workers in different industries had to pay compulsory war donations. Many industries, such as the industry of *bidi* (country cigar made of tobacco and *tendu* leaf) making, suffered, as importation of *tendu* leaves from India stopped.⁴⁵ This isolation and crisis disillusioned many among the East Pakistani intellectuals and politicians about the ability of the Pakistani army to provide East Pakistan with security. While during the war patriotism had surged in East Pakistan and nearly two million ordinary East Pakistani citizens had registered their names as volunteers for civil defence training, soon after the war the Awami League working committee criticized the Pakistani government for leaving East Pakistan unprotected.⁴⁶ Indeed, during the war Awami League leaders had in private maintained that the outcome of the war would not provide East Pakistan with autonomy, though they supported Pakistan unconditionally.⁴⁷ Soon after the ceasefire, the Awami League working committee claimed that a much stronger and independent defence was required for East Pakistan. They further added that East Pakistan was left untouched because of Indian goodwill.⁴⁸ Such a sentiment was in marked contrast to that of other political parties. The NAP did not provide any response, though Bhashani supported the war efforts in an ardent manner and emphasized national unity and integrity.⁴⁹ On 10 November 1965, in a public meeting, Awami League leaders criticized the Pakistani government for leaving East Pakistan unprotected and ridiculed the idea of national unity and integrity as a false slogan.⁵⁰ The fact that East Pakistan was unprotected during the war came from Ayub Khan himself. In a meeting in Dacca on 24 December, Ayub Khan admitted that the defence system of East Pakistan was very weak, and he promised to strengthen it in the future.⁵¹ The Awami League stood vindicated in its accusation that East Pakistan had remained without any defence during the war. On 25 December Ayub Khan held a meeting with provincial political leaders in the governor's house. Here, too, Sheikh Mujib complained about the marginalization of East Pakistan in the current constitutional arrangement.⁵² It was clear that Sheikh Mujib and his close colleagues in the Awami League were moving towards a more concrete demand charter for provincial autonomy. In the meeting with Ayub Khan, Nurul Amin, the leader of the NDF and the former chief minister of East Pakistan, presented his seven-point charter of demands to Ayub Khan.[53] Apparently, Khairul Kabir – a noted journalist and founder editor of the Bengali daily *Sombad* – had provided this demand charter to Amin. It is interesting that the programme was nearly identical to the later six-point programme presented by Sheikh Mujib. In the seventh point, Amin's programme was different, as he wanted to limit franchise on the basis of educational qualifications and the payment of certain amount of taxes.[54] This was the original recommendation of the Constitutional Commission appointed by Ayub Khan in 1960. But in the end this seventh clause was a rehash of the colonial argument about the devolution of power to people in the early twentieth century.[55] Yet the similarity between the two demand charters indicates a wider consensus among intellectuals and political activists about constitutional progress and provincial autonomy in East Pakistan. Despite such an apparent consensus, it was clear that Sheikh Mujib wanted to invest his time and efforts in upholding this programme even at the expense of his personal liberty, while Amin made little effort to own and support his own programme. That is why Sheikh Mujib attracted Ayub Khan's attention and hostility, as well as people's admiration for his tenacity in pursuing a programme of autonomy for East Pakistan, while Amin was simply ignored by the masses.

Politics in East Pakistan started taking a more menacing shape in the days following Ayub Khan's visit. In January 1966, as the Tashkent declaration became an important subject of political conversation in East Pakistan, the Awami League welcomed the Tashkent declaration and the coming of peace.[56] In East Pakistan, the Awami League became alarmed when, on 13 January, governor Monem Khan circulated a notice concerning the application of the Enemy Property Act.[57] Political activists, including Sheikh Mujib, were aware of the divisive potentials of such a move by the government.[58] On 18 January Sheikh Mujib demanded that all wartime regulations restricting freedom of speech, public meetings, processions, public debates and newspaper reportage had to be rescinded.[59] The government was becoming wary of such demands made by Sheikh Mujib, and soon, on 10 and 17 January, Sheikh Mujib was summoned to court for his speech during the ceasefire negotiations. On 28 January he was sentenced to two years of imprisonment on various charges of violation of national security, but he was provided with a bail after a legal appeal.[60] Meanwhile, as the Ayub Khan government witnessed fissures within its administration, opposition political parties sought to galvanize the movement for democracy. Chaudhry Muhammad Ali, who was then the leader of the Nizam-e-Islam party, called for a national convention of the opposition political parties. Noticing the unpopularity of the Tashkent declaration in West Pakistan, he stood for rescinding the declaration. Four parties agreed to join the convention. It included the Nizam-e-Islam, the Muslim League (Council), the Jamaat-e-Islami and the Awami League. On 5 and 6 February 1966, they organized an opposition conclave in Lahore. Nearly 740 delegates attended the convention, of which 21 were from East Pakistan.[61] The reasons for the poor representation of East Pakistan could be located in the reluctance of major East Pakistan-based political parties to join the convention. For instance, the NAP refused to join the conclave, and even the moderate NDF decided not to attend it.[62] Yet Sheikh Mujib accepted the invitation and went to Lahore with his colleague Tajuddin Ahmad. Sheikh Mujib did not seek the permission of the Awami League working committee to present his opinion. He was afraid that many within his party would not accept it.[63] He raised his programme to the subject committee of the convention on 6 February for its inclusion on the agenda. Political leaders in Lahore, however, did not allow Sheikh Mujib to table those proposals in the convention. Even Nawabzada Nasarullah Khan, the president of the national committee of the Awami League, refused to support it. Frustrated, Sheikh Mujib returned to Dacca and held a press conference on 11 February in which he presented his six-point programme formally. These six points include the following:

1. The constitution should provide for a Federation of Pakistan in its true sense on the basis of the Lahore resolution, and Parliamentary form of government with supremacy of legislature directly elected on the basis of adult franchise.
2. Federal government shall deal with only two subjects, viz. Defense and Foreign Affairs, and all other residuary subjects shall vest in the federating states.
3. (*a*) Two separate but freely convertible currencies for two wings may be introduced, or (*b*) one currency for the whole country may be maintained. In this case effective constitutional provisions are to be made to stop the flight of capital from East to West Pakistan. Separate Banking reserve is to be made and separate fiscal and monetary policy to be adopted for East Pakistan.

4. The federating states shall retain all power to tax and levy duties. The central government shall have no power of taxation but shall draw working revenues from the federating states.
5. (*a*) There shall be two separate accounts for foreign exchange earnings of the two wings.
   (*b*) Earnings of the East Pakistan government shall be under the control of East Pakistan government and that of West Pakistan under the West Pakistan government.
   (*c*) Foreign exchange requirements of the federal government shall be met by the two wings either equally or in a ratio to be fixed.
   (*d*) Indigenous products shall move free of duty between the two wings.
   (*e*) The constitution shall empower the unit governments to establish trade and commercial relations with, set up trade missions in and enter into agreements with foreign countries.
6. Setting up of a militia or a para-military force for East Pakistan.[64]

The six-point programme ostensibly refers to the original Lahore Resolution. But in 1946, during the Delhi session of the elected Muslim League members, when the resolution was revised for a single state, it was Suhrawardy who had moved the resolution, and there had been not a single murmur of protest from within the Bengal Muslim League.[65] At that time, the imminent departure of colonial rulers, Jinnah's magnetic charm as the sole spokesperson of Muslim public opinion in colonial India, and Muslim nationalism had led Bengali Leaguers to ignore the implications of the resolution. Yet the idea of two different economic policies for two different wings of Pakistan had originated in the decade of the forties. Economist Abdus Sadeque had actually presented a critical understanding of the economy of Pakistan in the forties, during the heyday of the East Pakistan Renaissance Society. Both Suhrawardy and Nazimuddin had rejected this proposal, as the map prepared by Sadeque in his booklet did not include West Bengal.[66] After independence, Sadeque further proposed that, in a bi-territorial state such as Pakistan, there was no alternative but to develop two different set of economic policies for the two wings.[67] This idea was known as the theory of two economies. It had been proposed in the 21-point manifesto of the United Front in the 1954 elections. As time passed, the idea of two economies gained currency among economists in East Pakistan. On 16 and 17 January 1956,

Abul Mansur Ahmad presented a critique of the Pakistani government's position in the Pakistan national assembly in Karachi. He suggested that a central government should keep foreign policy, defence and currency in their hands and all other subjects should be transferred to the provinces. A few professors of Dacca University including Abdus Sadeque, Muzzaffar Ahmed Chowdhury, Sadeque and A. F. A. Husain assisted Abul Mansur Ahmad in the research for and preparation of his speech.[68]

This became more evident in the sixties. Nurul Islam, who was the deputy chairman of the first Planning Commission of Bangladesh, recalled that in 1956, on the eve of the First Five-Year Plan of Pakistan, the government called for a conference of economists of East Pakistan. A group of economists published a report based on the discussions in the conference. Members of this group included M. N. Huda, A. F. A Husain, Mazaharul Haque, M. T. Haq, Abdus Sadeque, M. A. Razzaq and A. Farouk. East Pakistani economists who subscribed to the idea of two economies for the two wings of Pakistan argued that a relatively limited circulation of trade, mobility of labour and higher transportation costs of goods between the two wings had made the inter-wing trade more akin to international trade. A higher degree of investment in West Pakistan generated employment only in the western wing. Consequently, it was impossible for the labour force in East Pakistan to participate in the economy. Thus, the report recommended that for the purpose of development there should be two economic units in Pakistan. Primary economic activities such as statistics collection and tabulation of national income, the current-account loans and dues, and internal and foreign assets should be performed on a regional basis.[69]

In the years following, there developed a deep division between West Pakistani and East Pakistani economists regarding the theory of two economies for a bi-territorial state. Many West Pakistani government officials suspected that this would eventually result in the secession of East Pakistan.[70] In 1960, facing a significant degree of inflation, the government employed a commission to investigate into the causes of rapid price rise. This commission was headed by veteran Muslim League politician I. I. Chundrigarh. It comprised of two male economists, three businessmen and a woman representing consumers. Harvard University-trained East Pakistani economist, Nurul Islam, represented East Pakistan in this commission. Nurul Islam disagreed with the main report of the commission and argued for a different reason for the higher rates of inflation in East Pakistan. Finally, the commission agreed to include an appendix in which Nurul Islam was allowed to include his own analysis of the causes of different rates of inflation in the two wings. But when the government circulated the report widely among educationists, it excluded the appendix.[71] Ayub Khan was fully aware of the economic differences between the two wings of Pakistan. He invited East Pakistan-based economists for a breakfast in Dacca on 24 June 1961. M. N. Huda, A. F. A. Husain, A. Farouk and Nurul Islam were included in this team. Ayub Khan was accompanied by his secretary, Kiu Sahab, and possibly the information secretary, Gauhar. Governor Azam Khan encouraged the economists to articulate their opinions freely. When this team finished their discussion, Ayub Khan asked them to give their individual opinions to him in a written form. These economists prepared a written memorandum whereby they argued for two sets of economic policies for the two wings of Pakistan. But at the end the report recommended a separation of the economies of two wings of Pakistan. The central government, in their opinion, would control defence, foreign policy and inter-wing communication and transportations. Though there could be a single currency in the two wings of Pakistan, policies concerning loans, debts and currency reserves would be taken by the autonomous regional governing bodies of state banks in the respective provinces. All revenues and foreign currencies would be deposited in the respective provinces. According to their economic and fiscal abilities, and in proportion to the opportunities offered by the central government, the provinces would contribute to the expenses of the central government.[72] Nurul Islam maintained that this memorandum was drafted without any consultation with politicians.[73] Throughout the sixties, East Pakistani economists combated policy makers of the praetorian economy. Thus, it was the economy that took the front seat in the politics of the autonomy movement.

The idea of two economies for the bi-territorial state of Pakistan also entered the academic curriculum of Dacca University. In 1961, younger faculty like Rehman Sobhan and Nurul Islam convinced the Economics Department chair, M. N. Huda, to introduce a course on Pakistan's economies.[74] As there were few textbooks on Pakistani economics, both Islam and Sobhan started doing research based on data supplied by the newly established Pakistan Development Economics Institute.[75] They started developing theories about the political economy of regional discrimination and educated students about it. Sarwar Murshid, a faculty member of the English Department, started a journal called *New Values*. Sobhan and Murshid also ran a colloquium sponsored by the journal. Abdur Razzak, a respected faculty member of the Political Science Department, had once argued in a colloquium entitled 'Army in Politics' that in any family the less intelligent boys would join the army, thus indicating that they were not the competent people required to run the country.[76] In 1959 Sobhan published a critique of the Pakistani government's policies towards East Pakistan in the Bureau of National Reconstruction (BNR). Despite assurances from Kabir Chowdhury, who encouraged free and frank criticism, the article had earned the displeasure of higher authorities.[77] Islam, Sobhan and Habibur Rahman, who was then the deputy chairman of the Planning Commission, organized a seminar at Dacca University. Sobhan presented an article on the two economies of Pakistan. *Daily Observer*, a major English-language daily, made this article a headline piece on their front page. Sobhan, who was a young academic then, to his surprise found that Ayub Khan retorted in the newspaper that there existed only one economy in Pakistan.[78] Even in a BNR-organized seminar on the united economy of Pakistan, Sobhan presented a paper on Pakistan's dual economics. He argued in his paper that Pakistan's economy and integrity could be strengthened if the government gave the two units enough autonomy to control their fiscal policy, income from foreign trade and other associated economic issues. The *Pakistan Observer* published this entire article. In this context, East Pakistani economists had to confront the World Bank observers and the Harvard Advocacy group.[79] In 1961, in the National Finance Commission of Pakistan, East Pakistani economists and senior government employees had raised the issue of economic discrimination. D. K. Power, who was the additional chief secretary to the East Pakistani government, played a crucial role in highlighting regional discrimination. He was severely reprimanded by the central government for this role.[80] Meanwhile, the six-point programme consolidated the findings and ongoing debates about the political economy of Pakistan. Awami League leader Tajuddin Ahmad and government officer Ruhul Quddus, possibly in consultation with CSP officials Khan Mohammad Shamsur Rahman, Sanaul Haq and A. K. M. Ahsan, veteran politician Abul Mansur Ahmad, as well as Pakistani ambassador to Myanmar and former labour leader Kamruddin Ahmad, and Khairul Kabir drafted the document.[81] Sheikh Mujib invested energy and political capital in upholding the document. Thus, the six-point programme originated in the efforts of young economists, bureaucrats and politicians. It had a long history of its making, and its propagation stirred Pakistani politics and reshaped the autonomy question.

The announcement of the six-point programme invited intense scrutiny and provoked opposition and severe criticism. Within the Awami League there were hesitations, and many of the working committee members were not willing to commit themselves to such a radical programme. Sheikh Mujib called for a working committee meeting on 20 February. According to one anecdote, Serajul Alam Khan, who was the former general secretary of the Chhatro League, had encircled the meeting with students carrying sticks, thus forcing dithering members to either leave the place in fear or accept the six-point programme as the official programme of the Awami League.[82] Veteran Awami Leaguer Abdur Rashid Tarkabagish left the Awami League organization for his differences with the six-point programme. The working committee formed a new sub-committee comprising Sheikh Muijib, Tajuddin Ahmad and four other members, for the publication of the six-point programme as a booklet. Soon a booklet was published in Bengali and English signed by Sheikh Mujib. Abdul Momin, the campaign secretary of the Awami League, published this booklet from 51 Purana Paltan in Dacca. The booklet clearly declared that the Awami League did not hold ordinary West Pakistanis responsible for the exploitation of East Pakistan, but rather, they argued, the capitalist system was responsible for such a situation.[83]

On 18 March the Awami League council met under the presidentship of Syed Nazrul Islam in Hotel Eden in Dacca. The meeting was inaugurated with Tagore's song 'My Golden Bengal'. Zahidur Rahim sang that song indicating its prominence in the movement.[84] It indicated the new status of the song and the new confidence of the Awami League as a Bengali nationalist party. The council elected Sheikh Mujib as its president and Tajuddin Ahmad as the general secretary of the organization. Nazrul Islam became one of the vice-presidents. On the third day of the conference, Sheikh Mujib addressed a public meeting.[85] This council session adopted socialism as the main goal of the movement and the six-point programme as the first step towards securing an exploitation-free socialistic pattern of society.[86] It was a crucial development for a centrist organization such as the Awami League. In many ways, this resolution was the outcome of intense student and labour movements in the provinces and a global trend towards socialism in the majority world. Many student supporters of the Awami League had read Fanon, knew about the Algerian and Palestinian struggles, and were aware of Chinese experiments with agrarian socialism. They were radicalized by the Cuban Revolution, the Vietnam War and Congo's struggle for national emancipation and the ongoing anti-colonial struggles in Africa. They preferred a commitment towards the socialistic pattern of society. Indeed, this was a period of intense resistance in Dacca. The government-sponsored NSF attacked and beat up

Abu Mahmud Sarkar, a Marxist professor of the Economics Department at Dacca University.[87] On 16 February students demonstrated against this attack and called for a strike throughout East Pakistan on 22 February.[88] This student protest soon developed into a movement for the resignation of professor Osman Ghani, the vice chancellor of Dacca University, and went on strike on 7 March 1966.[89] At the same time Sheikh Mujib supported the students and tried to answer criticisms of the six-point programme[90]. Thus, the six-point programme became linked with student agitation.

The publication of the six-point programme placed Sheikh Mujib at the centre of political conversation in Pakistan. Ayub Khan criticized the programme on 8 March indirectly in the inaugural session of the national assembly. On 18 March he attacked the followers of the six-point programme as being opposed to national unity and integrity.[91] Federal ministers of Ayub Khan's cabinet asserted that this would lead them towards civil war and that it was the reflection of the demand for a greater Bengal. His foreign minister, Bhutto, even challenged Awami Leaguers that he would prove that the six-point programme was baseless. On 22 March the Awami League accepted Bhutto's challenge through a press declaration.[92] Throughout April, Sheikh Mujib toured different districts of Bengal and held massive meetings in support of the six-point programme. He was repeatedly arrested under the National Security Act. But his arrests made him more popular, and he gained a wider mass support. He famously described the six-point programme as a charter of liberty for Bengalis. On 8 May 1966, he held his last meeting on the six-point programme in the industrial township of Narayanganj. Here, in a mass meeting, he released six doves as a symbol of the six-point programme.[93] On the night of 8 May, the government arrested him from his residence at 32 Dhanmondi, Dacca. On the same night, the government arrested other top-ranking leaders such as Tajuddin Ahmad, Zahur Ahmad Chowdhury, Mansur Ali and others. Finally, in protest against the random arrests of their activists and their leader, the Awami League called for a total strike on 7 June 1966. While the Awami League prepared for the general strike to make it a success, they were not sure of its outcome. Sheikh Mujib and the six-point programme had evolved through intellectual conversation among political elites and the intelligentsia, primarily economists. Sheikh Muijib sought to make it a 'charter of liberation of East Pakistanis'. The abstract constitutional document, based on the idea of a minimalist federal state and economic autonomy, was translated into bread-and-butter terms for the masses through the speeches of Sheikh Mujib. He thus steered the political conversation in a new direction, but subsistence peasants and industrial workers had little understanding of the complex political reasoning embedded within the constitutional discourse. The Awami League attracted the support of intellectuals and the members of the salaried classes but did not fully capture popular imagination. Students sought to emerge as interlocutors of the six-point movement, but most students came from middle peasant and surplus farmers' families, and the remaining few hailed from professional families of urban centres. The politics of a deeply class-divided society could not transcend such limitations automatically. Yet there were political constituencies among the subaltern social classes that experienced a critical decline in their living standards despite the expansion of economic opportunities during the years of praetorian capitalism.

During the initial period of the conversation over the six-point programme, 12,000 autorickshaw drivers went on strike from 15 February onwards.[94] They withdrew their strike after government officials promised to look into some of their grievances. But as their grievances were ignored, they went on strike from 1 March 1966. They were joined by rickshaw pullers.[95] Dacca city's normal transportation system was disrupted by intense industrial action by these subaltern labouring classes. This created an environment of popular resistance to praetorian rule. Workers employed in railway, jute and cotton textile concerns had experienced a decline in their living standards due to inflation and the systematic suppression of wages as it was believed by policymakers that functional inequality would always accompany economic growth.[96] Apart from workplace issues, the quotidian sufferings of the Bengali working class, in the hands of a non-Bengali supervisory staff, slumlords and goons hired by factory managers, furthered coloured their experience of class oppression with an anti-Bengali racial prejudice. In 1965, before the war, railway workers, electricity workers and central government employees had organized a strike.[97] Thus, not surprisingly, on 7 June 1966, when the Awami League observed a total strike, there took place massive protests among workers in Tejgaon and Narayanganj. Police fired upon the workers, and soon Manu Mian, a worker of the Bengal beverage industry, was killed in the firing.[98] Angry and agitated workers marched to the Dacca city centre and moved on to the high court and Curzon Hall of Dacca University where students received the workers.[99] Nonetheless, neither Awami League leaders nor student radicals were prepared for the workers' militant participation. They did not even announce the future course of action, and the workers returned to their neighbourhoods.[100] The first phase of intense campaigning concerning the six-point programme ended on 7 June 1966. Despite various shortcomings, the Awami League under the leadership of Sheikh Mujib could transform a dry-as-dust constitutional document into a lively political conversation. Sheikh Mujib lost his personal freedom to promote this so-called 'charter of liberty' for East Pakistanis.

The six-point programme was a product of the long-existing discourse about economic well-being and constitutional power-sharing among Pakistanis. It was natural that the architects of praetorian capitalism criticized this set of demands as it directly challenged the Ayub Khan regime's politics of developmentalism. Yet surprisingly enough the most strident critique of the six-point programme came from the NAP, the second largest political organization of East Pakistan. As a party opposed to military dictatorship, this move of the NAP could be located in international politics and the growing distance between the Communist Party of the Soviet Union (CPSU) and the Chinese communists over the strategies for global revolutionary struggle from 1956 onwards. Bhashani, who headed the NAP in East Pakistan, was not a communist but was clearly a fellow traveller of the communists. The underground Communist party organization in East Pakistan operated largely within the NAP and provided cadres, finances and programmatic direction to the NAP. From 1961 onwards a growing split between the Soviet Union and China impacted debates within the Communist party in East Pakistan. Throughout Asia and Africa, anti-colonial struggles witnessed a growing divergence of opinion over forms of revolutionary strategies in the wake of the Sino-Soviet ideological debate. In neighbouring India, the communist movement experienced intense debates within its rank and file that led to the party's splitting in 1964.[101] In East Pakistan, too, the communists developed differences among themselves, and at the centre of it stood the left-leaning peasant populist leader Bhashani.

Bhashani had differed from the Awami League leadership over its position in global politics in 1957. Radicalized by the Suez Crisis, Bhashani had been supportive of Egypt and the Non-Aligned Movement. He had opposed Pakistan joining US-sponsored military pacts. In 1958, during the military takeover of the administration, both communists and the NAP moved underground. Bhashani and several other communists were arrested and sentenced to long imprisonment, and many were detained without trial. As noted earlier, the Algerian War of Independence and Congo's decolonization had deeply inspired the revolutionary youth movement in East Pakistan. Therefore, unsurprisingly, Bhashani and the NAP remained steadfastly committed towards the national liberation struggle in Asia, Africa and Latin America. As a peasant leader, Bhashani was far more impressed with the idea of agrarian revolution along the Chinese line.[102] This was the time when Sino-Soviet differences were slowly becoming apparent to the communist movements in Asia, Africa and Latin America. Bhashani was not a stranger to international political debates. He had attended the Stockholm Peace Conference in 1954, organized by the World Peace Council, as a member of presidium and spent a considerable time in London too.[103] His communist supporters were in tune with the developments in the international communist movement. To the discomfort of East Pakistani communists, the two major communist parties in the Soviet Union and China clashed with each other over the ideological tenor of the international communist movement. From 1963 onwards there took place debates about the Sino-Soviet split among communist prisoners in East Pakistani jails.[104]

The Russian Revolution had primarily originated in the working-class movement and was directed against capitalism. The Chinese Revolution was a product of anti-colonial peasant insurrection.[105] Thus, the two revolutions had two ideological orientations. From the summer of 1957, Chinese communist leaders had been critical of de-Stalinization, particularly as Mao Zedong became wary of criticism of the party policies in China during his Hundred Flowers Movement.[106] The CCP was also suspicious of Nikita Khrushchev's policy of peaceful coexistence with the US and Western countries. In the late fifties and throughout the sixties, the UN did not open its doors to the PRC. The US, the UK and their Western allies restrained revolutionary China from becoming a member of this international architecture of diplomacy. China was represented by the nationalist republic, a regime confined to the tiny island of Taiwan.[107] For the Chinese leadership, thus, any peaceful coexistence was meaningless as it was treated as a pariah nation. During the 22nd Congress of the CPSU, held in Moscow from 17 to 31 October 1961, in his formal report, Khrushchev explained the idea of an 'all people's state' and an 'all people's party'.[108] He condemned Joseph Stalin and criticized Enver Hoxha of the Albanian Labor Party[109]. Chinese communists believed that such an idea diluted the role of communist parties as an international vanguard of the proletarian movement and also sought to fracture relationships with fraternal communist parties. More problematic from the Chinese perspective was the idea of peaceful coexistence, peaceful transition, and peaceful competition. The Chinese were particularly opposed to the newly propounded Soviet doctrine of 'national democracy'. According to the idea of national democracy, post-colonial nations in Asia and Africa could formulate a non-capitalist path of growth through a 'state of national democracy'. National democracy would comprise a broad national front of several classes. At the centre of this development would be the class of the national bourgeoisie. As a class the national bourgeoisie could be distinguished from the comprador bourgeoisie and the monopolist capitalist because of their anti-imperialist commitment due to competition with the metropolitan capitalist class. Rather than the complete annihilation of private property, a worker-and-peasant coalition would compel the national bourgeoisie to pursue left policies and lead towards a peaceful transition towards a non-capitalist path of development, in alliance with the socialist bloc.[110] This policy thrust of the Soviet Union directly contradicted the Chinese idea that Asia, Africa and Latin America would be the arena of the revolutionary armed struggle of the peasantry. According to the CCP, through this revolutionary struggle a broad united front would emerge against the imperialist power bloc.[111] In the sixties, China increasingly became isolated in global politics, developed a more radical programme, warned the US against attacking North Vietnam and truly believed that she was the beaconing light of world revolution. In 1965, Zhou Enlai even communicated to the US that they were ready for a war.[112] As China became radicalized, its differences with the Soviet Union became sharper and Chinese leaders accused the Soviet Union of being a revisionist party.[113] As elsewhere, these debates and developments in international politics impacted the communist movement in East Pakistan. In neighbouring India, the CPI witnessed a vertical split in 1964, though not entirely over the Sino-Soviet split.[114] In East Pakistan, too, communists engaged in debates over the Sino-Soviet ideological divergence. The idea of the centrality of class struggle and the necessity of armed revolution divided opinion in the communist movement.[115] Meanwhile, the critical issue that impacted the NAP and its policies was the Sino-Indian war.

Previously, in the late fifties, Pakistan was regarded as the most devoted among the allied nations of the US, and unsurprisingly communist China had been critical of Pakistan. The Baghdad Pact and the SEATO, Beijing remarked, had enabled the US to build large-scale military bases openly in Pakistan and to use them against neighbouring, peace-loving countries. China believed that within Pakistan people of all strata were mounting a resistance to the state's current policies and charged that the rulers of the country, in their reliance upon American power to maintain their unstable control and suppress the struggle waged by the people at home, were deepening instability.[116] For communists and members of the NAP in East Pakistan, who were opposed to the Ayub Khan regime, this was a further vindication of their belief that Ayub Khan was an agent of the imperial powers. Yet the India–China war altered this easy equation. The Pakistani dictator was surprised by the outpouring of international sympathy for India and the flow of arms from the US and the UK to India. Pakistani public opinion expressed dismay with Ayub Khan for his pro-Western stance when it was announced in Washington that 525 million dollars in military aid would be extended to India.[117] Pakistan concentrated on improving its ties with China. The first Sino-Pakistani Trade Agreement was signed in Karachi on 5 January 1963. This treaty provided for an exchange of Chinese-manufactured goods for Pakistani cotton, jute and leather goods. Pakistan and China also signed a Boundary Agreement, with provisions for a Joint Boundary Demarcation Commission, on 2 March 1963. Pakistan's foreign minister, Bhutto, met with the Chinese foreign Minister, Chen Yi, to this effect.[118]

As the Sino-Pakistani relationship warmed up, Pakistan cast her vote for the PRC's admission to the UN in October 1963. Indeed, when premier Zhou Enlai visited Pakistan in February 1964, a China–Pakistan Joint Communique declared: '… the United Nations could not be considered to be fully representative of mankind until the rightful place of the People's Republic of China in the organisation was restored.' China issued a cautious statement about Kashmir, stating that the Kashmir dispute would be resolved in accordance with the wishes of the people of Kashmir as pledged to them by the people of India and Pakistan.[119] President Ayub Khan made a state visit to China in March 1965, accompanied by foreign minister Bhutto. Ayub Khan addressed a mass rally of 10,000 people in Beijing. In 1965 a Chinese team of journalists visited Pakistan. They declared that China would always be supportive of Pakistan. Throughout East Pakistan there was a significant degree of support for China. Popular opinion was as much anti-India as it was against the US. In April 1966, when president Liu Shao Qi visited Dacca, there was significant outpouring of support for China, though pro-Soviet communists withdrew from the reception committees of Qi.[120]

These twists in the foreign policy of Pakistan caused a problem for the NAP and the Communist party of East Pakistan. Between 1958 and 1962 Bhashani was imprisoned. He observed a hunger strike from 26 October 1962 for several demands of East Pakistan including the granting of 25 million rupees for flood victims and the implementation of the report of the Cruge Commission for flood control.[121] Finally, on 3 November 1962 he was released from prison. On 22 August 1963 Ayub Khan met Bhashani. On 24 September 1963 Bhashani was invited to China to attend the celebration of the Chinese Revolution.[122] In China he met with Mao Zedong and Zhou Enlai. According to an anecdotal reconstruction by Pakistani ambassador general Nadeem Raza, Enlai told Bhashani that he would welcome rapprochement between the NAP and Ayub Khan. Enlai further warned him about the US plot to ensure secession of Bengal from Pakistan.[123] Mao even went further and told that Bhashani's struggle against the Ayub Khan regime would strengthen the hand of Russia, America and India. He advised Bhashani to proceed carefully and slowly so that communist China could deepen its relationship with the Ayub Khan regime.[124] After returning from China, Bhashani wrote a travelogue on his visit in China. It was published in the Bengali periodical *Janata*.[125] While facing criticism for his visit to China in the midst of the anti-Ayub Khan struggle, Bhashani defended his position by claiming that China was the centre of anti-imperial struggle throughout Asia, Africa and Latin America. Thus, he regarded his visit to China as a pilgrimage.[126] Bhashani remained deeply committed to his anti-imperialist political agenda. In 1966 Bhashani attended the Tricontinental Conference in Havana, Cuba, between 3 January and 16 January. At the conference attended by Fidel Castro, Amilcar Cabral and Salvador Allende, Bhashani spoke against imperialism and even met Aruna Asaf Ali, the legendary Indian communist leader. True to their pro-Ayub Khan sympathies, Bhashani and the pro-Chinese wing in the CPP (East Pakistan Provincial Committee) viewed the six-point programme with suspicion.[127] Oli Ahad, a former radical and a veteran of the language movement, went a step ahead and called the document a product of US, Indian and Jewish conspiracy.[128] But more significant were the efforts of the veteran pro-Chinese communist trade union leader Mohammad Toaha's attempt to dissuade workers from joining the 7 June strike against the Ayub Khan government.[129] Most pro-Chinese communists considered the six-point programme as a conspiracy hatched by the CIA.[130] Interestingly, in 1966, at the very moment when pro-Chinese communists were condemning the six-point programme of the Awami League as a CIA-crafted document, the CIA, in its internal report, appeared to be the least sympathetic to Bengali demands. It stated quite unequivocally:

> The difficulty of solving many of East Pakistan's problems would hinder even the most capable and dedicated government. The lower educational level among Bengalis makes it inevitable that they will receive less than

their 'rightful' share of high government positions. The terrain of East Pakistan makes any development project much more expensive than an equivalent project in West Pakistan. Foreign aid suppliers are less interested in such projects and even with an equitable distribution of aid funds, the lack of results would probably leave the Bengalis feeling cheated. Ayub knows that equal defense forces for East Pakistan would make both provinces too weak to resist an Indian attack and has chosen to defend the western province. Should the government grant Mujib's six points or the programmes of his competitors, the central government would become powerless.[131]

The US thus remained committed to supporting Ayub Khan's praetorian regime while pro-Chinese communists were busy discovering Ayub Khan's anti-imperialist characteristics. It became clear that Sheikh Mujib was more prescient in his analysis when he had said earlier that the entire capitalistic development was directed towards hampering the progress of industrialization in East Pakistan. Sheikh Mujib maintained that this was according to the planning of three partners: the government of Ayub Khan, the industrialist lobby in West Pakistan and the foreign-aid donor agencies and their experts.[132]

The CPP (East Pakistan Provincial Committee) and the NAP: Ideological Conflicts, Split and Continued Subaltern Militancy

The NAP, weakened by internal dissensions within the ranks of the CPP (East Pakistan Provincial Committee), remained idle during the six-point programme mobilization by the Awami League between January and June 1966. In May 1966 the NAP observed an anti-price rise week. It held several meetings, organized processions and tried to mobilize the peasantry. Between 4 June and 7 June 1966, the central committee of the NAP met in Dacca for a conference. The conference decided to adopt a 14-point programme that was more focused on the restoration of democracy and the federal restructuring of the polity, whereby the central government would control foreign policy, military and currency. They also demanded the withdrawal of laws restricting individual freedom, the cancellation of pacts with the US, the recognition of trade union rights, the implementation of land reforms and the cancellation of taxes for small farmers.¹³³ The difference between this list of demands and the Awami League's six-point programme could be located in keeping the currency in the hands of the central government. But more importantly, the six-point programme emphasized changes in the taxation process and placed taxes under the control of federating units rather than the central government. The NAP's programme was more directed towards peasants and workers' demands. On 1 July Bhashani appealed for a united movement of political parties. The NAP's programmes were supported by two newspapers, *Sombad* and *Janata*. Yet as the NAP's programme did not include any reference to the six-point programme, the Awami League did not respond to the call. Undeterred by this lack of action on the part of the Awami League, Bhashani travelled in north Bengal in October and November of 1966 and held a series of public meetings despite his ill health. Meanwhile, the NAP and Bhashani were alarmed by the developments in Indonesia in the wake of the failure of the 30 September movement.¹³⁴ The genocide of the members of the Communist Party of Indonesia alarmed the pro-Chinese faction of the East Pakistani communists and encouraged their resolve to steer their propaganda against imperialism. Bhashani sent a telegram to Indonesia to spare the lives of Subandrio, the left-leaning foreign minister of Indonesia, who had been responsible for Indonesia's alliance with communist China.¹³⁵ On 10 November, in a massive peasant gathering in Rangpur, Bhashani said that the establishment of a socialist state was the only solution to the sufferings of peasants.¹³⁶ Bhashani devoted a substantial amount of time towards explaining the international situation. Bhashani and the NAP thus tried to bring the peasantry to the wider movement against praetorian capitalism and 'US imperialism'. Nonetheless, few NAP leaders who were also members of underground pro-Chinese groups in the CPP (East Pakistan Provincial Committee) such as Anwar Zahid took a pro-Ayub Khan stand, and in an article in the weekly newspaper *Janata*, Zahid described there were two voices of Pakistan: Ayub Khan and Bhashani. In another editorial he claimed there took place a silent revolution in Pakistan and Ayub Khan was its hero.¹³⁷

During this time, the CPP (East Pakistan Provincial Committee) witnessed a severe ideological debate within their ranks in the wake of the Sino-Soviet split. Within the underground party there developed two different political theses. The British intelligence report estimated the membership of the CPP (East Pakistan Provincial Committee) in East Pakistan to be 700.¹³⁸ The central leadership of the party remained pro-Soviet, but within the party there had developed another alternative thesis proposed by three prominent Maoist activists: Basir (Sukhendu Dostidar), Mohammed Toaha and Abdul Haque. The party sought to discuss these issues in a plenum in 1965, but the plenum was postponed due to war. In November 1966 the party again called for a plenum. Even before the plenum pro-Chinese communists had developed an alternative structure of command stretching from party units and district committees to province-wide committees. There existed a clandestine political centre of pro-Chinese communists. In many districts such as Chittagong, party district committees were dominated by pro-Soviet members, but workers' and peasants' organizations were dominated by pro-Chinese communists.[139] Bhashani was the president of peasant associations and Abdul Haque, a pro-Chinese communist, was the general secretary. Similarly, Mohammad Toaha was the president of the workers' federation and the popular Maoist-inclined labour leader Abul Bashar was the secretary. At the November plenum the CPP (East Pakistan Provincial Committee) was vertically divided. Many veteran communists felt sad about bidding farewell to their old comrades, but loyalty to their respective ideologies trumped over such emotional ties.[140] Even before the formal split in November, pro-Chinese communists had met in a plenum in August 1966 and elected a clandestine party centre. They called the new party the East Pakistan Communist Party (Marxist–Leninist), or the EPCP-ML.[141] Yet from the inception the new party had two different political theses. The first thesis stressed the necessity of the people' democratic revolution against feudalism, imperialism and the comprador bourgeoisie. This line was supported by Mohammad Toaha and Sukhendu Dostidar, while a second thesis was put forward by the Deben–Matin–Alauddin group that aimed at a socialist revolution led by the working classes.[142] These internecine squabbles over the heuristic analysis of class alignment led towards a split in the new organization, but that split acquired many permutations and combinations between different groups. Every group presented their own interpretations of national and international situations.[143] Thus the efficacy of the new party remained doubtful.

The NAP, supposedly a social democratic organization, had a significant presence of communists within its leadership as well as in its rank and file. The NAP witnessed tensions as soon as the CPP (East Pakistan Provincial Committee) underwent a split because of ideological divisions. This affair in the NAP came to the forefront in 1967, in the month of October. On 10 October 1967 the NAP provincial council expelled a few members of the Mymensingh district and issued a show-cause notice against two of the provincial leaders, Muhiuddin Ahmad and Pir Habibur Rahman. These two leaders were known to be connected with pro-Soviet communists. Soon, 139 members of the NAP's provincial council demanded a requisition meeting in Dacca from the NAP president, Bhashani, and the secretary, Muhammad Sultan. Bhashani did not respond to the requisition notice and called for a provincial council meeting in Rangpur on 30 November, where he expelled five prominent leaders of the NAP. His opponents called for another meeting on 16 and 17 December 1967. After this open fighting between the leaders of the NAP, the formal split came on 10 February 1968, when Muzaffar Ahmad and Syed Altaf Hossain formed a new provincial committee, appointing themselves as president and secretary. On 30 June, the all-Pakistan NAP elected Wali Khan as president and Mahmudul Haq Osmani as secretary. Meanwhile, on 24 and 25 February, Bhashani became the president and Mohammad Toaha became the general secretary of the pro-Chinese NAP.[144] The tendency towards splitting also touched the student wing of the party. Chhatro Union, a powerful student wing of the CPP (East Pakistan Provincial Committee), witnessed a split before the formal separation of the two parties. Many argued that such splits were due to personality clashes among student leaders. In 1965 the party circulated a notice against five pro-Chinese student leaders. These included Kazi Zafar Ahmad, Rashed Khan Menon, Haider Akbar Khan Rono, Mohiuddin Ahmad and Abdul Halim. All of them were previous office bearers of the Chhatro Union. On 1 April 1965 a Chhatro Union conference witnessed a significant degree of fist-fighting and scuffles. Gradually, the Chhatro Union got divided into two wings – one loyal to Matia Chowdhury, the first woman student of provincial eminence, and the other loyal to Kafi Zafar and Menon.[145]

The Krishak Samiti also witnessed similar divisions. The Samiti had had a long history in East Pakistan, and Bhashani had played a crucial role in establishing it. Between 31 December 1957 and 3 January 1958, Bhashani had established a peasant union, named East Pakistan Krishak Samiti, and had become the president of the new organization. The rest of the office bearers of this organization came from the clandestine CPP (East Pakistan Provincial Committee), though they were officially associated with the NAP.[146] Within a few months, the Krishak Samiti was able to establish units in all districts of East Pakistan. After the declaration of martial law, the Samiti was paralysed as most of its leaders, including Bhashani, were arrested. After the establishment of a civilian regime under military-bureaucratic rule, the Samiti started functioning again. On 1 November 1963 the Samiti celebrated Peasant Day, and nearly 25,000 peasants joined the festivity. In 1964, on 27 and 28 April, the Samiti held a provincial conference. Nearly 1,500 delegates attended the conference. They adopted a 15-point programme demanding ceilings on landholdings and the redistribution of surplus land among landless peasants, loans at low interest to small peasants, the establishment of factories for modern agricultural implements, the rescinding of treaties with the US and expansion of trade with the Soviet Union and China, the fixing of a lower support price for sugar cane and jute, restrictions on arbitrary collection of taxes in village markets, and provisions of boats for fishermen and ordinary villagers.[147] Despite its history of mobilization against dictatorship, in 1966, the Samiti was divided into two camps. In the Samiti segments influenced by the pro-Chinese wing, Bhashani remained the president and Abdul Haque the secretary. In the organizations influenced by pro-Soviet ideology, Amzad Hossain became the president and Hatem Ali Khan the general secretary.[148] Soon the pro-Chinese wing witnessed further splits when Abdul Haque and Moahammad Toaha, following in the footsteps of Indian Maoist Charu Majumdar, withdrew from mass organizations in order to prepare for revolution.[149] Notwithstanding such splits, Bhashani played a pivotal role in organizing a conference for jute peasants. In 1967 Bhashani and his associates organized a peasant march from Rangpur in north Bengal to Dacca. Organizers of the march planned to surround the governor's house in Dacca. But on the way to Dacca, at a place called Madhavdi, the police attacked the peasants at night and killed a few of them. The peasants got dispersed.[150] Thus, despite splits, peasant activists tried to organize a movement against praetorian capitalism and expanded the horizon of democratic activities.

Throughout the sixties, East Pakistan had a history of labour militancy against the military-bureaucratic regime. Workers even joined the student movement in 1962, and in 1963, in the Tongi industrial area, cotton textile workers observed a 40-day long strike for wage increase. This was followed by a strike in the Karnaphuli Paper Mill in the Chittagong district. In 1963 a massive railway strike paralysed the rail transportation system in East Pakistan.[151] It was during this time that railway workers published a weekly periodical called *Saptahik Probhati*. Two veteran communists, Harun-or-Rashid and Deben Shikdar, edited this magazine.[152] In 1965 there occurred another railway strike. The strike was accompanied by workers' unrest in the Chittagong port and in the power sector. In 1966 many workers marched against the US' involvement in military conflicts in Vietnam. International solidarity thus informed the workers' movement too.[153] In 1964, as discussed in the previous chapter, there took place a strike in the jute mills. Despite such militant history, in the wake of the split in the CPP (East Pakistan Provincial Committee), there took place splits in the labour organizations too. In 1966 experienced communist trade unionist Mohammad Toaha, popular peasant leader Bhashani, trade unionist Sirajul Hossain Khan[154] and communist labour leader Abul Bashar played a crucial role in developing the East Pakistan Labour Federation. Abul Bashar was the general secretary of this organization. In May 1967 three well-known communist student leaders, Zafar, Rono and Menon, were active in the Tongi industrial area. This had started in 1965, when, after his release from prison, Zafar went to the Tongi industrial area and became involved with the labour movement through a strike in a Benta Pharma Industries drug factory. He settled down in the Mill Bazaar, a nerve centre of the labour movement in Tongi. He built up organizations in the Satrong and Meghna textile mills through a successful strike. These leftists established nearly 105 study-circle units among workers. In these study circles, they discussed with workers their economic demands and sought to educate them on larger political issues and tried to convince them of the necessity of establishing a socialist political system.[155]

Despite splits in the NAP, labour resistance to praetorian capitalism escalated. Throughout the late sixties, industrial workers fought against inflation and decline in real wages and for the democratization of workplace administration. On many occasions workers revolted against the police and the paramilitary when trade union leaders were arbitrarily arrested. For example, on 6 April 1967, when armed police came to arrest Zafar, workers surrounded the police, snatched him from the custody of armed constabulary and enabled him to escape. This incident led to a battle between police forces and workers throughout the Tongi industrial area.[156] The jute mill workers threatened to go on strike against the mill owners in January 1967. The Maoist-led East Pakistan Workers' Federation supported the strike, and the independent left, mainly Saidur Rahman and Abdul Mannan's trade union, also assisted. This support was followed by the announcement of a demand charter in the newspaper that included provisions for additional benefits, just wages for 'piece rate' workers and the supply of rice and wheat to workers at a subsidized fixed price. Even before the strike, government and mill owners had sat with workers and agreed to provide additional benefits and promised a further round of negotiations after two months.[157] Soon employees in government-owned, self-governed institutions threatened to go on strike against draconian workplace laws. Meanwhile, transportation workers went into strike that again paralysed transportation in Dacca city.[158] Thus, despite splits in the ranks of the communists, the workers' and peasants' movement created an environment of opposition to the government. It was this subaltern militancy that kept opposition to the military-bureaucratic regime alive when most leaders were behind bars. Yet such a resistance lacked a coordinated political goal because of the fragmentation of the communist movement.

Repression and Resistance: Permutation and Combination among Political Parties

From 1966 onwards, the government arrested and put Sheikh Mujib and his close associates such as Tajuddin Ahmad behind bars. The government accused Sheikh Mujib of treason though they could not prove such allegations in the court. They kept him imprisoned on various pretexts. Ayub Khan regarded the six-point programme as a challenge. On 15 June 1966 the government arrested Tofazzal Hossain, popularly known as Manik Mian, who was the editor of the most popular Bengali daily *Ittefaq*.[159] Next day the government took control of the printing press of *Ittefaq*, known as the New Nation Printing Press. Though the government lost the case in court, it amended the ordinance and announced a new national security law to continue the control over the press and the ban on *Ittefaq*. Tofazzal Hossain was released again on 28 March 1967.[160] Meanwhile, centrist and faith-based politicians circulated a proposal among the opposition parties to unite. They were strengthened by the simple fact that, as a British diplomatic correspondence, put it:

> With the expiration on December 31, 1966, of the provisions of the Elective Bodies Disqualification (EBDO) approximately 80 politicians barred from public life on charges of graft, corruption or misuse of public office, were once again free to take active political roles.[161]

In a meeting on 30 April 1967, the Pakistani Nizam-e-Islam party, the Jamaat-e-Islami, a breakaway fraction of the Awami League led by Abdur Rashid Torkabagish, and the Pakistani Muslim League (Council) formed a new front called the Pakistan Democratic Movement (PDM). The movement adopted an eight-point charter emphasizing the restoration of the 1956 Constitution.[162] The demand charter of the PDM actually left a significant number of subjects in the central hand. All these parties and the former NDF had become rather moribund organizations. Among these old established parties, Nurul Amin, the former Muslim League chief minister, sought to raise issues concerning the restoration of democracy and provincial autonomy in the legislative assembly. Golam Azam, the leader of the Jamaat-e-Islami, wrote a booklet entitled 'What Is the Path for Emancipation of East Pakistan?'[163] These political leaders were searching for an alternative to the six-point programme and tried to walk a thin line between the Awami League and the government. Though no doubt propelled by the repression of the Awami League, the announcement of the eight-point programme by the PDM and the absence of major leaders outside jail attracted many Awami Leaguers to the PDM. Finally, on 14 August 1967, 14 PDM adherents within the Awami League requisitioned a working committee meeting of the Awami League. Before such a development, the Awami League, in a meeting on 23 and 24 July 1966, had decided to appoint Syed Nazrul Islam as the acting president and Amena Begam as the acting general secretary. Amena Begam continued her determined effort to continue with the six-point programme, and on 19 August 1967, in an Awami league council session, nearly 886 among the 950 councillors showed up and thus defeated the PDM adherents within the party.[164] Among the left parties, the pro-Soviet NAP and the underground pro-Soviet CPP (East Pakistan Provincial Committee) supported the six-point programme.[165] Politics in East Pakistan was then fragmented along three different lines: the PDM and its constituent organizations proposed a middle path, the Awami League and the pro-Soviet NAP supported radical autonomy, and the pro-Chinese NAP concentrated on mobilizing along anti-imperialist lines emphasizing supporting workers' and peasants' demands, though occasionally soft pedalling the opposition to the Ayub Khan regime. Thus, East Pakistani politics stood at a crossroad in a volatile period of the global sixties. International political circumstances, the hyper-masculine nationalism of the praetorian regime and the popular labour resistance against praetorian capitalism created a combustible political environment.

The government took initiative in recovering its popularity and legitimacy. In 1967 Ayub Khan wrote his autobiography, *Friends Not Masters*. The book had been translated into Bengali and was included in school curricula as a textbook. Despite the provocative title of the book, it narrates the story of a pro-Western military dictator's disenchantment with his mentors. The book contains disparaging, racially tinged references to Bengali Muslims and their supposed inferiority complex.[166] Ayub Khan also decided to celebrate

10 years of development since his military coup. Moving a step forward, in Dacca, Monem Khan, the governor of East Pakistan, at a Muslim League youth volunteer's meeting, introduced a green book containing Ayub Khan's sayings. He maintained that, just as people respect Mao Zedong in China, in Pakistan there should be a similar attempt at respecting the country president, Ayub Khan. Even a British diplomat, who was generally supportive of Ayub Khan, in his diplomatic correspondence, commented:

> It remains to be seen whether this sickening sycophancy is the beginning of some ghastly adulatory campaign or merely a creepy part of Monem Khan's efforts to retain his office.[167]

But such efforts did not improve the image of the government for the simple fact that the economy stood in the way. Massive inflation was corroding the real income of the salaried middle classes and the burgeoning working classes. Also, there had taken place a significant degree of the siphoning of capital from East to West Pakistan. The Awami League's six-point programme and Bhashani's 14-point programme challenged that. As this entire economic mechanism was dependent on foreign aid provided by Western countries, Ayub Khan could ill afford to keep the seemingly pro-Chinese Bhutto's services. Yet Bhutto's exit partially dented the image of a progressive foreign policy of Pakistan. International geopolitics and radical revolutionary developments sent mixed signals to various constituents of Pakistani political society. The regime started losing its legitimacy when it could not subsume within its overarching ideology of modernizing Islamic nationalism the question of national self-determination. Yet in response to the demand for democracy, the government was adopting a more Islamic–nationalistic posture. The government tried to prohibit the singing of Tagore's songs on Dacca radio. In 1967 this move was opposed by intellectuals, and on 13 August 1967 the judge, Hamoodur Rahman, in a discussion on 20 years of Bengali literature, announced that for the two national languages of Pakistan, the introduction of the Arabic script would help in national integrity.[168] All these provoked more opposition from the Bengali intelligentsia.

Confident that their repressive measures had subdued the movement for the six-point programme, the government moved a step ahead in 1968. In December 1967, the government launched a case against a few Bengali soldiers and lieutenant commandant Moazzem Hossain for their alleged involvement in a plot to separate East Pakistan in connection with an organization called the Bangladesh Liberation Front. It was further alleged that these soldiers had planned to assassinate Ayub Khan. On 6 January 1968 the Home Ministry of the Pakistani government announced the case in a press note. On 18 January, in another press note, the government announced the names of 35 prisoners accusing Sheikh Mujib as the prime conspirator in the infamous Agartala conspiracy case.[169] Sheikh Mujib was released from Dacca Central Jail and was taken into the custody of the army. As the case proceeded, the journalists who attended the case vividly described Sheikh Mujib's trial. In June 1968 Sheikh Mujib provided a long testimony. He highlighted the exploitation of East Pakistan and the oppression of the Awami League by the government. His long testimony was published as a booklet. The Awami League circulated the booklet among the people of East Pakistan. They even prepared a donation coupon for the expenses of Sheikh Mujib's defence.[170] Sheikh Mujib increasingly captured the popular imagination of many among East Pakistanis. His absence became more eloquent than his presence. Yet there prevailed calmness among people. It appeared that this was a lull before a storm. Indeed, the British Foreign Office despatch noted as early as 1967:

> The situation in East Pakistan, where extremist Awami League leaders are still in jail, it is a continuing problem for the government. But many people in the East Wing have vested interest in the continuance of the present regime and most of the people there want only a fairer deal and a greater say in policy decisions at the centre, not independence or greater Bengal.[171]

Global 68 and Pakistan: The Democratic Revolution

The year of 1968 heralded a period of crisis for the established political parties. The Awami League witnessed a split between the supporters of the PDM and the six-point programme. Most leaders of the six-point Awami League were in prison. The Agartala conspiracy case unnerved even the most ardent Awami Leaguers. Convinced of further attempts of state repression, many activists went underground. They prioritized the release of Sheikh Mujib as their immediate programme.[172] The NDF underwent a split, and old Awami Leaguers such as Ataur Rahman and Abul Mansur Ahmad wanted to join the Awami League but could not do so.[173] The communists and the NAP were divided, and the Maoist communists witnessed mind-boggling splits within their ranks. Within the PDM, the Jamaat-e-Islami was not prepared to work with the pro-Soviet NAP, though the latter was ready to work within the PDM. The Awami League was ready to work with both factions of the NAP, but the pro-Soviet NAP refused to work with the pro-Chinese NAP.[174] Ayub Khan's ruling formation, the CML, witnessed a split. Bhutto, once his trusted foreign minister, became his most vehement critic. He floated a new political party known as the People's Party of Pakistan (PPP) on 30 November 1967. He travelled widely in West Pakistan, highlighted the idea of Islamic socialism and even invoked Mao in his inner-party discussions.[175] Socialism was in vogue. Even the Council Muslim League adopted a radical programme calling for bank nationalization, progressive taxation, land reforms, cooperative farming, and minimum wages for agricultural workers.[176] But none of these political parties, either in the east or in the west, had a clear vision of the past, and they were not confident of pushing Pakistan towards a parliamentary democracy. Yet there were signs of resistance, not within the formal political movement, but outside its parameters.

In 1965–66, Mao had supported students in China who had unleashed a process of reform, and then a rebellion, based on the idea of revolutionary morality and the eradication of bourgeois values. Students and youths became the bearer of a revolutionary transformation that had its origin in the power struggle within the leadership of the CCP.[177] The news of the student revolution reached East Pakistan by 1967. The Naxalite rebellion across the border in West Bengal attracted the attentions of a section of youth in East Pakistan. Slogans related to Naxalbari were popular in East Pakistan among student circles. Student, and later labour leaders such as Rono, Zafar and Menon, were aware of the cultural revolution and the associated youth movement. China, perceived as a friendly country, could export books to Pakistan, and these generated interest in Mao Zedong thought.[178] Most students, who were untouched by Maoist or even Marxist politics, had some knowledge of events in North Vietnam. The US bombing campaign in North Vietnam aroused intense sympathy among students. So powerful was the perception of the plight of North Vietnam that even in the most unlikely quarters sympathies were articulated. The chief justice of Pakistan, Alvin Robert Cornelius, in a speech, spoke of the plight of North Vietnam during the Tet Offensive.[179] Many among the youth also had news of events in Latin America. Bhashani, the most widely travelled politician, in speech after speech reminded his listeners about Beijing's centrality to the world revolutionary process.[180] Diverse impacts of the events of the global sixties created a discursive political space among students. The news of Che Guevara's assassination on 9 October 1967, in La Higuera in Bolivia, spread in East Pakistan. In left-leaning newspaper, Ranesh Dasgupta wrote about political struggles in Latin America. It inspired many, and Che Guevara's dairy was published as a book in 1968. Many students read the diary and about Che Guevara.[181] The news of the civil rights movement in the US reached Dacca by 1968, while various newspapers like *Sombad* and *Ittefaq* carried word of a global revolution stretching from Palestine to Paris. The year 1968 witnessed an outburst of protests all over the world, stretching from Bangkok to Berlin, from Cairo to Calcutta. Student leaders like Tariq Ali carried the news of the Paris 1968 movements to Pakistan,[182] while in neighbouring Calcutta, a Bengali rhyme captured the mood: from Sorbonne to Jadavpur (a prominent university in West Bengal), the same tune was hummed by students.[183] The causes for the rise of these student movements in each location were different, but the students, workers and peasants felt the necessity to rebel, to push their agenda and to feel united with a global transformative moment for justice.

In 1968 labour militancy became acute in East Pakistan. The rail and port workers started agitating against price rises. From 8 April workers in the Bawani jute mill started a militant strike. Transport workers in Dacca claimed that despite increases in the bus fares, they did not have any increase in their salary. For a week the entire transportation system in East Pakistan remained paralysed.[184] In July 1968 floods devastated East Pakistan. It seemed a famine could break out in the province. The pro-Chinese NAP demanded that East Pakistan be declared a famine-struck area. In August and September, they tried to build up a movement. On 3 November 1968, they started moving towards a unified protest against the government.[185] Meanwhile, Ayub Khan, in a speech on 24 September, declared that Pakistan in the future would have one language.[186] Students started agitating against such a remark, and four student unions together issued a statement. Bhashani, who was then the president of the pro-Chinese NAP, issued a statement condemning Ayub Khan's rhetoric. Ayub Khan indicated that he would participate in the presidential election through Basic Democracy in the next decade. Students in the well-known Jagannath University in Dacca started agitating against the government takeover of the college administration. Even students of the Art College of Dacca protested against government policies.[187] In such an environment, in Dacca University, Saidur Rahman, a student leader of the pro-Ayub Khan student organization, the NSF, was killed in a local brawl.[188] The university had to be closed due to ensuing tensions. Ayub

Khan's government tried to celebrate a decade of development, and many became angry with such pomp and splendour in the midst of inflation and food crises in the province.[189] In October, the Awami League, in its council session, announced that the agitation for the six-point programme would continue and increasingly started criticizing the stranglehold exercised by the monopoly industrial houses over the economy in Pakistan. They also suspended their decision to participate in the election of Basic Democrats. They demanded representation according to the population distribution in the two units of Pakistan.[190] In 1968, on 3 November, the octogenarian red Bhashani[191] held a public meeting in Dacca's Paltan Maidan. He now openly endorsed the demand for regional autonomy and self-government. He claimed that in 1940, in the original Lahore Resolution, there had been a call for a two-state solution. He asked for a divorce from Pakistan. This marked a change in the tune of the pro-Chinese NAP. Many of his political critics alleged that Bhashani was also aware that Ayub Khan was alienated from the army.[192] Ayub Khan became a desperate, lonely soldier embraced by none, except his close confidants among bureaucrats.

Meanwhile, in West Pakistan students started organizing mammoth protests. The protests started on 13 October in Karachi where the police arrested 30 students and closed educational institutions. On 15 October angry students set fire to public buses. Bhutto, the leader of the newly formed PPP, supported the students. The government drafted a 21-point chargesheet against Bhutto. On 1 November students gave an ultimatum to the authorities that they would organize strikes and agitate if their demands were not met. Bhutto decided to tour the entirety of West Pakistan. His meetings attracted a large number of people. On 4 November 1968 the police used teargas to disperse the crowds attending Bhutto's meeting.[193] From 6 November new student protests destabilized Pakistan. These protests started due to a quarrel between law-enforcement agencies and the students of Gordon College in Pakistan over the purchase of smuggled goods from a market in an unregulated 'tribal' area. When the police tried to arrest the students, it led to massive protests. The students demanded that Ayub Khan and his family be punished for misappropriation of a vast amount of wealth. The students also gathered to welcome the rebel member of Ayub's erstwhile kitchen cabinet, Bhutto, on 7 November. Bhutto was scheduled to visit a polytechnic in Rawalpindi, but he was not allowed to speak there. He then relocated to the Intercontinental Hotel where the Gordon College students assembled. There, the police opened fire to disperse students. On the next day, students from local colleges gathered in the government college. Faced with police encirclement, they sneaked through the back door and assembled in the city centre. In the bazaar, students were joined by unemployed workers, and members of the public also joined the march. Soon Rawalpindi, the headquarters of the army and the interim capital of Pakistan, was witnessing massive protests.[194] Thus began the global 1968 in Pakistan.

Political parties in East Pakistan issued statements supporting the student revolt in West Pakistan. In November the pro-Soviet NAP tried to organize a programmatic unity with the Awami League.[195] Meanwhile, the pro-Chinese NAP and various factions of Maoist communist organizations became involved in mass protests against the autocracy. They were inspired by events in neighbouring West Bengal. In 1967 the Maoists in West Bengal started a peasant rebellion. *People's Daily*, the mouthpiece of the CCP, welcomed this development through an editorial on 5 July 1967 by declaring:

> A peal of spring thunder has crashed over the land of India. Revolutionary peasants in the Darjeeling area have risen in rebellion. Under the leadership of a revolutionary group of the Indian Communist Party [Transcriber's note: This group comprised the radical members of the erstwhile undivided Communist Party of India (Marxist), a forerunner of Communist Party of India (Marxist–Leninist), see above], a red area of rural revolutionary armed struggle has been established in India. This is a development of tremendous significance for the Indian people's revolutionary struggle.[196]

Maoists of various factions in East Pakistan steadily developed the notion that East Pakistan was progressing towards a revolution. In such circumstances, on 28 November 1968, the pro-Chinese NAP, along with affiliated peasant associations and workers' federations, called for an all-party meeting to develop a strategy for united political action. Yet they excluded the pro-Soviet NAP from this meeting. The Awami League, which was close to the pro-Soviet NAP, boycotted the meeting for this reason. As they failed to develop political unity, the pro-Chinese NAP moved alone. Bhashani toured the rural areas of north Bengal. With his uncanny ability to read the popular mentality, on 23 November he openly declared, in a meeting, that his party had initiated a political struggle to remove the Ayub Khan-led military regime from power.[197] On 6 December Bhashani called for a mass meeting in Dacca.[198] He tapped into the growing subaltern militancy in the city. At that time autorickshaw drivers were on strike, which had caused a near-collapse of the transportation system in the city. On 1 December the pro-Soviet NAP and the PPP organized a massive rally in West Pakistan. But the police attacked the rally and mercilessly beat up people with staves.[199] The Awami League called for the observance of a 'resist oppression day' on 13 December.[200] Meanwhile, former air marshal of Pakistan, Asghar Khan from West Pakistan, lieutenant general Azam Khan from East Pakistan, and justice S. M Murshed from East Pakistan became active in politics.[201] This was because the government had announced that in 1969–70 there would be a presidential election based on the Constitution of Basic Democracy. As Ayub Khan became unpopular and his regime became isolated from both the army and the bureaucracy, prominent figures tried to throw their hats into the ring. But centrist establishment-oriented political figures were more marginalized in this situation of revolutionary anger from below.

In Dacca, a massive crowd had gathered on 6 December to listen to Bhashani. Striking autorickshaw drivers requested Bhashani to announce a total strike the next day. He agreed with their demands and made the announcement. He also added that people would lay siege to the governor's palace.[202] To everybody's surprise, the next day a strike was observed in Dacca with the massive participation of the people. The success of this strike actually convinced people that Ayub Khan's days were numbered. In Chittagong, in a procession, Maoist communist activists raised slogans about workers and peasants picking up arms to liberate Bangladesh.[203] Indeed, in their clandestine meeting, the East Bengal Communist party, a Maoist faction, had already adopted a resolution about an independent democratic people's republic of East Bengal. Siraj Sikdar, a radical Maoist, led the East Bengal Workers' Movement. This group had already resolved in their 'revolutionary council' that 'East Bengal' (and not the official name, East Pakistan) was a colony of Pakistan. They identified the national question as the principal contradiction of Pakistan and thus launched a people's struggle for independence.[204]

The success of the strike on 7 December announced the arrival of global 1968 in Dacca. It opened the floodgate of protests in the following days. Even during the month of Ramadan, people observed a partial strike on 8 December.[205] On the eve of 13 December, when the Awami League called for a 'resist oppression day', the police arrested a significant number of activists and created an environment of terror. Consequently, on 13 December, fewer people came to attend offices and banks. Normal life in Dacca came to a halt.²⁰⁶ Bhashani now sought to extend the movement to rural areas. He called for a strike in the rural areas of East Pakistan, primarily trying to stop the functioning and transactions in village markets on 29 December. He also added the programme of laying siege to the government offices by peasant activists in rural areas.²⁰⁷ The pro-Chinese NAP did not have the strength to organize successful strikes in rural East Pakistan. Doubtful of the efficacy of his strategy, the underground EPCP-ML decided to distance themselves from the movement. Even then, the pro-Chinese NAP held numerous meetings, roadside gatherings and organized processions.²⁰⁸ But there took place sporadic clashes between the NAP activists and peasants on one side and the police on the other. In Hatirdia Bazaar the police fired at a gathering of peasants and students, and three people died. Similarly, the police fired into a crowd in the Narail area due to which two people were critically injured. They also attacked the Narail College student dorm and arrested students who were reading for their classes.²⁰⁹ Throughout rural areas, such clashes took place. Political parties condemned such instances of police atrocities. Radicalized by the momentum of peasant resistance and angry with the police firing, under the leadership of Bhashani, the pro-Chinese NAP declared that Bhashani would boycott the coming presidential election under the present Constitution of Basic Democracy. He further announced that the need of the hour was to build up a powerful democratic movement for a new Constitution. He claimed that in the new Constitution there would be the recognition of the right for self-government of various nationalities in Pakistan, and that the government would be elected on the basis of universal adult franchise. Bhashani demanded limits on the power of the federal government and a socialistic pattern of economy.²¹⁰ But conservative political parties became nervous at these radical utterings by Bhashani. British diplomatic observers still hoped

> [t]he government can therefore enter the New Year with a feeling of some satisfaction that things might be a great deal worse. True sporadic demonstrations of a more or less violent nature are likely to continue: but without a unified opposition those are unlikely to cause regime much loss of sleep.²¹¹

This was a fond hope of the international Anglo-American bloc supporting Ayub Khan and its moderate right-wing opposition, but the turn of events proved them wrong.

While the political parties were pursuing their own agenda, two fractions of the Chhatro Union and the Chhatro League met in the historic *bottola* (the shade of a banyan tree) near the Arts building of Dacca University. Students demanded political action, though the pro-Soviet Chhatro Union was slightly worried about the consequences of student militancy.[212] But the students tried to organize a procession violating a prohibitory order against large gatherings. The police tear-gassed students. Excited students gathered again on 2 January 1969 in the Dacca University campus. They had protested police atrocities on the previous day.[213] As students became more adamant for a confrontation with the authorities, different student associations and their leaders sat for a discussion among themselves for a common programme. Between 2 and 5 January, student leaders of the Chhatro League sat with both the pro-Chinese and pro-Soviet Chhatro Unions. Prolonged discussions followed, as Chhatro League leaders were not interested in pushing forward the demands of the various minority provinces of West Pakistan. On the other hand, the pro-Chinese Chhatro Union did not agree with the six-point programme, while the Chhatro League considered the six-point programme as basic to any future common programmatic action. Various former student union leaders such as Mohammad Farhad played a crucial role from the backstage in these discussions. Finally, on 6 January, *Dainik Sombad*, the pro-Soviet CPP (East Pakistan Provincial Committee)-affiliated newspaper published an 11-point programme that incorporated the six-point programme without calling it as such and included the specific demands of the student community, such as solvent colleges of East Pakistan not being brought within the control of the provincial government and students who passed with third class to be admitted to higher grades in academic institutions, as well as demands specific to engineering, technical, medical and agricultural students. Other demands included a reduction in student fees, rescission of the Acts restricting student activities and autonomy for higher educational institutions, as well as an increase in women's educational opportunities. There were additional demands, such as the scrapping of the one-unit policy and provisions for the autonomy of West Pakistani provinces, the nationalization of the banking sector, insurance and heavy industries, a reduction of taxes for peasants, just wages for workers and provisions for their housing and healthcare and their right to form unions, flood-control policies for East Pakistan, the release of political prisoners, the scrapping of emergency ordinances, and a non-aligned foreign policy.[214] Students formed the Student Action Committee (SAC) based on such programme.

As the major students' organizations united on one platform under a common list of demands, political parties started moving in that direction as well. Meanwhile, the government asked Mohammad Toaha and Abdul Haque, two senior leaders of the pro-Bhashani NAP, to appear in court.[215] On 4 January 1969, eight political parties – the Nizam-e-Islam, the Jamaa-ul-Ulema-e-Islam, the Jamaat-e-Islami, the Pakistan Muslim League (Council), the Awami League (PDM), the Awami League (six-point), the NDF and the NAP (pro-Soviet) formed the Democratic Action Committee (DAC).[216] The pro-Bhashani NAP and the PPP remained outside this coalition.[217] The DAC held a press conference at Sheikh Mujib's residence to indicate their solidarity with him. The DAC then announced an eight-point programme that included the election of a parliament based upon universal adult franchise, the formation of a federal government, the release of all political prisoners, rescinding of the emergency, a repeal of undemocratic ordinances, the restoration of press freedom and the withdrawal of prohibitory orders on *Ittefaq*, and the workers' right to form trade unions.[218] Conservative parties within the DAC did not accept the students' 11-point programme. But the Awami League and pro-Soviet NAP, despite being members of the DAC, extended their support to the students' demands. On the same day, the pro-six-point Awami League decided to boycott the elections being held under the Constitution of Basic Democracy.[219]

The students moved ahead with their programme. They organized meetings in colleges and also appealed to workers, and in some areas they even held meetings with peasants. On 10 January, Dacca University students held a meeting at the *bottola* in the Arts campus. In the meantime, the news of a hunger strike by political prisoners reached the students; angered, they tried to organize a procession and clashed with the police and the East Pakistan Rifles.[220] In protests against police atrocities, students observed a strike in all colleges and universities. Though students were united, the different student unions raised different types of slogans. The Chhatro League raised slogans to free Shiekh Mujib and for the scrapping of the Agartala conspiracy case, while the pro-Soviet Chhatro Union raised slogans heralding the victory of the proletariat and the pro-Chinese Chhatro Union raised slogans in favour of the Naxalbari rebellion in India and against social imperialism.[221] Yet the common students were more interested in the restoration of democracy, the release of political prisoners and regional autonomy for East Pakistan. The SAC issued a statement proclaiming 11 January as a day of protest.[222] Meanwhile, the Writers' Rights Association issued a leaflet on 14 January condemning censorship, press gagging and restrictions on publishing books.²²³ On 14 January Bhashani threatened to start a no-tax movement if the government refused to either accept the demand of autonomy for East Pakistan or pay heed to the economic demands of the people. As the political temperature increased on 17 January, both the SAC and the DAC organized protests. Once again, students clashed with the police in the Dacca University campus.²²⁴ The DAC tried to hold a public *namaz* (prayer), but the police stopped them from holding such religious processions. Finally, they held a protest meeting in the Bar Library.²²⁵ On 18 January the students observed a strike and fought with the police to hold a procession, and even the teachers joined them. The police entered the student dorms, and even the professors' residences, and fired tear gas into the women students' dorm, known as Rokeya Hall.²²⁶ To protest these police atrocities that took place on 18 January, the students decided to hold a strike in all the educational institutions in East Pakistan on 20 January 1969. Throughout East Pakistan students formed action committees and contacted the central leaders of other such committees. Iqbal Hall, a student dorm in Dacca University, became the nerve centre of the students' protests.²²⁷

On 20 January 1969 strikes spread through all the educational institutions in East Pakistan. A huge number of students had gathered in the Dacca University campus. The students brought their procession and the police clashed with them throughout the morning. This resulted in the student procession getting bifurcated when they tried to enter the city, as the police beat up the students with staves and fired tear gas. But the students also retaliated against the police by throwing stones. With thousands of students pouring into the procession at around 2 p.m., the police fired into a crowd of protesting students.²²⁸ Asaduzzaman, a communist student activist of the Law Department died in police firing.²²⁹ Asaduzzaman had previously participated in the organization of strikes among peasants in Hatirdia at the call of Bhashani. He was injured there too. He had come to Dacca and gone to meet Nirmal Sen, a left-leaning prominent journalist, of the *Doinik Pakistan*. Asad had told Sen that the police had indulged in stave-beating in Hatirdia and people had gotten injured. He then opened his headgear and showed his bloody wounds. Sen told Asad that he could not publish the news as the owners of the press had a policy of every news piece being verified by the police. Asad then quietly left the place. Sen quipped in his autobiography that Asad had come to get news published, but he soon became the news himself.²³⁰

The news of Asad's death spread throughout the city. Thousands of grief-stricken students gathered in the Dacca University campus. They were joined by leaders of opposition political parties. At 2.37 p.m., students, led by the female students, staged a black-flag demonstration. The East Pakistan Rifles tried to form a barricade to stop the students, but the female student carrying the black flag marched through the soldiers' barricades, and the soldiers strangely did not try to charge at the students with their bayonets. A very long procession marched through the street. Throughout Dacca city the mood of the people turned insurrectionary. On 21 January there took place a spontaneous strike in Dacca city. Indeed, the sentiment of the people was articulated by a 60-year-old man who was returning from the mosque after performing *namaz*. He inquired if the people had been paying taxes so that the army could be well-equipped to fire bullets into 'our children's chests'. A rickshaw puller reacted by noting: 'We lived hungry every day. What can we really earn by plying the rickshaw? We shall go hungry but shall observe strikes for next ten days.'[231] On 21 January a public funeral prayer, or *janaja*, was held in Paltan Maidan. The police and students fought pitched battles throughout the day. In many instances the police fired into the crowd. But more ominously for the government, the workers from the industrial areas and villagers joined students.[232]

In the evening of 23 January students gathered to organize a procession with burning torches. When the procession came out on the street people from all walks of life joined the students. Nearly 30,000 people marched through the streets.[233] On 24 January a large crowd, according to an estimate of nearly half-a-million people, gathered in the city.[234] It was ordinary people who took the real leadership. When the procession reached the central secretariat, many employees tried to join as well, but the police closed the gates and opened fire on the procession. A few young boys between the ages of 13 to 17, such as Maitiur, Maqbul and Rustam, died in the police firing.[235] Hearing this news of firing, thousands of workers and boatmen from the Buriganga River and peasants from villages surrounding Dacca joined the procession. The police lost control over the city, and an angry mob set fire to pro-government newspapers offices.[236] Student leaders now came out from underground. Mahabub Ullah, a student leader of the pro-Chinese Chhatro Union, later wrote in his memoir that the crowd was waiting in the field opposite the governor's house where the army was standing by with machine guns and cannons; if the student leaders had indicated, these people would have demolished the governor's house.[237] But the student leaders were not sure about the strategy.²³⁸ Even the maulvi, who led the prayer of the *janaja*, said, 'Oh Allah, you destroy the dictatorship of Ayub Khan', and the assembled crowd repeated his words.²³⁹ On both 24 and 25 January urban life was paralysed in Dacca. The government announced night curfew and deployed the army. On both 27 and 28 January the government clamped a night curfew, but people tried to violate it and held protests.²⁴⁰ Soon the student unrest had triggered a wider response in the countryside. Every district witnessed angry processions and the police retaliated with firing. Many people died in the confrontation. On the evening of 26 January factory workers clashed with police. Paramilitary forces fired at the workers and sporadic clashes ensued.²⁴¹ A. A Halliley, the British diplomat who at the beginning of the year predicted that the government was unlikely to face significant challenge, observed how

> the immense crowds ... came out in the streets after a student was killed on 20 January. Students expected about 200,000, in the event there may have been something of the order of 500,000. It is estimated that some 30,000 villagers joined the demonstration and that processions during the week 20–25 January were joined by numbers of white-collar workers and trade unionists.²⁴²

In the meantime, newspapers published a testimony of Sheikh Mujib, where he provided a clear outline of his stand and the government's baseless persecution of him and his group.²⁴³ On 30 January Bhashani called for peasant support for the 11-point programme, and asked for the withdrawal of curfew during the evening and vehemently criticized the Ayub Khan government.²⁴⁴ In the meantime, thousands of volunteers of the Krishak Samiti, affiliated to both wings of the NAP, started mobilizing peasants in rural areas. In the industrial areas of Chittagong workers organized an unprecedented strike.²⁴⁵ The entire East Pakistan witnessed a mass upheaval. Leaders of the SAC, the two NAPs and the Awami League led this struggle. But conservative faith-based parties in the DAC remained inactive, or rather lukewarm, to such a mass awakening. This was tacitly recognized in British diplomatic correspondence: 'In the context of the current political movement in the Province, left wing radicals consider DAC almost irrelevant.'²⁴⁶

Ayub Khan decided to adopt a more conciliatory position. On 1 February he announced that there would be discussion with the responsible leaders of the opposition political parties. He also released a few political prisoners and withdrew the night curfew from various towns.²⁴⁷ On the same day, students met with 37 workers' trade union federations. The students and workers formed a united platform. On 4 February the SAC called for the observance of a strike all over East Pakistan, which was held the following day.[248] On 6 February Ayub Khan visited Dacca to attend the CML's working committee meeting. On the same day Ayub Khan sent a letter to DAC leader Nasrullah Khan, inviting him and other political parties to a round table conference on 17 February, and announced that he would consider the withdrawal of national security regulations and the emergency.[249] Unimpressed with such developments, the SAC observed a black-flag day in Dacca. According to several eyewitness accounts, Dacca had become an ocean of black badges and flags.[250] The SAC also proposed a public oath-taking, insisting that till the 11 points were accepted, they would continue their struggle. Tofail Ahmed, the leader of the SAC, led the oath-taking ceremony. Thousands gathered to take oaths in Paltan Maidan in Dacca.[251] On that day, the crowd of students and workers returning from the oath-taking ceremony gathered in front of the central jail and proposed to liberate the prisoners forcefully by breaking the gate. Oli Ahad, a conservative politician, recalled in his autobiography how he, at the request of a nervous jailor and his cellmate, Awami League leader Tajuddin Ahmad, had lectured the crowd at the jail gate to desist from taking such an action from inside the prison.[252] On 7 February thousands of women marched on the streets in Dacca. Indeed, the mass insurrection of 1969 was marked by large participation of women in the protests.[253] On 13 February a representative of the rickshaw drivers' association declared that 30,000 rickshaw drivers would go on strike if Sheikh Mujib and other political prisoners were not released immediately.[254] On 14 February, in West Pakistan, the government released Bhutto and Wali Khan from prison. The next day, even the timid and rather conservative DAC called for a strike, and it was observed everywhere in the province.[255] In public meetings organized by the DAC, people in Dacca did not want to listen to anybody except those who supported the 11-point programme and demanded the release of Sheikh Mujib.[256]

Yet all was not good among the radicals. The situation in Chittagong illustrates this. After a week-long strike, workers wanted to return to work as they did not have much to eat, and the peasants yearned to go back to the farms, while the students got tired of marching and could not give up their studies altogether. Trade unionists, peasant activists and student leaders told veteran Maoist communist Sharadindu Dostidar in Chittagong to either order an insurrection or allow them to return to normal life. Dostidar approached Bhashani for direction. Bhashani listened to Dostidar and asked: 'Are you ready for revolution? Can you start an armed struggle for capturing power?' Dostidar realized that they did not think in those terms. In fact, in reality, divided into several competing Maoist groups, the EPCP-ML did not have the ability to initiate an armed struggle.[257] The pro-Soviet communists were more cautious and also vacillated in their response to the situation; a few became nervous and inactive, while others became elated and thought that they could transform this into a revolutionary uprising. Meanwhile, established political parties and Islam-oriented political organizations felt that East Pakistan was going through a revolutionary process and that a communist takeover was imminent. This was a conative reaction of the conservative forces that were apprehensive of any mass uprising. The Jamaat-e-Islami had always insisted on cautious legal methods of resistance. Their slogan was about the leadership of the Prophet, and they claimed that neither Moscow nor Beijing but Mecca was the centre of world emancipation.[258] But the popular slogan among students was 'Keu khabe, keu khabe na; ta hobe na, ta hobe na' (Hunger for some, while some others eat; that can't be, that can't be).[259] Students were impatient and intolerant towards the conservative faith-based leadership. Nurul Amin, a former Muslim League leader and the NDF chairman, who was presiding a public meeting, was not allowed to speak on 14 February in Dacca by students because in the past, as a Muslim league chief minister of the province, he had ordered police firing at the student movement of 1952.[260]

On 15 February a prisoner of the Agartala conspiracy case, Zahurul Haq, was killed by the army. Gauhar, Ayub's information secretary, suspected that Yahya Khan, who was the commander-in-chief of the army, had ordered his murder to frustrate Ayub Khan's attempt to find a political solution. Yahya Khan was waiting impatiently for political power to be transferred to him.[261] Complex twists and turns of events made matters worse for the Ayub Khan regime. No doubt, because of the division within the army and the bureaucracy, Ayub Khan's hold on power was tenuous. Even then many workers, peasants and students died in police firing, some were even bayoneted and other succumbed to their wounds from stave beatings. The revolutionary climate created by radical students, striking workers and rebellious peasants had made both the government and the non-communist faith-based political opposition nervous. Despite the complex political tug of war between the conservative, aged leaders of mostly faith-based political formations on the one hand and the radical students on the other, hundreds of thousands of people gathered for meetings and prayers for Zahurul Haq on 15 February. The students renamed Iqbal Hall, a student dorm that was the centre of the SAC in Dacca University campus, after Zahurul Haq.[262] Bhashani declared in a meeting that within two months the government would have to accept the 11-point programme and release political prisoners. He further emphasized that if Sheikh Mujib was not released, the people would snatch him from the prison.[263] An angry mob then targeted the red-coloured mansion where S. A. Rahman, the judge who was presiding over the Agartala case, used to live. The crowd set this house on fire, and Rahman saved his life by escaping from the house. Deeply shaken by this event, he closed the proceedings of the Agartala case and returned to West Pakistan on 17 February.[264] But the clashes continued on 18 February at Rajshahi University, where East Pakistan Rifles soldiers bayoneted university proctor Mohammad Shamsuzzoha.[265] The news of this death provoked thousands of students to violate the night curfew and hold processions in Dacca. The police clashed with angry students and workers in various places in East Pakistan. University teachers immediately went on strike throughout the province in protest against the killing of Shamsuzzoha. Rono recalled the evening he was sitting with Bhashani in a house in Dacca when a young man entered the house and asked Bhashani: 'Can you provide us with arms? The army is killing Bengalis. I know you have a connection with China. Please give us arms.' On investigation, Bhashani's associates found out that ordinary working-class people who lived in slums on the roadside had spontaneously decided to hold a procession as they were suffering from a lack of employment during the curfew. They invited the people who lived in the mansions next to the streets, and these relatively affluent people also joined them. Many among these middle-class people had their own guns, and when the army fired into the crowd, they fired back. Next day, when Bhashani went to visit hospitals, an old man told him that the army had murdered three of his sons. 'Nobody knew,' wrote Rono, 'how many were killed that night.'[266] In the meantime, 21 February, which was Language Martyrs' Day, approached, and students were ready to celebrate the occasion to further their protest. Yet they also longed to celebrate a victory. It came on 21 February, when dictator Ayub Khan declared that he would not be a candidate in the next elections, which would be held under the Constitution of Basic Democracy.[267]

As students, workers and peasants were determined to obtain their demands, from the second week of February the government started negotiations to release Sheikh Mujib, the president of the Awami League. Sheikh Mujib reminded the DAC convenor, Nasarullah Khan, that without the Awami League, the round table conference would be meaningless. Khan contacted the government officials and obtained the release of Tajuddin Ahmad on the night of 12 February.[268] The problem arose when the release of Sheikh Mujib was discussed, since he was a prisoner under a treason case. The government was ready to release him on parole. But senior Awami League leaders and leaders of the SAC were opposed to his being released on parole. Bhashani also demanded the scrapping of the conspiracy case.[269] Finally, Sheikh Mujib's wife, Begum Fazilatunnesa, met Sheikh Mujib in his special prison in the military cantonment and told him that his acceptance of the parole would be a betrayal of his people. Sheikh Mujib realized the issue and refused to be released on parole.[270] On 22 February the government released all the prisoners detained under the Agartala conspiracy case, and Sheikh Mujib was also unconditionally freed from prison. In the afternoon of 22 February 1969, Sheikh Mujib's neighbour, the communist leader Rono's father, spotted a military van slowly moving on the street. Rono's parents were driving their car and wondering the person in the van was. Suddenly the van stopped, and a passenger disembarked from it in front of Sheikh Mujib's house. To their delight, Rono's parents noted it was Sheikh Mujib himself. Excited by this incident, they jumped out of the car. Sheikh Mujib embraced Rono's father and returned to his house.[271] As news spread of his release, thousands rushed to his house to celebrate the occasion. The masses of East Pakistan had successfully freed their leader from prison through insurrectionary force. Military authorities also released Moni Singh, one of the founders of the communist movement in East Pakistan, and also Nagen Sarkar, the leader of the pro-Chinese faction of the CPP (East Pakistan Provincial Committee). The nervous government had released their prime suspects in a treason case without trial. This marked a new phase in the political journey of East Pakistan.

The Mass Insurrection of 1969, the Round Table Conference and Martial Law

On 12 March 1969 a secret CIA document provided a clue to the 1969 mass insurrection in Pakistan against praetorian capitalism through a schematic class analysis. The document prepared for secret foreign circulation stated unambiguously:

> East Pakistanis, the urban proletariat and certain elements of the middle class, subsistence farmers, and landless laborers are among those who have lost out in the distribution of economic gains in Pakistan. A few dozen families engaged in industry have done exceptionally well. Many wealthier and more progressive farmers, the civil service and the armed forces have also made absolute and relative gains. Students, drawn now in larger numbers from economic groups lower down the scale, are as a group troubled by economic anxieties.[272]

The document provided a class analysis of the developmental regime that Ayub Khan had put into place. Institutionally, the system prioritized the needs of the military-bureaucratic regime aligned with the US and the West, which poured foreign aid into Pakistan. The model of functional inequality that economists deployed to defend the regime was not politically sustainable.[273] Students who were exposed to international politics had cultural capital to conceptualize changes, and their connections with rural society acted as the vanguard of social protests. Workers, who faced a decline in real wages, revolted to defend their living standards. In 1968–69 widespread revolts, led by students and workers, against the status quo took place. Though economic anxiety and a desire for emancipation from a situation of internal colonization informed their core beliefs, they also had a wider vision of social justice and political activism, combined with the impatience of youth.

It was this sense of social justice, deprivation and impatience of the youth that both Sheikh Mujib and Bhashani appealed to. Yet politics has strange facets. After being released, Sheikh Mujib went straight to meet Bhashani and conferred with him about the possibility of attending the round table conference. Sheikh Mujib probably requested Bhashani to attend it, and Bhashani already recognized that the Ayub Khan regime was a spent force.[274] To Bhashani, going to Ayub Khan's conference would be akin to what Gandhi had once famously quipped about the Cripps Mission – that it was a post-dated cheque drawn on a failing bank. Sheikh Mujib believed that through negotiations he could secure his six-point demand charter, though in a private conversation he had once confided to communist youth leader Rono that the first meeting of the cabinet of independent Bangladesh would be held in the veranda of his house at Dhanmondi.²⁷⁵ Yet Bhashani's refusal caused a bitterness in the relationship with Sheikh Mujib. The respective paths chosen by the most ardent Bengali nationalist and the radical peasants and workers' activist would never meet again.

Incidentally, West Pakistani PPP leader Bhutto also boycotted the round table conference. Bhutto was present in Dacca at that time and met with Bhashani and Sheikh Mujib. Bhutto might have obtained information from the army that they would not like Ayub Khan to continue in power. Sensing popular disenchantment, Bhashani continued his movement to 'burn the organs of the state power and ruling establishments'.²⁷⁶ Though pro-Chinese communists officially supported Bhashani, their internal documents classified him as a vacillating petite bourgeois leader.²⁷⁷ Indeed, on 21 February, when the working classes were organizing massive processions in Khulna, Maoist communists were engaged in a party meeting to discuss the efficacy of West Bengal's Naxalite leader Majumdar's doctrine in East Pakistan. They were surprised by mass participation of working classes in the region.²⁷⁸ It seemed that the pro-Chinese communists were living in their own self-imagined reality. In such complicated political circumstances, Sheikh Muijib remained wedded to his own agenda.

On 23 February the SAC decided to invite Sheikh Mujib and other recently released political prisoners to a historically unprecedented mass gathering. Tofail Ahmed, the vice-president of the Dacca University student union and a Chhatro League leader, conferred the title 'Bangabandhu' (Friend of Bengal) on Sheikh Mujib, an appellation that has stuck with his name forever in history.²⁷⁹ Many debated whether this announcement was made in consultation with the non-Chhatro League members of the SAC, and the NAP-affiliated Chhatro Union remained angry with Tofail Ahmed for his 'hasty declaration'.²⁸⁰ Yet public approval of Sheikh Mujib was phenomenal at that time. Within the Awami League, the left-leaning nucleus group, which was working towards an independent Bengal, promoted Sheikh Mujib as a rallying figure for East Pakistanis.²⁸¹ Sheikh Mujib gave a stirring speech on 23 February and made it clear that he would attend the round table conference. Soon after the public reception, Sheikh Mujib met with Chhatro League leaders at his home at Dhanmondi.²⁸² On 24 February Sheikh Mujib started towards Rawalpindi. He was accompanied by senior Awami League leaders, including Tajuddin Ahmad, Syed Nazrul Islam, Mizanur Rahman Chowdhury, the leading constitutional expert Kamal Hossain, Amirul Islam and Khan Sarwar Murshid, among others.²⁸³

The round table conference involved 16 representatives of the DAC and 15 representatives of Ayub Khan and his administration. Asghar Khan, the former air force chief of Pakistan, and S. M. Murshed attended as independent experts.[284] The conference began on 26 February, but it was postponed till 10 March due to Eid.[285] Sheikh Mujib then returned to East Pakistan to meet his parents. As the conference was postponed, on 4 March the SAC announced another strike. It had given a call to the Basic Democrats and the members of the national assembly to resign from their respective positions, though they agreed to exclude national assembly members after talking with Awami League leaders. Thousands of Basic Democrats resigned from their position, making Ayub Khan's political system a defunct organization.[286] As violence spread, international supporters of the Ayub Khan regime became nervous.

Peter Hazelhurst of the *London Times* wrote how 'riots cripple East Pakistan' and described how Muslim League offices came under attack from people in some areas.[287] Meanwhile, it became clear that DAC representatives from Punjab were not ready to support Sheikh Mujib. On 9 March Sheikh Mujib issued a press statement supporting his six-point programme. Ayub Khan was under pressure from the anti-six-point lobby in Punjab.[288] On 12 March Yahya Khan, the then commander-in-chief of the armed forces, met with Sheikh Mujib. In a speech on 10 March, during the round table conference, Sheikh Mujib emphasized three critical problems:

> The first is that of deprivation of political rights and civil liberties. The second is the economic injustice suffered by vast majority of the people, comprising workers, peasants, low and middle income groups, who have had to bear the burden of the costs of development in the form of increasing inflation while the benefits of such development are increasingly concentrated in the hands of few families, who in turn are concentrated in one region. The third is the existing constitutional arrangements, their basic interests have consistently suffered in the absence of effective political power being conferred upon them. The former minority provinces of West Pakistan feel similarly aggrieved by the present constitutional arrangements.[289]

Despite pressure from Sheikh Mujib, Ayub Khan announced that he would not accept the proposal for autonomy or the scrapping of the one-unit policy. Ayub Khan was supported by delegates from Punjab and possibly by a section of the Bengali delegates. At the end of the conference, Ayub Khan had a long dinner with Sheikh Mujib. But Sheikh Mujib withdrew from the DAC and decided to continue his movement in favour of the six-point programme. On 14 March Sheikh Mujib returned to Dacca. He called for the struggle to continue. At his insistence Monem Khan was withdrawn as governor on 21 March, and Nurul Huda replaced him on 23 March. Monem Khan rushed to Rawalpindi after this news.[290]

Meanwhile, Bhashani, accompanied by Mohammad Toaha, went to Rawalpindi and met with Bhutto. He travelled throughout West Pakistan. In Shahiwal, in Punjab, the Jamaat-e-Islami supporters attacked him.[291] The Jamaat was increasingly asserting itself against any talk of socialism. Bhashani continued to deploy socialist slogans and rallied people against the military-bureaucratic regime. In the meantime, from the last week of February, workers, under their own initiative, introduced a new method of organizing strikes by laying siege to a factory management. Popularly known in Bengali as *gherao*, it entered into the English language because of the popularity of the tactic of encirclement introduced by Subhodh Banerjee, a member of the Socialist Unity Centre in India (SUCI). In 1969 Banerjee was the labour minister in the communist-led United Front government of West Bengal.[292] He introduced a method of protest in which workers prevented employers from leaving a place of work until their demands were met. From February onwards workers, had started using this tactic. Rono, who was then organizing workers in the Tongi industrial area, described the beginning of the *gherao* movement. One evening it came to light that the workers had confined the management to a room in the factory and were threatening to not release them till their demands, of raising the minimum salary and bonuses as well as the re-employment of workers dismissed for political activities, were met.[293] On 15 March Roy Fox, the deputy high commissioner, in a telegram, said that *gherao*s continued, with the latest long one being at Pakistan Tobacco Company. He noted about the possibility of serious disturbances on the street. He was also worried about references to Anglo-American imperialism by British Pakistani student leader Tariq Ali.[294] C. S. Pickard, the British high commissioner to London, meanwhile, wrote to his home office:

> The situation in East Pakistan is remarkably brittle. The workers are very restive and are pressing for wage increases. I suspect they will

prove themselves to be quite as difficult to handle as their West Bengal counter parts.[295]

As the police and administration had been demoralized through constant insurrection, the management had to accept the demands of the workers. Rono recalled how in the aftermath of the 1969 uprising there took place a transformation in the Tongi industrial area. In slums after slums, workers were flying red flags and there existed unprecedented solidarity among them. Employees dismissed for political reasons were re-employed in their jobs. In collective bargaining the workers prevailed in most instances.[296] In rural areas, too, the pro-Bhashani NAP initiated a popular struggle. When the SAC gave a call for Basic Democrat members to resign, the pro-Chinese NAP activists visited rural areas to tackle cattle thieves. For peasants in an agrarian society, cattle being stolen implied the loss of one of their most important economic assets. In many instances cattle thieves were patronized by powerful members of rural society, primarily rich peasants who operated with the tacit approval of the police. Bhashani and his associates organized the peasants, established a people's court and tried to punish cattle thieves. There were excesses, and, in some instances, unfortunate cattle thieves were murdered.[297] This movement was primarily organized by the middle peasants whose children were students, and thus they had been radicalized by the 1969 mass uprising. More importantly, the peasants seized land records and set them on fire. This was a deliberate attempt to stop tax collection. This event drew international attention. On 19 March *The Guardian* reported:

> There are reports of setting up in parts of Pakistan of 'people's courts' which were meting out instant executions to scores of wrong doers before mobs of wildly applauding peasants. In Kurigram, 250 miles north of Dacca, mobs opposed to President Ayub Khan were reported to have seized public records. Armed troops were said to be trying to restore order to the area.[298]

Peter Hazelhurst, a veteran reporter of *The Times*, also spoke of the people's courts and wildly applauding peasants present in the so-called people's courts. He further noticed: 'Poster[s] similar to those deployed during China's "cultural revolution" were appearing on walls in many parts of the country.'[299] The uprising was turning towards a social revolution.

It was clear that in such circumstances Ayub Khan had a limited choice. Many feared that East Pakistan would witness a communist revolution. Apparently, Bhashani's influence in the countryside and his invocation of socialism had attracted international attention. Newsmagazine *Time* had already called Bhashani a prophet of violence.[300] Bhashani, on his return from West Pakistan, announced that he would burn down voters' booths if elections were held under the Ayub Khan Constitution, rejecting the document vehemently. To his own supporters he confided in private that there would be martial law again very soon.[301] Indeed, Ayub Khan requested Yahya Khan to extend martial law in the country. But the latter informed him that only the armed forces could promulgate martial law. Ayub Khan took the hint, and on 24 March he wrote to Yahya Khan:

> It is with profound regret that I have come to the conclusion that all civil administration and constitutional authority have become ineffective. If the situation continues to deteriorate at the present alarming rate all economy, life, indeed the civilised existence will become impossible. I am thus left with no option but to step aside and leave it to the Defense Forces of Pakistan which today represent the only effective and legal instrument to take full control of the affairs of this country....[302]

Ayub thus transferred power not to the speaker of the Pakistani national assembly, according to his own Constitution, but to the chief of the armed forces. He knew that his Constitution was a mere façade to military rule. He also knew that a civilian government would not be able to control the popular rebellion in East Pakistan, which could transform itself into a socialist revolution. Thus, the students' and workers' uprising ended a phase of military rule in Pakistan. Discounting the theory of Chinese money supporting the pro-China group and US money for the Awami League, British diplomat R. F. N. Skillbeck wrote in his despatch, titled 'Student Power':

> For the January–February 1969 student movement in East Pakistan, at any rate, no conceivable amount of foreign money could have induced the scale and sustained power of demonstrations. This was a popular uprising, in which students spontaneously played the leading co-ordinating role.[303]

Political Parties in East Pakistan after the 1969 Mass Uprising

The declaration of martial law obviously relieved industrialists, foreign capitalists and landed families. Indeed, from 16 March 1969 onwards, even before the declaration of martial law, the government had increased troop presence in East Pakistan. A British diplomat, D. M. March, noted:

> We now have reliable evidence that the government of Pakistan has been quietly reinforcing its forces in East Pakistan over the last two months. We believe that at least a division (and probably two) is being formed in East Pakistan under the command of Lieutenant-General Tikka Khan. It is difficult to be precise as to the extent to which this will increase military forces at the disposal of the Government in the province because part of the exercise is probably designed to guard against any reluctance on the part of Bengali troops to enforce law and order in a situation where the military have to called in by the civil authorities.[304]

Indeed, the government had reasons to be worried. Rono, our known communist protagonist, observed that on 19 February, when he was travelling from the Tongi industrial estate to Dacca, several Bengali police officers shared a ride with him, though they did not know who he was. These Bengali officers were extremely critical of the Punjabi militia and were badmouthing them.[305] A sense of Bengali nationalism had spread among the police too. Yet many political activists found this martial law different from the one imposed in 1958. Back then martial law had been imposed when civilian politicians had discredited themselves through politicking and palace intrigues. In 1969 martial law was imposed against the background of a mass uprising. The martial authorities were restrained and did not want to be proactive in establishing strict regulations. They requested the politicians to confine their activities to the indoor space of homes. They did not want large processions in public places like streets, parks and open fields. They also announced that industrial agreements reached at the height of the *gherao* movement would be respected. Indeed, the government soon passed the Industrial Relations Ordinance, specifying minimum wages and providing benefits to workers. Many regarded this as one of the most progressive legislations in the field of industrial relations in Pakistan.[306] The Maoist trade unionists organized a strike. Zafar and Rono organized a go-slow in a mill in the Tongi industrial area and refused to accept wages till they were awarded with pay raise and a bonus. The martial law administration sent a small armed force under colonel Akkbar Hossain who arrested a few workers. The workers surrounded them and confined them to the Meghna Mill. The colonel negotiated with the workers that they would accept part of their salaries till the final pay award and that the martial law authorities would not send the army to mill areas. Yet as mill owners did not accept higher wages, the workers went on strike. These Maoists had a presence in every shift of work in every factory, and they formed shift committees and factory committees. Suddenly they declared a strike in the cotton textile mills in the Tongi area. The strike continued for two months.[307] Even then the government did not take steps against the strikers. Rao Farman Ali, who was a martial law administrator in Dacca, had once brought Rono and Zafar to the governor's building and negotiated with them.[308] In other words, the social movement encompassing the urban proletariat continued under martial law, though various interest groups and foreign powers, including the British, expressed dissatisfaction with the government for reinforcing the wage increase agreements signed 'under duress' during the *gherao* movement of 1969.[309] But Fox observed possibly aptly in a secret note:

> It was not known for certain that the army withdrew in the face of the mob and perhaps the hungry and passionate Bengali is not as 'afraid of the bayonet' as has been said.[310]

While Sheikh Mujib did not violate martial laws, he also did not abide by them entirely. He was with Badruddin Umar when martial law was imposed. Umar recalled that Sheikh Mujib was upset and lamented that all his political works had been wasted. But in all probability he had already guessed at the coming of martial law. He was active in his six-point programme, and in an unbridled emotional moment he also talked about independent Bengal. Rono recalled how once he and Menon were returning home, which was next to Sheikh Mujib's residence. Both of them were associated with the pro-Bhashani NAP and were thus critical of Sheikh Mujib. Sheikh Mujib was then engaged in conversation with the district leaders of the Awami League. He introduced them to Menon and Rono, and when these leaders left, an emotional Sheikh Mujib asked Rono and Menon whether they would like to liberate Bengal.[311] But apparently there persisted a calm in East Pakistan. Major political parties, more or less, accepted the martial law regime's declaration that democracy would be restored.

In 1969 there persisted four different trends in East Pakistani politics. The largest among them was the organization of the Awami League. Led by a charismatic leader, the Awami League had a clear political programme and aimed at transforming Pakistan to a confederation as they believed that was the original intention of the Lahore Resolution of 1940. Within the Awami League, a group called Bengal Nucleus was also actively organizing students for an armed struggle for independent 'Bengal'. These young men were inspired by the ideas of the Bengali nationalist revolutionary tradition of the twenties and thirties and, in particular, those of Subhas Chandra Bose. They listened to Trailokyanath Chakravarty, a nationalist revolutionary of the colonial period. People even read Shailesh Chakrabarty's *Ami Subhas Bolchi* (I Am Subhas Speaking).[312] Many Chhatro League members used to say: 'Sheikh Mujib Is Our Subhas.' Many of them were independent Marxists and thought highly of Che Guevara, having read his *Reminiscences of the Cuban Revolutionary War* and *Guerilla Warfare*. Impressed by Guevara, a Chhatro League activist even composed poems in his memory. Regis Debray's *Revolution in the Revolution?* was also popular among the students. Certain factions of the Chhatro League, though, were more conservative and even opposed to the Bengal Nucleus group.[313] Though vaguely socialist, the Chhatro League was more inclined towards an open economy, capital reinvestment and the industrialization of East Pakistan through private capital. Indeed, the six-point programme reflected the dream of an incipient and aspiring Bengali bourgeoisie. They ridiculed the international commitment of the Maoist Marxists and mocked them with the racially tinged slogan: 'Ho ho, Mao Mao, go to China and eat frog'. They called the pro-Soviet Chhatro Union agents of Russia, in response to which the Union branded the Chhatro League as agents of the CIA.[314] On 31 May 1969 one of the most articulate anti-Marxist intellectuals and the eminent journalist who founded the popular Bengali daily news *Ittefaq*, Tofazzal Hossain, popularly known as Manik Mian, passed away in Rawalpindi.[315] His death deprived Sheikh Mujib of a moderate and intellectually sharp non-communist advisor. Sheikh Mujib increasingly relied upon young leaders like Serajul Alam Khan, an activist dedicated to the idea of an independent 'East Bengal' who followed the tradition of the secret society movement in colonial Bengal.[316] Composed of diverse political lines, the Awami League and its powerful student wing, the Chhatro League, had various factions and remained a broad, united platform of the nationalist-minded autonomist political programme. Sheikh Mujib, with his championing of the cause of East Pakistan, could address

Bengali sensitivity. He also made repeated attempts to appeal to the goodwill of West Pakistanis. Between 6 and 14 August 1969 he toured West Pakistan and emphasized the scrapping of the one-unit policy, highlighting the discrimination against East Pakistan.

The second most important political organization in East Pakistan was the leftist NAP. But the NAP was a divided house. Bhashani retained his popularity. He organized a peasant convention at Shahpur in the Pabna district, contravening the martial law regime's regulations of not organizing public meetings. His convention attracted thousands of peasants who came with their raw food and utensils to cook. They gathered in the designated place of convention, cooked, sang songs and listened to several political speeches. This peasant convention appeared more like a village fair, but the disorganized organization appealed to peasants who felt empowered by such conventions. Bhashani, to put his pro-socialist stamp on the peasant movement, asked the peasant volunteers to wear red caps. Thousands of red-cap-wearing peasant volunteers marched through the countryside with red flags in hand.[317] This caused anxiety to the martial law regime, and even the Awami League and the pro-Soviet NAP, including the clandestine pro-Soviet CPP (East Pakistan Provincial Committee), were concerned about such peasant conventions. Impressed by the success of the peasant convention, Abdul Matin, an underground Maoist organizer, demanded the constitution of a peasant army.[318] Despite the continuation of the peasant movement, there were little efforts to organize political protests against the martial law regime. Bhashani became increasingly isolated from his NAP activists as they were mostly members of factions of various underground groups of Maoist communist organizations, and they did not have a clear programme of political movement. There were four broad groups among the Maoists. First was the group centred on the East Pakistan Communist Party (Marxist–Leninist), led by Mohammad Toaha and Sukhendu Dostidar. Influenced by the ideas of Charu Majumdar, the Indian Bengali Maoist, this group wanted to withdraw from all open trade union activities and believed in the annihilation of class enemies. They did not support the organization of movements geared towards economic goals. Second, there existed the Deben–Bashar–Matin–Alauddin group, which did not agree with the interpretation of Maoist doctrine by the Toaha group and thus wanted a different type of revolution. Third, Zafar, Rono and Menon organized a coordination committee of communist revolutionaries, who later became close to the Communist Party of India (Marxist) (CPI[M]) of West Bengal.[319]

Lastly, there existed the independent Marxist–Leninist organization of Siraj Sikdar.[320] The Maoist groups were vehemently criticized by Moni Singh's pro-Soviet Communist Party and the pro-Soviet NAP. Despite having a tight-knit organization, the pro-Soviet Communist Party was not popular among the masses. It had sided with Sheikh Mujib on the question of maintaining peace and law and order.[321] Also, Bhashani's doctrine of Islamic socialism, which he had developed in response to the Jamaat's criticism of him as a false Muslim, was not approved by Marxist intellectuals such as Umar.[322] Bhashani was so exasperated by the desertion of his supporters on a heuristic theoretical debate concerning Marxism and the correct revolutionary path that he once lamented:

> I supported Jinnah and Pakistan during Shylet referendum and Jinnah arrested me when I came to Pakistan, but I was not hurt…. I worked so hard for the foundation of Awami League and then when I left the organization, Sheikh Mujib, whom I loved so much, went against me but I was not sad. But I get truly depressed, when those who transformed me into a socialist from a diehard Muslim cleric, spread innuendos about me.[323]

In many ways, ironically, the global sixties, the Sino-Soviet split and the international political climate that had enabled the mass uprisings of 1969 also undermined the possibilities of a left alternative to the rising tide of Bengali nationalism, spearheaded by Sheikh Mujib. Soon, from July onwards, the martial law regime started arresting the leading communists, particularly those of Hindu origins such as Moni Singh and Deben Sikdar.[324]

Apart from these two larger conglomerations of leftist political groups, there also existed free-floating politicians, the past masters of political intrigues and both parts of the official Muslim League or breakaways from the Awami League. Records of British diplomatic despatches indicate British support to these individuals, though both the British and the Americans recognized that they were simply relics of the past.[325] The most prominent and intelligent among them were Nurul Amin, the former Muslim League chief minister and governor of East Bengal; Hamidul Haq Chowdhury, a minister in various Muslim League ministries; Mahbub Murshed, who had technical expertise in constitutional law and hoped that in the midst of political bickering he might be selected as a constitutional expert; and Oli Ahad, a former radical who turned neo-conservative. All of them criticized Sheikh

Mujib and feared that he would guide the movement towards the break-up of Pakistan, or that his 'demagogy' would enable the military to return to power.[326] On 24 June the breakaway the pro-PDM Awami League, the NDF, the Nizam-e-Islam and the Justice Party of Asghar Khan formed a united platform and elected Nurul Amin as its chairman. On 20 July, Ahad and Khairat Hossain constituted another centre–right political formation known as the National Progressive League, later known as the National League.[327] Yet all these formations had a skewed presence in the overall politics of the country.

A fourth, small but assertive group of politicians belonged to radical Islamic parties. Foremost among them was the Jamaat-e-Islami. The Jamaat had a tight-knit organization, a clear formulated ideology and a vision for Pakistan. The Jamaat was emphatic that a country that was established as a Muslim homeland should follow Islamic principles. In 1969 it participated in the DAC, though its role in the 1969 mass uprising was not very prominent. It criticized Ayub Khan's regime for the only progressive law the regime had enacted, known as the Muslim Family Laws Ordinance (MFLO), in March 1961, which provided preliminary protection to women in matters of marriage, divorce, custody and inheritance. The Jamaat were vociferous in their opposition to this law.[328] They opposed to any secularization of the educational system and remained determined to introduce Islamic rule in Pakistan. They were hostile to the idea of ethnic nationalism as it followed that there would not be any restriction among Muslims based on ethnic distinctions. The Jamaat also denounced the idea of Islamic socialism and maintained that socialism was foreign to Islam.[329] They regularly clashed with the supporters of the Bengal Nucleus within the Chhatro League and also with the two NAP-affiliated student organizations.[330]

The initial days of martial law were not entirely free from political activities and tensions. On 22 April, Yahya Khan announced that he would hold the first general election in Pakistan, and yet, at the same time, the court cases against Sheikh Mujib, based on his speech on 20 March 1966, were revived, and he was sentenced again to 15 months of imprisonment. Sheikh Mujib appealed to the high court.[331] On 24 April, Yahya Khan came to Dacca and students held a meeting at the *bottola* in the Dacca University campus. The student leaders warned that they would not accept martial law and held a procession in Dacca city.[332] On 7 June Sheikh Mujib remembered the police massacre of workers in a public meeting.[333] The government announced a new educational policy in July, and the SAC rejected it. During discussions, the Jamaat vehemently objected to pro-Soviet Chhatro Union leader Matia Chowdhury's argument for the secularization of the education system.[334] There took place a clash between the martial law administration and the SAC over the holding of procession on 22 April. On 26 September student leaders of the SAC were invited to the governor's house, and then they were asked to meet brigadier Majid ul-Haque. Meanwhile, this news caused tensions, and students in Dacca University waited with anxiety. They were ready to revolt if these student leaders were arrested, but the tension disappeared when the student leaders finally were allowed to return to the university dorm.[335] When the government appointed vice air marshal Nur Khan as the governor of West Pakistan, and vice admiral Syed Mohammad Ahsan as the governor of East Pakistan, the latter held talks with the pro-Soviet NAP and the Awami League regarding the Constitution. Soon the Awami League started preparing for elections. Sheikh Mujib started touring East Pakistan. Everywhere he was accorded wildly jubilant receptions, and the crowds in his meetings exceeded any previous mass meetings held in the country.[336] Thus, martial law could not curb political activities, even though it did put a lid on it.

Election and the Victory of Bengali Nationalism in East Pakistan

On 28 November 1969, martial law administrator Yahya Khan announced the conditions for the first general election of Pakistan, which was scheduled to be held in October 1970. He accepted several demands of the opposition and tried to move away from the errors committed in the 1956 Constitution as well as during the Ayub Khan years. The martial law regime dissolved the one-unit policy in West Pakistan, and separate provinces came into being. It declared unambiguously that elections would be held on the basis of universal adult franchise. This implied representation based on population, whereby the majority of seats in the national assembly would go to East Pakistan. It promised provincial autonomy, stating that the centre–province relationship would be worked out through constitutional power-sharing, including control over economic resources consistent with national integrity and effective working of a national government at the centre. It sought to establish a timetable for transfer of power to a constitutional government.[337] The government permitted full political activity from 1 January 1970 and promised to announce a provisional legal framework for holding elections by 31 March 1970. But it kept the trump card for the military regime in its hand by making it clear that martial law would remain supreme until a government was formed under the new Constitution. More precisely, it declared that general elections would be held on 5 October 1970 to a national assembly charged with framing a Constitution within 120 days, after which the constitutional government would take over.[338]

This announcement introduced new political life in the country. On 5 December 1969, Sheikh Mujib, on the death anniversary of Suhrawardy, demanded that East Pakistan be called Bangladesh.[339] This was a qualitative jump in political thinking since even few years ago, student activists of the Awami League had insisted on using the name East Pakistan. They even opposed using the name East Bengal.[340] The very use of the term 'Bangladesh' suggested a significant transformation in the national political consciousness. On 15 December, Sheikh Mujib, in an election meeting in New Market in Dacca, rhetorically asked: 'Sonar Bangla shoshan keno?' (Why has the golden Bengal become a crematorium?).[341] This rhetorical question would become the most important slogan of the Awami League during the elections and would be the header of their most famous leaflet. The Awami League captured the momentum of the electoral campaign. On 7 June 1970, addressing a mammoth public meeting in Racecourse Maidan in Dacca, Sheikh Mujib appealed for a vote for the six-point programme to eradicate the discrimination between East Pakistan and West Pakistan.[342] In its manifesto, the Awami League assured people that it would adhere to the principles of Islam, the protection of minorities, equality before the law, and the preservation of democratic rights of freedom of speech and press and the right to assemble peacefully, and stated that except for situations of emergency, such as wartime, these rights could not be suspended. The manifesto promised complete freedom to the Justice Department to remove economic discrimination.[343] On 17 November 1970, Sheikh Mujib, now popularly known as Bangabandhu, adopted the country boat as his symbol and started his campaign from Dholaikhal in the Dacca district.[344] Since then, in speech after speech, Sheikh Mujib promised to wipe out the remnants of praetorian capitalism by highlighting the contradiction between the prosperity of Pakistan-based monopoly capitalists and the poverty of the masses of Bangladesh. He emphasized experimenting with participatory forms of democracy, promised to strengthen the role of the state in the economy and touched on the issue of the cultural emancipation of Bengalis. His inclusionary populist appeal, grounded in the idea of democratizing polity, appealed to many Bengalis. After a decade of military dictatorship and shambolic façades of democracy, these populist ideals resurrected the nationalitarian notion of emancipation, offered new meanings to these ideals and gave birth to new strategies of political mobilization. Borrowing from Ernesto Laclau's notion of populism, it could be argued that Sheikh Mujib's nationalitarian, populist rhetoric articulated popular democratic interpellations as antagonistic to the dominant developmentalist ideology of the military-bureaucratic regime. To the vast masses he appeared different from quotidian mundane administrative politics.[345] Sheikh Mujib's campaign created an exceptional moment of a populist rupture. His invocation of the idea of a mythical golden Bengal further invoked Bengali patriotism.

As Sheikh Mujib gained political momentum, Bhashani could not negotiate a unified stand in the pro-Chinese NAP. A massive ideological and factional fight broke out in their council meeting in Khulna in August 1970. Bhashani supported the election boycott programme. Finally, the pro-Chinese NAP council adopted resolutions to demand change in the Legal Framework of Order, to release all political prisoners punished under martial law and to hold the election in March 1971. Bhashani tried to resurrect a utopia of social justice, called for a resolution of mass hunger before the vote and emphasized the purity of Islamic culture by removing corruption and establishing a socialist regime. His supporters among the various factions of Maoists withdrew active support from Bhashani.[346] Calling for boycotting the vote in a radio and TV address, Bhashani spoke about the need for the creation of an exploitation-free society according to the tenets of Islam and Pakistan's withdrawal from various US-sponsored military pacts. Based on the notion of the Islamic process of character-building, he talked about the stranglehold exercised by monopoly capitalists over the resources of the country and how the time had come for the poor to unite against the capitalists and feudal lords. He also appealed to Pakistani patriotism and said that the Pakistani army was an asset to the nation, but that they should not be dragged into everyday civil administration.[347] Despite Bhashani's lofty rhetoric, a shift had occurred in the ground reality of the politics in East Pakistan – it had developed from a class-based mobilization into a nationalist one. This transformation was evident in the changes to popular slogans. In 1969 the mass uprising popular slogan had been about workers and peasants picking up arms and liberating Bangladesh. This was now replaced by the slogan 'Valorous Bengali, pick up arms and liberate Bangladesh'. Another popular slogan, one that rhymes in Bengali, was 'What is our address? The farms and the factories!' but it too had been replaced by slogans that changed the 'address' part to 'Padma, Meghna and Jamuna', the three major rivers of Bangladesh. The reference to the three rivers contained an emotive reference to the riverine natural landscape that constituted the distinctive feature of the land of Bengal.

Despite such references to nature in the popular rhetoric of mobilization, nature appeared to have conspired against the holding of elections in East Pakistan in October. A devastating flood disrupted normal life. The government moved the date of the elections of the national assembly to 7 December 1970 and those of the provincial assembly to 17 December 1970. But on 12 November 1970, the Bhola cyclone devastated the south-eastern coastline of East Pakistan. According to Edris Alam and Dale Dominey-Howes, winds of over 200 kilometres per hour and a storm surge up to 10 metres high inundated over 4,000 square kilometres (1,700 square miles) and devastated the agricultural land and the built environment.[348] Millions of people were affected and rendered homeless. Officials estimated the death-toll range to be between 250,000 and 500,000 people. The East Pakistani news media alleged that, despite warnings from the US meteorological department, the government of Pakistan did not caution the people of East Pakistan. There were several allegations of the mishandling of relief distribution, and there was no attempt to declare an emergency in East Pakistan. Despite international relief operations, even the British Foreign Office and the US State Department diplomats had become exasperated with the lackadaisical attitude of the martial law administration. During this time president Yahya Khan was actually engaged in a much greater diplomatic mission, in relation to the US and China rapprochement at the request of the US president. He finally visited East Pakistan on 17 November on his way to China and on 23 November on his way back from China. In a press conference he admitted that there were some errors committed during the relief operations, and he communicated that there would be maximum autonomy for East Pakistan.[349]

The Bhola cyclone undermined people's trust in the Pakistani administration. There was serious negligence in communicating danger signal to the coastal community, and the government also neglected cyclone centres. Even after the disaster, the government adopted a lackadaisical attitude towards relief. In contrast to the government's paltry relief operations, various organizations, student groups and political activists in East Pakistan offered their services, money and resources to assist relief operations.[350] Zainul Abedin, a famous painter, drew his painting, *Manpura*, to capture the disaster and communicate his anguish to the spectators.[351] On 23 November 1970, Bhashani addressed a crowd in Paltan Maidan and accused the government ministers of not visiting the disaster sites. He then called for the independence of East Pakistan. His speech made newspaper headlines and captured the imagination of poet Shamsur Rahman, who composed a poem called 'Safed Punjabi' (White Shirt) to refer to the occasion.[352] Bhashani thus mobilized the anger and frustration of Bengalis into a particular direction. On 26 November, Sheikh Mujib held a press conference, in which he highlighted the neglect and argued that such a disaster would not be repeated in Bangladesh if the six-point programme was adopted. Archer Blood, the US deputy high ambassador in Dacca, called his performance memorable.[353] Sheikh Mujib increasingly appeared like a statesman who commanded respect from his people and even in international circles. Political parties other than the Awami League demanded the postponement of elections. Ahad, who was stridently critical of the Awami League, mentioned sarcastically that this was because all other political parties had little prospects of winning the election.[354] The Awami League demanded that the election be held on schedule. At the final moment, various centrist candidates withdrew from the election. Only a few centrist politicians, such as Nurul Amin, remained in the fray. On 7 December, when the electorate voted in the first general election of Pakistan, Sheikh Mujib became an icon of Bengali aspirations in East Pakistan. As the election results poured in, the Awami League had won 167 seats out of the 169 in the national assembly.[355] Its success in the provincial assembly was no less spectacular.

The victory of the Awami League clearly vindicated Sheikh Mujib's uncompromising stand since 1961 for the autonomy of East Pakistan. The left's international commitment and the pro-Chinese left's reluctance to endorse the six-point programme had initially caused their decline. The splintering of the left in general, the blind emulation of the pro-Chinese left's strategies of Naxalbari, as well as their confusion over the pro-Pakistan foreign policy of China further cost them political support. The underground pro-Soviet Communist Party could not retain the loyalty of the youth. The rest of the youth, though attracted by Marxism and the idea of solidarity in Asia, Africa and Latin America, became more inclined to support the Awami League and its gestures towards an independent Bengal. In the final stage, the youth found it hard to distinguish between the Awami League's political position and that of the pro-Soviet left. More importantly, they preferred an international commitment based on the analysis of the political economy, culture and social context of East Pakistan rather than what they perceived as a clientelist position of a major global power. Their support to the Awami League was conditional. They wanted the Awami League to deliver on what it had promised: complete provincial autonomy and democratic freedom both in the normative and the substantive senses. Normative freedom implied the right to vote, to organize and to express opinions. Substantive freedom implied freedom from poverty, hunger and a new type of education that would provide a meaningful path in life.

The Awami League thus became a prisoner of its promises. The people and the youth would not accept a digression from the six-point programme. The Awami League had to deliver its promises. Bangabandhu, as Sheikh Mujib was called, became an icon of the liberation of Bengal, and people could not see him in a different role. His long imprisonment, booming voice, soaring rhetoric and earthy sense of humour endeared him to the population. The myth and reality surrounding his sacrifices transformed him into a person that far exceeded the real-life politician. Yet his successful electoral strategy, his stubborn loyalty to the idea of full autonomy as envisaged in the six-point programme and his understanding of sentiments at the grassroots level enabled him to direct a non-violent path for the transfer of power to an elected authority. He was aware that his failure could lead him into a political abyss from which he might never recover. Despite his popularity, in high politics, the decks were stacked against him. He did not command the armed forces, and he had to negotiate with West Pakistan-based politicians such as Bhutto, who were products of a military-bureaucratic regime and had deep connections with the army. Bhutto was popular, a maverick and an unpredictable politician who wanted to come to power at any cost. Sheikh Mujib was more reliant on the legal advice of Kamal Hossain, a barrister and legal luminary, of Nurul Islam and Rehman Sobhan, two young academic economists, and of a large number of young student leaders such Serajul Alam Khan, Sheikh Moni and Tofail Ahmad. Yet his towering popularity exposed him to nearly utopian popular expectations.

Towards the National Liberation War: The Conclusion of the Global Sixties in Bangladesh

The election of the Pakistani national assembly dashed the expectations of the Pakistani army. Its ability to manipulate politicians had become almost negligible. In both the eastern and western wings of the country, two popular forces emerged completely victorious. The PPP secured 81 seats out of 138 for the national assembly. Bhutto's slogan 'Islam is our religion; socialism is our economy; democracy is our politics' captured the imagination of the urban and peri-urban electorate in West Pakistan, particularly in Sindh and Punjab. In West Pakistan, Bhutto represented the political constituency of the global 1968, who wanted a change. It would be futile for the army to contest with a movement from the core areas of Pakistan where soldiers were recruited.[356] The Awami league had secured 160 seats out of 162. Yet the absolute majority of the Awami League in the national assembly of Pakistan became a hurdle for the PPP, a representative organization of the urban petite bourgeoisie and the rural landed gentry, to imprinting their presence on the constitutional process. They were not willing to dismantle the colonial relationship with East Pakistan. East Pakistan constituted a captive market for West Pakistani industrial products. According to a cost–benefit analysis by the Foreign and Commonwealth Office in the context of a split in Pakistan, it was estimated that the western wing would lose substantially. The document, prepared by the high commissioner, argued that West Pakistan then accounted for over 50 per cent of Pakistan's total exports, but it had always enjoyed a disproportionate share of total imports and, as a consequence, had a trade deficit of about 270 million dollars, about 80 per cent of Pakistan's total trade deficit. But West Pakistan also exported goods worth of 272 million dollars to East Pakistan and ran a surplus of 100 million dollars in the intra-wing trade. In the event of split it was unlikely that West Pakistan would be able to find an alternative market, whereas it would presumably have to purchase more than half of its commodities through foreign exchange. West Pakistan imported from East Pakistan goods worth 180 million dollars. Thus, an independent West Pakistan could approximately run a trade deficit of about 300 million dollars, though the British government was convinced that economically East Pakistan would be in desperate state.[357] Yet the analysis provides a clue to the intransigent mentality of both Bhutto and the army in negotiating on the six-point programme, as this would involve dismantling the process of internal colonization.

The Awami League was aware that its transition towards forming the government would not be easy. Bhutto, now a recognized elected leader of West Pakistan, demanded that the PPP be a partner in the government. On 20 December he demanded that two different parties win in Pakistan: the PPP and the Awami League. As Punjab and Sindh had been traditional centres of power in Pakistan, he demanded that he should be part of the government. Indeed, the general election in 1970 gave a verdict for the coexistence of two countries in Pakistan. Except for the Jamaat-e-Islami, there did not exist a common political party in the two wings of Pakistan. Bangladesh and West Pakistan elected two different political parties with two different ideological inclinations. Bhutto demanded a recognition of this fact. Yet he refused to accept the six-point programme which demanded a constitutional recognition of this same reality.[358] On 24 December he further asserted that he should be included in the government. Concerned with these utterings, Sheikh Mujib called a public session of the elected members of the Awami League, and in that session in Dacca's Racecourse Ground, they took a public oath to defend the six-point programme before a jubilant crowd.[359] Martial law administrator Yahya Khan came to discuss with Bangabandhu the possible consequences of the six-point programme on 12 and 13 January 1971. During discussion, Yahya Khan made it clear that the Pakistani army could not be dependent upon the provinces for its military budget.[360] This was the most critical threat to the military–industrial complex of Pakistan. After the discussion with Sheikh Mujib, general Yahya Khan declared him the future prime minister of Pakistan. General Yahya Khan returned to West Pakistan and met with Bhutto in Sindh on 17 January.[361]

In the meantime, there took place a dramatic turn of events. On 30 January 1971, two hijackers of Kashmiri origin took over an Indian Airlines plane to Lahore. Bhutto negotiated the release of the crew and the passengers, but the hijackers did not agree to hand over the plane to the Indian authorities. On 2 February the plane was burnt with much fanfare. An angry India demanded an apology and compensation from the Pakistani government. They also demanded that the government send those hijackers to India. Pakistan refused to abide by the Indian request. India prohibited the flying of Pakistani planes over Indian skies. This event created a significant disturbance in the process of the transfer of power. Yahya Khan declared that the country was facing an external crisis and that a war could be imminent.[362] Sheikh Mujib demanded an investigation into the incident, but the Pakistani martial law administration refused. To Sheikh Mujib it appeared that this was an unnecessary diversion from the process of transfer of power.[363]

As these events were taking place against the background of the Cold War, the US and the UK, two major powers, were taking a keen interest in the affairs in South Asia. It had become clear to the US administration that the division of Pakistan was imminent. The UK also prepared a memorandum about the economic consequences of the division. The UK believed that an independent East Pakistan would be a basket case, and the US had long held such beliefs.[364] Despite this Anglo-American preparation for the division of Pakistan, negotiations for power-sharing continued in Pakistan itself. Bhutto came to Dacca and held a three-day-long discussion with Sheikh Mujib. On 30 January he declared that the negotiation for a Constitution was not impossible but that he needed time. As an astute observer of politics, Bhutto recognized that it was impossible for him to come to power in a united Pakistan with the numbers stacked against him. He started playing second fiddle to the military and contributed to their anguish about the unity of Pakistan in the event of the implementation of the six-point programme. Bhutto was acceptable to the army as he had nurtured his connections with a section of military establishment. His opposition to the Tashkent Agreement, his pro-China policies and his emphasis on military solutions to the Kashmir problem endeared him to many in the armed forces. He became further alarmed when Yahya Khan announced on 13 January that the session of the newly elected national assembly would start in Dacca from 3 March onwards. On 15 February Bhutto declared that he would not accept a weak centre under the six-point Constitution. He also threatened that if other elected members from West Pakistan attended the Dacca session, they should remember that they would have to return to West Pakistan. By 17 February, escalating his attack, he remarked that the national assembly session in Dacca would become a slaughterhouse. He also added that there were three different powers in Pakistan: the army, the PPP and the Awami League, and that Sheikh Mujib had to negotiate with these powers.[365] Finally, on 28 February, at a mass meeting in Lahore, he said that there were two alternatives before the martial law authorities: either they could postpone the session of the national assembly to reach a compromise among the leaders in a private discussion, or the 120-day limit imposed by the Legal Framework Order promulgated in March 1970 should be discarded so that differences could be aired and solutions sought in public on the floor of the house. He further threatened that if the assembly met without the participation of the PPP, he would launch a movement 'from the Khyber to Karachi'. He warned that if elections to women's seats took place as planned on 2 March, in the absence of his party, there would be a complete strike in West Pakistan. In a meeting with Yahya Khan, Bhutto advised him to use the military to unleash repression in Bangladesh. On 1 March, Yahya Khan postponed the opening session of the assembly sine die. He further announced the removal of the popular vice admiral Ahsan as the governor of East Pakistan.[366] Bhutto's intransigence provided hope to the military to play the role of an honest broker and thus help the army retain its influence.

This announcement triggered mass discontent in Dacca. At the time of general Yahya Khan's announcement, Sheikh Mujib and the Awami League members were preparing for national assembly sessions in Purbani Hotel in Dacca. Thousands of people had gathered on the streets and asked Sheikh Mujib for guidance. In a press conference in Purbani Hotel, Sheikh Mujib announced that on 2 March there would be a total strike in Bangladesh[367] and 3 March would be observed as a day of national mourning. On that day the Chhatro League decided to hold a meeting in Paltan Maidan in Dacca. More ominously, the government deployed the army to suppress the strike and processions. This led to the death of strikers in clashes with army.[368] Soon the Awami League formed two committees. The first was a political committee, which came to be known as the High Command and included Sheikh Mujib, Tajuddin Ahmad, Syed Nazrul Islam, Mansur Ali, H. M. Qamaruzzaman and Khondakar Mostaq Ahmad. The military committee included Tajuddin Ahmad, retired colonel M. A. G. Osmani, major general Mazid, lieutenant commander Moazzem Chowdhury, lieutenant colonel M. R. Chowdhury and major Khaled Mosharraf. An advisory committee comprising Kamal Hossain, Rehman Sobhan and Amirul Islam was also formed.[369] Students moved a step ahead. On 2 March they prepared a flag. According to an eyewitness account, Serajul Alam Khan told students to put a map of 'Bangladesh' at the centre of the flag so that there could not be any confusion that the Bengali nationalist movement in East Pakistan was a movement for greater Bengal.[370] In a handwritten manifesto students declared independence, and on the next day, in a mass meeting, they read it in front of Sheikh Mujib and held a flag march during which female students marched with dummy rifles. Finally, it was decided by students that Tagore's song 'My Golden Bengal' would be the national anthem of the new nation of Bangladesh.[371] In many ways, in the students' minds, Bangladesh had now become a reality and the symbols of a new nation were selected. On the other hand, the martial law authority had already started mobilizing troops. These troops were deployed in various sensitive locations; people clashed with them, and a curfew was imposed. Many died in military firing while violating the curfew.

Meanwhile, Sheikh Mujib called for a non-cooperation movement to demonstrate the Awami League's hold over the province. Sheikh Mujib refused to attend a round table conference called by Yahya Khan as only two representatives were invited from Bangladesh. On Sunday, 7 March, Sheikh Mujib addressed a mammoth rally, probably the largest mass meeting in Dacca. In a remarkable speech, he declared that from now onwards the struggle of the Bengali people would be a struggle for emancipation and liberty, though he refrained from declaring independence. Through a series of directives issued in the mass rally, Sheikh Mujib demonstrated his hold on the masses in East Pakistan. It was from him and not from the member of the military junta that the East Pakistani central secretariat, the police, the judiciary, posts and telegraphs and the railways took their orders. The government and administration came to a virtual standstill except where Sheikh Mujib expressly ordered it to continue. On his instructions, taxes were withheld and remittances, even by the State Bank to West Pakistan, ceased. Only in cantonments the army was in control. Sheikh Mujib now imposed conditions for attending the national assembly. He claimed that the withdrawal of martial law, the return of the army to the barracks, an enquiry into killings and the transfer of power to the representatives of the people would have to take place in advance of the framing of the Constitution.[372] The British diplomats, who were known for their sneering dismissal of Sheikh Mujib as a political leader, wrote with grudging admiration of his role during the final moments of negotiations with Bhutto and Yahya Khan. In a letter to the former British prime minister, Alec Douglas Home, R. A. Burrow, writing for the British high commissioner to Pakistan, observed:

> Throughout the crisis of the Yahya–Mujib–Bhutto triangle, only Mujib has pursued a constant and undeviating line. Faced by the mistakes and inconsistencies of his political opponents his demands have gone beyond the degree of autonomy subsumed in the six-points. This is probably due more to response to pressures from his own radicals than his own desire. Nevertheless, he has played skilful game and has not crossed the Rubicon of a UDI as many of his party wished. On this his position is still reserved; meanwhile he has been able to produce dramatic evidence of his ability to control public life in East Pakistan and, conversely, of the impotence of the Martial Law Administration in the face of more than 70 million dissidents.[373]

Yahya Khan criticized Sheikh Mujib in a radio address on 6 March, though he announced the national assembly session would start on 25 March.

On 9 March, Yahya Khan softened his tone.[374] He announced that he would come to Dacca soon to negotiate with the Awami League. At the same time, on 7 March, he sent Tikka Khan, who was known for his brutality against rebels in Baluchistan, as the governor and commander of Pakistani troops in East Pakistan.[375] Meanwhile, in a meeting at Paltan Maidan in Dacca, Bhashani declared that Pakistan should free East Bengal. On 16 March, Yahya Khan held a discussion with Sheikh Mujib and his associates. After this, Yahya Khan sent a telegram to Bhutto to come to Dacca. He met with Sheikh Mujib again on 17 and 18 March. On 19 March the army ordered East Bengal regiment soldiers to surrender their weapons, and the people came forward to support the regiment.[376] Worried, Sheikh Mujib held a discussion with colonel Osmani to prepare for a precautionary measure. Meanwhile, troops started taking positions. On 21 March retired Bengali soldiers marched with the Bangladesh flag.[377] On 23 March, which was observed from 1965 onwards as Pakistan Day, the SAC held a march of the Jay Bangla (Hail Bengal) brigade of students, and at the end of the parade, female students marched with dummy rifles and went to Sheikh Mujib's house with the flag of independent Bangladesh, which they handed over to him.[378] Sheikh Mujib hoisted that flag on the rooftop of his house. On 23 March, Bhutto, Yahya Khan and Sheikh Mujib held a meeting again. There was a sudden quietness on 24 March 1971. The Pakistani government deployed troops in commercial flights through Sri Lanka, and two ships carrying troops reached Khulna and Chittagong. At the Chittagong port the workers refused to unload weapons. Pakistani soldiers opened fire on the workers at the port. On 24 March 1971, Tajuddin Ahmad announced Yahya Khan's reluctance to continue with negotiations.[379] It was clear that the negotiation was over. Even before 24 March, various left-wing forces had felt that the day of liberation had come, and many of them decided to start a revolutionary war. Many among the leftists felt disappointed that the revolution had come before they could prepare for it.

Finally, on 25 March, Yahya Khan announced in a radio address that Sheikh Mujib had tried to undermine national unity and that he had to be punished for his treason. In a meeting at his house in the afternoon, Sheikh Mujib instructed members of his political committee and military committee to leave Dacca. By the middle of the night, the Pakistani army attacked civilians in Dacca city as well as a police station at Rajarbag. At 1 a.m. in the morning, they arrested Sheikh Mujib from his residence and sent him to West Pakistan. Resistance took place all over the country. Liberation war had begun in East Pakistan. On 25 March, a pre-recorded message of Sheikh Mujib's declaration of independence was sent through a telegraphic system by Subedar Major Sher Ali. International press claimed that they had heard the announcement of Sheikh Mujib.[380] On 27 March, Ziaur Rahman read his own message of independence from Chittagong radio.[381] Thus, the global sixties in East Pakistan ended in a war of national liberation.

Conclusion

Politics in East Pakistan underwent a complex process of transformation in late sixties. It was neither unilinear nor a homogenous monolith of Bengali masses demanding independence. Rather, it was a long, complex and bloody struggle waged by several political forces in different contexts. This transformation was also informed by the intricate manoeuvrings of global powers in the context of the Cold War. The process began with general Ayub Khan losing his political legitimacy to govern when, after massive wartime propaganda about an imminent victory, he had signed a treaty in Tashkent reinforcing the status-quo antebellum. War also exposed him to intense Cold War powerplays. His tilt towards China lost him his patronage from the US and the Western power bloc. On the other hand, China did not have the resources to fund his model of praetorian capitalism, and members of his kitchen cabinet, who, for both personal calculations and ideological reasons, started deserting the sinking ship. The crisis in the ruling establishment weakened their hold and political legitimacy among the masses. In East Pakistan, the isolation during wartime and decades of discrimination led towards the rise of the new autonomy movement. The six-point programme provided a path for East Pakistanis to challenge the process of internal colonization. Sheikh Mujib, through his constancy and consistency in propagating the issue of autonomy, captured the popular imagination of the masses. The global sixties and the revolutionary wave of the eros effect hit Pakistan with all their contradictions, whereby a divided left fought among themselves even as they fought against the military junta. Bengali nationalists, too, fought against the left and the military junta. Subaltern social classes revolted to preserve their declining living standards.

The inflationary pressures on the economy and the decline in real wages triggered workers' protests in factories, offices and the transportation industry. The communist student leaders, who graduated from the student movement to trade union organizing activities, pioneered new techniques in organizing the trade union movement. Veterans of the 1962 student uprising now became organizers of the mass uprising of 1968–69. Yet debates, discussions, dissensions and the war among the global communist powers of China and the Soviet Union cast a long shadow over the reception and organization of the global 1968–69 in East Pakistan. As China projected itself as the centre of global revolution, and Mao Zedong, with the help of the Chinese youth, unleashed the Cultural Revolution, the reception of this new revolution led to splits in the underground communist movement in East Pakistan. This had a repercussion on the workers' movement, the students' movement and even on the NAP, a social democratic platform through which underground communists operated in public politics in East Pakistan. All these frontal affiliated organizations experienced splits. The pro-Chinese communists overcame their initial hesitation in joining the six-point movement. Yet the principal antagonistic contradiction between the West Pakistan-based praetorian capitalist mechanism of governance and the masses of East Pakistan influenced the emerging mass movement. Bhashani recouped his image by directing the 1969 mass uprising. Yet, in the complex whirlpool of East Pakistani politics where political parties underwent splits and changed their positions, the consistency of Sheikh Mujib in his advocacy of the six-point programme, even at the expense of his personal liberty, made him more like the Pole Star. Bhashani and his associates, despite their active participation in the 1969 uprising, innovating new modes of protests and bringing in the peasantry in the movement, lost their opportunities. They wasted their efforts in heuristic debates over doctrines of revolution, and thus the masses left them behind in their opposition to the military junta. This not only divided the Maoist communists from others but also divided the Maoists themselves. Their withdrawal from the trade union movement and their espousal of the annihilation line of class enemies led to their self-marginalization. This took place at a time when Sheikh Mujib emerged as 'Friend of Bengal', or Bangabandhu. His populist appeal, soaring rhetoric and booming voice, combined with his stubborn adherence to his programme in the midst of the inertia of the martial law to deliver relief during a natural disaster, transformed him into an icon of the popular struggle. During electioneering, and even during discussions with Yahya Khan and Bhutto, Sheikh Mujib remained wedded to his own plan when others wavered, dilly-dallied and tried to stall the negotiations. In the final run, the responsibility of breaking Pakistan and unleashing violence was the product of the policies of the martial law administration. Thus, ironically, the military which wanted to preserve Pakistan as a unified political entity shredded its unity. The national liberation war triumphed in Bangladesh with the support of the indomitable will of people.

Notes

1. Following Herbert Marcuse and rejecting the sociological contagion theory, George Katsiaficas coined the term eros effect. For detailed description of the eros effect, see George Katsiaficas, *The Imagination of the New Left: A Global Analysis of 1968* (Boston: South End Press, 1987), p.19.
2. Katsiaficas, *The Imagination of the New Left*.
3. James Krapfl, *Revolution with a Human Face: Politics, Culture, and Community in Czechoslovakia, 1989–1992* (Ithaca, NY: Cornell University Press), pp. 8–9.
4. For details, see Sharif al-Mujahid, 'Pakistan: First General Elections', *Asian Survey* 11, no. 2 (1971): 159–71.
5. Frantz Fanon, *The Wretched of the Earth*, trans. Constance Farrington (London: Grove Press, 1968 [1961]), p. 179.
6. Klaus H. Pringsheim observed: 'President Johnson's cancellation (postponement) of President Ayub Khan's visit to the United States can be seen in a new light when it is pointed out that he may have known of certain Sino-Pakistani understandings which have not as yet reached the public domain.' Klaus H. Pringsheim, 'China's Role in the Indo-Pakistani Conflict', *China Quarterly* 24, no. 24 (1965): 170–75, p. 173.
7. In a telegram sent to the US ambassador to Pakistan, Walter McConaughy, and the US ambassador to India, Chester Bowles, later that day, Dean Rusk confirmed that the US would refuse all requests from India and Pakistan for military assistance while war continued in the subcontinent. The US publicly announced on 8 September its neutrality. Paul M. McGarr, *The Cold War in South Asia: Britain, the United States and the Indian Subcontinent, 1945–1965* (Cambridge: Cambridge University Press, 2013), p. 326.
8. A CIA report says: 'Communist China has issued another statement in support of Pakistani position and strongly condemning "Indian aggression." The Chinese statement claims that India continues to occupy Chinese territory and that India cannot evade the responsibility for having taken the first step in committing aggression against Pakistan.' CIA, Office

of Current Intelligence, 7 September 1965, Declassified CIA Documents, CIA Online Archives, p. 2.

9. 'On 18 September, Nikolai Fedorenko, the Soviet representative on the Security Council, condemned Mao Zedong's regime for pursuing a "criminal policy of driving the world's people to serve their own imperialist and expansionist aims"', and 'Arthur Goldberg, America's ambassador to the United Nations, cautioned Beijing that dire consequences would follow were it "to spread the [Indo-Pakistan] conflict and exploit what was already a tragedy"'. For details, see McGarr, *The Cold War in South Asia*, p. 330.

10. CIA Office of National Estimates, 24 September 1965, Special Memorandum Subject: India Pakistan War – A Preliminary Assessment, CIA Online Archives, pp. 4–5.

11. A CIA document notes: 'Ambassador McConaughy comments that during his meeting with President Ayub yesterday, Ayub seemed generally calm but was clearly under great strain. The ambassador says that Ayub is presently preoccupied with winning US and other allied support in the immediate crisis by invoking agreements and demanding their fulfillment. He is apparently determined to gain all-out US support: for a final settlement of the Kashmir problem.' CIA, Office of Current Intelligence, 7 September 1965, Declassified CIA documents, CIA Online Archives, p. 2.

12. CIA Office of Current Intelligence, 21 September 1965 (Approve 0027-525X1OCI No. 2014-65) (State Department review completed), Intelligence Memorandum, 'The India–Pakistan Situation' (Report #58 as of 6:00 AM EDT), p. 2, https://bhutto.org/wp-content/uploads/2021/01/CIA-Intelligence-Memorandum-India-Pakistan-Situation-21-Sep-65.pdf (accessed on 17 February 2021).

13. CIA Office of Current Intelligence, 'The India–Pakistan Situation', p. 2.

14. CIA Office of Current Intelligence, 'The India–Pakistan Situation', p. 2.

15. CIA Intelligence Report, Memorandum for Director, 3 September 1965, 'Problems of the Subcontinent', p. 17.

16. OCI No. 2005/65, CIA Office of Current Intelligence, 16 September 1965, Intelligence Memorandum, 'The India–Pakistan Situation' (Report #43 as of 6:00 A. M EST).

17. CIA Office of Current Intelligence, 21 September 1965 (Approve 0027-525X1 OCI No. 2014-65) (State Department review completed), Intelligence Memorandum, 'The India–Pakistan Situation' (Report #58 as of 6:00 AM EDT), p. 2, https://bhutto.org/wp-content/uploads/2021/01/

CIA-Intelligence-Memorandum-India-Pakistan-Situation-21-Sep-65.pdf (accessed on 3 May 2022).
18. CIA Office of National Estimates, 24 September 1965, Special Memorandum Subject: Indo-Pakistan War – A Preliminary Assessment, https://bhutto.org/wp-content/uploads/2021/01/CIA-Memorandum-The-Indo-Pak-War-A-Preliminary-Assessment-24-Sep-65.pdf (accessed on 3 May 2022).
19. Zubeida Hasan, 'Pakistan's Relations with the U.S.S.R. in the 1960s', *World Today* 25, no. 1 (1969): 26–35, p. 29.
20. Hasan, 'Pakistan's Relations with the U.S.S.R. in the 1960s'.
21. *The Dawn*, 24 November 1965
22. *The Dawn*, 16 November 1965.
23. Foreign and Commonwealth Office, File no, PL44/9, Part A DO133/79, From New York to Foreign Office, 13 October 1965, Confidential Routine.
24. *The Dawn*, 24 November 1965.
25. Foreign and Commonwealth Office, CRO to UK MISS, New York, 13 October 1965, 3765, 06 hours IST, Telegram DO133/179 449A.
26. Foreign and Commonwealth Office, CRO to UK MISS, New York, 13 October 1965, 3765, 06 hours IST, Telegram DO133/179 449A.
27. CIA Office of National Estimates, Special Memorandum Subject: Indo-Pakistan War – A Preliminary Assessment.
28. CIA Office of National Estimates, Special Memorandum Subject: Indo-Pakistan War – A Preliminary Assessment.
29. CIA Office of National Estimates, Special Memorandum Subject: Indo-Pakistan War – A Preliminary Assessment.
30. Foreign and Commonwealth Office, 'President Ayub's Visit to United States 12–16 December 1965'.
31. Foreign and Commonwealth Office, 'President Ayub's Visit to United States 12–16 December 1965'.
32. Foreign and Commonwealth Office, 'President Ayub's Visit to United States 12–16 December 1965'.
33. Based on diplomatic correspondence, historian Paul M. McGarr suggests: 'British and American officials viewed Bhutto as the sort of "reckless" and "crooked" manipulator that could lead Pakistan, and its president, to the brink of disaster.' McGarr, *The Cold War in South Asia*, p. 313.
34. Foreign and Commonwealth Office, File no. FO 371, J. L. Stevenson to P. M. Nixon, Far Eastern Department, London, 22 December 1965.

35. Foreign and Commonwealth Office, File no. FO 371, P. M. Nixon to J. L. Stevenson, 10 January 1966.
36. According to Gauhar, 'Ayub's Foreign Minister, Zulfikar Ali Bhutto, who had been closely connected with the strategy of mounting commando raids inside Kashmir, and had convinced Ayub that India would never cross the international boundary in retaliation, knew that his days in the cabinet were numbered. He was as anxious as the generals to divert all possible criticism from his conduct during the war. This convergence of interests made Bhutto a convenient ally for the army. Together they started criticising Ayub for not having had the courage to stand up to Shastri in Tashkent. Bhutto spread the rumour that there were certain secret clauses in the Tashkent Declaration which he would expose at the appropriate time. Since it originated with Ayub's own Foreign Minister, people accepted the rumours without question.' Altaf Gauhar, 'Pakistan: Ayub Khan's Abdication', *Third World Quarterly* 7, no. 1 (1985): 102–31, p. 114.
37. Ataur Rahman Khan, *Swaiiracharer Dosh Botsor* (Dacca: Naoroj Kitabistan, 1970), p. 266.
38. A. R. Khan, *Swaiiracharer Dosh Botsor*, p. 266.
39. Gauhar, 'Pakistan: Ayub Khan's Abdication', p. 114.
40. Tariq Ali, *Pakistan: Military Rule or People's Power* (New York: William Morrow and Company, 1970), p. 145.
41. Omar Noman, *The Political Economy of Pakistan, 1947–85* (London: KPI Limited, 1988), pp. 41–43.
42. Ishtiaq Ahmed, 'The Rise and Fall of the Left and the Maoist Movements in Pakistan', *India Quarterly* 66, no. 3 (2010): 251–65, p. 257.
43. Ataur Rahman, the former chief minister of East Pakistan, mentioned in his autobiography the isolation of East Pakistan from the rest of the world. A. R. Khan, *Swaiiracharer Dosh Botsor*, pp. 263–65.
44. Morshed Safiul Hasan, *Swadhinotar Potobhumi: 1960r Doshok* (Dhaka: Anupom Prokashoni, 2014), p. 103.
45. Sekhar Dutta, *Shaater Doshoker Gono Jagoron: Ghotona Probaho Parjyalochona Probhab* (Dhaka: Somaj Bigyan Prokashoni, 2015), p. 235.
46. Lenin Azad, *Unosottorer Gonoobbhuththan: Rastro Somaj o Rajniti* (Dhaka: Jatio Sahitya Prokash, 2019 [1997]), p. 452.
47. M. A. Aziz, a close associate of Sheikh Mujib, in a conversation with Sharadindu Dostidar, told the latter that India would not attack East Pakistan. 'What benefits would this war bring to the people of East

Pakistan? Can we obtain full autonomy?' Sharadindu Dostidar, *Jibon Smriti* (Akhanda Purnango Rup) (Dhaka: Sahitya Prokash, 2019), p. 172.

48. Azad, *Unosottorer Gonoobbuththan*, p. 452.
49. Azad, *Unosottorer Gonoobbuththan*, p. 453.
50. Azad, *Unosottorer Gonoobbuththan*, p. 453.
51. Azad, *Unosottorer Gonoobbuththan*, p. 453.
52. Oli Ahad, *Jatio Rajniti: 1945 theke 75* (Fourth Edition) (Dhaka: Bangladesh Co-Operative Book Society, 2004), p.283.
53. Ahad, *Jatio Rajniti*, p. 284.
54. Ahad, *Jatio Rajniti*, p. 289.
55. The seventh clause refers to educational qualification and financial status. In the colonial period, too, India's colonial rulers emphasized franchise being limited to people with educational qualification and property. Thus, this attitude contradicted the principle of universal adult franchise.
56. Dutta, *Shaater Doshoker Gono Jagoron*, p. 246.
57. Azad, *Unosottorer Gonoobbuththan*, p. 453.
58. Azad, *Unosottorer Gonoobbuththan*, p. 453.
59. Dutta, *Shaater Doshoker Gono Jagoron*, p. 249.
60. Dutta, *Shaater Doshoker Gono Jagoron*, pp. 248–49.
61. Siraj Uddin Ahmed, *Jatir Janak Bongobondhu* (Dhaka: Kamala Printers, 2016), p. 139. Also see Rangalal Sen, *Political Elites in Bangladesh* (Dhaka: University Press Limited, 1986), p. 286.
62. Dutta, *Shaater Doshoker Gono Jagoron*, p. 249.
63. Shyamali Ghosh, *Awami League 1949–1971*, trans. Habib ul-Alam (Dhaka: University Press Limited, 2007), p. 129.
64. '6-Points', *Pakistan Forum* 1, no. 4 (1971): 8–9.
65. Shila Sen has provided a detailed discussion of this issue in Bengal Muslim League. Shila Sen, *Muslim Politics in Bengal, 1937–1947* (New Delhi: Impex India, 1976), pp. 207–09.
66. Abul Kalam Shamsuddin, *Otit Diner Smriti* (Memories of Old Days) (Dhaka: Khosroj Kitab Mohal, 2019 [1968]), pp. 180–81.
67. Abdus Sadeque, *The Economic Emergence of Pakistan*, vol. 2 (Dacca: East Bengal Government, 1956), pp. 1–49.
68. Abul Mansur Ahmad, *Amar Dekha Rajnitir Ponchas Botsor* (Dhaka: Prothoma Prokashan, 2018), p. 317.
69. Nurul Islam, *Bangladesh: Jati Gothonkale Ek Orthinitibider Kichu Kotha* (Bangladesh: Few Words from the Days of Nation Formation) (Dhaka: University Press Limited, 2018), pp. 21–23.

70. Islam, *Bangladesh*, pp. 21–23.
71. Islam, *Bangladesh*, pp. 23–25.
72. Islam, *Bangladesh*, pp. 27–30.
73. Islam, *Bangladesh*, p. 30.
74. Rehman Sobhan, *Utal Romanthan: Purnatar Sei Bochorgulo* (Untranquil Recollections : The Years of Fulfillment) (New Delhi: SAGE Publications, 2018), p.183.
75. Sobhan, *Utal Romanthan*, p. 183.
76. Sobhan, *Utal Romanthan*, p. 187.
77. Sobhan, *Utal Romanthan*, pp. 229–30.
78. Sobhan, *Utal Romanthan*, p. 232.
79. Sobhan, *Utal Romanthan*, pp. 233–34, 238.
80. Islam, *Bangladesh*, pp. 43–49.
81. Hasan, *Swadhinotar Ptobhumi*, p. 106 (footnote).
82. Mohiuddin Ahmad, *Jasoder Utthan Poton Osthir Somoyer Rajniti* (Dhaka: Prothoma Prokashon, 2015), p. 16.
83. Dutta, *Shaater Doshoker Gono Jagoron*, p. 264.
84. Harun-or-Rashid, *Mul Dharar Rajniti: Bangladesh Awami League Council 1949–2016* (Mainstream Politics: Bangladesh Awami League Council 1949–2016) (Dhaka: Bangla Academy, 2019), p. 87.
85. Harun-or-Rashid, *Mul Dharar Rajniti*, pp. 94–99.
86. Harun-or-Rashid, *Mul Dharar Rajniti*, pp. 94–99.
87. Sobhan, *Utal Romanthan*, pp. 224–25.
88. *Dainik Sombad*, 16 February 1966.
89. *Dainik Sombad*, 4 March 1966.
90. Azad, *Unosottorer Gonoobbuththan*, p. 454.
91. Azad, *Unosottorer Gonoobbuththan*, p. 455.
92. Dutta, *Shaater Doshoker Gono Jagoron*, p. 284.
93. Dutta, *Shaater Doshoker Gono Jagoron*, p. 284.
94. Azad, *Unosottorer Gonoobbuththan*.
95. Azad, *Unosottorer Gonoobbuththan*, p. 455.
96. Omar Noman succinctly points out that 'the doctrine of functional inequality was based on the premise that initial stages of capitalist development required a high degree of inequality'. Noman, *The Political Economy of Pakistan*, p. 40.
97. See Chapter 5 for details.
98. Dutta, *Shaater Doshoker Gono Jagoron*, p. 292.
99. Dutta, *Shaater Doshoker Gono Jagoron*, p. 292.

100. Azad, *Unosottorer Gonoobhuththan*, p. 458.
101. Subho Basu, 'Manufacturing Radicals: The Sino-Indian War and the Repression of Communists in India', in *The Sino Indian War of 1962 New Perspectives 197–214*, ed. Amit R. Das Gupta and Lorenz M. Luthi, pp. 197–214 (London: Routledge, 2017).
102. Bhashani compared his visit to China to a pilgrimage. He called China the greatest comrade of the struggle for the emancipation of oppressed people. Syed Abul Maksud, *Maulana Abdul Hamid Khan Bhashani* (Dhaka: Agami Prokashani, 2014), p. 259.
103. Maksud, *Maulana Abdul Hamid Khan Bhashani*, pp. 140–46.
104. Dostidar, *Jibon Smriti*, p. 164; Haidar Akbar Khan Rono, *Shotabdi Perie* (Dhaka: Tarafdar Prokashani, 2012), p. 84.
105. Jeremy Scott Friedman, 'Reviving Revolution: The Sino-Soviet Split, The "Third World," and the Fate of the Left', vol. I, PhD Thesis, Department of History, Princeton University, Princeton, NJ, 2011, pp. 4–6.
106. Lorenz M. Luthi, *The Sino-Soviet Split: Cold War in the Communist World* (Princeton Studies in International History and Politics) (Princeton, NJ: Princeton University Press, 2008), pp. 47–48.
107. Increasingly, in the sixties, the US remained the only great power state that withheld recognition of the PRC. Lincoln P. Bloomfield, 'China, the United States, and the United Nations', *International Organization* 20, no. 4 (1966): 653–76.
108. Roger E. Kanet, 'The Rise and Fall of the "'All People's State'": Recent Changes in the Soviet Theory of the State', *Soviet Studies* 20, no. 1 (1968): 81–93.
109. Friedman, 'Reviving Revolution', p. 123.
110. Friedman, 'Reviving Revolution', p. 82; Philip E. Mosely, 'Soviet Policy in the Developing Countries', *Foreign Affairs* 43, no. 1 (1964): 87–98.
111. Luthi, *The Sino-Soviet Split*, pp. 303–04; George T. Yu, 'China and the Third World', *Asian Survey* 17, no. 11 (1977): 1036–48.
112. Conversation between Zhou Enlai and Ayub Khan, Karachi, 2 April 1965, in Odd Arne Westad, Chen Jian, Stein Tønnesson, Nguyen Vu Tung and James G. Hershberg, '77 Conversations Between Chinese and Foreign Leaders on the Wars in Indochina, 1964–1977', Working Paper No. 22, Cold War International History Project, Woodrow Wilson Center for Scholars, Washington, DC, 1998; *The Sino-Soviet Split*, p. 306.

113. Ylber Marku, 'Communist Relations in Crisis: The End of Soviet–Albanian Relations, and the Sino-Soviet Split, 1960–1961', *International History Review* 42, no. 4 (2020): 813–32.
114. Basu, 'Manufacturing Radicals', pp. 197–214.
115. Dostidar, *Jibon Smriti*, p. 181.
116. Vidya Prakash Dutt, 'China and Indo-Pakistani Relations', *International Studies* 8, nos. 1–2 (January 1966): 126–33, p. 129.
117. George J. Lerski, 'The Foreign Policy of Ayub Khan', *Asian Affairs* 1, no. 4 (1974): 255–273.
118. Pringsheim, 'China's Role in the Indo-Pakistani Conflict'.
119. Pringsheim, 'China's Role in the Indo-Pakistani Conflict'.
120. *The Dawn*, 16 April 1966.
121. Dostidar, *Jibon Smriti*, p. 163.
122. Maksud, *Maulana Abdul Hamid Khan Bhashani*, p. 258.
123. 'Record of Conversation between Zhou Enlai, Chen Yi and Head of Pakistan's Delegation Participating in the PRC's National Day Celebration, Maulana Abdul Hamid Khan Bhashani', https://digitalarchive.wilsoncenter.org/document/121573.pdf (accessed on 24 May 2021).
124. Ali, *Pakistan*, pp. 140–41.
125. Bhashani named his travelogue *Mao Tse Tunger Deshe* (In the Land of Mao). Maksud, *Maulana Abdul Hamid Khan Bhashani*, p. 258.
126. Maksud, *Maulana Abdul Hamid Khan Bhashani*, p. 259.
127. Maksud, *Maulana Abdul Hamid Khan Bhashani*, pp. 284–85.
128. Ahad, *Jatio Rajniti*, p. 284.
129. Dutta, *Shaater Doshoker Gono Jagoron*, p. 290.
130. In his autobiography, Kazi Zafar, a prominent student and labour leader, wrote that the pro-Chinese communists considered the six-point programme as a document prepared by the CIA. He further asserted that one of the weaknesses of the communist movement in East Pakistan was to theorize any movement without looking at it from a clear perspective. Kazi Zafar Ahmad, *Amar Rajnitir 60 Botsor: Joar Bhatar Kothon* (Sixty Years of My Politics: Stories of Ebb and Flow) (Dhaka: Torofdar Prokashoni, 2017), p. 154.
131. CIA Online Archives, Current Intelligence, Weekly Special Report, 'Pakistani President Ayub's Problems', CIA Directorate of Intelligence, 29 July 1966, OCI Number O300/66A, Copy No. 46.
132. *Ittefaq*, 7 November 1964.

133. Azad, *Unosottorer Gonoobbuththan*, p. 457.
134. Maksud, *Maulana Abdul Hamid Khan Bhashani*, p. 293.
135. Maksud, *Maulana Abdul Hamid Khan Bhashani*, p. 293.
136. Maksud, *Maulana Abdul Hamid Khan Bhashani*, p. 294.
137. Rono, *Shotabdi Perie*, p. 153.
138. Foreign and Commonwealth Office, FCO 2/3/67, Pakistan General Politics, DO134.32, File begins 5/12/66, 2-INT RAW, 6/60/1/D.
139. Dostidar, *Jibon Smriti*, p. 182.
140. Dostidar, *Jibon Smriti*, p. 183.
141. Dostidar, *Jibon Smriti*, p. 184.
142. Dostidar, *Jibon Smriti*, p. 185.
143. For details, see Nurul Amin, 'The Pro-Chinese Communist Movement in Bangladesh', *Journal of Contemporary Asia* 15, no. 3 (1985): 349–60.
144. Azad, *Unosottorer Gonoobbuththan*, pp. 482–88.
145. Rono, *Shotabdi Perie*, pp.73–75, 103–08.
146. Also see Mohammed Ayoob, 'Pakistan's Political Development, 1947 to 1970: Bird's Eye View', *Economic and Political Weekly* 6, nos. 3–5 (1971): 199–204.
147. Maksud, *Maulana Abdul Hamid Khan Bhashani*, pp. 245–48, 273–75.
148. Dostidar, *Jibon Smriti*, p. 183, 191–93; Hasan, *Swadhinotar Potobhumi*, p. 193.
149. Hasan, *Swadhinotar Potobhumi*, p.193.
150. Azad, *Unosottorer Gonoobbuththan*, p. 477; Hasan, *Swadhinotar Potobhumi*, pp. 192–93.
151. Hasan, *Swadhinotar Potobhumi*, pp. 196–97.
152. Hasan, *Swadhinotar Potobhumi*, p. 197.
153. Hasan, *Swadhinotar Potobhumi*, p. 201.
154. Kamruddin Ahmad, *Labour Movement in East Pakistan* (Dacca: Progoti Publishers, 1969), p. 51.
155. K. Z. Ahmad, *Amar Rajnitir 60 Botsor Botsor*, pp. 164–69.
156. K. Z. Ahmad, *Amar Rajnitir 60 Botsor Botsor*, pp. 171–72.
157. Azad, *Unosottorer Gonoobbuththan*, pp. 470–72.
158. Azad, *Unosottorer Gonoobbuththan*, p. 471.
159. Ahad, *Jatio Rajniti*, p. 310. Foreign and Commonwealth Office, DO 134/32, Pakistan General Politics, 2-INT/RAW 6/60/1/D of R. Hayward to R. Hickling, British High Commission, Rawalpindi, 29 March 1967, 1-D/C.6/145/1.

160. Foreign and Commonwealth Office, FCO 29/3/67, Pakistan General Politics, DO134.32, File Begins 5/12/66, 2-INT RAW 6/60/1/D of R. Hayward, Dacca, to R. Hickling. Rawalpindi.
161. Foreign and Commonwealth Office, FCO 2/7/67, Pakistan General Politics, DO134.32, File begins 5/12/66, 2-INT RAW 6/60/1/D.
162. Ahad, *Jatio Rajniti*, pp. 310–14.
163. Dutta, *Shaater Doshoker Gono Jagoron*, p. 299.
164. Ghosh, *Awami League*, p. 149.
165. Dutta, *Shaater Doshoker Gono Jagoron*, p. 290.
166. See Chapters 4 and 5 for details.
167. Foreign and Commonwealth Office, FCO 3/4/1967, P-INT RAW 6/60/1, R. J. Stratton, Rawalpindi, British High Commission, to A. A. Duff, Commonwealth Office, Pakistan General Politics, DO 134/32.
168. See Chapter 3 for details.
169. Ghosh, *Awami League*, pp. 158–59.
170. Azad, *Unosottorer Gonoobbuththan*, p. 495.
171. Foreign and Commonwealth Office, FCO 7/2/67, Pakistan General Politics, 'Note on Internal Situation in Pakistan', DO134.32, File begins 5/12/66 2-INT RAW 6/60/1/D.
172. Ghosh, *Awami League*, pp. 158–59.
173. Azad, *Unosottorer Gonoobbuththan*, p. 489.
174. Ahad, *Jatio Rajniti*, pp. 319–20.
175. Khalid B. Sayeed, 'How Radical Is the Pakistan People's Party?', *Pacific Affairs* 48, no. 1 (1975): 42–59.
176. Ali, *Pakistan*.
177. Xing Li, 'The Chinese Cultural Revolution Revisited', *China Review* 1, no. 1 (2001): 137–65.
178. I. Ahmed, 'The Rise and Fall of the Left'.
179. Foreign snd Commonwealth Office, FCO 7/2/67, Pakistan General Politics, 'Note on Internal Situation in Pakistan', DO134.32, File Begins 5/12/66, 2-INT RAW 6/60/1/D, The Supreme Court Judge and Bhutto by MFH Beg, a letter sent to *Daily Telegraph*, London. A copy of this letter was obtained by the British High Commission in Pakistan.
180. In a speech at Havana, Bhashani told his audience that events in Vietnam, Congo, Dominican Republic, Mozambique Israel, Aden and occupied Kashmir demonstrate how old and new imperial powers are playing with lives of people. Maksud, *Maulana Abdul Hamid Khan Bhashani*, p. 287.

181. Matiur Rahman, 'Che Ek Kinbdonti Purush' (Che a Legenda), *Kali o Kolom*, 22 August 2016, https://www.kaliokalam.com/%E0%A6%9A%E0%A7%87-%E0%A6%8F%E0%A6%95-%E0%A6%95%E0%A6%BF%E0%A6%82%E0%A6%AC%E0%A6%A6%E0%A6%A8%E0%A7%8D%E0%A6%A4%E0%A6%BF-%E0%A6%AA%E0%A7%81%E0%A6%B0%E0%A7%81%E0%A6%B7/ (accessed on 21 May 2022).
182. The British Embassy in Pakistan was watching Tariq Ali's movements in Pakistan. On 6 March m A. A. Halliley gleefully wrote to Miss Judy Walker: 'JIC(69) (W51)10, dated 6 March, devotes a whole paragraph to Tariq Ali but I think you should know that he has cut very little ice here so far. Pakistan students have been at pains to point out to him that he has arrived in his native land at the end of the struggle to secure the end of the Ayub regime: they and not he have shed their blood and have risked arrest and beatings up by the police.' Foreign and Commonwealth Office, FCO 37/469, FSP1/1, Part D, 'Pakistan Internal Political Situation', A. A. Halliley to Judy Walker, 6 March 1969.
183. Interview with Santosh Rana, 8 May 2016.
184. Azad, *Unosottorer Gonoobbuththan*, p. 493.
185. Azad, *Unosottorer Gonoobbuththan*, p.500.
186. Azad, *Unosottorer Gonoobbuththan*, p. 493.
187. Azad, *Unosottorer Gonoobbuththan*, p. 493.
188. Sobhan described Saydur Rahman as a thug loyal to Monem Khan, the governor of East Pakistan. In a colourful language Sobhan described him as *passpattur*, or a guy who passed Part II (there are three parts in a Bachelor of Arts exam: Part I, Part II and Part III). He led a group of students who created an environment of fear among common students. Most colourful among these student groups was Khoka who used to roam around with a snake tied to his neck. Sobhan, *Utal Romanthan*, p. 223.
189. Many seats in the government-organized functions remained vacant as people did not participate in such absurd display of pomp and splendour in the midst of a famine-like situation in East Pakistan. *Sombad*, 3 November 1968.
190. Azad, *Unosottorer Gonoobbuththan*, pp. 502–04.
191. Bhashani was nicknamed 'Red Maulana'.
192. Oli Ahad claimed that in a meeting with Bhashani, on 10 October, the latter claimed that Ayub Khan did not have the support of the army. General Yahya Khan and general Hamid would not allow the army to be used in law and order within the country. Ahad, *Jatio Rajniti*, p. 319.

193. Rafi Raza, *Zulfikar Ali Bhutto and Pakistan 1967–1977*, reproduced by Sani H. Panhwar, Member of Sindh Council, PPP, pp. 6–9, https://bhutto.org/wp-content/uploads/2020/12/Zulfikar-Ali-Bhutto-and-Pakistan-1967-1977.pdf (accessed on 20 May 2020).
194. This description of events in West Pakistan was based upon Tariq Ali's description. Ali, *Pakistan*, pp. 156–62.
195. Dutta, *Shaater Doshoker Gono Jagoron*, p. 386.
196. 'Spring Thunder over India', first published as an editorial in *People's Daily*, an organ of the central committee of the CCP, on 5 July 1967, and reproduced in *Liberation*, vol. 1, no. 1, November 1967, https://www.marxists.org/subject/china/documents/peoples-daily/1967/07/05.htm (accessed on 27 July 2020).
197. Azad, *Unosottorer Gonoobbuththan*, p. 506.
198. Dutta, *Shaater Doshoker Gono Jagoron*, p. 388.
199. Azad, *Unosottorer Gonoobbuththan*, p. 507.
200. *Sombad*, 7 December 1968.
201. Foreign and Commonwealth Office, FCO 37/467, Pakistan Political Affair,s Internal Situation, FSB1/1, Part B, Confidential Extract from IPBA Report on Pakistan, December 1968.
202. Dostidar, *Jibon Smriti*, pp. 204–05.
203. Dostidar, *Jibon Smriti*, p. 206.
204. Mesbah Kamal, *Unosottorer Gonoobbuththan: Shahid Asad o Shreni Rajniti Prosonge* (Dhaka: Shrabon Prokashoni, 2006), pp. 42–43.
205. Maksud, *Maulana Abdul Hamid Khan Bhashani*, p. 315.
206. *Azad*, 14 December 1968.
207. Bhashani called for remission of land revenue for those who hold land below 15 *bigha* and a minimum wage of 200 taka. He also demanded complete autonomy for East Pakistan. *Azad*, 7 December 1969.
208. Azad, *Unosottorer Gonoobbuththan*, p. 549.
209. *Azad*, 30 and 31 December 1968.
210. Maksud, *Maulana Abdul Hamid Khan Bhashani*, p. 318.
211. Foreign and Commonwealth Office, FCO FSP1/1, Part B, Pakistan Political Affairs Internal Situation, A. A. Halliley, Rawalpindi to Lynton Jones, South Asian Department.
212. Dutta, *Shaater Doshoker Gono Jagoron*, pp. 411–12.
213. Dutta, *Shaater Doshoker Gono Jagoron*, pp. 411–12.
214. *Azad*, 6 January 1969; Hasan Hafijur Rahman (ed.), *Bangladesher Swadhinota Juddho, Dolilpotro* (Documents Concerning the Liberation

Struggle of Bangladesh) (Dwitio Khondo) (Dhaka: Government of Bangladesh, 1985), pp. 405–08.
215. Dutta, *Shaater Doshoker Gono Jagoron*, p. 419.
216. *Azad*, 5 January 1969.
217. Dutta, *Shaater Doshoker Gono Jagoron*, p. 419.
218. *Azad*, 9 January 1969.
219. Dutta, *Shaater Doshoker Gono Jagoron*, p. 420.
220. Dutta, *Shaater Doshoker Gono Jagoron*, pp. 421–22.
221. Dutta, *Shaater Doshoker Gono Jagoron*, p. 421.
222. *Azad*, 18 January 1969.
223. Dutta, *Shaater Doshoker Gono Jagoron*, p. 425.
224. *Azad*, 18 January 1969.
225. Dutta, *Shaater Doshoker Gono Jagoron*, p. 427.
226. *Azad*, 19 January 1969.
227. Azad, *Unosottorer Gonoobbuththan*, p. 565.
228. *Azad*, 21 January 1969.
229. *Azad*, 21 January 1969.
230. Nirmal Sen, *Amar Jobanbondi* (Dhaka: Ityadi Grontho Prakashani, 2012), pp. 262–63.
231. *Azad*, 22 January 1969.
232. *Azad*, 22 January 1969.
233. *Azad*, 25 January 1969.
234. *Azad*, 25 January 1969.
235. Mahbub Ullah, *Shater Doshoker Chatro Andolon o Onyanyo Prosongo* (Dhaka: Islam Gyan Bitoroni, 2001), p. 35.
236. Sen, *Amar Jobanbondi*, p. 266.
237. Ullah, *Shater Doshoker Chatro Andolon*, p. 35.
238. Ullah, *Shater Doshoker Chatro Andolon*, p. 36.
239. Ullah, *Shater Doshoker Chatro Andolon*, p. 36.
240. *Azad*, 25 January 1969.
241. *Azad*, 25 and 26 January 1969.
242. Foreign and Commonwealth Office, FCO 37/438, FSP1/1, Part C, Pakistan Political Affairs Internal Situation, A. A. Halliley, 12 February 1969 to A. A. Duff, South Asia Department, Commonwealth Office, London.
243. Azad, *Unosottorer Gonoobbuththan*, p. 588.
244. *Azad*, 31 January 1969.
245. Dostidar, *Jibon Smriti*, p. 208.

246. Foreign and Commonwealth Office, FCO 37/438, FSP1/1, Part C, Pakistan Political Affairs Internal Situation, A. A. Halliley, 12 February 1969 to A. A. Duff, South Asia Department, Commonwealth Office, London.
247. On 30 January 1969, Z. A Shuleri published an op-ed in the *Pakistan Times* indicating that Ayub Khan would invite leaders of opposition to a round table conference. *Azad*, 30 January 1969; Azad, *Unosottorer Gonoobbuththan*, p. 590.
248. Mohammad Farhad, *Unoshottorer Gonoobuththan* (Mass Uprising of 1969) (Dhaka: Jatio Sahityo Prokashoni, 2019), p. 95.
249. Ahad, *Jatio Rajniti*, p. 333.
250. *Azad*, 7 February 1969.
251. Azad, *Unosottorer Gonoobbuththan*, p. 597.
252. Ahad, *Jatio Rajniti*, p. 335.
253. Azad, *Unosottorer Gonoobbuththan*, p. 593.
254. *Azad*, 13 February 1969.
255. *Azad*, 16 February 1969.
256. *Azad*, 16 February 1969.
257. Dostidar, *Jibon Smriti*, p. 210.
258. Abdul Rashid Moten, 'Mawdudi and the transformation of Jamaat-e-Islami in Pakistan', *Muslim World* 93, no. 3 (2003): 391–413.
259. Rono, *Shotabdi Perie*, p. 167.
260. Ahad, *Jatio Rajniti*, p. 337.
261. Nurul Kabir, *Deposing of a Dictator Revisiting a Magnificient Mass Uprising after 50 Years* (Dhaka: Samhati Publications, 2020), p. 95.
262. Kabir, *Deposing of a Dictator*, p. 96.
263. *Azad*, 17 February 1969.
264. 'We have received reports, so far, unconfirmed, but from reliable sources, to the effect that the burning of the state Guest House in Dacca on 16 February was because Chief Justice Rahman was accommodated there. We hear that he managed to escape and he has returned to Lahore. It seems that in the fire he lost not only his personal effects but his notes of the trial. Understandably, he is reluctant to return to Dhaka.' A. A. Halliley wrote to Lynton Jones on 20 February 1969. Foreign and Commonwealth Office, FCO 37/438, FSP1/1, Part C, Pakistan Political Affairs Internal Situation, A. A. Halliley, British High Commission, Rawalpindi, to Lynton Jones, Commonwealth Office, London, Agartala Conspiracy Case, 20 February 1969.

265. Ahad, *Jatio Rajniti*, p. 340.
266. Rono, *Shotabdi Perie*, pp. 179–81.
267. Dutta, *Shaater Doshoker Gono Jagoron*, p. 467.
268. Kabir, *Deposing of a Dictator*, p. 99.
269. Kabir, *Deposing of a Dictator*, p. 100.
270. Rono, *Shotabdi Perie*, p. 182.
271. Rono, *Shotabdi Perie*, pp. 183–84.
272. Foreign and Commonwealth Office, FCO 37/471, Pakistan Internal Political Situation, File No. FSP1/1, Part F (281–334), US Department of State Director of Intelligence and Research, RNA-15, 12 March 1969, FSP1/1.
273. Foreign and Commonwealth Office, FCO 37/471, Pakistan Internal Political Situation, File No. FSP1/1, Part F (281–334), US Department of State Director of Intelligence and Research, RNA-15, 12 March 1969, FSP1/1.
274. According to Rono, Sheikh Mujib visited Bhashani soon after his release and had a discussion in a closed-door meeting with Bhashani. Rono, *Shotabdi Perie*, p. 184.
275. Rono, *Shotabdi Perie*, p. 221.
276. Rono, *Shotabdi Perie*, p. 222.
277. Dutta, *Shaater Doshoker Gono Jagoron*, p. 472.
278. Azad, *Unosottorer Gonoobbuththan*, pp. 596–97.
279. Tofail Ahmed later recalled in a reminiscence that on 23 February the mass meeting became an ocean of humans. He was deeply moved by the mass gathering and then addressed Sheikh Mujib as an informal *tumi* instead of the formal *apni* as is the custom in Bengali and conferred the title 'Bangabandhu' (Friend of Bengal) on him. He called this the best day in his life. Tofail Ahmed, 'Unoshottorer Gonoobbuththan O Bangabandhu', in *Unoshottorer Gonoobbuththaner Mohanyaok Tofail Ahmed*, ed. Din Islam Rubel, pp. 15–23 (Tofail Ahmed: The Great Hero of Mass Insurrection of 1969) (Dhaka: Bornomala, 2019), p. 19.
280. Dutta, *Shaater Doshoker Gono Jagoron*, p. 470.
281. M. Ahmad, *Jasoder Utthan Poton*, pp. 22–23.
282. Dutta, *Shaater Doshoker Gono Jagoron*, p. 473.
283. Monem Sarkar, *Bangabandhu Sheikh Mujibur Rahman Jibon Kotha* (Kolkata: Soptaho Publications, 2015), p. 230.
284. Ahad, *Jatio Rajniti*, p. 342.
285. Ahad, *Jatio Rajniti*, p. 342.

286. Azad, *Unosottorer Gonoobbuththan*, p. 607.
287. *The Times*, 19 March 1969. This issue was preserved in Foreign and Commonwealth Office files, and D. M. March, a British diplomatic official, wrote also about a *Daily Telegraph* article on which the foreign minister issued a statement. FCO 37/469, FSP1/1, Part D, Pakistan Internal Political Situation, D. M. March to Judy Walker, 19 March 1969.
288. Kabir, *Deposing of a Dictator*, p. 123.
289. Ahad, *Jatio Rajniti*, pp. 342–48.
290. Ahad, *Jatio Rajniti*, p. 351; Rono, *Shotabdi Perie*, p. 185. Nurul Kabir further argued that general Ayub consulted his cabinet and was hopeful that many DAC leaders issued a press statement supporting him. He dismissed two governors. Kabir, *Deposing of a Dictator*, pp. 129–30.
291. Rono, *Shotabdi Perie*, p. 193.
292. Subho Basu and Auritro Majumder, 'Dilemmas of Parliamentary Communism', *Critical Asian Studies* 45, no. 2 (2013): 167–200.
293. Rono, *Shotabdi Perie*, pp. 188–90.
294. Fox states: 'The trouble now is that in East Pakistan opinion will harden against West Pakistanis. While West Pakistani leaders have by and large hailed President's decision no one here is happy. Pamphlets were being distributed in streets yesterday calling for early introduction of Bengale [*sic*] into cinema, bus steamer tickets, bank cheque books etc. Tariq speech yesterday referring to Anglo-American imperialism may have little effect but will not help.' Foreign and Commonwealth Office, FCO 37/469, FSP1/1, Part D, Pakistan Internal Political Situation, Telegram 179, Roy Fox to Rawalpindi from Dacca, 14 March 1969.
295. Foreign and Commonwealth Office, FCO 37/469, FSP1/1, Part D, Pakistan Internal Political Situation, Sir Cyril S. Pickard, High Commissioner of UK, to Sir John Johnston, 5 March 1969.
296. Rono, *Shotabdi Perie*, pp. 188–90.
297. Rono, *Shotabdi Perie*, pp. 191–92.
298. *The Guardian*, 19 March 1969. This issue was preserved in Foreign and Commonwealth Office files as controversy erupted over an article in the *Daily Telegraph*. FCO 37/469, FSP1/1, Part D, Pakistan Internal Political Situation, D. M. March to Judy Walker, 19 March 1969.
299. Pater Hazelhurst, 'Army out to Quell Riots in East Pakistan', *The Times*, 18 March 1969.
300. 'As much as any one man, Bhashani inspired the riots that last month forced President Ayub Khan to step down from the presidency. Now Bhashani is

the most severe single threat to a fragile peace brought to the troubled and geographically divided land by the imposition of martial law. Under fear of harsh penalties, Pakistan's other politicians, including Bhashani's chief Bengali rival, moderate Sheikh Mujibur Rahman, have kept silent. Not Bhashani, who continues to receive newsmen and followers at his bamboo-walled hut. "What have I to fear?" he asked TIME Correspondent Dan Coggin, as he adjusted his soiled straw skull cap and straightened the green sweater that he wore inside out. "I would welcome being hanged for my people."... Would the Pakistanis really revolt against the army? "Is it possible for the army to kill 125 million Pakistanis?" counters Bhashani angrily. "Have the North Vietnamese quit fighting? We are Southeast Asians like them. When the flame of discontent is lit, the people will stop at nothing."' 'Pakistan: Prophet of Violence', *Time*, 18 April 1969, https://content.time.com/time/subscriber/article/0,33009,844753,00.html (accessed on 19 May 2021).
301. Rono, *Shotabdi Perie*, p. 195.
302. Ayub Khan's letter to Yahya Khan, published in Ahad, *Jatio Rajniti*, pp. 352–54.
303. 'Student Power', FCO 37/469, FSP1/1, Part D, Pakistan Internal Political Situation, R. F. W. Skilbeck, 26 February 1969.
304. Foreign and Commonwealth Office, FCO 37/469, FSP1/1, Part D, I3/1 208, Pakistan Internal Political Situation, D. M. March to W. K. Slatcher, British High Commission, New Delhi, 19 March 1969. Later, major Horbrick, assistant military advisor in Pakistan, wrote to the British High Commission confirming this story of troop deployment. Horbrick wrote: 'The general but still unsubstantiated opinion amongst the military attache group is that approximately 4 Brigades have been sent as reinforcements, less their administrative and supporting arms. This would give approximately 12 battalions, say 10,000 troops, carrying small arms only, which correlates fairly closely to the figures or reinforcements reported. I am yet unable to confirm that brigades have left 11 Div and 16 Div (2) but these formations are frequently mentioned.' FCO, 37/469, FSP1/1, Part D, Pakistan Internal Political Situation, From Major A. I. A. Hobrick, 22 April 1969, British High Commission.
305. Rono, *Shotabdi Perie*, p. 178.
306. Rono, *Shotabdi Perie*, p. 204.
307. Rono, *Shotabdi Perie*, pp. 204–06, 209–11.
308. Rono, *Shotabdi Perie*, pp. 209–11.

309. In a rather surprising proclamation on 29 March, Yahya Khan instructed employers to pay the increases which they had awarded their workers, often under threat of strike and *gherao* during the previous month. 'Although we should still expect a ruthless approach from General Yahya in the face of opposition- and few early examples are quoted above – such concessions indicate more a conciliatory approach, possibly over if the fruits of gheraos are so easily to be retained.' Foreign and Commonwealth Office, FSP1/1 (Part F 281-334), R. F. W. Skilbeck, British High Commission, Rawalpindi, to Miss. J. M. H. Walker, South Asia Desk, Foreign and Commonwealth Office, 9 April 1969. The British high commissioner C. S. Pickard called on Yahya Khan and mentioned that British managers were concerned that no encouragement should be given to those who had been responsible for *gherao*s, and he articulated his strong opposition to the demand for the nationalization of jute trade. FCO, FSP1/1 (Part F 281-334) Telegram 341, 7 April 1969.
310. Foreign and Commonwealth Office, FSP1/1 (Part F 281-334), Roy Fox, Deputy High Commissioner, to Sir Cyril Pickard, High Commissioner to Pakistan, 2 April 1969.
311. Rono, *Shotabdi Perie*, p. 221.
312. Mohiuddin Ahmad, *Ei Deshe Ekdin Juddho Hoechilo* (Dhaka: Prothom Prokashan, 2019), pp. 56–57.
313. M. Ahmad, *Ei Deshe Ekdin Juddho Hoechilo*, pp. 56–57.
314. M. Ahmad, *Ei Deshe Ekdin Juddho Hoechilo*, pp. 56–59.
315. Abdur Rahman Chowdhury, 'In Remembrance of Tofazzul Hossain Manik Mia', *Financial Times*, 31 May 2022.
316. M. Ahmad, *Ei Deshe Ekdin Juddho Hoechilo*, pp. 58–59; M. Ahmad, *Jasoder Utthan Poton*, pp. 19–22.
317. Rono, *Shotabdi Perie*, pp. 224–25.
318. Rono, *Shotabdi Perie*, p. 225.
319. Rono, *Shotabdi Perie*, pp. 212–14; Dostidar, *Jibon Smriti*, pp. 226–30.
320. Talukdar Maniruzzaman, 'Bangladesh: An Unfinished Revolution?', *Journal of Asian Studies* 34, no. 4 (1975): 891–911. Also see Mohiuddin Ahmad, *Lal Sontras Siraj Sikdar o Sorbohara Rajniti* (Red Terror: Siraj Sikdar and 'Proletarian' Politics) (Dhaka: Batighar, 2021).
321. Farhad, *Unoshottorer Gonoobuththan*, pp.145–51.
322. Badruddin Umar, *Ekattorer Swadhinota Juddher Pothe* (Dhaka: Jatio Sahitya Prokash, 2015), pp. 34–36.
323. Rono, *Shotabdi Perie*, p. 220.

324. Dutta, *Shaater Doshoker Gono Jagoron*, p. 506.
325. When Hamidul Haq Chowdhury told Roy Fox, UK's Deputy High Commissioner, that centre parties, the NDF and the PDM, with anyone else who would like to join them, was the only viable alternative to what he regarded as anarchy, Fox retorted: 'I was often told this would not succeed as old guard had failed the people. He agreed that some names were anathema but insisted this was only answer.' Foreign and Commonwealth Office, 37/471, Pakistan Political Affairs Internal Situation, Roy Fox to Rawalpindi, Telegram no. 279, 2 May 1969, FCO FSP1/1 (Part F 281-334).
326. In a meeting with Fox, Hamidul Haq Chowdhury condemned Sheikh Mujib as a fascist, only comparable to Hitler. Foreign and Commonwealth Office, 37/471, Pakistan Political Affairs Internal Situation', Roy Fox to Rawalpindi, Telegram no. 279. 2 May 1969, FCO FSP1/1 (Part F 281-334). In a meeting with Fox, Nurul Amin said, to some extent prophetically: 'Unless Mujib were ready to compromise to a much greater extent than appeared likely now his actions could result in separation of the two wings.' He also alleged that 'Mujib's action in submitting constitutional amendments to the President on his return from the RTC may well have been the last straw which brought in Martial Law'. Justice Murshed confided to Fox of his desire to become the prime minister of Pakistan. He said: 'Mujib should concentrate on East Pakistan and he was one of the few uncommitted leaders who would be acceptable to both wings.' He then added Sheikh Mujib was impossible to deal with and he had cut a very poor figure at the round table conference. Murshed further claimed that Sheikh Mujib was a rabble rouser. Foreign and Commonwealth Office, 37/471, FSP1/1 (Part F 281-334), Roy Fox, Deputy High Commissioner, to Sir Cyril Pickard, High Commissioner to Pakistan, UK, 25 April 1969. Fox in a secret dispatch noted: 'Examination of the possibilities a third force led by such as Nurul Amin, Hamidul Haq Chowdhury and their lieutenants presents a rather barren picture. For there is little imagination or drive, poor organization and almost certainly a potential return to the former fratricidal warfare which consumed these organizations and their leaders. ...Time is on the side of the extreme left and external developments may well help them too.' Foreign and Commonwealth Office, FSP1/1 (Part F 281-334), Roy Fox, Deputy High Commissioner, to Sir Cyril Pickard, High Commissioner to Pakistan, 2 April 1969. Fox and the entire British embassy staff thoroughly disliked Sheikh Mujib because of his assertiveness

and bold and fearless political assertions in favour of Bengalis. Fox wrote in his despatch: 'He has indeed a goonda touch himself and it is so difficult to see him as a responsible, mature and balanced prime minster.' Foreign and Commonwealth Office, 37/471, FSP1/1 (Part F 281-334), Roy Fox to British High Commission, 11 April 1969.

327. Ahad, *Jatio Rajniti*, pp. 364–65.
328. Mumtaz Ahmad, 'The Muslim Family Laws Ordinance of Pakistan', *International Journal on World Peace* 10, no. 3 (1993): 37–46.
329. Muhammad Rizwan, 'The Elections 1970: From Ballot to Nowhere', *Asian Journal of Social Sciences and Humanities* 3, no. 4 (2014): 28–36.
330. Dutta, *Shaater Doshoker Gono Jagoron*, pp. 511–12.
331. Dutta, *Shaater Doshoker Gono Jagoron*, p. 502.
332. Dutta, *Shaater Doshoker Gono Jagoron*, pp. 502–03.
333. Dutta, *Shaater Doshoker Gono Jagoron*, p. 504.
334. Dutta, *Shaater Doshoker Gono Jagoron*, pp. 510–12.
335. Dutta, *Shaater Doshoker Gono Jagoron*, pp. 517–18.
336. Umar, *Ekattorer Swadhinota Juddher Pothe*, p. 32.
337. Imran Khan and Karim Haider Syed, 'Constitutionalism in Pakistan: The Yahiya Khan Interregnum', *Pakistan Language and Humanities Review* 5, no. 2 (2021): 1–14.
338. Lawrence Ziring, 'Militarism in Pakistan: The Yahya Khan Interregnum', *Asian Affairs: An American Review* 1, no. 6 (1974): 402–20.
339. Abdur Rauf Chowdhury, *Swayotto Shashon, Swadhikar o Swadhinota* (Dhaka: Kotha Prokash, 2010), p. 247.
340. Rono said that on two occasions he faced significant resistance from students loyal to the Chhatro League in the sixties for using the term 'East Bengal' in Bramanbaria instead of 'East Pakistan'. In Dhaka, too, students belonging to the NSF came to attack him for saying 'East Bengal' rather than 'East Pakistan'. Rono, *Shotabdi Perie*, p. 138.
341. Dutta, *Shaater Doshoker Gono Jagoron*, p. 529.
342. Chowdhury, *Swayotto Shashon*, pp. 247–49.
343. Nuh uul-Alam Lenin, *Bangladesh Awami League: Songkhipto Itihas o Nirbachito Dolil* (Bangladesh Awami League: A Short History and Selected Documents) (Dhaka: Somoy Prokashon, 2015), pp. 257–66.
344. Chowdhury, *Swayotto Shashon*, p. 250.
345. Ernesto Laclau, *On Populist Reason* (London: Verso, 2005).
346. Rono, *Shotabdi Perie*, pp. 219–21.
347. Chowdhury, *Swayotto Shashon*, pp. 251–54.

348. Edris Alam and Dale Dominey-Howes, 'Review: A New Catalogue of Tropical Cyclones in the Northern Bay of Bengal and the Distribution and Effects of Selected Landfalling Events in Bangladesh', *International Journal of Climatology* 35, no. 6 (2015): 801–35, p. 824, cited in Sravani Biswas and Patrick Daly, '"Cyclone Not above Politics": East Pakistan, Disaster Politics, and the 1970 Bhola Cyclone', *Modern Asian Studies* 55, no. 4 (2021): 1382–1410.
349. This entire section is based on Biswas and Daly, 'Cyclone Not above Politics'.
350. Biswas and Daly, 'Cyclone Not above Politics', pp. 1396–99.
351. See Chapter 3 for details.
352. Biswas and Daly, 'Cyclone Not above Politics', p. 1403.
353. Biswas and Daly, 'Cyclone Not above Politics', p. 1405.
354. Ahad, *Jatio Rajniti*, p. 368.
355. Craig Baxter, 'Pakistan Votes – 1970', *Asian Survey* 11, no. 3 (1971): 197–218.
356. Mohammed Ayoob, 'Profile of a Party: PPP in Pakistan', *Economic and Political Weekly* 7, nos. 5–7 (1972): 215–19.
357. Foreign and Commonwealth Office, 36/686, FSP1/9, 'Roundup Reports from High Commission of United Kingdom on Political Situation in Pakistan', Viability of Independent Wings, 27 August 1970, Sir Cyril Pickard, British High Commissioner of Pakistan, to Bank of England, Foreign and Commonwealth Office, Overseas Development Ministry.
358. Khalid B. Sayeed provided a detailed analysis of the West Pakistani elite's attitude. Khalid B. Sayeed, 'The Breakdown of Pakistan's political system', *International Journal* 27, no. 3 (1972): 381–404.
359. Ahad, *Jatio Rajniti*, p. 371.
360. Abul Maal Abdul Muhith, *Bangladesh: Jatirastrer Udbhob* (Bangladesh: Emergence of a Nation State) (Dhaka: Sahitya Prokash, 2017), p. 175.
361. Muhith, *Bangladesh*, p. 176.
362. Muhith, *Bangladesh*, p. 176.
363. Muhith, *Bangladesh*, pp. 177–78.
364. See note 359 for the British High Commission's report.
365. Muhith, *Bangladesh*, pp. 177–79.
366. Muhith, *Bangladesh*, p. 179.
367. Chowdhury, *Swayotto Shashon*, p. 292.
368. Chowdhury, *Swayotto Shashon*, p. 295.
369. Chowdhury, *Swayotto Shashon*, p. 292.
370. M. Ahmad, *Jasoder Utthan Poton*, pp. 29–30.

371. M. Ahmad, *Ei Deshe Ekdin Juddho Hoechilo*, pp. 80–81.
372. Foreign and Commonwealth Office, 37/870, F8 P1/2, Part A, Mr R. A. Burrow to Sir Alec Douglas Home, Former Prime Minister of UK, 23 March 1971.
373. Foreign and Commonwealth Office, 37/870, F8 P1/2, Part A, Mr R. A. Burrow to Sir Alec Douglas Home, Former Prime Minister of UK, 23 March 1971.
374. Foreign and Commonwealth Office, 37/870, F8 P1/2, Part A, Mr R. A. Burrow to Sir Alec Douglas Home, Former Prime Minister of UK, 23 March 1971.
375. Chowdhury, *Swayotto Shashon*, p. 307.
376. Chowdhury, *Swayotto Shashon*, p. 319.
377. M. Ahmad, *Ei Deshe Ekdin Juddho Hoechilo*, pp. 84–85.
378. Chowdhury, *Swayotto Shashon*, p. 321.
379. Chowdhury, *Swayotto Shashon*, p. 324.
380. *The Guardian*, 27 March 1971; *New York Times*, 27 March 1971.
381. This is a controversial topic in contemporary Bangladesh. Many claimed that Sheikh Mujib did not issue any statement and that it was prepared afterwards to enhance his status. Awami League leaders, on the other hand, claimed that Sheikh Mujib ordered the announcement of independence. But there is no doubt that Ziaur Rahman announced a statement of independence in his name on 27 March 1971.

Conclusion

The birth of Pakistan, in the wake of the transfer of power in 1947, had once provided hopes to millions of East Pakistanis. Yet in economic, cultural and political terms, the vast majority of East Pakistanis had been disappointed by the gradual deepening of inequalities between the two wings of Pakistan. In the colonial era, Bengali Muslims had sought to escape from the internal colonization of the eastern part of Bengal by the Calcutta-centric, Hindu landholding and service elites. They had invested their hopes and aspirations in the Pakistan movement. To them, the Pakistan movement came to signify the possibility of emancipation from the class structure that had evolved in response to the introduction of the Permanent Settlement. Many cultural and literary personalities, as well as journalists, had wanted to make a new beginning with literary–cultural experiments. This hope was encapsulated in the East Pakistan Renaissance Society movement. The very name of this group suggested its aim – the total rebirth of culture and civilization. Yet such hopes were belied. In cultural terms, from the very inception of Pakistan, the middle classes of East Bengal had faced contests over the national language, and, more importantly, their very Muslimness had been questioned because of the shared register of their language with non-Muslims. Soon the promised land of 'eternal Eid' became a site of poverty and hunger. The partition confined the spatially mobile, densely populated East Bengal society to the demarcated international border. The closing of the frontier had led to border skirmishes among peasants. The devaluation of the Indian rupee soon after the transfer of power, and Pakistan's refusal to follow suit, led towards further crisis. Smuggling, shrinkage in trade and commerce, a critical absence of infrastructure and sectarian violence along religious lines became the new reality of Pakistan. The economy of East Pakistan was characterized predominantly by subsistence peasant agriculture, with jute being the primary cash crop. In the early fifties, jute earned foreign exchanges for Pakistan, but those hard-earned foreign exchanges were spent on the building-up of the defence industry, primarily located in West Pakistan. In spatial terms, East Pakistanis were isolated from the other provinces of Pakistan by 1,400 kilometers. Thus, the historical experience of quotidian reality among the East Pakistanis did not correspond to their horizons of expectations.

While Pakistan was witnessing inter-wing rivalry, a silent social revolution was building up in East Pakistan. The new politicians who came to dominate the political parties were educated in Bengali and came from rich peasant households or the incipient stratum of Bengali Muslim professionals. The earlier generation of Muslim politicians from Bengal had come from Urdu-speaking, *ashraf* landowning families, such as Suhrawardy and Nazimuddin, who were educated at Oxbridge and became leaders because of their birth and familial connections. It was Fazlul Huq, who also came from a landowning *ashraf* family and spoke both Urdu and Bengali, who brought in the upper stratum of the Bengal peasantry and the incipient Muslim middle classes into politics. The process of recruitment of Bengali Muslims under the leadership of Suhrawardy and Abul Hashim came from the ranks of what Rounak Jahan calls 'vernacular elites'. This new generation of politicians were more committed to local issues in East Bengal politics and wanted to gain access to political power through democratic means. This includes veteran Congress–Khilafat movement activist Abul Mansur Ahmad; the new chief minister of East Pakistan, Ataur Rahman; and youth activist and party organizer Sheikh Mujibur Rahman. As these leaders were embedded in the incipient Muslim middle classes of Bengal, they were adamant about having their share of power and resources in Pakistani politics. Bhashani came from the ranks of the peasantry. He remained a peasant activist and tried to promote the rights of Bengali Muslim peasant settlers in Assam and later on became active in peasant issues in East Pakistan. His radicalism, peasant-populist approach and simple dress earned him moral capital among peasants. The peasant-populist approach also brought Bhashani close to the clandestine communists. His connection with the nationalist revolutionaries and Khilafatists made him an instinctive anti-imperialist. As African and Asian countries gained independence in the fifties and the sixties, the struggle for decolonization acquired a new intensity in Congo, in South

Africa, in Vietnam, Laos and Cambodia. Modernizing, republican, anti-capitalist movements became involved in conflicts with the West-backed oil-rich monarchies. Bhashani advocated tri-continental solidarity and an end to the neo-colonial domination of Asia and Africa. His politics, speeches and rhetoric connected issues in rural East Pakistan with global issues such as the Non-Aligned Movement, the peace movement in relation to Vietnam and the national liberation struggles in Africa. He thus also put East Pakistan on the global map of resistance to colonial capitalism and neo-colonial domination.

Politics in East Pakistan revolved around three main trends. The first trend was represented by faith-based political parties. The largest among them was the Muslim League. The Muslim League was a Muslim nationalist organization that viewed itself as the natural ruling party of Pakistan and had presence in both the wings. The Muslim League lost its steam in East Pakistan as most of its youth cadres, and even the middle-ranking leaders, defected to a new political formation – the Awami Muslim League. The other faith-based organizations, such as the Nizam-e-Islam and the Jamaal-ul-Ulema, were too small in East Pakistan. The Jamaal was initially a West Pakistan-based organization but had steadily gained adherents in East too. It had a political programme, ideologically-oriented cadres and a firm worldview based on the rule of sharia. It was not a loosely organized Muslim nationalist organization like the Muslim League. Apart from these faith-based political parties, the second trend was that of the several centrist political organizations, more or less autonomist in orientation. The largest among them was the Awami Muslim League till it dropped the word 'Muslim' in 1955 at the stubborn insistence of Bhashani and its rank-and-file activists. Since its inception the Awami League had adopted a regional tone. Built up mainly by Bengali Muslim followers of Suhrawardy and Hashim, this group presented itself as a party looking after Bengali interests in Pakistan. Led by Suhrawardy and Bhashani, the party formed an alliance with Fazlul Huq's Krishak Shramik Party and several smaller outfits in East Bengal. The Krishak Shramik Party was a pocket borough of Huq, a charismatic leader of East Bengal. The third trend included the clandestine communist network. Despite being severely repressed, the communists tried to operate in East Pakistani politics through frontal parties such as Ganatantri Dal. The idea was to promote the frontal party of social democratic orientation, and the communists worked within the organization. In 1954, in the first provincial elections held in East Pakistan on the basis of universal adult franchise, a united front of the Awami League and the Krishak Shramik Party swept aside the Muslim League from Bengal, primarily due to the former's autonomist charter of demands. However, the central state dismissed this government within two months. In 1956, during the era of palace intrigues, Awami League leader Suhrawardy became the prime minster of Pakistan, and his colleague Abul Mansur Ahmad also joined the central government. In East Pakistan, too, the Awami League was able to form a government. But soon the fact of Pakistan's presence in the Baghdad Pact, earned Bhashani's displeasure when a signatory of the pact, the UK, was engaged in war with Egypt. An ageing Bhashani vehemently promoted Afro-Asian solidarity, and on this issue, he broke away from the Awami League. The new outfit Bhashani formed, the NAP, had the support of the clandestine CPP (East Pakistan Provincial Committee) and came to constitute the powerful third stream in East Pakistani politics. Despite the appointment of Suhrawardy as the prime minister, democracy was a mere façade in Pakistan. Meanwhile, the social composition of West Pakistani elites and the institutional balance in the polity of West Pakistan actually stood in the way of a fully functioning democracy in Pakistan.

In West Pakistan the landholding elites constituted the backbone of the army and had also dominated the Constituent Assembly of Pakistan, elected in 1946, on the basis of limited electorate. In 1946 voting rights were limited to approximately 14 per cent of the adult population of British India. The military as an institution remained deeply embedded in the social fabric of Punjab, the largest province of West Pakistan. From the moment of its birth, West Pakistan had experienced bloody conflicts with India over Kashmir. It also had a very high proportion of refugees among its population. These refugees had experienced ethnic cleansing during the communal holocaust of 1947. They had a deeper insecurity with respect to India. In such circumstances, the army acquired a new potency in West Pakistani political life. Army officers were highly trained professionals who had a global experience of serving in different war theaters during the Second World War. Though they came from landholding social classes, they were more exposed to international affairs. The bureaucracy, meaning the elite members of the CSP, constituted the other pillar of the state. The bureaucracy was recruited primarily from the middle-class Muslim refugees who had migrated from what became India. High-ranking bureaucrats of the elite CSP also married into landholding families. Consequently, in West Pakistan, the political culture was very different from that in East Bengal, renamed as East Pakistan in 1956. In East Pakistan, most politicians, except for the three big players – namely Fazlul Huq, Nazimuddin and Suhrawardy – came from the ranks of rich peasants who had made their career by fighting against the large landholding families of upper-caste Hindu origin. Thus, the very social foundations of political elites in East and West Pakistan were different.

The founding political figure of Pakistan, Jinnah, had had his own dislike for mass politics. He also had little confidence in his colleagues among the politicians. He relied primarily on bureaucrats to run the administration of the country and acquired viceregal authority to concretize decisively his writ over the administration. These bureaucratic and military elites had a complete distrust of politicians. Socialized in the colonial school of governance, these bureaucrats believed that they were the custodians of the interests of the masses. A paternalistic despotism was apparent in their policymaking process, and soon they established political control over the governor general's office through the appointment of a series of bureaucrats after Nazimuddin stepped down to become the prime minister. It was during this period of palace intrigues that Ayub Khan became the first Pakistani commander-in-chief of the army. He was ambitious and figured out a way forward for strengthening the Pakistani army, and later he staged a coup d'état for Pakistan's economy. Ayub Khan shrewdly read the Cold War situation and sought the US's friendship. The US supported Pakistan as a critical ally against the expanding communist 'empire' in Asia. Ayub Khan soon took power and introduced his model of praetorian capitalism. The US and other countries in the West liberally provided Pakistan with foreign aid while the Harvard Economic Group acted as a consultant to Ayub Khan's development policies. US policymakers thought that Pakistan could act as the perfect case of a non-communist developmental model. Ayub Khan used these loans to promote industrialization in West Pakistan through various industrial houses. His policymakers believed that functional inequality was necessary during the early stages of industrialization. As a result, social inequality and regional inequality became hallmarks of the new system. Domestically, Ayub Khan sought to build up a constitutional façade for the military-bureaucratic regime. He thus created a system of Basic Electorate, composed primarily of rich peasants in rural areas who had some access to developmental funds under the guidance of bureaucrats. Ayub Khan's model of praetorian capitalism placed the army as an economic corporate organization, put substantial resources in the hands of a few industrial houses and made the bureaucrats and rich peasants a subordinate partner in the process. Ayub Khan's international alliances placed Pakistan at the heart of the Cold War in Asia. Yet such calculations were lost when the Sino-Indian war broke out and Ayub found, to his discomfort, that the very forces that had financed the Pakistani army and economy were now sending armaments to India, its regional rival. Increasingly, Ayub Khan moved closer to China, and the US was alarmed by Pakistan's China policy. Thus, Ayub Khan's model of governance and diplomacy had entered into crisis. This model, centred on international alliance, reached a final crisis point when Ayub Khan launched a war with India to wrest control over Kashmir. His failure to successfully do so, however, exposed his vulnerability. At the same time, his adherence to the Tashkent Declaration created dissension within his administration. Many officers were disappointed, and his close confidante, the foreign minister Bhutto, who had socialist leanings and was the architect of the alliance with China, became a rebel. China was forthcoming with its support for Pakistan. But China's involvement would increase Pakistan's international isolation from the western donor countries. Ayub Khan had to tread a balanced path. As Bhutto resigned, Ayub Khan's became a more isolated regime. Wartime strains on the economy unleashed an inflation that led to a decline in real wages. The workers became restive and political parties held conclaves to signal their opposition. The Awami League, under the charismatic leadership of Sheikh Mujib, adopted a six-point programme demanding a confederation of Pakistan. Students demanded academic freedom, the reduction of fees and an improvement in technical education. The Ayub Khan regime adopted stern measures to deal with these demands.

Students in any developing society, like East Pakistan, act as the bridge between the future and the present, the rural interior and the urban centre, folk culture and the supposedly chic middle-class aesthetic sensitivities. They view themselves as conscious harbingers of change. Concentrated in dorms in pivotal nerve centres of main cities, universities offered a critical space for them to think, organize and assert themselves. More importantly, students were aware that in a mostly pre-literate society, they were collectively perceived by various segments of the society and the subaltern masses as the future of the nation. Many among them read, discussed and debated the implications of international events. They also experimented with novel literary, cultural and aesthetic forms. A vast majority of the students came from middle peasant families, and they were also anxious about their future, since they wanted their family's investment in education to provide them with access to a meaningful livelihood. Both from pragmatic considerations and emotional as well as ideological perspectives, students resisted the declaration of Urdu as the state language in Pakistan. Their protests had significant practical reasons too. The use of Urdu as a national language would disadvantage them in comparison to native speakers in competitive exams for government jobs. But as they faced state repression in articulating their opinions, they became more radicalized and gave birth to a rebellious literary activism through the publication of an anthology of poetry celebrating the Language Martyrs' Day. They wrote poetry celebrating the national liberation struggles in Congo and articles on Algerian and Palestinian liberation struggles, and protested against the Vietnam War. They read Che Guevara's writings and Regis Debray's theorization of revolution, and went back to Bengal's history of secret society movements and national revolutionary struggles against colonial rule. Increasingly, the new generation of intelligentsia moved away from the writing of poems suffused with Muslim nationalist imagery and focused more on quotidian issues, rural landscape and urban decay as themes. Progressive cultural activists staged and composed plays on burning social issues of Bengal, starting with Munier Chowdhury's landmark play *Kabar*. They composed new revolutionary songs, staged dance dramas and waged a cultural war to question the commonsensical understanding of Bengali identity in Pakistan. There existed a vigorous conversation about what constituted Pakistani–Bengali identity and the cultural autonomy of Bengali Pakistanis, both from Indian and the Muslim nationalist Pakistani traditions of the Bengali language. In films, paintings, sculptures and newer art forms, there took place a gradual assertion of artistic freedom drawing upon both global and local folk traditions of Bengal. This became a long-drawn cultural battle that could be characterized in terms of changes in the commonsensical understanding of what it meant to be from East Bengal.

In 1966 Sheikh Mujib emerged as the votary of the six-point programme. This was an attempt to transform Pakistan into a confederation. The six-point programme had a long period of gestation, from the 21-point of the United Front in 1954, via the economic doctrine of the two economies to the final formulation of a precise document for a confederal constitutional transformation. It was Sheikh Mujib, through his earthy sense of humor, soaring rhetoric and booming voice, who made it a lively document for political conversation. The document, though criticized for being a reflection of the demands of the incipient bourgeoisie of East Pakistan, had conceptualized the necessity of the economic autonomy of the region from Pakistani polity and thus challenged the process of the internal colonization of East Pakistan. This was a period of uncertainty in East Pakistan, as well as in Pakistan in general as a country. The Ayub Khan regime was increasingly isolated from people of both the wings. The decade of development had generated economic inequality and the suppression of the voice of the subaltern social classes. Despite impressive economic growth, the burgeoning working classes had experienced a decline in their real incomes. Hyper-nationalist propaganda and sacrifices made during the 1965 war exposed the empty boastings of the ruling military junta about their ability to wrest Kashmir from India through military intervention. The gap between the ultranationalist rhetoric during the war and the cold reality of the Tashkent Declaration undermined confidence in the administration in West Pakistan. In East Pakistan, political elites who were divorced from any substantive access to power realized that they had been left unprotected during the war, though the East Bengal regiment contributed towards the defence of Lahore. Surrounded by India on three sides, East Pakistan remained isolated during the war. Its economy was devastated by this wartime isolation. In such circumstances, industrial workers became active in fighting for the preservation of their basic living standards. It was the resistance of the working classes that provided support to the six-point programme agitation on 7 June 1966. Trade unions guided by left-wing activists mounted resistances and strikes. Yet state repression undermined effective resistance on the part of the Awami League. The military regime promptly arrested Sheikh Mujib, lodged a treason trial against him and put the six-point Awami League on the defensive. There took place defections in the ranks of the Awami League. Opposition parties, including faith-based parliamentary parties, came together in the PDM, a platform for legal parliamentary opposition. They argued for the restoration of parliamentary democracy in Pakistan. Nonetheless, they were hesitant to launch any mass struggle against the military junta. Many Awami Leaguers who were opposed to the six-point programme joined the PDM.

Meanwhile, global political debates and splits between the Soviet Union and China impacted the world communist movement. The communist movement in East Pakistan and the NAP faced a split in their ranks. Bhashani was released from prison in 1961, and in 1963 he went to China, where he met Zhou Enlai and Mao Zedong. Both of them requested Bhashani to go slow on Ayub Khan. Nonetheless, Bhashani supported the common opposition candidate against Ayub Khan in 1965 and remained committed to the organization of peasant and labour movements against landlordism, monopoly capitalist houses and imperialism. He was suspicious of the six-point programme and categorized it as a CIA-sponsored document. As a consequence, the Awami League and the NAP were on a collision course.

But inside the NAP and the CPP (East Pakistan Provincial Committee)-affiliated student movements, too, there took place splits, and pro-Chinese activists moved away from the pro-Soviet ones. Bhashani headed the more popular pro-Chinese NAP. He and his associates sought to mobilize peasants and workers against the military regime on a class-based demand charter. The NAP particularly emphasized the problem of inflation. Two pro-Chinese communists, Kazi Zafar and Rono, built up a powerful trade union organization in the Tongi industrial area. In Chittagong, the pro-Chinese communists had a presence among the industrial workers through Abul Bashar and Deben Sikdar. The labour movement started gaining momentum under the leadership of various left factions of the splintered CPP (East Pakistan Provincial Committee). That actually established the momentum of a struggling class. Yet there persisted a calm as the military-bureaucratic regime unleashed repression.

As the political parties were divided, the Awami League was bewildered by the arrest of Sheikh Mujib. All their front-ranking leaders, as well as students in West Pakistan, started protests against the military regime, and they were joined by workers. Students were aware of the student movements all over the world. A large number of them were inspired by the Cultural Revolution in China and the war of resistance in Vietnam. Chinese communist literature was available in West Pakistan. As the news of student unrest in West Pakistan reached East Pakistan, students in Dacca entered into a dialogue. Meanwhile, Bhashani came to Dacca and, at the request of the union of autorickshaw drivers, declared a total strike on 7 December within 24 hours. The strike was successful, and it started a series of protests, marches and further strikes. In January 1969 the students formed the SAC comprising of the two factions of the pro-communist Chhatro Union and the Awami League's student organization, Chhatro League. On 20 January 1969, when police bullets killed a communist student activist, East Pakistani students and workers erupted in rebellion. The SAC led a massive uprising. In the midst of the student uprising Bhashani announced a *gherao*, or encirclement movement, that led to a massive spurge in industrial strikes in Dacca. The workers went on offensive, and collective bargaining enabled them to achieve some of their long-standing demands. Bhashani also took the movement to the countryside. Thousands of peasants attacked government offices and put up summary trials of cattle thieves. It was feared that the communists would take over the country. But the Maoist communists were divided into several warring groups with different political agenda and were unable to lead the movement. Pro-Soviet communists, meanwhile, extended support to Sheikh Mujib.

Sheikh Mujib steered the movement of 1969 towards electoral politics. His stubborn refusal to surrender his six-point programme, even at the expense of personal liberty, his articulation of the pains and anguish of East Pakistan and his attempt to rename East Pakistan as Bangladesh obviously endeared him to the masses. In the final years of the global sixties in East Pakistan, Sheikh Muijb emerged as the sole spokesperson of Bengali nationalism. His rhetoric, his earthy style of speaking and his critical commitment to the cause transformed him into an icon. The inadequate relief efforts for the devastating cyclone of 1970 revealed the callousness of the ruling military junta. Yet students enforced his agenda too. On 3 March students declared Tagore's 'My Golden Bengal' as the national anthem of Bangladesh. It was the SAC that designed the flag of Bangladesh. They provoked the Pakistani army through dummy rifle marches of female students. It was a challenge to a praetorian capitalism that had international origins, and this challenge encapsulated the spirit of the global sixties, which also had an international origin. The workers' militancy had definitely been inspired by a vision of social justice derived from the global socialist movement. The global sixties thus transformed the political landscape of East Pakistan into Bangladesh. It is clear that the way national liberation was achieved had not been envisaged or desired by those student and labour activists. Genocide, rape, ethnic cleansing, foreign invasion and the pain it caused were beyond the imaginations of the votary of the 1969 mass uprising. This circumstance evokes Marx's famous dictum:

> Men make their own history, but they do not make it as they please, they do not make it under self-directed circumstances existing already, given and transmitted from the past. The traditions of all dead generations weigh like a nightmare on the brains of the past.[1]

Note

1 Karl Marx, 'Chapter1', in *The Eighteenth Brumaire of Louis Bonaparte* (Moscow: Progress Publishers, 1937 [1852]), https://www.marxists.org/archive/marx/works/1852/18th-brumaire/ch01.htm (accessed on 20 February 2021).

Bibliography

Archives

National Archives of Bangladesh

Census of India, 1941, Volume IV: Bengal (Delhi, 1942).
Government of East Bengal, Home Department (CR), Political Branch, 1950–56.
Government of East Bengal, Home Department, Political Branch, B Proceedings, 1950–56.
Government of East Bengal, Home Political Branch Leaflet.
Government of East Bengal, Political Department.
Government of Bangladesh, *East Bengal Language Committee Report* (Dacca, 1949).

National Archives of the United States

Bator, Francis, Richard Blackmer, Richard Eckaus, Everett Hagen, Daniel Lerner, Max Millikan, Ithiel de Sola Pool, Lucian Pye, Paul Rosenstein-Rodan and Walt Whitman Rostow. 'Economic, Social, and Political Change in the Underdeveloped Countries and Its Implications for United States Policy'. A study prepared for the Senate Committee on Foreign Relations, MIT Center for International Studies, Massachusetts Institute of Technology, Cambridge, MA, 30 March 1960.
Department of State, Central Files, 611.93/12–1256, Secret; Priority.
Department of State, Central Files, Personal and Confidential.

McGill University Library, Montreal, Quebec

Central Statistics Office, *Economic Survey of East Pakistan* (Karachi: Government of Pakistan, 1957).
Foreign and Commonwealth Office Files, 1950–71 (Adam Matthew Collection).
Foreign Office Files, 1950–71 (Adam Matthew Collection).
Pakistan Commission on National Education, *Report, January–August 1959* (Karachi: Manager of Publications, 1961).

Online Archives

Marxists Internet Archives, https://www.marxists.org (accessed in November 2022).
Central Intelligence Agency (CIA) Archives, United States, https://www.cia.gov/resources/publications/publications-list (accessed in November 2022).
Cold War International History Project, Woodrow Wilson International Center for Scholars, Washington, DC, https://www.wilsoncenter.org/program/cold-war-international-history-project (accessed in November 2022).

Periodicals

American Spectator.
Azad, 1947, 1962–69.
Daily Star, 1998–2015.
Ittefaq, 1965, 1969–71.
Ittehad, 1947.
Kali o Kalam.
Moslem Bharot, 1947–51.
Nao Belal, 1951.
Newsweek, New York, 1950.
New York Times.
People's Daily, 1967.
Prothom Alo, 2002–20.
Samakal.
Saogat, Aswin, 1354.
Sombad, 1966–69.

The Dawn, 1950–71.
The Guardian.
The Statesman, Calcutta, 1948–56.
The Times, London, 1950–69.
Statistical Digest of Bangladesh, no. 8, Dhaka.

Memoirs

Ahad, Oli. *Jatio Rajniti 1945–75* (Sixth Edition) (Dhaka: Bangladesh Co-Operative Book Society Limited, 2015).
———. *Jatio Rajniti: 1945 theke 1975* (Fourth Edition) (Dhaka: Bangladesh Co-operative Book Society, 2004).
Ahmad, Abul Mansur. *Amar Dekha Rajnitir Ponchas Botsor* (Dhaka: Prothoma Prokashan, 2018).
Ahmad, Kamruddin. *Banglar Ek Modhyobitter Atmokahini* (Dhaka: Prothoma Prokashon, 2018).
Ahmad, Kazi Zafar. *Amar Rajnitir 60 Botsor Joar Bhatar Kothon* (Sixty Years of My Politics: Stories of Ebb and Flow) (Dhaka: Torofdar Prokashoni, 2017).
Ahmad, Mohiuddin. *Ei Deshe Ekdin Juddho Hoechilo* (Dhaka: Prothoma Prokashan, 2019).
Ahmad, Muzaffar. *Amar Jibon o Bharater Communist Party* (Calcutta: National Book Agency, 1969).
Ahmed, Mughees. 'Relationship between Political Parties and Non-Political Powers: An Analysis with Reference to Pakistan'. *Pakistan Journal of Social Sciences* 29, no. 1 (2009): 107–15.
Ahmed, Tofail. 'Unoshottorer Gonoobbuththan O Bangabandhu'. In *Unoshottorer Gonoobbuththaner Mohanyaok Tofiel Ahmed*, edited by Din Islam Rubel, pp. 15–19 (Dhaka: Bornomala, 2019).
Anisuzzaman. 'Claiming and Disclaiming a Cultural Icon: Tagore in East Pakistan and Bangladesh'. *University of Toronto Quarterly* 77, no. 4 (2008): 1058–69.
———. *Kal Nirobodhi* (Dhaka: Sahitya Prokash, 2019 [2003]).
Bhutto, Zulfiqar Ali. *The Myth of Independence* (Oxford: Oxford University Press, 1969).
Dostidar, Sharadindu. *Jibon Smriti* (Akhanda Purnango Rup) (Dhaka: Sahitya Prokash, 2019).

Dutta, Dhirendranath. *Shahid Drindronath Dotter Atmokotha*, edited by Anisuzzaman, Rashid Haidar and Minar Mansur (Dhaka: Bangla Academy, 1995).

Islam, Nurul. *Bangladesh: Jati Gothonkale Ek Orthinitibider Kichu Kotha* (Bangladesh: Few Words from the Days of Nation Formation) (Dhaka: University Press Limited, 2018).

Khan, Abdul Ghaffar Khan. *My Life and Struggle: Autobiography of Badshah Khan* (as narrated to K. P. Narang), translated by Helen Bouman (New Delhi: Hind Pocket Books, 1969).

Khan, Ataur Rahman. *Ojarotir Dui Botsor: Mukhkho Montritter Dinguli, 1956–1958* (Dhaka: Prothoma, 2017).

———. *Swaiiracharer Dosh Botsor* (Dacca: Naoroj Kitabistan, 1970).

Khan, Mohammad Ayub. *Friends Not Masters: A Political Autobiography* (New York: Oxford University Press, 1967).

Khan, Shahadat H. *The Freedom of Intellect Movement (Buddhir Mukti Andolan) in Bengali Muslim Thought, 1926–1938* (Lewiston, NY: Edwin Mellen Press, 2007).

Menon, Rashed Khan. *Ek Jibon: Swadhinotar Surjodoy* (A Life: Dawn of Independence) (Dhaka: Batighor, 2021).

Rahman, Sheikh Mujibur. *Asomapto Atmojiboni* (Dhaka: University Press, 2018).

———. *Amar Dekha Noya Chin* (Dhaka: Bangla Academy, 2020).

Rono, Haidar Akbar Khan. *Shotabdi Perie* (Dhaka: Tarafdar Prokashani, 2012).

———. *Uttal Shater Doshok* (Dhaka: Punthi Niloy, 2016).

Roy, Manoranjan. *Songramer Tin Doshok* (Dhaka: Jatio Prokashoni, 1986).

Sen, Nirmal. *Amar Jobanbondi* (Dhaka: Ityadi Grontho Prakashani, 2012).

Shamsuddin, Abul Kalam. *Otit Diner Smriti* (Memories of Old Days) (Dhaka: Khosroj Kitab Mohal, 2019 [1968]).

Singh, Moni. *Jibon Songram* (Prothom Khondo) (Dhaka: Jatio Sahitya Prokashoni, 1983).

———. 1992 *Jibon Songram* (Dwitio Khondo) (Dhaka: Jatio Sahitya Prokashoni, 1992).

Sobhan, Rehman. *Utal Romanthan: Purnatar Shei Bochorgulo* (Untranquil Recollections: The Years of Fulfillment) (New Delhi: SAGE Publications, 2018).

Ullah, Mahbub. *Shater Doshoker Chatro Andolon o Onyanyo Prosongo* (Dhaka: Islam Gyan Bitoroni, 2001).

Umar, Badruddin. *Ekattorer Swadhinota Juddher Pothe* (Dhaka: Jatio Sahitya Prokash, 2015).

Interviews

Mainul Hasan, Dhaka, 28 January 2020.
N. N. Tarun Chakrabarty, Montreal, 9 March 2021.
Rafiq Azad, Dhaka, 26 January 2020.
Santosh Rana, 8 May 2016.
Sirajul Islam Chowdhury, Dhaka 20 February 2020.

Books, Journal Articles and Unpublished Works

'6-Points'. *Pakistan Forum* 1, no. 4 (1971): 8–9.
Abdel-Malek, Anouar. *Nation and Revolution*, translated by Mike Gonzalez (*Social Dialectics*, vol. 2) (Albany, NY: State University of New York Press, 1981).
Abdullah, Abu. 'Land Reform and Agrarian Change in Bangladesh', *Bangladesh Development Studies* 4, no. 1 (1976): 67–114.
Abdullah, Abu, Mosharaff Hossain and Richard Nations. 'Agrarian Structure and the IRDP Preliminary Considerations'. *Bangladesh Development Studies* 4, no. 2 (1976): 209–66.
Ahmad, Kamruddin. *Labour Movement in East Pakistan* (Dacca: Progoti Publishers, 1969).
———. *A Social History of Bengal* (Dacca: Raushan Ara, 1970).
———. *Swadhin Banglar Obhyudyoy Ebong Otopor* (Dhaka: Dhrupad Sahityoangon, 2018).
Ahmad, Mohiuddin. *Jasoder Utthan O Poton Asthir Smoyer Rajniti* (Dhaka: Prothoma Prokashon, 2015).
———. *Lal Sontras Siraj Sikdar o Sorbohara Rajniti* (Dhaka: Batighar, 2021).
Ahmad, Mumtaz. 'The Muslim Family Laws Ordinance of Pakistan'. *International Journal on World Peace* 10, no. 3 (1993): 37–46.
Ahmad, Mushtaq. 'Land Rforms in Pakistan'. *Pakistan Horizon* 12, no. 1 (1959): 30–36. https://jstor.org/stable/41392253. Accessed on 4 May 2020.
Ahmad, Nafis. 'Industrial Development in East Bengal (East Pakistan)'. *Economic Geography* 26, no. 3 (1950): 183–95.
Ahmad, Tajuddin. *Tajuddin's Diary*, vol. 1, edited and translated by Simin Hossain Rimi (Dhaka: Protibhas, 2014 [1999]).
———. *Tajuddin's Diary*, vol. 2, edited and translated by Simin Hossain Rimi (Dhaka: Protibhas, 2014 [1999]).

Ahmed, Faisal, and Md Ismail Hossain. *A Study Report on Working Conditions of Tea Plantation Workers in Bangladesh* (Dhaka: ILO Country Office for Bangladesh, 2016).

Ahmed, Ishtiaq. 'The Rise and Fall of the Left and the Maoist Movements in Pakistan'. *India Quarterly* 66, no. 3 (2010): 251–65.

Ahmed, Istiaque, Khandaker Asif Mahmud and Shaila Islam. 'A Study on Historical Transformation of the Urban Integration Core of Khulna City, Bangladesh'. *International Journal of Innovation and Applied Studies* 8, no. 4 (2014): 1410–17.

Ahmed, Nazneen. 'The Poetics of Nationalism: Cultural Resistance and Poetry in East Pakistan/Bangladesh, 1952–71'. *Journal of Postcolonial Writing* 50, no. 3 (2014): 256–68.

Ahmed, Siraj Uddin. *Jatir Janak Bongobondhu* (Dhaka: Kamala Printers, 2016).

Aiyar, Sana. 'Fazlul Huq, Region and Religion in Bengal: The Forgotten Alternative of 1940–43'. *Modern Asian Studies* 42, no. 6 (2008): 1213–249. www.jstor.org/stable/20488062. Accessed on 9 July 2020.

Alam, Edris, and Dale Dominey-Howes. 'Review: A New Catalogue of Tropical Cyclones in the Northern Bay of Bengal and the Distribution and Effects of Selected Landfalling Events in Bangladesh'. *International Journal of Climatology* 35, no. 6 (2015): 801–35.

Alam, M. Shahid. 'Economics of the Landed Interests: A Case Study of Pakistan'. *Pakistan Economic and Social Review* 12, no. 1 (1974): 12–26. www.jstor.org/stable/25824782. Accessed on 4 May 2020.

Alamgir, Mohiuddin. 'Some Aspects of Bangladesh Agriculture: Review of Performance and Evaluation of Policies', *Bangladesh Development Studies* 3, no. 3 (1975): 261–300. http://www.jstor.org/stable/40794100. Accessed on 11 June 2021.

Alavi, Hamza. 'Authoritarianism and Legitimation of State Power in Pakistan'. In *The Post-Colonial State in Asia: Dialectics of Politics and Culture*, edited by Subrata Kumar Mitra, pp. 19–71 (New York: Harvester Wheatsheaf, 1990).

———. 'Class and State in Pakistan'. In *Pakistan: The Unstable State*, edited by Hasan Gardezi and Jamil Rashid, pp. 40–93 (Lahore: Vanguard, 1983).

———. 'The State in Post-Colonial Societies: Pakistan and Bangladesh'. *New Left Review* 1, no. 74 (1972): 59–81.

———. 'The State in Postcolonial Societies: Pakistan and Bangladesh'. In *Imperialism and Revolution in South Asia*, edited by Kathleen Gough and Hari P. Sharma, pp. 145–73 (New York: Monthly Review Press, 1973).

Ali, Kamran Asdar. 'Progressives and "Perverts": Partition Stories and Pakistan's Future' *Social Text* 29, no. 3 (2011): 1–29.

Ali, Murad. *The Politics of US Aid to Pakistan: Aid Allocation and Delivery from Truman to Trump* (Routledge Studies in South Asian Politics) (Abingdon, Oxon: Routledge, 2019).

Ali, Syed Azhar. 'Unicameralism in United Pakistan: Why and How?'. *Pakistan Horizon* 48, no. 3 (1995): 69–80. www.jstor.org/stable/41393529. Accessed on 8 July 2020.

Ali, Tariq. *Pakistan: Military Rule or People's Power* (New York: William Morrow and Company, 1970).

Ali, Tariq Omar. *A Local History of Global Capital: Jute and Peasant Life in the Bengal Delta* (Princeton, NJ: Princeton University Press, 2018).

———. 'Technologies of Peasant Production and Reproduction: The Post-Colonial State and Cold War Empire in Comilla, East Pakistan, 1960–70.' *South Asia: Journal of South Asian Studies* 42, no. 3 (2019): 435–51. DOI: 10.1080/00856401.2019.1590788.

Allen, B. C. 'Assam.' *Journal of the Royal Society of Arts* 75, no. 3892 (1927): 764–86.

al-Mujahid, Sharif. 'Pakistan's First Presidential Elections'. *Asian Survey* 5, no. 6 (1965): 280–94.

———. 'Pakistan: First General Elections'. *Asian Survey* 11, no. 2 (1971): 159–71.

Althusser, Louis. *For Marx* (London: Verso, 1990).

Amin, Nurul. 'The Pro-Chinese Communist Movement in Bangladesh'. *Journal of Contemporary Asia* 15, no. 3 (1985): 349–60.

Amin, Shahid. 'Gandhi as Mahatma: Gorakhpur District, Eastern UP, 1921–2'. In *Selected Subaltern Studies*, edited by Ranajit Guha and Gayatri Chakravorty Spivak, pp. 288–342 (New York: Oxford University Press, 1989).

Amjad, Rashid. 'Industrial Concentration and Economic Power'. In *Pakistan: The Roots of Dictatorship*, edited by Hassan Gardezi and Jamil Rashid, pp. 228–69 (London: Zed Press, 1983).

———. *Private Industrial Investment in Pakistan 1960–1970* (Cambridge: Cambridge University Press, 1982).

Andrus, J. Russel, and Azizali F. Mohammed. *The Economy of Pakistan* (London, Karachi and Dacca: Oxford University Press, 1958).

Arendt, Hannah. I963. *On Revolution* (New York: Viking Press, 1963).

Arnold, David. 'Famine in Peasant Consciousness and Peasant Action: Madras, 1876–8'. In *Subaltern Studies: Writings on South Asian History and Society*, vol. 3, edited by Ranajit Guha (Delhi: Oxford University Press, 1984).

Asadullah, Mohammad Niaz. 'Educational Disparity in East and West Pakistan, 1947–71: Was East Pakistan Discriminated Against?'. *Bangladesh Development Studies* 33, no. 3 (2010): 1–46.

Ayoob, Mohammed. 'Pakistan's Political Development, 1947 to 1970: Bird's Eye View'. *Economic and Political Weekly* 6, nos. 3–5 (1971): 199–204.

———. 'Profile of a Party: PPP in Pakistan'. *Economic and Political Weekly* 7, nos. 5–7 (1972): 215–19.

Azad, Humayun. 'Bhasha Andoloner Sahityik Potobhumi (Literary Background of Language Movement)', vol. 5, in *Bhasha Andoloner Artho Samajik Potobhumi (Socio-Economic Background of Language Movement)* (Combined 5 Volumes) (Dhaka: University Press Limited, 2000).

Aziz, K. K. *The Murder of History: A Critique of History Textbooks Used in Pakistan* (Delhi: Renaissance Publishing House, 1998).

Azad, Lenin. *Unosottorer Gonoobbuththan: Rastro Somaj o Rajniti* (Dhaka: Jatio Sahitya Prokash, 2019 [1997]).

Bahar, Abid S. 'The Religious and Philosophical Basis of Bhashani's Political Leadership', PhD dissertation, Concordia University, Montreal, 2003, pp. 43–45. https://spectrum.library.concordia.ca/id/eprint/2294/. Accessed on 6 August 2018.

Bajwa, Farooq. *From Kutch to Tashkent: The Indo-Pakistan War of 1965* (London: Hurst, 2013).

Balibar, Etienne. 'The Nation Form: History and Ideology'. *Review (Fernand Braudel Center)* 13, no. 3 (1990): 329–61. http://www.jstor.org/stable/40241159. Accessed on 20 April 2021.

Bandyopadhyay, Manik. *Granthaboli*, vol. 8 (Calcutta: Granthalaya, 1963).

Banerjee, Mou. 'The Tale of the Tailor: Munshi Mohammad Meherullah and Muslim–Christian Apologetics in Bengal, 1885–1907'. *South Asian Studies* 33, no. 2 (2017): 122–36.

Banerjee, Sandeep. *Space, Utopia and Indian Decolonization: Literary Pre-Figurations of the Postcolony* (Edinburgh South Asian Studies Series) (London: Routledge, 2019).

Banerjee, Sandeep, and Subho Basu. 'The City as Nation: Delhi as the Indian Nation in Bengali Bhadralok Travelogues 1866–1910'. In *Cities in South Asia*, edited by Crispin Bates and Minoru Mio, pp.125–142 (London: Routledge, 2015).

Banerjee, Sumanta. 'Bangladesh's Marxist–Leninists: I', *Economic and Political Weekly* 17, no. 32 (1982): 1267–71.

Bari, Syed Irfanul. 'Asamprodaikota o Maulana Bhashani'. In *Nanan Matray Maulana Bhashani* (Dhaka: Papyrus, 2018).

Baruah, Sanjib. *India against Itself: Assam and the Politics of Nationality* (Philadelphia: University of Pennsylvania Press, 1999).

Bass, Garry J. *The Blood Telegram: India's Secret War in East Pakistan* (New York: Random House, 2013).

Basu, Manoj. *Chin Dekhe Elam* (Dwitio Porbo). (Calcutta: Metropolitan Printing and Publishing House Limited, 1955).

Basu, Subho. *Does Class Matter? Colonial Capital and Workers' Resistance in Bengal, 1890–1937* (New Delhi: Oxford University Press, 2004).

———. 'Manufacturing Radicals: The Sino-Indian War and the Repression of Communists in India'. In *The Sino Indian War of 1962 New Perspectives 197–214*, edited by Amit R. Das Gupta and Lorenz M. Luthi, pp. 197–214 (London: Routledge, 2017).

———. 'The Dialectics of Resistance: Colonial Geography, Bengali Literati and the Racial Mapping of Indian Identity'. *Modern Asian Studies* 44, no. 1 (2010): 53–79.

Basu, Subho, and Auritro Majumder, 'Dilemmas of Parliamentary Communism'. *Critical Asian Studies* 45, no. 2 (2013): 167–200.

Baxter, Craig. 'Pakistan Votes – 1970'. *Asian Survey* 11, no. 3 (1971): 197–218.

Bertocci, Peter J. 'Community Structure and Social Rank in Two Villages in Bangladesh'. *Contributions to Indian Sociology* 6, no. 1 (1972): 28–52. DOI: 10.1177/006996677200600102.

———. 'Elusive Villages: Social Structure and Community Organization in Rural East Pakistan'. PhD thesis, Department of Anthropology, University of Michigan, 1970.

Beteille, André. 'Class Structure in an Agrarian Society: The Case of the Jotedars'. In *Studies in Agrarian Social Structure*, pp. 117–141 (Delhi: Oxford University Press, 1974).

Bhattacharjee, G. P. *Renaissance and Freedom Movement in Bangladesh* (Calcutta: Minerva Associates, 1973).

Bhattacharjee, Jayanta Bhusan. 'Genesis and Patterns of British Administration in the Hill Areas of North Eastern India'. *Proceedings of the Indian History Congress* 36 (1975): 409–30.

Bhattacharyya, Jnanabrata. 'An Examination of Leadership Entry in Bengal Peasant Revolts, 1937–1947', *Journal of Asian Studies* 37, no. 4 (1978): 611–35.

———. 'Language, Class and Community in Bengal'. *South Asia Bulletin* 7, nos. 1–2 (1987): 56–63.

Bhattacharya, Sabyasachi. *Vande Mataram: The Biography of a Song* (New Delhi: Primus Books, 2013).

Bhattacharya, Sanjay. *Propaganda and Information in Eastern India 1939–45: A Necessary Weapon of War* (Richmond, VA: Curzon Routledge, 2001).

Biswas, Sravani, and Patrick Daly. "Cyclone Not above Politics': East Pakistan, Disaster Politics, and the 1970 Bhola Cyclone'. *Modern Asian Studies* 55, no. 4 (2021): 1382–1410.

Blackwell, Stephen. 'A Desert Squall: Anglo-American planning for Military Intervention in Iraq, July 1958–August 1959'. *Middle Eastern Studies* 35, no. 3 (1999): 1–18. DOI: 10.1080/00263209908701276.

Blair, Harry W. 'Rural Development, Class Structure and Bureaucracy in Bangladesh'. *World Development* 6, no. 1 (1978): 65–82. DOI: 10.1016/0305-750X(78)90025-6.

Bloomfield, Lincoln P. 'China, the United States, and the United Nations'. *International Organization* 20, no. 4 (1966): 653–76.

Bose, Neilesh. *Recasting the Region: Language, Culture, and Islam in Colonial Bengal* (New Delhi: Oxford University Press, 2014).

Bose, Swadesh R. 'Trend of Real Income of the Rural Poor in East Pakistan, 1949–66', *Pakistan Development Review* 8, no. 3 (1968): 452–88, http://www.jstor.org.proxy3.library.mcgill.ca/stable/41981663. Accessed on 14 June 2021.

Baranov, Sergei Stepanovich. *East Bengal: Characteristics of Economic Development, 1947–1971*, translated from Russian by Tajul Islam, Abaul Barakat, Abdus Sabur, Abdul Momin, Kairul Hossain, Shoeb Ali Shikdar and Bau Naser Khan, edited by Tajul Islam (Dhaka: Jatiya Sahitya Prakashani, 1986).

Briggs, Charles L. 'The Politics of Discursive Authority in Research on the "Invention of Tradition"'. *Cultural Anthropology* 11, no. 4 (1996): 435–69.

Burki, Shahid Javed. 'Twenty Years of the Civil Service of Pakistan: A Re-evaluation'. *Asian Survey* 9, no. 4 (1969): 239–54. DOI: 10.2307/2642543.

———. 'Fall of East Pakistan: Some Economic Consequences'. *Pakistan Economic and Social Review* 10, no. 1 (1972): 9–16. http://www.jstor.org/stable/25824725. Accessed on 8 June 2021.

Casanova, Pablo Gonzalez. 'Internal Colonialism and National Development'. *Studies in Comparative International Development* 1 (1965): 27–37.

Chakrabarty, Dipesh. *Provincializing Europe: Postcolonial Thought and Historical Difference* (Princeton, NJ: Princeton University Press, 2008 [2000]).

Chatterjee, Partha. 'The Colonial State and Peasant Resistance in Bengal, 1920–1947'. *Past & Present* 11, no. 1 (1986): 169–204.

Chatterji, Joya. *Bengal Divided: Hindu Communalism and Partition, 1932–1947* (Cambridge: Cambridge University Press, 1994).

———. 'Secularisation and Partition Emergencies: Deep Diplomacy in South Asia', *Economic and Political Weekly* 48, no. 50 (2013): 42–50.

Chatterji, Kedar Nath (ed.). *The Modern Review: A Monthly Review and Miscellany*, vol. 88 (July–December 1950) (Calcutta: Modern Review Office, 1950).

Chaudhri, Mohammed Ahsen. 'Pakistan and the Muslim World'. *Pakistan Horizon* 10, no. 3 (1957): 156–66.

Chowdhry, Prem. 'Militarized Masculinities: Shaped and Reshaped in Colonial South-East Punjab'. *Modern Asian Studies* 47, no. 3 (2013): 713–50.

Chowdhury, Abdur Rauf. *Swayotto Shashon, Swadhikar o Swadhinota* (Dhaka: Kotha Prokash, 2010).

Connery, Christopher. 'The End of the Sixties', *Boundary 2* 36, no. 1 (2009): 183–210.

Constituent Assembly of India, *Population of India According to Communities Based on the 1941 Census* (Delhi: Government of India, 1947).

Costa, Thomas, and Anindita Dutta. *The Khasis of Bangladesh: A Socio-Economic Survey of the Khasi People*, edited by Philip Gain and Aneeka Malik (Dhaka: Society for Environment and Human Development [SEHD], 2007).

Crehan, Kate. *Gramsci, Culture and Anthropology* (Berkely: University of California Press, 2002).

———. *Gramsci's Common Sense: Inequality and Its Narratives* (Durham, NC: Duke University Press, 2016).

Cudjoe, Selwyn Reginald. *Resistance and Caribbean Literature* (Athens, OH: Ohio University Press, 1981).

Custers, Peter. 'Secular Democracy, Socialism and Bhasani'. *Frontier Weekly* 41, no. 11 (2008). https://www.frontierweekly.com/archive/vol-number/vol/vol-41-2008-09/vol-41-11-14%20Sep%2028-Oct%2025%202008/bhasani-41-11-14.pdf. Accessed on 15 March 2020.

Das, Debarshi, and Arupjyoti Saikia. 'Early Twentieth Century Agrarian Assam: A Brief and Preliminary Overview'. *Economic and Political Weekly* 46, no. 41 (2011): 73–80.

Dasgupta, Rajarshi. 'The People in People's Art and People's War'. In *People's Warrior: Words and Worlds of PC Joshi*, edited by Gargi Chakrabartty, pp. 443–56 (Kolkata: Tulika, 2014).

Das, Mayurakshi. 'Calcutta Cauldron: City-Life during the January 1964 Riots'. *Proceedings of the Indian History Congress* 78 (2017): 1147–54.

Dastidar, Sachi G., *Empire's Last Casualty: Indian Subcontinent's Vanishing Hindu and Other Minorities* (Kolkata: Firma KLM, 2008).

Das, Tulshi Kumar, Ritupurna Bhattacharyya and Pranjit Kumar Sarma. 'Revisiting Geographies of Nationalism and National Identity in Bangladesh'. *Geojournal* 87 (2022): 1099–1120.

David M. Laushey. *Bengal Terrorism & the Marxist Left: Aspects of Regional Nationalism in India, 1905–1942* (Calcutta: Firma K. L. Mukhopadhyay, 1975).

Debray, Regis. *Revolution in the Revolution?: Armed Struggle and Political Struggle in Latin America* (Harmondsworth, Middlesex: Penguin Books, 1968).

DeNardo, James. *Power in Numbers*. Princeton, NJ: Princeton University Press, 1985.

Devji, Faisal. *Muslim Zion: Pakistan as a Political Idea* (London: Hurst & Company, 2013).

———. 'End of the Postcolonial State'. *Economic and Political Weekly* 56, no. 44 (2021): 67–72.

Dey, Goutam Kumar. 'The Formation of Bengal Provincial Kisan Sabha and the Roll of Communist Party', *Proceedings of the Indian History Congress* 75 (2014): 623–27.

Dhanagare, D. N. 'Peasant Protest and Politics: The Tebhaga Movement in Bengal (India), 1946–47'. *Journal of Peasant Studies* 3, no. 3 (1976): 360–78.

Dixit, J. N. *India–Pakistan in War and Peace* (London: Routledge, 2002).

Dohrn, Bernardine. 'Sixties Lessons and Lore'. *Monthly Review* 53, no. 7, December 2001, p. 12.

Dorner, Peter, and William C. Thiesenhusen. 'Selected Land Reforms in East and Southeast Asia: Their Origins and Impacts'. *Asian-Pacific Economic Literature* 4, no. 1 (1990): 65–95.

Duara, Prasenjit. *Rescuing History from the Nation: Questioning Narratives of Modern China* (Chicago and London: University of Chicago Press, 1998).

Dutt, Vidya Prakash. 'China and Indo-Pakistani Relations'. *International Studies* 8, nos. 1–2 (1966): 126–33.

Dutta, Shekhar. *Shaater Doshoker Gono Jagoron: Ghotona Probaho Parjyalochona Probhab*. (Dhaka: Somaj Bikash Prokashoni, 2015).

Easterly, William. 'The Political Economy of Growth without Development: A Case Study of Pakistan'. Paper for the Analytical Narratives of Growth Project, Kennedy School of Government, Harvard University, 2001.

Egan, Daniel. 'Rethinking War of Maneuver/War of Position: Gramsci and the Military Metaphor'. *Critical Sociology*, 40, no. 4 (2014): 521–38.

Esack, Farid. *Qur'an, Liberation and Pluralism: An Islamic Perspective of Interreligious Solidarity against Oppression* (Oxford: Oneworld Publications, 1997).

Falcon, Walter P., and Gustav F. Papanek (eds.). Development Policy: The Pakistan Experience, vol. 2 (Cambridge, MA: Harvard University Press, 1971).

Fanon, Frantz, and Adolfo Gilly. *A Dying Colonialism*, translated by Haakon Chevalier (New York: Grove Press, 1967).

Fanon, Frantz, and Anthony Appiah. *Black Skin, White Masks*, translated by Richard Philcox (New York: Grove Press, 2008 [1952]).

Fanon, Frantz. *The Wretched of the Earth*, translated by Constance Farrington (London: Grove Press, 1968 [1961]).

———. *Toward the African Revolution: Political Essays*, translated by Haakon Chevalier (New York: Monthly Review Press, 1967).

Farhad, Mohammad. *Unoshottorer Gonoobuththan* (Mass Uprising of 1969) (Dhaka: Jatio Sahityo Prokashoni, 2019).

Faruqi, Shamsur Rahman. 'A Long History of Urdu Literary Culture'. In *Literary Cultures in History: Reconstructions from South Asia*, edited by Sheldon Pollock, part-i.î (Berkeley: University of California Press, 2003).

Feldman, Herbert, 2016. *From Crisis to Crisis: Pakistan 1962–1969* (London: Oxford University Press, 1972).

Førland, Tor Egil. 'Cutting the Sixties Down to Size: Conceptualizing, Historicizing, Explaining'. *Journal for the Study of Radicalism* 9, no. 2 (2015): 125–48.

France, Mireille Fanon-Mendès, and Donato Fhunsu. 'The Contribution of Frantz Fanon to the Process of the Liberation of the People'. *Black Scholar* 42, nos. 3–4 (2012): 8–12.

Franda, Marcus F. 'Communism and Regional Politics in East Pakistan'. *Asian Survey* 10, no. 7 (1970): 588–606.

Friedman, Harry J. 'Notes on Pakistan's Basic Democracies'. *Asian Survey* 1, no. 10 (1961): 19–24.

Friedman, Jeremy Scott. 'Reviving Revolution: The Sino-Soviet Split, the "Third World," and the Fate of the Left'. vol. I, PhD Thesis, Department of History, Princeton University, Princeton, NJ, 2011, pp. 4–6.

Gankovsky, Yu V., and L. R. Gordon-Polonskaya. *A History of Pakistan, 1947–1958* (Lahore: People's Publishing House, 1972).

Gardezi, Hassan N., and Soofia Mumtaz. 'Globalisation and Pakistan's Dilemma of Development [with Comments]'. *Pakistan Development Review* 43, no. 4

(2004): 423–40. http://www.jstor.org/stable/41260697. Accessed on 4 June 2021.

Gasiorowski, Mark J. 'U.S. Perceptions of the Communist Threat in Iran during the Mossadegh Era'. *Journal of Cold War Studies* 2, no. 3 (2019): 185–221.

Gassah, L.S. 'Trade Routes and Trade Relations between Jayantia Hills and Sylhet District in the Pre-Independence Period'. In *Proceedings of North East India History Association*, 9th session, Gauhati University, Guwahati, 1988, pp. 202–08 (Shillong: North East India History Association, Department of History, North-Eastern Hill University, 1988).

Gauhar, Altaf. 1985. 'Pakistan: Ayub Khan's Abdication'. *Third World Quarterly* 7, no. 1 (1985): 102–31.

———. *Ayub Khan: Pakistan's First Military Ruler* (New York: Oxford University Press, 1996).

Geertz, Clifford. 'Form and Variation in Balinese Village Structure'. *American Anthropologist* 61, no. 6 (1959): 991–1012.

Ghosh, Amitav. *The Glass Palace* (New York: Random House, 2001).

Ghosh, Anindita. 'Valorising the "Vulgar": Nationalist Appropriations of Colloquial Bengali Traditions, c. 1870–1905'. *Indian Economic & Social History Review* 37, no. 2 (2000): 151–83.

Ghosh, Subhasri. 'The Working of the Neheru Liaqat Pact: A Case Study of Nadia District, 1950'. *Proceedings of the Indian History Congress* 68, no. 1 (2007): 853–62.

Ghosh, Rajani. *Bhugol Vidyasar (Core of Geographic Knowledge): Containing a General Account of Asia, Europe, Africa, America and Oceania, A Detail of India, Great Britain, Ireland and a Particular Description of Bengal Especially, with an Appendix of Ancient Names of the Countries and Towns and Compiled from Recent Authorities* (Kati Para, Jessore: Rajcumar Ghosh, 1871).

Ghosh, Shyamali. *Awami League 1949–1971*, translated by Habib ul-Alam (Dhaka: University Press Limited, 2007).

Ghoshal, Anindita. 'The Invisible Refuges: Muslim "Returnees" in East Pakistan, 1947–1971'. *Journal of the Asiatic Society of Bangladesh (Humanities)* 63, no. 1 (2018): 59–89.

Glassie, Henry, and Feroz Mahmud. *Living Traditions* (Cultural Survey of Bangladesh Series, vol. 11) (Dhaka: Asiatic Society of Bangladesh, 2008).

Gottschalk, Peter. *Religion, Science, and Empire: Classifying Hinduism and Islam in British India* (New York: Oxford University Press, 2013).

Gramsci, Antonio. 'Note 18: History of the Subaltern Classes'. In *Quaderni del Cacere* (Prison Notebooks), vol. 3, edited by V. Gerratana (Turin: Giulio Einaudi Editore, 1975).

———. *Selections from the Prison Notebooks* of Antonio Gramsci, edited and translated by G. Nowell (New York: International Publishers, 1971).

Greenough, Paul R. *Prosperity and Misery in Modern Bengal: The Famine of 1943–1944* (Oxford: Oxford University Press, 1982).

Guevera, Che, and David Deutschmann. *Che Guevara Reader: Writings by Ernesto Che Guevara on Guerrilla Strategy, Politics & Revolution* (Melbourne: Ocean Press, 1997).

Guha, Amalendu. 'East Bengal Immigrants and Maulana Abdul Hamid Khan Bhasani in Assam Politics, 1928–47'. *Indian Economic and Social History Review* 13, no. 4 (1976): 419–52.

Guha, Ranajit. *Dominance without Hegemony: History and Power in Colonial India* (Cambridge, MA: Harvard University Press, 1997).

Guhathakurta, Meghna. 'Sonar Bangla: Inspiration, Illusion and extortion'. *Humboldt Journal of Social Relations* 23, nos. 1/2 (1997): 197–217.

Gunn, Christopher. 'The 1960 Coup in Turkey: A U.S. Intelligence Failure or a Successful Intervention?'. *Journal of Cold War Studies* 17, no. 2 (2015): 103–39.

Hanifa, Abu Md Noman, Md Aslam Mia, Hasanul Banna, Md Sohel Rana, A. S. A. Ferdous Alam, Chan Sok Gee, Che Ruhana Isa and A. C. Er. 'City Profile: Narayanganj, Bangladesh', *Cities* 59 (November 2016): 8–19.

Hannan, Mohammad. *Bangladesher Chatro Andoloner Itihas, 1830–1971* (Dhaka: Agami Prokashoni, 2013).

Haque, Abu Saeed Zahurul. 'The Use of Folklore in Nationalist Movements and Liberation Struggles: A Case Study of Bangladesh'. *Journal of the Folklore Institute* 12, nos. 2–3 (1975): 211–40. DOI: 10.2307/3813927.

Haque, Muhammed Shahriar. 'Early Life of an Accidental Actor: Before Nayak Raj Razzak'. *East West Journal of Humanities* (Special Issue) 6–7 (2016–17): 121–36.

Harlow, Barbara. *Resistance Literature* (New York: Methuen, 1987).

Hasan, Morshed Safiul. *Swadhinotar Potobhumi:1960r Doshok* (Dhaka: Anupom Prokashoni, 2014).

Hasan, Morshed Safiul, 2017. *Purbo Banglay Chinta Chorcha 1940–70: Dwondwo o Potikria* (Dhaka: Anupom Prokashoni, 2017).

Hasan, Parvez. 'Balance of Payments Problems of Pakistan'. *Pakistan Development Review* 1, no. 2 (1961): 15–48. www.jstor.org/stable/41258033. Accessed on 9 July 2020.

Hasan, Zubeida. 'Pakistan's Relations with the U.S.S.R. in the 1960s'. *World Today* 25, no. 1 (1969): 26–35.

Hashmi, Bilal, 'Dragon Seeds: Military in the State'. In *Pakistan, the Roots of Dictatorship: The Political Economy of Praetorian State*, edited by Hassan Nawaz Gardezi and Jamil Rashid, pp. 148–58 (London: Zed Press, 1983).

Hashmi, Sohail H. '"Zero Plus Zero Plus Zero": Pakistan, the Baghdad Pact, and the Suez Crisis'. *International History Review* 33, no. 3 (2011): 525–44. www.jstor.org/stable/23033197. Accessed on 6 June 2020.

Hashmi, Taj ul-Islam. *Pakistan as a Peasant Utopia: The Communalization of Class Politics in East Bengal, 1920–1947* (Boulder, CO: Westview, 1992).

Hebbert, Michael. 'The Street as Locus of Collective Memory'. *Environment and Planning D: Society and Space* 23, no. 4 (August 2005): 581–96.

Hendrickson, Burleigh. 2012. 'March 1968: Practicing Transnational Activism from Tunis to Paris'. *International Journal of Middle East Studies* 44, no. 4 (2012): 755–74.

Herring, Ronald, and M. Ghaffar Chaudhry. 'The 1972 Land Reforms in Pakistan and Their Economic Implications: A Preliminary Analysis'. *Pakistan Development Review* 13, no. 3 (1974): 245–79. www.jstor.org/stable/41258246. Accessed on 4 May 2020.

Hobsbawm, E. J., and Terence Ranger (eds). *The Invention of Tradition* (Cambridge: Cambridge University Press, 1983).

Hoek, Lotte. 'Cross-Wing Filmmaking: East Pakistani Urdu Films and Their Traces in the Bangladesh Film Archive'. *BioScope: South Asian Screen Studies* 5, no. 2 (2014): 99–118.

———. 'Urdu for Image: Understanding Bangladeshi Cinema Through Its Theaters'. In *South Asian Media Cultures: Audiences, Representations, Contexts* (Anthem South Asian Studies), edited by Shakuntala Banaji, pp. 73–90 (London: Anthem Press, 2010).

Hoodbhoy, Pervez. 'Jinnah and the Islamic State: Setting the Record Straight'. *Economic and Political Weekly* 42, no. 32 (2007): 3300–03.

Horowitz, Andrew W. 'Time Paths of Land Reform: A Theoretical Model of Reform Dynamics'. *American Economic Review* 83, no. 4 (1993): 1003–10. https://jstor.org/stable/2117592. Accessed on 17 May 2020.

Huntington, Samuel P. *Political Order in Changing Societies* (New Haven: Yale University Press, 2006).

Huq, Sabiha. 'A Liminal Bengali Identity: Film Culture in Bangladesh', in *Media Culture in Transnational Asia: Convergences and Divergences*, edited by Hyesu Park, pp. 162–80 (Rutgers: Rutgers University Press, 2020).

Huq, Sabiha, and Srideep Mukherjee. 'Guns in Bangla Cinema across Borders: Perspectives on Cultural Evolution'. *Palgrave Communications* 6, no. 1 (2020): 1–12. https://www.nature.com/articles/s41599-019-0379-6. Accessed on 28 April 2021.

Ikramullah, Shaista Suhrawardy. 1991. *Huseyn Shaheed Suhrawardy: A Biography* (Karachi: Oxford University Press, 1991).

Ishaque, A. H. M. *Agricultural Statistics by Plot-to-Plot Enumeration in Bengal 1944–45* (Calcutta: Department of Agriculture, Forest and Fisheries, Government of Bengal).

Islam, G. M. R., M. Iqbal, K. G. Quddus and M. Y. Ali. 'Present Status and Future Needs of Tea Industry in Bangladesh'. *Proceedings: Pakistan Academy of Sciences* 42, no. 4 (2005): 305–14.

Islam, Mozaharul. *Bongo Bondhu Sheikh Mujib* (Dacca: Bangla Academy, 1974).

Islam, Rafiqul. 'The Bengali Language Movement and the Emergence of Bangladesh'. *Contributions to Asian Studies* 11 (1978): 145–46. https://proxy.library.mcgill.ca/login?url=https://www-proquest-com.proxy3.library.mcgill.ca/scholarly-journals/bengali-language-movement-emergence-bangladesh/docview/1307833941/se-2?accountid=12339. Accessed on 12 February 2020.

Islam, Sirajul, and Ahmed A. Jamal (eds.), *Banglapedia: National Encyclopedia of Bangladesh* (Dhaka: Asiatic Society of Bangladesh, 2012 [2003]).

Jalal, Ayesha. 'Towards the Baghdad Pact: South Asia and Middle East Defence in the Cold War, 1947–1955'. *International History Review* 11, no. 3 (1989): 409–33.

———. *The State of Martial Rule: The Origins of Pakistan's Political Economy of Defence* (Cambridge South Asian Studies) (Cambridge: Cambridge University Press, 1990).

Jameson, Fredric. 'Periodizing the 60s', *Social Text* 9, no. 10 (1984): 178–209.

Jannuzi, F. Tomasson, and James T. Peach. 'Note on Land Reform in Bangladesh: The Efficacy of Ceilings'. *Journal of Peasant Studies* 6, no. 3 (1979): 342–47.

Jessop, Bob. 'Gramsci as a Spatial Theorist', *Critical Review of International Social and Political Philosophy* 8, no. 4 (2005): 421–37.

Joseph, Gilbert M. 'What We Now Know and Should Know: Bringing Latin America More Meaningfully into Cold War Studies'. In *In from the Cold: Latin America's New Encounter with the Cold War*, pp. 3–46 (Durham, NC: Duke University Press, 2008).

Harun-or-Rashid. *Mul Dharar Rajniti: Bangladesh Awami League Council 1949–2016* (Dhaka: Bangla Academy, 2019).

———. *The Foreshadowing of Bangladesh: Bengal Muslim League and Muslim Politics, 1936–1947* (Dhaka: Asiatic Society of Bangladesh, 1987).

Kabir, Alamgir. *Cholochitro o Jatio Mukti: Rochona Songroho* (Films and National Emacipation: Collected Works) (Dhaka: Agami Prokashoni, 2018).

Kabir, Nurul. *Deposing of a Dictator Revisiting a Magnificient Mass Uprising after 50 Years* (Dhaka: Samhati Publications, 2020).

Kaderi, Baitullah. *Shater Doshoker Kobita Bishoy o Prokoron* (Poems of the 1960s: Subject and Structure) (Dhaka: Nobojug Prokashoni, 2009).

Kadri, Shahid. *Tomake Obhibadon Priotoma* (Salute to You, My Darling) (Dacca: Progoti Prakashoni, 1974).

Kamal, Ahmed. *State against the Nation: The Decline of the Muslim League in Pre-Independence Bangladesh 1947–54* (Dhaka: University Press Limited, 2009).

Kamal, Mesbah. *Unosottorer Gonoobbuththan: Shahid Asad o Shreni Rajniti Prosonge* (Dhaka: Shrabon Prokashoni, 2006).

Kamran, Tahir. 'Early Phase of Electoral Politics in Pakistan: 1950s'. *South Asia: Journal of South Asian Studies* 24, no. 2 (July–December 2009): 257–82.

———. 'Punjab, Punjabi and Urdu the Question of Displaced Identity: A Historical Appraisal'. *Journal of Punjab Studies* 14, no. 1 (2008): 11–25.

Kanet, Roger E. 'The Rise and Fall of the "All-people's State": Recent Changes in the Soviet Theory of the State'. *Soviet Studies* 20, no. 1 (1968): 81–93.

Kanth, Idrees. 'The Social and Political Life of a Relic: The Episode of the Moi-e-Muqaddas Theft in Kashmir, 1963–1964'. *Himalaya: The Journal of the Association for Nepal and Himalayan Studies* 38, no. 2 (Article 10, 2018): 61–75.

Katsiaficas, George. *The Imagination of the New Left: A Global Analysis of 1968* (Boston, MA: South End Press, 1987).

Kaur, Rajender. 'The Vexed Question of Peasant Passivity: Nationalist Discourse and the Debate on Peasant Resistance in Literary Representations of the Bengal Famine of 1943'. *Journal of Postcolonial Writing* 50, no. 3 (2014): 269–81.

Kaushik, Susheela. 'Constitution of Pakistan at Work'. *Asian Survey* 3, no. 8 (1963): 384–89. DOI: 10.2307/3023649.

Kautsky, John H. 'Indian Communist Party Strategy since 1947', *Pacific Affairs* 28, no. 2 (1955): 145–60.

Kay, Cristóbal. 'Why East Asia Overtook Latin America: Agrarian Reform, Industrialisation and Development'. *Third World Quarterly* 23, no. 6 (2002): 1073–102. https://jstor.org/stable/3993564. Accessed on 13 May 2020.

Kazi, Aref Ahmed. *Nucleus, BLF, Swadhinota: Bangalir Jatio Rastro* (Dhaka: Ankur Prokashoni, 2014).

Kazi, Aref Ahmed, Abdur Rajjak and Serajul Alam Khan. *Bangalir Jatio Rastro* (Dhaka: Ankur Prokashoni, 2014).

Khan, Azizur Rahman. 'What Has Been Happening to Real Wages in Pakistan?', *Pakistan Development Review* 7, no. 3 (1967): 317–47.

Khan, Hafeez-ur-Rahman. 'Pakistan's Relations with the U.A.R.'. *Pakistan Horizon* 13, no. 3 (1960): 209–26. www.jstor.org/stable/41392373. Accessed on 4 July 2020.

Khan, Imran, and Karim Haider Syed. 'Constitutionalism in Pakistan: The Yahiya Khan Interregnum'. *Pakistan Language and Humanities Review* 5, no. 2 (2021): 1–14.

Khan, M. H. *The Role of Agriculture in Economic Development: A Case Study of Pakistan* (Wageningen: Centre for Agricultural Publications and Documentation, 1966).

Khan, Muhammad Fahim. 'The Life and Times of Ḥaji Sahib of Turangzai'. *Islamic Studies* 16, no. 1 (1977): 329–41.

Khan, M. Mahmud. 'Labour Absorption and Unemployment in Rural Bangladesh', *Bangladesh Development Studies* 13, nos. 3–4 (1985): 67–88. http://www.jstor.org/stable/40775791. Accessed on 14 June 2021.

Khan, Mushtaq. 'The Political Economy of Industrial Policy in Pakistan 1947–1971'. Working Paper No. 98, Department of Economics, SOAS, University of London. https://eprints.soas.ac.uk/9867/1/Industrial_Policy_in_Pakistan.pdf. Accessed on 12 January 2020.

Khan, Rafique Ullah. *Bangladesher Uponyas ebong Shilporup* (Dhaka: Bangla Academy, 1997).

Khan, Serajul Alam. *Swadhinata -Sososhtro Songram ebong Agamir Bangladesh* (Dhaka: Ankur Prokashoni, 2019).

Khan, Zillur R. 'Leadership and Political Opposition in Bangladesh', *Asian Affairs* 5, no. 1 (1974): 41–50.

King, Christopher. 'The Hindi–Urdu Controversy of the North-Western Provinces and Oudh and Communal Consciousness'. *Journal of South Asian Literature* 13, nos. 1–4 (1977–78): 111–20.

King, Robert D. 'The Poisonous Potency of Script: Hindi and Urdu'. *International Journal of the Sociology of Language* 150 (2001): 43–59.

Kling, Blair B. *Partner in Empire: Dwarkanath Tagore and the Age of Enterprise in Eastern India* (Berkeley: University of California Press, 1976).

Kokab, Rizwan Ullah, and Mahboob Hussain. 'National Integration of Pakistan: An Assessment of Political Leadership of Huseyn Shaheed Suhrawardy'. *Journal of Political Studies* 24, no. 1 (2017): 315–31.

Krapfl, James. *Revolution with a Human Face: Politics, Culture, and Community in Czechoslovakia, 1989–1992* (Ithaca, NY: Cornell University Press, 2016).

Kumar, B. B. 'The Border Trade in North-East India: The Historical Perspective'. In *Border Trade: North-East India and Neighbouring Countries*, edited by Gurudas Das and R. K. Purkayastha, pp. 3–11 (New Delhi: Akansha Publishing, 2000).

Kumarasingham, H. 'A Transnational Actor on a Dramatic Stage: Sir Ivor Jennings and the Manipulation of Westminster Style Democracy in Pakistan.' In *Constitution-Making and Transnational Legal Order* (Comparative Constitutional Law and Policy Series), edited by Gregory Shaffer, Tom Ginsburg and Terence C. Halliday, pp. 55–84 (Cambridge: Cambridge University Press, 2019).

Laclau, Ernesto. *On Populist Reason* (London: Verso, 2005).

Lambert, Richard D. 'Factors in Bengali Regionalism in Pakistan', *Far Eastern Survey* 28, no. 4 (1959): 49–58. DOI: 10.2307/3024111.

Law-Smith, Auriol. 'Response and Responsibility: The Government of India's Role in the Bengal Famine, 1943'. *South Asia: Journal of South Asian Studies* 12, no. 1 (1989): 49–65.

Lazarus, Neil. 'Disavowing Decolonization: Fanon, Nationalism, and the Problematic of Representation in Current Theories of Colonial Discourse', *Research in African Literatures* 24, no. 4 (1993): 69–98. https://jstor.org/stable/3820255. Accessed on 28 April 2020.

Leffler, Melvyn P. 'The American Conception of National Security and the Beginnings of the Cold War, 1945–48'. *American Historical Review* 89, no. 2 (April 1984): 346–81.

Lelyveld, David. 'The Fate of Hindustani: Colonial Knowledge and the Project of a National Language'. In *Orientalism and the Postcolonial Predicament: Perspectives on South Asia*, edited by Carol A. Breckenridge and Peter van der Veer, pp. 189–214 (Philadelphia: University of Pennsylvania Press, 1993).

Lenin, Nuh ul-Alam. *Bangladesh Awami League Songkhipto Itihas o Nirbachito Dolil Dolil* (Bangladesh Awami League: A Short History and Selected Documents) (Dhaka: Somoy Prokashon, 2015).

Lerner, Daniel. Lucille W. Pevsner and David Riesman. *The Passing of Traditional Society: Modernizing the Middle East* (New York: The Free Press, 1964).

Lerski, George. J. 'The Foreign Policy of Ayub Khan'. *Asian Affairs* 1, no. 4 (1974): 255–73.

Lewis, Stephen R. *Economic Policy and Industrial Growth in Pakistan* (London: Allen & Unwin, 1969).

Li, Xing. 'The Chinese Cultural Revolution Revisited'. *China Review* 1, no. 1 (2001): 137–65.

Lifschultz, Lawrence, and Kai Bird. *Bangladesh: The Unfinished Revolution* (Asia Series, vol. 2) (London: Zed Press, 1979).

Luthi, Lorenz M. *The Sino-Soviet Split: Cold War in the Communist World* (Princeton Studies in International History and Politics) (Princeton, NJ: Princeton University Press, 2008).

MacLennan, Hugh. *Two Solitudes*, edited by Michael Gnarowski (Montreal: McGill-Queen's University Press, 2018).

Mahmud, Tayyab. 'Praetorianism and Common Law in Post-Colonial Settings: Judicial Responses to Constitutional Breakdowns in Pakistan'. *Utah Law Review* 4 (1993): 1225–305.

Majumder, Auritro. *Insurgent Imaginations: World Literature and the Periphery* (Cambridge: Cambridge University Press, 2020).

Maksud, Syed Abul. *Maulana Abdul Hamid Khan Bhasani* (Dhaka: Agami Prokashoni, 2014).

Malik, Hafeez. 'The Marxist Literary Movement in India and Pakistan'. *Journal of Asian Studies* 26, no. 4 (1967): 649–64. DOI: 10.2307/205124.

Moniruzzaman, Talukder. 'Group Interests in Pakistan Politics, 1947–1958'. *Pacific Affairs* 39, nos. 1–2 (1966): 83–98.

———. 'Bangladesh: An Unfinished Revolution?'. *Journal of Asian Studies* 34, no 4 (1975): 891–911.

Mann, Michael. *The Dark Side of Democracy: Explaining Ethnic Cleansing* (New York: Cambridge University Press, 2005).

Marku, Ylber. 'Communist Relations in Crisis: The End of Soviet–Albanian Relations, and the Sino-Soviet Split, 1960–1961'. *International History Review* 42, no. 4 (2020): 813–32.

Maron, Stanley. 'The Problem of East Pakistan', *Pacific Affairs* 28, no. 2 (1955): 132–44.

Marwick, Arthur. 'The Cultural Revolution of the Long Sixties: Voices of Reaction, Protest, and Permeation'. *International History Review* 27, no. 4 (2005): 780–806.

Marx, Karl. 'Contribution to the Critique of Hegel's Philosophy of Right'. In *Early Writings*, p. 244 (New York: Vintage, 1974).

———. Chapter1'. In *The Eighteenth Brumaire of Louis Bonaparte* (Moscow: Progress Publishers, 1937 [1852]). https://www.marxists.org/archive/marx/works/1852/18th-brumaire/ch01.htm. Accessed on 20 February 2021.

Mason, Edward S. 'Economic Development of India and Pakistan', Occasional Paper No. 13, Harvard Center for International Affairs, Harvard University, Cambridge, MA, September 1966.

Mazumder, Rajit K. *The Indian Army and the Making of Punjab* (New Delhi: Permanent Black, 2003).

McGarr, Paul M. *The Cold War in South Asia: Britain, the United States and the Indian Subcontinent, 1945–1965* (Cambridge: Cambridge University Press, 2013).

McMahon, Robert J. 'United States Cold War Strategy in South Asia: Making a Military Commitment to Pakistan, 1947–1954'. *Journal of American History* 75, no. 3 (1988): 812–40.

McPherson, Kenneth. *The Muslim Microcosm, Calcutta, 1918 to 1935* (Beitrage Zur Sudasienforschung, vol. 8) (Wiesbaden: Steiner, 1974).

Mellema, R. L. 'The Basic Democracies System in Pakistan', *Asian Survey* 1, no. 6 (1961): 10–15.

Metcalf, Barbara. 'The Madrasa at Deoband: A Model for Religious Education in Modern India'. *Modern Asian Studies* 12, no. 1 (1978): 111–34.

Misra, Udayon. 'Immigration and Identity Transformation in Assam', *Economic and Political Weekly* 34, no. 21 (1999): 1264–71.

Misztal, Barbara A., 'Durkheim on Collective Memory'. *Journal of Classical Sociology* 3, no. 2 (2003): 123–43.

Mitra, Asok. *Census of India, 1951: District Census Handbook* (Delhi: Manager of Publications, Government of India, 1953).

Mitra, Priti Kumar. *The Dissent of Kazi Nazrul Islam: Poetry and History* (New Delhi: Oxford University Press, 2007).

———. 'Bangladesher Mukti Songramer Itihas 1958–1966'. In *Bangladesher Mukti Sangramer Itihas 1947–1971*, edited by Salahuddin Ahmad, Monem Sarkar and Nurul Islam Monjur, pp. 82–150 (Dhaka: Agami Prokashoni, 2013).

Mohiuddin, Md. 'Film Business in Bangladesh: A Historical Account'. *Journal of Humanities and Social Science* 19, no. 1 (2014): 33–36.

Mookherjee, Nayanika. 'The Aesthetics of Nations: Anthropological and Historical Approaches', *Journal of the Royal Anthropological Institute* 17, no. 1 (2011): S1–S20.

———. 'Gendered Embodiments: Mapping the Body-Politic of the Raped Woman and the Nation in Bangladesh'. *Feminist Review* 88, no. 1 (2008): 36–53.

———. *The Spectral Wound: Sexual Violence, Public Memories and the Bangladesh War of 1971* (Durham, NC: Duke University Press, 2015).

Mosely, Philip E. 'Soviet Policy in the Developing Countries'. *Foreign Affairs* 43, no. 1 (1964): 87–98.

Moten, Abdul Rashid. 'Mawdudi and the Transformation of Jamaat-e-Islami in Pakistan'. *Muslim World* 93, no. 3 (2003): 391–413.

Mufti, Aamir R. *Enlightenment in the Colony: The Jewish Question and the Crisis of Postcolonial Culture* (Princeton, NJ: Princeton University Press, 2007).

Muhith, Abul Maal Abdul. *Bangladesh: Jatirastrer Udbhob* (Bangladesh: Emergence of a Nation State) (Dhaka: Sahitya Prokash, 2017).

Mukherjee, Projit Bihari. 'Technospatial Imaginaries: Masud Rana and the Vernacularization of Popular Cold War Geopolitics in East Pakistan, 1966–1971'. *History and Technology* 31, no. 3 (2015): 324–40.

Mukherji, I. N. 'Agrarian Reforms in Bangladesh', *Asian Survey* 16, no. 5 (1976): 452–64.

Mukhopadhyay, Kali Prasad. *Partition, Bengal and After: The Great Tragedy of India* (New Delhi: Reference Press, 2007).

Mukhopadhaya, Subhas. *Nirbachita Nazim Hikmet* (Calcutta: Nazim Hikmet er Kibitz Eagle Publishing Company, 1952).

———. *Nazem Hikmet er Aro Kobita* (Calcutta: Viswabani, 1974).

Mukul, M. R. Akhtar. *Ponchaser Doshoker Rajniti o Sheikh Mujib* (Dhaka: Bikash Mudron, 2011).

Muniruzzaman, A. N. M. *The Living and Working Conditions of Students of the University and Colleges of Dacca 1957* (Dacca: University of Dhaka, 1961).

Murshid, Ghulam. 'Indian Sub-Continent: Bangladesh: Modern Bangladeshi Writing'. *Wasafiri* 10, no. 21 (1995): 66–69.

Newbold, Thomas. 'Beyond the Break with the Past: Reckoning with Literary Pakistanism in East Bengal'. *Economic and Political Weekly* 56, no. 44 (2021): 60–66.

Newman, Karl J., Heinz, Pankalla, and Robert Krumbein-Neumann. *Pakistan under Ayub Khan, Bhutto and Zia-Ul-Haq* (München: Weltforum Verlag, 1986).

Nimni, Ephraim. 'Marx, Engels and the National Question'. *Science & Society* 53, no. 3 (1989): 297–326.

Noman, Omar. *The Political Economy of Pakistan 1947–85* (London: KPI Limited, 1988).

Palmer, Norman D. *South Asia and United States Policy* (Boston, MA: Houghton Mifflin, 1966).

Pandey, Gyanendra. *The Construction of Communalism in Colonial North India* (New Delhi: Oxford University Press, 2006 [1990]).

Panjabi, Kavita. '"Otiter Jed" or Times of Revolution: Ila Mitra, the Santals and Tebhaga Movement'. *Economic and Political Weekly* 45, no. 33 (2010): 53–59.

Papanek, Gustav F. 'Squeezing the Peasant'. In *Pakistan's Development: Social Goals and Private Incentives*, pp. 184–225 (Karachi: Oxford University Press, 1968).

Park, Richard L. 'East Bengal: Pakistan's Troubled Province', *Far Eastern Survey* 23, no. 5 (1954): 70–74.

Park, Richard L., and Richard S. Wheeler, 'East Bengal under Governor's Rule', *Far Eastern Survey* 23, no. 9 (1954): 129–34.

Patnaik, Arun K. 'Gramsci's Concept of Common Sense: Towards a Theory of Subaltern Consciousness in Hegemony Processes'. *Economic and Political Weekly* 23, no. 5 (January 1988): PE2–PE5, PE7–PE10.

Porath, Yehoshua. 'Nuri al-Sa'id's Arab Unity Programme'. *Middle Eastern Studies* 20, no. 4 (1984): 76–98. DOI: 10.1080/00263208408700600.

Prashad, Vijay. *The Darker Nations: A People's History of the Third World* (New York: New Press, 2007).

Pringsheim, Klaus H. 'China's Role in the Indo-Pakistani Conflict'. *China Quarterly* 24, no. 24 (1965): 170–75.

Quadir, S. A., *Village Dhaniswar: Three Generations of Man-Made Adjustment in East Pakistan Village* (Comilla: Pakistan Academy for Village Development, 1960).

Qureshi, Saleem M. M. 'Party Politics in the Second Republic of Pakistan'. *Middle East Journal* 20, no. 4 (1966): 456–72. http://www.jstor.org/stable/4324059. Accessed on 22 August 2021.

Raghavan, Pallavi. 'The Making of the India–Pakistan Dynamic: Nehru, Liaquat, and the No War Pact Correspondence of 1950', *Modern Asian Studies* 50, no. 5 (2016): 645–78.

Raghavan, Srinath. *1971: A Global History of the Creation of Bangladesh* (Cambridge, MA: Harvard University Press, 2013).

Rahman, Hasan Hafizur (ed.). *History of Bangladesh War of Independence Documents*, vol. 1. (Dhaka: Government of Bangladesh, 1982).

———. *Bangladesher Swadhinota Juddho, Dolilpotro* (Dwitio Khondo) (Dhaka: Government of Bangladesh, 1985).

Rahman, Matiur. 'Che Ek Kinbdonti Purush' (Che a Legenda). *Kali o Kolom*, 22 August 2016. https://www.kaliokalam.com/%E0%A6%9A%E0%A7%87-%E0%A6%8F%E0%A6%95-%E0%A6%95%E0%A6%BF%E0%A6%82%E

0%A6%AC%E0%A6%A6%E0%A6%A8%E0%A7%8D%E0%A6%A4%E0%A6%BF-%E0%A6%AA%E0%A7%81%E0%A6%B0%E0%A7%81%E0%A6%B7. Accessed on 21 May 2022.

Raju, Zakir Hossain. *Bangladesh Cinema and National Identity: In Search of the Modern?* (Routledge Contemporary South Asia Series) (London: Routledge, 2015).

Ramaswamy, Sumathi. *The Goddess and the Nation: Mapping Mother India* (Durham, NC: Duke University Press, 2010).

Rasel, Azizul. 'Experiencing the Border: The Lushai People and Transnational Space'. In *Borders and Mobility in South Asia and Beyond*, edited by Reece Jones and Md. Azmeary Ferdoush, pp. 81–97 (Amsterdam: Amsterdam University Press, 2018).

Rashed, Mohammad Emdadur. 'The Emergence and Development of Academic Fine Arts: Perspective Bangladesh'. *Thespian Magazine* 4, no. 1 (September–October 2016): 34–39.

Rashid, Jamil. 'Pakistan in a Debt Trap'. In *Pakistan: The Roots of Dictatorship: The Political Economy of Praetorian State*, edited by Hasssan N. Gardezi and Jamil Rashid, pp. 173–91 (London: Zed Press, 1983).

Rashid, Jamil, and Hassan N. Gardezi. 'Independent Pakistan: Its Political Economy'. In *Pakistan, the Roots of Dictatorship: The Political Economy of Praetorian State*, edited by Hassan N. Gardezi and Jamil Rashid, pp. 4–11 (London: Zed Press, 1983).

Rashiduzzaman, M. *Politics and Administration in the Local Councils: A Study of Union and District Councils in East Pakistan* (London and Karachi: Oxford University Press, 1968).

———. 'The National Assembly of Pakistan under the 1962 Constitution'. *Pacific Affairs* 42, no. 4 (1969): 481–93.

———. 'The National Awami Party of Pakistan: Leftist Politics in Crisis', *Pacific Affairs* 43, no. 3 (1970): 394–409.

———. 'The Awami League in the Political Development of Pakistan', *Asian Survey* 10, no. 7 (1970): 574–87.

Rasul, Muhammad Abdullah. *Krishak Sabhar Itihas* (Calcutta: Nobojatok Prakashan, 1969).

Raychaudhury, Anasua Basu. 'Nostalgia of "Desh", Memories of Partition', *Economic and Political Weekly* 39, no. 52 (2004): 5653–660.

Ray, Rajat K. 'Masses in Politics: The Non-Cooperation Movement in Bengal 1920–1922'. *Indian Economic & Social History Review* 11, no. 4 (1974): 343–410. DOI: 10.1177/001946467401100401.

Razi, G. Hossein. 'Legitimacy, Religion, and Nationalism in the Middle East'. *The American Political Science Review* 84, no. 1 (1990): 69–91.

Rizwan, Muhammad. 'The Elections 1970: From Ballot to Nowhere'. *Asian Journal of Social Sciences and Humanities* 3, no. 4 (2014): 28–36.

Robinson, Warren C. '"Disguised" Unemployment Once Again: East Pakistan, 1951–1961'. *American Journal of Agricultural Economics* 51, no. 3 (1969): 592–604. DOI: 10.2307/1237911.

Roniger, Luis. 'Political Clientelism, Democracy, and Market Economy'. *Comparative Politics* 36, no. 3 (2004): 353–75.

Rose, Leo E., and Margaret W. Fisher. *The Politics of Nepal: Persistence and Change in an Asian Monarchy* (New York: Cornell University Press, 1970).

Rostow, Walt Whitman. 'The Stages of Economic Growth', *Economic History Review* (New Series) 12, no. 1 (1959): 1–16.

Roy, Anuradha. *Cultural Communism in Bengal, 1936–1952* (New Delhi: Primus Books, 2014).

Roy, Tirthankar. 'Where Is Bengal? Situating an Indian Region in the Early Modern World Economy', *Past & Present* 213, no. 1 (November 2011): 115–146.

Rupert, Mark. 'Globalising Common Sense: A Marxian-Gramscian (Re-)Vision of the Politics of Governance/Resistance'. *Review of International Studies* 29 (December 2003): 181–98.

Sadeque, Abdus. *The Economic Emergence of Pakistan*, vol. 2 (Dacca: East Bengal Government, 1956).

Safa, Ahmad. *Shotoborsher Pherari: Bankim Chandra Chattopadhaya* (Dhaka: Khan Brothers and Company, 2009).

Saikia, Yasmin. *Women, War, and the Making of Bangladesh: Remembering 1971* (Durham, NC: Duke University Press, 2011).

———. 'Ayub Khan and Modern Islam: Transforming Citizens and the Nation in Pakistan'. *South Asia: Journal of South Asian Studies* 37, no. 2 (2014): 292–305.

Sarkar, Monem. *Bangabandhu Sheikh Mujibur Rahman Jibon Kotha* (Kolkata: Soptaho Publications, 2015).

Sarkar, Sumit. *The Swadeshi Movement in Bengal 1903–1908* (New Delhi: People's Publishing House, 1973).

Sarkar, Tanika. 'Rabindranath's "Gora" and the Intractable Problem of Indian Patriotism', *Economic and Political Weekly* 44, no. 30 (2009): 37–46.

Sartori, Andrew. *Bengal in Global Concept History: Culturalism in the Age of Capital* (Chicago Studies in Practices of Meaning) (Chicago: University of Chicago Press, 2008).

Sartre, Jean-Paul. *No Exit, and Three Other Plays* (New York: Vintage International, 1989).

Sayeed, Khalid B. 'How Radical Is the Pakistan People's Party?'. *Pacific Affairs* 48, no. 1 (1975): 42–59. https://doi.org/10.2307/2755447.

———. 'Pakistan's Basic Democracy'. *Middle East Journal* 15, no. 3 (1961): 249–63. http://www.jstor.org/stable/4323370. Accessed on 28 May 2021.

———. 'The Breakdown of Pakistan's Political System'. *International Journal* 27, no. 3 (1972): 381–404.

———. 'The Political Role of Pakistan's Civil Service'. *Pacific Affairs* 31, no. 2 (1958): 131–46. DOI: 10.2307/3035208.

Schendel, Willem van. 'Working through Partition: Making a Living in the Bengal Borderlands'. *International Review of Social History* 46, no. 3 (2001): 393–421.

———. *A History of Bangladesh* (Cambridge: Cambridge University Press, 2013 [2009]).

Selim, Lala Rukh, 'Art of Bangladesh: The Changing Role of Tradition, Search for Identity and Globalization'. *South Asia Multidisciplinary Academic Journal* 9 (2014): 10–19.

Sen, Amartya. 'Starvation and Exchange Entitlements: A General Approach and Its Application to the Great Bengal Famine'. *Cambridge Journal of Economics* 1, no. 1 (1977): 33–59.

Sen, Dwaipayan. *The Decline of the Caste Question: Jogendranath Mandal and the Defeat of Dalit Politics in Bengal* (Cambridge: Cambridge University Press, 2018).

Sen, Rangalal. *Political Elites in Bangladesh* (Dhaka: University Press Limited, 1986).

Sen, Shila. *Muslim Politics in Bengal, 1937–1947* (New Delhi: Impex India, 1976).

Sen, Sudipta. *Distant Sovereignty: National Imperialism and the Origins of British India* (New York: Routledge, 2002).

Sharma, Jayeeta. *Empire's Garden: Assam and the Making of India* (Durham, NC: Duke University Press, 2011).

Shastropani, Mohosin. *Lal Potakar Niche Sanskritik Andolon* (Cultural Movement under the Red Banner) (Dhaka: Porua, 2017).

Shepherd, George W. 'Suez: Touchstone of Colonialism'. *Africa Today* 3, no. 5 (1956): 6–7. www.jstor.org/stable/4183826. Accessed on 4 July 2020.

Shih, Shu-Mei. 'Race and Relation: The Global Sixties in the South of the South', *Comparative Literature* 68, no. 2 (2016): 141–54.

Shikdar, Md Kayum, Amitkumar Biswas and Ripon Mollick. 'The Socio-Economic Background of Khasia Ethnic Community of Bangladesh'. *IOSR Journal of Humanities and Social Science (IOSR-JHSS)* 7, no. 4 (January–February 2007): 58–72.

Siddiqa, Ayesha. *Military Inc.: Inside Pakistan's Military Economy* (London: Pluto Press, 2007).

Siddiqi, Dina M. 'In Search of Sonar Bangla (Golden Bengal)' *Himal*, May 2003. http://www.himalmag.com/component/content/article/146/18u-In-Search-of-Shonar-Bangla.html. Accessed on 3 February 2011.

Singh, Chaitram. 'Military Coups in Pakistan and the Corporate Interests Hypothesis'. *Journal of Third World Studies* 28, no. 1 (2011): 47–59.

Sinha, Manish. 'The Bengal Famine of 1943 and the American Insensitiveness to Food Aid'. *Proceedings of the Indian History Congress* (2009): 887–93. http://www.jstor.org/stable/44147736. Accessed on 17 January 2021.

Siraji, Syed Abu Mohammad Ismail Hossain. *Turaska Bhraman* (Calcutta: Sahjahan Company, 1913).

Sisson, Richard, and Leo E. Rose. *War and Secession: Pakistan, India, and the Creation of Bangladesh* (Berkeley: University of California Press, 1990).

Sobhan, Rehman. *Basic Democracies Works Program and Rural Development in East Pakistan* (Dacca: Bureau of Economic Research, Dacca University and Oxford University Press, 1968).

Stevenson, Richard. *Bengal Tiger and British Lion: An Account of the Bengal Famine of 1943* (Bloomington, IN: iUniverse, 2005).

Suhrawardy, Huseyn Shaheed. 'Political Stability and Democracy in Pakistan'. *Foreign Affairs* 35, no. 3 (1957): 422–31. DOI: 10.2307/20031239.

Sultana, Shaila. 'Problematising the Popular Discourses about Language and Identity of Young Adults in Bangladesh'. *3L: Language, Linguistics, Literature* 18, no. 4 (2012): 49–63.

Sunderason, Sanjukta. 'Shadow-Lines: Zainul Abedin and the Afterlives of the Bengal Famine of 1943'. *Third Text* 31, nos. 2–3 (2017): 239–59.

Sur, Milani. 'Battles for the Golden Grain: Paddy Soldiers and the Making of the Northeast India–East Pakistan Border, 1930–1970', *Comparative Studies in Society and History* 58, no. 3 (July 2016): 804–32.

Tepper, Elliot L. 'The New Pakistan: Problems and Prospects', *Pacific Affairs* 47, no. 1 (1974): 56–68.

Thiong'o, Ngũgĩ wa. *Decolonising the Mind* (London: Heinemann, 1986).

Toor, Saadia. *The State of Islam: Culture and Cold War Politics in Pakistan* (London: Pluto Press, 2011).

Tripathi, Salil. *The Colonel Who Would Not Repent: The Bangladesh War and Its Unquiet Legacy* (New Haven, CT: Yale University Press, 2016).
Uddin, Layli. '"Enemy Agents at Work": A Microhistory of the 1954 Adamjee and Karnaphuli Riots in East Pakistan', *Modern Asian Studies* 55, no. 2 (2021): 629–64.
Ullah. Mahfuj. *Purbo Pakistan Chatro Union: Gourober Dinguli* (Dhaka: Adorn Publications, 2012).
Umar, Badruddin. *The Emergence of Bangladesh*, vol. 1: Class *Struggles in East Pakistan, 1947–1958* (Karachi: Oxford University Press, 2004).
———. *The Emergence of Bangladesh*, vol. 2: *The Rise of Bengali Nationalism, 1958–1971* (Karachi: Oxford University Press, 2006).
———. *Purbo Banglar Bhasha Andolon o Totkalin Rajniti* (Dhaka: Subarna, 2011).
Veer, Peter van der. *Religious Nationalism: Hindus and Muslims in India* (Berkeley and Los Angeles: University of California, 1994).
Vorys, Karl von. *Political Development in Pakistan* (Princeton, NJ: Princeton University Press, 1965).
Weingrod, Alex. 'Patrons, Patronage and Political Parties'. *Comparative Studies in Society and History* 10, no. 4 (1968): 377–400.
Westad, Odd Arne, Chen Jian, Stein Tønnesson, Nguyen Vu Tung and James G. Hershberg. '77 Conversations Between Chinese and Foreign Leaders on the Wars in Indochina, 1964–1977', Working Paper No. 22, Cold War International History Project, Woodrow Wilson Center for Scholars, Washington, DC, 1998.
Westergaard, Kirsten. *State and Rural Society in Bangladesh: A Study in Relationship* (London: Curzon Press, 1985).
Wittfogel, Karl. *Oriental Despotism: A Comparative Study of Total Power* (New Haven: Yale University Press, 1957).
Wolf, Eric. 'Peasant Rebellions'. *International Social Science Journal* 21, no. 2 (1969): 286–93.
Wolpe, Harold. 'The Theory of Internal Colonization: The South African Case'. In *Societies of Southern Africa in the 19th and 20th Centuries*, vol. 5, pp. 105–120 (London: Institute of Commonwealth Studies, University of London, 1974).
Woodward, John Thomas. 'The Rural Works Programme in East Pakistan'. In *Development Policy*, vol. 2: *The Pakistan Experience*, edited by Walter P. Falcon and Gustav F. Papanek, pp. 186–236 (Cambridge: Harvard University Press, 1971).

———. 'Development Institutions, Projects, and Aid: A Case Study of the Water Development Programme in East Pakistan'. *Pakistan Economic and Social Review* 12, no. 1 (1974): 77–103. http://www.jstor.org/stable/25824787. Accessed on 22 June 2021.

Yong, Tan Tai. Maintaining the Military Districts: Civil–Military Integration and District Soldiers' Boards in the Punjab, 1919–1939'. *Modern Asian Studies* 28, no. 4 (1994): 833–74. DOI: 10.1017/S0026749X00012555.

Yu, George T. 'China and the Third World'. *Asian Survey* 17, no. 11 (1977): 1036–48.

Yuval-Davis, Nira. 'Belonging and the Politics of Belonging'. In *Contesting Recognition: Culture, Identity and Citizenship*, edited by Janice McLaughlin, Peter Phillimore and Diane Richardson, pp. 20–35 (New York: Palgrave Macmillan, 2011).

Zinkin, Taya. *Reporting India* (London: Chatto & Windus, 1962).

Ziring, Lawrence. 'Militarism in Pakistan: The Yahya Khan Interregnum'. *Asian Affairs: An American Review* 1, no. 6 (1974): 402–20.

———. *Pakistan in the Twentieth Century: A Political History* (Karachi, New York and Delhi: Oxford University Press, 1997).

———. *The Ayub Khan Era: Politics in Pakistan, 1958–1969* (Syracuse, NY: Syracuse University Press, 1971).

Zedong, Mao. *On Practice and Contradiction*, with an introduction by Žižek Slavoj (London: Verso, 2007).

Životić, Aleksandar, and Jovan Čavoški. 'On the Road to Belgrade: Yugoslavia, Third World Neutrals, and the Evolution of Global Non-Alignment, 1954–1961'. *Journal of Cold War Studies* 18, no. 4 (2016): 79–97. DOI: 10.1162/JCWS_a_00681.

Online Resources

Chowdhury, Kabir. 'Liberation War and Creative Writing'. Muktomona, 16 December 2006. https://mm-gold.azureedge.net/Special_Event_/16December/kabir_chowdhury161206.html. Accessed on 27 April 2021.

Islam, Mufassil. 'Rabindranath, Jatiyo Songit o Dhormo'. YouTube. https://www.youtube.com/watch?v=rU17IsWSmqw. Accessed on 26 August 2019.

Raza, Rafi. *Zulfikar Ali Bhutto and Pakistan 1967–1977*, reproduced by Sani H. Panhwar, Member of Sindh Council, PPP, pp. 6–9. https://bhutto.org/

wp-content/uploads/2020/12/Zulfikar-Ali-Bhutto-and-Pakistan-1967-1977.pdf. Accessed on 20 May 2020.

'Record of Conversation between Zhou Enlai, Chen Yi, and Head of Pakistan's Delegation Participating in the PRC's National Day Celebration, Maulana Abdul Hamid Khan Bhashani'. https://digitalarchive.wilsoncenter.org/document/121573.pdf. Accessed on 23 June 2021.

Sharafat, Sumel. 'Mongla Port Capacity Expanding'. *Prothom Alo*. http://en.prothom-alo.com/economy/news/132991/Mongla-port-capacity-expanding. Accessed on 12 February 2021.

'Spring Thunder over India'. https://www.marxists.org/subject/china/documents/peoples-daily/1967/07/05.htm. Accessed on 27 July 2020.

Index

21 February 1952, 56–57, 123, 142–43, 145, 149–50, 155, 251, 310, 313
    Ekushe (anthology of poems, essays and short stories), 150

Abdel-Malek, Anouar, 8, 63*n*15, 111–12
Abedin, Zainul, 155, 161–62, 176*n*50
    Manpura '70 (scroll), 162, 327–28
Adamjee Jute Mills, 36, 42, 59, 196, 244–46
Africa, 2, 19, 56, 76, 111–12, 113*n*3, 128, 156, 220–21, 231, 279, 282–84, 286, 328, 361–62
    North Africa, 85
    South Africa, 36, 97
Afro-Asian solidarity, 77, 112, 121*n*135, 151, 363
Agrani, 147
Ahad, Oli, 54, 73*n*136, 95, 99, 103–04, 107–10, 135, 141, 143, 286, 308, 322, 348*n*192
Ahamad, Khondakar Mostaq, 55, 333
Ahmad, Ziauddin, 137
Ahmad, Abul Mansur, 43, 54, 57, 87, 91, 95–96, 101–02, 109, 118*n*70, 118*n*82, 132, 138, 154, 189, 222, 224, 229, 233, 255*n*29, 276, 278, 296, 361, 363
Ahmad, Aziz, 44, 59

Ahmad, Faiz, 147, 246
Ahmad, Farrukh, 138, 149
Ahmad, Kamruddin, 54, 101, 108, 228, 253*n*1, 278
Ahmad, Mohiuddin, 290
Ahmad, Muhiuddin, 165, 289
Ahmad, Muzaffar, 50, 61*n*2, 119*n*94, 290
Ahmad, Najir, 183*n*173
Ahmad, Safiuddin, 161
Ahmad, Tajuddin, 31–32, 42–43, 54, 63*n*16, 73*n*136, 229, 274, 278–80, 293, 308, 311, 313, 333, 335
Ahmed, Ekram, 157
Ahmed, Kazi Faruk, 240
Ahmed, Kazi Zafar, 231, 256*n*40
Ahmed, Tofail, 308, 313, 329, 352*n*279
Ahsan, A. K. M., 278
Ahsan, Syed Ali, 153
Akash ar Mati (film), 166
al-Azad, Alauddin, 151, 153
Algeria, 1, 3, 63*n*15, 106, 221, 231, 266, 279, 366
    War of Independence (1954–62), 2, 112, 168, 230, 282
al-Hasan, Mahmud, 97, 119*n*90
Ali, Aftab, 246
Ali, Captain Mansur, 189, 280, 333

Ali, Chaudhry Muhammad, 81, 84, 94–95, 208, 274
Ali, Korban, 189
Ali, Mahmud, 104, 225
Ali, Mansur, 189, 280, 333
Ali, Rao Farman, 319
Ali, Syed Mujtaba, 138
Ali, Tariq Omar, 9, 205, 298, 315, 348n182, 353n294
Al-Jamia al-Islamiya, 209
Allende, Salvador, 286
All India Student Federation, 236
al-Muti, Abdullah, 153
All Pakistan Trade Union Federation, 246
All-Party State Language Action Committee, 142–43
Alo Aschhe (play), 157
Alor Poth Jatri (play), 156
Al-Azhar University, Cairo, 209
al-Said, Nuri, 89, 105
Amin, 196
Amin, Nurul, 32, 43, 57, 164, 225, 241, 249, 254n13, 273, 294, 309, 322–23, 328, 356n326
Anisuzzaman, 130, 147–50, 154–155, 166, 176n49, 251
Asad, Ali, 233, 305–06
Asad's shirt, 158
Asaduzzaman, 305
ashraf, 53, 90, 92–93, 142, 150, 245, 361
Ashram, Abhoy, 205
Asia, 2, 5, 19, 56, 76–77, 112, 113n3, 156, 221, 231–32, 244, 283–84, 286, 328
South Asia, 7–10, 17, 30, 61n7, 75, 77–78, 83, 85–87, 98, 105, 109, 111, 123, 126, 129, 131, 137, 168, 190, 268, 282, 331
Asian Tide (journal), 231
Asiya (film), 166
Assam, 29–30, 32, 37, 44, 49–50, 55, 97–99, 130, 134–35, 248, 361
Awami League, 4, 10–11, 15, 17, 20, 57, 61, 76–78, 87, 92–93, 95–104, 106–11, 118n68, 123, 148, 154, 164, 189, 221–23, 225, 227, 229–30, 233, 235–36, 239, 248, 253n1, 255n29, 258n88, 263, 272–74, 278–82, 286–88, 293–97, 299–01, 304, 307–08, 311, 313–14, 317, 319–25, 328–35, 362–63, 365, 367–68
Awami Muslim League, 55–58, 90, 92–96, 99, 103–04, 143, 362
Azad (newspaper), 57, 134, 148, 154, 177n55, 243
Azam, Golam, 142, 294

Baghdadi, Nasiruddin, 96
Bahar, Habibullah, 139, 177n53
Baitul Mukarram mosque, 156, 251
Bakerganj, 43
Balibar, Etienne, 133
Bandyopadhaya, Tarashankar, 109
Bandung Conference (1955), 105, 112, 151
Banga Bahini
    'What do Bengalis Want?', 234
    'Bengal Again under Attacks by Jackals and Vultures', 234
    'Bengali in History', 234
Bangadarshan (journal), 29
Bangla Academy, 153
Bangladesh liberation struggle in 1971, 6, 10–11, 29, 158, 163, 264
Barisal, 41, 43–45, 51, 70n73
Braque, Georges, 163
Bashar, Abul, 289, 292, 368
Basic Democracy, 5, 185–95, 204–07, 211, 213n22, 214n33, 220, 225, 238, 249, 270, 298, 301–02, 304, 310
Basu, Ganesh Charan, 145, 180n107
Basu, Manoj, 148
Basu, Manoroma, 51
Baudelaire, Charles, 159
Baul (journal), 29
Bawani jute mill, 298
Bawani, 196, 246
Bawani, Yahya, 246

Bay of Pigs invasion, 230
Begam, Amena, 294
Begum, Rizia, 157
Beijing, 148, 284–85, 297, 309, 339n9
Bhagirathi River, 134
Bharat Mata, 29
Bharatnatyam (novel), 168
Bhashani, Maulana Abdul Hamid Khan (also known as Red Maulana), 4, 10, 20, 55–56, 59, 75–78, 90, 96–01, 104, 106–12, 113n3, 117n56, 118n86, 119n92, 120n97, 143, 148, 151, 162, 181n119, 222, 249, 251, 263, 272, 282–83, 285–86, 288–92, 295, 297–02, 304–05, 307, 309–13, 315–17, 319, 321–22, 326, 328, 335, 337, 344n102, 347n180, 348n192, 349n207, 352n274, 353n300, 361–63, 367–68
Bhattarcharrya, Bijon
  Joban Bondi (play), 147
Bhola cyclone, 264, 327, 358n348
Bhorer Obhijatri, 156
Bhutto, Zulfiqar Ali, 226, 249–50, 262, 266–70, 280, 285, 295, 297, 299, 308, 313, 315, 329–35, 337, 341n36, 347n179, 365
Bogra, Mohammad Ali, 81, 91, 138, 193, 238
Bolivia, 298
Bose, Buddhadev, 158
Bose, Nandalal, 163
Bose, Sarat, 135
Bose, Subhas Chandra, 109, 232, 320
bottola (the shade of a banyan tree), 303–04, 323
Buriganga River, 306

Cabral, Amilcar, 286
Calcutta (present-day Kolkata), 5, 32–33, 37, 39, 41–42, 44–45, 52, 54, 58, 60, 73n124, 93, 98–99, 130–32, 134, 138–39, 150–51, 159, 161, 164–66, 174n26, 181n119, 196, 234, 244, 248, 251, 253n1, 298, 360
Cariappa, Kodandera Madappa, 233
Castro, Fidel, 230, 286
Central Intelligence Agency (CIA), 89, 117n56, 265–66, 268–69, 286, 311, 320, 338n8, 367
Chakravarty, Trailokyanath, 320
Chatkal Shramik Federation, 246
Chattogram, 32
Chattopadhyay, Sarat Chandra, 132
Chattopadhyaya, Debiprasad, 148
Chayanat, 154
Chhatro League, 235–37, 240, 242–43, 279, 303–04, 313, 320, 323, 333, 357n340, 368
Chhatro Union, 103, 235–43, 290, 303–04, 306, 313, 320, 324, 368
Chatterjee, Bankim Chandra, 124–25, 132, 172n12
  'Vande Mataram' song, 61n2
Chatterjee, P. L., 137
Chaudhury, Mofazzal Haidar, 207
Chittagong Steel Mills, 245
Chittaranjan Cotton Mill, 244
Chittoprosad, 161
Chowdhury, Abdul Gaffar, 145, 151
Chowdhury, Abdul Halim, 232
Chowdhury, Amir Hossain, 247
Chowdhury, Anis, 151
Chowdhury, Asad, 231
Chowdhury, Hamidul Huq, 225, 254n13
Chowdhury, Kabir, 180, 278
Chowdhury, Kamal, 133
Chowdhury, Matia, 290, 324
Chowdhury, Mizanur Rahman, 313
Chowdhury, Moazzem, 232, 333
Chowdhury, M. R., 333
Chowdhury, Munier, 149, 153–54, 251, 366
Chowdhury, Muzzaffar Ahmed, 143
Chowdhury, Zahur Ahmad, 280
Chowdury, Nuruddin Shaben, 189
Chundrigarh, I. I., 276

Civil Service of Pakistan (CSP), 80–82, 191, 211, 278, 363
Colombo Powers, 108, 121n135
Comilla, 34, 66n35, 202–03, 205, 209
Commonwealth Summit, 233
Communist Party of India (CPI), 51–52, 61n2, 176n50, 236, 245, 284
Communist Party of India (Marxist) (CPI[M]), 300, 321
Communist Party of India (Marxist–Leninist), 300
Communist Party of Pakistan (CPP), 41, 58, 90, 99, 141, 146–47, 156–57, 221–22, 232, 234–36, 244, 246, 286–94, 303, 311, 321, 363, 368
Congo-Brazzaville, 231
Convention Muslim League (CML), 226, 247–48, 297, 308
Cornelius, Alvin Robert, 297
cotton textile mills, 245, 319
Council Muslim League, 226–27, 297
Cripps Mission, 312
Cuban Revolution of 1958, 1, 230–31, 279
Curzon Hall, 139, 281

Dacca (present-day Dhaka), 14, 24n27, 31–32, 36, 42–43, 45, 53–56, 59, 64n17, 90, 92, 99–101, 103, 105–07, 123, 126, 128, 138–39, 141–45, 148, 150, 152–53, 155–56, 158–59, 161, 164–68, 172n5, 179n84, 193, 198, 223–24, 226, 229, 232–38, 240–41, 244–48, 253n1, 272, 274, 277, 279–81, 285, 287, 290–92, 295–96, 298–301, 305–10, 313, 315–16, 318–19, 323, 325, 328, 331–35, 351n264, 368
Dacca College, 240, 242
Dacca East Bengal Cinematograph Society, 164
Dacca University State Language Action committee (Dhaka Bishyaviddalay Rastro Bhasha Songram Committee), 142–43
Dahomey, 231
Daily Hilal (journal), 208
Dalai Lama, 232
Danesh, Haji Ahmad, 103–04
Das, Chittaranjan, 92, 109
Dasgupta, Ranesh, 149, 153, 157, 298
Das, Jibanananda, 18, 158
Daulatpur, 247
Daultana, Mian Mumtaz Muhammad Khan, 226
Dawood, 196
Deben–Bashar–Matin–Alauddin group, 289, 321
Debi, Radharani, 109, 148
Degree Student Forum, 240
Democratic Action Committee (DAC), 304–05, 307–08, 311, 314–15, 323, 353n290
devaluation of currency, 36
devaluation of the rupee, 196
Dhakeshwari Cotton Mill, 244
Dhanmandi, 229
Dhansho Pahar (novel), 168
Dhirendranath Dutta, 141, 178n75
Dholaikhal, 325
District Soldiers' Boards, 83, 399
Dostidar, Sharadindu, 308–09, 321, 341n47
Dostidar, Sukhendu, 289, 308–09, 321
Doxiadis, Constantinos, 205
Dukkhe Jader Jibon Gora (film), 164
Dulles, John Foster, 88, 187
Dutta, Michael Madhusudan, 155

East Bengal Liberation Front, 231
East Pakistan Communist Party (Marxist–Leninist) (EPCP[M-L]), 289, 302, 309, 321
East Pakistan Film Development Corporation (EPFDC), 164–65

East Pakistan Industrial Development Corporation (EPIDC), 197
East Pakistan Mazdoor Federation, 246
East Pakistan Muslim Student League, 141–42
East Pakistan Renaissance Society (EPRS), 126, 131–34, 138, 144, 222, 275, 360
East Pakistan Rifle, 304, 306, 310
East Pakistan Trade Union Federation, 245
East Pakistan Workers' Federation, 292
Eastern Bengal and Assam, 29
Edu, Golam Mohammad, 157
Egypt, 76, 85, 104–05, 107–08, 116n45, 208, 231, 282, 363
Eisenhower, Dwight D., 88, 106, 186–88, 212n10
Elective Bodies (Disqualification) Ordinance, 1959, 189, 226–27, 293
export bonus, 197

Faiz, Faiz Ahmad, 166
famine, 49–50, 96, 131, 146–47, 161–63, 298, 348n189
  Bengal, 176n50
  line, 207
Fanon, Frantz, 1, 8, 16, 31, 63n15, 112, 126, 128–29, 152, 167, 230, 264, 279
Farhad, Mohammad, 303, 236–37, 242, 303
Farrukh, Mohammad, 239
Faruq, Shamsur Rahman, 178n70
Fauji Foundation, 19, 185
Fazilatunnesa, Begum, 311
Fazli, Fazl Ahmad Kariim, 139
Floud Commission, 46
Førland, Tor Egil, 1

Ganatantri Dal, 58, 89, 103, 362
Gandhara Motors, 245

Gandhi, Mohandas Karamchand, 75, 109, 136, 143, 204–05, 312
Garo, 32, 248
garrison state, 5, 87, 197, 220
Gauhar, Altaf, 214n32, 270–71, 277, 309, 341n36
Ghalib, Mirza, 155
Ghana, 112, 231
Ghani, Osman, 280
Goon, Nirmalendu, 18, 159
Gordon College, 299
Gorky, Maxim, 148, 156
  The Mother (novel), 155
Government College of Art and Craft, Calcutta, 161
Gramsci, Antonio, 13–16, 27n64, 129, 151–52
Guha, Ajit Kumar, 153
Gunj, Gopal, 92
Gupta, Ambuj, 164
Guru, Khalid Rashid, 157

Hafizuddin, A. K. M., 153–54
Haidar, Syed, 144
Hajari, Abdul Gani, 151
Hajongs, 32, 51
Halbwachs, Maurice, 140
Halim, Abdul, 50, 290
Halliley, A. A., 307, 348n182, 351n264
Hall, Iqbal, 305, 310
Hamoodur Rahman Commission, 158
Haq, Abdul, 207
Haq, M. T., 276
Huq, Obaidul, 164
Haq, Sanaul, 278
Haque, Abdul, 289, 291, 304
Haque, Abu Saeed Zahurul, 169
Haque, Amanul, 156
Haque, Anwarul, 161
Haque, Mazaharul, 276
Haque, Syed Shamsul, 151, 251
Harun-or-Rashid, 291
Harvard advisory group, 199

406 Index

Hasan, Quamrul, 161
Hashim, Abul, 9, 53–54, 135, 143, 154, 232, 361–62
Hatirdia Bazaar, 302, 305
Hazelhurst, Peter, 314, 316
Hazrat Bal, 250
Hill, Basil J. Green, 223
Hildreth, Horace, 105–06
Hindu Mahasabha, 42, 92
Hindustani, 136
Hindui (or Hindvi), 135, 178*n*70
Home, Sir Alec Douglas, 334
Hoque, Mofidul, 161, 183*n*164
Hossain, Akhtar, 157
Hossain, Kamal, 313, 329, 333
Hossain, Khairat, 323
Hossain, Mahmood, 242
Hossain, Syed Altaf, 290
Hossain, Syed Sajjad, 132
Hossain, Talim, 133–34
Hoxha, Enver, 283
Huda, M. N., 276–77
hukumat-i nafsdnyiat (the order of the tyrants), 97
hukumat-i-rabbani (the just order of god), 97
Humayun Kabir, 109
Huq, Abdul, 137
Huq, A. K. Fazlul, 43, 54, 57–59, 90–92, 166, 220, 225, 249, 252, 361–63
Huq, Syed Azizul, 225
Husain, Qazi Motahar, 138
Hussain, A. F. A., 276–77
Hussain, Qazi Anwar, 168
Hussain, Tofazzal, 101, 110, 151, 235, 239, 254*n*13, 293, 320

Iftikharuddin, Mian, 110
import-export control, 195
Indian Jute Manufacturer's Association, 33
Indian People's Theatre Association (IPTA), 162–63

industrial houses, 5, 196–98, 200, 221, 299, 364
Iqbal Films, 165
Iran, 26*n*57, 85, 88–89, 104, 116*n*48, 196, 208, 266
Ishaque, A. H. M., 46
Ishaque, Abu, 146
Iskra (journal), 231
Islam, Aminul, 151
Islam, Amirul, 313, 333
Islam, Kazi Nazrul, 18, 125, 128
Islam, Mazharul, 161
Islam, Nurul, 276–77, 329
Islam, Rafiqul, 156, 179*n*92, 251
Islam, Sirajul, 150, 182*n*146, 292
Islam, Syed Nazrul, 279, 294, 313, 333
Islam, Zahurul, 156
Ispahani, 53, 196, 246–47
Itehad-e-Muslimeen, 135
Ittefaq (newspaper), 101, 109–10, 149, 154, 172*n*6, 239, 243, 248, 251, 293, 298, 304, 320

Jabbar, Sheikh Abdul, 156, 165
Jadavpur, 298
Jago Hua Sabera (film), 166
Jahan, Rounak, 361
Jahangir, Burhanuddin Khan, 151
Jamaat-e-Islami, 293–94, 297, 304, 309, 315, 322–23
Jamauluddin, 151
James, Morrice, 227
Janata (newspaper), 286, 288
Jasimuddin, 154
Jayantia, 32, 64*n*20
Jennings, Sir Ivor, 81, 114*n*19
Jibon theke Neya (film), 167
Jinnah, Fatima, 220, 223, 248–49, 252
Jinnah, Mohammad Ali, 8–9, 80, 84, 109, 111, 137, 141–42, 164, 178*n*75, 189, 207, 213*n*24, 220, 275, 322, 364
Joar Elo (film), 167

Kabar (play), 149–50, 366
kabi gan (rural bard's recital of poems), 210
Kabir, Alamgir, 165, 231
Kabir, Khairul, 273, 278
Kaderia, 245
Kader, K. A. Abdul, 245–46
Kagmari Convention (1957), 151
Khasi, 32, 245
Khunla, 245
Kaiser, Shahidullah, 167
    Sareng Bou (novel), 160
Kaler Kalosh (anthology of poems), 159
Kamal, Sufia, 147, 251
Kardar, A. J., 166–67
Karim, 196, 246
Karnaphuli Paper Mill, 59, 245, 291
Kashem, Abul, 138
'Kashmir Medina ba-shud az moi-e-nab', 247
Kerala, 231
Khalequzzaman, Chowdhury, 59, 135, 226
Khan, Abdul Ghaffar, 110
Khan, Abdul Jabbar, 165
Khan, Abdul Qayum, 226
Khan, Abdus Sabur, 238, 247
Khan, Akhter Hameed, 204
Khan, Asghar, 301, 314, 323
Khan, Ataur Rahman (also known as 'mancha sarothi'), 92–93, 95–96, 100, 102, 106–07, 150–51, 222–23, 225, 229, 251, 254n13, 296, 361
Khan, Ayub, 5, 7, 19, 61, 81, 84, 87–88, 93, 110, 167, 169, 185–95, 197, 204–05, 207–09, 213n25, 220, 223, 225–26, 228–29, 232–33, 236–39, 242, 244–52, 255n29, 262–74, 277, 280, 282, 285–87, 293–02, 307–10, 312–17, 323–24, 336, 338n6, 341n36, 348n192, 351n247, 353n300, 364–67
    Friends Not Masters (autobiography), 294

Khan, Kamrul Ahsan, 157
Khan, Liaquat Ali, 41, 80–81, 84, 86, 141–42, 178n75
Khan, Manzurul Ahsan, 157
Khan, Maulana Akram, 54, 226
Khan, Mostofa Wahid, 157
Khan, Mukul, Abdus Samad, 156
Khan, Nawabzada Nasarullah, 274
Khan, Sardar Bahadur, 226
Khan, Sirajul Hossain, 292
Khan, Tikka, 318, 335
Khan, Wali, 290, 308
Khan, Yahya, 20, 163, 263–64, 309, 314, 317, 323–24, 327, 331–35, 337, 348n192, 355n309
Khan, Azam, 238, 277, 301
Khasru, Amir, 156
Khrushchev, Nikta, 283
Kibria, Ghulam, 51
Kissinger, Henry, 264
Koibarto Bidroho (novel), 157
Korean War, 86, 106, 196, 244
Kranti, 156
Krishak Samiti, 290, 307
Krishak Sramik Party, 227

La Higuera, 298
Lahiry, Tulsi, 147
Lahore Resolution of 1940, 92, 299, 320
Lahore, 164–65, 226, 232, 251, 271, 274–75, 331–32, 351n264, 367
Lal Salu (novel), 146
Land Reforms Act
    of 1964, 47
Lhasa, 232
Lohani, Fateh, 165–66
Lohani, Fazle, 151
Lohani, Kamal, 156, 172n6
Lumumba, Patrice, 221, 231
Luxmi Narayan Cotton Mill, 244

Madarsha Union, 53
Madhavdi, 291

Mahe Nao (magazine), 133
Maheshwarpasha School of Fine Art, 161
Mahmud, Al, 18, 159
Mahmud, Altaf, 145
Maitiur, 306
Majlis, Tamaddun, 14, 138
Majumdar, Charu, 291, 321
Malay Peninsula, 130
Mannan, Abdul, 159, 246, 292
McLennan, Hugh, 125
Mali, 231
Malik, A. M., 70n73, 245
Mann, Michael, 37–38, 67n44
Maqbul, 306
March, D. M., 318, 353n287, 354n304
martial law, 20, 23n27, 110, 189, 192, 222–25, 227, 234–46, 252, 263–64, 290, 311–19, 321–26, 333–34, 337, 354n300, 356n326
martial law administration, 79, 223, 319, 324, 326–27, 331, 334, 338
Matin, Abdul, 321
Mecca, 309
Meghna, 200, 245, 292, 319, 327
Menon, Rashed Khan, 231, 290
Mian, Manu, 281
Middle East Treaty Organization (METO) (also known as Baghdad Pact), 4, 89, 103–05, 107–09, 116n48, 236, 284, 363
Mirza, Iskandar, 59, 81–82, 84, 89–90, 93–95, 100–02, 105, 108–10, 187
Mitra, Ila, 52, 149
Mitra, Ramen (Ramzan Miah), 149
Modabber, Mohammad, 165
Montu, Mozzammel Hossain, 155
Mogultully, Dacca, 31, 54
Mohammadi (magazine), 28, 133,
Mohanagar (film), 167
Mongla port, 245, 247
Mosadegh, Mohammad, 89
Moscow, 105, 267, 283, 309
  International Film Festival, 167
Mosharraf, Major Khaled, 333
Muhammad, Ghulam, 80–81, 84, 92–94
Mukh o Mukhosh (film), 165
Mukhopadhyaya, Subhas, 148–49
Mukul Bahini, 134
Mukul, M. R. Akhtar, 45, 151
Muladi, 43
Murshed, Justice Sayed Mahbub, 301, 314, 356n326
Murshid, Justice Ghulam, 153
Murshid, Khan Sarwar, 313
Muslim Family Laws Ordinance (MFLO), 323
Mustafa, Golam, 181n131
Myanmar (erstwhile Burma), 48, 64n17, 121n135, 130, 228, 278
Mymensing, 43, 51, 57, 289
My Sorrowful Alphabet, 158

Nabanna (scroll), 161–62
Nabwi, Moi-e-Muqaddas, 247
Nadia, 38, 40, 45, 67n49
namasudra, 41
Narail, 302
Narayan, Jayaprakash, 233
Narayanganj, 36, 59, 244, 248, 280–81
Nasser, Gamal Abdel, 104–05, 108
nastaliq (Arabic script), 14, 26n57
national anthem, 29, 62n10, 155, 234, 333, 369
National Awami Party (NAP), 4, 10–11, 78, 102–10, 113n3, 227, 253n1, 272, 274, 282, 284–94, 296–302, 304, 307, 313, 316, 319, 321–24, 326, 337, 363, 367–368
National Democratic Front (NDF), 227–30, 252, 273–74, 294, 296, 304, 309, 323, 356n325
National Student Federation (NSF), 237, 243, 279–80, 298, 357n340
Nazimuddin, Khawaja, 32, 36, 54, 67n41, 67n42, 80–81, 90, 142, 220, 226, 248–49, 252, 275, 361, 363–64

Nehru, Jawaharlal, 41, 44, 105–10, 136, 231–33
Nixon, Richard Milhous, 88, 264, 269
Non-Aligned Movement, 4, 104–05, 282, 362
North Vietnam, 284, 297, 354*n*300
North-West Frontier Province (NWFP), 79, 95, 97, 136, 190, 213*n*25
Notre Dame College, 248

Obaidullah, Abu Zafar, 151
Odud, Abdul, 109
Odud, Kazi Abdul, 109
Operation Gibraltar, 250–51
Opurbo Sansad, 234
Osmani, M. A. G., 93, 110, 290, 333, 335
Osmani, Muhammad, 93, 110
Osmani, Mahmudul Haq, 290
Ottoman Turkey Khilafate, 28

Pakistan Democratic Movement (PDM), 293–94, 296–97, 304, 323, 356*n*325, 367
Pakistan Industrial Development Corporation, 196–97, 244, 251
Pakistan National Congress (PNC), 42–43, 58, 95
Pakistan Observer (newspaper), 278
Pakistan Oxygen, 245
Pakistan Sahitya Sansad (Pakistan Literary Association), 147
Paltan Maidan, 242, 299, 306, 308, 328, 333, 335
Palestine, 1, 298
Panni, Khurram Khan, 55
Parichoy (magazine), 151
Paris, 3, 168, 298
Pasha, Salah al-Din, 104
Patel, Vallabhbhai, 41
Paul, Shashi Bhushan, 161
People's Party of Pakistan (PPP), 297, 299, 301, 304, 313, 330, 332

People's Republic of China (PRC), 77, 106, 199, 283, 285, 344*n*107
People's Daily (newspaper), 300
Picasso, Pablo, 163
Pickard, Sir Cyril S., 24*n*27, 315–16, 355*n*309, 356*n*326
Podochihno (novel), 160
Power, D. K., 278
Prantik, 146
Pratham Gan Dwitiya Mrittur Age (anthology of poems), 158
pro-Chinese National Awami Party (NAP), 288, 294, 297–300, 302, 316, 326, 368
Progressive Writers and Artists Association, 153
pro-Soviet National Awami Party (NAP), 11, 288, 290, 294, 297, 300–01, 304, 321–22, 324
Provisional Legal Framework, 325
Punjab, 37, 79, 83, 135, 137, 314–15, 330–31, 363
Punthi literature, 177
Punthi Potro, 151
Purbo Bangla, 230–36
Purbo Pakistan, 126, 153
Purbo Pakistane Dos Din (documentary film), 164

Qadir, K. M. M., 246
Qadri, Shahid, 159–60
Qamaruzzaman, H. M., 333
Qi, Liu Shao, 285
Quddus, Ruhul, 278
Qudrat-i-Khuda, 154

Radio Pakistan, 154
Rahim, Zahidur, 279
Rahman, Akhlaqur, 153
Rahman, Fazlur, 142, 209, 226
Rahman, Hasan Hafizur, 150–51, 155, 251
Rahman, Mashiur (also known as Jadu Mian), 229, 239

Rahman, Pir Habibur, 289
Rahman, S. A., 310
Rahman, Saidur, 292, 298
Rahman, Saydur, 348n188
Rahman, Shamsur, 18, 158, 328
Rahman, Sheikh Mujibur (Sheikh
    Mujib), 10–11, 20, 23n27, 54–55,
    57, 89, 92–100, 102, 110, 141–42,
    148, 162–64, 172n6, 180n117, 189,
    221–23, 225, 228–30, 232–33,
    235–36, 244, 248, 251–52, 253n1,
    254n13, 263–64, 272–74, 278–80,
    282, 287, 293, 296, 304, 307–08,
    310–15, 319–20, 322–26, 328–29,
    331–37, 341n47, 352n274, 352n279,
    354n300, 356n326, 359n381, 361,
    365–69
Rahman, Sydur, 246
Raihan, Zahir, 167
    Behula (film), 175n35
    Hajar Bochor Dhore (novel), 160
Rajshahi University, 242, 310
Raju, Zakir Hossain, 166, 183n164
Ranadive, B. T., 52
Rana, Masud, 168
Rangpur, 108, 147, 288, 290–91
Rann of Kutch, 250
Rawalpindi, 267, 299–300, 313, 315, 320
Ray, Kiran Shankar, 135
Ray, Satyajit, 166–67, 176n50
    Mohanagar (film), 167
    Pather Panchali (film), 166
Razzak, Abdur, 277
Republican Party, 95, 100–01, 227
Revolutionary Socialist Party, 245–46
riots, 30, 37, 40–45, 59, 61n2, 135, 180n107,
    245, 247–52, 314, 353n300
Rokeya Hall, 305
Ronangon (book), 251
Rono, Haidar Akbar Khan, 231
Rostow, Walt Whitman, 212n14
    *The Stages of Economic Growth: A
    Non-Communist Manifesto*, 187

round table conference, 228, 308, 311–17,
    334, 351n247, 356n326
Roy Fox, 315, 356n325
Roy, Jamini, 163
Roy, Khoka, 150, 235, 248
Roy, Manoranjan, 257n60
Roy, Rammohan, 128, 153
Rupban (film), 167
Rural Public Works Program, 204–05
Rusk, Dean, 265, 338n7
Rustam, 306

Sadeque, Abdus, 134, 276
Sahabuddin, Khwaja, 154
Saha, Indu, 156
Sahitya Bisharad, Abdul Karim, 14, 147,
    174n26
Saigol, 196
Salahuddin, 167
Salamat (documentary), 164
Samad, Abdus, 246
samaj (society), 202
Samakal (magazine), 208
Sandipon, 157
Sanskriti Parishad, 146
Santiniketan, 138
Sanyal, Probodh, 109
Saptahik Probhati (periodical), 291
Sarkar, Abu Hossain, 94, 225
Sarkar, Nagen, 311
Sarkar, Sushobhan, 153
Sarwar, Ghulam, 59, 277
Sastropani, Mahasin, 156
Satrong cotton textile mills, 245, 292
Sen, Bhavani, 153
Senegal, 231
Sen, Nirmal, 305
Shahidullah, Muhammad, 137
Shahnur studio, 164
Shah, Sultan Alauddin Hussain,
    22n12
Shamsuddin, Abul Kalam, 57, 144–45,
    154, 177n53, 222, 254n3

Shamsuzzoha, Mohammad, 310
Shapath Nilam (play), 157
Sharif, Ahmad, 209, 234
Shariff, S. M., 239
Shastri, Lal Bahadur, 271, 341*n*36
Shikha (journal), 126, 231
Shoaib, Muhammad, 266
Shober Michile Jiboner Joygan (play), 156
Siddiq, Abdur Rahman, 233
Sikdar, Deben, 289, 322, 368
Sikdar, Siraj, 301, 322
Simanto Shibir (book), 251
Sindh, 37, 250, 330–31
Singh, Moni, 51, 117*n*55, 235–36, 244, 311, 322
Singh, Sachindra Lal, 233
Siraji, Abu Mohammad Ismail Hossain, 28, 61*n*1
six-point program, 264, 273–75, 278–82, 286–88, 291, 293–96, 299, 303, 314–15, 319–20, 325, 328–32, 336–37, 345*n*130, 365–69
Skillbeck, R. F. N., 317
Sobhan, Rehman, 200–03, 205–06, 277–78, 329, 333, 348*n*188
Sombad (newspaper), 154, 231, 243, 273, 288, 298, 303, 348*n*189
Sorbonne, 298
South-East Asia Treaty Organization (SEATO), 4, 88, 105, 109, 116*n*47, 231, 236, 284
South Korea, 78
Soviet Union, 11, 77, 88, 105, 116*n*45, 155, 199, 250, 265, 267–68, 282–84, 291, 337, 367
Srijoni Sahityk Gosthi, 155
Stalin, Joseph, 72*n*114, 109, 283
Stassen, Harold E., 88
Student Action Committee (SAC), 303–05, 307–08, 310–11, 313–14, 316, 323–24, 335, 368–69
Subandrio, 288
Suez Crisis, 76, 102–11, 151, 222, 282

Suhrawardy, Huseyn Shaheed, 4, 9, 20, 51, 54, 56, 90–95, 99–101, 103, 106–10, 118*n*68, *n*70, 135, 141, 189, 220, 222, 224, 227–29, 233, 235, 237, 240–42, 249, 252, 255*n*29, 275, 325, 361–63
Sukanto, 148
Sukumari (film), 164
Sulaiman, 155
Sultan, Mohammad, 151
Surbitan, 157
Surjya Dighal Bari (novel), 146
Swadhin Bangla Biplobi Parishad, 234
'Swadhinota' (poem), 158
Syed, G. M., 110
Sylhet Sahitya Sansad, 138
Sylhet, 32, 52, 64*n*20, 173*n*15, 232, 245

Tagore, Abanindranath, 29
Tagore, Dwarkanath, 124, 132, 172*n*8
Tagore, Rabindranath, 18, 28–29, 138, 152–55, 295
  Dublin-based academic accusation against, 62*n*10
  nationalism, 62*n*9
'O My Golden Bengal' (O Amar Sonar Bangla) (song), 28–29, 62*n*10, 155, 234, 279, 325, 333, 369
Tanzania, 231
Tarkabagish, Maulana Abdur Rashid, 144, 230, 279
tebhaga movement, 51–52
Tejgaon industrial area, 247
Tet Offensive, 2, 297
The Guardian (newspaper), 42, 316, 353*n*298, 359
The Times, 316
Thiong'o, Ngũgĩ wa, 128
Toaha, Mohammad, 246, 286, 289–92, 304, 315, 321
Tongi industrial area, 244–45, 259*n*119, 291–92, 315–16, 318–19, 368
Tripura, 32–35, 37, 66*n*35, 232–33, 248

Turkey, 28, 84, 88–89, 104, 108, 116*n*48, 208, 224, 266

Uddin, Layli, 75
Uddin, Pir Mohsin, 225
Udichi, 157
ulema(s), 209–211
Ullah, Mahabub, 306
United Front of 1954, 2, 20, 57–58, 89, 91, 94, 99, 101, 148, 207, 221, 224, 229, 275, 284, 315, 362, 366
United States of America, 18, 87–90, 106, 130, 144, 168, 188, 207, 230, 235, 247–48, 265–66, 268–69, 284, 286, 322, 339*n*9
Unmesh Sahitya o Sanskriti Sansad, 156
Urdu, 11, 14, 17, 26*n*57, 53, 55–56, 90, 92–93, 126–28, 135–39, 141–42, 148, 164–67, 173*n*15, 174*n*31, 175*n*35, 177*n*57, 178*n*70, *n*75, 245, 252, 361, 365–66

Vidyasagar, Ishwar Chandra, 132
Village Self Government Act (1919), 190
Vivekananda, 153

Waliullah, Syed
  Chander Amabosya (novel), 160
Wilhelm, Van Schendel, 49, 71*n*99
World Peace Conference, Beijing, 148
Writers' Guild, 155

Youth League, 58, 103–04, 107–08, 138
Yusuf Ali Chowdhury

Zaman, Q. M., 165
Zedong, Mao, 1, 109, 122*n*144, 234, 271, 283, 286, 295, 297, 337, 339*n*9, 367
Zhdanov, Andrei Aleksandrovich, 52, 72*n*114
Zinkin, Taya, 42–45, 89